MUTINY
and Romance in the
SOUTH SEAS
A Companion to the Bounty Adventure

By the same author:

Family Communication: A Guide To Emotional Health

Excuses: How To Spot Them, Deal With Them, And Stop Using Them

MUTINY
and Romance in the
SOUTH SEAS

A Companion to the Bounty Adventure

Sven Wahlroos
("Taote Tivini")

Foreword by Rolf Du Rietz

SALEM HOUSE PUBLISHERS
TOPSFIELD, MASSACHUSETTS

Library of Congress Cataloging-in-Publication Date

Wahlroos, Sven.
    Mutiny and Romance in the South Seas: A Companion
to the Bounty Adventure/by Sven Wahlroos.
        p. cm.
    Bibliography: p.
    ISBN 0-88162-395-4 :
    1. Bounty Mutiny, 1789. 2. Pitcairn Island.
        I. Bounty (Ship)
II. Title.
DU800.W34 1989
996.18—dc19   88-38362

Maps and map keys conceived by David Evans.

The author thanks Glynn Christian for use of the Fort
George and Tubuai maps, modified here and taken from
Fragile Paradise (Little, Brown and Company, 1984).
Printed in the United States of America

In memory of my friend

Captain Malcolm Sword
AVARUA, RAROTONGA

who has left on the Great Adventure

Acknowledgments

"Huzzah for Tahiti" the crew cried out
When the ship they had taken by force.
"Huzzah for my friends" is what I am about
To proclaim in this little discourse.

I will start with a Club to which I belong;
To me it has meant a great deal.
In its praise I would like to begin this song
With describing the way I feel:

The Adventurers' Club is the place to be
If excitement you want — and mirth;
With ideas the members bombard you, you see!
And that's how this book had its birth.

I had finished a talk on the South Sea isles
('way to Pitcairn I'd sailed on a barque);
Now my friends crowded round, and they were all smiles;
What they said then provided the spark:

"Write a book," they said, "on the Mutiny,
Write a book on Adventure, Sven.
For we all like to read of romance at sea
And the Bounty should sail again."

Where came it from, this idea to write
About Christian and about Bligh?
Was it South Seas music that played in the night
Or had drinks made some Club member high?

Or was it the tiki that stared at us all
Or perhaps the old shrunken head?
I don't know, but I certainly felt the call;
My decision was: Full Speed Ahead.

My thanks then to all my Adventurer mates
For providing the spark for this book.

ACKNOWLEDGMENTS

Every member in my mind most surely rates
On a par with good old Captain Cook.

But I certainly could not have written this tale
Were it not for my faithful First Mate:
My wife can be counted on never to fail
And to work as a team's our fate.

Countless hours she spent hunting books for me
And in reading the manuscript, too.
That her love is as strong for ships and the sea
As my own, is abundantly true.

Rolf Du Rietz is the foremost of those who know
The true story of Bounty*'s ill fate.*
For his help, I now wish that fair winds'll blow
On his ship — and will never abate.

To Bengt Danielsson herewith a heartfelt thanks
For old friendship, now tried and true.
Among South Seas experts he certainly ranks
Number one, I don't need to tell you.

And others have helped, all too many to name,
Good friends all, with a common goal:
To promote the old story of Bounty*'s fame,*
To them all I direct my Skål!

To Tahitian friends a mauruuru *I give*
For their joy of life and their zest.
I will never forget them as long as I live;
Among friends they are surely the best.

Fletcher Christian and William Bligh, I say,
And also the crew of the ship
Have my thanks, and this is my simple way
To toast them: I'll do it with flip.

Hearty cheers to the Bounty *and to her crew*
And a toast to the South Seas also!
Their memory lingers in anyone who
Loves Adventure; I'm sure that you know.

So then lastly a toast to Adventure, mate
(That's the purpose of life, you'll agree),
To the thrill of challenging one's own fate
And to Friends, wherever they be!

Foreword

We have frequently been told that the mutiny in the *Bounty* cannot be considered an "important" historical event, and that the quantity of the literature dealing with it is out of all proportion to the real "importance" of the subject. However, the criteria for determining the degree of "importance" of historical events are usually rather vague, and the eternal competition for funds and academic status is very often allowed to influence our opinions as to the relative importance (or lack of importance) of various subjects. In the end, all questions dealing with the degree of "interest" and "importance" in scholarship are highly subjective matters of opinion. It is also reasonable to assume that intellectually sound scholars would not gladly waste precious time and effort on certain fields of research if they did not really find those fields "interesting" and "important" to themselves, and thus by implication, to at least some few other intellectually sound human beings.

Historians of scholarship, however, might agree that there is at least one objective criterion available in this context, namely, the "posthumous" importance that may be attached to an historical event merely through the actual quantity of the existing literature on the subject. The indisputable impact of the event on contemporary and later mankind is reflected in the literature relating to that event. The "importance" may thus be said to be created by the literature itself, the mere quantity of that literature bearing witness to the fact that the "mind of man" has found the subject to be "interesting," "fascinating," "significant," and "important." Independent scholars and researchers do not choose their subjects for the lack of those qualities, they choose their subjects because they find them attractive and maybe also saleable.

During the forty years I have been interested in the subject of the *Bounty* a very large number of books and articles have been added to the most considerable number that have been contributed in this field even before 1949 (when I first read Nordhoff & Hall's trilogy and thus became irrevocably "lost" in the subject for the remainder of my life). An alarming number of the books may be dismissed as potboilers, and some of them are downright irresponsible. But there have also appeared writings that have added most significantly to *Bounty*–Bligh–Pitcairn scholarship. None are flawless (such writings do not exist, of course), but some of them are very good indeed, and it is a pleasure to mention here accomplished scholars and writers such as Harry Maude, John Beaglehole, Andrew David, David Mackay, Alexander

McKee, Bengt Danielsson, and Glynn Christian. As for the pioneers, Owen Rutter and George Mackaness, *Bounty* scholars will always remain in debt to those two industrious enthusiasts, who laid the solid foundations of *Bounty* scholarship for all times to come.

Finland-born Californian writer Sven Wahlroos is now joining company with the persons listed above. He is well-read, he has a good deal of that uncommon quality common sense, he is an expert sailor, he is a great *Bounty* enthusiast, he is a kind, pleasant, charming man. One of his most valuable qualifications as a *Bounty* scholar is his close acquaintance with the Pacific islands: he has traveled widely in the South Seas, has visited Tahiti (many times), Tubuai, Pitcairn, and other islands central to the *Bounty* story, and he is familiar with the Tahitian language.

Last, but certainly not least, he is also a trained psychologist (that is how he has earned his living for the last thirty years). Now, the book he has written is by no means entirely devoted to the psychological aspects of the *Bounty*–Pitcairn drama (after all, it is a story of high adventure), but a good deal of his knowledge and experience as a professional psychologist has got into the book, and this I consider to be one of the most valuable features of his achievement. True, psychological writing is not an entirely new phenomenon in *Bounty* scholarship, but so far the results have not inspired confidence. The subject itself, however, is so psychologically fascinating, and is so full of tantalizing psychological problems, that competent psychological treatment has long been overdue. Now, at long last, Dr. Wahlroos enters the field, and I can only hope that he will return to it again and again and perhaps also find time to contribute one or two more detailed pieces for professional journals. The historian who specializes in *Bounty*–Pitcairn studies needs to know quite something of the human mind and of human behaviour in general, and no true *Bounty* enthusiast will be able to avoid a sense of exhilaration when balanced and responsible psychological scholarship is now beginning to be applied to the problems of the *Bounty*–Pitcairn drama.

Another feature in the present book that I consider most useful and rewarding is the strict chronology of the narrative section, enabling us to follow, month by exciting month, exactly what went on *simultaneously* on the various stages of the drama. Those stages were constituted by ships and boats, and by islands and cities, all widely scattered on the surface of the globe.

Another welcome aspect of this work is that Dr. Wahlroos — in contrast to most earlier writers of the *Bounty* story — chronicles the second breadfruit expedition which, of course, is of great relevance to the subject.

Invaluable to the reader of a book (or the viewer of a movie) about the *Bounty* mutiny is the "Bounty Encyclopedia" which forms the second part of the present work. This is the real "companion" feature of the book, giving us the background and more detailed information about the *dramatis personae* and about the islands and ships relevant to the story. In addition, Dr. Wahlroos gives us — often humorous, sometimes moving — explanations of nautical terminology and Tahitian words and concepts.

The mutiny took place 200 years ago. Today, the drama has long since faded into history, the participants, their friends and their relations are long since dead, and many (far too many!) of their journals and letters are apparently lost forever. It is to be hoped that those few things that can still be saved for posterity will be discovered and made available for those who need them for their research. Bengt Danielsson recently traced Bligh's cave on the island of Tofua. The Queensland Maritime Museum in Brisbane is painstakingly and expertly taking care of what remains of the wreck of the *Pandora*. Booksellers and collectors are trying to bring to light as yet hidden historical manuscripts relating to the voyages of the *Bounty* and the *Pandora* and to the early history of Pitcairn Island. Scholarly editors are making more and more surviving documents available to a wider public. But what wouldn't we be prepared to pay for but an hour's personal transfer back to the actual events, enabling us, at long last, to perceive what the persons involved really looked like, what words were actually said, what actions were really taken, what feelings were really burning, what realities were really prevailing — in the *Bounty*, in the launch, in the *Resource*, in the *Pandora*, in the *Providence*, on Tahiti, on Tofua, on Tubuai, on Pitcairn, or during the various courts-martial in Portsmouth! How much wouldn't we be willing to give for but a few minutes' intense conversation with Captain Peter Heywood, R.N., with James Morrison, with John Fryer, with Sir Joseph Banks, with the Rev. John Howell, with the ageing John Adams on Pitcairn, or with William Bligh, Fletcher Christian, and Edward Edwards themselves, perhaps even some of the Polynesian ladies who went ashore on Pitcairn in January 1790! The Polynesian version of the *Bounty*-Pitcairn drama has never been told, but how shall we find means ever to tell it, fully and reliably?

Sven Wahlroos enables us to advance a bit further in the historian's eternal struggle to recover as many fragments as possible of the lost past, of the sunken treasure-laden ships resting in deep, tantalizing silence on the dark floor of the immeasurable ocean of History.

Rolf E. Du Rietz
Uppsala, Sweden

Contents

Introduction

...🚢...

*W*hy has the story of the mutiny on the *Bounty* become so well known? Why have more than 2500 books and major articles been written about this truly minor event in the history of the world? Why have five feature-length motion pictures and dozens of documentary films been made about an occurrence which was insignificant in the annals of the British Admiralty? What is it about this tale that has touched so many millions of people all over the world?

The mutiny was not an important event from a military or political perspective. From the standpoint of the Admiralty, all that was lost was a small converted merchant ship loaded with plants and useless for fighting. The only reason why the Admiralty did send out a warship to hunt down the mutineers was that it would have set a dangerous precedent to let *any* uprising go unpunished.

The mutiny on the *Bounty* was not a spectacular event by any means. A truly spectacular mutiny with tremendous military and political implications occurred at the Nore (a naval anchorage at the mouth of the Thames) from May 12 to June 13, 1797, when *fifty thousand* seamen in *one hundred and thirteen* ships deposed their commanders and set up ships' democracies. But, with the exception of maritime history buffs, who has ever heard about the great mutiny at the Nore?

The *Bounty* mutiny was not a bloody or gruesome occurrence. The only physical violence involved was that Captain Bligh's fists got a little chafed by being bound too tightly. There was a great deal of verbal violence, of course, but much of it came from Bligh himself.

For a truly bloody and gruesome event, consider the mutiny on HMS *Hermione* on September 21, 1797. The commander of the 180 men on board was Captain Hugh Pigot, a true sadist who flogged his men frequently and severely for insignificant offenses and had killed at least two seamen with the cat-o'-nine-tails. He often shouted to the men in the rigging that the last man down would be flogged. A dozen men flogged in a day was not unusual on the *Hermione* under his command.

On one such occasion, three seamen fell from the topmast in their anxiety not to be last; one died immediately and two were badly injured. Captain Pigot ordered all three thrown overboard.

This atrocity triggered one of the bloodiest mutinies in history. Captain Pigot was hacked and slashed until he was dying and then thrown overboard screaming "Have mercy, my lads." Nine other officers were killed by the mutineers.

The Lords Commissioners of the Admiralty viewed this mutiny as so serious that they pardoned forty of the men who had not taken an active part in it on the condition that they seek out the mutineers and deliver them for trial and execution. For nine years these men combed the major harbors of the world to find the mutineers. The last one captured was hanged and gibbeted in 1804. Yet who — except for those knowledgeable in maritime history — has ever heard of the mutiny on the *Hermione*?

In contrast, almost all people who read books or watch movies know about — or have at least heard about — the mutiny on the *Bounty*. How can this be explained?

I think there are at least four important reasons for the worldwide and lasting fame of the story.

One reason is Tahiti. By the time the *Bounty* sailed for the South Seas, accounts of the Polynesian islands written by Wallis, Bougainville and Cook had been widely read, and Tahiti had already acquired the aura of romance and adventure that has lasted to this day. Despite its noisy freeway, its shopping centers, gasoline stations and international airport, Tahiti remains a symbol of romance. All you need to do is open the travel section of a newspaper and the enticing advertisements will immediately make you aware of the power and magic Tahiti has today as a romantic destination.

The *Bounty* story is inextricably tied in with Tahiti, so profoundly, in fact, that Captain Bligh was convinced, to his dying day, that the irresistible allure of that lovely island was the sole cause of the mutiny. Many of the books, articles and movies of today take the same position. Even though these publications and movies — and Bligh — are demonstrably wrong, as we shall see in this book, the romance of Tahiti still accounts for much of the spell the *Bounty* story casts on everyone who will listen to it.

Another reason for the fame of the story is Bligh's extraordinary feat in navigating the *Bounty*'s 23-foot launch — with a freeboard of only seven to eight inches — 3618 nautical miles from Tofua to Timor. This voyage will forever remain one of the most magnificent achievements in maritime history.

Bligh's narrative of the voyage appeared in June 1790 and immediately became a bestseller. Even though the biases and distortions and, especially, the omissions in his account of the mutiny and the open-boat voyage were eventually exposed, the undeniably superb navigational skill and the extraordinary seamanship he manifested on the voyage assured him a place in the annals of the sea. They also added a spectacular sequel to the mutiny.

A third reason for the everlasting fame of the mutiny is inherent in the secret dream most of us have had of one day finding an exotic desert island where we can create our own paradise, a perfect existence with happiness reigning forever.

The *Bounty* mutineers had the opportunity of realizing this dream when they landed on Pitcairn. It would have been hard to imagine a lovelier uninhabited island. It had everything a dream island should have: lush vegetation, fertile soil, water, delicious tropical fruits and — above all — exquisite beauty. Had it not been for the fact that some of the mutineers were brutal and ruthless troublemakers and scoundrels, the dream may to some extent have been fulfilled. Instead, the early years of settlement were filled with murder and mayhem, ending with the violent deaths of thirteen of the fifteen men who first set foot on the island.

Around the turn of the eighteenth century, ten years after the *Bounty* was burned, Pitcairn did become the paradise it could have been from the outset and — with the exception of a few unhappy years — has remained so until today. Those who have been fortunate enough to visit *Fenua Maitai* (The Good Land, the name given to the island by the Polynesians who arrived on the *Bounty*) can testify to the aura of romance that still permeates Pitcairn. That romantic aspect may not be so evident to the Pitcairners themselves who have to face the arcane daily problems of making a living on the most remote and isolated inhabited island in the world. But they still love Pitcairn.

The settlement of Pitcairn, the island that every true romantic dreams about, and today the last surviving British Crown Colony in the South Pacific, is an important reason for the *Bounty* epic remaining so vivid and fascinating to this day. The very name Pitcairn has become a symbol for the haunting attraction that the story of the *Bounty* continues to have on the adventurous mind.

A fourth reason for the surviving fame of the mutiny is the magnificent trilogy by Charles Nordhoff and James Norman Hall, published in the early 1930s: *Mutiny on the Bounty, Men Against the Sea,* and *Pitcairn's Island.* Even though their facts are sometimes wrong (we know more about the mutiny today than half a century ago), Nordhoff's and Hall's intuitive insight into the forces which caused the protagonists to act as they did is probably the closest we will ever come to an appreciation of the emotional reality of what happened. The Nordhoff and Hall story of the *Bounty* cuts straight through to our yearnings for adventure and romance, excitement and beauty; it carries us on the ship to the islands and makes us experience the adventures ourselves. It is this fulfillment of our secret dreams which causes the *Bounty* to sail forever.

The present volume is intended for *Bounty* buffs, those in the making and those already "hooked." Although it can stand on its own (the story is told fully in Part I), it has been conceived primarily as a *companion* to reading about the *Bounty.*

In Part I, "A *Bounty* Chronicle," the story is told month by month. As a result, the reader can find out what Fletcher Christian was doing while Captain Bligh sailed from Batavia to Cape Town, and what the *Bounty* men who remained on Tahiti were up to at the same time. Or we can learn about Bligh's activities in England while the *Pandora* was in the South Atlantic, and about what was happening with

Christian and his men on Pitcairn at that time. Part I gives a perspective to the story which I hope will enrich the reader's understanding of the events and contribute to his enjoyment.

Where there is not too much to report in a certain month, I may have focused on some aspects of the story that are usually not covered in the literature. Alternatively, I have tried to provide a new view of an event so that it appears in a different light from the traditional view, or so that the reader has a deeper understanding of the dynamics of the protagonists. Specifically, when it comes to the forces that accounted for the actions of Christian and Bligh, I have tried to draw on whatever expertise I have as a professional psychologist.

In Part II, "A *Bounty* Encyclopedia", I have attempted to give some background details which may not be readily available to the average reader: brief biographies of the personages involved, short descriptions of the ships and the islands, and some explanations of nautical terminology and Tahitian words and concepts. Part II, then, comprises the real "'companion" feature of the book.

"A Sample of Literature on the *Bounty* and Related Subjects" contains almost 600 titles. But for a truly comprehensive bibliography on the *Bounty* we will have to wait for the eminent Swedish historian and *Bounty* scholar, Rolf Du Rietz, to publish the results of his lifelong and exhaustive investigations of the literature.

Anyone who picks up this book and thinks that the word "romance" in the title refers to torrid love scenes will be disappointed. We do not know the details of the amorous relationships between the crew of the *Bounty* and the Polynesian women, so any such elaboration will have to be made by writers of fiction.

By the word "romance" in the title I mean the romance of adventure and of the South Seas, the kind of romance involved in the very idea of sailing in unknown waters, of making a landfall on a beautiful island, of getting to know exotic people with different customs; the romance that can be felt in the caress of the trade wind, in the sight of palms and lagoons and spray-enveloped reefs, in the sounds of Polynesian chants, and in the smell of Tiare Tahiti. A reader who can see romance in Polynesian names like Mauatua and Teehuteatuaonoa, or in ships' names like *Lady Penrhyn* and *Seringapatam*, or in islands like Rarotonga and Tematangi, will enjoy this book.

So, mate, set sail with me and let us embark on an expedition two hundred years back in time, a voyage that will lead us to Adventure!

PART I

A
Bounty
Chronicle

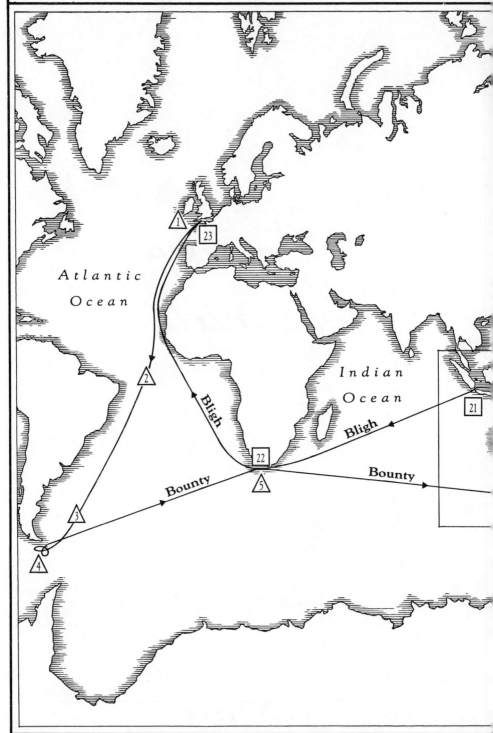

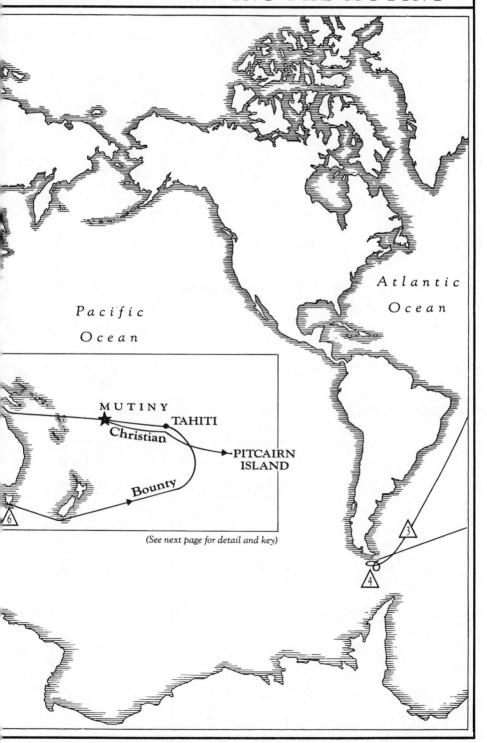

Atlantic

Ocean

Pacific

Ocean

MUTINY

TAHITI

Christian

PITCAIRN
ISLAND

Bounty

(See next page for detail and key)

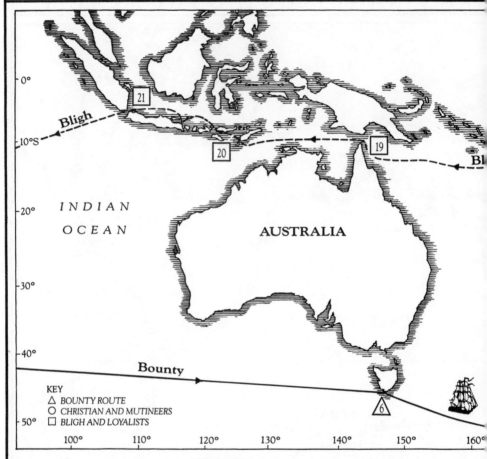

CHRONOLOGICAL MAP KEY FOR THE VOYAGE OF HMS *BOU*

Location or Event	*Bounty* Mission		Christian & Mutineers		Bligh & Loyalists		Remarks
	Arrive	*Depart*	*Arrive*	*Depart*	*Arrive*	*Depart*	
England	Start	12.23.87					*Bounty* sails (46 men)
Equator crossing	2.7.88	→					Traditional ceremonies
First flogging	3.11.88	→					Hard times begin
Cape Horn	3.24.88	4.22.88					Storm (No passage)
Cape of Good Hope (Cape Town)	5.22.88	7.1.88					Major repairs
Van Diemen's Land (Tasmania)	8.20.88	9.4.88					Supply stop
Bounty Islands	9.19.88	→					Discovered
Course change	10.3.88	→					For favorable winds
Tahiti	10.26.88	4.4.89					23 weeks (Breadfruit)
Aitutaki Island	4.11.89	→					Discovered
Nomuka Island (Annamooka)	4.23.89	→	[18 Mutineers —				Shore party (attacked)
Mutiny	April 28, 1789		12 Active]		[19 Men]		[7 Loyalists on *Bounty*]
Tubuai Island			5.30.89	5.31.89			First Refuge
			6.23.89	9.17.89			<Fort George>

KEY
△ BOUNTY ROUTE
○ CHRISTIAN AND MUTINEERS
□ BLIGH AND LOYALISTS

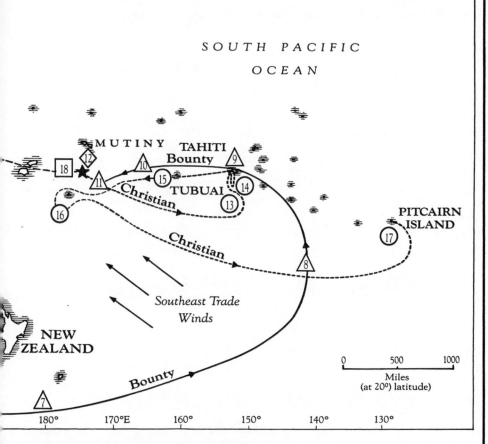

SOUTH PACIFIC

OCEAN

MUTINY TAHITI
Bounty

TUBUAI

PITCAIRN
ISLAND

Christian

Christian

Christian

Southeast Trade
Winds

NEW
ZEALAND

Bounty

0   500   1000

Miles
(at 20°) latitude)

180°   170°E   160°   150°   140°   130°

⊃ THE ROUTES OF BLIGH AND CHRISTIAN ✱

Location or Event	Bounty Mission		Christian & Mutineers		Bligh & Loyalists		Remarks
	Arrive	Depart	Arrive	Depart	Arrive	Depart	
Tahiti			6.5.89 9.22.89	6.18.89 9.23.89			Return to Tahiti <Supply stops>
Rarotonga			10/89	→			Discovered
Ono-I-Lau & Tongatabu Islands			11/89	12/89			Two days trading
Pitcairn Island			January 15, 1790				Bounty Burns on 23rd
Tofua Island					5.2.89	→	Supply stop
Cape York Peninsula (Australia)					6.3.89	→	Great Barrier Reef
Timor (Coupang)					6.14.89	8.20.89	Recuperation
Batavia (Djakarta)					10.1.89	10.16.89	Await passage home
Cape of Good Hope (Cape Town)					12.16.89	1.2.90	Await passage/write
England					3.14.90	Stop	Bligh Home (Trial begins)

✱(dates are in the 1700s)

Prologue

hen the British lost the American colonies, their possessions in the West Indies increased in importance. Almost all of England's sugar, for example, came from Caribbean islands under British rule.

The plantations in the West Indies used slave labor, and the feeding of the slaves was of course a major concern of the owners. Yams and bananas were staple foods, but banana trees were often destroyed by hurricanes. For bread, the islands were dependent on importing expensive corn from the American mainland.

When the early European explorers of the South Pacific came back from their voyages telling about bread growing on trees, the perfect solution seemed clear to the plantation owners: import this miraculous plant to the West Indies. There would then be no need to buy expensive flour and no more need for huge bakeries; all that was required was to pick the bread from the trees, roast it, and eat it!

Sir Joseph Banks, who had visited Tahiti on Cook's first voyage and who himself had large holdings in the West Indies, became enthusiastic about the project and — having access to the Court — soon interested George III in the project. The planned expedition was to be the first time the Royal Navy had engaged in a purely commercial venture.

The Admiralty did not have a ship which met the projected requirements of the expedition. For economic reasons the vessel had to be small, yet spacious enough to accommodate hundreds of breadfruit plants in addition to the crew. A cramped warship would not do; a suitable merchant ship had to be found.

Six ships were considered and of them, the *Bethia*, belonging to the family of Elizabeth Bligh, was chosen. It was renamed *Bounty* and Elizabeth's husband William was chosen, on August 16, 1787, to command the expedition.

Our story begins with an incident which happened a month before the departure of the *Bounty* for the South Seas.

November

1787

The *Bounty* was moored at Spithead outside Portsmouth getting readied for her long voyage to the South Seas. Most of the crew had been mustered, and master's mate Fletcher Christian, who was destined to become the world's most famous mutineer, had been on board since September.

A few weeks before the *Bounty* sailed, an event occurred which we have not known about until recently; it was discovered by Glynn Christian, a descendant of Fletcher's, in 1981, and reported in his book *Fragile Paradise* (1982).

On November 14, the East Indiaman *Middlesex* arrived in Spithead with Charles Christian, Fletcher's brother, his senior by two years, on board. In his eagerness to see his brother, Fletcher hired a small boat and boarded the *Middlesex* while she was still sailing. The brothers had always had a great deal of affection and respect for each other, and it is certain that they had many long discussions together before the *Bounty*, delayed by the bureaucratic slowness of the Admiralty, finally sailed at the end of December.

Why is this significant? Because Charles Christian, who had served as the ship's surgeon, had participated in a mutiny on the *Middlesex*! The mutiny had failed and the captain had regained control. If the ship had been part of the Royal Navy, Charles Christian may well have been hanged for his crime. However, the mutiny was not against the King, nor was it a civil offense since it took place on the high seas, and so Charles was merely suspended from the East India Company for two years.

It is difficult to believe that Charles and Fletcher Christian would not have had discussions on the topic of mutiny before the departure of the *Bounty*. This is not to imply that the discussions played a direct role in Fletcher Christian's decision one and a half years later to take over the *Bounty*. It is entirely possible, however, that the action of his brother could have influenced Fletcher's thinking, making the idea of mutiny something conceivable, rather than utterly unthinkable.

For hundreds of years the mere thought of mutiny had been dangerous. In the British Navy even a hint of it could be punished severely; in wartime it could lead to a sentence of death. But during the 1780s, mutiny was "in the air."

THE COMPLEMENT
OF
THE *BOUNTY*

Lieutenant William Bligh
COMMANDER

John Fryer
SAILING MASTER

William Cole
BOATSWAIN

William Peckover
GUNNER

William Purcell
CARPENTER

Thomas Huggan
SURGEON

Thomas Denman Ledward
SURGEON'S MATE

Fletcher Christian
MASTER'S MATE

William Elphinstone
MASTER'S MATE

Thomas Hayward
MIDSHIPMAN

John Hallett
MIDSHIPMAN

George Stewart
ACTING MIDSHIPMAN

Peter Heywood
ACTING MIDSHIPMAN

Edward Young
ACTING MIDSHIPMAN

Peter Linkletter
QUARTERMASTER

John Norton
QUARTERMASTER

George Simpson
QUARTERMASTER'S MATE

James Morrison
BOATSWAIN'S MATE

John Mills
GUNNER'S MATE

Charles Norman
CARPENTER'S MATE

Thomas McIntosh
CARPENTER'S CREW

Lawrence Lebogue
SAILMAKER

Joseph Coleman
ARMORER

Charles Churchill
MASTER-AT-ARMS
(Ship's Corporal)

John Samuel
CLERK AND STEWARD

Thomas Burkett
ABLE-BODIED SEAMAN

Michael Byrne
ABLE-BODIED SEAMAN
(Fiddler)

Thomas Ellison
ABLE-BODIED SEAMAN
(Boy)

Thomas Hall
ABLE-BODIED SEAMAN
(Ship's Cook)

Henry Hillbrant
ABLE-BODIED SEAMAN
(Cooper)

Robert Lamb
ABLE-BODIED SEAMAN
(Butcher)

Isaac Martin
ABLE-BODIED SEAMAN

William McCoy *
ABLE-BODIED SEAMAN

John Millward
ABLE-BODIED SEAMAN

William Muspratt
ABLE-BODIED SEAMAN
(Tailor and Assistant to the Cook)

Matthew Quintal
ABLE-BODIED SEAMAN

Richard Skinner
ABLE-BODIED SEAMAN
(Barber)

John Adams * *
ABLE-BODIED SEAMAN

John Smith
ABLE-BODIED SEAMAN
(Commander's Servant)

John Sumner
ABLE-BODIED SEAMAN

Robert Tinkler
ABLE-BODIED SEAMAN
(treated as acting midshipman)

Matthew Thompson
ABLE-BODIED SEAMAN

James Valentine
ABLE-BODIED SEAMAN

John Williams
ABLE-BODIED SEAMAN

David Nelson
BOTANIST

William Brown
GARDENER

* The name appears as Mickoy in the muster book of the *Bounty*. However, the descendants use the spelling McCoy, and I have therefore used it throughout this book.

** The name appears as Alexander Smith in the muster book. The real name was John Adams and that is how he is known on Pitcairn today. For that reason — and to avoid confusion with John Smith — the name Adams has been used throughout this book.

December
1787

To understand what Christmas must have been like on the *Bounty*, it is first necessary to consider the size of the ship. Those who visit the *Bounty* replica, which Dino de Laurentiis used for the 1983 movie, are generally struck by her smallness. It is difficult to imagine that she could have accommodated 46 men in addition to over 1000 breadfruit plants.

The *Bounty* was actually only 90 feet 10 inches long with a beam of 24 feet 4 inches. Her tonnage was given as 215.

Even her deck was crowded, because she carried three boats, one of which was 23 feet long. She had no superstructures. All nonsailing activities took place below and in virtual darkness since she had no portholes. The only light that seeped down came from the three-foot-wide hatches to the ladderways and they were open only when conditions allowed.

Light entered the main cabin from the stern windows, but this cabin was reserved solely for the storage of the breadfruit plants. For this purpose too, the size of the cabin had been almost trebled, from eleven feet to thirty, contributing to the incredibly cramped conditions on board.

The *Bounty* was actually both overcrowded and undermanned. Of the forty-six men on board nineteen were able-bodied seamen, and of those, only thirteen worked in the rigging.

After long delays, first because of the Admiralty's tardiness in sending Bligh his sailing orders and then because of contrary winds, the *Bounty* finally got under way on Sunday morning, December 23, 1787.

The atmosphere on board was permeated by excitement and anticipation among the crew, all of them volunteers. And of course there was a touch of melancholy, and even apprehension, among some of them; who could say when — or if — they would return? But there was nothing like an old shanty to keep such thoughts away. To quote from Alexander McKee's *H.M.S. Bounty* (1962):

As the men walked the capstan bars round, and the dripping anchor ropes came inboard, the half-blind Irish fiddler, Michael Byrn, struck up the traditional air, "Drops of Brandy," and the men hummed the words to themselves.

And Johnny shall have a new bonnet
And Johnny shall go to the fair,
And Johnny shall have a blue ribbon
To tie up his bonny brown hair.
And why should I not love Johnny
And why should not Johnny love me,
And why should I not love Johnny
As well as another bodie.

The weather was stormy. On the very first afternoon a seaman fell from a yard while unfurling the main t'gallant, but miraculously he managed to grab a stay and break his fall. On Christmas Eve it blew a full gale. By Christmas Day, however, the storm had abated somewhat and Christmas was celebrated with an extra issue of rum in addition to beef and plum pudding.

On Boxing Day the wind increased to full storm and on December 27 the stern windows collapsed under the weight of gale-driven water. The main cabin was flooded and the water broke an azimuth compass. Bligh could barely save the all-important chronometer and other instruments. There was a great deal of damage to the ship, but as far as the crew was concerned the greatest disaster was probably that seven full hogsheads of beer, lashed together on deck, had broken loose and gone overboard. In addition, two casks of rum had split and their contents were lost in the bilge.

The Christmas season was rough on the crew of the *Bounty*, but it paled by comparison with what awaited them at Cape Horn.

January

1788

...⛵...

The *Bounty* was sailing the Atlantic on a south-south-westerly course for Cape Horn. She stopped at Santa Cruz harbor, Tenerife, for five days to water and take on additional supplies; among these were several casks of "very good wine" (Madeira). Despite the additional provisions, Bligh cut the ship's company's allowance of bread by one third, justifying his decision by the fact that he planned to sail directly for Tahiti without stopping.

Bligh's character was an interesting mixture of highly admirable qualities and pernicious flaws. Certainly he was a man of great courage. He was also one of the finest navigators in maritime history and a superb cartographer. He was a man of boundless energy, had a strong sense of duty, and was totally dedicated to his profession. He was diligent and conscientious in the extreme and took every opportunity to add to the knowledge of the seas he traversed and the places he visited. There is no finer testimony to his qualities as a seaman than the fact that Captain Cook had selected him as sailing master of the *Resolution* on his third voyage.

But Bligh had a disastrous flaw in his character. Although in most respects he showed evidence of superior foresight, he had no understanding of the impact his frequent emotional outbursts and insulting accusations had on other people. He could call someone, even an officer, an "an infernal scoundrel" or a "contemptible thief" or an "incompetent mongrel" or a "cowardly rascal" in front of the whole ship's company, yet a short while later behave as if nothing had happened.

Language in the British Navy was rough. Swearing and cursing were common, even expected, so that was not the problem. The problem was that Bligh was a petty faultfinder who had a special knack of humiliating those with whom he found fault. Yet throughout his life he never realized this fact about himself. Long after the *Bounty* mutiny, in 1805, he was court-martialed for "oppression and *abusive language*," found guilty, and reprimanded. We can only imagine what it would have taken, in the harsh and authoritarian British Navy, for a post captain to be court-martialed for abusive language!

Another problem, seldom mentioned in the *Bounty* literature, was Bligh's appearance. He was short, chubby, and small-featured, his lips were of the "Cupid's bow" variety, his skin is variously described as pallid or like ivory or marble, his hair was short and curly, and his eyes were clear blue. The total impression was that of a doll. Additionally, Bligh's habit of wild gesticulation was unusual among the normally reserved British officer class. Yet, neither his appearance nor any of his mannerisms might have given him trouble if he had stayed calm. But his frequent and uncontrolled outbursts of temper, often over petty matters, made him look ridiculous rather than instilling respect.

Bligh admired and imitated his mentor, Captain James Cook. However, although Cook frequently lost his temper and was also petty at times, he always commanded the respect of those around him because of his commanding presence. Perhaps the most important difference between the two men was pointed out by David Howarth in his book *Tahiti: A Paradise Lost* (1983): "Cook looked for and brought out the best in men; Bligh looked for and brought out the worst."

Bligh's lack of understanding of his impact on others, his pettiness, and his very appearance must be taken into account in any serious attempt to explain the eventual mutiny.

February
1788

he ceremonies connected with crossing the equator stem back at least to the early 1500s. The custom seems to have originated on French ships (the oldest preserved account is dated 1529) but spread rapidly to other nations and survives in good health to this day. It was certainly firmly entrenched in the British Navy by the time HMS *Bounty* crossed the Line on her way to Cape Horn on February 7, 1788. Such ceremonies were often cruel procedures, but on the *Bounty* the event seems to have been all fun. Bligh would not allow the customary ducking (he considered it brutal), but the men were properly tarred and then shaved with a piece of an iron hoop. The officers had to pay forfeits of rum to the men (Bligh agreed to reimburse them) and there was a great deal of dancing to the fiddle of Michael Byrne, the almost blind seaman Bligh had signed on just for that purpose.

Undoubtedly all of the crew enjoyed the mildness of the horse latitudes after the cold storms they had just been through. And in his *Narrative* Bligh portrays the voyage to the Horn as a totally happy one. But the boatswain's mate, James Morrison, (who also wrote a narrative of the voyage) does not agree that all was well. In fact, according to Morrison, the now famous cheese incident had already taken place.

This incident was related to the fact that Bligh was not only captain of the ship but also purser. The Admiralty apparently expected him to make a profit from this position; they had reduced his salary precisely because he could make an extra income by being purser. To ensure everything would be fair, however, all supplies were to be opened in the presence of the whole ship's company. One day when a casket of cheese was opened, two cheeses were found to be missing. Instead of blaming this on the supplier (the suppliers were notoriously dishonest) and noting the fact in the log, Bligh for some inscrutable reason asserted that someone on board had stolen the cheeses. When a seaman named Hillbrant then ventured to say that the cheeses had been sent to Bligh's own residence on the orders of John Samuel, the ship's clerk and Bligh's personal servant, the captain flew into a rage and threatened to flog Hillbrant or anyone else making such allegations.

This was just the first of several similar episodes on board. It was important, however, in that it marked the beginning of a continuing diminution of respect for the captain among the crew — and the officers. In fact, it was just such an episode that triggered the eventual mutiny.

Hillbrant, a German, was the only crew member born in a non-English speaking country. There is a controversy, however, as to whether there were one or two Americans on board — if any at all. Isaac Martin, an able-bodied seaman who later ended up with Fletcher Christian on Pitcairn, was from Philadelphia. Most researchers accept that he was American, but the issue is confused by the existence of a small English community also called Philadelphia. In his book *Fragile Paradise*, Glynn Christian claims that Lawrence Lebogue, the sailmaker, was from Annapolis, USA, but I do not know his source for this allegation, nor have I encountered it elsewhere.

March

1788

... 🚢 ...

*T*hree significant events occurred on the *Bounty* in March, 1788: Bligh promoted Christian to acting lieutenant, able-bodied seaman Matthew Quintal was flogged, and the attempt to round the Horn had an inauspicious start in heavy gales off Tierra del Fuego.

The subject of punishment on board is important because so much of the popular *Bounty* literature — and four of the five motion pictures — have portrayed Bligh as a cruel commander, a monster who took pleasure in having his men flogged. Nothing could be further from the truth.

The Royal Navy of two hundred years ago was indeed a cruel institution, much more so than the Army. In fact, one of the most feared punishments in the Army was to be transferred to the Navy. Not only were seamen flogged mercilessly for minor infractions, but, as described by Scott Claver in his *Under the Lash* (1954), individual commanders actually designed their own instruments of torture to keep crews in line.

Floggings of one hundred lashes or more were not unusual. In fact, as late as 1807, George III saw fit to intervene in Navy affairs by setting an upper limit of one thousand lashes! Bligh is not known to ever have punished any member of his crew with more than four dozen lashes — and that was for desertion (for which the sentence was often death by hanging).

The frequently reviled Bligh was actually not as harsh a commander as the widely respected Cook. In the seventeen months that Bligh was in command of the *Bounty*, he ordered eleven floggings with a total of 229 lashes. Cook flogged at the rate of once or twice a week. (Even when we take into account that Cook had a larger crew, it is still clear that he flogged more frequently than Bligh.)

The two dozen lashes that Matthew Quintal had to endure on March 11, 1788, were for "insolence and mutinous behavior" toward the sailing master, John Fryer. Many captains of the time would have given Quintal an even stiffer punishment.

There are some *Bounty* researchers who feel that the mutiny, far from being caused by Bligh's cruelty, was partially due to his softness when it came to corporal punishment. To what extent such an allegation is valid is always debatable. What is not debatable is that, as far as corporal punishment is concerned, Bligh was less harsh than most of the Navy commanders of his time. It was not his physical cruelty but, rather, his humiliating tongue — in an era when a man's honor was more important than his life — that contributed heavily to the most famous mutiny of all time.

April

1788

...⛵...

The *Bounty* was engaged in a desperate attempt to round Cape Horn against prevailing westerly gales. A letter written from Cape Town by midshipman Peter Heywood gives some idea of what it must have been like:

> During the 29 days we were beating off the Cape, we had to encounter the most violent storms that I suppose were ever experienced. I suppose there never were seas, in any part of the known world, to compare with those we met for height, and length of swell; the oldest seamen on board never saw anything equal to them, yet Mr. Peckover (our gunner) was all three voyages with Captain Cook.

A less duty-conscious captain than Bligh would have given up much sooner. When Bligh finally did give up, it was primarily because he simply did not have enough men left to work the rigging. He wrote:

> Having maturely considered all circumstances, I determined to bear away for the Cape of Good Hope; and at five o'clock on the evening of the 22d [of April, 1788], the wind then blowing strong at W, I ordered the helm to be put aweather, to the great joy of every person on board. Our sick list at this time had increased to eight . . .

One of the eight was the ship's surgeon, Dr. Huggan; the others were seamen. Since there were only thirteen able-bodied seamen to man the rigging in the first place, this would have left only six men to handle the sails which were so weighted down by snow and ice and so stiff that it was well-nigh impossible to haul them up to be furled. The men were exhausted and weakened and their hands were bleeding. Bligh, in fact, had no choice but to give up.

Bligh was a superb foul-weather captain and a poor fair-weather captain. When things were rough, he showed his best qualities: bravery, excellent seamanship, strong sense of duty, resolution, perseverance and concern for his men. In fair weather, on the other hand, his worst qualities came to the fore: he was prissy and intolerant, petty and irritable, insulting and humiliating, picky and condescending.

The mutiny, which took place a year after the storms of Cape Horn, did not occur as a result of the crew having gone through any physical hardships. On the contrary, by that time everyone on board had experienced almost half a year of a paradisiacal existence on Tahiti, and the weather after leaving the island had been perfect. The mutiny, in fact, took place in the most wonderful tropical weather imaginable. But Bligh had also been on his very worst "fair-weather behavior" in the preceding weeks.

May

1788

*T*he *Bounty* was now sailing eastward from Cape Horn to the Cape of Good Hope. For almost the whole voyage there was a strong westerly wind which often propelled the ship to her maximum speed of nine knots (although midshipman Heywood tells us that she sometimes went to ten). Everyone on board was happy to get away from the storms of Cape Horn, but there was also a great deal of frustration: the *Bounty* was as far from Tahiti as when she had first sailed from England, so four months of incredible hardship and effort had been completely futile.

Table Mountain was sighted on May 22 and the next evening the ship anchored in False Bay (now known as Simonstown) for extensive repairs. The *Bounty* had to be completely recaulked; the leaks she had sprung at Cape Horn were so bad that it had been necessary to man the pumps every hour for the whole voyage to the Cape of Good Hope. The rigging and the sails also needed to be completely overhauled and, since large amounts of supplies had been damaged, there was a lot of reprovisioning to be done. All in all the *Bounty* spent 38 days refitting, which gives some idea of the damage she had received at the Horn.

The delay was certainly not due to any inefficiency or lack of assistance on the part of the authorities. Nearby Cape Town, from which the materials and supplies were obtained, had been established in 1652 by the Dutch East India company and was run very efficiently by the Dutch settlers.

The composition of the *Bounty*'s crew makes an interesting study. The first thing that is striking is that — contrary to what we see in the 1935 movie — there were no pressed men on board. Actually, the *Bounty* is thought to have been the first ship in the Royal Navy to sail without pressed men. The fact that all were volunteers is something that needs to be taken into account when evaluating the subsequent mutiny. Volunteers are more likely to be footloose and adventurous or dissatisfied with their present states of affairs than are men who are forcibly taken from their families and daily routines.

The crew was also very young. At the time of the departure, no one was older than forty and there were three fifteen-year-olds on board (midshipmen Heywood and Hallett and the "boy" Ellison). The average age of the ship's complement was 26.4 years. An age comparison between the future mutineers and the loyalists shows that the average age of future mutineers was 24.2 years and of loyalists 28 years.

Whether this difference is significant or not is debatable, but the loyalists almost certainly included a much greater proportion of married men. The records are unclear when it comes to the marital status of the crew members, but, as far as can be ascertained, there may have been only one married man who remained on board the *Bounty* at the time of the mutiny (carpenter's mate Charles Norman), and he was forcibly retained by Christian.

Several of the crew had sailed with Bligh before. Master's mate Christian, quartermaster Norton, sailmaker Lebogue, and able-bodied seaman Ellison had all been with Bligh on the *Britannia*. The gunner Peckover, and the botanist Nelson, had both been with Bligh on Cook's third voyage (although they had sailed in different ships: Bligh in the *Resolution*, Peckover and Nelson in the *Discovery*). Of the six, only Christian and Ellison became mutineers.

$\mathcal{June}$

1788

... ⛵ ...

$\mathcal{T}$he *Bounty* spent the whole month of June 1788 refitting and provisioning at False Bay. Most of the literature on the mutiny dismisses this period with a few sentences. Yet it is possible that something occurred during this time that has a bearing on the causes of the mutiny.

In 1825, John Adams, the only surviving mutineer on Pitcairn, told Captain Beechey of HMS *Blossom* that Christian had been under some obligation to Bligh, and that their "original quarrel" had happened at the Cape of Good Hope and "was kept up until the mutiny occurred" to a greater or lesser extent.

Christian was of course obligated to Bligh for two reasons before the arrival at Cape Town: for having been posted to the *Bounty* in the first place and for his promotion to acting lieutenant. But what could have happened at Cape Town that started a long-term quarrel?

In his book *Fragile Paradise*, Glynn Christian proposes that the dispute was about money. Fletcher's family had lost its fortune before the departure of the *Bounty* and it is probable that Fletcher was in need of money. In examining Bligh's papers in the Mitchell Library in Sydney, Glynn Christian discovered that Bligh had indeed lent money to Christian in Cape Town.

Considering what money can do to undermine a friendship, and keeping in mind that the party under obligation not infrequently becomes hostile to the benefactor, this could have been what Adams referred to in his statement to Beechey. It should be added that Christian had shown himself to be highly conscious of his dignity and his competence, and the respect and recognition he felt he deserved. We know that when he first sought a position with Bligh in the *Britannia*, he asked to be entered as a midshipman (not an unreasonable request, since he had essentially performed the duties of a lieutenant on HMS *Eurydice*). However, he had to settle for the formal position of a gunner (although he was actually treated as a midshipman). On the second voyage with Bligh in the *Britannia* he was promoted to second mate.

Bligh was an astute business man, a highly acquisitive person, and always on the lookout for a profit or a saving. In a letter from Cape Town addressed to his wife's uncle, Duncan Campbell, he wrote:

My transactions here have enabled me to realize a little cash, for which I beg leave to transmit to you an indorsed Bill to you by Christoffel Brand, Esqr. on the Victualling Board for 1,236 Rix Dollars which will be paid immediately as it becomes due.

To get an idea of the value of 1236 Rix Dollars, we can compare the amount with what Bligh later paid for the 34-foot schooner *Resource* in Coupang in July 1789 — 1000 Rix Dollars. There was probably no harm in Bligh's transactions in Cape Town but we know that he was ruthless when it came to money, especially in the case of loans, as exemplified by his treatment of acting surgeon Ledward in Batavia (see the November 1789 commentary).

Considering Bligh's and Christian's personality characteristics from the perspective of a clinical psychologist, I would venture the following observations, based on what we know of their behavior.

Bligh probably did not have any clear-cut mental or emotional illness, but he did show prominent compulsive, narcissistic, histrionic and somewhat paranoid tendencies. A major part of his interpersonal problems lay in his almost total lack of understanding of the emotional impact he had on others. His focus was always on himself.

However, if Bligh had developed an emotional or mental illness, he would have been either untreatable or extremely difficult to treat — the issue is of course academic, since a century was still to pass before the birth of psychotherapy. The reason for such a gloomy prognosis is simply that Bligh could not conceive of any imperfections in himself: he felt he had absolutely nothing to do with the misfortunes that befell him during his life. As Richard Humble put it in his *Captain Bligh* (1976):

> . . . a man who is *pathologically unable* to accept imperfection is a permanent martyr to himself: he has an enormous cross to bear. Bligh was such a man. But he had quite enough human weaknesses to make serious mistakes, and he was not only unable to face up to this, he recoiled from the very idea. From this mental block sprang his tendency to arrogance and diversion of the blame on to others; whatever went wrong, it could never be his fault. Inconsistent though he was, he was never inconsistent in this.

In other words, a psychotherapist's nightmare!

Christian, on the other hand, may have suffered from what today would be called borderline personality disorder. Note the clinical description of this condition:*

> Interpersonal relations are often intense and unstable with marked shifts of

---

Diagnostic and Statistical Manual of Mental Disorders, Third Edition, Revised (Washington: American Psychiatric Association, 1987).

attitude over time. Frequently there is impulsive and unpredictable behavior that is potentially physically self-damaging. . . . The borderline person will often go from idealizing a person to devaluing him.

This fits Christian and would partially explain why he alone reacted so drastically to Bligh's humiliating tongue-lashings, of which there were many other victims. These victims — especially sailing master John Fryer in the *Bounty* and first lieutenant Francis Bond in the *Providence* — must often have felt just as humiliated as Christian but, being more stable and level-headed, did not react aggressively or self-destructively to the provocations.

For the sake of completeness, it should be pointed out that Bligh described Christian as sweating profusely, so that he "soils anything he handles." On the basis of this description, H. S. Montgomerie in his book *William Bligh of the Bounty in Fact and in Fable* (1937) suggested that Christian suffered from hyperhidrosis, a condition "often associated with mental instability." A less speculative interpretation of the sweating would be that Christian was simply a very emotionally reactive man, and the tendency to perspire easily was part of the bodily adjustments associated with processes in the autonomic nervous system. It is well known, for example, that sweating would be expected in an individual who is tense, physically active, and experiencing stress.

July
1788

On July 1, 1788, Bligh left False Bay and set an east-south-easterly course for Adventure Bay in Van Diemen's Land (now Tasmania). This, the longest leg on the voyage to Tahiti, was well over 6000 miles. By the end of the month, having had strong westerly winds most of the time, the *Bounty* sighted St. Paul Island, actually just a little rock which Bligh wanted to reach on his way in order to test his navigational skill (superb as always).

This part of the voyage was essentially uneventful and I will therefore devote this commentary to a discussion of the general atmosphere of unrest and the quest for freedom from oppression, which were spreading in Europe in the last decades of the eighteenth century and ultimately led to several insurrections and mutinies.

This movement received tremendous impetus from an event which could be said to be distantly related to the mutiny on the *Bounty* — the American revolution. The mutiny of the American colonies (as it was viewed in England) had enormous repercussions in Europe, having demonstrated that it was possible to overthrow an authority that was unresponsive to its subjects' will. One consequence was the strengthening of republican sentiments in England, especially through the writings of Thomas Paine. Paine's *Common Sense,* which had played an important role in the American revolution, was also widely read and discussed in England, and this at a time when literacy was spreading among the "lower" classes. We do not know how many of the seamen on the *Bounty* could read, but it must have been a significant number, as shown by the fact that Bligh put his rules for the crew's expected conduct in Tahiti in writing and had them nailed to the foremast. It should be remembered too that probably at least one crew member of the *Bounty*, Isaac Martin, a future mutineer (and perhaps one more, Lawrence Lebogue, a loyalist), was American. We can be sure that not only the officers but also the able-bodied seamen on board had been exposed to discussions of ideas which challenged the rights — indeed the very existence — of royal authority and its manifestations in the Navy.

This, then, was a time when mutiny was "in the air." Many respected men openly advocated a political revolution. Robert Burns, for example, when called upon to toast William Pitt, the then prime minister, instead proposed a toast to George Washington, "a better man!"

The tendency was evident on the continent as well as in England. Strong anti-monarchistic forces were operating in France, culminating in the storming of the Bastille only a few months after the mutiny on the *Bounty*. There had been severe riots in the Austrian Netherlands. In 1780 the worst riots in British history — then and now — had taken place, during which 50,000 people had stormed Parliament; more than 700 were killed. During these so-called Gordon riots (named for Lord George Gordon who led the mob) a third of London was destroyed or damaged and not just one bastille, but *five*, were stormed and the prisoners let free: Newgate, the Fleet, Bridewell, King's Bench, and the Borough Clink.

In January 1788 the First Fleet, its transport ships crowded with convicted criminals, landed in Australia. The fleet had left England some months before the *Bounty* and it is interesting to note that the main reason for deporting the convicts was the overcrowding of the prisons and the concomitant fear of prison mutinies.

There had also been mutinies in the Navy. In fact, the harsh and unfeeling Captain Edward Edwards — who was to become known for capturing the *Bounty* men who remained on Tahiti — had been the object of a mutiny in 1782. And only eight years after the *Bounty* mutiny, in 1797, the biggest insurrection in naval history, the mutiny at the Nore, occurred. In this momentous event, as we mentioned in the Introduction, over 50,000 men serving in 113 ships refused to obey orders, expelled their officers, and set up ships' democracies.

It is quite ironic in this connection that William Wilberforce, member of Parliament and William Pitt's good friend, founded his Abolition Society (the main purpose of which was to terminate slavery in the West Indies) in 1787, the very year when the *Bounty* set out on an expedition designed to make ownership of slaves more cost-effective.

August
1788

ifty-one days out of False Bay, on August 20, 1788, Bligh sighted Mewstone Rock outside Adventure Bay in Van Diemen's Land. This was a remarkable feat of navigation considering the equipment then available.

Bligh wooded and watered in the bay and planted fruit trees and vegetables for the use of aborigines as well as for future ships. The stay would have been uneventful had it not been for an incident which dealt a severe blow to his authority.

William Purcell, the cantankerous and argumentative ship's carpenter, had been ordered to assist with hoisting water into the hold but refused "in a most insolent and reprehensible manner" on the grounds that, as a warrant officer, he could not be made to do the work of a common seaman. Technically Purcell was within his rights, but refusal to obey an order was still a severe offense, second only to outright mutiny. In home waters, he could have been severely punished; in time of war he could have been hanged. Everyone on board the *Bounty* must have expected that the carpenter would be in serious trouble.

Bligh, however, was faced with a dilemma. If Purcell had been an ordinary seaman, he would have been flogged and that would have put an end to the matter. But as a warrant officer Purcell could not be flogged without the authority of a court-martial. He could be put in irons until the ship returned to England where he could be tried, but the *Bounty* was not due back for another fifteen months and Bligh needed the skills of the carpenter for the successful outcome of his expedition.

In the end Bligh decided to withhold provisions from Purcell until he agreed to obey orders. The carpenter was "immediately brought to his senses," but denial of provisions was no punishment for mutinous behavior and everyone on board knew it. There is a vast psychological difference between a negative incentive and a punishment. One is a method of persuasion, blackmail in a sense, the other an enforcement of discipline.

In order to assert his authority and preserve discipline on board, Bligh should have put Purcell in irons, at least until the arrival in Tahiti. As it was, he was to be plagued with continuous problems from Purcell who was something of a "sea lawyer" and knew exactly how far he could go in insisting on his rights without getting into serious trouble.

When the mutiny took place, Purcell joined the loyalists who went with Bligh. But during the long and heroic voyage in the small launch from Tofua to Timor Bligh must often have wished that his carpenter had remained on the ship, because he continued his peskiness to the end. When he returned to England Purcell was highly instrumental in helping Fletcher Christian's older brother, Edward, in the latter's efforts to bring out those antecedents to the mutiny that Bligh had left out of his account. (As a result of Bligh's charges against him, Purcell was the only one of the loyalists to be court-martialed on their return; he received only a reprimand.) It may also be of interest to note that Purcell seems to have ended his days in an insane asylum.★

No doubt the officers and crew alike talked a great deal about the highly unusual occurrence of orders being disobeyed in the Royal Navy with no resulting punishment of the culprit. It must have had a negative effect on the discipline on board and on the crew's perception of Bligh as a commander.

★Sir John Barrow, in *The Eventful History of the Mutiny and Piratical Seizure of H.M.S. Bounty* (1831) states: "Purcell is said to be at this time in a madhouse." George Mackaness, in *The Life of Vice-Admiral William Bligh* (1951) quotes an obituary notice in the *Gentleman's Magazine* (in 1834): "March 10th, 1834, at Haslar Hospital, Mr. William Purcell, the last survivor of the *Bounty*."

September

1788

... 🚢 ...

*B*ligh left Adventure Bay in Van Diemen's Land on September 4, 1788. He rounded the southern tip of New Zealand and discovered thirteen small rocky islands which to this day are called the Bounty Isles. The *Bounty* was now heading for Tahiti with no further landfalls. On that beautiful island the main objective of the expedition, the breadfruit, was growing in abundance on countless trees.

Breadfruit (in Tahitian *'uru*) is a roundish-shaped fruit some four to eight inches in diameter. The color of the skin is green to brownish green and the inside is composed of a white, somewhat fibrous pulp. It grows on a tall (30–60 feet) tree with large, dark-green, leathery leaves. The breadfruit cannot be eaten raw. Traditionally, it was baked in ground ovens or roasted over hot coals, but today it is often steamed or fried. It tastes like something between potato and bread.

The breadfruit does not propagate through seeds but through shoots, and that is why the ship had to be modified rather drastically to accommodate all the pots for the shoots. The overcrowded condition which resulted certainly was one of the factors that played a role in the subsequent mutiny.

There are several varieties of breadfruit, the two best known being *Artocarpus incisa* and *Artocarpus altilis*. It first became known to Europeans during the voyage of Mendana de Neyra in 1598. William Dampier praised its food value in his *New Voyage Around the World* in 1697. But it was the popularity of Hawkesworth's account (1773) of Cook's first voyage that aroused real interest in the breadfruit plant. Later, in 1776, the Swedish botanist on that voyage, Dr. Daniel Solander, lauded it as "one of the most useful vegetables in the world."

Following the loss of its North American colonies, it was clearly in England's interest to have the West Indies less dependent on North America for food. And as far as feeding the slaves was concerned, it was of course desirable that the food be nutritious, cheap, and easily obtainable.

As far as we know, the first person to advocate the transplantation of the breadfruit to the West Indies was Valentine Morris who, in 1771, was appointed Captain-

General of the British West Indies. Being a friend of Sir Joseph Banks, who was later to become President of the Royal Society, Morris turned to him with his proposal. Banks, who himself had extensive holdings in the West Indies and was a botanist besides (he had also been on Cook's first voyage), embraced the idea with enthusiasm and elicited the support of George III.

So enthusiastic were some of the promoters of the project that Dr. Betham (Bligh's father-in-law), for example, compared the importance of the expedition to Sir Walter Raleigh's bringing the potato plant from Virginia to Great Britain. Bligh may or may not have shared this enthusiasm, but there is no doubt that he saw the project as important, perhaps for the good of England or the furtherance of his career, or both.

Long afterwards, even Lord Byron would write a poem on the subject, one of the worst that ever flowed from his pen, *The Island, or Christian and his Comrades*:

> *The Breadtree, which, without the ploughshare, yields*
> *The unreap'd harvest of unfurrow'd fields,*
> *And bakes its unadulterated loaves*
> *Without a furnace, in unpurchased groves,*
> *And flings off famine from its fertile breast,*
> *A priceless market for the gathering guest.*

Such a poem deserves a mutiny.

$$\mathscr{O}ctober$$

$$1788$$

...⛵...

$\mathscr{T}$he *Bounty* was sailing eastward in the Roaring Forties on her voyage from Adventure Bay to Tahiti. On October 3, 1788, being by that time south-east of the Society Islands, Bligh changed to a northerly course in order to catch the south-east trades and so sail westward to fetch Tahiti.

On Thursday, October 9, the expedition experienced its first casualty: one of the most robust of the able-bodied seamen, James Valentine, died. The cause of his death was blood poisoning which had set in after he had been bled — for a "slight indisposition" — by the alcoholic ship's surgeon, Thomas Huggan. Bligh was furious, because he had not even been told that Valentine was gravely ill until three days earlier. The incident illustrates how extremely isolated Bligh was, even from his officers, and how little he knew about what happened on board his ship, even though it was so small.

The very same day an incident took place which tended to further undermine Bligh's discipline, already damaged by the carpenter's open defiance of his captain's orders while the *Bounty* was at Adventure Bay. This time it was none other than the sailing master, John Fryer, who openly defied Bligh.

Fryer had not got along with Bligh ever since the latter had promoted Christian to acting lieutenant in March, 1788. Christian had not been promoted "over the head" of Fryer, as some students of the *Bounty* history have claimed. The distinguished *Bounty* scholar, Rolf Du Rietz, has pointed out that masters were promoted by rate, not by rank, and were never expected to become acting lieutenants when at sea. Nevertheless, it may have irked Fryer to be subordinate to Christian because of the latter's age (Fryer was thirty-three, Christian twenty-three).

Contrary to common *Bounty* lore, Fryer appears to have been (as Du Rietz has pointed out) a very competent man, and we know that Bligh could not tolerate any rivalry in competency on board his ships. He took every opportunity to "put down" officers who measured up to his own skills and talents. On the other hand, the master, a few years senior to Bligh, was not a man who easily accepted insults to his dignity and by late September he had declined to continue dining with Bligh. On October 9 he brought matters to a head by refusing to sign the monthly expense books unless Bligh would sign a certificate confirming Fryer's good behavior during the voyage so far.

Bligh would not stand for any conditional obedience. He had the ship's company assembled on deck and read the Articles of War. Fryer signed, but not before he had made clear — in a loud voice — that "I sign in obedience to your orders, but this may be canceled hereafter."

This, then, was the second time a warrant officer had openly defied Bligh in front of the whole crew. (The boatswain's mate, Morrison, says in his narrative that this was only one of many conflicts between Bligh and Fryer before the arrival in Tahiti.)

Another instance of disobedience was recorded ten days later when the gunner's mate, John Mills, and the botanist's assistant, William Brown, refused to take part in the daily dancing that Bligh had ordered for exercise. Both had their grog stopped, a punishment second only to flogging in severity.

In the early morning of Saturday, October 25, having altered course to the west, the *Bounty* sighted the small island of Mehetia (then populated, but now uninhabited), 70 miles east of Tahiti. Tahiti was sighted in the evening, and on Sunday morning, fifty-two days out of Van Diemen's Land, the ship dropped anchor in Matavai Bay surrounded by hundreds of outrigger canoes filled with wildly shouting and waving Tahitians. They soon climbed on board "in vast numbers," so that Bligh "could scarce find my own people." The total distance the *Bounty* had sailed since leaving England on December 23, 1787, was 27,086 miles by the log (108 miles for each 24 hours).

November 1788

The *Bounty* had arrived at one of the most beautiful islands in the world. The cloud-enveloped peaks of the towering mountains of Tahiti had been seen from far away, grandiose and green with graceful waterfalls cascading into the lush valleys. The spectacular, spray-spewing, thunderous reefs, the gentle emerald lagoons, the tender and beckoning palm-studded beaches, the haunting, exotic fragrance of the flowers wafting far out to sea, all blended into an experience never to be forgotten, a treasure to keep for the rest of one's life.

No one on board the *Bounty* except for Bligh, Nelson, and Peckover, all of whom had been there before, had ever seen such beauty. And yet, the physical characteristics of the island were as nothing compared with those of the inhabitants. Alexander McKee (in his *H.M.S. Bounty*, 1962) quotes an early account describing the Tahitians:

> The shape of the face is comely; the cheekbones are not high, neither are the eyes hollow, nor the brow prominent; the nose is a little, but not much, flattened; but their eyes, and more particularly those of the women, are full of expression, sometimes sparkling with fire, and sometimes melting with softness; their teeth also are, almost without exception, most beautifully even and white, and their breath perfectly without taint. In their motions there is at once vigour as well as ease; their walk is graceful, their deportment liberal, and their behaviour to strangers and to each other affable and courteous. In their dispositions they appear to be brave, open, and candid, without suspicion or treachery, cruelty or revenge.

To this should be added the extraordinary kindness and hospitality described by George Hamilton, the surgeon of the *Pandora*:

> A native of this country divides every thing in common with his friend, and the extent of the word friend, by them, is only bounded by the universe, and was he reduced to his last morsel of bread, he cheerfully halves it with him; the next that comes has the same claim, if he wants it, and so in succession

to the last mouthful he has. Rank makes no distinction in hospitality; for the king and beggar relieve each other in common.

Despite the onslaughts of all the representatives of modern civilization — beachcombers, whalers, missionaries, bureaucrats, frustrated artists, and spoiled tourists — the Tahitians have not lost the characteristics described above. It is difficult to imagine the "culture shock" the seamen of the *Bounty* must have experienced when they arrived on the island. At least half of the ship's complement came from poor and squalid circumstances where harshness and inhumanity were taken for granted. Suddenly they were confronted with the gentlest people in the world, handsome, beautiful, intelligent, compassionate, tactful, fun-loving, meticulously clean, and aristocratic in bearing. And this in a surrounding which to this day is described as the most beautiful in the world.

Even the climate was heavenly compared to the cold rains and the fogs of England. There were no poisonous insects, not even mosquitoes at that time, and no dangerous animals. And the sailors of the *Bounty* were to stay in this paradise for almost half a year! Moreover, the Tahitians welcomed their European visitors even though they were dirty and stank to high heaven, had coarse manners and often behaved in a cruel manner. Only a week after the *Bounty*'s arrival, the islanders received a lesson in European civilization. On November 3, 1788, Bligh writes:

> Several petty thefts having been committed by the natives owing to the negligence and inattention of the Petty Officers and men, which has always more or less a tendency to alarm the chiefs, I was under the necessity this afternoon to punish Alex^r Smith 12 lashes for suffering the gudgeon of the larger cutter to be drawn out without knowing it.

The flogging took place despite the entreaties of the Tahitians that Bligh show mercy.

The islanders certainly admired their guests for their high technical accomplishments, but they could not get over the latter's strange spiritual beliefs. How could the *popa'a*s (as they did, and still do, call the whites) have a god who was not married and yet had a son who also did not have a wife?

The sex-starved men of the *Bounty* had no trouble finding lovely accommodating Tahitian *vahines*. (In Tahitian, *vahine* means woman and *tane* means man.) Many of the crew members, perhaps most, had never known any other women than the garishly painted coarse prostitutes of the harbors; now, for the first time, they experienced what a loving relationship with a woman could be like.

Soon each member of the ship's company also had his *taio* or *hoa* (special friend) which meant that he had the use of the latter's house and possessions, including his wife. Being treated like kings, with lovely *vahines* all around who had no sexual inhibitions, with abundant, delicious food, and with exciting entertainment, the crew members were in for twenty-three weeks of paradisiacal existence. This fact plays a decisive role in explaining why Christian later found as many followers as he did at the time of the mutiny.

When Bligh had visited Tahiti with Cook eleven years earlier, he had met the chief of the neighboring district of Pare who had then called himself Tu, but who now bore the name Teina. Bligh had no difficulty persuading Teina that a large quantity of breadfruit would be a good way of repaying King George for the gifts he had sent along with Bligh.

Christian was put in charge of shore operations and a camp was established on Point Venus, a peninsula forming the eastern shore of Matavai Bay. On November 7, 1788, work began on collecting breadfruit plants. The work was apparently very easy. In just eight days, 774 shoots, all that there was room for in the main cabin, had been collected.

Then why did Bligh stay on Tahiti for five and a half months? Students of the *Bounty* story can only speculate since, unfortunately, Bligh gives no reason for it in his log. Dr. Bengt Danielsson, one of the world's foremost experts on the *Bounty* adventure, has given what is probably the simplest and most plausible explanation for Bligh's delay. Bligh's orders called for him to sail home through Endeavour (now Torres) Straits, and Bligh was a person who followed orders, no matter what. These dangerous straits, however, could not be negotiated during the period of November to April, since the winds then blew constantly from a westerly direction. Moreover, this was also the hurricane season when, even today, smaller craft tend to avoid voyages in the South Pacific.

I do think there is an additional reason, however. Bligh was a very conscientious person — compulsive, in fact — and he wanted to be double-sure and triple-sure that enough plants would survive the voyage to the West Indies. So he waited until he was certain that the shoots had taken root properly. On at least one occasion he made the botanist, David Nelson, throw away a number of actually healthy plants merely on the suspicion that there was something wrong with them. In the end he took with him 1015 plants, many more than he had planned.

There is no doubt that the long stay in Tahiti made it easier for Christian to find a following. Even today, as all Transpac skippers know, crew members are likely to desert in Tahiti!

December
1788

$\mathscr{S}$ ince the first purpose of the *Bounty* expedition, to gather breadfruit plants for transport, had been essentially completed the previous month, December 1788 was rather leisurely, as were all the months until the *Bounty*'s departure in April, 1789. Repairs on the ship continued and sickly plants were exchanged for healthy ones, but on the whole there was not much else to do but to enjoy the earthly paradise called Tahiti.

Discipline problems continued, however. Bligh had commanded the carpenter, Purcell, to make a grindstone for one of the chiefs. Purcell, who did not want to ruin his own personal tools, refused, saying: "It will spoil my chissel." And he added: "Though there is a law to take away my clothes, there is none to take away my tools." He was within his rights and Bligh knew it. Purcell was arrested but released the next day; Bligh simply could not do without his carpenter.

On December 9 the ship's surgeon, Thomas Huggan, died. There is no doubt that he drank himself to death. But the Tahitians had liked him and were sorry to see him go.

Bligh added to the dislike his crew had developed for him by starting to appropriate some of the gifts that the seamen received from their *taios*. He made a special point of confiscating the hogs. Morrison writes:

> The market for hogs beginning now to slacken Mr. Bligh seized on all that came to the ship, big & small, dead or alive, taking them as his property, and serving them as the ship's allowance at one pound pr man pr day. He also seized on those belonging to the master, & kill'd them for the ship's use . . . and when the master spoke to him, telling him the hogs were his property, he told him that "He, Mr. Bligh would convince him that evry thing was *his*, as soon as it was on board, that he would take nine tenths of any man's property and let him see who dared say anything to the contrary." Those of the seamen were seized without ceremony, and it became a favour for a man to get a pound extra of his own hog.

There is no doubt that these measures, which the men of the *Bounty*, officers and crew members alike, saw as grossly unfair, created at least as much resentment as the floggings.

On Christmas Day the *Bounty* was moved from Matavai to the more sheltered Toaroa harbor three miles west of Point Venus. For some reason, the ship ran aground. It was refloated without significant damage, but Bligh blamed the incident on his officers even though he was on board and in charge of the operation. He was more convinced than ever that he had a set of worthless and incompetent officers to work with.

Christmas was celebrated on Sunday, December 28, by "demonstrating the power of the ship's weapons," a show that made a deep impression on the Tahitians.

The paradisiacal existence on the island was not only marred by Bligh's confiscation of gifts; his physical punishments seemed to increase in frequency once the *Bounty* had reached her destination, and December was a month of floggings on Tahiti. On December 5, Matthew Thompson was given "twelve lashes for insolence and disobedience of orders," on December 27 William Muspratt got the same punishment for "neglect of duty" and on December 29 Robert Lamb, the ship's butcher, got the same for "suffering his Cleaver to be stolen."

It may be of interest to note that of the three men who were constantly ashore during the five and a half months the *Bounty* spent in Tahiti, two became mutineers (Fletcher Christian and William Brown, the gardener). Both developed a deep identification with the Tahitian way of life. The third, botanist David Nelson, who was older and had visited Tahiti before during Cook's third voyage, remained loyal to Bligh.

We know that Christian was genuinely liked by the Tahitians. They did not like Bligh, probably because they considered him *fa'a'oru* (conceited) and *piripiri* (stingy), but they did respect him for his power and his "riches" and his supposed relationship with King George.

Did Christian form a permanent attachment with a Tahitian woman at this time? We will never know for sure, but the likelihood is that he did not. Fryer later wrote:

> I can only say that Christian was not particularly attached to any Woman at
> Otaheite; nor any of them, except Mr. Stewart and James Morrison, Boatswain's
> Mate — who were the only two that had there particular Girls.

Both Stewart and Morrison were loyalists, although they remained in the ship after the mutiny. The likelihood is that Christian knew his future wife Mauatua (also referred to as Maimiti, Isabella, and Mainmast) before the *Bounty* left Tahiti, but if he had had a deep involvement with her, he would have headed straight for Tahiti to pick her up after the mutiny, instead of sailing to Tubuai. There is no way of knowing how deeply attached to her he subsequently became.

Despite what the movies of the *Bounty* story have claimed, however, it is most unlikely that a specific attachment to a Tahitian woman had anything to do with his decision to take over the ship.

January
1789

On New Year's Day 1789, the *Bounty* was securely anchored in Toaroa harbor, not far from present-day Papeete. The day was celebrated with the issuance of a double ration of grog to the ship's complement. It was, however, an ordinary working day, so only two sailors got shore leave in the usual manner of rotation.

The month of January provided an ominous preview of what was to come. Monday, January 5, at the relief of the night watch (4:00 a.m.), it was discovered that the small cutter was missing. Bligh mustered the ship's company and found that three had deserted. One was Charles Churchill, the ship's corporal, whose very duty it was to uphold discipline and prevent desertions! Another was William Muspratt, able-bodied seaman and Bligh's own steward. The third was John Millward, able-bodied seaman. They had taken with them eight stand of arms with ammunition.

The Tahitians informed Bligh that the deserters had left the cutter in Matavai and were now on board a sailing canoe headed for Tetiaroa, an atoll 30 miles north of Tahiti (now owned by Marlon Brando).

Bligh managed to get a contingent of Tahitians — led by Teina's younger brother, Ari'ipaea, and another chief named Moana — to promise to sail to Tetiaroa and capture the run-aways by pretending to be friendly and then grabbing their arms and binding them. However, before the pursuers could get under way the weather turned bad and the expedition had to be postponed.

On January 17 the sun came out again and Bligh ordered all sails out to be weathered. It was then that he discovered the *Bounty*'s set of new sails had been mildewed and was in a rotting condition. This was a most serious matter since sails could not be replaced for many months to come. The men Bligh held responsible for this calamity were the sailing master, John Fryer, and the boatswain, William Cole. Bligh was furious, but all he felt he could do was to give Fryer and Cole one of his famous tongue-lashings and leave it at that. Nevertheless, the incident shows how much naval discipline and routine on board the *Bounty* had deteriorated.

The incident also shows something else: Bligh's tendency to blame everyone else for whatever went wrong and take all the credit for whatever went well. Bligh had been in Tahiti before and he should have known how quickly canvas or any cloth mildews in the rainy season — yet he had not ordered the new set of sails to be weathered. Also, because Bligh insisted on personally seeing to every single detail, the men were left with the expectation that he had everything under control. However, when he left a detail unattended, he blamed someone else.

The deserters were captured toward the end of the month, an incident during which Bligh showed his bravery: he walked up to them alone, armed only with a cutlass. The men claimed they had given themselves up, but it turned out that their gunpowder was wet, a fact that Bligh did not know.

In the Royal Navy deserters were severely punished. In wartime they were usually hanged. In peacetime, too, they stood a chance of being condemned to death, or they might be given 500 lashes. With mitigating circumstances, they might get away with a gross (twelve dozen) lashes.

Bligh sentenced Muspratt and Millward to four dozen lashes, Churchill to two dozen. It remains a mystery why the deserters were dealt with so leniently and especially why Churchill, their leader, received a lesser punishment. (Midshipman Thomas Hayward who was asleep on watch when the desertion took place had earlier been sentenced to eleven weeks' confinement in irons.)

So unusual was the mild sentence when compared to the Navy standards of the time that the three culprits actually wrote Bligh a thank-you letter which reads as follows:

> ON BOARD
> THE *BOUNTY*,
> AT OTAHEITE

January 26, 1789

SIR,

We should think ourselves wholly inexcuseable if we omitted taking this earliest opportunity of returning our thanks for your goodness in delivering us from a trial by Court Martial, the fatal consequences of which are obvious, and although we cannot possibly lay any claim to so great a favour, yet we humbly beg you will be pleased to remit any further punishment and we trust our future conduct will fully demonstrate our deep sense of your clemency, and our steadfast resolution to behave better hereafter.

> C. Churchill
> Wm. Muspratt
> John Millward

TO CAPTAIN BLIGH.

The letter was written after the first half of the punishment had been administered. Probably because the sentence had been so light, Bligh was not "pleased to remit" the second half. Three months later the promise "to behave better hereafter" was broken, and the trio turned into hard-core mutineers.

It is true that Bligh did not punish his men harshly compared to other commanders; no one who sailed with him ever accused him of physical cruelty. However, he was what psychologists call a "crazy-maker." What I mean by this is that he often gave orders which were of the "damned if you do and damned if you don't" variety. For example, a seaman could be flogged if he was responsible for something having been stolen by natives, yet he would also be flogged if he struck a native. On January 30, Isaac Martin, the American, was sentenced to nineteen lashes for striking a Tahitian who had tried to steal an iron hoop from him. The sentence had been twenty-four lashes, but the Tahitians, led by chief Teina, had begged Bligh to reduce it if he could not dispense with it, and Bligh grandiosely obliged them by decreasing the number of lashes by five. (Martin later joined the mutineers.)

This crazy-making tendency has not been pointed out in the *Bounty* literature, perhaps because no psychologist has written about Bligh so far. Yet I think it is of importance, because Christian had been a victim of Bligh's crazy-making shortly before the mutiny, and this could well have been one of the factors setting the stage for his fateful decision.

On January 26, 1788, the First Fleet had reached Australia and established the original penal colonies in Botany Bay (actually Port Jackson, today's Sydney) and on Norfolk Island. In January 1789, some newly-transported convicts on Norfolk conspired to capture the next ship to arrive and sail her to Tahiti. They were discovered before they could carry out their scheme, but it is interesting to consider what would have happened if they had succeeded. They would then have arrived in Tahiti while Bligh was still there and would probably have been captured and returned to Norfolk on the already overcrowded *Bounty*. In such a case, with all of the attention of the ship's complement being focused on the convicts — and with a second ship involved — it is probable that no mutiny would have occurred. Or, on second thought, might the would-be deserters on the *Bounty* have made common cause with the convicts? We will never know.

February
1789

On February 4, 1789, the deserters — Churchill, Millward and Muspratt — received the second half of their punishment: a dozen lashes for Churchill and two dozen each for the other two. There had barely been time for a thin scab to form on the exposed raw flesh. Not surprisingly, all three of the deserters were to become mutineers.

During the night between February 5 and February 6 the *Bounty* was subjected to sabotage. In the morning the anchor cable was found almost cut through at the water's edge; only one strand remained whole. With any wind at all the cable would have parted and the ship would either have drifted ashore or onto the reef of the lagoon.

Some writers have speculated that there may not have been any sabotage at all and that the cable may simply have chafed against sharp coral. These writers cannot be sailors themselves, since any sailor would know the difference between a cut and a chafed cable. Bligh himself never mentioned any possibility of the cable being chafed.

Bligh's original theory was that the cable had been cut by a Tahitian who wanted the ship to remain at the island. After the mutiny it occurred to him that the culprit could have been one of the *Bounty*'s crew who, like the deserters Churchill, Millward and Muspratt, wanted to stay in Tahiti.

Bligh's first theory was correct, but for a reason he had not considered. As described in the January 1789 commentary, midshipman Hayward had been put in irons for sleeping on duty. Like all on board the *Bounty*, Hayward had a *taio* ashore. This special friend was the local chief's brother, Vaetua, and he wanted Hayward released. It was Vaetua who had ordered the anchor cable cut, expecting the ship to drift ashore with resulting evacuation of the whole crew, including Hayward.

Vaetua divulged his plan long afterwards to those mutineers and loyalists who had remained on Tahiti when Christian sailed away with the *Bounty* for the last time.

Bligh did not know how close he had come to being killed by Vaetua. At the time Hayward was sentenced, Vaetua had been on board the ship standing directly behind Bligh with a war club, ready to crush the captain's skull if he had ordered Hayward flogged.

Vaetua despised Bligh. In fact, the *Bounty*'s boatswain's mate, Morrison, writes in his narrative that Vaetua had "cursed Mr. Christian for not killing Lieut. Bligh which he said he would do himself if ever he came to Taheite." Vaetua must have changed his mind, however, because when Bligh did show up again in the *Providence* on the second breadfruit expedition, Vaetua dined with him occasionally and often told him how superior British spirits were to the Tahitian *'ava* (Oliver 1988, pp. 193 and 200).

In attempts to explain why Christian encountered little trouble finding crewmen to join him in the mutiny, *Bounty* scholars have concentrated on the allure of the Tahitian women and the influence it had on the crew. In this they are correct; there is no doubt that the attraction of the Tahitian women was a powerful magnet for many members of the crew. But the significance of the *taios* should not be forgotten.

The word *taio* is no longer used in Tahiti, having been replaced by the more comprehensive and general word *hoa* (friend) or *hoa rahi* ("great" friend). But the principle remains the same even today.

If a Tahitian *hoa* exchanges names with you (the custom is rarer today but still exists), he will be your friend forever, through thick and thin, no matter what you do, short of betrayal. You will be considered not only as part of his family, but actually as more important than his family, because he *chose* you.

Many of the mutineers had no close family ties and probably not much in the way of close friendships either. The fact that each man on the *Bounty* had a *taio* — and thereby also a loving family — is an additional factor that should be taken into account in explaining the positive reaction of some crew members to Christian's proposal of mutiny with the attendant hope of returning to Tahiti.

March
1789

The *Bounty* was coming to the end of its long (over five months) stay in Tahiti, and the loading of the breadfruit plants its crew had gathered now began. The discipline had become extremely lax during these months, not only among the seamen but also among the officers. Examples of this deterioration have been mentioned in previous commentaries, for instance the neglect of Fryer, the sailing master, which resulted in the *Bounty*'s new sails being destroyed, and the fact that midshipman Hayward was sleeping on duty when three crew members deserted.

On March 2, 1789, there was yet another incident illustrating the lackadaisical attitude of the officers. That morning William Peckover, the gunner, had several articles stolen from him by a Tahitian. If he had been an ordinary seaman, he would have been flogged but, again, since he was a warrant officer Bligh did not feel he could punish him.

The thief was caught and Bligh had him flogged with 100 lashes "severely given." (This shows, by the way, that although Bligh was not the cruel monster that some have made him out to be, he certainly was not as humane as others have claimed. The reason he did not flog his own seamen severely was not necessarily that he had a kind disposition. From his own writings it is more likely that he merely wanted to keep them healthy and efficient, much as an engineer wants to keep his machine in good working order.)

After the flogging the islander was put in irons as a reminder to his compatriots of what would happen to them if they were to engage in similar pilfering. However, early in the morning of March 7 the prisoner managed to break his irons and escape while George Stewart, acting master's mate, was on watch. Again Bligh was exasperated but felt he could do nothing more than give Stewart one of his famous tongue lashings.

On the day the Tahitian prisoner escaped, Bligh wrote in his log: "Verbal orders in the course of a Month were so forgot that they [the officers] would impudently assert no such thing or directions were given, and I have been at last under the necessity to trouble myself with writing what by decent Young Officers would be complied with as the Common Rules of the Service." The fact that Bligh found it necessary to issue his orders in writing clearly illustrates the slackness to which his officers had succumbed.

In attempts to explain the subsequent mutiny, most writers have stressed the discontent of the crew and their supposed rebellion against the captain's discipline (even though none of the seamen ever complained about his floggings). But the fact is that Bligh also had officers who — in his opinion at least — did not do their duty conscientiously. Some of them, certainly Hayward, were lazy and careless; others, like Fryer, had been too demoralized by Bligh's frequent humiliating attacks to have any heart in their work. Paradoxically, the only officer Bligh trusted (and never mentions negatively in his log) was Fletcher Christian!

We know that Christian found it relatively easy to get seamen to join him in the mutiny. But what about the role of the officers? The fact is that none of the officers on board except the sailing master, Fryer (who, interestingly, had received as much abuse from Bligh as Christian had, although we do not know if he had been called a coward and a thief), made even a half-hearted attempt to assist their captain at the time of the mutiny.

One can have divergent opinions about whether such an attempt would have had a chance of success. (Morrison, the boatswain's mate, felt there was such an opportunity.) But it is clear from the record that no serious attempt to recapture the ship was made at all.

Ultimately, a realistic explanation of the mutiny would have to take into account not only the conflict between Christian and Bligh (which, as was mentioned earlier, may have started in Cape Town) and the long stay in Tahiti with its pleasures in contrast to the conditions on board, but also the fact that Bligh had no one on whom he could rely. There was no other commissioned officer on the *Bounty*, and the warrant officers were clearly not dependable. It is indeed ironic that the only officer in whom Bligh had felt he could place his trust, an officer whom he had promoted, was the very one who incited the mutiny.

April

1789

... ⛵ ...

Aue te mauiui rahi
i to revaraa na te ara;
Aue te arofa i to'u mau hoa
e ta'u i here . . .

Oh, how it hurts to leave for the vastness beyond; oh, how much love I feel for my friends and for my sweetheart . . .*

This haunting and nostalgic Tahitian song did not exist at the time of the *Bounty*'s departure from the island. But the sentiment must have been there. I have never been able to leave Tahiti without tears welling up in my eyes. It is difficult to imagine that anyone who had stayed on the island for almost half a year would not have strong feelings about leaving it.

Many close relationships had arisen between the men of the *Bounty* and the Tahitians. Each crew member had his *taio* and many had formed an intimate liaison with a *vahine*; several children were to be born who would never see their British fathers. Now when the *Bounty* was to sail, the genuine grief of the islanders over losing their friends was evident. Nor can there have been many men on the *Bounty* who were not sad to leave this island paradise.

On Saturday, April 4, 1789, the *Bounty* weighed anchor and sailed out from Toaroa harbor. On board were 1015 breadfruit plants in 774 pots, 39 tubs, and 24 boxes. In addition there were numerous samples of other South Seas plants (requested by Sir Joseph Banks), 25 live hogs, 17 goats, and a number of chickens. As if that were not enough, the deck was crowded with last-minute gifts from Tahitian *taios*: coconuts, plantains, breadfruit, yams, bananas, etc. The *Bounty* looked like a floating farm. Overcrowded before, it was now "bursting to the seams."

After briefly stopping at Huahine in the Leeward Islands, Bligh set course for

*My free and unauthorized translation of the first lines of the beautiful song *E Mauruuru a vau (Farewell for just a while)* by Jack Brooks and Eddie Lund. Copyright by Michael H. Goldsen, Criterion Music Corporation.

the Friendly Islands (Tonga). On April 11 he discovered Aitutaki (in what is now the Southern Cook group) but did not land. On April 23 the *Bounty* arrived at Nomuka in the Tongan (Friendly) Islands, 1800 miles west of Tahiti, where Bligh had landed once before in 1777, on Cook's third voyage. The very fact that he stopped here is of interest for two reasons.

First, it shows his extraordinary meticulousness. Bligh stopped at Nomuka primarily to replace one dead and two or three "sickly looking" breadfruit plants out of 1015! He also wanted to "wood and water," less than three weeks after leaving Tahiti.

Secondly, it was during and immediately after this stop that the incidents occurred which triggered the mutiny. Would the mutiny have occurred anyway? We will never know.

It may be useful to review some of the background. Bligh and Christian, who was the younger by ten years, had been friends on two previous voyages. As has been mentioned, Christian was the only one of the officers whom Bligh trusted, and this is why Bligh had promoted him to his second-in-command soon after the *Bounty* left England. We also know that a quarrel, probably over a loan, had started between them in Cape Town and had lasted throughout the voyage. Yet Bligh had given Christian the most important assignment in Tahiti — full command over shore operations. What had happened to their friendship that later caused it to deteriorate so badly?

It is likely that Bligh had felt left out in Tahiti. He probably sensed that the Tahitians did not like him and resented Christian's deep involvement with them. (Christian had totally immersed himself in Tahitian life to the point of being tattooed on both his chest and his buttocks.) Considering Bligh's later hatred of Peter Heywood, he may also have resented Christian's close friendship with the young midshipman.

But to read a homosexual conflict into the relationship, as Madge Darby has attempted to do in her book *Who Caused the Mutiny on the Bounty* (1965), goes against everything we know about Bligh and Christian. If there was any sexual element present at all (which is improbable), it is more likely that Bligh, unconsciously, was jealous of bachelor Christian's popularity with the Tahitian women when he himself felt bound by his marriage vows to stay chaste.

Whatever the precursors of it were, the conflict between Bligh and Christian was greatly exacerbated on the voyage from Tahiti, to the point that Christian told Bligh during the mutiny: "I have been in hell with you for weeks."

Bligh was definitely at his worst on the voyage from Tahiti, fault-finding, insulting, petty, and condescending. He seems to have relished humiliating all his officers. Yet it is clear that he went out of his way to torment Christian.

At Nomuka Bligh put Christian in an impossible position. He sent him in command of a watering party with orders not to use any weapons, but to leave them in the boat. When Christian then encountered hostile Tongan warriors who threatened him and his men with spears, clubs and rocks, he had to retreat to the boat, since he had no arms. An adze was stolen from one of his men.

On hearing of the theft, Bligh damned Christian for a "cowardly rascal," asking if he was afraid of "a set of naked savages while he had arms." To which Christian replied: "The arms are no use while your orders prevent them from being used." Not only was Bligh engaging in crazy-making (damned if you do — use arms — and damned if you don't), but more important, a gentleman simply did not call another a coward. Back in England the insult could well have resulted in a duel.

Only two days later, on Monday, April 27 (the day before the mutiny), Bligh accused Christian — in front of the assembled ship's company — of stealing some of his coconuts, calling him a thief and a hound.

This incident is extremely important, because it probably triggered the mental breakdown in Christian which would culminate in his decision to take over the ship. Morrison describes the incident in his narrative:

> In the Afternoon of the 27th Mr. Bligh Came up, and taking a turn about the Quarter Deck when he missed some of the Cocoa Nuts which were piled up between the Guns upon which he said that they were stolen and Could not go without the knowledge of the Officers, who were all Calld and declared that they had not seen a Man toutch them, to which Mr. Bligh replied then you must have taken them yourselves, and orderd Mr. Elphinstone to go & fetch evry Cocoa Nut in the Ship aft, which He obeyd. He then questioned evry Officer in turn concerning the Number they had bought, & Coming to Mr. Christian askd Him, Mr. Christian answerd "I do not know Sir, but I hope you don't think me so mean as to be Guilty of Stealing yours". Mr. Bligh replied "Yes you dam'd Hound I do — You must have stolen them from me or you could give a better account of them — God damn you you Scoundrels you are all thieves alike, and combine with the Men to rob me — I suppose you'll Steal my Yams next, but I'll sweat you for it you rascals I'll make half of you Jump overboard before you get through Endeavour Streights" — He then Calld Mr. Samuel and said "Stop these Villians Grog, and Give them but Half a Pound of Yams tomorrow, and if they steal then, I'll reduce them to a quarter". The Cocoa Nuts were Carried aft, & He Went below, the officers then got together and were heard to murmur much at such treatment, and it was talked among the Men that the Yams would be next seized, as Lieut. Bligh knew that they had purchased large quantitys of them and set about secreting as many as they Could.

We have to remember that this was a time when a man's honor was more valuable than his life. (This is why movie makers cannot show what actually happened; there is simply not enough time in a film to recreate the atmosphere of the era. Conse-

TONGAN ISLANDS

175°W

VAVA'U

KAO

TOFUA

HA'APAI

KOTU

20°S

SOUTH PACIFIC
OCEAN

NOMUKA

NUKUALOFA

TONGATABU

'EUA

N

quently, Bligh must be portrayed as a brutal and physically cruel tyrant, otherwise Christian's mutiny will simply not seem believable.) Christian came from an unbroken line of twenty-five generations of aristocracy and none of his forefathers would have let themselves be called cowards or thieves without exacting retribution.

Yet Christian's first reaction was to get away from Bligh at any cost. At this point he had obviously lost his judgment: he was trying to construct a raft from a few spare spars and planks in order to leave the ship. (He had also torn up his personal papers and given away his curios and mementos.)

As a psychologist, it is my opinion that Christian was at this time suffering from a brief reactive psychosis. Note the clinical definition of this condition:*

> The essential feature is the sudden onset of a psychotic disorder of at least a few hours' but no more than two weeks' duration, with eventual return to premorbid level of functioning. The psychotic symptoms appear immediately following a recognizable psychosocial stressor that would evoke significant symptoms of distress in almost anyone . . . Invariably there is emotional turmoil. . . . Suicidal or aggressive behavior may be present. . . . Individuals with . . . Borderline Personality Disorders [see the June 1788 commentary] are thought to be particularly vulnerable to its development. By definition situations involving major stress predispose to development of this disorder.

Christian's plan to leave the ship on a flimsy raft was certainly suicidal, even if he at the moment may consciously have believed that he might survive. When Christian mentioned his plan to his friend, midshipman George Stewart, the latter pleaded with him not to leave and then added a phrase which in all probability triggered a total change in Christian's plans: "The men are ready for anything!"

The crew was definitely in an ugly mood. Not only had they recently gone through the shock of leaving an island paradise where they had spent almost half a year, but they had come back to an atmosphere on board that was worse than at any period they had experienced on the voyage from England. If they had had any respect for their captain as a human being before, they would have lost it totally when they witnessed his hysteria over a few coconuts which could be bought at the price of twenty for a small nail. Not only had Bligh accused the popular Christian of being a thief, but he had also ordered the ration of yams to be cut in half and — even worse for a sailor — the grog to be stopped altogether. A sailor can starve if need be without too much complaint, but to have rations cut down in the midst of plenty — and the grog stopped on top of it — for a totally ridiculous reason must have been maddening.

Stewart's statement "The men are ready for anything" was almost certainly not

*Diagnostic and Statistical Manual of Mental Disorders, Third Edition, Revised (Washington: American Psychiatric Association, 1987).

THE MEN
ON
CHRISTIAN'S WATCH

Thomas Hayward MIDSHIPMAN	*Thomas Burkett* ABLE-BODIED SEAMAN
John Hallett MIDSHIPMAN	*Thomas Ellison* ABLE-BODIED SEAMAN
John Mills GUNNER'S MATE	*Isaac Martin* ABLE-BODIED SEAMAN
Charles Norman CARPENTER'S MATE	*Matthew Quintal* ABLE-BODIED SEAMAN

intended to suggest mutiny, as some writers have suggested, but rather to warn Christian that he was needed on the ship in case of problems with the crew. Stewart was a strict disciplinarian and, despite the fact that he eventually remained on the ship, was most probably a loyalist. (Stewart died when the *Pandora* foundered and what role, if any, he may have played in the mutiny may always remain uncertain.)

Yet his statement probably triggered the idea of mutiny in Christian's mind. Christian's great-great-grandfather had become a folk hero on the Isle of Man by mutinying against the British Crown and a popular ballad about him had been published in 1780. And, as we know, Christian's brother Charles had participated in a mutiny prior to the *Bounty*'s departure from England.

On the night between April 27 and April 28 Christian had probably had very little sleep. There are some indications that he had been drinking. In any case, when he was awakened for his 4:00 to 8:00 a.m. watch he felt his head "was on fire."

He made the impulsive decision to seize the ship. The fact that the most discontented seamen on board were on his watch probably helped trigger his action. When he approached them, he found little difficulty in getting accomplices.

Bligh later claimed there had been a conspiracy to mutiny ever since the *Bounty*'s stay in Tahiti. He may be partly correct; it is difficult to imagine that the idea of mutiny would not have arisen among the crew. After all, three had deserted (and been caught) in Tahiti. But it is highly unlikely that a definite plan to mutiny existed; the events during the takeover of the ship were simply too confused and haphazard for that to have been the case.

The actual details of the mutiny have been portrayed with various degrees of accuracy in numerous books and articles and in five feature-length films. Suffice it to say here that Christian and eleven of his shipmates — out of a complement of forty-four — managed to take over the vessel and set Bligh and eighteen loyalists adrift in the Pacific thousands of miles from any European settlement. (Other loyalists had to stay on board so as not to further overload the ship's launch.)

Twelve against thirty-two! Could the mutiny have been put down through determined action by the officers? Morrison thought there was a good chance:

> The behaviour of the officers on this occasion was dastardly beyond description, none of them ever making the least attempt to rescue the ship, which would have been effected had any attempt been made by one of them, as some of those who were under arms did not know what they were about, and Robt Lamb who I found centry at the fore hatchway when I first came on deck went away in the boat and Isaac Martin had laid his arms down and gone into the boat, but had been ordered out again.

Muspratt, the mutineer who was later found guilty and condemned to death (but was pardoned on the basis of a technicality), said in his defense speech at the court-martial:

> The great Misfortune attending this unhappy Business is that no one ever Attempted to rescue the Ship; it might have been done — Thompson was the only Centinel upon the Arm Chest.

A possible reason for the inaction of the officers is that having been almost as badly abused as the men by the captain, they felt no loyalty towards him and were not about to risk being shot to death in an attempt to free him.

Finally a few points that are often overlooked. The mutiny on the *Bounty* is one of the few bloodless ones in history. The harshest action, apart from setting the loyalists adrift, was that Bligh's wrists were bound hard enough to cause him pain. Most of the violence was verbal and much of it came from Bligh, although the mutineers certainly did a good deal of threatening.

Another point illustrates — one could almost say proves — that the mutiny was not planned, and that is that *three* boats were launched: first the jolly boat which was found to be rotten through with worms and would certainly have sunk, then the cutter which also leaked and simply would not hold the large number of loyalists who preferred to go with Bligh, and finally the launch.

The third point is that the poor condition of the ship's boats in itself illustrates the slackness of discipline that had prevailed during the stay in Tahiti. Not only had the new sails been allowed to rot, but two of the ship's boats had not been repaired and were in no condition to be used in an emergency.

When Bligh had been forced into the launch together with eighteen loyalists,

LOYALISTS WITH BLIGH
IN THE LAUNCH

John Fryer
SAILING MASTER

William Cole
BOATSWAIN

William Peckover
GUNNER

William Purcell
CARPENTER

Thomas Ledward
ACTING SURGEON

William Elphinstone
MASTER'S MATE

Thomas Hayward
MIDSHIPMAN

John Hallett
MIDSHIPMAN

Peter Linkletter
QUARTERMASTER

John Norton
QUARTERMASTER

George Simpson
QUARTERMASTER'S MATE

Lawrence Lebogue
SAILMAKER

John Samuel
CLERK AND STEWARD

Thomas Hall
ABLE-BODIED SEAMAN

Robert Lamb
ABLE-BODIED SEAMAN

John Smith
ABLE-BODIED SEAMAN
(Bligh's Servant)

Robert Tinkler
ABLE-BODIED SEAMAN
(Acting Midshipman)

David Nelson
BOTANIST

ACTIVE MUTINEERS

Fletcher Christian
ACTING LIEUTENANT

Matthew Quintal
ABLE-BODIED SEAMAN

Charles Churchill
MASTER-AT-ARMS

Richard Skinner
ABLE-BODIED SEAMAN

John Mills
GUNNER'S MATE

John Adams
ABLE-BODIED SEAMAN

Thomas Burkett
ABLE-BODIED SEAMAN

John Sumner
ABLE-BODIED SEAMAN

Thomas Ellison
ABLE-BODIED SEAMAN

Matthew Thompson
ABLE-BODIED SEAMAN

William McCoy
ABLE-BODIED SEAMAN

John Williams
ABLE-BODIED SEAMAN

INACTIVE MUTINEERS
(OR ACTIONS DURING MUTINY UNKNOWN)

Edward Young
ACTING MIDSHIPMAN
(role in mutiny unknown)

John Millward
ABLE-BODIED SEAMAN
(vacillating)

Henry Hillbrant
ABLE-BODIED SEAMAN
(actions unknown)

William Muspratt
ABLE-BODIED SEAMAN
(vacillating)

Isaac Martin
ABLE-BODIED SEAMAN
(vacillating)

William Brown
GARDENER
(apparently passive)

LOYALISTS REMAINING
ON BOARD THE *BOUNTY*

George Stewart
MIDSHIPMAN

Charles Norman
CARPENTER'S MATE

Peter Heywood
ACTING MIDSHIPMAN

Thomas McIntosh
CARPENTER'S CREW

James Morrison
BOATSWAIN'S MATE

Joseph Coleman
ARMORER

Michael Byrne
ABLE-BODIED SEAMAN

the freeboard remaining was less than the length of a man's hand. The boat was designed for a maximum of fifteen men and for short distances, not for nineteen men with belongings and supplies and destined to sail close to four thousand miles.

May

1789

··· ⚓ ···

*E*ighteen men had joined Bligh in the *Bounty*'s launch, most of them not from any personal loyalty but from their loyalty to the Crown and the wish to have a chance to return to England. On board the *Bounty* remained the seven loyalists who had not found room in the overcrowded launch, and Christian with seventeen mutineers (eleven of whom had played an active role in the mutiny).

What was the mood in the launch? With keen psychological insight, Rolf Du Rietz has described what it must have been (Du Rietz, 1965):

> When the *Bounty* had disappeared below the horizon, Mr. Bligh, in the launch, found himself watched by eighteen pairs of eyes, all of which presumably being almost as expressive as words would have been. And the look of the eyes expressed to him something like this: "You damned idiot, you went too far! And now we all have to suffer for it! Count yourself lucky that we are not throwing you overboard!"

This may have been one of the few times in Bligh's life when his inability to understand his impact on other people was a blessing for him rather than a curse.

The launch had very little in terms of provisions or water on board. This was not because Christian wished that the men would perish. It is clear from the accounts that the general assumption on board the *Bounty* — as well as in the launch — was that Bligh would sail to the nearby Tongan islands, specifically Tongatabu, and there wait for an English ship. If that had not been the case, the mutineers would not have shouted sarcastically: "You will not need any arms where you are going; you will be among *friends*" when Bligh asked for muskets. (The sarcasm was in reference to Bligh's order that the shore parties on Nomuka not use their arms when dealing with the "Friendly Islanders.") Nor would the mutineers have objected to Purcell, the carpenter, taking his tools along, and have feared he would build a ship with them, if they had thought the launch would head for Timor. The fact is that the launch had full provisions for only five days, but that was more than enough to reach Tongatabu.

As to navigational equipment, Christian had given Bligh his personal sextant, and there was a compass, a quadrant, and tables used for determining latitude and longitude, in addition to a time-keeper, on board. Without detracting from Bligh's extraordinary achievement on the open-boat voyage that lay ahead, it should be mentioned that Fryer could probably have performed the same feat, and probably some of the other men on board also.

Bligh set course for the island of Tofua, thirty miles distant, an active volcano, as it is to this day. He hoped to obtain provisions there since what he had on board the ship's launch was totally inadequate for nineteen men on a long voyage. He finally found a cave in the steep cliffs that marked the shore and sent out provisioning parties. (This cave was "rediscovered" and identified by Bengt Danielsson in 1985.)

The stores obtained were meager and the natives who gathered in increasing numbers grew more hostile by the hour, partly because Bligh had made the incredible blunder of telling them that he had been shipwrecked. The natives could see that the men were practically defenseless, having only four cutlasses between them.

They attacked on May 2, 1789, and the men barely made it to the boat. The natives tried to haul it to the shore. At this point, with magnificent bravery, quartermaster John Norton jumped out of the boat and ran up the beach to unfasten the line. He was killed in the attempt, while the rest of the boat's complement escaped miraculously — by throwing out pieces of clothing which the natives in the faster pursuing canoes stopped to pick up.

And then followed the most famous open-boat voyage in maritime history: 3618 nautical miles by Bligh's makeshift log from Tofua to Timor in a 23-foot launch with no more freeboard than the length of a man's hand, without charts, with meager provisions, and with the constant threat of imminent death.

For much of the voyage the weather was cold and stormy with copious rain and with high seas breaking over the stern, making it necessary for the men to constantly bail for their lives. The slightest inattention by the helmsman would have meant immediate disaster for them all. In the end, however, the rainy weather may have saved them, because they clearly did not have enough water on board at the outset to last through the voyage, even when minutely rationed.

On this voyage, the men in the launch became the first Europeans to ever sail through the Fiji islands. Bligh marked all the islands they passed, trying to chart them and give their positions as best he could; so well did he succeed that his chart of "Bligh Islands," as he called them, could be used for navigation today.

Bligh had heard from some Tongans that the Fijians were cannibals, so he did not dare to land on any of the lush, inviting islands. On one occasion, however, the launch was pursued by Fijians in fast sailing canoes and almost overtaken. A. B. Brewster in *The Hill Tribes of Fiji* (1922), has described what it must have been like:

From her bosom (the Pacific) rises the chain of the Yasawa Islands, whose jagged and fantastic forms are silhouetted against the northern sky, and beyond, looming on the far horizon, is Vanua Levu or the Great Land, the second in size of the group. A broad passage separates the Yasawas from Vanua Levu, marked on the southern side by Alewa Kalou, the Round Island of the Admiralty charts, through which the main ocean is reached. Captain Bligh, in his famous boat voyage in 1789, after the mutiny of the *Bounty*, escaped by it into the open sea, when he was chased by canoes from Waia, one of the Yasawa Islands. On its high volcanic peaks were always sentinels watching for canoes or other craft in distress. Such were lawful prey, "those with salt water in their eyes," being doomed by the ancient law to the bamboo knives, the heated stone ovens and the cannibal maw. With what pangs must those weary, sea-worn refugees from the *Bounty* have looked upon the cooling brooks falling in cascades over the volcanic cliffs, and the glossy, green groves of breadfruit, coco-nuts and bananas of the fair and fertile isles by which they passed. We can see by Bligh's charts how close they were to some of them, yet from the savage nature of the inhabitants they dared not land. Often and often, as I took my evening walk to the edge of the precipitous cliffs to watch the setting sun as it dipped away beyond the Yasawas, have I thought of that brave voyage of nearly 4000 miles in the *Bounty*'s boat.

Death by starvation was a constant threat, the ration, served twice daily, being only one twenty-fifth of a pound of bread and a gill (quarter pint) of water with occasional additions of half an ounce of pork and a teaspoonful of rum. Although a fishline was always out, no fish was ever caught. Towards the end of the month, the launch reached the Great Barrier Reef of Australia. When the men, more dead than alive, finally staggered ashore on a sandy islet which Bligh called Restoration Island, many of them could neither stand nor walk. And they still had 1300 miles to sail in order to reach Timor.

While Bligh and his crew were fighting for their lives, Christian was heading for Tubuai, an island 350 miles south of Tahiti. Cook had sighted the island in 1777 on his third voyage but had not landed. Here Christian planned to found a settlement, since he was reasonably confident that Tubuai would not be visited for a long time; it had poor anchorage and only one narrow passage through the surrounding reef.

Christian reached Tubuai at almost the same time as Bligh arrived at Australia. The *Bounty* met with a very hostile reception, however, and Christian felt forced to fire into the armada of about 50 attacking canoes carrying close to 1000 men. Eleven men and one woman were killed.

BLIGH'S OPEN-BOAT VOYAGE

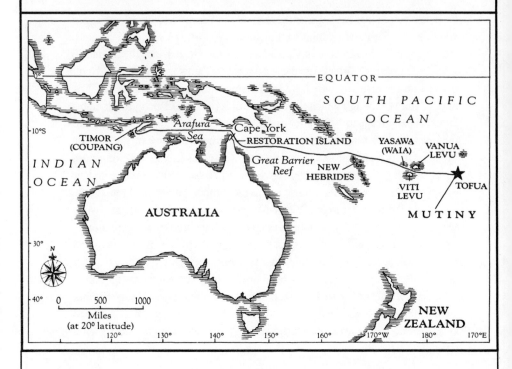

Nevertheless, Christian was determined to establish a colony on the island. To his astonishment, however, there were no mammals except rats on Tubuai, no pigs or goats, not even dogs. No one on board wanted to lead a vegetarian existence. Furthermore, the Tubuaian women were not as accommodating as their Tahitian counterparts. So Christian decided to sail to Tahiti to pick up women, pigs, goats, and chickens. The *Bounty* sailed on May 31, 1789.

June

1789

*B*ligh and his seventeen loyalists were safely inside Australia's Great Barrier Reef. Reading Bligh's account of the open-boat voyage from Tofua to Timor, one gets the impression that there had been little dissension on board, even though the men had undergone incredible hardships. But Bligh was always careful to omit any references to incidents where he may not have appeared in the best possible light.

According to John Fryer, the sailing master, Bligh "was as Tyrannical in his temper in the Boat as in the Ship, and . . . his chief thought was his own comfort . . ." Be that as it may, now when the immediate perils of the voyage were over (at least for the time being), trouble broke out. In fact, Bligh was faced with another mutiny!

On an islet which Bligh had named Sunday Island, Purcell, the carpenter, had been gathering clams under the impression that it was "every man for himself." When he returned to camp with his catch, Bligh proclaimed that all victuals were to be considered common property and demanded that Purcell hand over his clams. The latter refused, whereupon Bligh called him a scoundrel, adding: "If I had not brought you here, you would all have perished." Purcell replied: "Yes, sir, if it had not been for you, we should not have been here." At this, Bligh again called him a scoundrel. Purcell: "I am not a scoundrel, sir, I am as good a man as you."

This enraged Bligh who considered the statement mutinous. He grabbed a cutlass and told Purcell to take another and defend himself. At this point Fryer, the sailing master, gave an order to the boatswain: "Mr. Cole, please arrest both these men!"

The situation was critical for Bligh; he could have lost his command right then and there. Eventually, however, both Fryer and Purcell backed off when they saw that the captain was determined to preserve his authority or die in the attempt. If they had not given up, Bligh would have been in a weak position; there was a strong anti-Bligh faction among the loyalists consisting not only of Fryer and Purcell, but including quartermaster Linkletter and able seamen Hall, Lamb, and Tinkler as well. In fact, Bligh was so unpopular that he could not have counted on support from any of the loyalists, except possibly for botanist Nelson and sailmaker Lebogue, and they were in the weakest condition of them all.

Again, Fryer's recollection of the affair was quite different. In the words of his daughter, Mary Ann: ". . . the fact is Purcel [sic] had in some way offended Bligh and he as usual gave way to his ungovernable passions, and drew his Cutlass swearing at the same time he would kill him. My father wrested the weapon from him to prevent blood-shed and for this he was for ever after both hated and feared by Bligh."

Fryer told Bligh after this incident: "There are other methods in making people do as they are ordered, without fighting them, Sir. And you may rest assured that I will support you in that as far as lays in my power." Bligh's answer has not been recorded, but it can well be imagined.

After another two weeks of extreme suffering Bligh and his crew finally reached Coupang, a Dutch settlement on Timor, on Sunday, June 14. It is characteristic of Bligh's pedantry and compulsive insistence on protocol that, even though several of his men were dangerously close to dying, he insisted on hoisting a distress flag and waiting for permission to land. And when the boat finally docked, Bligh's petty vindictiveness again showed itself: he commanded Fryer to stay in the boat to "guard it," as if there had been anything to guard!

Meanwhile, Christian and his mixed crew of mutineers and loyalists were collecting the women (including Christian's consort Mauatua) and pigs, goats and chickens on Tahiti for their intended colony on Tubuai. During the stay on Tahiti, Christian made it known that any attempt on the part of a loyalist — or a mutineer for that matter — to remain on Tahiti would be severely punished. He did not want to take any risk of his planned refuge becoming known to pursuers.

Christian loaded the *Bounty* with 312 pigs, 38 goats, eight dozen chickens, and the bull and the cow that had been left by Cook in 1777. Dogs and cats were also taken along and some plants that had not been seen on Tubuai. Christian also took on board nine Tahitian men, eight boys, ten women, and a young girl as passengers. Add to this the *Bounty*'s remaining crew of twenty-five men and anyone who has been on board a 90-foot vessel can imagine how crowded it must have been.

Maneuvering out from Matavai Bay the *Bounty* came close to running aground on Dolphin Bank (so named after the ship in which the European discoverer of Tahiti, Samuel Wallis, arrived). In the process, one of the ship's anchors was lost. (It was later retrieved by Captain Edwards in the *Pandora*). Had the *Bounty* sustained major damage, it might still have been in Tahiti when the brig *Mercury* arrived on August 12; how that would have influenced the fate of Christian and his men is up to speculation.

On arrival at Tubuai on June 23, 1789 (nine days after Bligh reached Timor), Christian made friends with the most powerful chief of the island, Tamatoa, who reigned over the western half, the rest of the island being divided between two minor chiefs. He and Christian exchanged names and everything seemed to be working

TUBUAI ISLAND

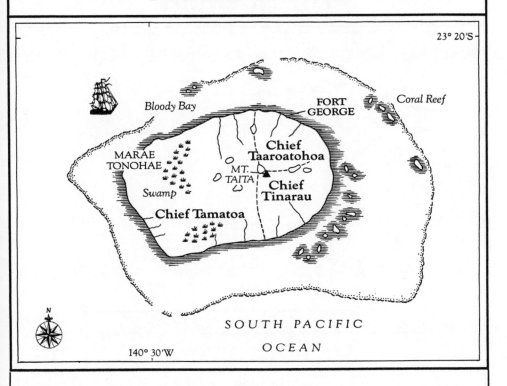

out for the best.

However, Christian now made two fatal mistakes which were to doom his little colony to failure. Even though Tamatoa had offered a large piece of beautiful land to the men of the *Bounty,* Christian — for some reason that will forever remain a mystery — preferred a site to the east of Tamatoa's chiefdom which belonged to a minor chief, Taaroatohoa. This was a humiliation which Tamatoa could never forget, and from then on he was Christian's sworn enemy.

Christian's second mistake was to let the 312 pigs loose on the island. All the Tubuaians had beautiful gardens which, since they had no animals, were not fenced in, and the pigs began to root them up.

Tamatoa and the third chief on the island, Tinarau, now formed an alliance against Christian and Taaroatohoa. Even the latter soon turned against Christian as the damage of the pigs became evident.

Christian had made plans to build a fort which, patriotically enough, was to be called Fort George. It is interesting to speculate about what would have happened had he built it on Tamatoa's property; it is possible that the colony might then have been successfully established on Tubuai. But, as it was, Christian now had most of the natives on the island against him and, as if that were not enough trouble, he started having severe problems with the discipline of his crew; in fact, he was

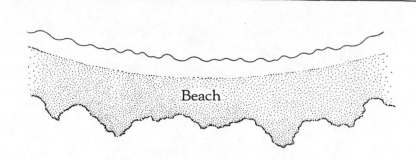

Beach

Palms and bush

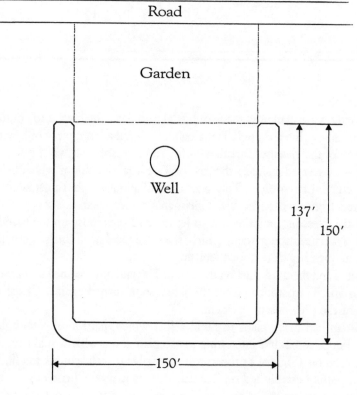

Road

Garden

Well

137′

150′

150′

N

soon to face some mutinies of his own.

Christian planned an elaborate fort which would have been the fulfillment of every boy's dream. Originally it was to have measured 100 yards square with walls 20 feet high and 18 feet thick at the base, surrounded by a moat crossed by a drawbridge. On each corner of the fort one of the *Bounty*'s cannons was to be mounted with the swivel guns placed on the sides.

The fort was never finished, but it must have been a very imposing structure even in its uncompleted state. The ruins could still be seen at the beginning of this century and even today you can see the outlines of the fort .

July
1789

ligh and his seventeen loyalists spent the month of July 1789 regaining their strength in the Dutch settlement of Coupang on Timor. And now when the perils and privations of the journey in the open boat were over, the same troubles surfaced as earlier on Tahiti and also on the islands within the Great Barrier Reef. Discipline disintegrated to the extent that Bligh again found it necessary to issue written orders, as he had during the last months on Tahiti.

According to Alexander McKee in *H.M.S. Bounty* (1962):

> Purcell, the carpenter, told Bligh to his face that, during the boat voyage, he had seen him frequently drop a piece of bread, while serving out the rations, and afterwards, when he thought no one was looking, pick it up and pop it in his mouth. Linkletter, one of the quartermasters, backed Purcell up: he, too, had seen Bligh conjuring an extra piece for himself. Bligh retaliated in the customary Service way: within twenty-four hours he had "picked on" Purcell and Linkletter, and had them imprisoned on board Captain Spikerman's ship.

(Captain Spikerman was the first officer to greet and help Bligh and his crew on their arrival at Coupang.)

Fryer, the sailing master, was again "insolent and neglectful" and, according to Bligh, had even told his brother-in-law, able seaman Robert Tinkler, to stick his knife into Cole, the boatswain!

Being anxious to get to Batavia (now Djakarta), 1800 miles distant, in time for the departure of the Dutch October fleet for Europe, Bligh bought a 34-foot schooner for 1000 Rix Dollars and named it HMS *Resource*. Because of the prevalence of pirates in the Java Sea, the vessel was armed with four swivel guns, and the crew with 14 stand of small arms.

After Norton's death on Tofua there had been no further casualties on the long voyage. But now the tropical fevers of Indonesia started taking their toll. David Nelson, the botanist, succumbed to an "inflammatory fever" on July 20. Others were to follow.

Meanwhile, Christian and his men on Tubuai began constructing Fort George. The land for it was purchased with "a quantity of red feathers" which Christian had prudently brought from Tahiti and which were highly prized by the natives of Tubuai who, amazingly, did not show any interest in iron tools or European clothes, preferring their own stone tools and clothing made of tapa.

The work on the planned, grandiose fort must have been exhausting in the extreme in the tropical heat and with unrelenting insects all around. (Tubuai was badly infested with mosquitoes.) Before the work began in earnest the Union Jack was hoisted on a makeshift flagpole; Christian's mutiny was against Bligh, not against the King.

Considering the explosive mix of his crew, a majority of mutineers who had already defied authority and a minority of loyalists who had been forced to come along, it is amazing that Christian had been able to preserve discipline as well and as long as he had. It is especially remarkable in view of the fact that many of the mutineers and all of the loyalists wanted to settle on Tahiti, a plan which Christian strongly opposed, knowing that a British warship would show up there sooner or later. Christian's authority over his men can only be explained by the fact that he had been liked by everyone on board. Now, however, when the shipboard routine was over, he faced the same discipline problems that Bligh had experienced on Tahiti and was now encountering on Timor.

It started with able seamen John Sumner and Matthew Quintal going ashore and staying overnight without leave. When Christian confronted them about this breach of orders, their reply was: "The ship is moored and we are now our own masters." Christian said he would show them who was master and had them put in irons for a few days. It was a minor incident, but it did show in what direction the wind was blowing.

The problems with the natives also worsened and, on July 25, a party of seamen collecting coconuts was ambushed. Although no one was seriously injured, this confrontation was another sign of further trouble ahead. On July 27, able seaman John Adams had to be rescued from the house of one of the chiefs where he had been overpowered and deprived of everything but his shirt. In reprisal Christian confiscated the chief's household gods (ancestor images most sacred to Polynesians) and burned down his house. There was now a clear escalation of hostilities and more and more of the men began to doubt the wisdom of remaining on Tubuai.

August 1789

*I*n early August 1789 Bligh and his loyalist crew were still in Coupang occupied with fitting out the 34-foot schooner Bligh had bought and named HMS *Resource*. They sailed for Java on August 20, having had a good two months to recuperate from the extreme privations of the open-boat voyage from Tofua to Timor. Because of the danger of attacks by pirates, they were escorted by two armed proas.

Christian, meanwhile, was facing mounting difficulties on Tubuai. He had both discipline problems with his crew and escalating hostilities with the natives. The pigs the mutineers has let loose on arrival had done terrible damage to the natives' gardens, but that was not the only cause of the unrest. The *tahu'as* (native priests), afraid of losing their power to the white men, had spread a rumor that the deep and wide moat which was being dug around Fort George was actually intended as a mass grave for the whole population of the island!

The existence on Tubuai was nothing like that on Tahiti. Here there was backbreaking work on the fort in the daytime and a constant fight against mosquitoes, fleas, lice, and rats at night. And the women, although quite as beautiful as on Tahiti, were not as accommodating. By the end of the month, most of the white men and some of their Tahitian companions were ready to leave. But Christian, who could be just as stubborn as Bligh, insisted on staying.

Christian never found out about it, but on August 9 his hide-out came close to being discovered. Late in the evening the 150-ton brig *Mercury*, under the command of Captain John Henry Cox, passed within two miles of Tubuai. Cox could not see the *Bounty* in the dark (if he had, he would certainly have stayed until morning), but he did see fires ashore and fired two guns — there was no response. If Christian and his men heard the shots, they must have thought it was thunder, because no mention of it is made in any account of their stay on the island.

Also, because of the dark, the *Mercury* was almost wrecked on the reef of Tubuai, and it is interesting to speculate about what would have happened had this been the case. Would the crews of the two ships have made common cause or would it have come to conflict between them? How would Christian have dealt with Cox and vice versa?

Such speculation is made even more interesting by the fact that the *Mercury*, although her crew was English, sailed under the Swedish flag. Many *Bounty* historians do not seem to know it, but the ship was in reality a privateer commissioned by the Swedish King and, with the commission, she had been re-christened *Gustaf III* in honor of the King. Her mission was to harass Russian settlements in Alaska, Sweden then being at war with Russia.

As it was, the *Mercury* continued north to Tahiti where she arrived on August 12. Captain Cox was thoroughly mystified by all the stories he heard there about Ra'atira Titerano (Captain Christian) and Ra'atira Parai (Captain Bligh); his lieutenant, George Mortimer, mentions the confusion and puzzlement in his narrative of the voyage.

Cox marooned one of his men on Tahiti, a seaman named John Brown (alias Bound) who had slashed one of his shipmates across the face with a razor. The *Mercury* sailed after a stay of three weeks.

September
1789

ligh and his loyalist crew were sailing westward on the schooner *Resource* on their way from Coupang to Batavia. The term "loyalist" may be a euphemism, because Bligh again faced a mutiny, albeit a minor one. Having reached Surabaya, a Dutch settlement on the north coast of Java, Bligh ordered Fryer, the sailing master and Bligh's nemesis, to take the *Resource* and meet him in the harbor at a point to which the governor of the district was going to take Bligh in the official launch. However, when the captain and the governor reached the place at the appointed time, the *Resource* was nowhere to be seen. Bligh, livid with rage over the embarrassment, finally found her snugly moored at the quay. He demanded to see Mr. Fryer.

When Fryer appeared, Bligh heaped even more than his usual abuse on him. Fryer: "You not only use me ill, but every man in the vessel will say the same." And the seamen who were standing around agreed: "Yes, by God, we are used damn ill, nor have we any right to be used so." At which point Bligh grabbed a bayonet and arrested Fryer and also Purcell (who had been the most vocal of the complainers) and had them put in irons.

In Surabaya Fryer had also accused Bligh of fraudulent dealings at Coupang, but he later retracted his allegations. After apologizing, Fryer was released when the party reached Samarang on September 22, but Purcell, who refused to apologize, was kept prisoner until the ship arrived in Batavia on October 1.

Christian was facing a mutiny at the same time. The cause for it, however, was not his personality — he was still well liked — but the conditions on the island which had reached a crisis point.

The natives of the neighboring districts on Tubuai had become so hostile that it came to outright battles. Although Christian and his men, armed with muskets as they were, emerged the victors (more than sixty natives were killed while the only casualty in Christian's party was seaman Thomas Burkett who received a slight wound), it was clear to the majority that Tubuai was not the place for them, especially since the native women refused to come and live with them.

The mutineers demanded that they be allowed to take women by force. Christian refused, whereupon the mutineers called a general strike, stopped working on the fort, and broke into the spirit room on board.

Having lost all authority, Christian called a meeting for September 10. A vote was taken (in which the seven loyalists who had been forced to remain on the *Bounty* were, incredibly, allowed to participate) which turned out 16 to 9 in favor of returning to Tahiti. Christian then made his famous speech, for modern ears quite melodramatic, but very much in character:

> Gentlemen, I will carry you, and land you, wherever you please. I desire none to stay with me, but I have one favour to request, that you will grant me the ship, tie the foresail, give me a few gallons of water, and leave me to run before the wind, and I shall land upon the first island the ship drives to. I have done such an act that I cannot stay at Otaheite. I will never live where I may be carried home to be a disgrace to my family.

Considering Christian's suicidal plan to leave the *Bounty* on a makeshift raft, there is no doubt that he meant what he said. However, when he was finished, midshipman Edward Young rose and said: "We shall never leave you, Mr. Christian, go where you will!" He was speaking for all who had voted against returning to Tahiti.

On September 17, after barely three months on Tubuai, Christian and his crew, together with their Tahitian companions and a few Tubuaians, left for Tahiti and anchored in Matavai on September 22 (the same day Bligh arrived at Samarang). The nine mutineers and seven loyalists who wanted to remain on the island were let ashore while Christian and the eight mutineers who had cast their lot with him prepared to leave.

We now know that the main reason Christian sailed immediately was that his consort, Mauatua, had discovered a plot among the Tahitians to capture the ship (which they could have done, since the *Bounty* now had a crew of only nine). Christian, in fact, spent only sixteen hours on Tahiti.

Because of his hasty departure, Christian never met John Brown, the troublemaker who had been marooned on Tahiti by the Swedish privateer *Mercury* only a month earlier. (The *Mercury* arrived in England several months before Bligh left on his second breadfruit expedition.) Accordingly, he never found out how close he had come to being discovered on Tubuai.

In order to be certain that enough women would be on board when he left, Christian pretended that he planned to stay a few days longer to take on more water and provisions. In the evening he gave a party on board at which nineteen women showed up. Drinks flowed freely and some time during the night Christian quietly slipped the anchor cable (leaving a second anchor in Tahiti; see the June 1789 commentary) and set sail. Some of the women noticed that the ship was under way,

THE *BOUNTY* MEN
WHO SAILED WITH CHRISTIAN

Edward Young
ACTING MIDSHIPMAN

Matthew Quintal
ABLE-BODIED SEAMAN

John Mills
GUNNER'S MATE

John Adams
ABLE-BODIED SEAMAN

Isaac Martin
ABLE-BODIED SEAMAN

John Williams
ABLE-BODIED SEAMAN

William McCoy
ABLE-BODIED SEAMAN

William Brown
GARDENER

but Christian assured them that he was merely moving the ship to the harbor at Pare.

Christian also seems to have tried to kidnap Coleman, the armorer, since his skills were important on a long voyage. Evidently he could not get Coleman drunk enough, however, and Coleman ran up on deck as soon as he noticed the ship was under way, jumped overboard, and swam ashore.

In the morning, the women could feel that the ship was outside the reef, and ran on deck. Although the distance to the reef was already a good mile, one woman jumped overboard and swam back but none of the others dared to try it (or perhaps they were hung over). Six of the women were considered "rather ancient" and were sent ashore in Moorea. That left twelve women, which would have been enough for the mutineers and the three Polynesians (two of them from Tubuai) who had been allowed to come along. Soon afterwards, however, three male Polynesian stowaways were discovered, and now Christian made a fateful mistake: instead of landing the stowaways on Moorea or some other island, he let them remain on board. It is entirely possible that the later tragedies on Pitcairn — which were caused partly by the lack of women — could have been avoided if the stowaways had been landed.

As it was, Christian left on his quest for a refuge with a time bomb aboard.

THE *BOUNTY* MEN
WHO REMAINED ON TAHITI

MUTINEERS

Charles Churchill
MASTER-AT-ARMS

John Millward
ABLE-BODIED SEAMAN

Thomas Burkett
ABLE-BODIED SEAMAN

William Muspratt
ABLE-BODIED SEAMAN

Thomas Ellison
ABLE-BODIED SEAMAN

Richard Skinner
ABLE-BODIED SEAMAN

Henry Hillbrant
ABLE-BODIED SEAMAN

John Sumner
ABLE-BODIED SEAMAN

Matthew Thompson
ABLE-BODIED SEAMAN

LOYALISTS

George Stewart
MIDSHIPMAN

Charles Norman
CARPENTER'S MATE

Peter Heywood
ACTING MIDSHIPMAN

Thomas McIntoshn
CARPENTER'S CREW

James Morrison
.BOATSWAIN'S MATE

Joseph Coleman
ARMORER

Michael Byrne
ABLE-BODIED SEAMAN

October
1789

On October 1, 1789, Bligh and his men arrived in Batavia in the *Resource.* Purcell, who had been in irons ever since the stop-over at Surabaya was now let free.

On the following day Bligh fell ill with malaria, an ailment which was to haunt him for the next few years and from which he suffered especially during the second breadfruit expedition.

The *Resource* was sold at auction on October 10, as was the launch, with which Bligh, for sentimental reasons, found it difficult to part.

On October 16, accompanied by his clerk Samuel and his servant John Smith, Bligh left for South Africa on the Dutch packet *Vlydte.* Before their departure, seaman Thomas Hall died from a tropical disease. The other crew members were left in Batavia to arrange for passage home in various Dutch ships. Many of them were ill; a few were dying. If Bligh had cared for his crew for any other reason than to keep them in effective working order on board, he would have seen to it that the sick were sent home first.

Christian, meanwhile, was faced with the problem of where to look for his island of refuge. He first considered the Marquesas but decided against it, because the islands in the group were populated and too vulnerable to discovery. The experience on Tubuai had taught him an important lesson. He needed an island which was uninhabited, fertile, remote, and difficult of access.

Pitcairn fits that description perfectly. Indeed, for many years it was widely assumed that Christian set out for Pitcairn immediately after leaving Tahiti. Not only is that a highly unlikely conjecture (it takes only two to three weeks, not four months, to sail the 1300 miles from Tahiti to Pitcairn), but we now know with certainty that Christian sailed westward on a voyage of exploration which covered thousands of miles before he arrived at Pitcairn. By then he had sailed approximately 7800 miles since the day of the mutiny.

How do we know?

In 1956 a discovery was made which created a sensation among *Bounty* historians. Professor H. E. Maude of the Australian National University found some newspaper articles from the 1820s which contained interviews with Teehuteatuaonoa (also called "Jenny"), consort of the mutineer Isaac Martin and the first of the original settlers to leave Pitcairn (in 1817).

From Teehuteatuaonoa's account it is clear, not only that Christian sailed westward, but that he discovered Rarotonga, the main island in what is now known as the Cook group. Until Professor Maude proved otherwise, it was thought that Rarotonga was discovered by Philip Goodenough in 1814, although island tradition and some statements by John Adams on Pitcairn hinted at the possibility that the *Bounty* had stopped at Rarotonga after leaving Tahiti for the last time.

Teehuteatuaonoa's account is also confirmed by a Rarotongan legend written down by the missionary John Williams in 1823. According to this island lore, Rarotonga had, two generations earlier, been visited by a floating garden with two waterfalls. The *Bounty* did indeed look like a garden and the waterfalls must refer to the pumps on board. A Polynesian generation is usually counted as fifteen to seventeen years, so "two generations ago" fits well with the time of the *Bounty*'s visit. In any case, even without confirmation of the validity behind the legend, Williams was always convinced that it referred to the *Bounty*.

Finally, we also know that it was the *Bounty* which introduced the orange to Rarotonga, the juice of which fruit today accounts for the island's main export.

November 1789

$\cdots \rightsquigarrow \cdots$

*B*ligh spent the month of November 1789 on the Indian Ocean on his way from Batavia to Cape Town. He certainly did not like being a passenger and least of all on a Dutch ship; his journal is full of contemptuous and sarcastic remarks concerning Dutch methods of navigation.

Meanwhile, the tropical diseases in the Dutch East Indies were wreaking havoc with the loyalists he had left behind to wait for transportation home. David Nelson, the botanist, had died in Coupang. Seaman Thomas Hall had died in Batavia before Bligh left. Now it was quartermaster Peter Linkletter's and master's mate William Elphinstone's turn to succumb to the "violent fevers." Seaman Robert Lamb died on the passage home and the acting ship's surgeon, Thomas Ledward, was never heard of again. The likelihood is that he was on board the ship *Welfare* which was lost without a trace. Some *Bounty* scholars, however, think he died in Batavia, others that he survived and is identical with a surgeon, also named Ledward, who allegedly was on George Vancouver's ship *Discovery* from 1791 to 1795 (Kennedy: *Bligh*, 1978).

One of Ledward's letters from Batavia has been preserved and it gives an excellent insight into Bligh's pettiness and meanness (the word "mean" was equivalent to stingy or ungenerous in the 1700s):

> The captain denied me, as well as the rest of the gentlemen who had not agents, any money unless I would give him my power of attorney and also my will, in which I was to bequeath to him all my property, this he called by the proper name of security . . . In case of my death I hope this matter will be clearly pointed out to my relations.

Eventually, only twelve of the nineteen men set adrift by the mutineers ever reached England (quartermaster John Norton having been killed by natives on Tofua).

Christian's adventures around this time are known only from Teehuteatuaonoa's accounts and from the contradictory stories told to various sea captains by John Adams on Pitcairn. Polynesians do not attach much importance to matters involving time, and Adams' memory was not very reliable, so exact dates are not known. We do know, however, that Christian, after discovering Rarotonga, sailed to the Lau group in the Fijis where he discovered the island Ono-i-Lau. He then sailed for Tongatabu where he stayed for two days and traded with the natives for provisions. Since Tongatabu is less than 100 miles distant from Tofua, the mutineers were now practically back at the place where the mutiny had taken place seven months earlier.

But what about the nine mutineers and seven loyalists who had chosen to remain on Tahiti when Christian and his men left the island? The accounts of boatswain's mate James Morrison and midshipman Peter Heywood reveal that the *Bounty* men had all been welcomed by their old *taios* and invited to stay in their households. William Muspratt and Henry Hillbrant, both mutineers, as well as the loyalists Michael Byrne, Thomas McIntosh, and Charles Norman stayed in Pare, chief Teina's district west of Matavai (although Teina himself was in Taiarapu, the south-east part of Tahiti). The others settled on Point Venus with chief Poino. There was no division among the *Bounty* men as far as mutineers and loyalists were concerned.

On November 11 several of the remaining seamen started to build a ship, a schooner which would enable them to leave the island. The initiator of the project, Morrison, claimed later, in the journal he reconstructed from memory, that he wanted to sail with the other loyalists to the Dutch East Indies and from there back to England. If so, it is very interesting that he confided his plan not only to the loyalist McIntosh, but to John Millward, a mutineer, both of whom agreed to help him and to keep the reason for the project a secret. To the other *Bounty* men they said they were building the ship in order to cruise among the islands.

McIntosh was a natural choice since his designation on board had been carpenter's crew. But it is difficult to understand why Morrison confided his plan to the mutineer Millward if he wanted to keep it a secret. Nor is it readily apparent why Millward agreed to help. He was one of the active mutineers and later, having survived the wreck of the *Pandora*, was eventually hanged from the yardarm of HMS *Brunswick* in Spithead. Perhaps he thought he could gain a pardon by his action, but he should have known better; there was no pardon for actively participating in a mutiny. On the other hand, maybe he thought he and the other mutineers could take over the ship and sail to another island, as Christian had done. No records have come to light that could give us an insight into his motivation.

The loyalist Norman, carpenter's mate on board, and the mutineer Hillbrant, who had served as cooper on the *Bounty,* also joined Morrison in the building project, unaware of its real purpose. Again, we can see that there was no real division between loyalists and mutineers on Tahiti.

December
1789

The Dutch East Indiaman *Vlydte* was nearing the African continent on her way from Batavia to Cape Town. A very impatient Bligh was complaining about the length of the voyage caused, in his opinion, by the Dutch "not carrying a sufficient quantity of sail."

On December 16 the ship finally anchored in Table Bay and Bligh immediately started dispatching letters to England explaining his view of the mutiny. He also sent letters to Port Jackson and even to India with descriptions of the *Bounty* and of the mutineers.

It must have been around this time that Christian decided on Pitcairn as a promising possibility for a permanent settlement. In Bligh's library he had read Hawkesworth's *Voyages* which contained Carteret's description of the discovery of Pitcairn in 1767:

> We continued our course westward till the evening of Thursday, the 2nd of July, when we discovered land to the northward of us. Upon approaching it the next day, it appeared like a great rock rising out of the sea: it was not more than five miles in circumference, and seemed to be uninhabited; it was, however, covered with trees, and we saw a small stream of fresh water running down one side of it. I would have landed upon it, but the surf, which at this season broke upon it with great violence, rendered it impossible. It lies in lat. 20° 2' south; long. 133° 21' west. It is so high that we saw it at the distance of more than fifteen leagues, and it having been discovered by a young gentleman, son to Major Pitcairn of the marines, we called it PITCAIRN'S ISLAND.

Pitcairn is one of the most remote islands in the world. It lies "in the middle of nowhere," 4650 miles from California, 4000 from Chile, and 3300 from New Zealand. The closest inhabited island is Mangareva in the Gambier group, 306 miles to the north-west. (Mangareva was not discovered until 1797 and no European is known to have landed there until 1825.)

Here, then, seemed to be the fulfillment of Christian's dreams, an island that fitted all of his requirements: it was remote, difficult of access, lush with vegetation, and apparently uninhabited. And, although Christian did not know about it at the time, Pitcairn had an extra bonus in store for him: Carteret had given it a position on his chart which was almost 200 miles off!

We do not know how Christmas 1789 was celebrated by either Bligh or Christian, but Morrison describes in his narrative how it was celebrated by the mutineers and loyalists who had remained on Tahiti:

> We kept the Hollidays in the best manner, killing a Hog for Christmas dinner, and reading Prayers which we never Omitted on Sundays, and having wet weather were not able to do anything out of doors for the remainder of the year. The natives were curious about the raising of the flag every Sunday, and we told them it was God's Day.

January 1790

*B*ligh, who had spent over two weeks in Cape Town dispatching letters right and left and who was eager to get home as soon as possible, sailed for England on January 2, 1790, on the same Dutch East Indiaman that had brought him from Batavia.

Christian, meanwhile, was sailing eastward, tacking against the south-east trade winds, on his search for Pitcairn. It was an arduous voyage and voices were heard on board clamoring for a return to Tahiti. Christian, knowing that such a destination would mean disaster for himself and the other mutineers, insisted on pressing on to Pitcairn.

It was not an easy task, since Carteret had charted the island so far to the west of its true position. But Christian guessed — rightly so — that the latitude would be approximately correct, and in the evening of January 15 Pitcairn appeared on the horizon 7800 miles and eight and a half months after the mutiny. Because of heavy weather, it was not until three days later that Christian, with some of his companions (Brown, Williams, McCoy, and three Polynesians), could land on what is now called Tedside on the west coast of Pitcairn. Two days were spent ashore and on January 20 Christian returned to the ship with good news: the island was well suited for a permanent settlement.

The *Bounty* was run up on the rocks close to the slight indentation in the shore line now known as Bounty Bay, and livestock and goods were shipped ashore. Most students of the *Bounty* story seem to assume that everything valuable and useful was salvaged from the vessel. That is highly improbable.

The *Bounty* carried pigs, goats, chickens, cats, dogs, and several varieties of plants. These all had to be ferried ashore (plus the Tahitian baby girl called Sully who was floated ashore in a barrel). Those who have visited Pitcairn know that even on the calmest day there is a heavy surf thundering into Bounty Bay and the waters there are extremely turbulent and dangerous. So it must have taken at least the best part of the day to get the animals and plants ashore.

PITCAIRN ISLAND

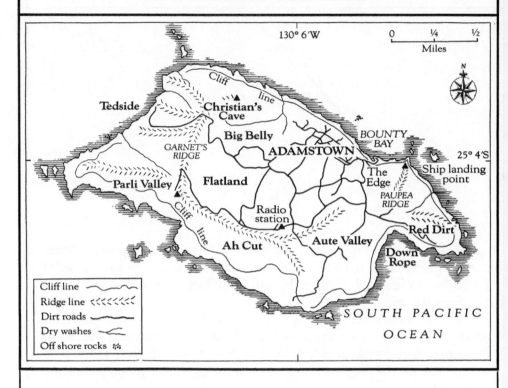

But the *Bounty* was burned on January 23, three days after it was beached. In this short time it would simply have been impossible to salvage everything valuable, let alone everything potentially useful.

One can only imagine what the feelings of the settlers may have been as they saw their last link with the outside world destroyed. It is difficult to imagine that anyone was elated, although some or all of the mutineers may have felt relief, while some or all of the Polynesian women who had been forced to come along may have been depressed.

Be that as it may, the fact that everything useful had not been salvaged must have created ill feeling. Tradition has it that Matthew Quintal, in a state of drunkenness, put fire to the ship. Since he was one of the most willful and undisciplined of the mutineers, the story is probably true. An accidental fire is unlikely, and so is a command by Christian to burn the ship before everything useful had been brought ashore. The theory that the ship was burned to prevent dissenters from leaving founders on the fact that it would have been impossible to refloat the *Bounty*. Even if it had been possible, it would have required the cooperation of everyone. The traditional story is more believable.

But the conclusion that can be drawn is that the very first days of the settlement on Pitcairn were probably marred by disappointment and frustration. It was an ill omen for the future.

February
1790

$\mathscr{B}$ligh spent the month of February 1790 sailing as a passenger from Cape Town to England. Most of his time was occupied with writing an account of the mutiny and of the open-boat voyage, to be used for the obligatory court-martial and also for a book that he published not long after his arrival.

On Pitcairn, Christian and his fellow mutineers and their Polynesian companions were busy hauling the goods salvaged from the *Bounty* up the steep slope which to this day is called the Hill of Difficulty. The task would be formidable under the best of climatic conditions, but January and February are the hottest and most humid months on Pitcairn. Today there is a narrow roadway leading up the Hill of Difficulty; it is strenuous enough to climb without carrying anything. We can only imagine the grueling effort it must have entailed to haul up heavy burdens through the dense undergrowth which then marked the place. Temporary living quarters, employing sails from the *Bounty*, were constructed on The Edge, the small plateau overlooking The Landing Place (now called Bounty Bay).

A watch had to be kept inland as well as towards the sea, since the island was so densely forested that no one could be sure that it was uninhabited. There were many signs of earlier habitation: maraes (Polynesian outdoor temples), tikis (godlike ancestor images), and stone tools, as well as the presence of breadfruit, bananas, and yams (which can only be transported to an island by humans). The stone structures and artifacts, however, seemed to be very old and were quite overgrown with vegetation, so the settlers soon became convinced that no one else lived on the island.

At some early stage of the settlement, the mutineers made a fateful decision that was to doom the small community to deadly strife in the future. They divided the island into nine parts, one parcel of land for each of the white men and none for the Polynesians.

For a Polynesian, the most important thing in life is land. Land gives prestige, importance, worth, and a sense of identity to the owner — the more of it the better. Without land a man is nothing. Two of the Polynesians now on Pitcairn were chiefs, accustomed not only to owning land but to controlling the lands of their subjects.

In view of this great injustice — understandable in terms of the then prevailing European view of the Polynesians as "savages," but totally incomprehensible to the islanders — it is indeed a wonder that they took the situation in stride for so long without open resistance. It is a tribute to the forbearance and good nature of these Polynesian men who, presumably, had all come along willingly. After all, not only were they now landless, but the six of them had to share three women and all of them seem to have been treated as "hewers of wood and carriers of water" rather than as *taios*.

On Tahiti, meanwhile, there was violence. On February 11 Matthew Thompson, one of the most brutal of the mutineers, had killed a Tahitian man and his child without any provocation other than that the man had not understood a command to leave. Fearing reprisals Thompson fled and, in company with his equally hotheaded mate Churchill, went to the district of Taiarapu where Churchill's *taio* Vehiatua was chief. Soon afterwards Vehiatua died and, since he left no children, his *taio* Churchill now became chief, marking the first time a white man had risen to such a position in the South Seas (the second was Will Mariner in Tonga in 1806) and the only time ever in Tahiti.

March
1790

··· ⛵ ···

*O*n March 14, 1790, Bligh arrived in England and on March 16 he presented his report to the Admiralty. As early as March 24, the King's decision to send out a ship to hunt down the mutineers (or pirates, as they were called) was announced.

Bligh also contacted Sir Joseph Banks, the initiator and principal patron of the failed breadfruit expedition. Understandably, Bligh was anxious to know what the reaction of this powerful man would be to the disastrous outcome of the project. He need not have worried: Sir Joseph gave him his full support and his backing for another expedition.

While Bligh was busy justifying his loss of the *Bounty* and rapidly becoming a national hero because of his outstanding feat of navigating the *Bounty*'s launch from Tofua to Timor, Christian and his fellow mutineers were settling down on Pitcairn.

On Tahiti, where the mutineer Churchill had become chief of one of the largest districts, Taiarapu, Matthew Thompson had become envious of the white chief. After a heated argument Thompson had moved to a neighboring district, but since Churchill did not trust Thompson, he ordered some of his servants to steal Thompson's firearms. Thompson suspected Churchill and confronted him, but the latter managed to make him believe that he had had nothing to do with the affair and the two of them moved back together.

Soon afterwards, however, when Churchill had mercilessly beaten one of his servants, Maititi, the latter took revenge by telling Thompson who was behind the theft of the muskets. At the first opportunity Thompson then shot down Churchill from the back, probably with one of Churchill's own muskets.

But Thompson had not counted on the fact that, although Churchill was unpopular with many of his subjects, he still had friends and supporters among them and they felt it was their duty to avenge the death of their chief. As soon as Thompson was off guard for a moment, some of them — led by Churchill's friend Patire —

attacked him and crushed his head with a rock.

Meanwhile, the *Bounty* men in Pare were at work on the schooner they had started building in November of the previous year. They had made good progress and the frame was completed on March 15 (one day after Bligh's arrival in England). When we consider that the builders had only a limited number of tools from the *Bounty* and no effective means by which to fashion planks, their achievement is truly astonishing. They did, of course, have a great deal of assistance from the ever-helpful Tahitians who wanted to learn how a European-type vessel was built.

The schooner was designed to measure 30 feet with a beam of 9 feet 6 inches. It eventually turned out to be a masterpiece of marine engineering, a fast and graceful vessel, a memorable tribute to British skill, resourcefulness, and ingenuity. But as destiny would have it, Morrison's dream would be only partially fulfilled.

April
1790

We do not know what the initial reaction of Fletcher Christian's family was when Bligh arrived in England. The newspapers of the time did not feature what are today called human interest stories and no reporters besieged the individuals involved in newsworthy events, much less their relatives. However, the recently widowed mother of midshipman Peter Heywood wrote to Bligh to enquire about the fate of her son who had been only fifteen years old when the *Bounty* left Portsmouth almost two and a half years earlier. In reply Bligh wrote what must be one of the cruellest letters a worried mother has ever received:

LONDON,
April 2, 1790

Madam,

I received your letter this day, and feel for you very much, being perfectly sensible of the extreme distress you must suffer from the conduct of your son Peter. His baseness is beyond all description, but I hope you will endeavour to prevent the loss of him, heavy as the misfortune is, from afflicting you too severely. I imagine he is, with the rest of the mutineers, returned to Otaheite.

I AM, MADAM,
Wm Bligh (signed)

This letter is of extreme interest from a psychological standpoint. In a sense, one could say that it contains the key to Bligh's problems in life, the essence of his main character defect, and, ultimately, the key to the mutiny.

Even Bligh's apologists consider the letter cruel. Mackaness writes: "It is impossible to excuse or even palliate the harshness of Bligh's reply." Some of Bligh's supporters, for example Gavin Kennedy, try to explain it by concentrating on Bligh's having felt betrayed by Heywood when he needed help most. But apart from the fact that there was nothing Heywood realistically could have done by the time he became aware that a mutiny had taken place, the feelings Bligh had towards Peter Heywood have little to do with the fact that he was dealing with a recently widowed mother who was worried about her son.

Bligh had not observed Heywood participating in any mutinous act. Officially he based his judgment of Heywood's "villainy" solely on the fact that the latter had done nothing to help him and had remained on board the *Bounty*. It is clear, however, that the hatred he felt towards Heywood stemmed from something quite different: the fact that Heywood and Christian had formed a close friendship. To the end of his life Bligh believed that Heywood had not only known about the mutiny in advance but had actively planned it together with Christian.

The most striking thing about this letter, at least to a psychologist, is the fact that Bligh truly believed that he was consoling a poor, unfortunate mother. Bligh was not a sadist, nor was he a person who would *consciously* try to hurt someone by sarcasm or by feigning compassion. He truly believed that Peter Heywood's mother must be suffering from the "baseness of her son's conduct." The fact is that the letter was cruel by impact, not by conscious intention. If anyone would have called the letter cruel, Bligh would have been uncomprehending: had he not clearly, demonstrably, undeniably, offered the widow his sympathy?

It was this inability to understand the impact his words had on others that accounted for most of Bligh's problems throughout his life. He could never understand that he, the most righteous, the most dutiful, the most efficient, the most caring of naval commanders, could not be recognized as benevolent by everyone. He had always done his best, and whatever negative consequences there had been were all due to the inefficiency, the incompetence, and — in the case of the mutiny — the treachery of the people around him.

Bligh never realized that most of his problems stemmed from his own limitations. In this sense, he is a tragic figure in maritime history. He possessed many of the positive qualities of his mentor and ideal, Captain Cook, but the psychological blind spot he had in his dealings with other people prevented him from becoming one of the truly great naval commanders in history.

May

1790

... 🚢 ...

*N*ot long after his return to England, Bligh had become something of a national hero because of his courage and skill in navigating the *Bounty*'s overladen launch 3618 miles from Tofua to Timor. The newspapers had reported on the mutiny as early as March 24, 1790, ten days after Bligh's arrival. But no extensive account of his epic voyage appeared until May when *Gentleman's Magazine* published an article describing it. Bligh's feat, however, was widely known by now and everyone was eager to read his book about the mutiny and the voyage, which was due to be published in June.

The fame of the event was considerably augmented by a dramatization produced by one of the largest theaters in London. The handbill for the production read:

ROYALTY THEATRE
Well-Street, near Goodman's-Fields.

— — — — — —

This present THURSDAY, May 6, 1790,

will be presented

A FACT, TOLD IN ACTION, CALLED

THE PIRATES!

or

The Calamities of Capt. BLIGH.

Exhibiting a full account of his Voyage from his taking
leave at the Admiralty.
AND SHEWING
The BOUNTY sailing down the River THAMES.

The Captain's reception at Otaheite and exchanging the *British Manufactures* for the BREAD-FRUIT TREES. With an OTA-HEITEAN DANCE

The Attachment of the OTAHEITEAN WOMEN to, and their Distress at parting from, the BRITISH SAILORS.

An exact Representation of
The Seisure of Capt. BLIGH in the cabin of the BOUNTY, by the pirates.

With the affecting Scene of forcing the Captain and his faithful Followers into the boat.

Their Distress at Sea, and Repulse by the Natives of One of the *Friendly Islands*.

Their miraculous Arrival at the *Cape of Good Hope*, and their friendly Reception by the Governor.

DANCES AND CEREMONIES of the HOTTENTOTS
On their Departure. And their happy Arrival in England.
Rehearsed under the immediate Instruction of a Person who was on-board the Bounty, Store-Ship.

The "Person who was on board the *Bounty*" remains anonymous — if he ever existed.

Meanwhile, Tahiti was experiencing a revolutionary change due to the presence of those *Bounty* men who had elected to remain on the island when Christian left it for good. This change was fully as important in the history of Tahiti as that brought on by the missionaries who arrived in 1797 and deserves to be given more emphasis in the *Bounty* literature than has so far been the case.

Before European contact, Tahiti was divided into several chiefdoms which sometimes warred with each other, but usually lived in peaceful and harmonious coexistence. As soon as one chief would become too powerful or warlike in the eyes of his neighbors, the latter would form a coalition with the purpose of keeping him in check. Thus, it was impossible for a central power to emerge on the island. The actual power of decision rested with the heads of the family-clans in the districts, even though the chiefs theoretically had absolute authority.

When the first European explorers arrived, they naturally tried to establish good relations with the main authority on the island. Matavai being the preferred harbor of the British, the contacts they made were with the chiefs of the surrounding districts, Pare and Haapape. For some reason, Cook assumed that Tu, the chief of Pare, was the paramount authority on Tahiti; this was probably due, to no insignificant extent, to Tu's cunning representations to that effect. Tu was a shrewd man who well understood the value European support and European possessions, especially firearms, would have in his attempts to increase his power. Actually, however, Tu was a minor chief of a small district and had little or no influence on the decisions of other chiefs. In fact, the latter tended to look down on him because he was a "foreigner," stemming from the Tuamotus, who had achieved his status merely by marrying the daughter of a chief.

Because of the gifts that were given to Tu by the European visitors, especially the firearms, his power was greatly augmented. But he still needed men accustomed to the use of the European weapons. There were fourteen well-armed *Bounty* men (Churchill and Thompson had been killed in March 1790) who remained on Tahiti for more than a year and a half. Most of them stayed in Pare and their presence tipped the scales of power, eventually resulting in Tu's ascendance to the position of supreme ruler of Tahiti under the name Pomare I. (Technically and traditionally the power resided in his son, also named Tu and six years old at the time, who later became known as Pomare II, the first chief on Tahiti to accept the Christian faith.)

Although this process probably was inevitable (in some respects it can be compared with Kamehameha's ascendance to power in Hawaii), it is still clear that the mutiny on the *Bounty*, an insignificant event in the eyes of the British Admiralty, had momentous significance in the history of Tahiti.

June

1790

ligh's book about the ill-fated *Bounty* expedition was published in June 1790, something of a record when one considers that Bligh had arrived in England only three months earlier. It bore the imposing title *A Narrative of the Mutiny on board His Majesty's Ship "Bounty"; and the subsequent voyage of part of the crew in the ship's boat from Tofoa, one of the Friendly Islands, to Timor, a Dutch Settlement in the East Indies* and immediately became a bestseller. The success of the book was one of the key factors in assuring the everlasting fame of the mutiny itself.

Meanwhile, the mutineers and loyalists on Tahiti were putting the finishing touches to the schooner they were building. The tremendous impact the men of the *Bounty* had on the history of Tahiti has already been described. It is worthwhile also to discuss the general impact European intrusion had on the Polynesians.

The first serious consequence was the introduction of transmittable maladies, especially venereal diseases in the beginning but soon followed by other contagious diseases to which the Polynesians had no immunity. The subject of whether transmittable diseases existed among the Polynesians before European contact is controversial; there may never be an answer to the question. The likelihood is that there were no venereal diseases and very little in the way of illness at all; only yaws and a disease of the throat or neck, which to the Europeans seemed similar to scrofula, appear to have been endemic in Tahiti. With the exception of some inhabitants of barren atolls who were threatened with starvation from time to time, the Polynesians were exceptionally healthy and their main problem therefore was overpopulation (which, incidentally, had been one of the reasons for their migrations).

Several of the men on the *Bounty*, including Christian, had been treated for venereal disease on board. The whole crew was pronounced free of disease by the drunken surgeon Huggan before arrival in Tahiti. However, apart from his judgment being questionable, the "cures" of that time were so primitive and unreliable that the *Bounty* men probably contributed to — as well as became victims of — the venereal diseases introduced earlier by the crews of Wallis, Bougainville, Cook,

Boenechea, Langara, and Watts.

All sorts of other diseases were brought by Europeans: tuberculosis, typhus (which the Tahitians called "ship's fever," adapting the English word to "fiva"), and measles being among the worst killers. The Polynesians died in droves and their populations were reduced to a fifth or a tenth or, in some cases, even a twentieth of what they had been. Missionaries unwittingly contributed to the carnage by their insistence on totally inappropriate clothing and their disregard for physical health. Whalers and beachcombers spread not only diseases but alcoholism and moral decay.

Dr. George Hamilton, surgeon on board HMS *Pandora*, wrote in his *A Voyage Round the World in H. M. Frigate Pandora* (1793):

> Happy would it have been for those people had they never been visited by Europeans; for, to our shame be it spoken, disease and gunpowder is all the benefit they have ever received from us, in return for their hospitality and kindness.

The most serious consequence of European contact, however, was cultural. The Polynesian cultural community, especially the one existing on what are now referred to as the Society Islands, had probably come closer to an earthly paradise than any other in history. It was a community ruled by commonly held ideals of kindness and generosity. A strong faith and equally strong bonds to the extended family, together with firmly entrenched custom and tradition, ensured that the ideals were followed.

This is no idealization of "the noble savage" or a romantic distortion of Polynesian society; there is universal agreement among the early visitors to Eastern Polynesia in particular that the inhabitants were happy and fun-loving, kind and generous, gentle and considerate. They had a supreme God (Te Atua) and many other gods, but no devil. They had a heaven, but no hell. The idea of sin was foreign to them; it had to be introduced — together with the idea of a devil — by European missionaries to whom even laughing was a sin.

In his excellent book on this subject *Tahiti: A Paradise Lost* (1983), David Howarth says:

> ... if the missionaries judged by St. Paul's three criteria, they found the Tahitians had perfect faith, though in their own version of God; they had not much need of hope [to this day, there is no word for "hope" in the Tahitian language], because they were not threatened by gods or men; and of charity, the greatest of the three, they had an abundance.

A visitor to the Tahiti of today will still find these qualities surviving — at least to a much greater extent than they could be found in other societies — despite the influence of whalers, beachcombers, missionaries, bureaucrats, and tourists. It is a tribute to the strength of a once flourishing civilization which in so many ways was far superior to our own.

July 1790

$\mathcal{T}$he news of the mutiny on the *Bounty* eventually reached the United States. It must have created considerable interest, because the *Columbian Centinel* of July 21, 1790, devoted more than a full column to the story.

This was also the month when the schooner which the *Bounty* men on Tahiti had built was launched. They had every reason to be proud of their accomplishment: they had built a beautiful two-masted vessel, 30 feet long with a beam of 9 feet 6 inches. The planks, laboriously fashioned with tools from the *Bounty*, had been caulked with gum from the breadfruit tree. James Morrison, especially, could be proud. It was he who had conceived the project, designed the vessel, and led the construction of it. The launching was indeed a historic occasion. The *Resolution*, as it was christened, was the first ship built by Europeans on Tahiti, if not on any South Sea island. It was named after Cook's ship on which, ironically, Bligh had been sailing master on the last voyage.

The Tahitians insisted on the *Bounty* men following the same ancient ceremonies in launching the *Resolution* as they themselves did when launching their own ocean-going canoes (called *pahis*). The ceremonies were led by Poino, the chief of the district of Haapape on the eastern shore of Matavai Bay. Morrison describes the ceremony in his narrative (the journal he later reconstructed from memory):

> All being ready on the 5th we applied to Poeno who told me that the priest must perform his prayers over her, and then he would have her carried to the sea, the priest being sent for and a young pig and a plantain given him when he began walking round and round the vessel, stopping at the stem and stern and muttering short sentences in an unknown dialect; and having a bundle of young plantain trees brought to him by Poenos order, he now and then tossed one in on her deck. He kept at this all day and night and was hardly finished by sunrise on the 6th. When Poeno and Tew, Matte's father, came with three or four hundred men, and having each made a long oration, their men were divided into two partys and the servants of Tew having received a hog and

some cloth which was provided by Poeno for the occasion, one of the priests went on board and several plantain trees were tossed to him from both sides. He then ran fore and aft and exorted them to exert themselves, and on a signal being given they closed in, and those who could not reach by hand got long poles, a song being given they all joined in chorus and she soon began to move and in half an hour she reached the beach where she was launched and called the *Resolution*.

The little ship floated beautifully and turned out to be a very fast sailer. The main problem was the sails. Christian had not left any of the *Bounty*'s sails, or sailcloth, on Tahiti when he left, so native matting had to be used instead. However, because the sails had to be so large, the heavy matting did not work as well as it did on the Tahitian *pahis*; in fact, it kept tearing in strong winds and it was therefore doubtful whether the schooner could be used for any long voyages.

For the time being then, the schooner was used for pleasure trips. Later it was to be used as a warship in military operations, engaged in by the *Bounty* men, which helped increase the power of chief Tu who was at that time called Mate (Morrison: Matte).

August
1790

*O*n August 10, 1790, the British Admiralty appointed Captain Edward Edwards commander of HMS *Pandora*; he thereby became leader of the expedition which was sent to hunt down Christian and the rest of the mutineers. The task involved was formidable, and so was the manning and provisioning of the ship, since England was expecting war at the time.

Christian and his eight fellow mutineers on Pitcairn were destined to face problems just as serious — and just as lethal — as the danger of being caught by the long arm of the British Admiralty. In fact, one could say that their colonization project was doomed from the start because of the three serious mistakes they had made at the outset.

The first mistake (mentioned in the September 1789 commentary) was to allow the three male Polynesian stowaways on the *Bounty* to stay on board, since this resulted in a shortage of women. The second mistake was to divide the land on Pitcairn only among the mutineers, making the Polynesians landless.

The third mistake — and probably the worst — was to treat the Polynesians as servants rather than as equals. Perhaps it was inevitable in view of the eighteenth century Zeitgeist that considered Polynesians, indeed all "savages," biologically, intellectually, and culturally inferior to Europeans. Be that as it may, it was certainly a blueprint for disaster.

Not only were the Polynesians treated as servants, they were actually mistreated by several of the mutineers. Christian, Young, Adams, and Brown, the gardener, were reasonably humane in their dealings with the "Indians," but the rest of the mutineers were not. Quintal and McCoy were outright cruel to the Polynesians, men and women alike.

In order to understand future developments on Pitcairn, let's look at how the colonists paired off on arrival; see the table on page 112.

In addition, Teio had brought with her a baby daughter whose father was Tahitian, although we do not know his identity. Nor do we know the Tahitian name

MUTINEERS AND THEIR CONSORTS

Fletcher Christian
MAUATUA
(Maimiti, Isabella, Mainmast)

William McCoy
TEIO
(Te'o, Mary)

Edward Young
TERAURA
(Taoupiti, Mataohu, Susannah)

John Mills
VAHINEATUA
(Paraha Iti, Balhadi)

John Adams
PUARAI
(Obuarei, Opuole)

Matthew Quintal
TEVARUA
(Sarah, Big Sullee)

William Brown
TEATUAHITEA
(Te Lahu, Sarah)

John Williams
FAAHOTU
(Fahutu, Fasto)

Isaac Martin
TEEHUTEATUAONOA
(Jenny)

POLYNESIAN MEN AND THEIR CONSORTS

Tararo
(Talalo, from Raiatea)

TOOFAITI
(Hutia, Nancy, from Huahine)

Manarii
(Menalee, from Tahiti)

MAREVA
(Malewa)

Titahiti
(Taaroamiva, from Tubuai)

TINAFANAEA
(Toholomota, from Tubuai?)

Teimua
(Teirnua, from Tahiti)

MAREVA
(Malewa)

Oha
(Oher, from Tubuai)

TINAFANAEA
(Toholomota, from Tubuai?)

Niau
(Nehow, from Tahiti)

MAREVA
(Malewa)

of the girl; the mutineers referred to her as "Sully" (variously Sally or Sarah). She was ten months old on arrival at Pitcairn.

So each mutineer had a woman, but the six Polynesian men had to share three women. The way they did it is of considerable interest.

The chief from Raiatea, Tararo, had a woman of his own, Toofaiti from Huahine. Together they formed a cultural entity, both being from the ancient Polynesian Holy Land today called the Leeward Islands. Titahiti and Oha were both from Tubuai and shared Tinafanaea who probably came from the same island. Manarii, Teimua, and Niau were all from Tahiti and shared Mareva.

It is clear, then, that the Polynesians separated themselves on the basis of cultural and linguistic origin. Many tellers of the *Bounty*/Pitcairn story have portrayed the Polynesians as one homogeneous unit; in fact, some refer to them simply as "the Tahitians" even though at least four, probably five, of them did not stem from Tahiti.

The fact is that the Polynesians from different island groups were in many respects as diverse as Europeans from different countries. It is true that they spoke similar languages, showed strong cultural similarities, and obviously had a common origin. Nevertheless, the fact that the early explorers were so impressed by their similarities has tended, to this day, to overshadow their differences.

Just as the German-speaking Swiss never have felt much in common with Germans, the Tubuaians saw the Tahitians as foreigners — and do so even today although they artificially and administratively "belong" to French Polynesia. And just as a northern German finds it difficult to understand Switzerdytsch, a Tahitian has difficulties understanding the Tubuaian dialect. (This dialect is now dying out due to the strong influence of Tahitian as a lingua franca of the region and to the efforts of the French to impose their language as the universal means of communicating within the region.) There were cultural and linguistic differences between Tahiti and the Leeward Islands, too. Even today the inhabitants of Huahine, for example, look down at the way Tahitian is spoken on Tahiti.

The fact that the six Polynesians had to share three women was not as much of a problem in the beginning as one might think. Polyandry, like polygamy, was not unusual in Polynesia; in the Marquesas it was even the preferred type of marriage. Nevertheless, the situation was precarious, because with this shortage of female companions, what would happen if one or more of the women died? This problem was soon to arise.

September 1790

*S*eptember 1790 saw the beginning of a momentous and historical change in the politics of Tahiti. For the first time the balance of power among the chiefdoms (described in the May 1790 commentary) was broken; the reason was that the men of the *Bounty*, instead of staying neutral, allied themselves with one chief against another.

Before Bligh sailed from Tahiti in April 1789, Tu, the chief of Pare (who called himself Teina during Bligh's visit), had begged Bligh to take him along, being afraid that the chiefs of the neighboring districts would attack him once his British supporters had disappeared over the horizon. Bligh had refused and Teina sought refuge with his more powerful brother-in-law, chief Vehiatua in Taiarapu (whose death led to his *taio* Churchill becoming chief until he was killed by Thompson). Now Tu was still in Taiarapu — calling himself Mate — and his brother Ariipaea exercised the power of regent in Pare.

On September 12, 1790, Ariipaea asked the *Bounty* men for assistance in what he claimed was an impending attack by the neighboring chiefdom of Te Fana (today's Faaa where the international airport is located). Without making any attempt to mediate in the conflict, Morrison and several of the other *Bounty* men — plus the bloodthirsty scallawag Brown who had been marooned by the *Mercury* the previous year — rushed to Ariipaea's defense. As it happened, they could not assist him with firepower, because they could not distinguish enemy from friend in the hand-to-hand fighting that took place. Nevertheless, their mere presence was sufficient encouragement to the Pare warriors to ensure victory.

Tepahu, the chief of Te Fana, now realized that there was nothing he could do against such a powerful enemy with his limited forces. But instead of suing for peace he followed the old Tahitian custom and formed an alliance with the two chiefs of the powerful Atehuru district to his south. The latter knew, of course, that should Te Fana come under the domination of Pare, they would be next.

The *Bounty* men were now in danger, because the chiefs of Atehuru had sworn

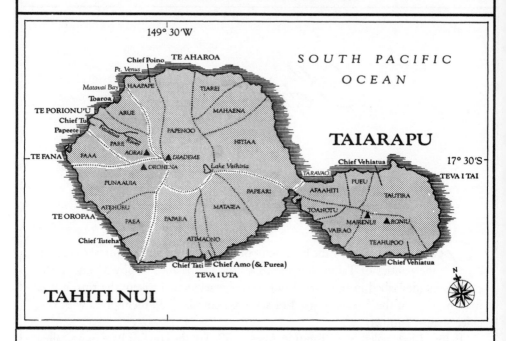

149° 30'W

Chief Poino TE AHAROA

Pt. Venus

SOUTH PACIFIC
OCEAN

Matavai Bay HAAPAPE

Toaroa

TE PORIONU'U ARUE TIAREI

Chief Tu

Papeete MAHAENA

PARE PAPENOO

AORAI HITIAA TAIARAPU

TE FANA FAAA DIADEME

OROHENA Lake Vaihiria Chief Vehiatua 17° 30'S

TARAVAO TEVA I TAI

PUNAAUIA FUEU

PAPEARI AFAAHITI TAUTIRA

ATEHURU TOAHOTU

TE OROPAA PAEA PAPARA MATAIEA MAIRENUI RONUI

VAIRAO

Chief Tuteha ATIMAONO TEAHUPOO

Chief Tati Chief Amo (& Purea) Chief Vehiatua

TEVA I UTA

N

TAHITI NUI

to kill the white intruders who had assisted Ariipaea in what had actually been an attack rather than a defense. Muskets were decisive in minor engagements but would not for long be a match against the mighty armies of Atehuru. The *Bounty* men had been foolish in taking sides in an internal Tahitian conflict and now had to pay the consequences. Their future well-being was, from then on, inextricably tied in with the survival of the Pare dynasty.

Since they could not rely on firepower alone against overwhelming numerical superiority, they had to resort to politics and strategy. Together with Ariipaea and Poino (the chief of the district of Haapape at Matavai) and Temarii (the chief of Papara to the south of Atehuru) they planned a pincer movement with a simultaneous thrust against Atehuru from the north and south. This was facilitated by the fact that two trigger-happy mutineers, Burkett and Sumner, were residing in Papara and they were reinforced by the presence of Brown, and the Tahitian Hitihiti (originally from Bora Bora) who had become an expert marksman.

The coordinated attack took place on September 22. Morrison advanced from the north with his two armies, and the troops from Papara attacked from the south. At the same time the best marksmen from the *Bounty* provided firepower from on board the *Resolution* in the lagoon. They were accompanied by a fleet of forty war canoes with two thousand men.

Against this powerful coalition and the murderous firepower of the Europeans the Atehuru warriors were doomed and finally capitulated. The victory was celebrated in Pare for a whole week, but Tu (Mate) was still too afraid to attend.

Tu provides, incidentally, a good example of the old Tahitian custom of changing and exchanging names, which can make for considerable confusion when one reads the accounts of the early visitors to the island. When Bligh first visited Tahiti with Cook in 1777, the name of the chief of Pare was Tu. When Bligh returned in the *Bounty*, Tu had changed his name to Teina. During the time the mutineers and loyalists stayed on Tahiti (after Christian's departure) Tu called himself Mate. When Bligh came back to Tahiti on his second breadfruit expedition, Tu had either reverted to the name Teina (which Bligh uses in his journal) or the captain simply insisted on referring to him by the older name. Eventually Tu adopted the name Pomare and is today referred to in Tahitian history as Pomare I.

To further complicate matters, Tu's father's name was Teu and his son was named Tu. The latter is often referred to as "Prince Tu" and later became Pomare II.

October 1790

*F*letcher Christian's and Mauatua's first child was born on Pitcairn on a Thursday in October 1790 — although the exact date is not known. It was a boy and Fletcher appropriately enough named him Thursday October Christian. He was the first child born to the newly founded colony and therefore also the first born on the island since the original Polynesian settlers had left.

According to the later visitors to Pitcairn, Thursday October grew up to be a fine man, both in looks and personality. He was one of the three youths who paddled out to greet Captain Folger when he "rediscovered" Pitcairn in 1808. He married the much older Teraura, the widow of Edward Young, and had six children with her. In the tragic migration of the whole population of Pitcairn to Tahiti in 1831, he was one of the seventeen who died from a disease (probably influenza or dengue) before they returned to Pitcairn. His house, weather-torn but still sturdy, can be seen on Pitcairn today.

On October 22, in England, Bligh faced his court-martial for losing the *Bounty*. Some authors have claimed that he asked for the trial to exonerate himself, which is nonsense since in the British Navy, as indeed in most navies, a court-martial was — and is — obligatory when a vessel is lost.

The trial was held at Spithead on board HMS *Royal William*, Admiral Samuel Barrington presiding. In Bligh's case the proceeding was just a formality and he was summarily acquitted from all responsibility for losing the ship. No attempt was made to discover the cause of the mutiny.

Another, more interesting, court-martial took place immediately afterwards. Bligh had proffered charges against Purcell, the *Bounty*'s carpenter, alleging disobedience and disrespect during the open-boat voyage. The court, after duly listening to the evidence, gave Purcell a reprimand. The fact that Bligh brought charges against his former carpenter shows his vindictiveness and pettiness. After all, Bligh could hardly have performed as well as he did on the mission without Purcell's skills. They had faced the dangers and endured the hardships of the open-boat voyage together and survived. A reasonable man would have let bygones be bygones. Moreover, the worst crime that Purcell had committed — but one that really riled Bligh — was that he had said "I am as good a man as you!" Bligh saw this as a mutinous utterance, but the reality was that Bligh could never acknowledge that there was anyone equal to him, even among officers, except perhaps Captain Cook.

Even more interesting is the fact that Bligh did not proffer charges against his sailing master, Fryer, with whom he had quarreled for most of the trip. Fryer had threatened to arrest both Bligh and Purcell when their conflict erupted on Sunday Island, but more important, he had disobeyed orders in Surabaya whereupon Bligh had put both him and Purcell in irons.

The most likely reason why Bligh left Fryer alone is that the latter knew too much about Bligh's affairs as a purser. That theory fits well with what we know: the famous cheese incident, Fryer's conditional refusal to sign Bligh's books en route to Tahiti, and his allegations of fraudulent accounting in Coupang. The two of them probably had an agreement, spoken or unspoken, to leave each other alone.

George Mortimer, the first lieutenant on the *Mercury*, arrived in England on October 25, but we do not know if he contacted Bligh to discuss his visit to Tahiti while Christian was at Tubuai.

Finally, this was the month when Robert Dodd's famous aquatint engraving of the mutiny was unveiled. It has served as an illustration for almost all books on the *Bounty*, inside, or on the cover, or both. It shows the *Bounty*'s stern crowded with mutineers and her launch filled with loyalists. The interesting question is: does the figure standing on the spot where Bligh's private privy should be shown, really represent a likeness of Fletcher Christian? There is no preserved, authenticated portrait of him and it is unlikely that one will ever be found. We will probably never know what the world's most famous mutineer looked like.

November 1790

The British Admiralty considered the mutiny on the *Bounty* a minor incident, an insignificant event indeed compared with the fact that England seemed to be on the verge of war with Spain and France. All of the resources of the Navy had to be mustered in order to meet the threat, and a huge fleet under the command of Lord Richard Howe (popularly referred to as "Black Dick" because of his swarthy complexion) was being mobilized. Among the officers eager to serve in that fleet, by the way, was Horatio Nelson, still a quite unknown aspirant for command.

The *Bounty* affair was simply a source of irritation to the Admiralty. On the one hand, all available ships were needed for the defense of the country but, on the other, a mutiny could not go unpunished. This would have created a dangerous precedent and would have reflected badly on national prestige. A well-armed and fast vessel was needed to catch the *Bounty*, and the Admiralty chose HMS *Pandora*, a three-masted, ship-rigged, 24-gun frigate with a complement of 160. Her mission was to capture the mutineers of the *Bounty* (and the ship too, if possible) and bring them back to England for trial.

Not surprisingly, provisioning and manning the ship turned out to be a difficult problem, since Lord Howe's fleet was commandeering all available men and supplies. Moreover, the *Pandora* also had to carry extra supplies for the *Bounty* in case she was captured. When everything necessary for the long voyage had been stored, the *Pandora* was almost as crowded as the *Bounty* had been three years earlier.

Unlike the *Bounty*, the *Pandora* was not undermanned. But her crew consisted almost entirely of landlubbers who had been rounded up by press-gangs, whereas the *Bounty* crew were all volunteers and, despite their youth, experienced seamen.

The commander of the *Pandora* was Captain Edward Edwards, forty-eight years old, one of the harshest and most unfeeling commanders in the British Navy. He was essentially an automaton, a "bureaucrat of the sea," to whom human beings existed only in terms of whether they facilitated or hindered him in the execution of his duty. Bligh was also a user of men, but he did have some capacity for compassion; Edwards had none. Bligh could be sentimental at times, even lyrical (as when he described the natives of Tahiti); Edwards never was.

Both men were martinets of sorts, but Bligh showed a great deal of foresight and imagination in the execution of his orders; Edwards showed very little of either. Bligh certainly far surpassed Edwards as a commander in terms of his seamanship and navigational skills. Bligh showed a great deal of curiosity for, and interest in, the places he visited, but Edwards showed none. Bligh was constantly on the lookout for something extra he could do that would be useful to seafaring or to science — or to his own advancement; Edwards merely followed orders to the letter. Both men put duty above everything else, but Bligh saw duty in personal and idealistic terms — as a principle; Edwards saw duty merely as a bureaucratic necessity.

Edwards had himself been the object of a mutiny in 1782 when he commanded HMS *Narcissus*. The mutiny was put down, six of the mutineers were hanged, one was sentenced to 500 lashes and another to 200. Edwards of course never forgot this event and the memory of it undoubtedly contributed to the extraordinary harshness and cruelty with which he treated the *Bounty* men he captured and the almost paranoid fear he had of their inciting his own crew to mutiny.

Among the officers on board the *Pandora* was first lieutenant John Larkin, a sadistic officer if there ever was one. The second lieutenant, Robert Corner, however, was not only competent and efficient but also a humane and reasonable man, often praised in the account which Dr. Hamilton, the surgeon on board the *Pandora*, later wrote of the voyage. The third lieutenant was Thomas Hayward, the former midshipman of the *Bounty*. He had been chosen partly because of his knowledge of Tahitian waters and partly because he could identify the mutineers. Contrary to the claims of many writers, including Geoffrey Rawson in *Pandora's Last Voyage* (1963), John Hallett, former midshipman on the *Bounty*, was not on board.

On November 7, 1790, HMS *Pandora* sailed from Jack-in-the-Basket outside Portsmouth. Her task was formidable: to search for a small ship among thousands of islands in the vast and mostly uncharted Pacific ocean. Edwards was well aware of the difficulty of his mission, as we can see from an excerpt of a report he later wrote to the Admiralty:

> Christian had been frequently heard to declare that he would search for an unknown or uninhabited island in which there was no harbour for shipping, would run the ship ashore, and get from her such things as would be useful to him and settle there, but this information was too vague to be followed by me in an immense ocean strewed with an almost innumerable number of known and unknown islands.

OFFICERS OF THE *PANDORA*

Edward Edwards
CAPTAIN

George Passmore
SAILING MASTER

John Larkin
FIRST LIEUTENANT

John Cunningham
BOATSWAIN

Robert Corner
SECOND LIEUTENANT

George Hamilton
SURGEON

Thomas Hayward
THIRD LIEUTENANT

Gregory Bentham
PURSER

Parker
(first name unknown)
GUNNER

December
1790

*O*n December 15, 1790, Bligh was finally appointed post captain, a promotion which he had wanted and expected before assuming command of the *Bounty* in 1787. He had become a man of considerable distinction in London and had been introduced to the King at Court, probably by his life-long benefactor, Sir Joseph Banks. He was not lacking for money, because — despite the failed breadfruit expedition — the members of the House of Assembly in Jamaica showed their appreciation for his efforts by voting him a gratuity of five hundred guineas.

The *Pandora* was on her way to Tahiti and reached Rio de Janeiro at the end of the month. An epidemic of a "malignant fever" had broken out on board shortly after the ship left England and illness was rampant among the crew until well into the new year.

On Tahiti this was a month of peace and tranquility. A daughter had been born to midshipman George Stewart and his Tahitian wife whom he called "Peggy" (we do not know her real name). This was probably the time when Peter Heywood started compiling his Tahitian dictionary which later, reconstructed from memory, would be so helpful to the first missionaries. All the men of the *Bounty* were enjoying the idyllic life on Tahiti to the fullest.

On Pitcairn there was the beginning of a crisis which would, ultimately lead to tragedy. The chronology of what happened is hazy, because neither Adams, nor Teehuteatuaonoa, on whose respective accounts we have to rely, are clear about dates. In any case, some time towards the end of the first year of the *Bounty*'s arrival, John Williams' consort Faahotu died from "a scrophulous disease of the neck."★

Williams now demanded that he be given one of the three women that were shared by the six Polynesian men. At first the rest of the mutineers were against the idea and suggested that Williams wait until Sully, the Polynesian girl who was

★This disease may have been common among the eastern Polynesians. Bligh writes in his journal of the second breadfruit expedition: "One of the natives [of Aitutaki] who came on board had a sore throat and neck, evidently the same disease as the Otaheitans are subject to."

now about two years old, reached womanhood. But Williams was not about to wait around in celibacy for over a decade, and finally the mutineers cast lots among the three women shared by the Polynesian men in order to choose a consort for Williams. The outcome was that Tararo, the chief from Raiatea, had to give up his woman, Toofaiti, and "hand her over" to Williams.

Toofaiti seems not to have been unhappy about this arrangement, because being the consort of a white man implied a higher status, but Tararo was humiliated and enraged and took to the hills.

Not long afterwards, Adams' consort Puarai was killed by falling from a precipice while hunting for birds' eggs. Adams then demanded that he, too, be given a new woman. This time the lot fell on Tinafanaea, the woman who was shared by the two men from Tubuai, and she was "given" to Adams.

This left only one woman to be shared by five Polynesian men (Tararo had not come back from his self-imposed exile): a totally untenable situation. The two Tubuaians, Titahiti and Oha, joined Tararo in the mountains and the three of them conceived a plan to kill the mutineers.

One evening Mauatua (Christian's consort) and Teatuahitea (Brown's) heard Toofaiti — who had been in contact with the conspirators — sing a song with strange words:

> *Why does black man sharpen axe?*
> *To kill the white men.*

Mauatua and Teatuahitea, who immediately understood the portent of the words, went straight to Christian and told him of the impending danger to the white men.

Christian and the other mutineers now sent the three Tahitians, under the leadership of Manarii and armed with muskets, into the mountains with orders to kill the conspirators from Tubuai and Raiatea. The first killed Tararo and shortly thereafter Oha. Titahiti surrendered without a fight and was taken back to the settlement to live more or less like a slave with Isaac Martin and his consort Teehuteatuaonoa.

This bloodshed was followed by a few years of an uneasy peace between the Polynesians and the mutineers. During this time the Polynesians were treated even worse than before, especially by McCoy, Quintal, and Mills. It was not a question of whether, but of when, violence would erupt again.

January

1791

On January 8, 1791, HMS *Pandora* left Rio de Janeiro on her way to Tahiti via Cape Horn. Because it was early enough in the season, Captain Edwards had no trouble in rounding the Horn, and once he had entered the Pacific and turned northward the weather became mild and the diseases which had up to then plagued his crew subsided.

The impact on Tahiti — and on all Polynesia — of the early European discoverers and explorers has been discussed earlier, but even people well familiar with the *Bounty* story often do not realize how frequently these islands were visited in the last three decades of the eighteenth century. Actually the *Bounty*'s visit to Tahiti was the thirteenth time a European ship touched at the island; the *Pandora*'s was the fifteenth.

The European discoverer of Tahiti was Captain Samuel Wallis in HMS *Dolphin*. He named it King George III Island. His sailing master, George Robertson, describes Tahiti as having "the most beautiful appearance its posable to Imagin."

The next visitor was Louis de Bougainville in 1768, in the French frigate *Boudeuse*, accompanied by the storeship *Étoile*. Being unaware of Wallis's visit, he thought he had discovered the island, claimed it for the King of France, and named it La Nouvelle Cythère.

The third visitor was Captain James Cook in HMS *Endeavour* in 1769. He had been sent out by the Admiralty ostensibly to observe the transit of Venus, but in actuality to search for the elusive *Terra Australis Incognita* — which the geographers still insisted must exist — and to make discoveries in the South Seas. It is interesting to consider that the gunner on the *Bounty*, William Peckover, was with Cook not only on this voyage but also on the next two. Since Cook visited Tahiti twice on his second voyage, Peckover's arrival in Tahiti in the *Bounty* was his fifth.

Next came Don Domingo de Boenechea in the Spanish frigate *Aguila* in 1772. Like Bougainville, he was unaware of previous contacts, claimed the island for Spain, and named it Amat after the Viceroy of Chile, Don Manuel de Amat.

Cook returned in 1773 in HMS *Resolution* on his second voyage to the South

Seas. By this time several Tahitians were suffering from diseases, primarily venereal and heretofore unknown in the islands. There was no doubt that these afflictions had been introduced by European seamen. Cook was accompanied by HMS *Adventure*, commanded by Tobias Furneaux, an explorer in his own right, who took on board Mai (Cook thought his name was Omai), a native of Huahine in the Leeward Islands who wanted to visit England.

The seventh visit was again by Cook in the *Resolution* in 1774, still on the second voyage but this time without the *Adventure*. The two ships had lost contact in October 1773, and the *Adventure* reached England one year before Cook, making Captain Furneaux the first British commander to circumnavigate the globe from west to east.

In late 1774 Boenechea came back to Tahiti in the *Aguila* accompanied by the storeship *Jupiter* commanded by Don Thomas Gayangos. This time the Spaniards had with them two priests who were left on the island in order to convert the heathen to the one and only True Faith. They took up residence on Tautira in Taiarapu where Vehiatua was chief. In early 1775 Boenechea died and was buried on Tahiti. Gayangos assumed command for the return voyage.

The *Aguila* was dispatched on a third expedition to Tahiti, this time to bring supplies to the priests. Under the command of Don Cayetano de Langara she arrived in Tahiti in October 1775. The Tahitians had not taken kindly to the missionaries, who constantly threatened them with hell and damnation if they did not accept the new religion. So, although the priests had not been harmed, they did go in fear of their lives and demanded to be taken off the island. So ended the first attempt at christianization on Tahiti.

In 1777 Captain Cook came back in the *Resolution* on his third voyage to the South Seas. His sailing master was William Bligh. Cook brought Mai back from England and set him ashore at his home island, Huahine. Cook also visited Taiarapu where he saw the house the missionaries had lived in and Boenechea's grave.

With Cook was Captain Charles Clerke in HMS *Discovery* and on this ship were two men who were to figure in the *Bounty* story: the botanist David Nelson and the future gunner of the *Bounty*, William Peckover.

The twelfth visit was made in July 1788 by Captain Sever in the transport *Lady Penrhyn*. He had told the Tahitians of Cook's death, thereby creating some trouble for Bligh who arrived a few months later and did not want the Tahitians to know that Cook was dead. Bligh felt he could count on more goodwill from them if they thought that "Tute," whom they held in high esteem, would still come back and visit them one day. Bligh did manage to convince the Tahitians that the story of Tute's death was just a rumor without foundation.

The thirteenth visitor was the *Bounty* and the fourteenth the *Mercury* (alias *Gustaf III*).

By this time, the Tahitians had had ample opportunity to observe that, although the *popa'as* were superior to them in technical achievements, they were inferior in human qualities such as kindness and generosity and in their spiritual life. However, it was only when the fifteenth visitor, the *Pandora*, arrived in Tahiti that the Tahitians got a clear picture of how inhuman and cruel white men could be.

February 1791

While the *Pandora* was sailing towards Tahiti on her mission to capture the mutineers, the *Bounty* men on Tahiti continued the peaceful life that had prevailed after the fighting against Atehuru in which, by the way, not a single white man had even been wounded.

Having, for the moment at least, achieved a position as the most powerful chief on Tahiti, Mate (earlier known as, first, Tu and then, Teina) wished to consolidate his power. He summoned all the chiefs of the island to a ceremony through which his son, also called Tu (actually Tu nui ae i te Atua), was going to receive tokens of submission from them all.

At this ceremony "Prince Tu" was going to be invested with the *maro ura* which had been captured in Atehuru. The *maro ura* or "Royal Sash," as Morrison calls it, consisted simply of a belt of plaited pandanus leaves decorated with red (sometimes also black and yellow) feathers, but it was fully comparable with a European crown as a sign of royalty. It was usually inherited, but it could also be acquired through conquest. In either case the ceremony of investiture was similar in significance to a European coronation.

As mentioned earlier, no Tahitian chieftain had ever achieved supremacy over the entire island. Mate was determined to accomplish this goal, knowing that he had the backing of most of the men of the *Bounty*.

At birth, Mate's son Tu, now seven years old, had technically and traditionally succeeded his father as chief. It was therefore "Prince Tu" who was now going to be invested with the *maro ura*.

Even before the ceremony, Mate had sent his son on a triumphal tour of the island to receive tokens of allegiance from the other chiefs. He had wisely avoided the mighty Taiarapu district however, since his influence there had vanished with the demise of his brother-in-law Vehiatua.

The banner carried at the head of the triumphal procession was, interestingly enough, the Union Jack, decorated with the red feathers so treasured by the Tahitians.

Morrison was very proud of this symbol and may even have been the instigator of its use. He says that the Tahitians interpreted the presence of the *Bounty* men as "a declaration on our part to support our flag in circumventing the island, as it was composed of English colours, and they made no scruple to say that war would be instantly made on those who should attempt to stop it."

Being intimidated by the military power of the men of the *Bounty*, the chiefs of the other districts on Tahiti (Taiarapu was of course not on the itinerary) allowed the procession to pass through, but this cannot be seen as a sign of true submission under Mate's rule.

The investiture ceremony was held on February 13, 1791, in Pare, close to Toaroa harbor where the *Bounty* had been anchored two years earlier. Morrison describes it as follows:

> Toonoeaiteatooa [Tu nui ae i te Atua] the young king being placed on the morai [marae], a priest making a long prayer put the sash around his waist and the hat or bonnet on his head and haild him king of Taheite . . . three Human Victims [corpses] were brought in and offered for Morea, the Priest placing them with their head towards the Young King and offered three young Plantain trees. He then took an Eye out of each, with a piece of split bamboo, and placing them on a leaf took a young plantain tree in one hand and the Eyes in the other, made a long speech holding them up to the Young King, who sat above him with his Mouth open.
>
> I enquired the Cause of the Eye being offered and was informed that the King is the Head of the People for which reason the Head is sacred; the Eye being the most valuable part is the fittest to be offered, and the reason that the King sits with his Mouth open, is to let the Soul of the Sacrifice enter into his Soul.

The ceremony stems back to times when ritualistic cannibalism existed and the chief actually ate the eyes of a sacrificial victim in order to absorb his *mana* (spiritual power).

Ominously, all the chiefs of Taiarapu had boycotted the ceremony. They had come to know Mate well during his self-imposed exile there under the protection of Vehiatua. They had seen through his megalomaniacal plans of being the sole ruler of Tahiti, and they would have nothing to do with it; in fact, they were violently opposed to any such development.

This meant war!

March 1791

··· 🚢 ···

*H*MS *Pandora* was entering eastern Polynesia, passing Easter Island on March 4. On March 16, Captain Edwards discovered Ducie Island and, had he continued on the same parallel, he would have seen Pitcairn and probably captured Christian and his men. His orders were, however, to head directly for Tahiti and, turning slightly north, he passed close to Pitcairn without seeing it. On March 17, he discovered Marutea which he named Lord Hood's Island — in honor of the British admiral who would later preside over the court-martial of the captured *Bounty* men.

The *Pandora* was now only a few days' sail from Tahiti where war was in the making. The fact that the chiefs on the Taiarapu peninsula refused to acknowledge Tu nui ae i te Atua's suzerainty grated on the latter's father, Mate (Tu, Teina), who decided to subjugate them by force. Since this was going to be purely a war of conquest without even a pretense of a need for defense, four of the *Bounty* men (midshipmen Heywood and Stewart, the armourer Coleman, and seaman Skinner) refused to have anything to do with Mate's schemes.

The other nine *Bounty* men (Michael Byrne did not count since he was nearly blind) promised their assistance, but the most eager promoter of the war was the bloodthirsty scallawag John Brown who had been marooned by the brig *Mercury*.

Temarii, the chief of Papara who had supported Mate in his war against Atehuru, came up with the best plan of attack. It had to be based on deception and surprise, because Taiarapu was powerful and the chiefs of the other districts on Tahiti could not be trusted as solid allies. If large troop concentrations were to amass close to the isthmus of Taravao, the news would immediately reach Taiarapu which could mount an effective defense on the narrow isthmus.

Temarii therefore proposed to call his and Mate's troops and their allies to a gigantic feast in Papara. When the feast had lasted long enough to convince the chiefs on Taiarapu that no danger was involved, the troops would be moved in forced marches under the cover of night to the isthmus, from where they could make a

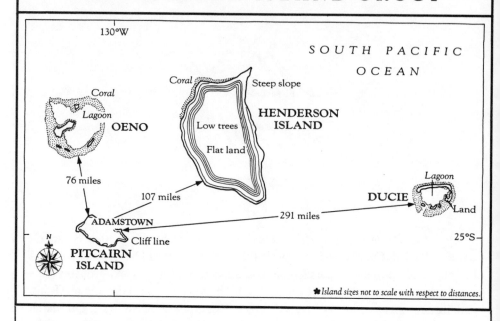

THE PITCAIRN ISLAND GROUP

130°W

SOUTH PACIFIC
OCEAN

Coral

Coral
Steep slope

Lagoon
OENO

HENDERSON
ISLAND

Low trees

Flat land

76 miles

Lagoon
DUCIE
Land

107 miles

291 miles

ADAMSTOWN

25°S

N
Cliff line

PITCAIRN
ISLAND

★ Island sizes not to scale with respect to distances.

surprise attack on the Taiarapuans.

The men of the *Bounty* sailed to Papara on the *Resolution* and arrived at the site of the feast on March 24. But before they had time to partake of the delicacies offered, a courier arrived with a message which came as lightning from blue sky: a British warship called HMS *Pandora* had anchored in Matavai Bay the day after they had left!

The swaggering confidence of the mutineers was suddenly changed into deadly fear and some of them at least must have regretted that they had not sailed away with Christian when they had the chance. Even the loyalists among them were stricken by panic, because they had learned from the courier that the four *Bounty* men who had stayed behind (three of whom were loyalists: Heywood, Stewart, and Coleman) had voluntarily boarded the ship and yet they had immediately been put in irons. And at this very moment two launches from the *Pandora*, under the command of Thomas Hayward, the former midshipman of the *Bounty*, were on their way to Papara to arrest all of them, mutineers and loyalists alike. (Hayward, by the way, had snubbed his former fellow midshipmen Heywood and Stewart and made it clear that he wanted nothing to do with them.)

The news created such a panic that even four loyalists, among them Morrison, attempted to escape with the mutineers in the schooner. Since the vessel had no provisions for a long voyage, however, they decided to return to Papara and hide in the mountains. Only Morrison and Norman decided to walk to Matavai and give themselves up (Byrne had already done so). On arrival they, too, were immediately put in irons.

The rest were betrayed by natives bribed by Brown who, as a typical psychopath, had no pangs of conscience in turning against his former comrades-in-arms.

With all *Bounty* men captured, Mate had lost the mainstay of his power and was faced with imminent danger from his enemies. He at first pleaded with Edwards to take him along to England, but when the captain refused, he fled to the mountains (soon afterwards changing his name to Pomare). He had come within a hair's-breadth of making himself absolute ruler over Tahiti and he had failed, due to the arrival of the *Pandora*, but he had shown his son how it could be accomplished — through alliances with the whites. Tu nui ae i te Atua did indeed eventually, with the help of the missionaries and only after much blood had been spilled and many cruelties committed, become the sole ruler of Tahiti and is known to posterity as Pomare II.

April
1791

Through the offices of his life-long patron, Sir Joseph Banks, Bligh was appointed commander of a second breadfruit expedition on April 15, 1791. No doubt the news gladdened him, but he would certainly have been even happier had he known that Captain Edwards in HMS *Pandora* had just captured those mutineers who had remained on Tahiti. In fact, by this time Bligh seems to have considered everyone who remained on board the *Bounty* after the mutiny, whether voluntarily or not, a villain, so he would undoubtedly have been pleased to learn that the loyalists, too, had been put in irons.

On the *Pandora*, anchored in Matavai Bay, construction had begun on what was soon to be called "Pandora's box," a dark cage measuring eleven by eighteen feet fastened to the quarter deck of the ship. The only entrance was from a small ceiling hatch which was usually closed and bolted on the outside. The only ventilation came from two nine-inch, heavily barred scuttles in the bulkhead of the box.

The fourteen *Bounty* men captured on Tahiti were shackled to the walls and floor of this cage by their ankles and wrists. The shackles were checked every day and were so tight that they led to hideous and dangerous swellings of the limbs. (The sadistic Lieutenant Larkin told the captives with a smile that the shackles were "not supposed to fit like gloves.") As if this did not constitute sufficient security, the box was guarded day and night by two heavily armed marines on top and one on deck. The prisoners' shackles were never removed, they were never allowed to exercise or even to get a breath of fresh air, and they had to perform all their natural functions in two buckets that were emptied twice a week. As Harry L. Shapiro says in his book *The Heritage of the Bounty* (1936): "No commentary is necessary on the character of a man capable of confining fellow creatures in such a cesspool."

The Tahitians were horrified at this inhuman treatment of their friends, many of whom had formed households and fathered children during the year and a half they had lived on the island. They came to the ship daily and brought the prisoners the best delicacies the island had to offer. We do not know whether or to what extent the *Bounty* men were allowed to partake of the island food brought to them. We do know that they were not allowed to see any of the Tahitians who came to visit them, not even their wives or *taios*. The only exception made was for the six prisoners who had fathered children: they were permitted to see and hold their babies. Apologists for Edwards have made much of this latter magnanimity, but the probability is that Edwards was afraid that the prisoners' island friends, many of whom were in powerful positions, would attempt to sabotage the ship or even to capture it, if he did not show some leeway in his harsh treatment of the captives.

The surgeon on the *Pandora*, George Hamilton, describes the scene:

> The prisoners' wives visited the ship daily and brought their children, who were permitted to be carried to their unhappy fathers. To see the poor captives in irons, weeping over their tender offspring, was too moving a scene for any feeling heart.

The most heartbreaking sight was that of midshipman Stewart's wife Peggy, the daughter of a chief, who brought their little daughter with her. She could not stop crying and, when forcibly removed from the ship, she would gash her head in the old ritual manner so that the blood was streaming down her face. The scene was so upsetting that Stewart had to request that she not be allowed on board. The missionaries who later arrived on the island — and who brought up Stewart's little girl — heard that Peggy had died "of a broken heart" only a few months after the departure of the ship.

The psychopathic blackguard John Brown, however, got along famously with Edwards; perhaps the two recognized in each other a sort of kinship of souls, if indeed souls they had. Anyway, Edwards offered to take Brown on board and Hamilton says the latter "rendered many eminent services, both in this expedition and the subsequent part of the voyage."

May

1791

$\cdots$ ⚓ $\cdots$

*W*hile Bligh was in England starting preparations for his second breadfruit expedition, Edwards was getting ready to sail from Tahiti. All *Bounty* men on the island had been rounded up and were languishing in the torture chamber which Edwards had constructed on the quarter deck of the *Pandora*. The ship had been fully provisioned and meticulous precautions had been taken against any attempt on the part of the Tahitians to liberate their friends by sabotaging or capturing the ship.

Edwards decided to use the *Resolution*, the beautiful schooner that the *Bounty* men had built under Morrison's direction, as an escort; he thought it would be especially useful as a lookout in negotiating Endeavour Straits (Torres Straits) because of its shallow draft. Although the *Resolution* was a fast vessel that could sail circles around the *Pandora*, she had not been capable of long voyages, since the *Bounty* men had no sailcloth and the native matting was too heavy and ripped too easily in strong winds. Edwards therefore had the schooner fitted out with sails sewn especially for her and he put on board a crew of nine, including the commander, master's mate William Oliver.

Brown was signed on the *Pandora* as an able-bodied seaman and even Hitihiti, the indefatigable traveler who had been seven months with Cook on the second voyage, was taken aboard for a trip to the island of his birth, Bora Bora.

On May 8, 1791, the two ships sailed out of Matavai Bay and Edwards' search for the *Bounty* and the nine missing mutineers began. His task was hopeless: the Pacific contained thousands of islands on which the mutineers could have hidden. He had already unknowingly passed Pitcairn where they actually were, and he was not likely to go back in his tracks against the prevailing trade winds. Moreover, the instructions from the Admiralty directed him to search in the Leeward Islands and then in island groups further to the west. Aitutaki (in what are now called the Cook Islands) and islands in the Tonga group were specifically mentioned in his orders.

Christian had indeed been clever in his choice of hiding place. He knew that the Admiralty would first send a ship to Tahiti and that it was unlikely that the ship would then turn back and sail eastward. Instead, it was likely that the search would be directed towards the west, farther and farther away from Pitcairn.

How very right Christian was can be seen from the fact that Pitcairn was not "re-rediscovered" until 1808.

Edwards started his futile search in the Leewards, where Hitihiti got drunk on Huahine and missed the ships when they continued on to Bora Bora. Edwards then sailed to Aitutaki which, of course, was an island that Christian never would have chosen since it had been discovered by Bligh and was certain to be investigated.

Edwards next sailed to Palmerston atoll — discovered by Cook on his second voyage — where a sensational discovery was made. A boat crew of the *Pandora*, under the command of Lieutenant Robert Corner (a highly competent and humane officer who despised Edwards and Larkin), discovered a yard marked "Bounty's Driver Yard" and some other spars marked "Bounty!" A thorough search was made of the atoll even though it was clear that the spars had been in the water a very long time (actually they had drifted all the way from Tubuai where they had been lost by the mutineers).

A tragic event occurred at Palmerston on May 24. A jolly boat with five men on board, commanded by midshipman John Sivall, was lost in a heavy squall and never seen again. Its loss was only the beginning of the tragic events that were to mark the voyage of the *Pandora*.

Edwards searched for the jolly boat for five days until he finally set sail for the next island group.

June

1791

... ⛵ ...

At the beginning of June 1791, the *Pandora*, accompanied by the *Resolution*, sailed from Palmerston atoll towards Duke of York's Island (Atafu) in the Union group (Tokelau). The reason for Captain Edwards' interest in this island was that one of the *Bounty* men confined in "Pandora's box," Henry Hillbrant, had told him that Christian had declared his intention to sail for Duke of York's Island and settle there with his fellow mutineers. We do not know what Hillbrant's motivation was for imparting this information to Edwards, but if he expected better treatment as a result, he must have been sadly disappointed. Edwards, however, fell for Christian's ruse and sailed even farther westward on his wild goose chase.

The island was sighted on June 6, and was thoroughly investigated. Having found no trace of any mutineers, Edwards sailed on and, on June 12, discovered Nukunono (also in the Tokelau group) and named it Duke of Clarence Island. He then headed for the Navigator Islands (the Samoas), passed Savaii on June 18 and, thinking that he had discovered it, named it Chatham's Island. (La Pérouse had discovered it in 1787.) Edwards passed Tutuila on June 21.

Still smarting from the loss of his jolly boat with five men the previous month, Edwards met with a new misfortune on June 22. In the evening, during a sudden rainstorm off the coast of Upolu, he lost contact with the *Resolution*. He searched for her for two days and then sailed to the previously agreed-upon rendezvous in the Tongan islands, Nomuka, where he anchored on June 29. There was no sign of the *Resolution* which, being a faster vessel, should have been there before the *Pandora*, had it not come to harm in some way. An additional worry was that the *Resolution* was out of food and water; it had been scheduled for reprovisioning the day after it became separated from the *Pandora*.

What had happened to the *Resolution*? On the night the ships lost contact the schooner was attacked by a large number of Samoans in war canoes. The nine men on board kept firing their muskets into the attacking fleet as fast as they could reload, but in the noise and confusion of the battle the Samoans did not seem to perceive any connection between the shots and the fact that some of their men were crumpling up or falling into the water. Fortunately, the *Resolution* was provided with boarding nets; without them she would have fallen victim to the overwhelming superiority in manpower. One warrior did succeed in climbing on board and would have killed the commander, master's mate William Oliver, with his war club, had he not been shot to death at the moment of striking.

The schooner spent two days in searching for the *Pandora*, but being without provisions and not being able to land in the hostile Samoan islands, Oliver decided to head for the rendezvous, Nomuka, which was 360 miles due south. That should not have been a problem for a fast schooner, but they had had no water since the day they were separated from the mother ship and they suffered horrible thirst on this voyage which, for some reason that has not been explained, took much longer than they had anticipated.

When they finally reached what they thought was their destination, it turned out — as they learned long afterwards — that they had mistaken Tofua for Nomuka; in other words they were forty-five miles from the *Pandora* without knowing it. If the larger ship had fired one of its guns, the *Resolution* would have been able to rejoin it, but Edwards did not think of the possibility that the schooner might be waiting at the wrong island.

Oliver traded some nails with the natives of Tofua for a little water and some food, but soon the natives — who had attacked Bligh and the loyalists in the *Bounty*'s launch — made an all-out assault on the schooner and again the nine-member crew, one of whom was seriously ill from dehydration, beat off the attackers with their firepower. Oliver had no choice but to leave, and he sailed away to the west with hardly any provisions and with very little water on board.

July

1791

$\mathscr{T}$he *Resolution*, having been separated from her mother ship the *Pandora*, and attacked savagely by the natives of Tofua, sailed westward on July 1, 1791. The commander, William Oliver, knew that Captain Edwards would eventually head for Endeavour Straits (Torres Straits) and, having the faster ship, he thought it best to wait for the *Pandora* there. But he had only enough water and food for a few days. And between Tofua and the Straits there was a distance of 2500 miles of unknown waters.

Oliver was lucky. After sailing only 300 miles, he sighted Matuku, one of the few islands in the Fiji group where the inhabitants were not fierce and warlike cannibals.

The men of the *Resolution* spent five weeks at this beautiful island, recuperating and getting ready for the long voyage ahead. The natives were almost as kind and hospitable as the Tahitians had been, there was plenty of good food and water, and a safe harbor for their little ship. Unknowingly, they were making history: they were the first Europeans to land on and have significant contact with the inhabitants of a Fijian island. And the *Resolution* was the first ship ever to anchor in the Fijis.

Edwards had meanwhile been waiting for the *Resolution* at Nomuka, but he finally gave up and sailed back to Upolu where the schooner had been separated from the *Pandora*. On the way, he visited Tofua, where the natives pretended they had never heard of the *Resolution* and were very sorry for what had happened during Bligh's visit. Hayward, the former midshipman of the *Bounty*, recognized some of the Tofuans as having been among those who murdered quartermaster Norton when Bligh and his men tried to escape in the open boat. Edwards, however, did not dare to take any punitive measures for fear of what would happen if the *Resolution* showed up after he left. If he had known about the attack on the schooner, he would probably have taught the Tongans a lesson that would long have been remembered and might have saved the lives of other ships' crews in the island group over the next years, notably those of the *Port au Prince* and the *Duke of Portland*.

Edwards arrived at Upolu on July 16. He made thorough inquiries about the *Resolution*, but was told it had not been seen. This is hardly surprising, because the natives were not about to confess that they had made a savage attack on the schooner. Nor had they seen anything of the *Bounty*.

For a last attempt, Edwards returned to Nomuka, where he arrived on July 28. Still no sign of the *Resolution*! The natives on Nomuka were hostile this time and robbed and stripped some crew members who had become separated from the landing party. One of the natives attacked Lieutenant Corner who was forced to kill him. Even with this provocation, Edwards did not engage in punitive action; his instructions from the Admiralty were to keep the friendliest of relations with the Friendly Islanders (so named — or rather misnamed — by Cook) in order to ensure a welcome reception of possible future settlers and to gain an advantage over competitive colonial powers.

The surgeon on board the *Pandora*, George Hamilton, had the following to say about the Nomukans and the Tongans in general:

> The people of Anamooka [Nomuka] are the most daring set of robbers in the South Seas; and, with the greatest deference and submission to Capt. Cook, I think the name of Friendly Isles is a perfect misnomer, as their behaviour to himself, to us, and to Capt. Bligh's unfortunate boat at Murderers' Cove, pretty clearly evinces. Indeed Murderers Cove, in the Friendly Isles, is saying a volume on the subject.

The *Bounty* men imprisoned in "Pandora's box" had now been chained in that torture chamber for four months. Not once had their shackles been removed or even loosened a little and not once had they been allowed to speak to anyone except the master-at-arms. They were not even allowed to use the Tahitian language among themselves lest they hatch a plot to take over the ship. They were fourteen men — of whom only seven were mutineers — against one hundred and sixty.

Morrison describes the conditions in the cage in these terms:

> The heat of the place when it was calm was so intense that the sweat frequently ran to the scuppers, and produced maggots in a short time, the hammocks being dirty when we got them we found stored with vermin of another kind which we had no method of eradicating but by lying on the plank; and tho' our friends [in Tahiti] would have supplied us with plenty of cloth, they were not permitted to do it, and our only remedy was to lay naked; these troublesome neighbours and the two necessary tubbs which were kept in the place helped to render our situation truly disagreeable . . .

Edwards' obsession with the idea that seven — or let us say fourteen — securely incarcerated and heavily guarded prisoners could cause a mutiny on board his ship can only be seen as paranoid in nature. His prohibition against their talking to the crew is understandable, but the cage was on the quarter deck, far away from the crew. The mounting of three guards, one of them a midshipman, is also understandable: the mutineers could conceivably have talked one or two guards into setting them free, but what could they — or the guards, for that matter — have done after that?

What is totally incomprehensible, and indefensible, is that the prisoners were allowed no fresh air and no exercise. What harm could it possibly have done to allow them a few minutes' walk once in a while, one at a time? Edwards' treatment of the prisoners went far beyond strict precautions. Perhaps his measures were based on a personal vendetta against all mutineers (as he had been the object of a mutiny in 1782), but he comes through as such an unfeeling automaton that even hatred seems unlikely in his case. Edwards' inhumanity is without a doubt the most unsavory aspect of the whole *Bounty* story.

August 1791

*C*aptain Edwards, having given up hope of the *Resolution* ever joining up with the *Pandora*, sailed from Nomuka on August 2, 1791. (At almost the same time, on August 3, Captain Bligh sailed from England in HMS *Providence* on his second breadfruit expedition, this time accompanied by a tender, HMS *Assistant*, commanded by Lieutenant Nathaniel Portlock.)

On the way to Endeavour Straits Edwards discovered some islands, among them Rotuma, which he named Grenville Island. Passing Vanikoro in the Santa Cruz group of the Eastern Solomon Islands on August 13, he saw smoke signals but did not bother to investigate and simply sailed on. If he had stopped and landed, he would have solved the riddle of the lost La Pérouse expedition.

La Pérouse with his two ships, the *Boussole* and the *Astrolabe*, had sailed from France in 1785 on a voyage of discovery. He had been in Port Jackson in New South Wales on January 26, 1788, when the First Fleet came in with convicts from England, but he had not been heard from since he sailed from there in February. The two ships had vanished in the South Seas and there were no clues to their disappearance.

It was not until 1826 that the English navigator-adventurer Peter Dillon found evidence which finally led to a reconstruction of what had happened. Both of La Pérouse's ships had foundered in a storm off Vanikoro three years before the *Pandora* passed the island, and at least two survivors were still there then. It is highly likely that the smoke signals Edwards saw were sent up by the castaways to attract his attention. But Edwards was neither curious nor imaginative, and definitely not compassionate; it was the mutineers he was after and they would certainly not have sent up any smoke signals. Edwards sailed on.

The *Pandora* was now approaching the Great Barrier Reef, one of the world's most dangerous areas for seafarers. On the evening of August 28, at about the same time as Bligh was anchoring in Tenerife, the *Pandora* struck the reef and immediately started to ship water. All available men were commanded to the pumps. The seriousness of the situation can be seen from the fact that three of the *Bounty* men,

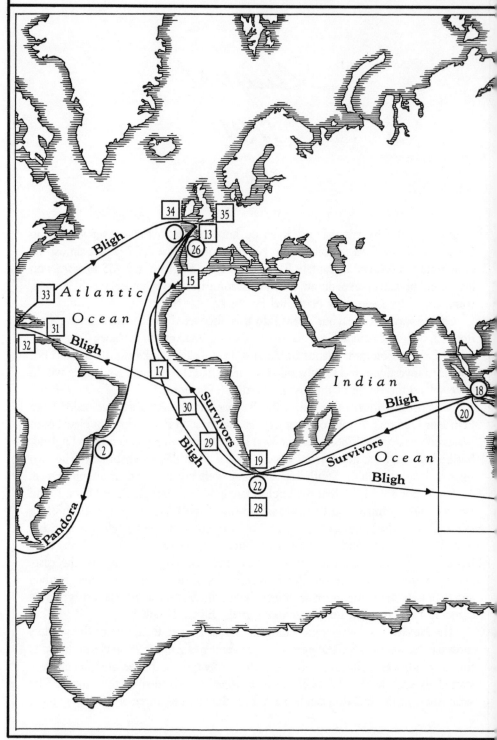

THE VOYAGES OF HMS PANDOR
AND OF HMS PROVIDENC

Bligh

33 *Atlantic*

Ocean

31

32

Bligh

17

30

Survivors

29

Bligh

19

22

28

Pandora

2

1

34

35

13

26

15

Indian

Bligh

Survivors

Ocean

Bligh

18

20

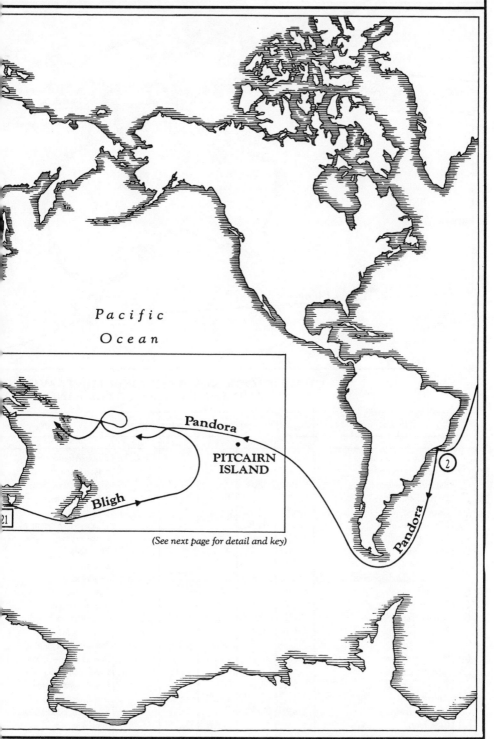

Pacific

Ocean

Pandora

PITCAIRN
ISLAND

Bligh

Pandora

Pandora

(2)

(See next page for detail and key)

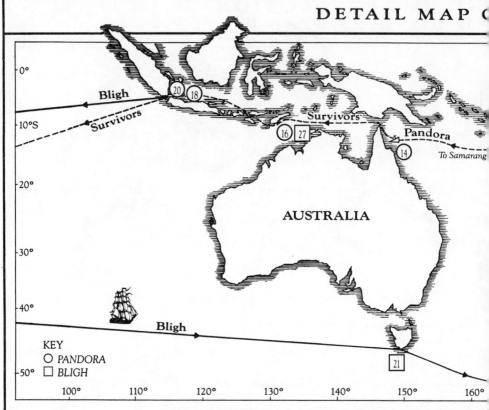

KEY
○ PANDORA
□ BLIGH

CHRONOLOGICAL MAP KEY FOR THE TRAVELS OF
AND THE TRAVELS OF THE *PANDORA* ON

	Location or Event	Pandora (& Resolution)		Providence & Assistant		Courts-martial	Remarks
		Arrive	Arrive	Arrive	Depart	Trial Dates	
—	Bligh's Court-Martial					10.22.90	Required formality
①	*Pandora* departs England	Start	11.7.90				Search for mutineers
②	Rio De Janeiro, Brazil	12.31.90	1.8.91				Malignant fever breakout
③	Easter Island	3.4.91	→				Nearing Polynesia
④	Ducie Island	3.16.91	→				Discovered
⑤	Matavai Bay, Tahiti	3.25.91	4.8.91				14 *Bounty* men captured
⑥	Palmerston Atoll	5.24.91	→				5 men lost in jolly boat
⑦	Duke of York's Island (Atafu)	6.6.91	→				Investigated
⑧	Nukunono Island	6.12.91	→				Discovered
⑨	Navigator Islands (Samoas)	6.18.91	→				Searching
⑩	Samoas	6.22.91	→				Lost contact with *Resolution*
⑪	Nomuka Island	6.24.91	→				Rendezvous point
⑫	Matuku Island, Fiji	7.3.91	8.10.91				*Resolution* stops 5 weeks
⑪	Nomuka Island	7.28.91	8.2.91				Return for *Resolution*
13	England			Start	8.3.91		2nd Breadfruit mission
⑭	Great Barrier Reef	8.28.91					*Pandora* sinks — 35 lost
15	Tenerife (Spain)			8.28.91	→		Supply stop
⑯	Timor (Coupang)	9.15.91	10.6.91				*Pandora* survivors rest
17	Equator			10.3.91	→		Breadfruit mission
⑱	Samarang (Java)	10.6.91	10.30.91				Survivors find *Resolution*
19	Cape Town			11.6.91	12.23.91		Supply/rest stop

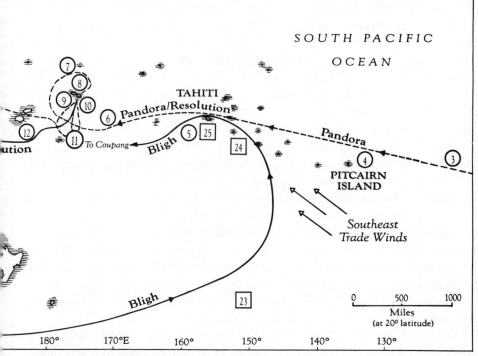

SOUTH PACIFIC

OCEAN

TAHITI

Pandora/Resolution

To Coupang

Bligh

Pandora

PITCAIRN
ISLAND

Southeast
Trade Winds

Bligh

0   500   1000
Miles
(at 20° latitude)

180°   170°E   160°   150°   140°   130°

TAIN BLIGH ON HIS SECOND BREADFRUIT MISSION
SEARCH FOR THE BOUNTY MUTINEERS ⋆

Location or Event	Pandora (& Resolution)		Providence & Assistant		Courts-martial	Remarks
	Arrive	Arrive	Arrive	Depart	Trial Dates	
Batavia	11.7.91	→				Resolution sold
Van Diemen's Land (Tasmania)			2.9.92	2.23.92		Adventure Bay
Cape Town	3.18.92	5.6.92				Change ships again
48th Parallel			3.18.92	→		South of Tahiti
Bligh's Lagoon Island (Tematangi)			4.5.92	→		Discovered
Tahiti			4.10.92	7.19.92		Collect Breadfruit trees
Spithead, England	6.19.92	End				Mutineers held
On board HMS Hector					9.12.92	Mutineers on Trial
On board HMS Hector					9.18.92	Trial ends — 6 guilty
Coupang, Timor			10.2.92	10.11.92		Supply/rest stop
England					10.24.92	2 pardoned/1 appealed
On board HMS Brunswick					10.29.92	3 executed (11 am)
Cape of Good Hope			11.19.92	→		No stop
Saint Helena Island			12.17.92	12.27.92		Supply stop
Ascension Island			1.1.93	→		Passed
Kingston Bay, Barbados			1.23.93	1.30.93		At anchor
Port Royal Harbor, Jamaica			2.5.93	6.15.93		Goal of expedition
Cape San Antonio, G. Caymans			7.20.93	7.21.93		Stop
Ireland			7.27.93	→		End of mission
Deptford, England			8.2.93	End		Arrive home
England					2/93	Appeal successful

⋆ (dates are in the 1700s)

Coleman, McIntosh, and Norman, whom Bligh had recommended for mercy (in addition to the almost blind seaman Byrne), were let loose and sent to the pumps.

The eleven remaining prisoners in "Pandora's box" went through a night of horror. It was clear even to them in the pitch dark cage that the *Pandora* was doomed and could sink at any moment, drowning them like rats. They were tightly shackled in their irons and the hatch cover above was bolted from the outside. By super-human efforts they managed to break their shackles and cried for someone to let them out. Edwards now got a chance to show what he was made of. As soon as he found out that the prisoners had broken their irons, he ordered them to be shackled again and this time so heavily and tightly that they would have no chance to repeat their feat. The hatch was then bolted from the outside and the guards were told to shoot to kill if there were any further attempt to remove the shackles. Meanwhile the ship was sinking. By dawn the *Pandora* was almost totally waterlogged and everyone knew the end would come soon. The water started pouring in through the gun ports, the pumps were abandoned and the order came to abandon ship; it was now every man for himself. Edwards was among the first of the officers to jump into the water to save himself. Only after giving the order to abandon ship had he told an armourer's mate to free the prisoners. Muspratt, Skinner, and Byrne were let out of the cage, Skinner in such a panic that he jumped into the water with his hands still manacled and immediately drowned.

The guards had evidently not heard Edwards' new orders and felt they should not have let the three prisoners escape, so they again shut the hatchcover and bolted it from outside even though the armourer's mate was still inside trying to free the prisoners from their shackles. The ship was now so deep in the water that only the quarter deck was above the surface. Suddenly it took a lurch and the guards fell into the sea.

In the cage there was the panic of imminent death. The water started gushing in through the small vents and it was clear that everyone would drown. Just then one of the *Pandora*'s bosun's mates, William Moulter, climbed up on the roof of the cage and called out that he would either free them or go down with them. He unbolted the hatch and the prisoners rushed through the opening, some still manacled. Hillbrant, who had still not been freed, went down with the cage.

The account above is based on an integration of Morrison's and Surgeon Hamilton's stories of what happened. Hamilton said that Edwards had ordered the release of the prisoners (albeit when it was too late for four of them). A more reliable witness — who had no need to defend the treatment of the prisoners, as did Hamilton — is second lieutenant Robert Corner who, according to Barrow (1831), claimed that Edwards never gave an order to release the prisoners and that Hamilton lied about the incident in his book:

> Three of the *Bounty*'s people, Coleman, Norman, and McIntosh, were now let

out of irons, and sent to work at the pumps. The others offered their assistance, and begged to be allowed a chance of saving their lives; instead of which, two additional sentinels were placed over them, with orders to shoot any who should attempt to get rid of their fetters. Seeing no prospect of escape, they betook themselves to prayer, and prepared to meet their fate. . . .No notice was taken of the prisoners as is falsely stated by the author of the *Pandora's Voyage* [Hamilton], although Captain Edwards was entreated by Mr Heywood to have mercy upon them, when he passed over their prison to make his own escape. . . . Among the drowned were Mr Stewart, John Sumner, Richard Skinner and Henry Hillbrandt, the whole of whom perished with their hands still in manacles.

Rolf Du Rietz (1965 and 1986) has pointed out that the passage quoted above was written by Marshall (1825), who took all the information from Morrison's narrative.

In his monumental work *The Life of Vice-Admiral William Bligh* (1951), George Mackaness comments on the fate of the prisoners:

A consideration of the foregoing statements, taken in conjunction with Edwards's own statement submitted to the court martial, wherein he makes scarcely any mention of the mutineers, leaves but one conclusion in the mind of a critical reader, namely, that he not only treated his prisoners with the grossest inhumanity, but also disobeyed his express orders from the Admiralty. He had been ordered to pay "proper regard to the preservation of their lives". To have kept eleven of them handcuffed, ironed, and securely confined, while the ship was actually breaking up, implies either that Edwards had so completely lost his head amid the disorder of the wreck that he did not know what he was doing, or else that he was entirely indifferent to the fate of the prisoners under his control. It must also be remembered that the ship did not sink for about eleven hours after she struck. Surely a capable officer, with a well-disciplined crew, such as Hamilton assures us the men of the *Pandora* were, should have been able in that space of time to complete his arrangements for the safety, not only of his crew, but of the prisoners under his guard. That any of the latter were saved was certainly due, not to the exertions of the commander, but to the humanity of the armourer and the boatswain's mate, who risked their lives to save some of the mutineers. The master-at-arms, who had dropped the keys through the scuttle, was himself drowned.

Edwards had not "lost his head." On the contrary, he had gathered his officers together to sign a paper he had drawn up to the effect that they agreed with him in his decision to abandon ship. That is not the behavior of a person in panic, it is the behavior of a coldly calculating automaton who is concerned only about himself, a "bureaucrat of the sea" to whom the fate of the prisoners was indeed a matter of indifference. In fact, in view of Edwards' paranoid fear of another mutiny, he would probably have welcomed the death of all the prisoners. His subsequent behavior towards the surviving prisoners strongly suggests that he was annoyed that they survived.

One loyalist, Stewart, and the three mutineers, Hillbrant, Skinner, and Sumner, who drowned when the *Pandora* foundered, left widows and children in Tahiti. Thirty-one of the *Pandora*'s crew also drowned; eighty-nine were saved plus ten of the men of the *Bounty*. Surgeon Hamilton wrote: "The cries of the men drowning in the water was at first awful in the extreme; but as they sunk and became faint, it died away by degrees."

The wreck of the *Pandora* was discovered in 1977 in seventeen fathoms of water on the outer edge of the reef near Cape York. The study of the wreck continues as this is being written and many interesting artifacts have been recovered.

September 1791

*W*hen the *Pandora* foundered on the Great Barrier Reef, the survivors gathered on a small sandy island without shade. Edwards ordered sails to be erected on spars in order to protect the ship's crew from the sun's rays, but the prisoners, who were all naked, were not given anything with which to protect themselves. Consequently, although they tried digging themselves into the sand for protection, they all received serious sunburns — yet another example of Edwards' callousness and insensitivity to human suffering.

Edwards' orders directed him to have "proper regard to the preservation of the prisoners' lives that they may be brought home to undergo the punishment due to their demerits." Being clearly responsible for the death of four prisoners, one of whom was a loyalist, Edwards cannot by any stretch of the imagination be said to have followed these orders conscientiously.

At about the same time as Bligh, on the other side of the world, sailed from Tenerife in the *Providence*, the shipwrecked men now set out on the same long and dangerous voyage to Timor which Bligh had undertaken more than two years earlier, the difference being that the men in the *Bounty*'s launch, even at the outset, were half-starved and totally exhausted by the long voyage from Tofua. Nevertheless, the voyage of the *Pandora*'s survivors was one of extreme suffering and hardship.

The men shipped into the four boats that had been saved from the *Pandora* and the mutineers were divided among them. Unluckily for Morrison — but fortunately for us — he was assigned to the boat commanded by Edwards. Through Morrison's subsequent account we can therefore get a close-up view of Edwards' ingrained brutality, although earlier evidence of it makes further examples superfluous. Suffice it to say that he did not even allow Morrison to pray.

The voyage to Coupang lasted close to two weeks, during which time some of the men suffered so horribly from thirst that they drank their own urine (those who did subsequently died). Timor was sighted on September 13 and Coupang reached on September 15. The survivors of the *Pandora* received the same gracious hospitality from the Dutch that had been extended to Bligh and his men. (The unfortunate Hayward who had been through both open-boat voyages was in a good position to compare!)

A few weeks earlier, a boatload of escapees from the penal colony at Port Jackson (today's Sydney) had arrived at Coupang, including a woman with two children. They claimed that they were survivors of an English ship that had foundered and that their captain had gone in another boat. They were now told the good news that their captain had finally arrived! Without thinking, one of them made the mistake of exclaiming: "What captain? Dam'me, we have no captain!"

That statement gave them away, of course, and the authorities realized that they were dealing with impostors. The escaped convicts soon confessed their true identities and were put behind bars. The woman, Mary Bryant, has earned a niche in literary history by eventually becoming a protegée of James Boswell. Accounts of her adventures are given in Geoffrey Rawson's *The Strange Case of Mary Bryant* (1935) and, more authoritatively, in F. A. Pottle's *Boswell and the Girl from Botany Bay* (1937). The story has also been told by Louis Becke and Walter Jeffery in *A First Fleet Family* (1896). Perhaps the most up-to-date and reliable book on the Bryant story is C. H. Currey's *The Transportation, Escape and Pardoning of Mary Bryant (née Broad)* (1963).

In maritime history the open-boat voyage of the escapees from Port Jackson to Timor deserves equal standing with the voyages of Bligh and Edwards. They rowed and sailed 3254 miles without anyone on board who could navigate and with a baby still at the breast, without losing a single member of their party. And, unlike the men in Bligh's and Edwards' boats, they had no home to go to, it was only the desire for freedom that drove them on.

October
1791

...⛵...

aving spent three weeks in Coupang regaining their strength after the open-boat voyage from the Great Barrier Reef, Captain Edwards and his men and the captured men of the *Bounty* sailed for Batavia on October 6 in the Dutch East Indiaman *Rembang*. (This was three days after Bligh with his ships *Providence* and *Assistant* had crossed the line on the way to Tahiti via Cape Town.)

The *Bounty* men, who had been virtually naked ever since the *Pandora* left Tahiti, had been given some clothes by the kindly citizens of the Dutch settlement. Joining them on board the *Rembang*, as prisoners, were the eleven escapees from the penal colony at Port Jackson. All prisoners except Mary Bryant and her two children were in irons, although they were in no condition to escape and certainly did not constitute any danger. Mary's husband William seemed to be dying and surgeon Hamilton advised Edwards of this fact, but the captain's attitude was true to character: "The only good convict is a dead one."

During the voyage Edwards came close to experiencing a second shipwreck. In a cyclone the *Rembang* was dismasted on a lee shore and, according to Hamilton, would have been stranded had it not been for the exertions of the English seamen. The Dutch sailors, who "would fight the devil should he appear to them in any other shape but that of thunder and lightning," had taken to their hammocks.

At the end of the month, on October 30, the *Rembang* anchored in Samarang on the north coast of Java and there a big surprise was awaiting Edwards and his men: riding safely at anchor in the harbor was the beautiful schooner *Resolution* which had been separated from them in the Samoas more than four months earlier. The Dutch had treated the crew hospitably, but they had placed them under house arrest. The reason was that Bligh had alerted all Dutch outposts to be on the lookout for the mutineers, should they attempt to touch at one of the ports, and the crew of the *Resolution* had no official papers with which to identify themselves. Moreover, the schooner was obviously built recently — clearly not on a wharf — and was composed of timbers from the South Seas, so it could very well have been built by the *Bounty* mutineers — as indeed it was.

Whether or not the captain of the *Resolution*, William Oliver, kept a journal, no detailed account of his extraordinary voyage has survived. (Midshipman David T. Renouard who was on board wrote a brief account which was published in 1842 by W. H. Smyth and in 1964 by Henry E. Maude; see "A Sample of Literature", under "Renouard.") Edwards, who had no curiosity or imagination — and evidently minimal interest in exploration — dismisses the voyage of the *Resolution* with a few lines. His brutal conduct against the men of the *Bounty* is inexcusable, but it is also difficult to excuse him for not letting us have a full account of the voyage of the *Resolution*.

*November
1791*

...⛵...

aptain Edwards in the Dutch East Indiaman *Rembang*, accompanied by the schooner *Resolution*, arrived at Batavia on November 7, 1791, one day after Bligh in the *Providence* with the tender *Assistant* had anchored in Table Bay outside Cape Town. Edwards now sold the *Resolution* (some writers claim she was sold in Samarang) and the money was divided among the crew of the *Pandora* to enable them to buy some clothes. Needless to say, the *Bounty* men who had built the vessel did not receive a penny from the sale.

Edwards divided his crew among various Dutch ships bound for Europe. He himself boarded the Dutch East Indiaman *Vreedenberg*, taking the ten *Bounty* men — whom he always referred to as "pirates" — with him on board. The convicts who had escaped from Port Jackson were divided between two other ships. Mary Bryant's husband William had died in Batavia, as had their little boy Emanuel.

Several weeks after Edwards' arrival in Batavia, the *Vreedenberg* sailed. By that time sixteen of the *Pandora*'s survivors had died from tropical fevers; this time, however, no *Bounty* men succumbed to them.

Mary Bryant and her daughter Charlotte sailed soon afterwards as prisoners on board the *Hoornwey* and witnessed some shocking and tragic scenes. One of the incidents throws additional light on the character of Thomas Hayward, the former midshipman on the *Bounty*, who was in charge of the prisoners on board the ship.

The *Hoornwey* was sailing in the middle of a four-mile wide stretch of the Sunda Straits. One of the escaped convicts from Port Jackson, James Cox, had been allowed to have his shackles removed in order to go to the canvas privy hanging over the railing. Suddenly he jumped overboard into the shark-infested waters where a strong current would have made it impossible for him to reach the shore two miles away.

It was either a desperate attempt to gain freedom at last or a deliberate suicide attempt. The ship's master ran to the stern and began to shout orders to put the helm down and launch a boat. Hayward, who had been promoted to lieutenant before sailing in the *Pandora*, contradicted him: "No, no! Sail on! He may escape the gallows, but not the sharks!"

It is no wonder that Hayward was the only one (except Samuel) that Bligh had praised upon his return to England.

December

1791

*O*n December 23, 1791, four years to the day since he left England on the ill-fated first breadfruit expedition in the *Bounty*, Captain Bligh sailed from Table Bay outside Cape Town. Again he was bound for Tahiti but this time in two ships, the *Providence* and the *Assistant*. Unknowingly, he was crossing the Indian Ocean in the opposite direction to that of Captain Edwards who had sailed from Batavia in the *Vreedenberg* bound for Cape Town.

Bligh had his course set on Van Diemen's Land where he planned to stop, so there was no chance that the two would meet on the ocean. Whether they met after both had returned to England is unrecorded, although it seems likely that they would have made an effort to get together and swap experiences. (We, in fact, do not even know for certain whether they met before the *Pandora* sailed from England, but it seems highly likely that Edwards would have consulted with Bligh before leaving for the South Seas.)

All the way from England Bligh had been suffering on and off from headaches and recurrent attacks of a tropical fever, probably malaria, which he had contracted in Java. For part of the voyage he had to give over command of the *Providence* to Lieutenant Nathaniel Portlock, the captain of the *Assistant*, sending his first lieutenant, Francis Bond, to relieve Portlock.

On Christmas Day supplies of fresh mutton, flour, pork, and onions, procured in Cape Town, were served to all hands. No other celebration of Christmas is mentioned.

At the end of the year, on December 29, Captain George Vancouver in HMS *Discovery* anchored in Matavai Bay in Tahiti. His armed tender *Chatham*, commanded by Lieutenant Broughton, had preceded him.

Vancouver had left England on April 1, 1791, so he knew about the mutiny on the *Bounty* and about the *Pandora* expedition which had left England five months before him, and he was very curious about what had happened to the mutineers and to the *Pandora*. As a midshipman he had sailed with Bligh on Cook's third voyage, although they had been in different ships, Vancouver in the *Discovery* which he now commanded and Bligh in the *Resolution*.

Tu, who now called himself Pomare, gave Vancouver a friendly reception and filled him in on past developments as best he could, considering the language barrier. During Vancouver's stay Pomare's power happened to be further augmented by the death of his father-in-law, a chief on Moorea, which brought that island under closer control of "King" Pomare. Vancouver's visit was of course also an important boost for the ambitious chief whose power and influence on Tahiti depended so much on the support of visiting British ships and therefore had waned since the departure of Edwards.

January

1792

Bligh started the new year, 1792, sailing almost due east from Cape Town to Van Diemen's Land. The *Providence* had some trouble keeping in touch with her tender, the *Assistant*, which was slower in strong winds and faster in light weather. In his log for January 6 Bligh writes, "When going above six knots, we sail faster than the *Assistant*, but when the wind will not carry us, she sails better than we do." This time around there was no chance of mutiny on Bligh's ships. The Admiralty had seen to that by implementing all precautionary measures which should have been taken on the first expedition. Not only had Bligh's authority been strengthened by his promotion to post captain, but he now had experienced commissioned officers around him and therefore had less direct contact with the men. The fact that two ships were employed would in itself have made a mutiny at sea very difficult, and now there was also a sizeable contingent of marines on board to keep order.

Bligh's tongue was as vicious, insulting and humiliating as ever, but this time there was no unstable and psychologically thin-skinned Christian to brood over the wrongs that had been inflicted on him. Even if someone like Christian had been on board, there were fellow officers whose company he could have sought and with whom he could have commiserated and let out his feelings. Finally, the *Providence* was almost double the size of the *Bounty* and, although modified to receive a large number of breadfruit shoots, was not as crowded.

One of Bligh's finest virtues was foresight (except that he never learned to foresee the reaction of other people to his humiliating remarks) and it is certain that he did not give any potential mutineer the slightest chance to take over his ship on this voyage. Never again, for example, did he sleep without a guard outside his cabin door.

But on this voyage, too, he managed to drive some of his officers to the point of desperation and there is no doubt that several of them gained a very good understanding of what it was that finally triggered the mutiny on the *Bounty*.

OFFICERS
OF
THE *PROVIDENCE*

William Bligh
CAPTAIN

Matthew Flinders
MIDSHIPMAN

F. G. Bond
FIRST LIEUTENANT

William Askew
MIDSHIPMAN

James Guthrie
SECOND LIEUTENANT

John Bushby
MIDSHIPMAN

George Tobin
THIRD LIEUTENANT

George Killsha
MIDSHIPMAN

William Nichols
MASTER

George Holwell
MIDSHIPMAN

John Impey
COMMANDER'S MATE

John Head
MIDSHIPMAN

Thomas Walker
MASTER'S MATE

Richard Franklin
MIDSHIPMAN

Thomas Gillespie
MASTER'S MATE

Edward Harwood
SURGEON

Edward Hume
MASTER'S MATE

Robert Ridgway
SURGEON'S MATE

R. Pearce
LIEUTENANT OF MARINES

Douglas White
SURGEON'S MATE

Robert Ogilvie
MIDSHIPMAN

Edward Hatfull
CLERK

John England
GUNNER

OFFICERS
OF
THE *ASSISTANT*

Nathaniel Portlock
LIEUTENANT

Andrew Dyce
ACTING MIDSHIPMAN

George Watson
SAILING MASTER

James Campbell
ACTING MIDSHIPMAN

David Gilmour
MIDSHIPMAN

James Norris
SURGEON'S MATE

John Gore
MIDSHIPMAN

Andrew Goldie
GUNNER'S MATE

Thomas England
MIDSHIPMAN

Robert Scott
ACTING CARPENTER

Francis Matthews
MIDSHIPMAN

Daniel Myers
CARPENTER'S MATE

John Lapenotiere
ACTING MIDSHIPMAN

Richard Wallace
SAILMAKER

Francis Wilson
BOATSWAIN'S MATE

NATURALISTS ON THE EXPEDITION

Christopher Smith
BOTANIST

James Wiles
BOTANIST

February 1792

While Captain Edwards was sailing towards Cape Town, Bligh was nearing Van Diemen's Land in a full gale from west-south-west. On February 4, 1792, a heavy cross sea almost swamped the smaller (110 tons) *Assistant* and even the *Providence* (420 tons) shipped a lot of water. On February 8, land was sighted and the next day the ships anchored in Adventure Bay.

To Bligh this was like coming home again. He had been here with Cook fifteen years earlier on Cook's third voyage. Then, and later, Bligh played an important part in the exploration of this part of Van Diemen's Land, although it was left to another explorer, Admiral Bruni d'Entrecasteaux, to discover that Adventure Bay was on an island (later named after the admiral and now known as Bruny) and not on the mainland of Tasmania. (D'Entrecasteaux, in fact, arrived only two months after Bligh had left in the *Providence*.)

Bligh's second visit to the bay had been in the *Bounty* in August 1788 and it was then that he had his first serious trouble with the carpenter, William Purcell. Also on that occasion, an old tree trunk had been found with the inscription "A.D. 1773." He knew that it must have been carved by someone sailing with Captain Tobias Furneaux who had discovered and named the bay in that year while commanding the *Adventure* on Cook's second voyage.

This, then, was Bligh's third visit to Adventure Bay and, as always, he made valuable observations and drew detailed maps for the benefit of future visitors. Considering his keen and constant desire for exploration, it is very possible that on this visit he might have made some of the discoveries that d'Entrecasteaux made a few months later, had the weather not been so rough.

On this last visit, Bligh ordered a statement carved into a tree which read: "Near this tree Captain William Bligh planted seven fruit trees:- Messrs. S. and W., botanists." (S. referred to Christopher Smith and W. to James Wiles.) This led the naturalist on d'Entrecasteaux's expedition, Jacques de Labillardière, to deplore "the despotism which condemned men of science to initials and gave a sea captain a monopoly of fame!"

Bligh left Adventure Bay for Tahiti on February 23. We do not know if he ever learned of Labillardière's comment, but if he did, he probably just shrugged his shoulders. Bligh was not one to accept criticism from anyone and certainly not from a Frenchman!

March
1792

... 🚢 *...*

On March 18, 1792, Edwards arrived in Cape Town on board the *Vreeden-berg* after a slow passage from Batavia. Even before the ship had anchored in Table Bay, Edwards saw a British warship in the harbor. It turned out to be HMS *Gorgon* en route from New South Wales to England. Although the commander, Captain John Parker, already had several passengers on board, including his own wife, other women and children, he agreed to make room for Edwards, the captured men of the *Bounty*, and the escaped convicts from Port Jackson.

Meanwhile, Bligh was sailing eastward in the South Pacific south of the 48th parallel and on March 21 he reached the longitude of Tahiti, whereupon he turned northward. He passed within a few days' sail of Pitcairn Island, the refuge of his old nemesis Fletcher Christian, unwittingly confirming the wisdom of Christian's choice: Pitcairn lay outside all shipping lanes, and remained so until 1914 when the Panama Canal opened and Pitcairn found itself in the path of traffic to and from New Zealand.

Bligh may have known from Lieutenant Mortimer of the *Mercury* (see the October 1790 commentary) that the mutineers had been on Tahiti, but he did not know whether they had stayed there, nor whether Edwards had been able to capture any of them. It was therefore with extreme interest and excitement that he looked forward to arriving.

Meanwhile there had been a shipwreck in the Tuamotus, one that was going to have some significance in the history of Tahiti. On the night of February 24, 1792, the British whaler *Matilda*, commanded by Captain Matthew Weatherhead, foundered in a storm on the reef of Mururoa. Incredibly, the whole ship's company survived and all four of the whaleboats remained intact.

The crewmen of the *Matilda* had heard that the natives on the Tuamotu islands were cannibals (some were) and they therefore set off immediately for Tahiti where they had stopped for provisions several days earlier. It was a distance of 640 nautical miles and they covered it in ten days.

As they had expected, the Tahitians welcomed them with open arms, although they did "confiscate" their muskets and pistols and money. "They" in this case means the inhabitants of Haapape (where Matavai Bay is located) and the theft — which it was — triggered a war with the adjacent district of Pare. The chief of Pare was Pomare (Tu, Teina, Mate) and as he wanted supremacy over the island he did not take kindly to other districts having European weapons.

The fact that money was also "appropriated" is highly significant and shows the degree to which the Tahitians had been "Europeanized." Even just a few years earlier, money would have meant nothing to them. But the steady stream of ships from Europe had given them a good understanding of what European values were and, unfortunately (some might say fortunately), they were not late in adopting them, at least superficially.

Most of the twenty-nine shipwrecked men from the *Matilda* seem to have been homesick and within a few months twenty-three of them had left Tahiti on various ships. The schooner *Jenny* from Bristol arrived in Tahiti on March 25 and when it sailed six days later Captain Weatherhead and four of his crew took passage on her for North America. On the same day three foolhardy members of the *Matilda*'s crew sailed for Port Jackson in Australia in one of the whaleboats. It is a virtual certainty that they perished on the voyage; at least there is no record of their having arrived at their destination.

Six of the crew, however, remained on Tahiti and took part in the war that was going on between Pomare and his enemies. Three of them allied themselves with Pomare and the other three with the opposing chiefs.

One of the three who cast their lot with Pomare was Anders Lind, a Swede who was an excellent marksman and also a good military tactician. Later on, in early 1793, he was joined by a Swedish-speaking Finn, Petter Hägersten, from Helsingfors (Helsinki), and the two of them played an important role in establishing Pomare's supremacy over the island. Petter Hägersten, by the way, was the first European to settle permanently on Tahiti and live out his days there. He served not only as Pomare's "general," but also as an interpreter for the missionaries who arrived in 1797 and for visiting sea captains.

April

1792

... ⛵ ...

*O*n Cape Town the captured men of the *Bounty* and the escaped convicts from Port Jackson had been taken on board HMS *Gorgon* bound for England. From this point on Captain Edwards had no authority over the captives; their treatment now depended on the commander of the *Gorgon*, Captain John Parker, who kept them in strict confinement but showed no deliberate cruelty towards them.

The *Bounty* men found their "accommodation" and treatment a vast improvement over what they had experienced on board the *Pandora* and the *Vreedenberg*. Even though they were at first put on the regulation two-thirds allowance of food and grog (changed to full allowance on April 10), Morrison says that this

> ... was now thought feasting. McIntosh, Coleman and Norman were at liberty, and the rest of us only one leg in irons and every indulgence given and Lieut. Gardner of this ship, in the absence of Capt. Parker, very humanely gave us a sail to lay on which by us was thought a luxury; and was indeed such as we had not enjoy'd for 12 months before.

There were six escapees from Port Jackson on board (the others had died), including Mary Bryant and her daughter Charlotte. They were similarly confined, except for Mary and her daughter who were at liberty. The *Gorgon* sailed on April 6, 1792.

At the same time, in the South Pacific, Bligh was nearing Tahiti in the *Providence* with the tender *Assistant*. On April 5 he discovered an atoll in the Tuamotus which he named Bligh's Lagoon Island but which is known today by its Tuamotuan name Tematangi (*te matangi* means the wind). The ships anchored in Matavai Bay in Tahiti on April 10.

Among the canoes that came out to the ship, Bligh was astonished to see a whaleboat full of Englishmen. They were, of course, the members of the crew of the *Matilda* which had foundered six weeks earlier. Eight of the crew, including the captain, had left eleven days earlier, but twenty-one were still on the island.

Bligh arrived at Tahiti in the middle of a war between the districts of Pare and Haapape over the weapons and the money that had been "confiscated" from the crew of the *Matilda* by the inhabitants of Haapape. He was asked to join forces with Pare whose chief was his old friend Teina (now called Pomare), but he wisely stayed out of the conflict, guaranteeing only that he would not let Pare be invaded by Haapape (whose chief was Teina's former friend Poino).

Among Bligh's first questions upon arrival was, of course, what had happened to the men of the *Bounty* — the "pirates," as he referred to them all, no matter whether they were mutineers or loyalists. He writes in his journal: "It may readily be believed that I found great satisfaction to hear of these men all being taken by Captain Edwards except two who were killed by the Indians" (see the March 1790 commentary).

Bligh was distressed by the changes he saw in the Tahitians: "Our countrymen have taught them such vile expressions as are in the mouth of every Otaheitan, and I declare that I would rather forfeit anything than to have been in the list of ships that have touched here since April, 1789." And later: ". . . but little of the ancient customs remain — all that was laid aside. It is difficult to get them to speak their own language without mixing a jargon of English with it, and they are so altered that I believe in future no Europeans will ever know what their ancient customs of receiving strangers were."

Bligh had come close to contributing to the drastic change on the island. Before his departure from England he had been persuaded to take with him two missionaries from the group which would later emerge as the London Missionary Society. The men chosen, however, had backed out in the last moment.

By the end of the month, 1090 breadfruit shoots and many other plants had been collected.

May
1792

... 🚢 ...

MS *Gorgon* was sailing for England with Captain Edwards, the captured men of the *Bounty*, and the escapees from Port Jackson on board. Mary Bryant, the unfortunate "girl from Botany Bay", had lost her husband and little boy to the fevers of Batavia. Now, on May 6, her little daughter Charlotte died from an unknown ailment. She was four and a half years old; she had come to the world on the convict transport *Charlotte* and she left it on the "convict transport" *Gorgon*.

On Tahiti Bligh was gathering breadfruit shoots for the second time around and by May 6 had completed his task. His botanists, however, wanted to be sure that the shoots would survive, and on their advice he stayed at Tahiti more than two months longer.

Meanwhile the war between the districts of Haapape and Pare was over, and their chiefs, Poino and Pomare, became friends again. However, the natives of Haapape had still not returned the weapons and money they had "confiscated" from the crew of the *Matilda* (although a considerable part of the property was returned on May 9).

Bligh of course had a keen interest in what the men of the *Bounty* had been up to during their stay on the island, and on May 2 he met a woman who had been the consort of Thomas McIntosh, carpenter's crew on board the *Bounty* and a loyalist. The European name he had given her (many of the seamen could not pronounce Tahitian names) was "Mary." Mary showed Bligh the child she had had with McIntosh, a girl who was now eighteen months old and called Elizabeth.

Among the old friends who came to visit Bligh was "Queen" Purea-Tetupaia (also called Peroa; Bligh spelled her name Obereeroah), Teina's mother, who was now living in Moorea.

Over several glases of good Madeira, Purea and her friend "Parai" — who could be sentimental at times — shared memories of the old times of beauty and wonder and dignity and mutual admiration, the times that would never come back, *te mau taime matamua, te tau i mairi.*

June 1792

HMS *Gorgon* arrived in Spithead on June 19, 1792, and two days later the captured men of the *Bounty*, all suspected mutineers in the eyes of the law, were transferred to HMS *Hector* where they were to await their court-martial.

The convicts who had escaped from Port Jackson were taken to Newgate Prison to be sentenced. Two of the four surviving men were sent back to the penal colony, one was allowed to enlist in the so-called Rum Corps, and the fate of the fourth is unknown.

Mary Bryant had lost everything that was dear to her in life, her husband, her two children, and her freedom. The probability is that Mary, too, would have been sent back to the colony had it not been for the fact that she had found two benefactors. One was a Captain of the Marines, Watkin Tench, who, by coincidence, had been on board the convict transport which brought her to New South Wales and now had traveled home in the *Gorgon* and befriended her on board. Captain Tench writes:

> I confess that I never looked at these people [the escapees] without pity and astonishment. They had miscarried in a heroic struggle for liberty after having combated every hardship and conquered every difficulty.
>
> The woman and one of the men had gone out to Botany Bay in the same ship which took me thither (*Charlotte*). They had both been distinguished for good behaviour and I could not but reflect with admiration the strange combination of circumstances which had again brought us together, to baffle human foresight and to confound human speculation.

One authority (Sir Basil Thomson in his Introduction to *Voyage of HMS* Pandora (1915) claims that Mary obtained a full pardon "owing chiefly to the exertions of an officer of marines [presumably Tench] who went home with her in the *Gorgon* and eventually married her.

Mary's other benefactor was none other than James Boswell. Professor F. A. Pottle of Yale University, in *The Girl from Botany Bay* (1937), has shown that Boswell took an interest — evidently purely platonic — in Mary, obtained a pardon for her, and provided her with an annuity of ten pounds a year. The two accounts of her fate are not necessarily contradictory.

In Tahiti, Bligh was busy making valuable ethnographic observations while making sure that the breadfruit shoots he had gathered would not only survive but thrive. His observations of the Tahitians included their children in whom he seems to have delighted, but he was never able to overcome the prejudice of his times. He writes, "Few more engaging children are to be met with could we divest ourselves of the dislike to the colour."

On June 4 King George's 54th birthday was celebrated and Bligh describes the occasion in his journal:

> In commemoration of our most gracious and good King, we held this day a Festival. At eight in the morning both ships were dressed to the delight of the natives. At noon the marines were drawn up under arms and fired three vollies, and the Indians joined their cheers with ours. At one the ships fired twenty-one guns each. To every person was served an allowance of liquor. At night I had a dozen sky rockets sent off, and Mr. Tobin having made two small balloons the whole were successfully displayed to the great pleasure of 600 persons. "Mahannah no Erree Britanee! King George."* (The King of England's birthday! King George!) was repeated every minute by men, women, and children. All the chiefs were collected around us, and drank to His Majesty's good health and afterwards dined with me.

*Actually: "*Mahana no te Arii Peretane, Arii Tihoti!*"

July

1792

$\mathscr{B}$ligh was preparing to leave Tahiti with his breadfruit plants all ready to be stowed on board. He wrote: "Monday, July 9th. My plants are now in such charming forwardness that the botanists have determined I need not be detained here any longer than a week or two."

The captain was besieged with requests by the Tahitians to take them along so they could visit England, as Mai had done several years ago when Cook took him aboard on his second voyage and returned him on the third. The man Bligh finally consented to take along was Maititi who was previously mentioned as Churchill's servant (see the March 1790 commentary).

Bligh also found out that many natives had asked crew members to hide them on board as stowaways. Actually, the Polynesians seem to have travel "in their blood" — a heritage, perhaps, from the time when they populated the vast Pacific while the Europeans were afraid to venture far from their shores. Even today, Polynesians love to visit new places whenever they can save up enough money to do it, and arrivals and departures remain of extreme importance in Tahiti. Close friends of visitors always go to the harbor or airport to meet and *faahei* them (give them a *hei tiare* or flower lei). Even casual acquaintances go to the departures of visitors they have met and present them with a *hei pupu* (shell lei). Not to go to the departure of a friend can be seen as an insult if there is not a good reason for it.

Although Bligh had not been well liked on the island during his visit in the *Bounty*, the Tahitians felt compassion for him when they heard the truth about what had happened to him, and this time they seem to have been sorry to see him leave. In fact, they promised to build a house where he could live when he came back (he never did), and after his departure they did indeed build a house for him close to his old breadfruit camp. The missionaries who arrived in 1797 saw it and described it as "a large oval-shaped native house . . . pleasantly situated on the western side of the river near Point Venus."

Before leaving, Bligh signed the back of a portrait of Cook. It had become a custom for all visiting captains to do so ever since John Webber had painted it in 1777 and given it to Tu (now Pomare). It was at this time in the custody of Poino, the chief of Haapape on the eastern shore of Matavai Bay. For many years it served as a Tahitian "guestbook" of sorts — now lost.

On July 19 Bligh sailed out of Matavai. To his astonishment one Tahitian had managed — despite a careful search of the vessel — to hide himself on board the *Providence*. Bligh wrote in his journal: "I had not the heart to make him jump overboard. I conceived he might be useful in Jamaica . . . therefore directed he should be under the care of the botanists." So Bligh left with two Tahitians on board.

He also brought with him fifteen of the crew members of the *Matilda*, two of whom were on board the *Assistant*. And he had with him 2126 breadfruit plants, 472 "other plants," and 36 "curiosity plants."

August
1792

... ⚓ ...

For Bligh, who had an inquisitive mind and was always looking for new discoveries, the month of August 1792 was one of exciting exploration. After leaving Tahiti he had touched at Aitutaki (in the Cook group) which he had discovered in the *Bounty* in 1789. He now checked some of Maurelle's discoveries in the Vavau and Haapai groups of Tonga and then continued westward through the Fiji islands.

Bligh had sailed through this group on his open-boat voyage and had made several sketches and maps even then. Now he was in a much better position to determine the exact locations of the islands and to chart them. Although Tasman and Cook before him had made some peripheral discoveries in the group, Bligh must be considered the principal European discoverer of Fiji and is so viewed by the Fijians today. He himself, never lacking in vanity, called them Bligh's Islands. From the Fijis Bligh sailed to the New Hebrides and by the end of the month he was nearing the dangerous Endeavour Straits.

What was Bligh like on this second breadfruit voyage? As far as we know, he was at least as irascible and faultfinding and petty as on the first, perhaps more so, since he was now chronically beset with headaches and recurring fevers. Thanks to the eminent historian and *Bounty* expert Rolf Du Rietz, who first realized the significance of the Bond material, we know what Bligh's step-nephew Francis Bond, first lieutenant on the *Providence*, thought of Bligh (see Du Rietz, 1965, pp. 28–31). He wrote the following in a letter to his brother:

> The very high opinion he has of himself makes him hold everyone of our profession with contempt, perhaps envy: nay the Navy is but [a] sphere for fops and lubbers to swarm in, without one gem to vie in brilliancy with himself. I don't mean to depreciate his exensive knowledge as a seaman and nautical astronomer, but condemn that want of modesty in self estimation. To be less prolix I will inform you he has treated me (nay all on board) with the insolence

and arrogance of a *Jacobs*; and notwithstanding his passion is partly to be attributed to a nervous fever, with which he has been attacked most of the voyage, the chief part of his conduct must have arisen from the fury of an ungovernable temper.

Every dogma of power and consequence has been taken from the Lieutenants, to establish, as he thinks, his own reputation — what imbecility for a post Capn! The inferior Warrants have had orders from the beginning of the expedition, not to issue the least article to a Lieut. without his orders so that a cleat, fathom of log line, or indeed a hand swab, must have the commander's sanction. One of the last and most *beneficent* commands was that the Carpenter's Crew should not drive a nail for me without I should first ask his permission — but my heart is filled with the proper materials always to disdain this humiliation.

. . . yet the company of a set of well informed messmates makes my moments pass very agreeably, so that I am by no means in purgatory . . .

Lieutenant Bond was not in purgatory, because he had fellow officers with whom to commiserate and, perhaps more importantly, he was not in the constant contact with Bligh that Christian had been on the small and overcrowded *Bounty*. Christian, however, had been not just in purgatory but in hell, as he said before and during the mutiny.

The majority opinion of Bligh on board the *Providence* is perhaps best summed up by the captain of the marines on the expedition: "[because of] Bligh's odious behaviour during the voyage, I would as soon shoot him as a dog, if it were not for the law!"

September 1792

... ⛵ ...

*A*s Bligh was navigating through the treacherous Endeavour Straits on his way from the Pacific to the West Indies, the long awaited trial of the captured men of the *Bounty* took place in England. It was preceded by Captain Edwards' obligatory court-martial for the loss of the *Pandora* at which he was acquitted of responsibility. The fact that he had flagrantly disobeyed his orders — which stated that he was to pay "proper regard to the preservation of [his prisoners'] lives" — never came up at the perfunctory trial.

The ten *Bounty* men had been kept waiting for almost three months on board HMS *Hector*. They had been given some privileges, such as the use of paper and pen, and Morrison especially had used his time well in writing his own defense, helping his shipmates write theirs, and reconstructing his journal from memory. He also sent a letter to a clergyman in Portsea near Spithead, Reverend William Howell, which was to be of importance for the eventual outcome of his case (see the December 1792 commentary). Heywood, with the help of his fellow prisoners, had worked on his Tahitian dictionary which would later be of great value to the missionaries. The court-martial opened on September 12 in the great cabin of HMS *Duke* at Spithead. Vice-Admiral Samuel Lord Hood presided over the proceedings with eleven captains as assistant judges, among them Captain Albemarle Bertie who was Peter Heywood's uncle by marriage. All prisoners had been charged with "mutinously running away with the said armed vessel and deserting from His Majesty's Service."

The public interest in the trial was keen, especially since Bligh's account of the mutiny had become a bestseller and there was a special aura of mystique surrounding the take-over of the ship.

The main interest centered on Heywood and Morrison. Bligh himself had made clear that Byrne, Coleman, McIntosh, and Norman had remained on board against their will, and there was little doubt concerning the guilt of Burkett, Ellison, Millward, and Muspratt.

Unfortunately for posterity, the court showed no interest in the causes of the mutiny, only in who was guilty and who innocent. There was no middle position that could be taken and the judgment would be either acquittal or death by hanging. Only Heywood and Muspratt had legal counsel during the proceedings; the others had to fend for themselves. Heywood felt legal counsel was rather useless, since lawyers were not allowed to speak at a court-martial anyway. What eventually happened in Muspratt's case proved Heywood wrong.

The first witness to be called was the sailing master of the *Bounty*, John Fryer. His testimony would have been damaging to Bligh, had the court been interested in the causes of the mutiny. As it was, Fryer testified that he had not seen Heywood during the mutiny and that he had considered Morrison someone he would have trusted if an opportunity to recapture the ship had presented itself.

The next witness was William Cole, boatswain of the *Bounty*. He had seen Heywood — in his bunk! This cast doubt on Bligh's accusation that Heywood had been one of the instigators of the mutiny. Later he had seen Heywood assisting with the lowering of the launch, but his impression was that Heywood had wanted to go with Bligh and had been kept on board against his will. As far as Morrison was concerned, Cole testified that he had no reason to believe that the accused had had any part in the mutiny.

The next witness was William Peckover, the gunner, who had been in his cabin during most of the action and therefore did not have much to say. Morrison did get Peckover to admit, however, that he had no reason to believe that Morrison was one of the mutineers.

William Purcell, the carpenter who could not stand Bligh, would undoubtedly have had some interesting caustic remarks to make regarding his former commander, but the court was not interested in what anyone thought about Bligh. Purcell had little to say about Morrison, but did not think that he had been one of the mutineers. As far as Heywood was concerned, Purcell testified that he had seen Heywood with his hand on a cutlass, although he had quickly removed his hand when Purcell called out to him "In the Name of God, Peter, what do you do with that?" This was highly damaging evidence, and it did not help much that Purcell said he thought Heywood had merely acted thoughtlessly and could not be considered as having been armed.

Former midshipman Thomas Hayward carefully neglected to mention that he had slept on duty the morning of the mutiny and that he had later cried and begged the mutineers to be allowed to stay on board. He made it clear that he thought Morrison was one of the mutineers. He had to admit that he had not seen Heywood actively assist in the mutiny, but he claimed that Heywood had remained on the ship of his own volition and therefore must be considered as having been on the side of the mutineers.

Midshipman Hallett, who also had cried and implored the mutineers to let him stay on board, gave even more damaging testimony against Heywood, claiming that Bligh had said something to Heywood and that the latter, instead of answering, had laughed in a derisive manner and gone away. His testimony against Morrison was devastating: he claimed he had seen him armed with a musket in the stern of the ship!

(Both Hayward and Hallett later admitted that they might have been mistaken and regretted their testimonies, but that was after the court-martial was over.)

Bligh's servant John Smith testified that he had seen neither Heywood, nor Morrison, under arms.

Captain Edwards and First Lieutenant Larkin of the *Pandora* were called and testified that Coleman, Heywood, and Stewart had given themselves up voluntarily in Tahiti. Second Lieutenant Robert Corner of the *Pandora* testified that Morrison, Norman, and Ellison had surrendered voluntarily.

On September 17 the accused were allowed to make speeches in their own defense and to cross-examine witnesses. Heywood's defense was astonishingly weak in view of the fact that he had the advice of legal counsel, a Mr. Aaron Graham who was experienced in naval courts-martial. Instead of focusing on the established fact that he had been prevented from going on deck when the loyalists went into the launch, his highly emotional and outright mawkish speech concentrated on his youth and inexperience, an argument almost guaranteed not to carry any weight with the court. (A clear presentation of the circumstances involved in Heywood's defense is found in Du Rietz, 1965.)

Morrison — who had no one to help him — put up a much stronger and much more cogent defense. On cross examination however, Cole damaged Morrison's case by testifying that the latter had had a derisive tone of voice when he shouted a request (to be remembered to his friends at home) directed to the men in the launch.

Muspratt, on the advice of his astute attorney, Stephen Barney, made the following petition, read by the Judge Advocate:

> It is every day's practice in the Criminal Courts of Justice on the Land when a Number of Prisoners are tried for the same facts, and the Evidence does not materially Affect some, for the Court to acquit those that are not Affected, that the other Prisoners may have an Opportunity to call them if advised to do so. I beg to have the Opportunity of calling Byrne and Norman.

The official record of the proceedings of the court-martial continues:

> The Court withdrew and agreed That the Court is of Opinion that they cannot depart from the usual Practice of Courts Martial and give Sentence on any particular Prisoner, until the whole of the Defences of the Prisoners, are gone through.

So the petition was denied, but that was exactly what Barney wanted. The testimonies of Michael Byrne and Charles Norman would not have been likely to make any difference in the case of Muspratt, but the denial of the petition provided

Barney with the opportunity to later appeal the verdict on the basis that his client's rights had been violated.

The verdicts and sentences were pronounced on September 18. The court first asked whether any one of the accused wished to say something on his own behalf. Heywood availed himself of this opportunity to again stress his youth. He produced a birth certificate showing that he had been only sixteen (actually he was almost seventeen) at the time of the mutiny. This did not make any impression on the court. The Navy had an abundance of young seamen and officers (the youngest crew member on HMS *Victory*, for example, was ten years old), so tender age was no excuse.

The first on the list of those pronounced guilty and condemned to death were Heywood and Morrison! The court had simply not been able to disregard Hayward's and Hallett's highly damaging testimonies. The rest on the list were expected: Burkett, Ellison, Millward, and Muspratt were all found guilty and condemned "to suffer death by being hanged by the neck" on board one of His Majesty's ships of war.

The verdict, of course, came as a tremendous shock for Heywood and Morrison who thought that they had been successful in their defense and had established their innocence. However, the court had something to add: "in consideration of various circumstances" it "did humbly and most earnestly recommend" Heywood and Morrison to His Majesty's mercy, meaning that they had a chance of being pardoned. Byrne, Coleman, McIntosh, and Norman were acquitted, as expected.

It is interesting to speculate about what would have happened if Bligh had testified at the court-martial. Since everyone accused would have had a chance to cross-examine him, it is possible that at least Heywood would have been acquitted (despite Bligh's post-mutiny hatred for the young man).

Why had the court not waited until Bligh returned and could testify? We will never know for certain, but it is entirely possible that the highly influential patron of Bligh, Sir Joseph Banks, did not want his protégé present at the trial where he would have been subject to cross-examination. It could even have been one reason why Bligh was sent off on the second breadfruit expedition long before the *Pandora* was expected to return.

It was not unusual in mutiny courts-martial to make counter-accusations and it had even happened on some occasions that a captain had been dismissed from the service as a result. Sir Joseph could not afford to take the risk of such embarrassment, since it would have reflected negatively on his choice and, ultimately, on that of the King. Even as it was, the trial had been damaging to Bligh, especially in view of the fact that no one had even attempted to act decisively in his defense during the mutiny. And people were starting to wonder what provocation there could have been for an officer of the Royal Navy, Fletcher Christian, to incite a mutiny, and for another officer, Edward Young, to join in it. It was unheard of.

For a detailed day-by-day account of the court-martial, consult Owen Rutter (ed.): *The Court-Martial of the "Bounty" Mutineers* (1931).

October

1792

*B*ligh had successfully negotiated Endeavour Straits in nineteen days. As was his custom, he had all the while been making valuable observations, sketches, and charts for future seafarers. On October 2, 1792, he reached Coupang on Timor where he found his old benefactor, Mynheer Timotheus Wanjon, who had been so kind and helpful to him and the loyalists when they arrived in the *Bounty*'s launch in 1789. Wanjon was now governor of the Dutch settlement and again received Bligh warmly.

From Governor Wanjon, Bligh found out about the foundering of the *Pandora* and about the fate of the captured men of the *Bounty* up until their departure for Cape Town. He was also told the story of the escaped convicts from Port Jackson and was shown a journal that had been kept by one of the escapees. Bligh had one of his fever attacks at the time and was too weak to copy the journal, which is a pity, because it is now lost.

By this time 224 of the breadfruit plants in pots had wilted and he replaced them with many of the exotic plants indigenous to Timor. He left Coupang on October 11 and, after passing Bengoar Island, set his course west-south-west-by-west for Madagascar.

In England the six condemned *Bounty* men were waiting to be either executed or pardoned. Morrison and Heywood busied themselves with writing; Morrison's accounts of the South Sea islanders and their customs were to become invaluable to ethnographers and historians, and Heywood's Tahitian dictionary was very helpful to the early missionaries on Tahiti.

On October 24 Heywood and Morrison received a Royal Pardon which, in fact, implied an overturning of the verdict. On the advice of his skillful lawyer, Stephen Barney, Muspratt appealed his verdict on a technicality. He had to wait until February 1793 before the court ruled on his appeal. He won!

The execution of Burkett, Ellison, and Millward had been set for October 29 on board HMS *Brunswick*. It was not going to be a hanging in the sense that we conceive of today. A Navy hanging was a particularly gruesome affair, since the condemned were not dropped so their necks would be broken, but were hoisted up. Consequently, it could take as long as twenty minutes before their twitchings and gaspings finally stopped.

The evening before the execution the prisoners were rowed over to the *Brunswick*. Ellison had been only sixteen when he joined Christian in the mutiny and now his life was to end before he had reached full adulthood. Yet he, as well as the other two condemned, seemed in good spirits. They spent the night in prayer led by Millward who was the best educated among them.

At nine o'clock in the morning a gun was fired from the *Brunswick* and a yellow flag hoisted as a signal to the other ships anchored at Spithead to send delegations to witness punishment. Boats immediately started to converge on the ship, the deck of which was already thronged with spectators. There were also huge crowds lining the shores and voices were heard among them expressing disappointment that only three men were to be hanged!

At eleven o'clock the prisoners were taken up on deck accompanied by four clergymen and by Morrison who wanted to give them his support in their last moments. Before the noose was put around his neck, Millward made a speech to the assembled men:

> Brother seamen, you see before you three lusty young fellows about to suffer a shameful death for the dreadful crime of mutiny and desertion. Take warning by our example never to desert your officers, and should they behave ill to you, remember it is not their cause, it is the cause of your country you are bound to support.

The nooses were now fitted around the necks of the prisoners and at the sound of a cannon, they were hoisted to their slow and agonizing deaths, one hanging from the starboard yard arm, two from the port.

November 1792

$\mathcal{O}$n board the *Providence* and the *Assistant*, sailing on the Indian Ocean, there was a great deal of illness that had been contracted in Timor. On November 6 one of the marines died, probably from a tropical disease, although the log book attributes his death to "catching cold and from an improper use of arrack before he embarked!"

The reason why Bligh had been instructed to consider St. Augustine's Bay on Madagascar rather than Table Bay as a stop-over for provisioning was the fact that the climate of the latter port might turn out to be too cold for the breadfruit plants. On November 10 Bligh informed his botanists that he could now set a course for St. Augustine's if they thought it best for the preservation of the plants. At this time of year, however, the bay was subject to heavy seas from the north-west and Bligh was short of anchors. He was therefore pleased when the botanists agreed with his preference which was to sail directly for St. Helena. The Cape of Good Hope was passed on November 19.

In England the court-martial of the ten accused mutineers was over. Four had been acquitted, two had been pardoned, one was waiting on the outcome of his appeal, and three had been hanged. Everyone now felt free to speak out about the causes of the mutiny without jeopardizing his own cause or anyone else's.

As early as November 5, midshipman Peter Heywood wrote to Fletcher Christian's older brother, Edward, who was a professor of the Laws of England at Cambridge:

> Excuse my freedom, Sir:- If it would not be disagreeable to you, I will do myself the pleasure of waiting upon you; and endeavour to prove that your brother was not that vile wretch, void of all gratitude, which the world had the unkindness to think him; but, on the contrary, a most worthy character, ruined only by the misfortune (if it can be so called) of being a young man of strict honour, and adorned with every virtue; and beloved by all (except one, whose ill report is his greatest praise) who had the pleasure of his acquaintance.

Meanwhile the former sailing master of the *Bounty*, John Fryer, had visited another relative of Fletcher's, Joseph Christian, and told him his view of what had happened on the *Bounty*.

Heywood's letter to Edward Christian was published in the *Cumberland Pacquet* which introduced it with an editorial comment:

> — For the honour of this county, we are happy to assure our readers that one of its natives FLETCHER CHRISTIAN is not that detestable and horrid monster of wickedness and depravity, which with extreme and perhaps unexampled injustice and barbarity to him and his relations he has long been represented but a character for whom every feeling heart must now sincerely grieve and lament. . .

The article also quotes Thomas McIntosh, carpenter's crew on the *Bounty*, as saying about Fletcher Christian: "Oh! he was a gentleman, and a brave man, and every officer and sailor on board the ship would have gone through fire and water to have served him."

Heywood's family, especially Peter's sister Nessy, had been very active in trying to secure his acquittal and, when that effort failed, his pardon. However, they had been forced to be careful about what was said lest it do damage to his cause. Now there was no reason to withhold the facts that Bligh had omitted from his account. The Heywoods, in effect, joined forces with the Christians in a campaign to tell the whole truth about the mutiny. The object was to fully vindicate Peter and to provide an understanding of why Christian had become a mutineer.

In this effort they got full cooperation from many of the loyalists, which is quite remarkable considering the sufferings they had gone through as a result of the mutiny. They clearly saw the tragic event as having been provoked by Bligh; not one member of the *Bounty*'s crew has ever been recorded as saying one negative word about Christian. If there was a retaliatory motive behind this campaign, especially as far as Heywood, Morrison, Purcell, and Fryer are concerned, it would not be surprising, but the conscious motivation, at least, was to set matters straight and if Bligh's reputation was hurt in the process, so be it. After all, he had not cared about the fact that he had blackened the reputations of many of his subordinates.

Bligh had left on his second breadfruit expedition as something of a national hero. Little did he know that he was to come home to a cold reception, in which even his fellow officers would avoid him.

December
1792

*B*ligh arrived at St. Helena on December 17, 1792, ten weeks after leaving Timor. He had lost 496 pots of breadfruit plants since leaving Tahiti and "655 vessels containing 830 plants" remained.

In accordance with the orders he had been given, he presented the governor of the island with ten breadfruit plants and one of every other kind he had brought with him. For this he was given a letter of thanks before he left on December 27, bound for the West Indies.

In England, meanwhile, Bligh's patron and benefactor Sir Joseph Banks had become aware of the incriminating statements that had been made against Bligh after the court-martial of the accused mutineers. In particular, he had read the letter that Heywood had written to Edward Christian, which had been reprinted by several newspapers. Without losing faith in his protégé, Sir Joseph nevertheless saved all the criticisms of Bligh for the time when he could get the latter's response.

Unlike Christian and Heywood, James Morrison, who had been pardoned at the same time as Heywood, had no important family connections to help bring to light all of the circumstances connected with the mutiny. His writings, however, were powerful in their indictment of Bligh and Edwards. The Morrison papers were not to be made public until 1825 (although his anthropologically valuable description of Tahiti was published by Haweis in 1799; see Du Rietz, 1986) and even then only in part, long after Bligh and Sir Joseph — and Morrison himself — had died. However, hand-copied versions, especially of his *Memorandum* with the motto *Vidi et scio* (I saw and I know), had probably circulated among Navy officers. On October 10 Morrison had written a letter, containing charges against Bligh, to Reverend William Howell who was Pastor at St. John's Chapel in Portsea near Spithead. It is likely that this minister helped Morrison by showing copies of the letter and the *Memorandum* to the Navy personnel with whom he associated daily.

As counter-suits were not unusual in mutiny trials and were sometimes successful, Morrison's charges against Bligh in the *Memorandum* were serious enough to warrant a court-martial and, had they been proved in court, could have led to Bligh's career being harmed or even stopped altogether.

Bligh would in that case not have been the only one hurt. A judgment against him would have been embarrassing for those who had sponsored him, including Sir Joseph and, ultimately, the King. It is therefore possible that the "various circumstances" mentioned in Morrison's pardon really referred to the possibility of a counter-suit.

Morrison had planned to publish his narrative in February 1793. It was not published during his lifetime. Why not? The likelihood is that someone in "high places" (perhaps Sir Joseph) intervened in order to avoid embarrassment. Morrison's writings were not published in their entirety until 1935!

January 1793

On New Year's Day 1793 the *Providence* and the *Assistant* passed Ascension Island on their way to the West Indies. Their crews were still suffering from diseases acquired in the Dutch East Indies and on January 7 a seaman on board the *Providence* died from "dysentery contracted at Timor."

The weather was rough and squally and on January 20 the *Providence* "carried away her main topgallant mast. At sunset on the 22nd Barbados was seen to the north-west, and next morning St. Vincent where, on the same evening, the ships anchored safely in Kingstown Bay."

It had been twenty years since Bligh had visited the island and he therefore used a pilot in entering the harbor.

On the morning of January 24 the unloading of some of the breadfruit plants began. In the *Bounty* saga, the arrival in the West Indies with the breadfruit would have been the climax of the story — but the *Bounty* never arrived. The mutiny which prevented the purpose of the first expedition from being achieved has also overshadowed the success of the second expedition. In fact, many people who have read about, or seen a movie about, the mutiny on the *Bounty* are unaware that there was a second expedition.

Although at least half the breadfruit was kept for Jamaica, Bligh left 544 plants at St. Vincent and "received, for His Majesty's Garden at Kew, 465 pots and 2 tubs containing botanic plants." Two men (one from the *Matilda*) deserted on this island and one fell overboard and drowned. On January 30 Bligh sailed for Jamaica to deliver the rest of the breadfruit plants on board.

In England, this month saw the publication of the (misnamed) book *A Voyage Around the World in His Majesty's Ship Pandora* by the surgeon of the ship, George Hamilton. His account makes interesting reading and is written in an almost ribald fashion, often rather risqué for the times, but there is not a word in it about the inhuman treatment of the prisoners. This is hardly surprising; why would Hamilton admit that the men of the *Bounty* were mistreated when it was partly his responsibility to see to it that they were not? It is significant, however, that although all other ship's officers are mentioned, several of them repeatedly, the name of the sadistic first lieutenant, John Larkin, does not appear once. It is as if Hamilton wanted to forget that such a monster was ever on board.

February 1793

On February 5, 1793, the *Providence* and the *Assistant* came to their moorings in Port Royal harbor in Jamaica, the actual goal of the expedition. The breadfruit plants were all unloaded in a condition which Bligh describes as "the highest perfection," although they had been on board for six and a half months. One of the botanists on board, James Wiles, disembarked with the task of taking care of replanting the trees, and Papo, the Tahitian stowaway, went with him as assistant and adviser.

In England, William Muspratt, the mutineer who had been condemned to death but had appealed the verdict, was still waiting for the outcome. On February 11 he was finally told that he was a free man.

Muspratt had one of Britain's finest attorneys, Stephen Barney, to thank for his new lease on life. It was Barney who had discovered the legal issue on which the appeal was based.

Early in the trial Barney had advised Muspratt to request that the court try separately the men previously certified by Bligh as innocent, so that they could become witnesses for his defense after being cleared of the charges. Specifically, he had asked for Norman and Byrne to be allowed to appear as his own witnesses. The court, however, refused to acquit anyone until it had heard testimony from all. This created the legal loophole through which Barney was able to get Muspratt freed.

Immediately after being sentenced to death, Muspratt — on the advice of Barney — charged that he had not been given a fair trial since he had been denied the testimony of witnesses cleared of any charges. In a civil court he would not have been denied this privilege, so he claimed his rights had been violated. The Judges on the King's Bench heard the appeal and ruled in favor of Muspratt.

Barney, a thorough and conscientious attorney, had taken copious notes during the proceedings of the court-martial. Edward Christian had asked the Admiralty for permission to print the official minutes but had been refused, so he asked Barney if he could publish his notes instead, and Barney had nothing against it.

Barney's *Minutes of the Proceedings of the Court-Martial* came out in mid-1794, published by Edward Christian who had attached an important *Appendix* which contained the result of interviews with eleven men of the *Bounty*. In this *Appendix* many of the facts omitted by Bligh were brought out for the reading public, and its publication ultimately led to a confirmation of the impression gained at the court-martial: that there were important reasons for the mutiny which Bligh had either attempted to conceal or simply had not understood.

March to August
1793

In recognition of the great service Bligh had rendered Jamaica in transporting the breadfruit from the South Seas, the island's House of Assembly voted a thousand guineas to be given to him as a token of appreciation. Lieutenant Portlock, commander of the *Assistant*, received five hundred guineas.

While Bligh was still anchored in Port Royal harbor, a ship arrived with the news that the National Convention of France had declared war on England. This delayed the departure of Bligh's ships, since Commodore Ford, the Naval Commander on the island, wanted to detain them "until more force had arrived at Port Royal."

Commodore Ford hoisted his pennant on board the *Providence* and often used the *Assistant* to convoy ships to ports in the vicinity. Several other ships of the Royal Navy soon appeared at the island and engaged in attacking French vessels in the Caribbean.

On June 10 Bligh received orders to sail for England. The *Assistant* was elsewhere at the time and Bligh decided to put to sea without his tender. He sailed on June 15, having taken on board all the plants intended for Kew Gardens. On June 17, at the Grand Cayman Islands, he met up with the *Assistant*.

Bligh and Portlock reached Cape San Antonio on June 20 and the next day sailed for England together with eight other ships. The voyage was uneventful and the convoy arrived off Ireland on July 27.

On August 2, the *Providence* and the *Assistant* reached the Downs and on August 7 anchored at Deptford. The expedition had lasted two years, almost to the day. The voyage had been eminently successful. The object of the expedition, to bring the breadfruit to the West Indies, had been accomplished and it was not Bligh's fault that the slaves for whom it was intended refused to eat it, preferring their own yams and bananas. Nevertheless, it was an ironic outcome of an endeavor that had taken five and a half years and had cost so many lives.*

* Gradually, however, the inhabitants of the West Indies got used to the breadfruit and today it forms a significant part of the diet.

September 1793

*M*aititi, the Tahitian who so fervently wanted to visit England and whom Bligh had brought with him in the *Providence*, had a horrible shock when he arrived. One of the first sights that greeted him in this civilized country was a number of men suspended in chains from gibbets lining the banks of the river Thames. Maititi was greatly alarmed and, having developed an illness earlier on the voyage, took a turn for the worse and had to be landed at Deptford. On September 4, 1793, the day the *Providence* struck her pennant and went out of commission, Maititi, in Lieutenant Tobin's words "struck his." Bligh does not mention the cause of his death.

With this poignant introduction to the blessings of civilization, Maititi must have wished himself back to the South Seas before he died, back to Tahiti of the golden sun, the emerald lagoons, the swaying palms, and, above all, its gentle, proud people. But even at this moment of his death on the other side of the world, Tahiti was changing; in fact, it was becoming "civilized" with all the meager advantages and all the ample curses that attended the process.

What must the former captain of the *Bounty* have felt upon his arrival in England? He had left his country as almost a national hero; now the Admiralty gave him the cold shoulder and even his fellow captains avoided his company. He was still sometimes called "Breadfruit Bligh," but there was now a pejorative connotation to this byname; in fact, he was now more often referred to as "that *Bounty* bastard." Bligh, the unsurpassed master of the art of humiliating others, was now himself humiliated daily by seeking an audience at the Admiralty without success. The First Lord of the Admiralty, Lord Chatham, refused to see him but gave an audience to Bligh's subordinate, Lieutenant Portlock, right away.

When Bligh had returned from his unsuccessful first breadfruit expedition, the Admiralty had rushed to publish his account of it; now, when he had been successful, the Admiralty was not interested in his writing a book and made it clear that they would not support its publication if he did write one.

To top it all off, Bligh was not given a command, not even kept in active service.

He was put on half pay even though the country was at war.

True enough, Bligh had received the coveted Gold Medal of the Royal Society of the Arts, and he had with him the one thousand guineas he had been given in Jamaica, but these recognitions could hardly make up for his being ignored and avoided. To Bligh it was all incomprehensible.

The first experiment in establishing a European/Polynesian community in the South Seas was approaching a cataclysmic climax on Pitcairn. We do not have a chronology of events on Pitcairn between the time of the deaths of two Polynesian women and the killing of two Polynesian men in December 1790 and September 1793. But from the accounts of Teehuteatuaonoa and from the last accounts of Adams (given when he no longer had any reason to lie), we know approximately what happened on or around September 20, 1793, a date which has gone down in Pitcairn history as Massacre Day.

On Pitcairn, as mentioned previously, the Polynesians were allowed no land of their own, the four Polynesian men who now remained had to share one woman, Mareva. They were treated more like servants than friends, and especially Quintal, McCoy, and Mills considered them as no more than slaves and dealt with them brutally. It was not a situation that could continue peacefully forever, and the fact that violence did not erupt earlier is probably due as much to the gentleness, good-naturedness, and patience of the Polynesians as to the fact that they were badly outnumbered. Nevertheless, everyone has a breaking point, even a Polynesian.

By this time several children had been born on the island. Fletcher Christian and Mauatua now had two sons, Thursday October and Charles; Quintal and Tevarua had a son, Matthew Jr.; McCoy and Teio also had a son, Daniel; and Mills and Vahineatua had a daughter, Elizabeth (who, was to live to the age of ninety-three).

The fact that no fullblooded Polynesian child was ever born on Pitcairn indicates almost certainly that the old Polynesian deep-massage method of abortion, or infanticide, or both, must have been employed in the Polynesian/Polynesian pregnancies that must have occurred. We can only guess why. The most likely reason is that there was a pro-European and anti-Polynesian sentiment on the island, certainly among the mutineers but, interestingly, also among some of the women. The extent of this bias can be seen clearly by the fact that the Tahitian language died out completely by the time the third generation was born, and in today's Pitcairnese language only a few Polynesian words survive, mostly referring to plants and fishes for which there were no English equivalents.

According to Teehuteatuaonoa, the trigger of the massacre that occurred on September 20 was that "Manarii stole a pig belonging to McCoy for which offence the European beat him severely. Teimua stole some yams, and was also chastised, so the natives again planned to murder the Englishmen."

Teimua and Niau took some muskets and fled to the mountains. Manarii and Titahiti remained in the village pretending solidarity with the mutineers. They kept

POPULATION OF PITCAIRN
AT THE BEGINNING OF SEPTEMBER 1793

Fletcher Christian

Consort:
MAUATUA

Children:
THURSDAY OCTOBER, CHARLES

Edward Young

Consort:
TERAURA

John Adams

Consort:
TINAFANAEA

William Brown

Consort:
TEATUAHITEA

William McCoy

Consort:
TEIO

Children:
SULLY*, DANIEL

John Mills

Consort:
VAHINEATUA

Children:
ELIZABETH

Isaac Martin

Consort:
TEEHUTEATUAONOA

Matthew Quintal

Consort:
TEVARUA

Children:
MATTHEW JR.

John Williams

Consort:
TOOFAITI

Titahiti

Consort:
MAREVA

Manarii

Consort:
MAREVA

Teimua

Consort:
MAREVA

Niau

Consort:
MAREVA

* Sully was a full-blooded Tahitian daughter of Teio (father unknown)
brought to Pitcairn as a baby.

secret contact with each other, however, and this time none of the women were apprised of their plans.

In the early morning of September 20, as previously planned, Teimua and Niau came down from the mountains armed with their muskets. Meanwhile Titahiti had borrowed a musket from Isaac Martin under the pretext that he was going to shoot a pig for supper. Instead he joined Teimua and Niau at a pre-arranged place.

The three now went to Williams' plantation knowing that he, like the other mutineers, would use the cool morning hours to work in his garden. They shot him dead without warning.

Manarii was working on Mills' plantation together with Mills and McCoy. The mutineers heard the shot and asked: "What was that?" According to plan, Manarii answered: "Oh, that's just Titahiti shooting a pig for supper," which reassured Mills and McCoy.

While Teimua and Niau kept themselves hidden, Titahiti now went to Mills' plantation and asked if Manarii could come and help him carry the pig he had just shot, to which the two mutineers had no objection. The four Polynesians now went to Christian's plantation and shot him from the back. He was only a few days from his twenty-ninth birthday and his consort, Mauatua, whom he regarded as his wife, was pregnant.

According to island tradition, Christian cried out "Oh, dear" as he died. Mills and McCoy heard the shot and also the sound of someone groaning, and McCoy said: "There was surely some person dying," but Mills replied: "It's only Mainmast (Mauatua) calling her children to dinner."

It now became necessary for the Polynesians to separate McCoy and Mills from each other and Titahiti therefore ran to them and said that he had seen the runaway Polynesians, Teimua and Niau, stealing things from McCoy's cabin.

McCoy immediately ran to his home. Meanwhile Teimua and Niau had hidden themselves in his house and, when he came running in, they both shot at him — and both missed!

McCoy ran out, only to be attacked by Manarii who was waiting outside. McCoy, however, was the stronger of the two and managed to throw the Polynesian into the pigsty. He then ran back to Mills to warn him, but Mills naively refused to believe that his servant Manarii would do anything to harm him.

McCoy now ran over to Christian's house where he saw the dead body and immediately understood what was going on. As confirmation he heard a shot from the direction of Mills' plantation and surmised correctly that his friend was being killed.

He now rushed to Quintal's house to tell him what was happening and the two of them ran up into the mountains to hide.

Meanwhile the Polynesians went to Isaac Martin's house and asked him: "Do you know what we are doing today?" "No," said Martin. "We are killing pigs," said the Polynesians and shot him dead.

Next they went to William Brown's plantation. It is said that Teimua, who liked Brown, shot at him with a powder charge only and told him to pretend to be dead. Brown, however, moved too early and was beaten to death by Manarii.

Adams, meanwhile, had been working on his plantation unaware of what was going on. Quintal's consort Tevarua ran past his house and shouted something like: "How can you keep working at a time like this?" Tevarua's English was poor and Adams' Tahitian was even worse, so he did not understand what she was saying, but he realized that something serious was happening and ran after her.

He was spotted at a distance by the Polynesians who fired at him. The ball hit him in the neck and shoulder. He fell and the Polynesians attacked him with the butts of their muskets; Adams broke two fingers trying to ward off the attack. They then tried to shoot him twice, and both times the gun misfired! Amazingly, Adams got to his feet and ran away.

Even more amazingly, the Polynesians shouted to him to give himself up, that they would do him no further harm. Adams, weak from loss of blood and not knowing how much longer he could last, surrendered and the Polynesians carried him to Ned Young's house.

Why was Young not attacked? There are two main theories to account for this strange circumstance. One is that Ned, being a favorite with the women, was protected by them and hidden from the Polynesian men. A more sinister theory is that Young had masterminded the massacre!

The second theory is supported by some plausible arguments. To begin with, Polynesian men would not take orders from women and it would have been impossible to hide Young for any length of time. Secondly, one of the Polynesians is said to have apologized to Adams for shooting him, adding that he had forgotten that Young had said Adams should be spared. Thirdly, it was known that the two fugitives, Teimua and Niau, had often visited Young and helped him in his garden. Most importantly, however, it was no secret that Young desperately wanted Christian's consort, Mauatua (with whom he had three children after Christian's death). Finally, although Young was educated as a gentleman, he was a mulatto, born in the West Indies, and had probably been the victim of some prejudice in his Navy career, so he may from the beginning have identified with the Polynesians.

An almost inescapable conclusion from the accounts we have of Massacre Day is that Young must at least have had foreknowledge of the plans of the Polynesians. However, his actual role in the events will probably never be known.

There were now only four Europeans left: Young and Adams in the village and McCoy and Quintal who were hiding in the mountains. Even though there were now more women than men on the island, the Polynesians started fighting among themselves about who should have which woman. Teimua and Manarii were both interested in Young's consort Teraura (Young had tired of her and wanted only Mauatua) and, one evening when Teimua was accompanying Teraura's singing on his nose flute, Manarii shot him dead. Titahiti and Niau resented this murder and Manarii felt it best to run into the mountains where he joined McCoy and Quintal who were suspicious of his motives and would only accept him if he first gave them his musket. Soon, however, the three of them quarreled — we do not know over what, but it could have been over some of the women who from time to time came to visit them — and the two mutineers killed Manarii.

Meanwhile the Polynesian women, many of whom had been strongly attached to their European men, decided to take revenge on the two surviving Polynesian men. Teraura lopped off Titahiti's head with an axe while he was sleeping with Teatuahitea, and then Ned Young — perhaps to accommodate the women — shot and killed Niau.

The massacre concluded with four mutineers and ten Polynesian women left alive, in addition to the children. All Polynesian men had been killed. It was a gruesome end to the hopes and dreams that the settlers had brought with them to this beautiful island.

After the deaths of McCoy and Quintal a few years later (see PITCAIRN in Part II) the island, despite its grim history, turned into a peaceful tropical paradise and so it has remained to this day.

Epilogue

*T*he death of Christian on Pitcairn concludes my chronicle of the *Bounty* adventure. For the subsequent fate of other protagonists, where known, I must refer the reader to the "*Bounty* Encyclopedia" which forms the second part of this book.

I would like to end my account with some "what ifs" and try to answer them. Would there have been a mutiny on the *Bounty* if Bligh had realized the impact his humiliating tongue had on other people? *No.* Would there have been a mutiny if the *Bounty* had had a typical British Navy commander? *No.* Would there have been a mutiny if Christian had not been on board? *No.*

Would Christian have found supporters among the crew if the *Bounty* had left Tahiti three weeks after her arrival (when the planned number of breadfruit shoots had been gathered)? Probably not. Perhaps there is an unending number of "what ifs."

For two hundred years *Bounty* historians have debated the question of what — or who — caused the mutiny on the *Bounty*. I do not expect that my answer will put an end to the controversy, but I will give my opinion nevertheless.

The mutiny was certainly not caused by one individual or by one circumstance. In this book a number of factors which, directly or indirectly, have causal significance have been discussed. But they all boil down to a seemingly simplistic answer: the mutiny on the *Bounty* was caused by *the interaction between Bligh and Christian.*

The birth of family psychology a few decades ago stemmed partly from a realization that family problems are not caused by one or two or three individuals: they are caused by an *interaction* between two or more individuals. In family therapy we do not treat just individuals, we treat the interaction. Anyone who has sailed on long cruises realizes how close the analogy is between a family and the crew of a ship.

Also, the severity of a problem is not determined objectively, but by how it is perceived. To Bligh, the loss of a few coconuts was an extremely severe problem. To Christian, being called a coward and a thief was worse than death. The interaction between Bligh and Christian *caused* the mutiny; the fact that Christian could perceive no constructive solution to the problem *triggered* the mutiny. That, in my opinion, is the basic explanation for what happened on the *Bounty* on April 28, 1789.

EPILOGUE

.. But let us consider the most important "what if". What if the mutiny on the *Bounty* had never taken place?

Can you imagine? If there had been no mutiny on the *Bounty*, if the first breadfruit expedition had been completed successfully, no one today — with the exception of a few experts in maritime history — would have heard of the *Bounty* or of Fletcher Christian. Bligh would be remembered, if at all, as an insignificant and unsuccessful governor of New South Wales.

And in that case we would all have lost something valuable, indeed priceless, something which makes life worth living. We would have lost a most enchanting tale of romance and adventure, one of the most intriguing yarns ever spun about good grappling with evil, a most exciting story of courage and determination, of passionate desires and fervent hopes, of treachery and savagery and kindness and gentleness and baseness and honor.

Above all, where else would we have looked for the fulfillment of our childhood dreams, for the glorious power of adventure over humdrum existence, for the thrill and excitement of wagering all in the quest for liberty? And where could there have been a more perfect setting than the South Sea islands with their haunting promise of everlasting happiness, the fulfillment of our deepest wishes, and for some, the Holy Grail finally found?

Scholars will always quarrel about what is true and not true in the various versions of the *Bounty* adventure. I have presented the truth as I see it. But I am reminded of the concluding words of one of my favorite books when I was a boy: "True are only the memories we carry within us, the dreams that we spin, and the longings that drive us." And therewith I will end my tale.

PART II

A
Bounty
Encyclopedia

*R*eading about the *Bounty* story can be confusing for many reasons. To begin with, two full years of the story are intimately involved with Tahiti, both half a year before, and one and a half years after, the mutiny. During this time the Tahitians who played a role in the story had a tendency to change and exchange names. For example, Tu, Teina, Mate, Vairaatoa, and Pomare I are all the same person, but that is seldom explained in the literature.

To add to the confusion, the European spellings of Tahitian names vary wildly. Who would know, for example, that Oberea is identical with "Queen" Purea or that Tullaloo is actually Tararo, the Raiatean chief who followed Christian to Pitcairn? Who knows that Whaeeahtuah is Vehiatua, after whose death Churchill became the first — and only — white chief in eastern Polynesia, or that Whyeadooa is Vaetua, Hayward's friend, who sabotaged the *Bounty* and was ready to kill Bligh?

Few people are aware that Navigator Islands refer to the Samoas, or that Rotterdam Island is Nomuka, where the fuse of the mutiny was lit. Or that Whytootackee refers to Aitutaki, the island Bligh discovered shortly before the mutiny.

In this *Bounty* encyclopedia I have attempted to clear up this confusion as well as to give a background to the events in the fascinating story of the *Bounty*.

HMS *ACTAEON* A British warship commanded by Captain Lord Edward Russell. It was the arrival at Pitcairn of the *Actaeon* on January 10, 1837, and Lord Russell's exposure of Joshua Hill as an impostor, which broke Hill's dictatorial power on the island. (See the entries for PITCAIRN ISLAND and HILL, JOSHUA.)

ADAMS, John, alias SMITH, Alexander ("Alec") Able-bodied seaman on the *Bounty*; mutineer; went with Christian to Pitcairn; died there in 1829.

Adams was from Hackney in London, an orphan who had been brought up in a poorhouse. He was twenty years old when he mustered on the *Bounty*. For some reason, probably desertion from another ship or some trouble with the law, he used a fictitious name, Alexander Smith, and did not change back to his real name until after the visit to Pitcairn of the *Topaz* in 1808.

Bligh's description of Adams, written after the mutiny, reads as follows:

> ALEXANDER SMITH. 22 years, 5 feet 5 inches high. Brown complexion, brown hair, strong made, pitted with smallpox. Very much tattooed, scar on right foot.

Adams was flogged (one dozen lashes) only one week after the *Bounty* arrived at Tahiti. His offense was that he had let a rudder gudgeon be stolen from one of the ship's boats. The punishment was carried out in full view of the Tahitians who had tried in vain to intercede for him and who cried as they witnessed the barbaric act.

Bligh based his disciplinary measure on the allegation that Adams had been lax in his attention. This was unfair. Bligh — and for that matter all the *popa'as* — did not realize that the Tahitians, because of their extraordinary swimming ability, had the ship and the boats at their mercy. (The later sabotage of the anchor cable gave evidence of this. See the February 1789 commentary in Part I.) Most of the British seamen were either poor swimmers or could not swim at all and diving was almost unknown to them. The fact that a Tahitian could swim long distances under water and could hold his breath for two and a half to three minutes seemed inconceivable. The explanation for the theft, therefore, had to be found in Adams' inattention, not in any superiority on the part of a Tahitian; the "Indians" were not supposed to be superior to the white men in any respect whatsoever.

Adams soon fell in with island life and was one of the first in the crew to have himself tattooed. It is probable that he at this time formed a relationship with Teehuteatuaonoa, whom he called Jenny.

Adams took an active part in the mutiny from its very inception (although he was later to tell sea captains visiting Pitcairn that he had been asleep at the time). He was with Christian when the latter went to Coleman to demand the key to the arms chest. And Bligh wrote later that when he was arrested by the mutineers ". . . Alexander Smith . . . assisted under arms on the outside."

When the *Bounty*, under Christian's command, sailed to Tahiti to pick up women and livestock for the intended colony on Tubuai, Teehuteatuaonoa came with Adams to that island. But, as we know (see the June to September 1789 commentaries in Part I), things did not turn out well on Tubuai. When the vote was taken on whether to stay or to leave, Adams was one of the mutineers who voted with Christian and who later sailed with him to Pitcairn. On arrival there, however, he had a new consort, Puarai.

When Edward Young died on Christmas Day 1800 Adams became the last survivor of the mutineers and a sought-out object for interviews by visiting sea captains. He could not feel secure, however, until after the visit in 1814 of HMS *Briton* and HMS *Tagus* whose captains, Staines and Pipon, assured him that he would not be taken to England for trial.

Many of the visitors seemed to revere the old patriarch, but a more realistic evaluation of him, I think, can be had from a modern writer, David Silverman, who in his book *Pitcairn Island* (1967) writes:

> The standard picture of Adams in Pitcairn literature as a completely regenerated rascal, benevolence and piety incarnate, while not without basis, is much too simplistic and pat to encompass the record, as it will appear. It should not be forgotten that, not only was he the leader of he community when the first ships visited Pitcairn, he was the only man on the Island who had experience of life off that tiny rock, that he monopolized the visitors, that he was unlikely to be contradicted in any statement he made, and that he had a shrewd sense of what the visitors might like to hear in response to their questions and the ability to project a sympathetic picture of the artless man of profound sincerity and good will.

Adams had five Tahitian consorts during his life: *(1)* Teehuteatuaonoa, who became Martin's consort before the arrival at Pitcairn. Adams had no children with her. *(2)* Puarai, with whom he landed on Pitcairn but who died within a year after the arrival. There were no children from this liaison. *(3)* Tinafanaea, the consort of Titahiti and Oha, who was "given" to him by vote of the mutineers when Puarai died. They had no children. *(4)* Vahineatua, who had been John Mills' consort and had borne him two children. She bore Adams three daughters, Dina, Rachel, and Hannah. *(5)* Teio, who had been the consort of Thomas McIntosh on Tubuai and of William McCoy on Pitcairn. She bore Adams his only son, George, who later married Polly Young, the daughter of Edward Young and Mauatua, Fletcher Christian's widow.

Teio and Adams were married by Captain Beechey during his visit in 1825. On March 5, 1829, John Adams died and was followed just nine days later by Teio. His grave can still be seen on Pitcairn; the resting places of the other mutineers and their consorts are unknown.

ADAMSTOWN Name of the center of the settlement on Pitcairn Island. It is by no means a town, and today — with the population of Pitcairn down to forty-eight (September 1988) — it could barely be called a small village. It consists of a widely spread cluster of houses and gardens, some occupied, some abandoned. These dwellings extend along the path that runs from Bounty Bay along the Edge (a narrow plateau approximately 200 feet above the Bay) and continue westward for about two thirds of a mile.

In the center of Adamstown is Bounty Square where one of the anchors of the *Bounty* is displayed. It was found and recovered by the crew of the *Yankee* under the command of Captain Irving Johnson in 1957. In the square is also a ship's bell which can be heard from far away; various strikes announce a call to prayer or to public work or other community activities; five strikes signify the arrival of a ship.

The square is bordered on three sides by one-story, verandah-shaded buildings. To the west is the court house, but as there is no crime to speak of on the island this is something of a misnomer. The building is used for community functions and for the meetings of the Island Council. To the south are the post office, library, and dispensary. The Seventh-day Adventist Church stands to the east; inside, mounted in a display cabinet, is the *Bounty* Bible. (Christian's Bible is in the rare books collection of the New York Public Library.)

The north side of the square is formed by a long bench where you can sit and socialize or just while the hours away dreaming.

One of the unforgettable moments of my life was when the Expedition Flag of my Club, the Adventurers' Club of Los Angeles, was hoisted on the flagpole in front of the Courthouse in Adamstown on April 17, 1987. To me, that is *romance*!

Afterwards the Flag was signed by Andrew Clarence Young, the oldest direct descendant of the mutineers — fifth generation from Midshipman Edward Young of the *Bounty*. I regret to report that Andrew Young passed away on Thursday March 17, 1988, one month before his eighty-ninth birthday. Everyone who met him will always remember him.

ADVENTURE BAY   A bay on the eastern shore of Bruny Island off Tasmania, thirty miles south of Hobart.

Adventure Bay was discovered in 1773 by Tobias Furneaux, commander of the *Adventure* on Cook's second voyage, who named it after his ship. None of the first four English expeditions that anchored in the bay realized that it was not part of the Tasmanian mainland. It was Rear Admiral (actually "Citizen Admiral") Bruni d'Entrecasteaux in the *Espérance* with the tender *Recherche* who found the channel between the island which is named for him, and the mainland of Tasmania. He made this discovery in April 1792, only a few weeks after Bligh was there in the *Providence*.

Bligh visited Adventure Bay three times in his life: in the *Resolution* on Cook's third voyage in 1777; in the *Bounty* in August 1788; and in the *Providence* in February 1792.

AGOODOO Bligh's spelling of KOTU.

AHIMA'A Tahitian word for earth oven. See HIMA'A.

AHU Tahitian for a walled-in, rectangular stone altar on a marae (open-air temple).

'AHU Tahitian for cloth or clothing (*'a'ahu* means clothes or dress).

AIMATA See POMARE IV.

AIMEO (Eimeo) Ancient name for MOOREA.

'AITO See IRONWOOD.

AITUTAKI Aitutaki is the most north-western of the southern Cook Islands and lies at 18⁰52'S., 159⁰45'W., 140 miles due north of Rarotonga and 680 miles west of Tahiti. It was discovered by Bligh on April 11, 1789, seventeen days before the mutiny.

When Christian returned to Tahiti in the *Bounty*, he told the Tahitians that he was going to sail to Aitutaki. Actually Aitutaki would have been out of the question as a refuge, since it was certain to be investigated by a ship searching for the mutineers. In fact Captain Edwards did sail to Aitutaki in the *Pandora*, arriving at the island on May 19, 1791.

Aitutaki is a volcanic island, about four miles long north to south and one and a half miles wide. It is surrounded by a reef and the fishing in the lagoon is among the best in the South Seas; the ocean immediately outside the reef is teeming with tuna, marlin, wahoo, and barracuda.

Aitutaki is not a particularly high island — Maungapu, the highest peak, rises to only 390 feet — but it is thickly wooded and well-watered. It can today be reached by air from Rarotonga; the inter-island aircraft landing on Aitutaki avail themselves of a huge airstrip which was constructed by New Zealanders during World War II for the use of the U.S. Air Force.

If you are an old South Seas hand and visit Aitutaki for the first time, you will immediately sense that something is different on the island, but what it is may not occur to you right away. It took me two days on the island until I realized what it was: there are no dogs! Some years back a little girl was bitten by a rabid dog and died; the islanders felt the best measure of prevention was to kill all dogs and prohibit the entry of canines in the future.

AMA Tahitian for outrigger float.

AMAE See MIRO.

AMAMOCKA See NOMUKA.

AMAT Domingo de Boenechea's name for Tahiti.

AMO (Tevahitua i Patea, "Oamo") In the *Bounty* story, Amo is known primarily as the husband of the dominating "Queen" Purea and the father of Temarii (who had succeeded his father as chief of Papara by the time the *Bounty* visited Tahiti).

AMSTERDAM ISLAND Tasman's name for TONGATABU.

ANAMOOKA, ANNAMOOKA See NOMUKA.

AOA See ORA.

AREEPAEEA, AREPAEA See ARI'IPAEA.

ARETU Tahitian for a species of sweet-smelling grass.

ARI'I Tahitian for chief or ruler.

ARI'I RAHI Tahitian for supreme chief or ruler or "king."

ARI'IFAATAIA See TEMARII.

ARI'IPAEA (Te Ari'i Faatou, "Areepaeea," "Oreepyah," "Urripiah") Ari'ipaea was born in 1758 and was a younger brother of Pomare I. He was one of the chiefs — the other was Moana — who brought back the deserters from Tetiaroa (see the January 1789 commentary in Part I). During the one and a half years that the men of the *Bounty* spent on Tahiti after the mutiny, Ari'ipaea was staying in Pare as regent for "Prince Tu" (later Pomare II) while Pomare I (called Mate at the time) was in Taiarapu. Ari'ipaea was Muspratt's *taio*. He died a few years before the arrival of the missionaries in 1797.

ARIOI Of all exotic phenomena that confronted the men of the *Bounty* when they arrived in Tahiti, the performances of the *arioi* society must have been among the foremost. The society was comprised of talented individuals from all social classes who worshipped 'Oro, the God of War, and had forsworn child-bearing (which in practice meant that pregnancies were terminated through deep-massage abortions or that the children were strangled at their birth). Teuira Henry describes the *arioi* in *Ancient Tahiti* (1928):

> From very ancient times the society of comedians, called *arioi*, had their sway
> throughout the Society Islands and neighboring islands. They were scholars
> and actors of no mean ability, chosen from all ranks of people, and held in high
> esteem by all classes. Their performances were connected with mysteries which
> they attributed to the god 'Oro, to whom they gave the special title of 'Oro-i-
> te-tea-moe ('Oro-of-the-spear-laid-down), the emblem of which was a triangle,
> somewhat masonic in appearance, made of spears, thus ▽, meaning that 'Oro
> was then a god of peace.
>
> The *arioi* went from place to place among the islands in flotillas of canoes
> as grand as those of royalty, the magnitude of such an expedition can be
> conceived from an account given by Captain Cook of the departure from
> Huahine of seventy canoes filled with *arioi*, and also by the immense houses,
> measuring from 180 to more than 300 feet in length, that were built on all the
> islands for their reception. Those houses built by the public were called *fare
> arioi* (comedians' houses), and also *fare manihini* (guests' houses), as they were
> held open also to visitors of note.

The flotilla of *arioi* witnessed by Cook in 1774 actually consisted of seven hundred
performers. There was no theater in London — or anywhere else in the world —
which could put on such a grandiose spectacle. The excitement caused by the arrival
of such a flotilla was described by William Ellis in *Polynesian Researches* (1829):

> Sometimes they performed in their canoes, as they approached the shore;
> especially if they had the king of the island, or any principal chief, on board
> their fleet. When one of these companies thus advanced towards the land, with
> their streamers floating in the wind, their drums and flutes sounding, and the
> Areois, attended by their chief, who acted as their prompter, appeared on a
> stage erected for the purpose, with their wild distortions of person, antic gestures,
> painted bodies, and vociferated songs, mingling with the sound of the drum
> and the flute, the dashing of the sea, and the rolling and breaking of the surf,
> on the adjacent reef; the whole must have presented a ludicrous imposing
> spectacle, accompanied with a confusion of sight and sound, of which it is not
> very easy to form an adequate idea.

The numerous actors and performers all took care in preparing themselves for
the spectacle. In the words of Teuira Henry again:

> Before acting, the chief comedians dyed their faces red with the sap of mati
> (*Ficus tinctoria*) and tou (*Cordia subcordata*) leaves. So also did all the other orders,
> in addition blackening themselves with soot from burnt *tutui* (candlenut), which
> some of the men, to create laughter in their plays, used for painting grotesque

figures over their bare bodies and limbs.

The amusements generally took place at night, when the great *arioi* house was illuminated with fires and candlenut tapers, so that it was called *rehu arui* (night daylight). On a high platform called a *raira'a-maro 'ura* (exalting-red-girdles), erected at one end of the house were placed high stools as seats for the chief *arioi* of both sexes. In the center of the building were the comedians, over whom presided the *arioi-hi'o-niao* (master-of-ceremonies). The royal family had their seats of honor, and within the building and outside upon the grass were the spectators. Even the crickets, it is said, cried with joy on these occasions.

The performances were a grand-spectacle/vaudeville/striptease combination. They were on such a grand scale that it would be difficult to top them today. Only Folies-Bergères could have a chance of competing with them and even that illustrious company would be hard-pressed to come up to the standards of the *arioi*.

What really impressed the sex-starved European sailors were the "lascivious" dances (Beaglehole, *Captain Cook and Captain Bligh*, 1967):

> Most of these were young women, who put themselves into several lascivious postures, clapp'd their hands and repeated a kind of Stanzas which every now and then began afresh. At certain parts they put their garments aside and exposd with seemingly very little sense of shame those parts which most nations have thought it modest to conceal, but in particular a woman more advanc'd in years who stood in front & might properly be calld the tutoress or prompter of the rest, held her cloaths continually up with one hand and dancd with uncommon vigour and effrontery, as if to raise in the spectators the most libidinous desires and incite her pupils to emulation in such a wanton exercise. The men flockd eagerly round them in great numbers to see their performance and express'd the most anxious curiosity to see that part just mentioned, at which they seem'd to feel a sort of rapture that could only be express'd by the extreme joy that appear'd in their countenances.

Morrison writes about

> Young Wantons, who stripping of their lower Garments Cover themselves with a loose piece of Cloth and at particular parts of the Song they throw Open their Cloth and dance with their fore part Naked to the Company making many lewd gestures — however these are not merely the effects of Wantoness but Custom, and those who perform thus in Publick are Shy and Bashful in private, and seldom suffer any freedom to be taken by the Men on that account.

The *arioi* also performed an important function in criticizing and even ridiculing the official functionaries. Neither the chiefs, nor the priests, were exempt from exposure. Henry writes: "In their plays the actors flattered or ridiculed with impunity people and even priests, from the greatest to the least, and they often did much good in thus causing faults to be corrected." Morrison writes about the

> Satyr, which is often directed at their Chiefs, and they never fail to expose such Charracters as draw their attention and tho they treat thier Chiefs with great freedom they incur no displeasure so long as they keep to the truth — by this Method they rebuke them for their faults in Publick, having first diverted them to draw their attention — this is done in a kind of Pantomime at which they are so good that any person who knows the Man they mean to represent may easily perceive who they are making the subject of their sport.

The missionaries saw the *arioi* as the incarnation of evil and made it one of their priorities to have the society abolished. In this they succeeded when Pomare II — who also was an *arioi* — formally converted to Christianity and in a bloody war christianized all of Tahiti in 1815.

AROMAITERAI See TEMARII.

ARRACK Arrack is an alcoholic drink distilled in the Far East, usually from palm toddy; its alcoholic content is around 70 volume per cent. Despite the fact that some mean tongues claim that its name comes from an Arabic word meaning "perspiration," arrack has a very fine and distinguished aroma. Improperly distilled and injudiciously enjoyed, however, it can be a dangerous drink.

On his way to the West Indies from Coupang on the second breadfruit expedition, Bligh wrote in his log on November 9, 1792: "Thomas Lackman, marine, a poor worn-out creature, died through catching cold and from an improper use of arrack before he embarked."

There are also quite proper uses of arrack. In fact, no traditional and festive Scandinavian dinner party is complete without coffee and arrack punch liqueur after the dessert.

ARUE A district on the north coast of Tahiti including most of the shoreline of Matavai Bay. Arue was bordered in the east by Haapape (today's Mahina) and in the west by Pare with which it formed the joint district called Te Porionuu.

HMS *ASSISTANT* The *Assistant* accompanied HMS *Providence* as tender on Bligh's second breadfruit expedition (August 3, 1791, to August 7, 1793). She was a brig of 110 tons burden, armed with four 4-pounders and eight swivel guns, and carrying a complement of twenty-seven. Her commander was Lieutenant Nathaniel Portlock.

ATAFU (Duke of York) ISLAND The smallest of the three large atolls in the

Tokelau (Union) group, situated at 8°32'S., 172°31'W.; discovered in 1765 by the British explorer John Byron.

In order to put pursuers on the wrong track, Christian "confided" to able seaman Henry Hillbrant, a mutineer who stayed on Tahiti, that he planned to settle on Atafu. The ruse worked: it sent Captain Edwards on a wild goose chase thousands of miles in the wrong direction.

There are today about 600 inhabitants on Atafu and they are rather traditional; there are more dugout canoes here than on the other two atolls (Fakaofo and Nukunono). The island is officially "dry," but there is a local homebrew of yeast and sugar which provides relief from essential thirst.

ATEHURU   An ancient district on the west coast of Tahiti Nui, roughly comprising the districts Punaauia and Paea of today.

ATIRA   Tahitian word for enough.

ATTAHOOROO   See ATEHURU.

ATUA   Tahitian for God or Deity.

AUTE   Tahitian for mulberry tree.

AUTE WALLEY (Aute Valley)   On Pitcairn: the area from the main ridge of the island to the cliffs on the southern side. The first gardens of the aute or mulberry tree, brought from Tahiti by the mutineers, were planted here.

'AUTE   Tahitian for hibiscus flower.

AVA   Tahitian for reef opening, pass, channel between lagoon and sea.

'AVA (kava)   A drink made from the roots of *Piper methysticum*, a plant related to the pepper bush. The roots of the plant are chewed by young virgins and spat into a wooden bowl. Water or coconut juice is added and sometimes crushed leaves of the plant are added. The mixture is then strained and ready to drink.

Douglas Oliver in *Ancient Tahitian Society* (1974) describes the sensation obtained from imbibing this remarkable drink:

> The effect, all observers reported, was befuddlement leading usually to sleep. According to some accounts the drink immobilized the limbs, especially the legs, but heightened mental activity for a while, before sleep or stupefaction set in. The capacity to arouse oneself to action quickly out of a kava-induced

stupor was regarded as an attribute of "heroes."

Although the men of the *Bounty* were all exposed to *'ava*, they seem to have preferred their rum. Eventually the Tahitians agreed with them and today the Tahitian word for alcohol is *'ava*.

AVAST   Stop, cease.

AZIMUTH COMPASS   The azimuth of a horizontal direction is its deviation from the north or the south. True north-south differs from magnetic north-south and the magnitude of the difference varies from place to place. An azimuth compass, then, is designed to measure the amount of magnetic variation, the degree to which magnetic north differs from true north at any given location.

The early navigators did not know that variation existed; they thought the compass needle always pointed to true north. It was only after Columbus, in 1514, that the first azimuth compass was constructed. Today there is no need to observe the amount of variation at any given place since it is recorded on every chart.

"BALHADI"   "Balhadi" was the closest John Adams could come to pronouncing one of the Tahitian names of his fourth consort: Paraha Iti. See VAHINEATUA.

BANKS, Sir Joseph   Patron of science, explorer, naturalist, principal instigator of the breadfruit expeditions and life-long supporter of Bligh.

Banks was born on February 2, 1743, and after attending school at Harrow and Eton studied the natural sciences at Oxford. He was a multi-talented man and also extremely wealthy, having inherited an enormous fortune from his father.

After having travelled to Newfoundland and Labrador, Banks joined Captain Cook on his first voyage (1768–1771). He had the *Endeavour* fitted out at his own expense and took with him a number of assistants, among them the Swedish botanist, Daniel Solander.

Banks clearly relished Tahiti and is said to have had a wild love affair with "Queen" Purea (see PUREA). Of the Tahitian women he wrote: "I have nowhere seen such Elegant women as those of Otaheite, such as might even defy the Chizzel of a Phidias or the Pencil of an Apelles." He thought they were perfect for love-making, being "modeled into the utmost perfection for that soft science." Another example of his enthusiasm for Tahiti is that he had one of his hands tattooed on the island.

In 1778, Banks became President of the Royal Society. He had always been interested in botany and especially in plants that were useful. This — together with his business interests in the West Indies — was why he was enthusiastic about transporting the breadfruit from the South Seas to the West Indies. He considered

Bligh as the best person to head such a project, since Bligh had had experience in Tahiti (on Cook's third voyage) as well as in the Caribbean (while being in the employ of Duncan Campbell). Being highly influential in Court circles and having access to the king, Banks had no difficulties in getting his desires realized as far as his projects — of which the breadfruit expedition was only one — were concerned.

Among the many important projects Banks became interested in was the establishment of a penal colony in New Holland (Australia). As early as 1779, Banks testified before a House of Commons committee in charge of looking into the conditions of the overcrowded prisons and into what could be done about transporting convicts out of the country. Banks stated as his opinion that it would be

> expedient to establish a colony of convicted felons in any distant part of the globe, from whence their escape might be difficult, and where, from the fertility of the soil, they might be enabled to maintain themselves, after the first year, with little or no aid from the mother country.
>
> If the people formed among themselves a civil government they would necessarily increase, and find occasion for many European commodities; and it was not to be doubted, that a tract of land such as New Holland, which was larger than the whole of Europe, would furnish matter of advantageous return.

Eight years later, on May 13, 1787, the First Fleet sailed to Botany Bay. Because of his early enthusiasm for this project, Banks has sometimes, perhaps with some exaggeration, been called "the father of Australia."

He became a Knight Commander of the Bath in 1795 and was admitted to the Privy Council in 1797. He was an honorary director of the Royal Botanic Gardens at Kew and, often at his own expense, sent out botanical collectors to distant countries.

Banks remained a faithful patron of Bligh's throughout the captain's career and was instrumental in arranging for Bligh's appointment as governor of New South Wales in 1805.

Banks died at Isleworth on June 19, 1820.

BANKS GROUP The northern part of Vanuatu (formerly New Hebrides) consisting of Vanua Lava, Mota, Valua, and Ureparapara. Bligh saw the group on May 14, 1789, from the *Bounty*'s launch on the voyage from Tofua to Timor and revisited the islands on his second breadfruit expedition. Not knowing that Pedro Fernandez de Quiros had seen the islands in 1606, he thought himself the discoverer and named them after his benefactor, Sir Joseph Banks.

BANYAN DAY A day on which no meat was served on board. The expression came from the service in East India where Hindu traders, called banyans, belonged to a caste forbidden to eat flesh. The practice was instituted during the reign of

Elizabeth I in order to save on the cost of meat; cheese or fish were served instead.

BANYAN TREE See ORA.

BARK CLOTH See TAPA.

BARNEY, Stephen Barney is prominent in the *Bounty* story for two reasons. His brilliant legal maneuver which saved mutineer William Muspratt from the noose (see the February 1793 commentary in Part I) is the first. The second is that he allowed Fletcher Christian's older brother Edward to publish his (Barney's) *Minutes of the Proceedings of the Court Martial held at Portsmouth 12th August* (should be September), *1792.* Christian added his famous *Appendix to the Proceedings* which finally confirmed what many had suspected, that there was a great deal more behind the events of the mutiny on the *Bounty* than Bligh had divulged.

BARQUE (bark) A sailing vessel with not less than three masts, square-rigged except for the after mast which is rigged fore and aft.

BARQUENTINE (barkentine) A sailing vessel with not less than three masts, square-rigged on the fore mast, the other masts being rigged fore and aft.

BARRINGTON, Samuel Admiral of the Blue; Second Officer in Command of His Majesty's Ships and Vessels at Portsmouth and Spithead; presided over Bligh's court-martial for losing the *Bounty*, October 22, 1790.

BARROW, Sir John Second Secretary to the Admiralty; was the first non-participant to write an account of the *Bounty* mutiny: *The Eventful History of the Mutiny and Piratical Seizure of H.M.S. Bounty: Its Cause and Consequences* (1831). An attractive re-issue of this volume, edited by Gavin Kennedy, appeared in 1980.

Barrow was the guiding force behind getting the Royal Navy involved in Arctic exploration in the first half of the nineteenth century. But his lasting fame has come from his book on the *Bounty* mutiny. About this work Rolf Du Rietz (1986) has commented: "Its influence assumed proportions on a really grand scale during World War I, in a book-shop in Paris, on that day in the late autumn of 1916 (a day now famous in Pacific literary history), when a young American named James Norman Hall acquired a copy of . . . Barrow's work and brought it home for immediate reading."

Barrow died in 1848.

BATAVIA Now called Djakarta (Jakarta); city on the north coast of West Java; capital of Indonesia.

Batavia (the Latin name of the Netherlands), was founded by the Dutch in 1618. It was the main port for the fleet of the V.O.C. (Vereenigde Oost-Indische Compagnie), the Dutch United East India Company.

Bligh arrived in Batavia on October 1, 1789, having sailed 1800 miles from Coupang in Timor in the schooner *Resource*. He lost four men to the tropical fevers of this settlement (one died at sea on the homeward voyage).

Edwards arrived in Batavia in November 1791 with the survivors of the *Pandora*, including the ten mutineers and loyalists he had captured on Tahiti (four had died when the *Pandora* foundered). We do not know how many casualties Edwards had among his crew due to the fevers, but all ten *Bounty* men reached England.

Nevertheless, Batavia at that time must have been a veritable hellhole. Here is how the surgeon of the *Pandora*, George Hamilton, describes his impressions of the place:

> In a few days we arrived at Batavia, the emporium of the Dutch in the East. Our first care was employed in sending to the hospital the sickly remains of our unfortunate crew. Some dead bodies floating down the canal struck our boat which had a very disagreeable effect on the minds of our brave fellows whose nerves were reduced to a very weak state from sickness. This was a *coup de grâce* to a sick man on his premier entrée into this painted sepulchre, this golgotha of Europe, which buries the whole settlement every five years.

Djakarta today is a booming metropolis with a population of four and a half million.

BECKE, Louis Australian adventurer and author of numerous books about the South Seas, among them *The Mutineer* (1898, co-authored with Walter Jeffery); lived 1855–1913.

Michener and Day, in their book *Rascals in Paradise* (1957), say the following about Becke: "Almost without fail, people who know the Pacific will choose as their favourite author Louis Becke. And equally without fail, those who do not know the great ocean will not have heard of Becke." And: ". . . if one wants an honest, evocative, unpretentious and at times fearfully moving account of the Pacific in its heyday, he must read Becke." And: "Around the world, men who have wandered the Pacific go back again and again to the works of Louis Becke, and as they leaf through the graceless stories of this awkward man, suddenly they are gripped in a veritable typhoon of nostalgia. For Becke could describe the grubby foreshore of an atoll, or the waters rushing into a lagoon through a break in the reef, or a trader's lonely shack, in such salt-stained and wind-ripped words as to make anyone who knows these things cry out in almost anguished recollection of his youth, 'Ah, that's the way it was!' "

Anyone interested in the *Bounty* adventure should be familiar with Becke, not only because of his recreation of the real romance of the South Seas, but also because of his theory about Christian's death which differs totally from the commonly accepted version that Christian was killed by the Polynesian men on Pitcairn.

Becke visited Pitcairn some time in the 1860s and claims that he was told the "true story" of Christian's death: that he had been shot by Adams while trying to escape the island in the *Bounty*'s boat to join a sailing ship that had been sighted. According to this version, Adams felt he had to prevent Christian from escaping in order to protect the island from discovery. Later Adams protected himself by claiming that Christian died at the hands of the Polynesian men.

We will never know the circumstances of Christian's death with certainty. Meanwhile, if you are interested in the *Bounty* and in the South Seas, you must read *The Mutineer*.

BEECHEY, Frederick W.   Captain Beechey commanded HMS *Blossom* in which he visited Pitcairn for sixteen days in December 1825. At that time there were thirty-six men and thirty women on Pitcairn; only six remained of the original settlers from the *Bounty* — five Tahitian women and John Adams who was then fifty-eight years old.

Beechey described his visit in *Narrative of a Voyage to the Pacific . . . in His Majesty's Ship Blossom* (1831). His story of the mutiny and of the early history of Pitcairn is considered among the most reliable. This is because Adams — who provided most of the information and had previously told contradictory stories — by this time knew that he would not be taken back to England for trial and therefore had no reason to consciously distort facts.

Beechey saw, and partially copied, Edward Young's journal which soon afterwards became lost.

BELCHER, Lady Diana   Lady Belcher, née Jolliffe, was born in 1806 and became the stepdaughter of Peter Heywood. She married Admiral Sir Edward Belcher, who as a lieutenant visited Pitcairn Island in 1825 in HMS *Blossom*, commanded by Captain Beechey. Upon the death of her stepfather she inherited one of the Morrison manuscripts (perhaps two). In 1870 she published *The Mutineers of the Bounty and Their Descendants in Pitcairn and Norfolk Islands*. She died in 1890.

HMS *BELLE POULE*   The frigate in which Bligh, as sailing master under Captain Philip Patton, served from February 14 to September 5, 1781, and in which he participated in the engagement against the Dutch at Dogger Bank on August 5 the same year.

BENTHAM, Gregory   Purser on the *Pandora;* a good choice, because he had visited Tahiti before on one of Cook's voyages.

BERTIE, Albemarle One of the judges at the court-martial of the accused mutineers of the *Bounty*. Captain Bertie was Peter Heywood's uncle by marriage and had helped him out with money while Heywood was a prisoner on board HMS *Hector*.

It was from Captain Bertie's command, HMS *Triumph*, that Bligh obtained Thomas Ledward as assistant surgeon for the *Bounty* in view of the chronic drunkenness of Surgeon Thomas Huggan.

HMS *BERWICK* A 74-gun ship commanded by Captain John Fergusson; the first ship in which Bligh served as a commissioned officer (fifth lieutenant) from September 5, 1781, to the end of December the same year.

BETHAM, Richard Richard Betham, LL.D., of Glasgow, was Bligh's father-in-law. He is described as a man of great erudition and an intimate friend of David Hume and Adam Smith. It was Betham who urged Bligh to accept Peter Heywood as midshipman on the *Bounty*.

BETHIA The merchant ship owned by Duncan Campbell which was selected for the first breadfruit expedition and renamed *Bounty*.

BIG SULLEE See TEVARUA.

BILGE The lowest inside part of a ship immediately above the keel where stale water and refuse tend to collect. Bilge or bilge water is also used to denote any stale or worthless remark or idea; nonsense, rubbish.

BISHOP OF OSNABURGH ISLAND The name Lieutenant Philip Carteret gave to MURUROA atoll when he discovered it in 1767.

(The name should not be confused with OSNABURGH ISLAND which refers to MEHETIA.)

HMS *BLENHEIM* The 74-gun HMS *Blenheim*, flagship of Admiral Sir Thomas Troubridge, sank with all hands in a storm off the Isle of Bourbon on February 1, 1807. The chief gunner on board was James Morrison, boatswain's mate in the *Bounty* and avid chronicler of the *Bounty* adventure.

BLIGH, Elizabeth (née Betham) Elizabeth Betham was born in 1754, the second daughter of Richard Betham, LL.D., who was Collector of Customs and Water Bailiff at Douglas on the Isle of Man. For a woman of her times she received an excellent education and has been described as "a cultured and accomplished lady." When she met William Bligh in 1780, soon after his return from Cook's third voyage, there seems to have been an immediate mutual attraction between the two. They were married on February 4 the next year at the Parish Church of Onchan in Douglas on the Isle of Man.

Through her family connections, Elizabeth was a tremendous help to Bligh in his career. Her uncle was Duncan Campbell who employed Bligh in his fleet of merchant ships and used his acquaintance with Sir Joseph Banks to either recommend or suggest Bligh for the position as commander of the breadfruit expedition.

It was also through Elizabeth's family that Bligh came to know the Heywoods. Peter Heywood, as well as Thomas Hayward and John Hallett, all came to the *Bounty* on her suggestion (Hallett's sister Ann was a bosom friend of Elizabeth's). The fact that Bligh was to hate Peter Heywood and his family for the rest of his life (being convinced that he had not only been a mutineer but one of the instigators of the mutiny) did not reflect on Elizabeth. Nor did the fact that her family knew the Christians (the Isle of Man is small) and that this connection had been a factor in Bligh's accepting Fletcher on board the *Britannia* for two voyages before the breadfruit expedition.

Betsy, as Bligh referred to her, bore her husband six daughters: Harriet, Mary, Elizabeth, Frances and Jane (twins born after Bligh had left on the first breadfruit expedition), and Anne. She also bore him a pair of boy twins in 1795, named William and Henry, but they died within twenty-four hours.

She was probably Bligh's only friend in life. He had two patrons who stood by him: Betsy's uncle Duncan Campbell and Sir Joseph Banks, but, as far as we know, he had no friends. Bligh did not have the kind of personality required to keep a friend; he was far too preoccupied with proving his own excellence and lack of faults to engage in the giving part of a give-and-take friendship.

Betsy, however, was devoted to him and stood by him through thick and thin. When stories began to arrive from New South Wales that were uncomplimentary to Bligh, to say the least, she actively campaigned on his behalf writing letters right and left to persons with influence, especially of course to Banks.

Most of their married life they had been apart from each other. When Bligh came back from New South Wales in 1810, his active career was finished and the two of them might have looked forward to spending his retirement years together. But Betsy's health was broken — some say as a result of the agony she had experienced when faced with stories about her husband which she could not or would not believe. She died on April 15, 1812, at the age of fifty-nine, and was buried in the family grave in Lambeth Churchyard where Bligh was to follow her five and a half years later.

BLIGH, William Bligh was born on September 9, 1754, in Plymouth in Cornwall, the son of a customs inspector. He was an only child and his mother died before he was sixteen.

The oft-repeated claim that Bligh went to sea at the age of seven stems from a misunderstanding of the workings of the Royal Navy of the time. Influential parents who wanted their son to have a naval career simply persuaded some captain to put him on the rolls of his ship. This gave the boy a marked advantage later on in his career when seniority was required for promotion. It was a corrupt and unfair practice, of course, but it was widely practiced. In Bligh's case, Captain Keith Stewart of HMS *Monmouth* agreed to nominally put the boy on the ship's rolls as his "servant."

It was not until 1770, when Bligh was sixteen, that he actually mustered on a ship, HMS *Hunter*. He enrolled officially as an able-bodied seaman, but the understanding was that he would be treated as an acting midshipman. Probably due to his outstanding abilities he was promoted to midshipman in just half a year.

After a year of service in the Irish Sea in the *Hunter*, Bligh was transferred to HMS *Crescent*, a 36-gun frigate. In her he spent three years sailing in the West Indies. In 1774 he was again transferred, this time to HMS *Ranger* in which he spent another two years (1774–1776) in the Irish Sea. He might have been further promoted had it not been for the fact that England was at peace and advancement in the Navy therefore was slow. In 1776 he passed the theoretical part of the examination for officer and soon afterwards was given the honor and distinction — at only twenty-one years of age — of being chosen by Captain Cook as sailing master on his flagship *Resolution*, bound for the Pacific on Cook's third expedition (1776–1780). During the six weeks spent at Tahiti, Bligh for the first time tasted the fruit which would later become part of his byname: "Breadfruit Bligh."

Cook soon became convinced that he had made a good choice and, among other indications of trust, gave Bligh the task of charting the just discovered Hawaiian Islands. Bligh was not only a skillful cartographer and navigator, he also possessed great courage, determination, and a strong sense of duty, and it is entirely possible that Cook might have been saved had Bligh been in charge of the launch that accompanied Cook to the beach at Kealakekua Bay the day the great explorer was killed by the Hawaiians (February 14, 1779).

Upon his return to England in 1780 Bligh took a trip to western England and also visited the Orkneys and the Isle of Man. On the latter island he met three families that were to become intricately involved with his destiny, the Bethams, the Christians, and the Heywoods. Bligh fell in love with Elizabeth ("Betsy") Betham, and they were married on February 4, 1781, at Kirk Onchan outside Douglas on the Isle of Man.

England was then at war with France, Spain, and the Netherlands, and only ten days after the wedding Bligh had to leave for Portsmouth. He was enrolled as sailing master on HMS *Belle Poule* (the ship had been captured from the French and, according to old Navy custom, had retained its original name). On board this ship Bligh took part in the battle against the Dutch at Dogger Bank on August 5, 1781.

Shortly after this engagement Bligh received his commission as officer and served then as a lieutenant on various ships. In the end of 1782 he was on board HMS *Cambridge* as sixth lieutenant in Lord Howe's successful relief expedition to Gibraltar.

Peace came in early 1783 and Bligh, together with hundreds of other officers, was dismissed with half pay. Since this amounted only to two shillings a day and the family meanwhile had been blessed with a daughter and Betsy was pregnant, Bligh was in need of work. Fortunately, Betsy's uncle Duncan Campbell owned a fleet of merchant ships which traded with the West Indies and was willing to offer Bligh the command of one of his vessels, the *Lynx*.

For four years Bligh stayed in the employ of Campbell and it was during his last two voyages to the West Indies (in the *Britannia*) that he came to know (and like) Fletcher Christian.

While Bligh was at sea on his last voyage Campbell had suggested him as the future commander of the breadfruit expedition initiated by Sir Joseph Banks. Banks knew and trusted Campbell and also knew of Bligh's record under Cook, so he was chosen for the position even before he returned from the West Indies (July 31, 1787). Bligh was of course thrilled with this new opportunity and accepted immediately. He was officially appointed commander of the expedition on August 16 but was not promoted to post captain as he had hoped.

Bligh's adventures during the next few years are told in Part I of this book. Following is a list of only the most important dates.

December 23, 1787:	Sails from Spithead in HMS *Bounty*.
October 27, 1788:	Arrives at Tahiti.
April 4, 1789:	Sails from Tahiti.
April 28, 1789:	Mutiny; is set adrift in the *Bounty*'s launch with eighteen men.
June 14, 1789:	Arrives at Coupang.
August 20, 1789:	Sails from Coupang in the *Resource*.
October 1, 1789:	Arrives at Batavia.
October 16, 1789:	Sails from Batavia as passenger in the *Vlydte*.
March 14, 1790:	Arrives at Portsmouth.
October 22, 1790:	Court-martialed for the loss of the *Bounty*; acquitted of responsibility.
December 15, 1790:	Promoted to post captain.
August 3, 1791:	Sails from Spithead in HMS *Providence* on the second breadfruit expedition.
April 10, 1792:	Arrives at Tahiti.

July 19, 1792:   Sails from Tahiti.

January 23, 1793:   Arrives at St. Vincent in the West Indies.

August 7, 1793:   Arrives at Deptford.

In Part I there are several quotations from Bligh's writings. It is important to keep in mind that Bligh often omitted highly significant details and sometimes distorted the truth considerably. On one occasion, at least, what he claims is totally impossible.

On March 2, 1789, Bligh had a Tahitian who was guilty of a minor theft from the shore station (most of the stolen objects were recovered) taken on board and "punished with a hundred lashes [!], severely given, and from thence into irons. He bore it surprizingly and only asked me twice to forgive him altho he expected he was to die." Bligh then adds: "His back became very much swelled, but only the last stroke broke the skin."

Now this is a complete impossibility. The cat-o'-nine-tails usually broke the skin on the fourth blow and by the twelfth the back was a bloody mess of raw meat. It is entirely reasonable to assume that the skin of a Tahitian in those times was tougher than that of a white man. But twenty-five times tougher? When Bligh is not speaking of matters directly related to navigation or geography or ethnography, we have to take what he claims with several grains of salt.

After being on half pay for over a year and a half — but managing on the money he had received from plantation owners in the West Indies for his successful mission — Bligh finally got a ship in the late spring of 1795. It was the *Warley*, an old merchantman which he was to convert into an armed cruiser. It was a hard and thankless job, but Bligh always performed his duties conscientiously and efficiently, and by August he had the ship, meanwhile renamed HMS *Calcutta*, ready for action.

This remarkable performance seems to have been appreciated by the Admiralty, and in January 1796 Bligh received his first important naval command, the 64-gun HMS *Director*. In May 1797, on board the *Director*, he experienced the momentous mutiny at the Nore when 50,000 seamen in 113 ships deposed their commanders and set up ships' democracies. Bligh's own crew joined the mutiny and sent him ashore. He had, according to the Admiralty, acquitted himself well, and reassumed command after the mutiny had been quelled.

In October the same year Bligh commanded the *Director* in the battle of Camperdown when Admiral Duncan defeated the Dutch under de Winter. In 1801 he commanded the 54-gun HMS *Glatton* at the battle of Copenhagen and was afterwards commended by Nelson. In 1805, while commanding HMS *Warrior*, Bligh was court-martialed for "tyrannical and oppressive behaviour" and for "abusive language." He was reprimanded by the court.

In 1806 Bligh arrived in New South Wales where he had been appointed governor. There he tried to abolish the lucrative rum trade engaged in by corrupt officers of the army, and his apologists claim that it was this effort on behalf of law and order that made him the object of yet another mutiny. There are indications, however, that Bligh abused his powers as governor and enriched himself in under-the-table transactions which, from a moral and ethical standpoint, were no more defensible than the rum trade. On January 26, 1808, he was taken prisoner by the new mutineers. He was put under house arrest and was not able to return to England for two years.

When the new governor arrived, Bligh returned to England. On April 27, 1810, he boarded HMS *Hindostan* and arrived at Spithead on October 25. He was exonerated for his efforts to stem the "rum rebellion," but the incident marked the end of his active career.

In March of the same year an extraordinary notice had appeared in the English *Quarterly Review* reporting on the American Captain Mayhew Folger's discovery of the hide-out of the *Bounty* mutineers on Pitcairn Island. Bligh must therefore have learned about it, but we have no knowledge of what his reactions and sentiments were when he found out.

Interestingly, Bligh had been aware of Folger and his ship *Topaz* in New South Wales several months before Folger "re-rediscovered" Pitcairn. In a dispatch to Viscount Castlereagh dated June 30, 1808, Bligh mentions the American sealer *Topaz* as having landed "rum and gin" in October of the previous year.

Through the customary advancement in terms of seniority Bligh achieved the rank of Rear Admiral of the White in 1812 and Vice-Admiral of the Blue in 1814. He died of cancer on December 7, 1817, at the age of sixty-three and is buried next to his wife in the churchyard of St. Mary in Lambeth. He left six daughters; his wife Betsy had died five years earlier and a pair of twin sons had died at birth.

Bligh was not the cruel monster he has often been portrayed as, nor was he the kind and considerate and righteous man of honor that recent efforts to whitewash him have claimed he was. For some observations on Bligh's personality and character, see the commentaries in Part I for January, April and June 1788; January and April 1789; April 1790; and August 1792.

When Bligh's third lieutenant on the *Providence*, George Tobin, heard about his death, he composed what will probably remain the most balanced epitaph that Bligh could ever have. In a letter to Francis Bond, Bligh's step-nephew, who had been first lieutenant on the *Providence*, he wrote:

> So poor Bligh, for with all his infirmities, you and I cannot but think of him otherwise, has followed Portlock*. He has had a busy and turbulent journey of it — no one more so, and since the unfortunate mutiny in the *Bounty* has

*In the letter Tobin was referring to Lieutenant Nathaniel Portlock who commanded the *Assistant* on the second breadfruit expedition. He had died on September 12, 1817.

been rather in the shade. Yet perhaps he was not altogether understood — I am sure my dear friend, that in the *Providence* there was no settled system of tyranny exercised by him likely to produce dissatisfaction. It was in those violent *tornados* of temper when he lost himself. Yet when all, in his opinion, *went right* when could a man be more placid and interesting? Once or twice I felt the *unbridled licence* of his *power of speech* yet never without receiving something like an emollient plaister to heal the wound. Let our old Captain's frailties be forgotten, and view him as a man of Science and an excellent practical seaman. He had suffered much, and even in difficulty, by labour and perseverance extricated himself. But his great quality was Foresight. In this I think, Bond, you will accord with me. I have seen many men in his profession with more resources, but never one with so much precaution — I mean chiefly as a Navigator.

For detailed biographies of Bligh, see those by George Mackaness, *The Life of Vice-Admiral William Bligh, R.N., F.R.S.* (1951) and Gavin Kennedy, *Bligh* (1978), and (the best of them all) Owen Rutter, *Turbulent Journey* (1936).

BLIGH BOAT ENTRANCE   A break in Australia's Great Barrier Reef through which Bligh and the loyalists passed on May 29, 1789, on their open-boat voyage from Tofua to Timor. The entrance is twelve miles north of the Second Three Mile opening in the reef and lies to the south of Providential Channel (12º34'S.) where Cook entered in the *Endeavour* on his first voyage.

BLIGH CHANNEL   Part of the western side of Endeavour (Torres) Strait.

BLIGH WATER   A sea area in the Fijis north of Viti Levu bounded on the north and north-west by the Yasawa Group and on the east by Vanua Levu.
    It was here that Bligh and his loyalists in the *Bounty*'s launch were pursued by Fijians (who were cannibals at the time) in two fast sailing canoes (see the May 1789 commentary in Part I).

BLIGH'S ISLANDS   In the log books of Bligh and his officers on the second breadfruit expedition, the Fiji Islands are referred to as Bligh's Islands. It was not an inappropriate appellation — the Fijians of today consider Bligh the principal European discoverer of Fiji — but it never caught on.

BLIGH'S LAGOON ISLAND   See TEMATANGI.

BLOODY BAY   Name given by Christian to the part of the lagoon at Tubuai where he had opened fire on a fleet of attacking canoes, killing eleven men and one woman (see the May 1789 commentary in Part I).

HMS *BLOSSOM* British frigate of sixteen guns with a complement of 100, commanded by Captain Frederick W. Beechey; visited Pitcairn from December 4 to December 20, 1825.

BOATSWAIN (bosun) A warrant officer on a warship or a petty officer on a merchant ship in charge of sails, rigging, boats, anchors, cables, cordage, etc. He is also in charge of all deckhands. The boatswain of the *Bounty* was William Cole.

BOLA BOLA See BORA BORA.

BOND, Francis Godolphin First Lieutenant (Bligh's second in command) in the *Providence* on the second breadfruit expedition (August 3, 1791, to August 7, 1793).

Bond was the son of Bligh's half-sister Catherine and was his protégé. In the history of the *Bounty* adventure, he is important for his candid and highly perceptive observations on Bligh as a commander (see the August 1792 commentary in Part I).

Bond's confidential communications regarding the voyage (they were obviously not meant for publication) are invaluable for our understanding not only of Bligh's personality, but of Fletcher Christian's. They show that Bligh had learned nothing from his experience on the *Bounty*; he was just as petty and humiliating and irrational (in Bond's words, "insane at times"). In fact, it seems as if Bond himself had been close to losing control in his role as victim of Bligh's abuse. However, because of the spaciousness of the ship (which provided him with privacy) and the company of his fellow officers (Christian, as acting lieutenant, had no fellow officers except Bligh), he was "by no means in purgatory." His use of the expression "purgatory" is in itself interesting — it was common knowledge that Christian had said: "I have been in hell for weeks!"

Some *Bounty* scholars feel that there could indeed have been a mutiny on the *Providence* if *(1)* there had been an officer as unstable as Christian on board; *(2)* there had not been a contingent of marines present; *(3)* there had not been an accompanying ship, and *(4)* the stay on Tahiti had been longer.

It is interesting to note that, upon his return from the expedition, Bond resolved never to sail with Bligh again. He had a successful career in the navy and distinguished himself as commander of the schooner *Netley*, 1799–1801, when he captured several French and Spanish privateers and recaptured English ships from the enemy.

BORA BORA (ancient name: Vavau) A volcanic island in the Leeward group of the Society Islands 160 miles west-north-west of Tahiti, situated at 16⁰30'S., 151⁰45'W. Once seen, the profile of this island is etched in the memory forever: the dominating mountain, Te Manu (2386 feet) looks like a high altar reaching into the sky assisted by the double-peaked Mount Pahia (2159 feet) one third of a mile westward.

Bora Bora is surrounded by a barrier reef which is covered by *motus* (islets) most of which are wooded. One of the islands in the lagoon is Motu Tapu where the famous movie, *Tabu*, was filmed in the 1930s.

As volcanic islands go, Bora Bora is relatively small, only about fourteen square miles. The current population is 3300. James Michener was stationed here briefly during World War II and many say that this is his Bali Hai (others say it is Moorea). It is indeed a breathtakingly beautiful island.

Hitihiti, the adventurer *par excellence* who sailed with Captain Cook, fought for Mate (Pomare I) together with the men of the *Bounty*, and sailed again with Captain Edwards, was born on Bora Bora and was related to its famous chief at the time, Puni.

During World War II American troops were stationed in Bora Bora and built an airfield on one of the *motus*. It is still in use for inter-island flights.

When I first visited Bora Bora in the early 1960s, there was one hotel and thirteen cars on the island. Today there are several hotels and close to 600 cars. But somehow the romance of the island is still preserved.

BOUGAINVILLE, Louis Antoine de   French navigator and explorer. As captain of the frigate *Boudeuse*, Bougainville became the second European (after Samuel Wallis) to visit Tahiti. He anchored in the lagoon of Hitiaa on April 6, 1768, and, thinking that he had discovered the island, claimed it for France and named it La Nouvelle Cythère. Bougainville lived from 1729 to 1811.

BOUND, John   See BROWN, JOHN.

HMS *BOUNTY* (ex *Bethia*)   In the late 1780s the British Navy was made up of more than 600 ships of various sizes and types. Yet the Admiralty must have considered none of them suitable for the planned breadfruit expedition. For that purpose a ship had to be found which could be converted to a floating greenhouse; carrying capacity in relation to size was the main criterion.

Six merchant ships were considered and of them the Admiralty chose the *Bethia* which was fairly new, having been built two and a half years earlier at Hull. She was a three-masted, full-rigged, snub-nosed ship of only 215 tons burden and had so far been used only for coastal trading. The Navy Board bought her on May 23, 1787, for £1950 and, on the suggestion of Sir Joseph Banks, renamed her *Bounty*. She was then immediately transferred to Deptford for refitting. (According to George Mackaness in *The Life of Vice-Admiral William Bligh*, the *Bethia* belonged to Duncan Campbell, the uncle of Bligh's wife Elizabeth. Campbell's influence may have played a role in the choice of Bligh as commander of the ship.)

The *Bounty* was incredibly small when one considers her mission. She was 90 feet 10 inches long with a beam of 24 feet 4 inches and a draft of 11 feet 4 inches.

She had no superstructures; all accommodations and facilities were below deck. Her three masts varied in height from 48 to 59 feet. There were three yards on the fore- and mainmasts, two on the mizzenmast. Under the bowsprit there was a figurehead portraying a woman in a blue riding habit.

The refitting was costly. The bottom of the hull was sheathed in copper plate to protect the wood from teredos and other wood-boring worms, a rather new and very expensive feature. The procedure had first been tried in 1761, but had failed because of the electrolysis which results when ferrous and nonferrous metals are put in salt water and which leads to corrosion of the iron. By now, however, designers had learned to use only copper and bronze for exposed underwater fittings, and the *Bounty* was constructed accordingly.

The great cabin aft, normally reserved for captain's quarters, was extended to a third of the length of the ship in order to house the pots for the breadfruit plants. Planks with holes for the pots formed a second deck within the cabin and the floor was covered with lead sheeting to prevent the excess water from leaking through to the deck below. Pipes were fitted which would lead the water to containers below, so that it could be re-used. All in all there was room for 626 pots in the cabin. A large coal-fired heater was also installed so that the plants would not freeze when the ship was sailing in colder latitudes.

For armament the *Bounty* received four short-carriage four-pounders and ten half-pounder swivel guns. Although the *Bounty* may have been small for her mission, it certainly appears that no expense was spared in preparing her for the voyage: the total bill for the refitting came to £4456, more than twice the purchase price.

The *Bounty* was commissioned on June 8, 1787, and Lieutenant William Bligh was appointed her commander on August 16. (A list of her entire complement appears in the November 1787 commentary in Part I.)

The history of the *Bounty* is told in detail in Part I of this book. Following is a list of only the most important dates:

End of 1784:	Built in Hull.
May 23, 1787:	Bought by the Navy Board.
June 8, 1787:	Commissioned.
August 16, 1787:	Bligh appointed commander.
December 23, 1787:	Sails from Spithead.
March 23, 1788:	Reaches Staten Land, encounters heavy gales off Cape Horn.
April 22, 1788:	Sets course for Cape of Good Hope.
May 23, 1788:	Anchors in False Bay.
July 1, 1788:	Sails from False Bay.

August 20, 1788:	Anchors in Adventure Bay.
September 4, 1788:	Sails from Adventure Bay.
October 9, 1788:	James Valentine dies.
October 26, 1788:	Anchors in Matavai Bay.
November 15, 1788:	Gathering of breadfruit completed.
December 9, 1788:	Thomas Huggan dies.
April 4, 1789:	Sails from Matavai Bay.
April 11, 1789:	Aitutaki discovered.
April 22, 1789:	Arrives at Nomuka.
April 28, 1789:	Mutiny; Christian assumes command.
May 24, 1789:	Arrives at Tubuai.
May 31, 1789:	Sails from Tubuai.
June 6, 1789:	Anchors in Matavai Bay.
June 16, 1789:	Sails from Matavai Bay.
June 23, 1789:	Arrives at Tubuai.
September 17, 1789:	Sails from Tubuai.
September 22, 1789:	Anchors in Matavai Bay.
September 23, 1789:	Sails from Matavai Bay.
October ?, 1789:	Rarotonga discovered.
January 15, 1790:	Arrives at Pitcairn.
January 23, 1790:	Burns and sinks.

Finally it should be mentioned that there are two *Bounty* replicas sailing today. One was built in Lunenburg, Nova Scotia, by Metro Goldwyn Mayer for the 1962 movie version of the mutiny. At the time of writing (September 1988), she is on exhibit at the Bayside Marketplace in Miami, but she still sails and, for example, took part in the Tall Ships Parade during the Statue of Liberty Centennial celebrations.

The second *Bounty* replica was used by Dino de Laurentiis for the 1983 movie. She was in Fremantle during the America's Cup races in 1987 and at that time was on her way around the world with passengers who also performed the duties of crew members. She also took part in the re-enactment of the sailing of the First Fleet to Australia in commemoration of the Bicentennial of the first settlement of the continent.

BOUNTY BAY A small cove on the north-eastern coast of Pitcairn; the mutineers called it the Landing Place, and the name Bounty Bay stems back to Captain

Beechey's visit in 1825. The cove or indentation in the shoreline that boasts this name has no protection against the raging surf except a jetty that was built a few years ago. Here is how Robert B. Nicolson described it in his book *The Pitcairners* (1965):

> The channel to Bounty Bay is narrow and rough and sweeps to the left to gain the pebbly beach. Two things could happen when entering: if the turn of the channel is not negotiated, a jumble of sharp, surf-washed rock is seconds dead ahead of an erring boat; or, beforehand, a miscalculation in entering the channel could swamp the craft. In either case, there is no time for a second chance. Even on a calm day, a big surf runs; and on the calmest day the sea is a continual churning surge of rough water.

In April 1987 I visited Pitcairn on a calm day. It was an awesome experience to say the least; I still cannot think of the waters of this "bay" without a shudder. But, needless to say, it was well worth it.

BOUNTY CHRONOMETER See FOLGER, MAYHEW.

BOUNTY DAY January 23, a holiday on Pitcairn Island. Interestingly, the Pitcairners do not celebrate the day the island was discovered by Carteret (July 2, 1767) or sighted by Christian (January 15, 1790), but the day the *Bounty* was burned (January 23, 1790).

Bounty Day was first celebrated in 1850 when one of the original settlers, Teraura, Edward Young's first consort and Thursday October Christian's wife, was still alive. It has been a Pitcairn holiday ever since. The highlight of the celebration is the burning of a large model of the *Bounty*.

BOUNTY ISLES Thirteen small rocky islands located south of New Zealand at 47⁰44'S., 179⁰09'E., discovered by Bligh on September 19, 1788, when he was on his way from Adventure Bay, Van Diemen's Land, to Tahiti.

BREADFRUIT ('uru) The various uses of the breadfruit tree are best described by Teuira Henry in *Ancient Tahiti* (1928):

> The large, handsome 'uru, or breadfruit, tree has heavy dark-green foliage, which turns yellow all the year round. In the bearing season its spherical fruit, some as large as a person's head, hang in all stages of development. The average size of the leaves, pinnately cleft to different depths in different species, is about 16 inches by 12 inches. The leaves are much used for wrapping food in cooking and for covering native ovens. Propagation is by roots and young shoots. The wood is red and durable and highly prized, in olden times being used for planks

for doors, house posts, and ridgepoles, for altars (*fatarau*), ornamental figures (*unu*), in temples, and canoes. The sap is very adhesive when fresh and was formerly spread on trees by natives for catching birds. It was also used as pitch with fine coconut fiber in calking canoes.

Henry describes forty varieties of breadfruit in Tahiti and also tells the legend of the origin of the breadfruit. The preparation of the breadfruit is described by Douglas L. Oliver in *Ancient Tahitian Society* (1974):

> The fruit was prepared for eating in several different ways. The simplest method, resorted to when traveling, was to roast it whole and then scrape off the charred rind. Usually, however, the fruit was baked in an earth oven . . . Most commonly the fruit was picked at its first stage of ripening and baked, either whole and in its rind or with rind and core removed and cut in large chunks. The rind was removed with a sharp-edged bivalve, and the pulpy fruit cut up with a special wooden splitter.

The role of the breadfruit in the *Bounty* story is discussed in the September 1788 commentary in Part I.

BRIG   A two-masted sailing vessel square-rigged on both masts.

BRIGANTINE   A two-masted sailing vessel square-rigged on the fore mast and fore-and-aft-rigged on the main mast.

BRITANNIA   Merchant vessel owned by Douglas Campbell, the uncle of Elizabeth Bligh. William Bligh commanded the ship on at least two voyages to the West Indies.

It was on this ship that Bligh accepted the ten-year-younger Fletcher Christian on board for two voyages; on the first as an ordinary seaman, although he messed with the midshipmen and officers, and on the second as second mate.

Lawrence Lebogue, later the sailmaker on the *Bounty*, also sailed with Bligh in the *Britannia*.

HMS *BRITON*   British warship of 44 guns and with a complement of 300 officers and men, commanded by Captain Sir Thomas Staines.

The *Briton* and her consort HMS *Tagus* were on a mission to track down the U.S. frigate *Essex*, under Commander David Porter, which had been attacking British shipping in the Pacific, when they sighted Pitcairn Island in the early morning of September 17, 1814. After establishing contact with the inhabitants they left the island the same evening.

On board the *Briton* was Lieutenant John Shillibeer who later wrote a narrative of the voyage.

See the entries for PIPON (the commander of the *Tagus*), SHILLIBEER, and STAINES.

BROWN, John, alias BOUND, John   A bloodthirsty scallawag who was marooned on Tahiti by Captain Cox of the *Mercury* (*Gustaf III*) when she left the island on September 2, 1789. On the ship he had cut up another crew member's face with a razor.

When the men of the *Bounty* who had voted to stay on Tahiti (see the September 1789 commentary in Part I) arrived three weeks later, Brown soon took up with the rowdiest of the mutineers and became part of a mercenary army. This group, in exchange for certain favors in terms of land, women, and special privileges, and also simply for the excitement of fighting, helped Mate (Pomare I) wage war against other districts on the island with the object of achieving supremacy. In fact, Brown became one of Mate's body guards.

When Captain Edwards arrived in the *Pandora* on March 23, 1791, he took an immediate liking to Brown — who must have been something of a "soul-mate" — and engaged him in betraying his former comrades-in-arms. Brown turned to the job with relish and, with the help of bribed natives, soon had everyone rounded up. Edwards then took the kindred spirit with him when he sailed on May 8.

Presumably Brown survived the wreck of the *Pandora*, but his subsequent fate is not known to me.

BROWN, William   Gardener and botanist's assistant on the *Bounty*; mutineer; went with Christian; was killed on Pitcairn.

Brown, born in Leicester, had an unusual background for a gardener. Although technically a civilian, he had seen service as a midshipman and had been acting lieutenant in HMS *Resolution* (Captain Lord Robert Manners) in the early 1780s. Why he changed his career is unknown, but it is likely that his naval background was one reason why he was chosen for the expedition.

Brown's physical description, written by Bligh after the mutiny, reads as follows:

> [WILLIAM BROWN]. Assistant botanist, aged 27 years, 5 feet 8 inches high, fair complexion, dark brown hair, strong made; a remarkable scar on one of his cheeks, which contracts the eye-lid, and runs down to his throat, occasioned by the king's evil; is tatowed.

The first significant mention of Brown on the voyage is on October 19, 1788 (only a week before the arrival at Tahiti), when he and John Mills refused to take part in the daily dancing that Bligh had ordered for exercise. Both men had their grog stopped as a consequence, the most severe punishment on board next to a flogging.

Brown was of course one of the men who were permanently stationed on Point

Venus in Tahiti to supervise the collection of breadfruit shoots (the others being Nelson and Christian).

He stayed below deck during the mutiny and seems to have joined the mutineers only afterwards. On Tubuai he voted with Christian and then joined him on his quest for an island refuge.

Brown arrived at Pitcairn with his consort Teatuahitea whom he called "Sarah." He was an obvious choice for the exploratory shore party and he liked what he saw on the island. The place where he found a well is to this day called Brown's Water.

On Massacre Day, September 20, 1793, Brown was the fifth and last mutineer to be killed by the Polynesians. Island tradition has it that Teimua, who liked Brown, shot at him with only a powder charge and told him to pretend he was dead. Brown moved too soon, however, and was beaten to death by Manarii.

Brown seems to have been the kindest and mildest of the white men on the island. He left no children.

BRUCE, H. W. Captain of HMS *IMOGENE*.

HMS *BRUNSWICK* The British warship on which the convicted *Bounty* mutineers, able-bodied seamen Thomas Burkett, Thomas Ellison, and John Millward, were hanged at Spithead on October 29, 1792.

BUFFETT, John Buffet was an English sailor born in Bristol on July 16, 1797. On December 10, 1823, he arrived at Pitcairn aboard the London whaler *Cyrus*. When John Adams, the only surviving mutineer, asked Captain Hall if one of his crew could stay on the island to help with the education of the children, Buffett volunteered; one of his shipmates, John Evans, jumped ship and also remained on Pitcairn. They were the first immigrants on Pitcairn since the arrival of the *Bounty* almost thirty-four years earlier.

Exactly two months later, on February 10, 1824, Buffett married Dorothy ("Dolly") Young, daughter of Edward Young and Christian's widow, Mauatua. She bore him five sons. "On the side," however, he was intimate with Mary ("Big Melly") Christian, the daughter of Thursday October Christian and Tevarua. She bore him first a daughter and later two sons. The daughter was born before Adams died, so the old mutineer — who professed to have become *very* religious — may well have regretted that Buffett had stayed on the island.

During the Hill dictatorship on Pitcairn 1832–1837 (see PITCAIRN ISLAND and HILL, JOSHUA) Buffett was sentenced to three dozen lashes (he received two dozen, necessitating his taking to bed for two weeks) and was ordered off the island. Hill's excuse for imposing this punishment was Buffett's extramarital relationship with Big Melly.

Buffett (together with John Evans and George Nobbs) sailed to Tahiti in March 1834 on the whaling ship *Tuscan*. He returned three months later in the barque *Pomare* in order to pick up his family; they settled on Tahiti for the time being, from where Buffett wrote to the British Government about Joshua Hill's usurpation of power on Pitcairn. On September 16, 1834, being certain that Hill's rule would now be short-lived, Buffett and his family returned to Pitcairn on the American brig *Olivia*.

John Buffett died on Norfolk Island on May 5, 1891, at the age of ninety-five.

BUMBOAT   A boat used to convey provisions, utensils, and clothing for sale to ships in port, a "floating chandler's shop." It was also used to carry prostitutes for hire.

BURAU   See PURAU.

BURGOO   Bligh several times mentions burgoo in his log entries. It was a porridge or gruel made of boiled oatmeal to which salt and sugar and sometimes butter was added. The stale, poor-quality oatmeal combined with bad-smelling ship's water made it a most unappetizing dish; in fact, one naval surgeon wrote that it was cruel to expect human beings to eat it. Nevertheless, burgoo was easy to make and was therefore served all too frequently, especially when the cook on board was lazy. Needless to say, it was not a popular food with seamen.

In one of his entries, Bligh writes that "wheat and barly were now boiled every morning in lieu of burgoo." Morrison, commenting on the same breakfast, writes: "The quantity was so small, that it was no uncommon thing for four men in a mess to draw lots for the breakfast."

Food was an extremely important concern to seamen and, as we have seen (in the April 1789 commentary in Part I), it was a controversy concerning food which triggered the mutiny on the *Bounty*.

BURKETT (Burkitt), Thomas   Able-bodied seaman on the *Bounty*; mutineer; stayed on Tahiti; survived the wreck of the *Pandora*; found guilty at the court-martial and hanged.

Burkett was born in Bath and was twenty-five years old when he joined the *Bounty*. There appears to be no significant reference to his pre-mutiny activities in the literature other than that he was one of the four able-bodied seamen permanently stationed ashore during the *Bounty*'s stay at Tahiti.

Bligh's description of Burkett, written after the mutiny, reads as follows:

> [THOMAS BURKETT] 26 years, 5 feet 9 inches high. Fair complexion. Very much marked with smallpox. Brown hair, slender made and very much tattooed.

Burkett was in Christian's watch and on the morning of the mutiny he was a lookout on the forepeak. He was from the very beginning an active participant in taking over the ship, in fact, he was one of the men who went below with Christian to arrest the Captain.

He seemed, however, to have had more compassion than most of the mutineers. It was he who adjusted Bligh's shirt so it would cover his exposed private parts and called down for clothes for the captain, and it was he who, over Quintal's objections, insisted on letting boatswain Cole take a compass into the launch.

On Tubuai Burkett got wounded in the side by a spear in one of the skirmishes with the natives and had a narrow escape. The wound, however, was not dangerous and healed quickly.

Burkett elected to stay on Tahiti when Christian sailed away on the *Bounty*. On the invitation of chief Temarii, he stayed in the district of Papara (together with his fellow mutineer John Sumner) and took part in the military campaigns against the enemies of Pomare I (then called Mate). It was he who buried Churchill after Thompson had murdered him. Before the *Pandora* arrived, his Tahitian consort — we do not know her name — bore him a son.

Burkett survived the *Pandora* but not the court-martial. Of course, being clearly an active mutineer he never had a real chance. And he had no clever attorney who could find a loophole for him, as Muspratt's lawyer did. To everyone's satisfaction, however, he did manage to bring out the fact that Hayward and Hallett had cried and begged to be allowed to stay on board the *Bounty* at the time of the mutiny. Ellison confirmed his testimony.

Burkett, together with Millward and Ellison, was hanged on HMS *Brunswick* at Spithead on October 29, 1792.

BURNEY, James   James Burney (1750–1821) was a member of Cook's crew on the *Resolution* during the second voyage (1772–1775) and a lieutenant in the *Discovery* during the third voyage (1776–1780); he was transferred to the *Resolution* after the deaths of Cook and Captain Charles Clerke. It was during this voyage that he became well acquainted with Bligh who was sailing master in the *Resolution*.

Burney authored a major work in five volumes: *A Chronological History of the Discoveries in the South Sea or Pacific Ocean* (published 1803–1817). He is best known in the *Bounty* story as the editor of Bligh's *A Voyage to the South Sea* (1792).

BYAM, Roger   In their magnificent work *Mutiny on the Bounty*, Nordhoff and Hall use the actual names of the crew members on board — with one exception: the narrator of the story is midshipman Roger Byam. There was no person with that name on the *Bounty*, but the fictional Roger Byam is identical with the real-life midshipman Peter Heywood who was a good friend of Fletcher Christian's but took no part in the mutiny.

There are two reasons why Nordhoff and Hall chose a fictional name for the narrator. One was that they wanted to avoid giving the impression that the story was an actual historical account, and the second was that the name Heywood can easily be confused with Hayward (midshipman Thomas Hayward was also on the *Bounty*).

BYRNE (Byrn), Michael Able-bodied seaman on the *Bounty*; loyalist; kept on board against his will; survived the wreck of the *Pandora*; acquitted at court-martial.

Michael Byrne was born in Kilkenny, Ireland, and was twenty-six years old when Bligh signed him on the *Bounty* for the express purpose of playing his fiddle while the sailors danced. Bligh explained his view in a letter to Sir Joseph Banks:

> Some time for relaxation and mirth is absolutely necessary and I have considered it so much so that after 4 o'clock the evening is laid aside for their amusement and dancing. I had great difficulty before I left England to get a man to play the violin and I preferred at last to take one two-thirds blind than come without one.

Bligh was a man without humor and he viewed his crew as an engineer views his machinery; therefore even the "mirth" had to be regulated. The mirth was in fact forced on the men: when Mills and Brown refused to dance, they were punished.

In the accounts of Bligh's second breadfruit expedition there is no mention of a fiddler or of dancing. Did Bligh consider the experiment a failure? No one knows.

After the mutiny, Bligh gave the following description of Byrne:

> [MICHAEL BYRNE] 28 years, 5 feet 6 inches high. Fair complexion and is almost blind. Plays the fiddle. Has the mark of an issue in the back of his neck.

There is not much mention of Byrne in the *Bounty* story; because of his handicap he simply had to "tag along." During the mutiny he was left in one of the ship's boats that had been launched and then rejected as a means of conveyance for the loyalists. He spent his time trying to keep the boat from banging into the ship's side and crying because he did not really know what was going on or what was going to become of him. He was probably kept on board for two reasons: he was popular because he provided music, and the launch was already overfilled when he was considered in terms of remaining or leaving.

Byrne gave himself up voluntarily when the *Pandora* arrived. It is amazing that he survived the shipwreck; probably someone helped him. At the court-martial he had little difficulty in clearing himself.

Rolf Du Rietz (1965) has described Bligh's efforts to get Byrne to give him a favorable affidavit. Byrne declined to cooperate and Bligh wrote to his step-nephew, Francis Bond (August 14, 1794):

> As to the blind scoundrel, I can only beg of you to make the best of him, &

get him flogged nobly whenever he deserves it, as he is certainly a very great Villain. . . . Dont let him get on shore for I am sure he deserves no leave.

When Byrne finally consented to cooperate, he (in Du Rietz's words) "with Irish stubbornness adhered strictly to the truth (as far as he had knowledge of it)."

I have seen no references to Byrne's later fate.

CABLE'S LENGTH   Nautical measure of distance, 608 feet in the British Navy, 720 feet in the U.S. Navy.

HMS *CALCUTTA* (ex *Warley*)   The old merchant vessel to which Bligh was assigned in 1795 in order to supervise its conversion to an armed cruiser (see BLIGH, WILLIAM).

CAMBRIAN   One of the merchant ships which Bligh commanded while in the employ of his wife's uncle, Duncan Campbell.

HMS *CAMBRIDGE*   The first-rate ship in which Bligh, as sixth lieutenant, served from March 20, 1782, to January 13, 1783. The *Cambridge* took a minor part in Lord Howe's relief expedition to Gibraltar in the end of 1782.

Interestingly, Fletcher Christian served in the *Cambridge* at the same time as Bligh, but it is not likely that the two would have known each other since Christian was enrolled as ship's boy, and a first-rate ship of the line carried a complement of about 850 seamen and officers.

CAMPBELL, Duncan   Duncan Campbell was the uncle of Elizabeth Bligh (her mother's brother). He was a wealthy shipowner who traded with the West Indies and owned several plantations there. When Bligh was released from the Navy on half pay in 1783, Campbell took him into his service and gave him command of his newest ship, the *Lynx*. Bligh remained in Campbell's service until 1787, commanding the *Cambrian* and the *Britannia*.

Campbell also owned the *Bethia* (named for Elizabeth's father's family, the Bethams) which was purchased by the Navy Board for the breadfruit expedition and renamed the *Bounty*. He knew Sir Joseph Banks well and it is likely that he either suggested or recommended Bligh for the position of commander of the expedition.

Bligh wrote to Campbell frequently and the letters that have survived give us information that is not always recorded in Bligh's log or journal.

CANDLENUT   See TUTUI.

CAPE YORK The northernmost tip of the Australian continent, forming the south side of Endeavour Strait. Bligh passed north of Cape York on June 3, 1789, on his open-boat voyage from Tofua to Timor.

CARTERET, Philip Carteret (1738–1796) sailed as first lieutenant of the *Tamar* in Byron's expedition; as captain of HMS *Swallow* he accompanied Samuel Wallis on his expedition to the South Seas 1766–1769; his "Account of a Voyage Round the World" in Hawkesworth's *Account of the Voyages by Byron, Wallis, Carteret, and Cook* was published in 1773.

Captain Wallis in HMS *Dolphin* and Captain Carteret in the sloop *Swallow* encountered heavy storms in the Straits of Magellan and spent four months before they reached the Pacific on April 10, 1767. On the following day, however, the two ships became separated in a fog and the *Swallow* was thought to have foundered. Actually she had been saved by Carteret's superb seamanship and sailed westward on the 25th parallel south of the equator.

Carteret is important in the story of the *Bounty*, because on July 2, 1767, he discovered Pitcairn (which he named after the young midshipman who had seen the island first). It was Carteret's account of this discovery in Hawkesworth's *Voyages* that persuaded Christian to look for Pitcairn as the ultimate hide-out. The island turned out to be even more ideal for this purpose than Christian could have hoped, because Carteret had put its position more than 200 miles west of where it actually is!

The *Swallow* was, in Carteret's words "an old ship, having been in the service thirty years, and was in my opinion by no means fit for a long voyage."

Sir Peter Buck (Te Rangi Hiroa) says in his small but excellent volume *Explorers of the Pacific* (1953):

> Though Carteret added little to Polynesian discovery, his voyage was one of the pluckiest in history. Not only should the *Swallow* have been relegated to the scrap heap instead of being sent out on an expedition, the Admiralty had refused to supply Carteret with an anvil and other equipment for repairs. The story of how he circumnavigated the world in a leaking tub and kept her afloat for two years and seven months will ever remain a record for endurance, courage, and skill.

CASUARINA See IRONWOOD.

CAT-O'-NINE-TAILS Dr William Burney, who edited an edition of *Falconer's Marine Dictionary* in 1816, described the cat-o'-nine-tails used in the Navy as being "composed of nine pieces of line, or cord, about half-a-yard long, fixed upon a piece of thick rope for a handle, and having three knots on each, at small intervals, the first being near the end." There were several variants on this instrument of torture, but the description above would probably apply to the cat-o'-nine-tails used on the *Bounty*. The expression "letting the cat out of the bag" stems from the grim ceremony of taking the cat-o'-nine-tails out from its bag of red baize.

A most graphic description of the use of the cat-o'-nine-tails is given by Vice-Admiral Sir William Kennedy, K.C.B., in his reminiscences *Hurrah for the Life of a Sailor* (1900).

See also FLOGGING.

CHARLES DOGGETT American brig, a 110-ton whaler from Salem commanded by Captain William Driver. The *Charles Doggett* carried the Pitcairners back to their island from Tahiti after the disastrous emigration attempt in 1831 (see PITCAIRN ISLAND).

CHINESE MULBERRY See MULBERRY TREE.

CHOKE ONE'S LUFF Feast on good food.

CHRISTIAN, Ann (née Dixon) Fletcher Christian's mother; born 1730; married to Charles Christian on May 2, 1751.

Ann bore her husband ten children, four of whom died before reaching adulthood. Fletcher was the seventh child.

Ann was widowed at the age of thirty-eight. Due to financial difficulties she lost the family home in Cumbria and in 1780 went to live in Douglas on the Isle of Man with Fletcher, his sister, and his younger brother.

Ann Christian lived to the age of 90, which means that she learned about Fletcher's fate and that she knew that, far away on an island in the South Seas called Pitcairn, she had three grandchildren whom she would never see. She died in Douglas on March 30, 1820.

For more information, see Glynn Christian: *Fragile Paradise* (1982).

CHRISTIAN, Charles Father of Fletcher Christian; born 1729; married to Ann Dixon on May 2, 1751.

Charles Christian was an attorney with a practice in Cockermouth in Cumbria. With Ann he had ten children, four of whom died before reaching adulthood. Fletcher was their seventh child.

Charles died on March 13, 1768, when Fletcher was only three and a half years old. He was buried in Brigham.

For more information, see Glynn Christian: *Fragile Paradise* (1982).

CHRISTIAN, Charles Brother of Fletcher Christian. Charles was born in 1762, the sixth child of Charles and Ann Christian. He was two years older than Fletcher and was six when the father died. In his late teens he joined the Yorkshire Militia in Liverpool and in 1780 he went to Leeds to begin his studies to become a surgeon.

It was as a surgeon on the East Indiaman *Middlesex* that Charles had participated in a mutiny (see the November 1787 commentary in Part I).

Charles Christian never married. His reaction to the news of Fletcher's mutiny has been preserved and is quoted by Glynn Christian (see reference below):

> I was struck with horror and weighed down with a Sorrow to so extreme a pitch that I became stupified. ... I knew that this unfortunate occurrence, following so close on the heels of my late eventful and disastrous voyage [in the *Middlesex*], would occasion the lies which had been spread abroad in consequence to assume the aspect of Truth.

Charles wrote to Bligh's father-in-law, Dr Richard Betham, and "firmly prophecied that it would be found that there had been some Cause not then known that had driven Fletcher to this desperate step. I was enabled to form the just presage from what I had so recently observed possible to occur on Board of Ship where Strife and Discord prevailed." Betham, however, had died long before the letter reached him.

After Bligh returned from his second breadfruit expedition, Charles had spoken to a captain of marines on the *Providence* who had said: "from Bligh's odious behaviour during the voyage, he would as soon shoot him as a dog, if it were not for the law."

Charles died on November 14, 1822, in the house on Fort Street in Douglas that he had shared with his mother.

It is exclusively due to Glynn Christian's investigative efforts that we know anything about Charles Christian, especially the discovery that Charles had participated in a mutiny and that Fletcher must have known about it — a major contribution to *Bounty* research. For more information, see Glynn Christian: *Fragile Paradise* (1982).

CHRISTIAN, Charles　Fletcher Christian's second-born son. Charles was born to Fletcher and Mauatua on Pitcairn in 1791 or 1792. In 1810 he married Sully, the Polynesian baby who had been the only child on board the *Bounty* when it arrived at Pitcairn in 1790. With her he had four sons: Fletcher, Edward, Charles Jr., and Isaac, and four daughters: Sarah, Maria, Mary and Margaret.

Sully died in 1826, leaving Charles to raise the children who then ranged in age from a little over one year old to fifteen.

Charles survived the disastrous emigration to Tahiti in 1831 (during which his older brother, Thursday October, was the first of seventeen to die). He was among the few on Pitcairn who actively opposed the dictatorial rule of Joshua Hill (1832–1837). He died on January 14, 1842.

Charles and Thursday October were the only sons of the mutineers who married fullblooded Tahitian women. The present-day descendants of Charles are on Norfolk Island.

CHRISTIAN, Edward   Fletcher Christian's brother. Edward Christian was born in 1758, the fourth child of Charles and Ann Christian. According to Glynn Christian (*Fragile Paradise*, 1982), he grew up to be Chief Justice of the Isle of Ely, Professor of the Laws of England at Cambridge, a founder of Downing College, Professor of Law at East India College, and Commissioner for Bankrupts.

Edward Christian is best known for his staunch defense of his younger brother Fletcher. Defense is perhaps not the best word, since Edward never tried to defend the crime of mutiny; what he wanted to make clear was that there were versions of what had taken place other than the one published by Bligh, and that there had been extraordinary provocation involved that could explain, even if it could not excuse, Fletcher's action.

Edward's efforts originated in a meeting he had with Peter Heywood who, soon after being pardoned, had asked to see him. In this meeting he learned that "the dreadful mutiny on the *Bounty* originated from motives, and was attended with circumstances, different from those which had been presented to the world."

His efforts culminated in the middle of 1794 when he published Stephen Barney's *Minutes of the Proceedings of the Court-Martial* and added *The Appendix* which contained the result of interviews with six loyalists who had returned with Bligh: Fryer, Hayward, Peckover, Purcell, Smith, and Lebogue, and four loyalists (Coleman, McIntosh, Byrne, and Heywood) and a mutineer (Muspratt) who had survived the wreck of the *Pandora*.

This *Appendix* caused quite a sensation and Bligh's reputation never recovered from the effects of its publication. Bligh followed with *An Answer to Certain Assertions Contained in the Appendix to a Pamphlet* which was weakly argued and based primarily on objections to Edward's method of gathering and presenting his material (Edward had not said which informant had said what; if he had not granted them anonymity, they would not have spoken up). Edward Christian countered with a *Short Reply to Capt. William Bligh's Answer* which even Bligh's apologists admit is brilliantly argued.

Edward died in 1823. No papers or correspondence have been preserved that contain his reaction to the news concerning Fletcher's fate after the mutiny.

CHRISTIAN, Fletcher   Fletcher Christian came from old gentry, a landed family with estates both on the Isle of Man and in Cumberland on the west coast of England. He was born to Charles and Ann (née Dixon) Christian on September 25, 1764, at Moorland Close near Cockermouth in Cumberland on the north-west coast of England. (The house of his birth still stands and was occupied as late as 1974.) He was the seventh of ten children, four of whom died before reaching adulthood.

When Fletcher was only three and a half years old, his father died. Ann Christian was a dedicated mother and, despite financial difficulties, saw to it that all her children got an excellent education. In 1780, having lost the family home in Cumbria, Ann took her daughter and her two youngest sons, Fletcher and Humphrey, and moved to Douglas on the Isle of Man. Fletcher may well have been proud of his Manx background, because in that year a popular ballad was published extolling the bravery of his great-great-grandfather, Illiam Dhone, who had led a mutiny against English rule over the island and had been executed in 1663.

Christian went to sea at the age of eighteen. By an interesting coincidence, his first ship was HMS *Cambridge* on which Bligh was sixth lieutenant at the time. Since Christian was enrolled as just a ship's boy, it is unlikely that the two had much contact.

The *Cambridge* took part in the successful relief expedition to Gibraltar in the end of 1782, commanded by Lord Howe. On the return of the ship, Christian was discharged.

It is probable that Christian at this time had a romantic interest in Isabella Curwen, a rich heiress who was also very beautiful, and that this is the reason why he later called Mauatua, his Tahitian consort, Isabella. The heiress, however, married one of Fletcher's distant cousins, John Christian, in October 1782.

On April 25, 1783, Fletcher signed on as midshipman on board HMS *Eurydice*, commanded by Captain George Courtney. For almost six months the ship lay at anchor in Spithead. Finally, on October 11, it sailed for India. In Madras, on May 24, 1784, Christian was made acting lieutenant after only one year's service. This fact is important, since so much has been made of Bligh's supposed benevolence in promoting him to acting lieutenant early in the voyage of the *Bounty*. It was Christian's competence, rather than his commander's kindness, that was the reason for the promotion. And Bligh needed a lieutenant.

Christian's idea of what it takes to be a good commander was rather different from Bligh's. His brother Edward quotes him as having said: "It was very easy to make one's self beloved and respected aboard a ship; one had only to be always ready to obey one's superior officers, and to be kind to the common men, unless there was occasion for severity, and if you are, when there is a just occasion, they will not like you the worse for it."

By June, 1785, the *Eurydice* was back home and Christian was paid off. He now had to start looking around for peace-time employment. His family was on friendly terms with the Bethams, the family of Elizabeth Bligh, and this is probably why Christian applied for a berth on the merchant ship *Britannia*, owned by Elizabeth's uncle Duncan Campbell and commanded by William Bligh. For the same reason, Bligh may have felt an obligation to accept Christian on board. They were to sail together on two voyages to the West Indies. On the first, Christian entered as an ordinary seaman, although he messed with the officers; on the second, Bligh made him second mate.

However, the contention — found in many publications on the *Bounty* story — that Bligh taught Christian the elements of navigation on these voyages, simply does not make sense. If Christian had not known the "elements" of navigation, he would not have been promoted to acting lieutenant on the *Eurydice*. This does not preclude the likelihood that Bligh, one of the master navigators of all time, helped Christian hone and perfect his skills.

Their relationship must have been friendly, otherwise Bligh would not have accepted Christian as master's mate on the *Bounty*, nor would he, being of a vindictive nature, have promoted him to acting lieutenant early in the voyage, competence or no.

There is no preserved portrait of Fletcher Christian, nor of his brothers and sisters, and it is doubtful that we can get a balanced impression of his appearance from the description Bligh wrote down for various port authorities after the mutiny:

> [FLETCHER CHRISTIAN] Master's mate, aged 24 years, 5 feet 9 inches high, blackish, or very dark complexion, dark brown hair, strong made; a star tatowed on his left breast, tatowed on his backside; his knees stand a little out, and he may be called rather bow legged. He is subject to violent perspirations, and particularly in his hands, so that he soils any thing he handles.

All others who knew Christian agreed that he was handsome and of an athletic build. He seems to have been an honest and forthright man, normally with a happy and friendly disposition, and very charming. He seems to have been liked by everyone on board the *Bounty* with the possible exception of Hayward and Hallett (whom nobody liked).

It is remarkable that none of the men, loyalists or mutineers, who went through so much suffering as a result of the mutiny, ever had one negative word to say about Christian. All of them saw their misfortunes as having been brought about by Bligh. Following are some of the statements that former *Bounty* crew members, all but one of them (Muspratt) loyalists, later made to Edward Christian after the court-martial of the mutineers:

> "He was a gentleman; a brave man; and every officer and seaman on board the ship would have gone through fire and water to have served him." — "I would still wade up to the arm-pits in blood to serve him." — "As much as I have lost and suffered by him, if he could be restored to his country, I should be the first to go without wages in search of him." — "Every body under his command did their duty at a look from Mr. Christian." — "Mr. Christian was always good-natured, I never heard him say 'Damn you,' to any man on board the ship."

In other words, Christian was a gentleman in the best sense of the word. How could any man wish for a better epitaph!

In Part I of this book I have commented on Christian's personality and his mental state during the mutiny (see especially the commentaries for June 1788 and April 1789). The only existing biography of Fletcher Christian is written by his descendant Glynn Christian: *Fragile Paradise: Fletcher Christian of H.M.S. Bounty* (1982). I have drawn upon it many times in writing this book and I recommend it highly to my readers.

The adventures of the world's most famous mutineer, from the time he sailed from England on the *Bounty* to his death on Pitcairn, are told in Part I of this book. He had three children with Mauatua: Thursday October, Charles, and Mary Anne (born after his death). His descendants live today on Pitcairn and on Norfolk Island and in many other places in the Pacific and the rest of the world. Since both of his sons were married to fullblooded Tahitian women (Thursday October to Teraura and Charles to Sully), the Tahitian genetic heritage is more noticeable in Fletcher's descendants today than in those of the other mutineers.

Christian's close friend Peter Heywood once told Sir John Barrow that he had seen — sometime in 1808 or 1809 — a person who looked exactly like Fletcher Christian on Fore Street in Plymouth Dock, but that the man had run away when he saw Heywood approaching. This claim, mentioned by Sir John in his book on the mutiny (1831) has led to wild speculations which will probably never cease. In my opinion it is quite unlikely that Christian left Pitcairn. There are three reasons for this: *(1)* If Christian's identity had been known on board a ship, it could not have been kept secret. *(2)* If Christian had managed to board a ship incognito, everyone on Pitcairn would still have known about it. Knowing the Tahitian fondness for gossiping and telling secrets, it is inconceivable that none of the Tahitian women on the island would have mentioned it eventually, especially since telling the absolute truth became a fetish on the island in the early 1800s. Adams never even hinted at such a possibility, and Teehuteatuaonoa, who had no reason to lie, stated definitely that Christian had been killed by a Polynesian. *(3)* It is improbable that Christian could have lived out his life incognito in England without giving rise to a family tradition about it.

"Sightings" of dead and missing persons are extremely common. Hitler, for example, was simultaneously "seen" in hundreds of locations after World War II. I once clearly "saw" a close friend who had just died. If I had not had the opportunity to go up and examine "him" closely and convince myself that it was merely someone who looked very much like him, it would forever have left me with an eerie feeling.

Christian's fate was tragic. Had it not been for that one moment of mental aberration, he would undoubtedly have gone on to a distinguished career in the Navy. But then again, he would hardly have achieved the immortality of which he is now assured. His name has become a symbol of adventure, of revolt against pettiness, and of the romance of the sea. For that we will always be grateful.

CHRISTIAN, Mary Ann   Fletcher Christian's daughter. Mauatua was pregnant with Mary Ann when Fletcher was killed on September 20, 1793. The child was born soon afterwards (Glynn Christian says she was born on the day of the massacre).

Mary Ann was in her youth known as the "Fair Maid of the South Seas," but she died a crabby old spinster (as Glynn Christian puts it) on January 2, 1866. She was the inspiration for Mary Russell Mitford's poem "Christina, The Maid of the South Seas" which was published in 1811.

CHRISTIAN, Parkin   A direct descendant of Fletcher Christian. In 1933, Parkin Christian brought up the rudder of the *Bounty* from six fathoms of water.

CHRISTIAN, Thursday October   Thursday October was Fletcher Christian's and Mauatua's first son and the first child to be born on Pitcairn (in October 1790). He was three years old when his father was murdered. At sixteen he married Teraura who was past 30 then, had been Edward Young's original consort, and had borne Matthew Quintal a son. With Teraura Thursday October had three sons: Charles, Joseph, and Thursday October II, and three daughters: Mary, Polly, and Peggy.

When the disastrous attempt to migrate to Tahiti took place in 1831, Thursday October was the first of the Pitcairners to succumb to the diseases on the island to which he and the others had no immunity. He died on Tahiti April 21, 1831.

Lieutenant Shillibeer of HMS *Briton* made a sketch of Thursday October in 1814, the only likeness of him known to exist. Shillibeer wrote under it "Friday October Fletcher Christian." This has been explained in the *Bounty* literature as stemming from Bligh's forgetting to correct for gaining a day when sailing eastward. If that were true, Thursday October's real name should have been "Wednesday October." It is more probable that the *Briton* had corrected for losing a day when sailing westward (the International Date Line was not officially established until 1883).

In any case, Thursday October soon went back to his given name and also gave it to his third son who was born in 1820 (although we do not know whether it was on a Thursday in October). His house still stands on Pitcairn and many of the Pitcairners today are his descendants. (The descendants of his brother Charles live on Norfolk Island.)

CHRISTIAN, Tom   Tom Christian, M.B.E., has for many years been the radio operator on Pitcairn Island; he is also a ham operator (VR6TC). He is the son of Fred and Flora Christian and is married to Betty Christian. Tom is an honorary member of the Adventurers' Club of Los Angeles.

CHRONOMETER   The *Admiralty Manual of Navigation* describes a chronometer as "simply an enlarged watch . . . and its mechanism is by no means complicated, although its construction demands the most accurate workmanship, and its adjustment requires a high degree of skill."

The chronometer shows Greenwich Mean Time. Local Mean Time is obtained through astronomical observation, for example of the height of the sun. The difference between Greenwich and local time is the longitude in time which can easily be changed into an arc with degrees, minutes, and seconds.

The first chronometers accurate enough to be used for navigation were constructed by John Harrison, a Yorkshire carpenter, between 1729 and 1760. Harrison's chronometers were copied by a London watchmaker, Larcum Kendall, and the *Bounty* carried a Kendall chronometer on her voyage.

It was the fact that Lieutenant Carteret's chronometer was inaccurate when he discovered Pitcairn which accounted for the island's position being indicated as almost 200 miles westward of its true position.

Today a marine chronometer can be made so accurate that it will not gain or lose more than a second per month. Ironically, chronometers are no longer needed, since radio time signals have taken over their function.

For the fate of the *Bounty*'s chronometer, see the entry FOLGER, MAYHEW.

CHURCHILL, Charles Master-at-Arms (Ship's Corporal) on the *Bounty*; mutineer; stayed on Tahiti and was killed there by fellow mutineer Thompson.

Churchill was born in Manchester and was twenty-eight years old when the *Bounty* left England. Bligh, after the mutiny, described his physical appearance as follows:

> [CHARLES CHURCHILL] Ship's Corporal, 30 years, 5 feet 10 inches high. Fair complexion, short light-brown hair. Bald headed, strong made. The forefinger on his left hand crooked, and the hand shows the mark of a severe scald. Tattooed in several parts of the body.

Churchill's attempt to desert the ship at Tahiti, together with Millward and Muspratt, was described in the January 1789 commentary in Part I. In view of the fact that he later took a highly active and decisive part in the mutiny, it is possible that he had toyed with the idea before Christian approached him with it.

During the mutiny Churchill was one of the first to join Christian and one of the men who went below with him to arrest Bligh. All through the morning he assumed the role of Christian's second-in-command, often answering for Christian when the latter seemed to hesitate.

Churchill was a coarse and brutal person with a real proclivity for violence. During the second stay in Tahiti he was eager to participate in the warfare between the districts and, with his training as a Royal Marine and with the muskets procured from the *Bounty*, he was instrumental in changing the relatively non-lethal nature of the conflicts between the chiefdoms into bloody carnage. Like his friend Thompson, he once killed an innocent Tahitian in cold blood.

A possible reason for Churchill's staying on Tahiti rather than sailing away with Christian was that he had a very powerful *taio*, Vehiatua, who was Teina's (Mate's) brother-in-law and chief of Taiarapu. Vehiatua may have made promises to Churchill that were difficult to turn down. As we have seen (in the commentaries for February and March 1790) he became chief of Taiarapu when Vehiatua died without a male heir, but was killed by his crony Thompson soon afterwards.

"CLOTH PLANT"   See MULBERRY TREE.

COCKPIT   In the old sailing navies the cockpit was a space below the waterline near the after hatchway and below the lower gundeck. This space was usually allotted to senior midshipmen for their messes. In times of action, it became the operating theater for the surgeon. (Nelson was carried to the cockpit of the *Victory* after he had been mortally wounded at the Battle of Trafalgar.)

In the *Bounty*, the cockpit was occupied by cabins for the steward, the surgeon, the clerk, the botanist, and the gunner. In addition, there were three store rooms.

COCONUT PALM (tumu ha'ari, niu, *Cocos nucifera*)   The coconut palm is the Polynesian's best friend. Every single part of it can be used. The nut itself contains deliciously flavored water. Coconut "milk" is produced by grating and squeezing the white meat inside the nut. The husk of the nut can be braided into sennit cord, provides the material for mats, brooms, and brushes, and makes good fuel. The smoke of the husks keeps mosquitoes away. A healthy coconut palm will produce about fifty nuts per year for over sixty years.

The oil pressed from the meat is used not only for nourishment but as scented hair and body oil (*monoi*). The oil pressed from dried coconut meat (copra) is shipped all over the world and is used in making high-quality soap.

The leaves or fronds make wonderful decorations. They are woven into durable baskets, fans, and hats, and are used for thatching roofs.

The trunk of the coconut palm provides building material, the bark and the roots are said to have medicinal properties. Most amazingly, Teuira Henry claims in *Ancient Tahiti* (1928) that the coconut shells were used as surgical prostheses:

> In former times the fractured human skull was mended with coconut shell in the *nia* stage, when it was of the same thickness as the skull, by carefully removing the splinters of bone, smoothing the edge of the broken part, nicely fitting in the shell, and then closing it over with the skin of the scalp. The bone of the skull gradually knitted itself round the shell, which lasted through the remainder of a man's lifetime and did not inconvenience him. Skulls thus mended have been seen and the settings found satisfactory by scientists of note.

The Tahitian word for coconut is *ha'ari* and for palm frond *ni'au*. A house thatched with palm fronds is *fare ni'au*.

COLE, William Boatswain on the *Bounty*; loyalist; was on the open-boat voyage from Tofua to Timor; arrived safely in England.

Bligh had been furious with Cole in Tahiti when it was discovered that a set of new sails had been allowed to mildew and rot. On January 17, 1789, he wrote in his log:

> This morning, the sail room being cleared to take the sails on shore to air. The new fore topsail and fore sail, main topmt stay sail and main stay sail were found very much mildewed and rotten in many places. If I had any officers to supercede the Master John Fryer and Boatswain William Cole, or was capable of doing without them, considering them as common sea men, they should no longer occupy their respective stations.

As we have pointed out in the January 1789 commentary in Part I, Bligh was the one who had been in Tahiti before and who should have known what the island's humidity can do to canvas.

Cole was one of the men on board in whom Christian had confided his plan to leave the ship on a raft shortly before the mutiny. He did not mention it when he came back to England, simply because it was dangerous to have even discussed desertion.

Cole certainly understood Christian well. During the mutiny he and Purcell urged Christian to stop what he was doing, and when Christian reminded them of how ill he had been treated by Bligh, Cole said: "I know it very well, Mr. Christian. We *all* know it, but drop it for God's sake!"

It was Cole who demanded that the loyalists be given the *Bounty's* launch rather than one of the two other boats which were not seaworthy. It was also he who demanded and — when Quintal refused — insisted, that they be given a compass.

At the subsequent court-martial, Cole confirmed Heywood's innocence, although in vain. He also spoke up for Morrison, also in vain. However, his testimony may have contributed to the pardon Heywood and Morrison were granted after being found guilty.

Cole's later activities are not known to me.

COLEMAN, Joseph Armorer on the *Bounty*; loyalist; kept aboard against his will; survived the wreck of the *Pandora*; was acquitted at the court-martial.

Coleman was born in Guildford and was thirty-six years old when he mustered on the *Bounty*. He was married and had children. Bligh's description of Coleman is as follows:

> [JOSEPH COLEMAN] Armourer, 40 years, 5 feet 6 inches high. Fair

complexion, grey hair, strong made, a heart tattooed on one arm. (Bligh adds to this description, "This man declared to me publickly when I was in the Boat that he knew nothing of the transaction and begged of me to remember he told me of it and that he was kept against his consent.")

The armorer on board a ship was an extremely important member of the crew. Not only did he keep the arms in repair, but he served as a highly skilled blacksmith who often had to manufacture gear that had been damaged or lost.

On Tahiti, Coleman was one of the busiest men on shore. He had to serve all the needs of the *Bounty*, but he also — as a gesture of goodwill towards the Tahitians — had to repair and sharpen the iron tools that they had received from previous visitors.

Christian, even though he was obviously in extreme emotional turmoil during the mutiny, probably experiencing a brief psychotic episode (see the April 1789 commentary in Part I), was not so out of touch with reality that he did not realize Coleman's importance for the ship and he therefore forbade him to go in the launch.

When Christian arranged his "farewell party" on Tahiti in order to kidnap enough women for the mutineers (see the September 1789 commentary in Part I), he had also planned to kidnap Coleman. However, he could not get Coleman drunk enough, and when the ship started moving, the armorer immediately became suspicious, jumped overboard, and swam ashore. It was a disappointment for Christian but not a disaster: John Williams, one of the mutineers who had cast their lot with Christian, was something of a blacksmith himself and had assisted Coleman on board the *Bounty*.

Coleman helped Morrison build the *Resolution*. When the *Pandora* arrived, he was the first one to go on board, happy in the knowledge that Captain Bligh had promised to do him justice. He was also the first one to be put in irons. However, when the *Pandora* was about to founder, he — together with Norman and McIntosh (who had also been promised "mercy" by Bligh) — was released from his shackles to help in manning the pumps.

Since there was no evidence against Coleman, and Bligh had stated that he had been detained in the *Bounty* against his will, he had no difficulty in getting acquitted at the court-martial. His later activities are unknown to me.

HMS *COMET* British sloop-of-war commanded by Captain Alexander A. Sandilands. The *Comet* escorted the transport barque *Lucy Ann* which moved the population of Pitcairn to Tahiti in 1831.

CON A verb meaning to direct the steering of a ship, to give the necessary orders to the helmsman. At the time when the mutiny broke out on the *Bounty*, gunner's mate John Mills was conning the ship with able seaman Thomas Ellison at the helm.

COOK, James (in Tahiti called Tute)   The most significant of the explorers of the Pacific; lived 1728 to 1779; made three voyages to the South Seas.

COOK'S VOYAGES
TO THE SOUTH SEAS

VOYAGE I
IN THE *ENDEAVOUR*
(1768–1771)

Participants of interest:

Joseph Banks, F.R.S.
BOTANIST

William Peckover
LATER GUNNER IN THE *BOUNTY*

Charles Clerke
MASTER'S MATE

John Gore
AMERICAN, HAD SAILED WITH WALLIS
IN THE *DOLPHIN*

Charles Green
ASTRONOMER

Sydney Parkinson
DRAFTSMAN, ARTIST

Daniel Solander
BOTANIST, FROM SWEDEN

Herman Spöring
SECRETARY, FROM ÅBO, FINLAND

VOYAGE II
IN THE *RESOLUTION*
AND THE *ADVENTURE*
(1772–1775)

Participants of interest:

Mai ("Omai")
FROM HUAHINE, VISITED ENGLAND

William Peckover
LATER GUNNER IN THE *BOUNTY*

Tobias Furneaux
COMMANDER OF THE *ADVENTURE*

James Burney
LIEUTENANT IN THE *ADVENTURE*

Charles Clerke
LIEUTENANT IN THE *RESOLUTION*

Johann Reinhold Forster
BOTANIST AND PASTOR

George Forster
BOTANIST

William Hodges
ARTIST

Anders Sparrman
BOTANIST, FROM SWEDEN

George Vancouver
SEAMAN

VOYAGE III
IN THE *RESOLUTION*
AND THE *DISCOVERY*
(1776–1780)

Participants of interest:

Mai ("Omai")
FROM HUAHINE,
RETURNED FROM ENGLAND

William Bligh
SAILING MASTER
OF THE *RESOLUTION*

David Nelson
BOTANIST

William Peckover
SAILED IN THE *DISCOVERY*

Nathaniel Portlock
LATER COMMANDER
OF THE *ASSISTANT*

James Burney
LATER EDITED BLIGH'S NARRATIVE
OF THE MUTINY

Charles Clerke
COMMANDER OF THE *DISCOVERY*

William Bayly
ASTRONOMER ABOARD THE *DISCOVERY*

Thomas Edgar
SAILING MASTER OF THE *DISCOVERY*

William Ellis
SURGEON IN THE *RESOLUTION*

John Gore
LIEUTENANT IN THE *RESOLUTION*
(Commander of the *Discovery* after Cook's death)

James King
LIEUTENANT IN THE *RESOLUTION*

John Rickman
LIEUTENANT IN THE *DISCOVERY*

Edward Riou
MIDSHIPMAN IN THE *DISCOVERY*

David Samwell
SURGEON'S MATE IN THE *RESOLUTION*

George Vancouver
MIDSHIPMAN IN THE *DISCOVERY*

John Watts
MIDSHIPMAN IN THE *RESOLUTION*
(Later lieutenant in the *Lady Penrhyn*)

John Webber
ARTIST

John Williamson
LIEUTENANT IN THE *RESOLUTION*

There are numerous biographies of Cook, so this entry will cover only a few facts which connect him and his voyages with the story of the *Bounty*.

Cook's botanists on the first voyage were Joseph Banks and Daniel Solander, the latter from Sweden. Both became important figures in the background history of the *Bounty* expedition because of their enthusiastic endorsement of the value of the breadfruit.

The fact that Cook on his second voyage brought Mai (in the literature consistently and erroneously referred to as "Omai") back with him to England created a widespread interest in — and often longing for — Tahiti and contributed to the fact that the *Bounty*'s crew consisted of volunteers only. The *Bounty* seems to have been the first ship in the Royal Navy to sail without any pressed men on board.

Cook was very popular with his men, partly because of his personality and partly because he realized that there was something about fresh food and lime juice that prevented scurvy, the dreaded disease that had killed so many sailors on long voyages in the past. The seamen sometimes complained about what he made them eat and drink, but in the end they were appreciative, as can be seen from this poem written by Thomas Perry, an able-bodied seaman who sailed with Cook on the second voyage:

> We were all hearty seamen, no cold did we fear
> And we have from all sickness entirely kept clear
> Thanks be to the Captain, he has proved so good
> Amongst all the islands to give us fresh food.
>
> And when to old England, my Brave Boys, we arrive
> We will tip off a Bottle to make us alive ...

Bligh was Cook's sailing master on the third voyage. Other *Bounty* men present were David Nelson, the botanist, who sailed in the *Discovery* and William Peckover, gunner on the *Bounty*, also in the *Discovery* (he sailed with Cook on all three voyages). Nathaniel Portlock, who would later command the *Assistant* on the second breadfruit expedition, served as master's mate, first in the *Discovery* and after Cook's death, in the *Resolution*.

On February 14, 1779, when Captain Cook was killed by the Hawaiians on the shore of Kealakekua Bay on the Big Island of Hawaii, Bligh was at the opposite side of the bay. The officer in command of the marines, Lieutenant John Williamson, was in a boat close to the shore; he lost his nerve at the critical moment and withdrew when he should have landed and attacked. It is entirely possible that Cook's life would have been saved if Bligh had been in command of the boat, because, whatever his faults, he always showed great courage and determination and never flinched from what he saw as his duty.*

As it happened, however, Bligh may have been partly responsible for Cook's death. Alexander McKee, in *H.M.S. Bounty* (1962), has described not only what occurred but also Bligh's typical reaction to it:

> When Cook went ashore in Hawaii to remonstrate with the chiefs about thefts by the natives, two boats were left in the bay to prevent canoes escaping; one commanded by Lieutenant Rickman, the other by Bligh. A chief tried to get away in a canoe, both boats fired, and the chief was killed. When the news reached the natives on the beach, they attacked and killed Cook. This sequence of events was testified to, independently, by Captain Clerke, Cook's second-in-command, Lieutenants King and Burney, Mr. Edgar, the master of the *Discovery*, and William Bayley, an astronomer aboard the *Discovery*. Bligh was one of the two culprits, and his account was a masterpiece of evasion: "Lieut. Rickman did fire, and it was said killed a man; but the attack (on Cook) was over and past before that was known." The blame for firing Bligh put on Rickman; the chief he described as a "man"; his death he tried to pass off as rumour; and he altered the time of firing to after the death of Cook instead of before, so that no blame could possibly be attached to himself.

Cook was probably the only man whom Bligh ever admired. Bligh always tried to imitate Cook, and the two men did have several traits in common: both were superb seamen, navigators, cartographers, surveyors; both had a desire for exploration and a strong sense of duty; both were resourceful and courageous and steadfast in emergencies. Bligh never realized, however, that he lacked some of the essential qualities which made Cook great: magnanimity, reasonableness, a keen sense of proportion, humor, forthrightness, an understanding of other people, and charisma.

In my opinion, the best epitaph for Cook was written by the surgeon's mate in the *Resolution* on the third voyage, David Samwell, in *A Narrative of the Death of Captain James Cook* (1786):

> Nature had endowed him with a mind vigorous and comprehensive, which in his riper years he had cultivated with care and industry. His general knowledge was extensive and various; in that of his own profession he was unequalled. With a clear judgment, strong masculine sense, and the most determined resolution; with a genius peculiarly turned for enterprise, he pursued his object with unshaken perseverance — vigilant and active in an eminent degree; cool

---

* In the Battle of Camperdown on October 11, 1797, Williamson, while commanding HMS *Agincourt*, was accused of cowardly behavior and was shortly afterwards dismissed from the service. Lord Nelson's opinion was that he should have been hanged.

and intrepid among dangers; patient and firm under difficulties and distress; fertile in expedients; great and original in all his designs; active and resolved in carrying them into execution. In every situation he stood unrivalled and alone; on him all eyes were turned; he was our leading-star, which at its setting left us involved in darkness and despair.

His constitution was strong, his mode of living temperate. He had no repugnance to good living, however. He always kept a good table, though he could bear the reverse without murmuring. He was a modest man and rather bashful; of an agreeable lively conversation, sensible and intelligent. In his temper he was somewhat hasty, but of a disposition the most friendly, benevolent and humane. His person was above six feet high, and though a good-looking man he was plain both in address and appearance. His head was small, his hair, which was a dark brown, he wore tied behind. His face was full of expression, his nose exceedingly well-shaped, his eyes, which were small and of a brown cast, were quick and piercing; his eyebrows prominent, which gave his countenance altogether an air of austerity.

He was beloved by his people, who looked up to him as to a father and obeyed his commands with alacrity. The confidence we placed in him was unremitting, our admiration of his great talents unbounded, our esteem for his good qualities affectionate and sincere.

COOK ISLANDS On September 23, 1773, on his second voyage to the South Seas, Captain James Cook sighted the small island Manuae and named it Hervey's Island after Captain Hervey, one of the Lords of the Admiralty and the Earl of Bristol. He was unable to find a suitable anchorage and sailed on.

Later in the second voyage, on his way westward from Tahiti, Cook discovered an uninhabited atoll, now part of the Cook Islands, which he named Palmerston.

On his third voyage, in March and April 1777, Cook discovered Mangaia and Atiu. Today these four islands, and eleven more, are part of Cook Islands. Those in the southern group (sometimes referred to as Hervey Islands) are: Rarotonga, Takutea, Mitiaro, Mauke, Atiu, Aitutaki, Mangaia, Manuae (Hervey), and Palmerston (Avarau). Those in the northern group (sometimes referred to as Manihiki Islands) are: Tongareva (Penrhyn), Nassau, Pukapuka (Danger Island), Manihiki, Rakahanga, and Suwarrow.

The largest and most important of the islands, Rarotonga, was discovered by Fletcher Christian, probably in October, 1789. Aitutaki had been discovered by Bligh on April 11, 1789.

The Cook Islands lie between the Societies (Tahiti) in the east and Samoa and Tonga in the west. They cover a vast area of ocean, stretching from 157⁰42'W. to 165⁰51'W. and from 8⁰59'S. to 21⁰56'S. Within these 850,000 square miles, the total land area of the islands is only 93 square miles, and the population barely 20,000, half of whom live on the main island, Rarotonga.

The islands were populated by Polynesians from the east between 600 and 800 A.D. They form the vast majority of the population today and are in charge of their own affairs, the Cook Islands being a self-governing nation in free association with New Zealand.

CORNER, Robert   Second Lieutenant on the *Pandora*. He was a courageous, humane, and efficient officer who is often praised in surgeon Hamilton's account of the voyage. He died in 1820.

Corner was in charge of all landings on the islands where the mutineers, or traces of them, were sought. Being third in command, there was not much Lieutenant Corner could do for the prisoners, but he did what he could. Morrison writes:

> . . . when the roughness of the weather gave the ship any motion, we were not able to keep ourselves fast, to remedy which we were threatened to be stapled down by the Captain, but Mr. Cornor [sic] gave us some short boards to check ourselves with, which he made the carpenters secure, and thereby prevented us from maiming each other and ourselves.

For Lieutenant Corner's important remarks on how the *Bounty* men were treated when the *Pandora* foundered, see the August 1791 commentary in Part I.

COUPANG (Kupang, Koepang)   Former Dutch settlement (founded in 1618) on Timor, located on the south-west coast of the island at $10^0 12$'S., $124^0 41$'E.; now part of Indonesia.

Bligh and the loyalists reached Coupang on Sunday, June 14, 1789, after having spent forty-one days in the *Bounty's* launch, traveling 3618 nautical miles according to their makeshift log (probably closer to 3800 miles). They were well taken care of by Mynheer Timotheus Wanjon, the son-in-law of Governor van Este who was fatally ill.

The *Bounty* men spent over two months in Coupang trying to regain their strength. It was not a good place to recuperate, however, because of rampant tropical fevers. On July 20 David Nelson, the botanist, died, probably from malaria. One month later Bligh and his men sailed for Batavia in the schooner which he had bought in Coupang and named HMS *Resource*.

Two years later, on September 15, 1791, the inhabitants of Coupang were again treated to the spectacle of ghost-like British seamen, hardly able to walk, dragging themselves up from the harbor. This time it was Captain Edwards and his crew from the *Pandora* and the captured men from the *Bounty* that taxed the hospitality of the Dutch. Governor van Este had died and Wanjon was the new governor. He treated the new contingent as kindly as he had Bligh and his men. On October 6 the *Pandora* survivors sailed for Batavia in the Dutch East Indiaman *Rembang*.

ENCYCLOPEDIA

Only one year later, on October 2, 1792, Bligh visited Coupang on his second breadfruit expedition in the *Providence* accompanied by the *Assistant.*

Today Kupang (modern spelling) has 125,000 inhabitants and is the capital of Timor.

COURTNEY, George   Captain of HMS *EURYDICE.*

COUVRET, Peter   Captain of the *VLYDTE.*

COX, John Henry   Captain of the *MERCURY.*

HMS *CRESCENT*   The 36-gun ship on which Bligh learned most of his seamanship. As a midshipman he served almost three years on the *Crescent* (from September 22, 1771, to August 23, 1774).

CUT AND RUN   To cut or slip the anchor cable and run before the wind; hence also: to leave in a hurry. This is what Fletcher Christian did in the night between September 22 and September 23, 1789, when he kidnapped Tahitian women and set sail in quest of an ultimate refuge.

CUTLASS   The British Navy cutlass was a slightly curved, heavy sword, only three feet long and with a black basket hilt.

CYRUS   A British whaler from London commanded by Captain John Hall. The *Cyrus* called at Pitcairn on December 10, 1823; two of its crew, John Buffett and John Evans, became Pitcairn's first immigrants since the arrival of the *Bounty* almost thirty-four years earlier.

HMS *DAEDALUS*   The *Daedalus,* commanded by Lieutenant James Hanson, was sent to Tahiti by Vancouver in order to pick up the shipwrecked men of the *Matilda* about whom he had heard from Captain Weatherhead in Alaska in October 1792. As mentioned in the July 1792 commentary in Part I, however, Bligh took with him most of the men when he left in the *Providence.*

When the *Daedalus* arrived in Tahiti on February 15, 1793, she found her mission already accomplished (the *Matilda* men who had remained on the island did not want to leave) and sailed on after a stay of only two weeks. One member of her crew, however, a Swedish-Finnish seaman from Helsingfors (Helsinki) by the name of Petter Hägersten, jumped ship and became the first white visitor in the history of Tahiti to settle permanently on the island.

One might say that Hägersten made the dream of the *Bounty* mutineers into reality.

DANGEROUS ARCHIPELAGO See TUAMOTU. The name Danger Islands refers to Pukapuka, Motu Ko, and Motu Katava in the Northern Cooks.

DELANO, Amasa Delano was a friend of Captain Mayhew Folger whom he had met in the year 1800 at the island of Massafuero off the South American coast, each as the commander of his own ship. Even then they were interested in what had happened to the *Bounty* and to Christian and his men and had had long discussions on the topic.

When Folger returned to Boston after having discovered the last hiding place of the mutineers, he met Delano and told him the story in detail. Folger never published his discovery, but Delano — who never himself visited Pitcairn — did devote considerable space to the story in his book *A Narrative of Voyages and Travels* (1817).

Delano was in a unique position to appreciate the story of the *Bounty*. He had been in Coupang on Timor from February to March 1792, only a few months after the *Pandora*'s crew and the men of the *Bounty* who were their prisoners had sailed for Batavia (in October 1791). Later, from 1803 to 1805, the gunner on Delano's ship was Charles Spence who had been a member of the crew of the *Pandora*.

DILLON, Peter Captain Peter Dillon, born on Martinique in 1788 of Irish heritage, was a colorful navigator-adventurer-trader who only recently became significant in the history of the *Bounty*. In 1957 Professor Henry E. Maude of the Australian National University found an interview with Teehuteatuaonoa (the mutineer Isaac Martin's consort who had left Pitcairn in 1817), given to Reverend Henry Nott in the presence of Captain Peter Dillon. It was Dillon who recorded it and had it published in the *Bengal Hurkaru* on October 2, 1826. It was later reproduced in the *United Service Journal* (1829).

It is primarily thanks to this recorded interview that we are able to reconstruct the events from Christian's last departure from Tahiti to the last years that Teehuteatuaonoa spent on Pitcairn. Her account must be considered more reliable than the accounts given by John Adams which are highly contradictory and tainted by his desire to paint himself in a favorable light.

Dillon's main claim to fame, however, is the fact that he solved the mystery of the disappearance of the La Pérouse expedition which had vanished without trace in 1788 (see the August 1791 commentary in Part I and the entry EDWARDS, EDWARD). In 1826 he found a French swordhilt (inscribed J. F. G. P. = Jean François Galaup de la Pérouse) in Tikopia in the Solomon Islands. It had been brought there from Vanikoro in the same group. Finding that the French showed little interest in helping him (they were sending out their own expedition under the command of Dumont d'Urville), Dillon persuaded the East India Company to place him in command of a search expedition, and in 1827 he found the remains of the *Boussole*, La Pérouse's ship; her consort, the *Astrolabe*, had sunk in deep water, according to the natives he interviewed.

In 1829 King Charles X of France conferred on Peter Dillon the Order of the Legion of Honor for his achievement in solving the mystery of the disappearance of the La Pérouse expedition. Peter Dillon died on February 9, 1847, almost exactly twenty years after he had solved one of the great riddles in maritime history.

HMS *DIRECTOR* Bligh's first important naval command. The *Director* was an old ship, rated 4th class, with 64 guns and 491 men. Bligh was in command of the *Director* for over five years (from January 4, 1796, to March 13, 1801), during the mutiny at the Nore as well as at the Battle of Camperdown when Admiral Duncan defeated the Dutch under Admiral de Winter.

DJAKARTA See BATAVIA.

DJAWA See JAVA.

DODD, Robert Robert Dodd (1748–1815) was a prominent British marine painter who often exhibited at the Royal Academy. He is famous for his paintings of naval engagements, including the Battle of Trafalgar.

Dodd's aquatint engraving "The Mutineers Turning Bligh and his Men Adrift in the *Bounty*'s Launch" has been used as an illustration for a multitude of publications on the *Bounty*. It was unveiled in October 1790 and now hangs in the British Museum.

DODDS, James Quartermaster on the *Pandora*, sailed with master's mate Oliver from Upolu in the Samoas to Rembang on Java in the schooner *Resolution*.

DOLPHIN BANK A reef off Point Venus on the northern coast of Tahiti, named after the ship *Dolphin* which carried the discoverer of Tahiti, Samuel Wallis, around the world.

Christian came close to running the *Bounty* aground on Dolphin Bank when he left for Tubuai on June 16, 1789. He lost an anchor in the process (which was later retrieved by the *Pandora*). It is interesting to speculate about what would have happened if the *Bounty* had foundered or been disabled. Less than two months later the brig *Mercury* arrived in Tahiti and if Christian had still been there, his whereabouts would soon have become known. Moreover, the delay involved in repairing the *Bounty* or in building a new ship could have enabled Captain Edwards to capture him.

"DOODOOEE" See TUTUI.

DRAM   A small drink of liquor.

DRIVER, William   The commander of the Salem whaler *Charles Doggett*. Captain Driver has gone down in history for two reasons: *(1)* He transported the sixty-five survivors of the disastrous 1831 migration from Pitcairn to Tahiti back to their home island. The ship was so small (110 tons) that Captain Driver slept on deck during the voyage (August 14 to September 4, 1831) in order to accommodate his passengers. *(2)* Captain Driver is said to have originated the term "Old Glory" for the American flag.

DUCIE ISLAND   Atoll 290 miles east of Pitcairn (24⁰40'S., 124⁰47'W.); uninhabited; discovered on March 16, 1791, by Captain Edward Edwards in the *Pandora* while searching for the mutineers. It was named after Baron Francis Ducie, a captain in the Royal Navy.

Christian and his fellow fugitives never knew how close they came to being discovered and returned to England for trial. If Edwards had continued his voyage on the same parallel he would have sighted Pitcairn and, since he made a point of investigating each island he passed, he would most probably have captured them. As it was, he turned northward and missed the island.

Ducie is about one and a half miles long, northeast to southwest, and about one mile wide. It is about twelve feet in height and the few trees there grow to about fourteen feet at the most. The lagoon is deep and noted for its poisonous fish and extremely dangerous sharks. The island is seldom visited.

DUFF   The 267-ton, three-masted, full-rigged ship which, under the command of Captain James Wilson, transported eighteen missionaries, some with wives and children, to Tahiti, arriving on Sunday March 5, 1797. A monument to the *Duff* can today be seen on Point Venus. See WILSON, JAMES.

HMS *DUKE*   The court-martial of the accused mutineers was held at Spithead in the great cabin of this ship from September 12 to September 18, 1792.

DUKE OF CLARENCE ISLAND   Captain Edwards' name for NUKUNONO.

DUKE OF YORK ISLAND   Commodore John Byron's name for ATAFU.

EAREE   See ARI'I.

EARTH OVEN   See HIMA'A.

EATOOA   See ATUA.

EBRIEL, Thomas Captain of the barque *MARIA*.

EDDIA, EDEA See ITIA.

THE EDGE On Pitcairn: the narrow plateau on top of the cliff 250 feet above Bounty Bay.

EDWARDS, Edward Captain of HMS *Pandora*. Edwards was one of the most ruthless commanders in the British Navy. Compared to him, Bligh was a prissy Sunday school teacher. As a direct result of his inhumanity, Edwards had been the object of a mutiny aboard HMS *Narcissus* in 1782 and he never forgot the experience, in fact he used it as an excuse for his continued inhumanity. His very harshness probably accounted for why he was appointed (August 10, 1790) to search for the mutineers of the *Bounty*.

Edwards sailed from Jack-in-the-Basket, Portsmouth, on November 7, 1790. On March 16, 1791, on his way to Tahiti, he discovered Ducie Island. If he had stayed on the same parallel, he would have sighted Pitcairn and probably captured Christian and the eight other mutineers who had sought refuge there. Instead he turned slightly northward and barely missed the island. The *Pandora* anchored in Matavai Bay on March 23 and Edwards went about capturing both the mutineers and the loyalists who had remained on Tahiti when Christian left with the *Bounty* one and a half years earlier. Not only did he put them all in irons, but he had his men build an 18 by 11 foot "cell" on deck which had minimal ventilation and in which the fourteen men of the *Bounty*'s crew were to remain chained in the tropical heat for four months while Edwards kept searching for the rest of the mutineers.

The *Pandora* sailed from Tahiti on May 8 in company of the *Resolution*, the small schooner which the loyalists had built and which Edwards had manned with nine men from his ship. He arrived at Palmerston Island on May 21, 1791, where he found some spars marked "Bounty" (they had drifted there from Tubuai). At Palmerston a sudden storm blew up and Edwards lost five of his men, including a midshipman, in the jolly-boat. They were never seen again.

On June 22, the *Resolution* became separated from the *Pandora*. Edwards looked for it for two days and then sailed on to Nomuka for another fruitless search for the mutineers.

Not only did Edwards miss out on capturing Christian and his fellow mutineers (if had succeeded, Pitcairn would probably have remained uninhabited to this day), but he missed an opportunity to become one of the heroes of maritime history. On August 13, 1791, the *Pandora* was sailing close to the island of Vanikoro in the Solomons and sighted smoke signals, but Edwards was interested only in mutineers and knew the signals would not have come from them, so he sailed on. We know today with virtual certainty that those were distress signals from the La Pérouse expedition which had not been heard from since it left Botany Bay in February 1788. The mystery of the missing expedition was not solved until thirty-six years later (see DILLON, PETER).

Edwards was not a skillful navigator, and the *Pandora* was wrecked on Australia's Great Barrier Reef on August 28 with the loss of thirty-one of her own crew and four from the *Bounty*. His cruelty is illustrated by the fact that, as the ship was sinking and the prisoners had managed to break their chains, he ordered them to be put back in irons. In the last moment one of his crew defied his orders and helped free the prisoners, but he did not have time to remove the irons from all.

In four boats Edwards and the rest of his crew with the remaining prisoners set out for Timor, much as Bligh had done two years earlier. On the way from there to Batavia they found the *Resolution* at Samarang. The survivors of the *Pandora* arrived at Spithead on June 19, 1792.

No competent commander loses thirty-five men when he has eleven hours to prepare for abandoning ship inside a reef. I can think of no other reason for Edwards getting away with this miserable performance during his obligatory court-martial than that the judges, too, were callous when it came to the question of saving human lives.

Having achieved the rank of Rear Admiral, Edwards died at the age of seventy-three in 1815. It is a pity that newspapers of the time did not conduct interviews, because before his death he may well have heard of the rediscovery of Pitcairn and the story of Christian and the other missing mutineers. If so, we will never know how he felt about finding out how close he had come to capturing them.

EHU   Tahitian word for fair, sandy, or reddish, especially as applied to hair.

EIMEO (Aimeo)   Ancient name for MOOREA.

HMS *ELEPHANT*   Admiral Nelson's flagship at the Battle of Copenhagen in 1801. It was on the quarterdeck of this ship that Nelson congratulated Bligh on his performance during the battle with the words: "Bligh, I sent for you to thank you. You have supported me nobly."

Harrison Fryer, the son of the old sailing master of the *Bounty* (who was now master in Sir Hyde Parker's flagship *London*), was a midshipman in the *Elephant* at this time.

ELIZABETH   English whaler commanded by Captain Henry King. King sighted Henderson Island in 1819 and named it after his ship, not knowing that Captain Henderson in the *Hercules* had discovered the island shortly before.

ELIZABETH ISLAND See HENDERSON ISLAND.

ELLIOTT, Russell Captain Elliott is important in the history of Pitcairn in that he helped establish an island government after the infamous dictatorial reign of the impostor Joshua Hill.

Elliott arrived at Pitcairn in November 1838 as commander of the British warship *Fly*. He formally declared the island to be under the protection of the British Crown on November 29, 1838.

A unique feature of the "regulations" drawn up by Elliott was that women were given the franchise. Pitcairn, then, was the first political entity in the world where women were guaranteed the right to vote. It was also the first to institute compulsory education.

ELLISON, Thomas Able-bodied seaman on the *Bounty*; mutineer; stayed on Tahiti; survived the wreck of the *Pandora*; found guilty at court-martial and hanged.

Ellison was born in Deptford and was only fifteen years old when he was entered on the rolls of the *Bounty*. Yet he had already sailed with Bligh on the *Britannia*. He was a protegé of Duncan Campbell, Mrs. Bligh's uncle, so it would have been difficult for the captain not to take him along.

Bligh's description of Ellison, written after the mutiny, reads as follows:

> [THOMAS ELLISON] 17 years, 5 feet 3 inches high. Fair complexion, dark hair, strong made. Has his name tattooed on his right arm, and dated "October 25, 1788".

In a letter to Campbell, written in the beginning of the voyage, Bligh stated: "Tom Ellison is a very good Boy and will do very well." He must often have regretted those words later.

Ellison was in Christian's watch and on the morning of the mutiny he was at the wheel. When the mutiny broke out, he was at first "Terrifyde," as he later testified during the court-martial, but — like several others among the crew — he soon became elated at the turn of events, in fact he lashed the wheel, took a bayonet and waved it in Bligh's face and shouted: "Damn him, I will be sentinel over him!"

Ellison remained on Tahiti when Christian sailed away and took part in the war against Teina's (Mate's) enemies. When the *Pandora* arrived, he gave himself up voluntarily together with Morrison and Norman. He survived the wreck of the *Pandora* and was in the same boat as Morrison on the voyage to Timor. He was treated as cruelly as Morrison being "pinnioned with a cord and lash'd down in the boat's bottom."

At the court-martial, Ellison tried to plead his youth at the time of the mutiny, but that did not impress the court: youth was no excuse for mutiny, there were thousands of young boys in the Navy. Ellison did have the satisfaction, however, of corroborating Burkett's testimony concerning Hayward and Hallett having begged to be allowed to stay on board the *Bounty*, and he added that they had "weep't bitterly" when they were ordered into the launch.

Together with Millward and Burkett, Ellison was hanged by slow strangulation on board HMS *Brunswick* on October 29, 1792.

ELPHINSTONE (Elphinston), William   Master's mate on the *Bounty*; loyalist; went with Bligh; died in Batavia. Elphinstone was born in Edinburgh and was thirty-six years old when he joined the *Bounty*.

Most authors who have written about the *Bounty* story have claimed that John Fryer, the sailing master on the *Bounty*, must have been hurt or offended when Fletcher Christian, a master's mate, was promoted to acting lieutenant by Captain Bligh. The falsehood of that argument was pointed out in Part I (the October 1788 commentary). Someone who did have cause to feel slighted was Elphinstone who was also a master's mate but thirteen years older than Christian and even three years older than Bligh. However, the likelihood is that he had no aspirations to become a lieutenant.

Elphinstone was asleep when the mutiny began and was put under guard, so he did not have much first-hand knowledge about what went on.

He seems to have been a supporter of Bligh at least until the open-boat voyage; there are indications that he started rebelling against Bligh's martinet style of authority by the time the loyalists reached Surabaya.

In Batavia Elphinstone died — probably of malaria — only a week after Bligh's departure.

EMEA (Eimeo)   See MOOREA.

ENDEAVOUR STRAIT (Torres Strait)   A dangerous passage, one hundred miles wide, between the Australian continent and New Guinea. Today it is named after Luis Váez de Torres who first sailed through it in 1606. It was called Endeavour Strait by Captain Cook who rediscovered it in 1770 on his first voyage (he did not know about Torres' voyage, because the British were unaware of the Spanish discovery).

The northernmost passage is called Bligh Channel; he discovered it on his second breadfruit expedition in 1792. The middle passage was discovered by Matthew Flinders in the *Investigator* in 1795. Flinders wrote of Endeavour Strait: "Perhaps no space of three and a half degrees in length presents more danger."

Today we can only imagine the courage it must have taken to navigate through these treacherous waters in a sailing ship. The last one to do so was Captain Korzeniowski, better known as Joseph Conrad, who in 1888 sailed the *Otago* through the Strait. In his article "Geography and Some Explorers" published in the year of his death, 1924, in the *National Geographic Magazine,* Conrad pays tribute to the explorers of old — and unwittingly to himself:

> What would the memory of my sea life have been for me if it had not included a passage through Torres Strait in its fullest extent . . . along the track of the early navigators?
>
> It was not without a certain emotion that I put her head at daybreak for Bligh Entrance and packed on her every bit of canvas I could carry. Windswept, sun lit, empty waters were all around me, half veiled by a brilliant haze. The first thing that caught my eye was a black speck — the wreck of a small vessel. . . . Thirty-six hours afterwards, of which about nine were spent at anchor, as I approached the other end of the Strait, I sighted a gaunt grey wreck . . . and thus I passed out of Torres Strait before the dusk settled upon its waters.
>
> The sea has been for me a hallowed ground, thanks to those books of travel and discovery which had peopled it for me with unforgettable shades of the masters in the calling which, in a humble way, was to be mine too. These were men great in their endeavour and in hard-won successes of militant geography; men who went forth, each according to his lights and with varied motives but each bearing in his breast a spark of the sacred fire.

ERREE See ARI'I.

ERREEOY See ARIOI.

ERREERAHIGH See ARI'I RAHI.

ETUATI The Tahitian name for Captain Edwards.

HMS *EURYDICE* On April 25, 1783, at the age of eighteen and a half, Fletcher Christian signed on board this ship as midshipman (see CHRISTIAN, FLETCHER).

The *Eurydice,* a sixth rater with 24 nine-pound guns, was a most interesting ship. Even though she was only two years old, she had been built to totally archaic specifications. She was 114 feet long with a beam of 32 feet and carried a complement of 140; in other words, she was considerably larger than the *Bounty.* Yet, she was the only ship in the Royal Navy which, in addition to being sailed, could be maneuvered by rowing! For this purpose she employed oars that were 113 feet long, approximately the length of the ship. I have not been able to ascertain how many pairs of oars she had or how many men were required to man them.

EVANS, John At the age of nineteen, John Evans arrived at Pitcairn on December 10, 1823, aboard the whaler *Cyrus* of London. When his friend and shipmate John

Buffett volunteered to stay on Pitcairn to help in the education of the children, Evans hid on the island until the *Cyrus* had left, thus becoming one of the two first immigrants since the arrival of the *Bounty* almost thirty-four years earlier.

On November 26, 1824, Evans married Rachel Adams, the daughter of John Adams and Vahineatua. She bore him three sons and three daughters.

Joshua Hill, the dictator on Pitcairn from 1832 to 1837 (see PITCAIRN ISLAND and HILL, JOSHUA), tried to persuade Rachel to leave her husband and to live with him instead, which infuriated both her and Evans. Later, when Evans requested a copy of Hill's "laws" for the island, the dictator flew into a rage and sentenced him to one dozen lashes.

Together with John Buffett, Evans left Pitcairn in March 1834 for Tahiti, returning three months later to pick up his family. For the time being they settled on Mangareva, 300 miles northwest of Pitcairn, together with George Nobbs and his family. After Nobbs had received a petition from the Pitcairners asking for his return, they all sailed for their home island on the American brig *Olivia*, arriving on October 13, 1834, against Hill's violent protests.

Evans died on Norfolk Island on December 30, 1891, "at a very advanced age."

FAAA See TE FANA.

FAAATA Tahitian clown (from *faa* meaning make and *ata* meaning laugh).

FAAHOTU ("Fasto") The first Tahitian consort of mutineer John Williams. She landed with him (we do not know whether she was kidnapped or came of her free will) on Pitcairn, but died within a year of the arrival. According to Teehuteatuaonoa, Faahotu succumbed to "a scrophulous disease which broke out in her neck" (it seems to have been a malady indigenous to eastern Polynesia). She left no children.

Faahotu's death led to Williams' demand that he be allowed to take one of the consorts of the Polynesian men for himself; he was eventually "given" Tararo's consort Toofaiti. Indirectly, then, Faahotu's death was a contributory cause of the subsequent violence on Pitcairn.

FAAONE A district on the east coast of Tahiti Nui, south of Hitiaa and north of Papeari. During the time of the *Bounty*'s stay at Tahiti, Faaone was a part of Hitiaa.

FAHUTU See FAAHOTU.

FARA (pandanus, screw pine) In its usefulness and value to the Polynesians, the *fara* or pandanus is surpassed only by the coconut palm. It provides wood and thatch for building, mats, leaves for rolling cigarettes (even many *popa'as* prefer them to paper), and food. Its fragrant, white flowers, called *hinano*, are used for decoration and the juice of the fruit stems can be made into an alcoholic beverage.

A house thatched with pandanus leaves (called *rauoro*) is known as a *fare rauoro*.

FARE   Tahitian for house. Also the name of the main community and harbor of Huahine.

"FASTO"   See FAAHOTU.

FATHOM   Six feet.

FEEJEE   See FIJI ISLANDS.

FE'I   The Tahitian word for plantain or cooking (red) banana (*Musa paradisiaca*). The *fe'i* bunches stand upright; the fruit is most nutritious and has a very pleasant taste when cooked.

FENUA   Tahitian for land or for large island.

FENUA MAITAI   Tahitian for Good Land, the name the Polynesian companions of the *Bounty* mutineers gave to PITCAIRN ISLAND.

FIGGY-DOWDY   Steamed fruit pudding, a rare treat on board.

FIJI ISLANDS   The Fijis constitute the easternmost island group in Melanesia ranging from 15⁰40' to 21⁰00' S., and from 178⁰00' W. to 176⁰45' E. The group comprises well over 300 islands, many of which are uninhabited. They are usually subdivided into four parts:

Viti Levu (largest, highest and westernmost) with neighboring islands; Lau or the Eastern Group with Lakemba and neighboring islands; Vanua Levu (second in size); and the Southern Group comprised of outlying islands of Viti Levu and the Eastern Group.

Some of the Fiji islands in the extreme north-east were sighted by Tasman in 1643. Vatoa, an island in the far south was seen by Cook in 1774 on his second voyage. Bligh, however, was the first European to sail through the group (in May 1789) on his open-boat voyage from Tofua to Timor. He is today considered, by the Fijians at least, as the principal discoverer of Fiji.

Christian stopped at Ono-i-Lau (in the Eastern Group) in late November or early December 1789 which makes him the European discoverer of the island. Prior to the finding (in 1956) of Teehuteatuaonoa's account of the voyage it was thought that Bellingshausen discovered it in 1820.

Master's mate Oliver of the *Pandora* and his crew in the schooner *Resolution* were

ENCYCLOPEDIA

the first Europeans to anchor at and land on a Fijian island (Matuku) and have close contact with the natives (in 1791).

Fiji became a British colony in 1874 and an independent nation in 1970. The seat of the government is in Suva on Viti Levu. There is an international airport at Nadi (pronounced Nandi).

FLINDERS, Matthew   Midshipman in the *Providence* on the second breadfruit expedition; later an important navigator and explorer who circumnavigated Australia in 1798; author of *A Voyage to Terra Australis.*

Flinders was born in 1774 and entered the Royal Navy at the age of fifteen. Some authors claim that he learned his first lessons in navigation from Bligh. Actually Flinders learned navigation aboard HMS *Bellerophon* in which he had been midshipman since July 1790 before joining the *Providence.* The commander of the *Bellerophon* was Sir Thomas Pasley who befriended Flinders and was the one who advised him to sail on the second breadfruit expedition. (Sir Thomas was an uncle of Peter Heywood, a judge at his court-martial, and asked him to serve as midshipman in the *Bellerophon* immediately after Heywood was pardoned.)

Flinders did not gain a very high opinion of Bligh during the two years he served under him. George Mackaness, in *The Life of Vice-Admiral William Bligh* (1931), quotes a contemporary of Flinders as writing:

> At the instance of Captain Pasley, he joined the *Providence*, Captain Bligh, appointed to convey plants of the bread fruit from the South Sea Islands to the West Indies. In this voyage he suffered much, especially from the short supply of water; he and others would lie on the steps and lick the drops of the precious liquid from the buckets as they were conveyed by the gardener to the plants. That he did not retain a respectful remembrance of his commander we may infer from the fact that, in after years, when they met at a soirée at the house of Sir Joseph Banks and Admiral Bligh asked Flinders to dedicate to him the important work on which he was engaged, the honour was declined. While on the *Providence*, he proved useful to Captain Bligh, being always ready to assist in the construction of charts and astronomical observations; the latter branch of scientific service and the care of the time-keepers were principally entrusted to our juvenile navigator.

After the expedition, Flinders rejoined the *Bellerophon* and served at the battle of the Glorious First of June in 1794. As a midshipman in the *Reliance* he sailed to New South Wales in 1795. On board he became friends with the surgeon, George Bass; the two shared an all-absorbing interest in exploration and, in 1798, proved that Van Diemen's Land (Tasmania) is an island. To achieve this they sailed through the strait, which today bears Bass's name, in the sloop *Norfolk.*

In the ancient and leaky sloop *Investigator* Flinders circumnavigated Australia

1802–1803 in a voyage of great hardships and with a loss of many of his men to scurvy; his own health was severely damaged on this expedition.

Flinders also made important contributions to navigation in general, especially through his studies of compass deviations caused by iron components of a ship. The soft-iron bars used for correction on binnacles today are named after him.

Flinders died in 1814 at the age of forty; his important work, *A Voyage to Terra Australis*, was published on the day he died.

FLIP   A mixture of beer, strong spirits, and sugar. It was introduced into the British Navy by Admiral Sir Clowdisley Shovel (what a wonderful name!) in the late seventeenth century and we have every reason to believe that it was as popular a drink among the officers of the *Bounty* as it was among officers of other ships in the fleet.

Today flip simply refers to beer liberally laced with rum, still a highly popular drink in the Navy. And who could resist it when listening to this old song:

> *A sailor's life's the life for me,*
> *He takes his duty merrily;*
> *If winds can whistle, he can sing;*
> *Still faithful to his friend and King;*
> *He gets belov'd by all his ship,*
> *And toasts his girl and drinks his flip.*

The obligatory toasts were, as quoted by Commander Geoffrey L. Lowis in *Fabulous Admirals* (1957):

Monday Night	Our ships at sea!
Tuesday Night	Our men!
Wednesday Night	Ourselves — as no one is likely to concern himself with our welfare!
Thursday Night	A bloody war or a sickly season!
Friday Night	A willing foe and sea room!
Saturday Night	Sweethearts and wives!
Sunday Night	Absent friends!

FLOGGING   In one of my lectures on the *Bounty* mutiny, I had just mentioned the fact that Captain Bligh used flogging rather sparingly in comparison with other naval commanders, when a young lady raised her hand and asked "Excuse me, but I don't know what flogging is." The question, I think, was a nice one to hear and bodes well for the future of the world.

In the last century it would not have been possible to find someone who did not know what flogging was. In the British Navy, for example, this punishment was not outlawed altogether until 1868 and even then only during times of peace. It was outlawed altogether in 1881, but there were instances of flogging even after it was officially prohibited.

Flogging as a punishment is probably as old as the inhumanity of humankind, but in the British Navy, at least, it did not become an official punishment until after the reign of William III, in the early 1700s. Extreme discretionary powers were invested in individual sea captains who literally decided over the life or death or permanent maiming of their seamen.

Fortunately, sea captains then, as now, were on the whole a quite decent and humane lot and tried their best to be fair. The times, however, were different and most people did not have the abhorrence of injury-producing physical punishment that we have today. For example, although Bligh flogged his crew during the voyage, none of them ever complained about his being physically cruel; in fact, flogging was never even mentioned as having had anything to do with the mutiny, it was just part of life in the Navy.

On one extreme, there were sea captains who disapproved of flogging and used it as little as possible; on another, there were sadists who used it at the drop of a hat (an example is Captain Hugh Pigot who was mentioned in the Introduction of this book in connection with the mutiny on HMS *Hermione*).

Flogging was inflicted on the naked back — sometimes on the breech — by means of the CAT-O'-NINE-TAILS. It was a cruel punishment indeed. The skin was usually broken by the fourth lash, and each lash after that drew more blood and tore at the flesh. Two dozen lashes, a very common punishment, would produce a condition where, according to a contemporary account, "the lacerated back looks inhuman; it resembles roasted meat burnt nearly black before a scorching fire."

Two dozen lashes were the punishment that Millward and Muspratt received *twice* (with a few weeks in between, just enough for a thin scab to form over the huge wound) for deserting on Tahiti. And that was considered a very mild punishment for desertion, so mild in fact that they wrote Bligh a thank-you note (see the January 1789 commentary in Part I).

What was it like to be flogged? Alexander McKee, in *H.M.S. Bounty* (1962) quotes a contemporary source:

> I felt an astounding sensation between the shoulders under my neck which went to my toenails in one direction, and my fingernails in another, and stung me to the heart, as if a knife had gone through my body . . . He came on a second time a few inches lower, and then I thought the former stroke was sweet and agreeable compared with that one . . . I felt my flesh quiver in every nerve, from the scalp of my head to my toenails. The time between each stroke seemed so long as to be agonising, and yet the next came too soon . . . The pain in my lungs was more severe, I thought, than on my back. I felt as if I would

burst in the internal parts of my body . . . I put my tongue between my teeth, held it there, and bit it almost in two pieces. What with the blood from my tongue, and my lips, which I had also bitten, and the blood from my lungs, or some other internal part, ruptured by the writhing agony, I was almost choked, and became black in the face . . . The time since they began was like a long period of life; I felt as if I had lived all the time of my real life in pain and torture, and that the time when existence had pleasure in it was a dream, long, long gone by.

In the MGM movie of 1935 there is a scene depicting "flogging 'round the fleet" at Spithead. The culprit is rowed to the *Bounty* and Bligh (Charles Laughton) orders him flogged even though he is already dead. The scene is totally unrealistic: such an event could never have occurred. Flogging around the fleet was not uncommon, but there was always a surgeon in the boat who would suspend the punishment if he thought the culprit could not take any more without endangering his life. "Suspend" is the key word in the last sentence. If the punishment was 200 lashes, it might have to be suspended twice or three times. But that was in itself cruel, because lashes on a barely healed wound were of course much worse than on an intact skin. Surgeons, out of compassion and knowing little about sepsis, would therefore often take the risk of having all the punishment inflicted at once. As a result, many culprits died shortly afterwards from various types of blood poisoning, infection, gangrene.

The following is a list of Bligh's floggings on board the *Bounty* and in Tahiti:

FLOGGINGS ON BOARD THE *BOUNTY*

Churchill
JANUARY 23, 1789
desertion, 12 lashes

Churchill
FEBRUARY 4, 1789
desertion (second installment),
12 lashes

Lamb
DECEMBER 29, 1788
"suffering cleaver to be stolen,"
12 lashes

Martin
JANUARY 30, 1789
striking a native,
19 lashes

Millward
JANUARY 23, 1789
desertion, 24 lashes

Millward
FEBRUARY 4, 1789
desertion (second installment),
24 lashes

Muspratt

DECEMBER 27, 1788
neglect of duty, 12 lashes

Muspratt

JANUARY 23, 1789
desertion, 24 lashes

Muspratt

FEBRUARY 4, 1789
desertion (second installment),
24 lashes

Quintal

MARCH 11, 1788
insolence and mutinous behaviour,
24 lashes

Adams

NOVEMBER 3, 1788
"suffering rudder gudgeon to be stolen,"
12 lashes

Sumner

APRIL 12, 1789
neglect of duty, 12 lashes

Thompson

DECEMBER 5, 1788
insolence and disobedience, 12 lashes

Williams

MAY 22, 1788
neglect of duty in heaving the lead,
6 lashes

Total number of lashes during the voyage — 229

The very fact that it was "worthwhile" to assemble the whole ship's company and read the articles of war in order to punish John Williams with six lashes shows how severe the punishment of flogging was. Six lashes would today be considered "cruel and unusual punishment." Imagine, then, a punishment of 500 or 1000 lashes!

The floggings were administered by the boatswain's mate. On the *Bounty* this was James Morrison who was well liked; no one resented him for having to carry out this unpleasant duty.

For a full account of the practice of flogging, see Scott Claver: *Under the Lash* (1954).

HMS *FLY*   British warship commanded by Captain Russell Elliott; arrived at Pitcairn in November 1838. See ELLIOTT, RUSSELL.

FOLGER, Mayhew   Captain of the American sealer *Topaz*. Folger was a skipper from Nantucket who worked for Messrs Boardman and Pope, dealers in seal skins. With their ship *Topaz* he had left Boston harbor on Sunday, April 5, 1807, to hunt for seals in the South Pacific.

On February 6, 1808, his entry in the log book reads:

> At ½ past 1 P.M. saw land bearing SW by W½ steared for the land. . . . at 2 A.M. the Isle bore south 2 leagues dis. Lay off & on till daylight. at 6 A.M.

put off in two boats to Explore the land and look for seals. On approaching the Shore saw a Smoke on the land at which I was very much surprised it [Pitcairn] being represented by Captain Carteret as destitute of Inhabitants, on approaching Still more the land — I discovered a boat paddling towards me with three men in her.

The boat was a Tahitian-style canoe and the dark-skinned "natives" hailed the captain in English:

"Who are you?"

"This is the ship *Topaz* of the United States of America. I am the master, Captain Mayhew Folger, an American."

"You are an American?" "You come from America?" "Where is America?" "Is it in Ireland?"

Folger was too taken aback by the "natives" speaking English to answer. Instead he asked:

"Who are you?"

"We are Englishmen."

"Where were you born?"

"On that island which you see."

"How can you be Englishmen if you were born on that island?"

"We are Englishmen because our father is an Englishman."

"Who is your father?"

"Aleck" (referring to Alexander Smith whose real name was John Adams, but who on the island was known as Aleck).

"Who is Aleck?"

"Don't you know Aleck?"

"How should I know Aleck?"

"Well, then, do you know Captain Bligh of the *Bounty*?"

All seafaring men knew about the *Bounty*, about the mutiny, and about Bligh's open-boat voyage. But no one in the world knew what had happened to Christian and the mutineers who had followed him in his quest for an island of refuge.

Imagine then the feelings that must have possessed Captain Folger when he realized that he was the first person in the world to find the hide-out of the mutineers of the *Bounty*! At the moment he did not know that all of them had died except one. He did not know whether he was in a dangerous situation or not. But the lads in the outrigger seemed very friendly and his curiosity overcame him. He told the youngsters in the canoe to ask "Aleck" to come on board.

The canoe went ashore, but soon returned without any extra passenger. Folger shouted:

"Where is Aleck?"

"Aleck does not want to come on board!"

No wonder. Folger immediately understood why "Aleck" would not want to come on board: he was afraid he would be arrested and taken to England to be hanged. But the youngsters in the canoe had an invitation:

"You are welcome to come ashore, Sir. Aleck and the women have prepared a meal for you."

Folger was somewhat apprehensive himself, but again his curiosity won out. He remembered how often he and his friend, Amasa Delano, had discussed the mystery of the missing mutineers of the *Bounty*. He decided to go ashore. His log reads as follows:

> I went on shore and found there an Englishman by the name of Alexander Smith, the only person remaining out of the nine that escaped on board the ship Bounty, Captain Bligh, under the command of the archmutineer Christian. Smith informed me that after putting Captain Bligh in the long boat and sending her adrift, their commander — Christian — proceeded to Otaheiti, then all the mutineers chose to Stop except Christian, himself and seven others; they all took wives at Otaheiti and Six men as Servants and proceeded to Pitcairn's Island where they landed all their goods and Chattles, ran the Ship Bounty on Shore and Broke her up, which took place as near as he could recollect in 1790 — soon after which one of their party ran mad and drowned himself another died with a fever, and after they had remained about four years on the Island their Men Servants rose upon and killed Six of them, Leaving only Smith and he desperately wounded with a pistol Ball in the neck, however he and the widows of the deceased men arose and put all the Servants to death which left him the only Surviving man on the Island with eight or nine women and Several Small Children. . . . he Immediately went to work tilling the ground so that it now produces plenty for them all and the[re] he lives very comfortably as Commander in Chief of Pitcairn's Island, all the Children of the deceased mutineers Speak tolerable English, some of them are grown to the Size of men and women, and to do them Justice I think them a very humane and hospitable people, and whatever may have been the Errors or Crimes of Smith the Mutineer in times Back, he is at present in my opinion a worthy man and may be useful to Navigators who traverse this immense ocean, such the history of Christian and his associates.

The garbled history in this account must be due partly to Adams hiding the truth (he was to tell widely differing stories to subsequent visiting sea captains) and partly to Folger's own distortions of memory.

Adams was understandably reluctant to talk about the mutiny. But he was eager to find out what had happened in England since he left it more than twenty years ago. And Captain Folger told him about the important changes in Europe over the last two decades: the French Revolution, Napoleon's rise to power, and the tremendous and protracted war against France. When he came to describe England's glorious victory in the Battle of Trafalgar in 1805, Adams rose and swung his hat three times over his head and called out: "Old England forever! Huzzah!"

Unfortunately, Folger remained at Pitcairn for only ten hours. As a parting gift, Adams presented him with the *Bounty*'s azimuth compass and with the Kendall chronometer which had served Bligh — and later Christian — so well. (An oft-repeated, but false, claim in the *Bounty* literature is that this chronometer had been used by Captain Cook in the *Resolution* on the third voyage. The fact is that Cook's chronometer was the one today referred to as K (Kendall) 1; the *Bounty* chronometer was K2.)

Folger sailed eastward to Juan Fernandez (Robinson Crusoe's Island) where the compass and the chronometer were both, for some unexplained reason, confiscated by the Spanish governor. Long afterwards, in 1840, the *Nautical Magazine* published this account of the chronometer, by Captain R. A. Newman of HMS *Sparrowhawk*:

MAY 18TH, 1840, MR MOUAT, CHRONOMETER-MAKER, &C., AT VALPARAISO, RECEIVED FROM CAPTAIN HERBERT, OF H.M.S. CALLIOPE, THE CHRONOMETER, LARCUM KENDALL, LONDON. A.D. 1771.

This chronometer was in H.M. late ship the Bounty, at the time of the mutiny, and has been in Chili since the time of the arrival of the American ship that first touched at Pitcairns Island, after the mutineers settled themselves there. It was stolen from the American captain on the ship's passage from Juan Fernandez to Valparaiso; and next made its appearance at Concepcion, where it was purchased for three doubloons by an old Spaniard of the name of Castillo, who kept it in his possession till his death, which happened lately at Santiago; when his family sent it to Capt. Herbert, to be conveyed to the British Museum. Capt. Herbert sent it to Mr Mouat to be put in order, and from his relation I am enabled to give these particulars.

On the chronometer being taken to pieces it was found to be in a complete state of preservation. . . .

The chronometer is six inches in diameter, with three dials on its face — one for hours, one for minutes, and one for seconds; with an outer silver case, made as the outer cases of pocket watches were sixty or seventy years ago; so that its appearance is that of a gigantic watch. . . .

On this day (23rd of June,) it was delivered to Capt. Herbert, being then fast on Greenwich mean time 0h. 0m. 26.5s. and losing daily 3.5 seconds. . . .

The Calliope sailed from Valparaiso for China, on the 1st of July, 1840; and thus will this, now very interesting instrument, in all probability, return to the place of its construction. . . .

The *Bounty* chronometer is today in the National Maritime Museum in Greenwich.

The Spanish governor on Juan Fernandez kept Folger and his crew in jail until some months later a new governor arrived and set the Americans free.

When Folger finally arrived in Valparaiso, he reported his momentous discovery to Lieutenant William Fitzmaurice of the Royal Navy who was serving on the naval station in Chile. Fitzmaurice forwarded this report, together with an extract of the log of the *Topaz*, to the commander of the British naval station in Brazil on October 10, 1808. The British Admiralty received the report on May 14, 1809.

The general public did not become aware of the discovery until March 1810 when a report of it appeared in the English *Quarterly Review* (Bligh was still in New South Wales then). The extract of the logbook of the *Topaz* also appeared in the *Sydney Gazette* for October 27, 1810 (two days after Bligh arrived in England).

Puzzled over the fact that the British Admiralty seemed to pay no attention to his discovery, Folger wrote a letter to Rear Admiral Hotham on March 1, 1813, in which he gave a more detailed report of his visit to Pitcairn and added: "I am sending you the azimuth compass which I received from Alex. Smith. I repaired and made use of it on my homeward passage. I now forward it to your lordship." It was clear, however, that the Admiralty considered the report unimportant and it was simply forgotten until 1814 when two British warships, HMS *Briton* (Captain Staines) and HMS *Tagus* (Captain Pipon) again "rediscovered" Pitcairn.

Captain Folger died on September 4, 1828, in Massillon, Ohio, without publishing his discovery. But his friend since 1800, Captain Amasa Delano, did publish what Folger had told him as part of his book *A Narrative of Voyages and Travels* (1817).

FORT GEORGE   The fort which Christian and his men started to build in chief Taaroatohoa's district Natieva (now called Taahuaia) on Tubuai. The structure was never completed. See the June 1789 commentary in Part I.

The ruins were still standing in 1902 when they were examined by Alvin Seale who wrote:

> The fort consists of the ordinary military square of earth work thrown up to the heights of perhaps 6–7 feet. Its open side faces the sea, about 300 feet distant; the size of the fort is 125 feet by 120 feet . . . It is now overgrown with trees and brush and a native house is in the open side.

The National Geographic Society has erected a wooden plaque at the site which reads:

FORT GEORGE

BUILT BY THE MUTINEERS OF H.M.S. BOUNTY
UNDER THE COMMAND OF FLETCHER CHRISTIAN
JULY 10, 1789

After a French translation follows a Tahitian:

PATUHIA E TE MAU ORU RE HAU O TE
PAHI RA BOUNTY I RARO AE I TE FAATERERAA
A FLETCHER CHRISTIAN I TE 10 NO TIURAI 1789.

FREEBOARD   The distance from the water level to the gunwale (upper edge of the side) of a boat or to the upper deck level in a ship. The measurement is taken at the waist (center) of the vessel.

FRIENDLY ISLANDS   See TONGA.

FRIGATE   A frigate of the late 1700s was a three-masted ship, fully rigged on each mast, smaller and faster than a ship of the line. Her rigging was lofty, since speed, not stability, was her main purpose. She was armed with from 24 to 44 guns carried on a single gundeck. She was often used in search of privateers and as an escort ship for convoys.

The *Pandora* was a frigate. Another famous frigate is the American ship *Constitution* (Captain Isaac Hull) which acquitted herself well against the British frigate *Java* on December 29, 1812.

In today's navies, the term frigate usually refers to any smaller warship with a general purpose capability.

FRYER, John   Sailing master on the *Bounty*; loyalist; went with Bligh; returned safely to England.

Fryer was born at Wells-next-the-Sea in Norfolk on August 15, 1752. He was two years older than Bligh. In the *Bounty* literature he has usually, and unfairly, been portrayed as incompetent and a cantankerous troublemaker by writers who have uncritically accepted Bligh's opinion. It is in fact highly unlikely that the Admiralty would have chosen an incompetent sailing master for the expedition. It is more likely that he was highly competent and that Bligh tried to defame him for exactly that reason; Bligh simply could not stand competition from colleagues and had a highly vindictive nature. As the distinguished *Bounty* historian Rolf Du Rietz has pointed out, Fryer is the one member of the *Bounty* complement who has suffered most unfairly in the later descriptions of the *dramatis personae*.

Fryer was appointed to the *Bounty* on August 20, 1787. He had served as Master in the Royal Navy since 1781 when he was in HMS *Camel*. He had risen to Master of the Third Rate.

In the beginning of the voyage, Bligh had approved of his sailing master: "The master is a very good man, and gives me every satisfaction." His feelings towards Fryer soon changed, however, and most probably because the master was not a yes-man; he had strong opinions of his own. Also, even though he was not as sensitive to insults as Christian, he was conscious of his dignity and his competence and let Bligh know, in no uncertain terms, that he was not going to take things "lying down."

During the mutiny, Fryer was the only officer who made a forceful attempt to talk Christian out of his hasty decision. When that failed, he made an earnest, although equally unsuccessful, attempt to mediate between Christian and Bligh. Finally, he was among those who most forcefully demanded that the loyalists be given the *Bounty*'s launch instead of one of the other two boats which were not seaworthy. At one point Christian pressed his bayonet against Fryer's chest and said he would run him through if he advanced one inch further.

During the open-boat voyage the men seem to have been divided in two parties: those who looked to Bligh for leadership and those who wished that Fryer were in command (see also the June 1789 commentary in Part I).

Although Bligh had just as low an opinion of Fryer as of Purcell, he brought charges against the latter but not against the former. The reason is probably that Fryer simply knew too much about Bligh's questionable financial transactions as purser, and Bligh could not afford to take the risk of these being exposed.

During the court-martial of the accused mutineers, Fryer testified that he had seen Burkett, Muspratt, and Millward under arms. His testimony regarding the rest of the accused was generally in their favor.

As soon as the court-martial was over, Fryer looked up Joseph Christian, a distant relation to Fletcher, in order to tell him about the facts that had not been divulged during the trial. Fryer was later instrumental in helping Fletcher's older brother, Edward Christian, gather the facts which had been omitted by Bligh and which Edward published in his *Appendix* to Steven Barney's *Minutes of the Proceedings of the Court-Martial*. He wrote an account of the mutiny in 1792.

Fryer went on to a distinguished and honourable career in the Royal Navy, reaching the top of his profession, Master of the First Rate, in 1798. Even before then his competence had been recognized by several commanders who wrote him letters of recommendation. Captain Thomas Foley of HMS *Britannia*, for example, wrote that

> he conducted himself with sobriety, diligence, and obedience in the execution of his duty, and that in every respect he shewed himself to be skilful Seaman and good Officer and that in the several difficult services there was to perform, he gave his assistance with a zeal and ardour, that calls on me to recommend him in the strongest terms to the favor of the Navy Board, as one worth any Promotion they may have to bestow.

(Bligh would have been totally incapable of writing such a letter of recommendation for anyone, no matter how talented.)

In the Battle of Copenhagen, Fryer was sailing master in Admiral Sir Hyde

Parker's flagship *London* (his son Harrison Fryer was midshipman in Nelson's flagship *Elephant*, his brother-in-law Robert Tinkler was a lieutenant in the *Isis*, and Bligh commanded the *Glatton*). He retired from the Navy in 1812 and died at Wells-next-the-Sea on May 26, 1817.

For the best summing up of Fryer the man and the sailor, we have to go to Rolf Du Rietz (1981): "John Fryer of the *Bounty* was . . . not a so-called historically important figure, and he will never get a full-dress biography. Nevertheless he was — as far as we know — a loyal and profoundly competent officer and an honest man, who deserved well of his country during the greatest and most crucial period of the naval history of Great Britain. As a moral character, there is every reason to suppose that he was far above Bligh, and we must never forget that a human being may, after all, be of great worth even if he does not become a Fellow of the Royal Society, or succeed in ending up in the *Dictionary of National Biography*."

FULL-RIGGED   Synonym for ship-rigged (square-rigged on all three or more masts).

FURLONG   Two hundred and twenty yards.

GALLEY   A kitchen aboard a vessel, also called the caboose in smaller merchant ships.

GAMBIER ISLANDS   See MANGAREVA.

GILL   One fourth of a pint.

HMS *GLATTON*   The 54-gun ship which Bligh commanded at the Battle of Copenhagen in 1801. The *Glatton* received severe damage during the engagement and was the only British vessel to lose a topmast.

HMS *GORGON*   Captain Edwards, Lieutenant Larkin, and the ten accused mutineers who had survived the wreck of the *Pandora* sailed on this 44-gun frigate from Cape Town on April 6, 1792, and arrived at Spithead on June 19. The commander was Captain John Parker.

GRAHAM, Aaron   Judge-advocate; Peter Heywood's counsel at the court-martial of the accused mutineers of the *Bounty*; a friend of Commodore Sir Thomas Pasley. It was also through Graham that Heywood was introduced to his future wife.

GRENVILLE ISLAND   See ROTUMA.

GROG Rum and water, named after "Old Grog," British admiral Edward Vernon, who was so nicknamed because of his grogram (a coarse fabric) cloak and who in 1740 ordered the daily ration of rum to henceforth be mixed with water. The daily issuance of grog in the British Navy survived until 1987.

A ballad illustrates the origin of the word:

> *A mighty bowl on deck he drew*
> *And filled it to the brink;*
> *Such drank the Burford's gallant crew,*
> *And such the Gods shall drink;*
> *The sacred robe which Vernon wore*
> *Was drenched with the same;*
> *And hence its virtues guard our shore,*
> *And Grog derives its name.*

GUDGEON A metal plate attached to the sternpost of a vessel and carrying an eye to receive the pintle of a rudder. Usually two gudgeons are employed in order to give the rudder stability. Gudgeons and pintles are today used only on boats and very small yachts, but their advantage lies in the ease with which the rudder can be unshipped.

GUNWALE (gunnel) A piece of timber going around the upper sheer strake (planking) of a boat to bind in the top work. Loosely: the upper edge of the side or the bulwarks of a vessel.

GUSTAF III His Swedish Majesty's Armed Brig *Gustavus III*, a Swedish privateer. See MERCURY.

GUTHRIE, James Second lieutenant in the *Pandora* on the second breadfruit expedition (August 3, 1791, to August 7, 1793).

HAAPAPE The name of a district on the north coast of Tahiti, east of Arue. It includes Point Venus and the eastern shore of Matavai Bay and corresponds roughly with today's Mahina. The chief of Haapape during the visits of the *Bounty* was Poino.

HAARI Tahitian for coconut.

HAEVA See HEIVA.

HÄGERSTEN, Petter (HAGERSTEINE, Peter) When the reports by Wallis, Bougainville, and Cook describing Tahiti — the Paradise Island — were read in

Europe, there were many who not only longed to go there for a visit, but who would have liked to settle there for life. Almost all of the ships that visited Tahiti had problems with deserters, as do visiting yachts to this very day. Those of the *Bounty* mutineers who elected to stay on Tahiti when Christian left certainly planned to end their days there (if indeed they did any planning at all), knowing that they would be hanged if they tried to get back to England. As we know, none of them were ever to see Tahiti again.

The first white man who succeeded in establishing himself permanently on the island was a Swedish-Finnish seaman from Helsingfors (Helsinki) called Petter Hägersten. He had been a crew member in HMS *Daedalus*, commanded by Lieutenant James Hanson, which visited Tahiti in February 1793. When the *Daedalus* sailed after a stay of only two weeks, Hägersten jumped ship. He was the first deserter from any ship visiting Tahiti up till then who succeeded; all others had been caught.

The Tahitian chiefs had always seen to it that deserters from the ships of the *popa'as* (white men) were rounded up and delivered to their captains. Why they did not do so with Hägersten we will never know. Perhaps they took a special liking to him. He certainly did to them. He learned the language with amazing speed and soon became an interpreter for Pomare I and later also for the missionaries who arrived in 1797. He also became Pomare's "general," thus following in the footsteps of the *Bounty* mutineers.

Peter Hägersten died on his beloved Tahiti, but we do not know when.

HALL, James Norman Author of many books about the South Seas; co-author (with Charles Nordhoff) of the magnificent trilogy *Mutiny on the Bounty, Pitcairn's Island,* and *Men Against the Sea,* all published in the early 1930s.

Hall was born in Iowa on April 22, 1887. During the first world war he served as a pilot in the famous Escadrille Lafayette. He achieved three combat victories and spent six months as a prisoner of war. After the war he was assigned the duty of writing a history of the Corps together with Charles Nordhoff who was destined to become his friend for life. In 1920 they left for Tahiti and — with an almost immediate intuitive understanding of the islands and the islanders — wrote what, in my opinion, is one of the best books ever written about Eastern Polynesia: *Faery Lands of the South Seas.*

Although both authors also wrote independently, their best works were produced jointly: the *Bounty* trilogy, *The Hurricane, The Dark River,* and *No More Gas.* They made a perfect writing team and integrated their material so skillfully that it seemed to have flown from one and the same mind.

In 1925 Hall married Sarah Marguerite Sophie Teraireia Winchester, the beautiful daughter of a Tahitian mother and an English sea captain. Sarah, affectionately called Lala, was only sixteen and Hall was thiry-eight when they met. With her he had a son, Conrad Lafcadio, and a daughter, Nancy Ella. In 1928 they moved into the house in Arue which is still standing.

The Tahitians knew that Hall loved them, and they loved him for his kindness and modesty and nobility of spirit. His death on July 6, 1951, was a cause for island-wide mourning, and older Tahitians revere his memory to this day.

Hall was buried on Herai (Ferai) Hill above his home on a spot from where one can see Matavai Bay where the *Bounty* anchored in thirteen fathoms of water on Sunday, October 26, 1788. At the funeral the chief of Papenoo, Teriieroo, delivered the eulogy:

> We all knew and loved Papa Hall. He was one of us in his interest in our sports and our activities. We knew him especially as a *kind* man, a simple man, to whom the interests of the poorest were more important than those of the rich and comfortable. No one ever in vain approached him with a request for aid. These things I knew and we all knew. But today my eyes are opened. When I look upon that cushion upon which are pinned his medals and decorations from the leading governments of the world, I for the first time realize that we have had living amongst us a great man. I know now, but never knew before, that in our midst dwelt a hero.

Lala had a bronze plaque made for her husband's grave; the inscription is a verse he himself had written:

> *Look to the northward, stranger,*
> *Just over the hillside, there;*
> *Have you in your travels seen*
> *A land more passing fair?*

Because of Hall and Nordhoff, the *Bounty* will sail forever in our imagination. In 1932, their editor, Ellery Sedgwick, wrote in his introduction to *Mutiny on the Bounty*: "... that story is of the primeval stuff that Romance is made of" and "Here is the book they have written. Read it, and you, too, will know that Romance has come into her own."

Hall's wife, Lala, lived until 1985. His son Conrad is now a cinematographer in Hollywood; his daughter Nancy lives in Tahiti and Hawaii.

HALL, Thomas   Able seaman and ship's cook on the *Bounty*; loyalist; went with Bligh; died in Batavia.

Hall was born in Durham and was thirty-eight years old when he mustered on the *Bounty*. Evidently it was not easy to be ship's cook under Bligh, because of the scanty rations he ordered to be issued to the men. Morrison writes: "The quantity was so small, that it was no uncommon thing for four men in a mess to draw for the breakfast, and to devide their bread by the well known method of 'who shall have this,' nor was the officers a hair behind the men at it. ... the division of [the] scanty allowance caused frequent broils in the gally, and in the present bad weather [off Cape Horn] was often like to be attended with bad consequences and in one of these disputes the cook, Tho^S Hall, got two of his ribbs broke & at another time Churchill got his hand scalded and it became at last necessary to have the M^{rs} mate of the watch to superintend the division of it."

On the morning of the mutiny, he was sitting with Muspratt, the assistant cook, by the starboard fore scuttle splitting wood for the galley. His actions during the mutiny seem to have involved bringing up provisions for the launch. Otherwise, there is very little mention of Hall in the literature on the *Bounty*. Weakened by the open-boat voyage he died from a tropical disease (probably malaria) in Batavia on October 11, 1789.

HALLETT, John   Midshipman on the *Bounty*; loyalist; went to England with Bligh.

Hallett was born in London and was only fifteen years old when he mustered on the *Bounty*. In many ways, he and Hayward were like peas in the pod. Both had come on board by the influence of Mrs. Bligh who knew their respective families well (Ann Hallett, John's sister, seems to have been a bosom friend of Betsy Bligh). Both were disliked on the ship because of snobbishness and arrogance, both had a tendency to sleep on duty, and when the mutiny broke out, both had tearfully begged to be allowed to stay on board the *Bounty* while other loyalists were going into the launch. Yet both later testified against those loyalists who had been forced to stay on board the ship.

When the mutiny broke out, Hallett had not even appeared on deck even though he was in Christian's watch. His — and Hayward's — disinclination to do any work clearly made it easier for Christian to take over the ship.

Hallett's testimony during the court-martial of the accused mutineers was highly damaging to Heywood. Hallett claimed that he had observed Bligh saying something to Heywood during the mutiny and the latter had just laughed and turned around and walked away. After the publication of Edward Christian's *Appendix*, Bligh needed help in defending himself against the charges that had been leveled at him, and he found a willing instrument in Hallett who claimed that, no matter what anyone else had said, Bligh had never accused anyone of stealing any coconuts.

Hallett later became a lieutenant and died on board HMS *Penelope*.

HAMILTON, George   Surgeon on the *Pandora*. The best description of Hamilton is by Sir Basil Thomson who reprinted Hamilton's *A Voyage Round the World in H. M. Frigate Pandora* (1793):

> Fortunately for us, the *Pandora* carried a certain rollicking, irresponsible person as surgeon. George Hamilton has been called "a coarse, vulgar, and illiterate

man, more disposed to relate licentious scenes and adventures, in which he and his companions were engaged, than to give any information of proceedings and occurrences connected with the main object of the voyage." From this puritanical criticism most readers will dissent. Hamilton was bred in Northumberland, and was at this time past forty.

[He was] a man of middle age, with clever, well-cut features, and a large, humorous, and rather sensual mouth. His book, with all its faults of scandalous plain speech, is one that few naval surgeons of that day could have written. The style, though flippant, is remarkable for a cynical but always good-natured humour, and on the rare occasions when he thought it professionally incumbent on him to be serious, as in his discussion of the best dietary for long voyages, and the physical effects of privations, his remarks display observation and good sense. It must be admitted, I fear, that he relates certain of his own and his shipmates' adventures ashore with shameless gusto, but he wrote in an age that loved plain speech, and that did not care to veil its appetite for licence. Like Edwards, he tells us little of the prisoners after they were consigned to "Pandora's Box." His narrative is valuable as a commentary on Edwards' somewhat meagre report, and for the sidelights which it throws upon the manners of naval officers of those days.

In his account, Hamilton tries to whitewash the cruel treatment of the prisoners, probably because the truth would reflect negatively on himself who did not, or could not, do more to intervene in their behalf. He does not comment on the harshness of Edwards and he avoids any mention of the sadistic Larkin.

HANSON, James   The lieutenant in command of HMS *DAEDALUS*.

HARWOOD, Edward   Surgeon on HMS *PROVIDENCE*.

HAVAIKI   The mythical ancestral island of all Polynesians. Also: the ancient name of Raiatea.

HAWKESWORTH, John   British writer; born 1715; succeeded Samuel Johnson as contributor to *Gentleman's Magazine*; started (with Johnson and others) a periodical called *The Adventurer*; edited the works of Swift and Cook's papers concerning his first voyage; died 1773.

Hawkesworth wrote *An Account of the Voyages by Byron, Wallis, Carteret, and Cook* which was published in the year of his death. It was in this book that Christian read of the discovery (by Carteret in 1767) of Pitcairn's Island, as it was then called. The description of the island and its remoteness made Christian decide to seek it out as a permanent refuge.

HAYWARD, Thomas Midshipman on the *Bounty*; loyalist; went with Bligh; arrived safely in England; shipped as third lieutenant on the *Pandora*, survived the wreck, and went back to England.

Hayward was born in Hackney and was twenty years old when he came on board the *Bounty*. Both he and his young friend Hallett came to the ship through the influence of Bligh's wife Betsy; the families of both had been friends of the Bethams for some time.

Hayward seems to have been lazy and undependable. He and Hallett were universally disliked on the *Bounty* because of their arrogance. Hayward had a propensity for sleeping on duty: on Tahiti Bligh put him in irons for having been asleep while on watch when the deserters left the ship.

Nevertheless Hayward and Bligh seem to have liked each other. After Bligh's hysterical outburst over the supposedly missing coconuts, the officers had agreed among each other not to accept a dinner invitation from the captain. Hayward broke the agreement and dined with him the evening before the mutiny. Bligh commended him highly after the open-boat voyage, and Hayward was totally in support of Bligh during the trial of the accused mutineers.

Hayward was the mate of Christian's watch. On the morning of the mutiny he was again sleeping on duty (on the arms chest) when Norman called out that he had seen a giant shark. This awakened Hayward and although he was at first interested in catching the shark, he soon noticed that some of the men came on deck armed and asked them what was going on. Christian told him "Mamu!" ("Shut up" in Tahitian) and that took care of Hayward; he never made any attempt to alert Bligh.

When the loyalists were to go into the launch he, and Hallett, tearfully begged to be allowed to stay on board. They were too disliked by the crew, however; nobody wanted them on board.

Not only did Hayward reach England safely, he soon returned as third lieutenant in the *Pandora* in search of his former shipmates. The dislike he had developed for them, even for the loyalists, was immediately evident when the ship reached Tahiti. Towards Heywood, especially, he seems to have developed feelings close to hatred. When Heywood — who had stayed on Tahiti with the other loyalists and some of the mutineers — came on board the *Pandora* and wanted to greet Hayward as an old shipmate, Hayward turned a cold shoulder and would have nothing to do with him. Heywood later wrote:

> Having learned from one of the natives that our former messmate, Mr. Hayward, now promoted to the rank of lieutenant was on board, we asked for him, supposing he might prove the assertions of our innocence. But he, (like all worldlings when raised a little in life) received us very coolly and pretended ignorance of our affairs. Appearances being so much against us, we were ordered to be put in irons and looked upon oh! infernal words! — as piratical villains.

At the trial of the accused mutineers, Hayward damaged Heywood's case by making it clear that he considered Heywood a mutineer because the latter had remained on board.

Hayward was later drowned in the China Sea while commanding the sloop-of-war *Swift* when she foundered in a typhoon.

HMS *HECTOR* British 74-gun warship, commanded by Captain (later Sir) George Montagu, on which the mutineers and other *Bounty* crew members who had survived the wreck of the *Pandora* were imprisoned at Spithead while awaiting their court-martial.

The court-martial of Captain Edward Edwards for the loss of the *Pandora* was held on board this ship on September 10, 1792.

HEDEEDEE, HEETE-HEETE See HITIHITI.

HEILDBRANDT Morrison's spelling of HILLBRANT (Heildbrandt was probably closer to the original spelling, since Hillbrant was born in Germany).

HEIVA The literal meaning of the Tahitian word *heiva* is amusement or entertainment. By the time the *Bounty* arrived in Tahiti, the actual meaning had become something like "dance concert with other entertainment interspersed." Bligh and Morrison witnessed several *heivas* on Tahiti and described them in their accounts.

Dancing was, and is, a way of life in Tahiti. There are no poor dancers on the island; the range is from good to superb. In the old days people danced every day, according to the historian Peter O'Reilly in *Dancing Tahiti* (n.d.):

> After meals, the sound of the flute and the drum soon got everyone on the move. They would soon begin singing and dancing and each day would pass in this manner with hour upon hour given to entertainment and the pleasures of which they were so enraptured . . . In every district there were daily meetings and dances where women would appear fully bedecked, graced with flowers and leis, drenched in perfumed oil and covered with the whitest of cloths. There were often dancing competitions and shows between districts. Challenges would be exchanged, in the presence of the chiefs and numerous spectators. One would try above all for agility and grace of movement . . . Children would take part from a tender age onward in each of these exercises . . .

Almost any occasion could provide a motive for dancing:

> It is quite apparent that the Tahitian would dance for any reason, from the impromptitude of a private meeting to the great solemn meetings on the *marae*. He would also dance for quite different reasons: to show his joy or to greet

ENCYCLOPEDIA

a visitor; to implore the gods or defy an enemy; to triumph in competition or just for the pure pleasure of showing his joy of living.

And that is what characterizes the Tahitians to this day: their joy of living.

HENDERSON (Elizabeth) ISLAND Henderson Island lies 107 miles east-north-east of Pitcairn (nearly 200 miles west-north-west-by-west of Ducie) at 24°22'S., 128°20'W. It is a flat limestone island about 100 feet high, five miles long, north to south, and two and three quarter miles wide, and is roughly rectangular in shape. It was discovered in 1819 by Captain James Henderson in the merchant ship *Hercules*. Shortly afterwards the island was sighted by Captain Henry King in the English whaler *Elizabeth* who named it after his ship. It was still known as Elizabeth Island to the Pitcairners when they first visited it in 1851.

Although Henderson is six times larger than Pitcairn, it is uninhabited. One reason is of course its isolation — Pitcairn might also be uninhabited today if it had not been for the mutiny on the *Bounty*. The main problem with living on Henderson, however, would be the difficulty in finding good fresh water (brackish water can be found in clefts and pools). The island is densely wooded and so thickly interlaced with shrubs that walking is not only difficult but dangerous, since the vegetation conceals the cavities in the coral. Professor Harold St. John, who explored the island botanically some years ago, reported that a false step could mean plunging into a jagged limestone crevasse to sudden death.

Incredibly, Henderson was nevertheless populated by Polynesians, possibly for generations, between approximately 1250 and 1425 A.D. In 1971, Professor Yosihiko Sinoto of the Bernice Pauahi Bishop Museum in Honolulu discovered small shelter caves in the base of a limestone cliff with evidence of human occupation.

The last human inhabitant on Henderson was Robert Tomarchin, an American eccentric, who in 1957 spent three weeks on the island with his chimpanzee, Moko, before he had to be rescued by a passing ship. In the early 1980s another American, millionaire Smiley Ratcliff, offered to buy the island and build an airstrip on it. He was turned down by the British government in 1983.

The Pitcairners visit Henderson from time to time in order to gather *miro* wood for their carvings. However, the voyage against the trade winds is difficult, and the Pitcairners deeply appreciate it when a visiting vessel will take on board their longboats and transport them to Henderson (coming back is of course not as difficult). The first such voyage recorded in the *Pitcairn Island Register* was undertaken on November 11, 1851, with the assistance of a ship named *Sharon*. Added to the entry in the *Register* is the following comment: "Eight human skeletons were found upon the island, lying in caves. They were doubtless the remains of some unfortunate ship-wrecked seamen, as several pieces of wreck were found upon the shore."

Captain Irving Johnson, who visited Pitcairn seven times in his voyages around the world in the schooner (later the brigantine) *Yankee*, made a special point of taking the islanders to Henderson.

HERCULES British East Indiaman from Calcutta in which Captain James Henderson discovered Henderson Island in 1819.

HERVEY ISLANDS In a strict sense, Hervey Islands refers only to Manuae and Auotu islands on the reef of Manuae atoll in the Southern Cook Group, but the term has in the past often been used to designate the whole group.

HETEE HETEE Morrison's spelling of HITIHITI.

HEYWOOD, Nessy A *Bounty* Encyclopedia would not be complete without an entry for Nessy Heywood, Peter Heywood's sister. Nessy never lost her belief in her brother's innocence and she was untiring in her efforts, first to have him acquitted and, when that had failed, to secure his pardon. An excellent account of Nessy's campaign on behalf of her brother can be found in Sir John Barrow's *The Eventful History of the Mutiny and Piratical Seizure of H.M.S. Bounty*, edited by Gavin Kennedy under the title *The Mutiny of the Bounty* (1980).

HEYWOOD, Peter Acting midshipman on the *Bounty*; kept on board against his will; survived the wreck of the *Pandora*; found guilty at court-martial but recommended for mercy and pardoned; went on to a distinguished career in the Navy.

Heywood was born in Douglas on the Isle of Man on June 6, 1772, and was therefore fifteen years old when he was entered on the rolls of the *Bounty*. He was "of excellent lineage in the north of England" according to Lady Belcher (his later stepdaughter) and was recommended to Bligh by Dr. Richard Betham, Bligh's father-in-law. On board the *Bounty* he ate in Christian's mess together with George Stewart and Robert Tinkler. Heywood and Christian (whose family was Manx) soon became good friends.

On Tahiti, Heywood was assigned to Christian's shore party and thus had an excellent opportunity to compile material for the Tahitian dictionary which would later prove so valuable to English missionaries. He adapted quickly to the Tahitian way of life, to the point of having himself heavily tattooed (the word tattoo, by the way, comes from the Tahitian *tata'u*).

During the mutiny he had run up on deck but had been ordered to go below and was there kept under guard together with George Stewart. From what we know today — which is more than the judges knew at the court-martial — it is clear that Heywood had nothing to do with the mutiny. Bligh, however, was always convinced that Heywood not only took an active part in the mutiny but had planned it together with Christian. Since this was a firm conviction, not just a suspicion, it is probable that it originated in Bligh's feeling hurt and left out by Christian and Heywood during the stay at Tahiti.

Bligh's description of Heywood, written after the mutiny, reads as follows:

> [PETER HEYWOOD] Midshipman, 16 years, 5 feet 7 inches high, fair complexion, light-brown hair, well proportioned. Very much tattooed, and on the right leg is tattooed the Legs of Man, as the impression on that coin is. At this time he had not done growing. He speaks with the Isle of Man accent.

Heywood kept a journal which he submitted to Edwards who made some abstracts from it. The original was lost with the *Pandora*, but the abstracts have survived among Edwards papers and support the contents of Morrison's narrative.

During his second stay on Tahiti, from Christian's departure to the arrival of the *Pandora*, Heywood wisely refrained from taking an active part in the island's wars. There is no doubt that he loved the Tahitians; in a letter to his mother he later wrote:

> Whilst we remained there we were used by our Friends (the Natives) with a Friendship, Generosity, & Humanity almost unparallelled, being such as never was equalled by the People of any civilised Nations, to the Disgrace of all Christians.

When the *Pandora* arrived, he was one of the first to go on board and — like the other loyalists — was shocked to find himself treated as if he were a mutineer.

Heywood received strong support from his family on his return to England. His sister Nessy and his mother spared no effort in trying to see to it that he would be acquitted and — when he was found guilty and condemned to death — to obtain the King's pardon for him.

Heywood's mother had wanted to engage two of England's most eminent attorneys for her son's defense, but she was advised against it by Commodore Thomas Pasley, Peter's uncle, who knew the prejudice captains sitting as judges at a court-martial had against lawyers. Pasley instead recommended a friend of his, Mr. Aaron Graham, who had extensive experience as a judge advocate at naval courts-martial.

It may nevertheless have been a mistake, because Graham, instead of advising Heywood to concentrate on the hard fact that he had been kept below deck by force, suppressed Heywood's own defense speech and, together with his associate Mr. Const, wrote a rambling speech which was mawkish and over-emotional and hardly likely to have a positive influence on the captains sitting as judges. Youth was a poor defense in any case, as shown by the fact that Ellison, who was about the same age as Heywood, also emphasized his tender age at the time of the mutiny and was hanged nevertheless.

It is possible, however, that a different defense would not have led to acquittal; the testimony of Hayward and Hallett — which both afterwards said they regretted — was highly damaging and could not be ignored by the judges.

After obtaining the King's pardon, Heywood was highly instrumental in helping Edward Christian in his efforts to have the whole story of the mutiny told.

Although the judges at the court-martial could not ignore Hayward's and Hallet's testimony, it is clear that they had a favorable impression of Heywood. On the very day that the pardon was issued, the President of the court-martial, Admiral Lord Hood, wrote to Heywood's uncle, Commodore Pasley, offering his nephew a berth as a midshipman on board his own flagship, HMS *Victory*. Pasley, however, wanted Heywood on board his own ship, HMS *Bellerophon*.

Many years later, Heywood thought he saw Fletcher Christian on a street in Plymouth. The man had run away, however, which Christian would hardly have done. Nevertheless, the fact that Heywood talked about the incident with his friends has led to many fanciful speculations concerning Christian's supposed departure from Pitcairn and later adventures.

Heywood had a highly distinguished career in the Navy. He beame a post captain in 1803 and his rising to the rank of Admiral was prevented only by his death on February 10, 1831, at the age of fifty-eight (he had, however, retired from active service in 1816).

Sir John Barrow, First Secretary of the Admiralty, wrote about Heywood: "Having reached nearly the top of the list of captains, he died in this present year, leaving behind him a high and unblemished character in that service, of which he was a most honourable, intelligent, and distinguished member."

HILL, Joshua   The dictator of Pitcairn from 1832 to 1837; his self-proclaimed title was "President of the Commonwealth." He was born on April 15, 1773.

Under the entry PITCAIRN ISLAND there is a summary of Hill's dictatorial reign (see also BUFFETT, EVANS, and NOBBS). But how did Hill happen to come to Pitcairn?

Hill had left England in June 1830. In Hawaii he had been refused a grant of land by the governor of Maui. He left for Tahiti where he arrived in October 1831, a few weeks after the Pitcairners had left for home after their disastrous attempt at emigration. Moerenhout describes Hill's behavior in Tahiti (at the same time getting in some digs against his arch-enemy Pritchard):

> The man gave himself airs of importance, and pretended to have been sent by the British Government to arrange for the transportation of the Pitcairners to some other island, and let it be understood that he was in charge of some secret mission, concerning the state of all the islands. The missionaries, Pritchard more than the rest, believed him to be a person of importance. He was presented

> to the queen, and, with the missionaries as interpreters, questioned her concerning her government with all the gravity of a diplomatic envoy. . . . This man, during his residence at Tahiti, showed a childlike vanity, a boundless pride, a dangerous fanaticism, and an implacable hatred for whosoever dared to oppose him. As he never gave the least proof concerning his pretended mission, people came to realize he was an impostor; but for more than a year, he lived wholly at Pritchard's expence, who was even obliged to pay his laundress. At last he got rid of the man when an English captain offered to take him to Pitcairn where Hill had long wanted to go.

This describes the psychopathic confidence artist *par excellence*. If Hill could dupe the sophisticated Pritchard, who was soon to become the Consul of Britain, how easy must it have been for him to gain power over the trustful Pitcairners who could not even imagine that anybody would lie.

Hill's psychopathology, however, went beyond the tricks of a skillful confidence artist, as shown by the fact that when Charlotte Quintal (the daughter of Matthew Quintal's youngest son, Arthur) had stolen some yams, Hill sentenced her to be executed; she was twelve years old! (Her father prevented the sentence from going into effect.)

As to Hill's later activities, Robert B. Nicolson in *The Pitcairners* (1965) tells us that

> Hill was put ashore at Valparaiso and eventually made his way back to England.
>
> In 1841 Captain Hill wrote another "Memorandum", this time to the British Government, claiming payment for the time he had spent attending to the needs of the Pitcairn Islanders. In this document he included a vitriolic attack on George Hunn Nobbs and John Buffett, accusing them of the most outrageous deeds since they had arrived on the island.
>
> The last public record of Joshua Hill appears to be in 1844, when at the age of seventy-one he wrote to the Government a bitter condemnation of the morals of the missionaries who had been at Tahiti during his visit there twelve years before.

Perhaps Hill never heard of the pot and the kettle.

HILL OF DIFFICULTY   On Pitcairn: the steep slope extending from Bounty Bay to the plateau called The Edge. The path leading up this "hill" can today be negotiated by terrain motorcycles.

HILLBRANT, Henry (HEILDBRANDT, Heinrich)   Able-bodied seaman and cooper on the *Bounty*; mutineer; stayed on Tahiti; drowned when the *Pandora* foundered. Hillbrant was born in Hanover and spoke English poorly and with a heavy accent. He was twenty-four years old when he signed on the *Bounty*.

Bligh's description of Hillbrant, written after the mutiny, reads as follows:

[HENRY HEILDBRANDT] 25 years, 5 feet 7 inches high. Fair complexion, sandy hair, very strong made. His left arm shorter than the right, having been broke. Is an Hanovarian and speaks bad English. He is tattooed in several places.

Hillbrant triggered Bligh's first major temper tantrum when, during the famous cheese incident, he said that the ship's clerk, John Samuel, had ordered the cheeses — which Bligh claimed had been stolen — to be taken to the captain's residence before the *Bounty* sailed. Bligh screamed at Hillbrant that he would get "a damn'd good flogging" if he ever said anything like that again.

Hillbrant's role in the mutiny could not have been very active, since his participation is not detailed in any of the accounts. He stayed on Tahiti, as did eight of the other mutineers, taking the chance of being discovered by a British warship. Being a skilled craftsman, he was of great help to Morrison in building the schooner *Resolution*. He also took an active part in the wars on the island.

When the *Pandora* arrived, Hillbrant was one of the Bounty men who took to the mountains. Like the others, he was soon captured and confined to "Pandora's box," chained to hands and feet.

On May 14, 1791, six days out of Tahiti, he asked if he could speak with Captain Edwards. What he told him was that, the evening before Christian had left Tahiti for good, he had told Hillbrant his destination: an uninhabited island to the west of Danger Island discovered by John Byron. Edwards knew that must be Duke of York's Island (Atafu), but he should have known it was a ruse designed by Christian. Nevertheless he sailed there, stopping at Aitutaki and Palmerston on the way, all the time getting farther away from Christian.

If Hillbrant had hoped he would get any advantage from divulging this "secret" to Edwards, he must have been bitterly disappointed. Not only did he remain shackled in "Pandora's box," but — due to Edwards' inhuman orders to keep the prisoners chained while the *Pandora* foundered — Hillbrant went down with the ship without a chance to save himself. His fate is a testimony to the unspeakable callousness of the ship's commander.

HIMA'A (ahima'a, earth oven) The best description I have found of the old Tahitian earth ovens called *hima'a* (which are in use even today for *ma'a Tahiti*, Tahitian food) is in Douglas L. Oliver's *Ancient Tahitian Society* (1974), a monumental three-volume work which I recommend to anyone interested in the rich cultural heritage of Tahiti:

> The Maohi oven (for the average size household) was a simple but highly effective affair, which consisted of a pit about one to two feet deep and five to six feet across. To prepare an oven, layers of firewood and stones were stacked

in the pit and the wood burned to ash. One layer of hot stones was then left on the bottom of the pit and covered with leaves. On this was placed the food to be cooked, another layer of leaves, and the whole thing covered with ash, dirt, and sometimes more leaves. Such was the most common practice; in some instances, however, the food was placed directly on the hot stones. Unprocessed breadfruit, tubers, and roots were usually placed in the oven without additional wrappings, as were large cuts of pork and dog flesh, but fish, fowl, and vegetable puddings were usually baked in leaf wrappings, and other more liquid foods were baked in halves of coconut shell. Some oven pits were dug to dimensions required for the occasion, but in addition every household had one or more permanent ovens.

The earth oven was what the settlers on Pitcairn used to prepare their food and the custom survived long after the last original Tahitian settler had died. (*Maohi* means indigenous to the archipelago; Tahitian. In an extended sense it means Polynesian.)

HITIAA   District on the east coast of Tahiti Nui. It was in the lagoon of Hitiaa that Bougainville anchored during his visit in April, 1768.

HITI-AU-REVAREVA   According to Teuira Henry, the old Tahitian name for *Pitcairn*. The literal meaning is "border of passing clouds."

HITIHITI ("Odiddy," "Oedideedee," "Heete-Heete," "Hedeedee")   Hitihiti was originally from Bora Bora, a relative of that island's famous chief Puni. He was Pomare I's uncle by marriage.

He was an avid traveler and a true adventurer in the best sense of the word. He was also a friend of Captain Cook who wrote (in connection with his second voyage to Tahiti): "Heete-heete, who is a native of Bolabola, had arrived in Otaheite, about three months before, with no other intention, that we could learn, than to gratify his curiosity, or, perhaps, some other favourite passion; which are, very often, the only objects of the pursuit of other travelling gentlemen." I cannot think of a better definition of an adventurer.

Hitihiti sailed with Cook for part of the second voyage during which he visited Tonga, New Zealand, Easter Island, and the Marquesas and learned many valuable skills. He was exceedingly well liked on board during the seven months that he was part of the crew.

Being fascinated with fire-arms, Hitihiti soon became an excellent marksman and soon advanced to a position of principal aide to Pomare I. He became a skillful commander of troops and was successful in several campaigns, some of them under the tutelage of the men of the *Bounty* who stayed on Tahiti when Christian left.

Nor did Hitihiti "spit in the glass," as the Scandinavian saying goes. Cook wrote (about a dinner party or *tamaaraa* in Raiatea) that "Poor Odiddy had drunk a little too freely either of the juice of peper ['*ava*] or our Grog or both and was brought into the boat dead drunk." That this was not a once-in-a-life-time occurrence we know from the fact that Hitihiti also sailed with Captain Edwards to the Leeward Islands in order to visit his native Bora Bora, but he got drunk in Huahine and missed the ship!

In Nordhoff and Hall's trilogy, Hitihiti appears as the chief of Haapape (the actual chief of the district was Poino). The same is the case in some of the movie versions.

HITIMAHANA   Community in the district of Mahina (the old Haapape) immediately east of Point Venus. The literal meaning of *hitimahana* is sunrise.

HOA   Tahitian for friend.

HOA RAHI   Tahitian for special ("great") friend (*taio*).

HOGSHEAD   A large cask containing anywhere from 63 to 140 gallons.

HOOD, Lord Samuel   Admiral of the Blue; Commander-in-Chief of His Majesty's Ships at Portsmouth harbor 1786–1789 and 1791–1793; presided over the court-martial of the accused *Bounty* mutineers September 12 to 18, 1792.

Hood was born in 1724 and reached the rank of post captain in 1756. He fought in the American War of Independence and distinguished himself in the crucial battle of the Chesapeake in 1781. The next year he was given a peerage as Lord Hood. Nelson considered him one of the greatest of England's admirals. Hood died in 1816 at the age of ninety-two.

When Peter Heywood, after having been found guilty and condemned to death at the court-martial, received a King's pardon, Hood immediately offered him a berth in his flagship HMS *Victory* (Heywood's uncle, Sir Thomas Pasley, however, insisted on having his nephew aboard his ship, HMS *Bellerophon*).

HOOKER   Any old-fashioned or clumsy vessel (from the Dutch *hoeker*); a sailor's term for an old prostitute. Also: a large drink of liquor.

HORUE   Tahitian word for surfing, a sport which was very popular during the time of the early European visitors to the island. Surfing died out on Tahiti and the other Polynesian islands after the arrival of the missionaries (1797) who considered all entertainment sinful. Only in the last decades has surfing again become popular in Tahiti.

HOWELL, William   Reverend William Howell was Minister of St. John's Chapel in Portsea near Spithead at the time of the court-martial of the alleged *Bounty* mutineers. He attended to the prisoners from the time the court-martial ended (September 18, 1792) to the execution of the three condemned mutineers (October 29, 1792).

Reverend Howell may also have played an indirect role in securing a Royal Pardon for James Morrison by circulating the latter's writings among Navy personnel (see the December 1792 commentary in Part I). He died in 1822.

HUAHINE   Huahine, the easternmost of the Leeward group of the Society Islands, is situated at 16º45'S., 151º00'W. It is approximately eight miles long, north to south, and five miles wide. It is divided into two parts, Huahine Nui (big Huahine) in the north and Huahine Iti (small Huahine) in the south.

Huahine is a volcanic island; the highest peak is Mount Turi on Huahine Nui which attains a height of 2331 feet. The main harbor and settlement is Fare in the northwest. The current population of the island is approximately 4000.

Huahine was the home of Mai ("Omai") who went to England with Cook on the second voyage and returned on the third. Toofaiti, who sailed to Pitcairn with Christian as Tararo's consort and was later "given" to John Williams (the action that triggered the trouble on Pitcairn), was also from Huahine.

In modern times, the national hero of the Society Islands, Pouvanaa a Oopa, was born on Huahine (in 1895). Because of his desire for independence from France, he was arrested by the authorities on trumped-up charges, shipped to France, and imprisoned until he was too old to constitute a real threat.

Because Huahine has always been fiercely independent, it has been neglected by the French autocrats in Papeete and was therefore the last of the big islands to be allowed tourism. Consequently, it is the most "virgin" of the larger Society Islands to visit. In addition, it has the largest number of restored maraes (open-air temples).

To illustrate the (until relatively recently) total neglect of Huahine, we can take the *Official Directory and Guide Book of French Polynesia* for 1974. In chapter 11, entitled "Other Islands of French Polynesia" almost all islands are mentioned except Huahine. Whereas Marlon Brando (whose misportrayal of Fletcher Christian as being sissified and effete in the 1962 MGM motion picture still rankles *Bounty* enthusiasts) gets almost a full page pushing his exorbitantly priced hotel on Tetiaroa, Huahine is mentioned only incidentally in a list as being one of the islands in the Leeward group!

HUGGAN, Thomas   Surgeon on the *Bounty*; died on Tahiti December 9, 1788. Bligh had noticed Huggan's chronic drunkenness long before the *Bounty* sailed from Spithead and had tried to have him replaced, but the Admiralty had either refused or not been able to find a replacement. Bligh had therefore taken on board a surgeon's mate, Thomas Ledward, an action which showed considerable foresight.

There is little doubt that it was Huggan's fault that able-bodied seaman James

Valentine died. Valentine had been suffering from asthma, Huggan bled him — a common enough procedure at the time — and the wound became infected. Evidently gangrene set in because of mismanagement and neglect. Huggan did not even notify Bligh of the severity of Valentine's situation until the latter was already on the point of death.

Huggan was very much liked by the Tahitians during the six weeks they got to know him. As far as I can determine, he was the first Englishman to be buried on Tahiti (Domingo de Boenechea being the first European to be buried there, in 1775).

HUMPUS-BUMPUS A Pitcairn Island dish made of mashed bananas with manioc, prepared by baking or sometimes frying. It is similar to the Tahitian *po'e* from which it most probably stems.

HMS *HUNTER* A small 10-gun sloop, the ship in which Bligh started his naval career on July 27, 1770, shortly before his sixteenth birthday.

HUPE In Tahiti, the wind that blows from off the land in the early morning hours.

HURA Ancient Tahitian dance performed by pairs of women. Although the word has acquired a slightly different meaning, it is identical to the Hawaiian *hula*.

HUTIA See TOOFAITI.

IDDEA, IDEEAH See ITIA.

HMS *IMOGENE* The British warship which, under the command of Captain H. W. Bruce, arrived at Pitcairn on December 6, 1837, and removed Joshua Hill, the "dictator of Pitcairn," to Valparaiso.

IRONWOOD The ironwood referred to in books on the *Bounty* and Pitcairn is actually the beefwood (*Casuarina equisetifolia*; in Tahitian *toa* or *'aito*), a hard wood excellent for carving. Many of the artifacts made on Pitcairn are of this material.

The ancient maraes (open-air temples) were often built in groves of ironwood. Teuira Henry, in *Ancient Tahiti* (1928), tells us this story:

> In the reign of King Pomare V 1877–1880, a white man obtained the King's consent to sell him some fine 'aito trees that shaded the central cape at Papa'oa, where the national marae, Tara-hoi, had stood, and where the royal tomb of the Pomares now stands. The idea greatly shocked the people of the neighborhood, and they warned the foreigner not to commit such depredation.

But he derided them as superstitious, felled the trees, and disposed of the beautiful wood for cabinet work. Soon the white man was covered with a loathsome, incurable disease, from which he died about a year afterwards — a fate that the natives firmly believed to have been in consequence of the act.

Sometime in the 1700s the Pomare family adopted the name Vairaatoa (grove of *toa* trees) which made the word *toa* taboo. The name of the tree was changed to *'aito* and was adopted for use by the whole population.

"ISABELLA"   See MAUATUA.

ITAETAE   Tahitian word for a small, white tern (*Sterna alba*).

ITIA (Tetuanuireia i te Rai Atea, "Itea," "Eddia," "Edea," "Iddea," "Ideea")   Itia was the wife of Pomare I and stemmed from Moorea. She is described as a large, rather manly woman of great courage and with masculine tastes. She was reputed to be a warrior, a surf-riding champion, and an expert wrestler. She also became a master in the use of fire-arms.

Itia bore Pomare I four children. The first two were killed at birth, because Pomare belonged to the *arioi* society whose members were not allowed to have children. Probably because he wanted a successor, he resigned from the society and the next child was the boy, "Prince Tu," who succeeded him under the name of Pomare II.

Itia's fourth child was also a boy, named Teriitapunui. He succeeded his uncle, Vehiatua, as chief of the Teva i Tai clan on Taiarapu (actually he succeeded Vehiatua's *taio*, Charles Churchill, who had been chief for a few weeks until he was murdered by Matthew Thompson).

JAKARTA   See BATAVIA.

JAUNTY   A ship's master-at-arms (from the French *gendarme*). Charles Churchill was the *Bounty*'s jaunty.

JAVA (Djawa)   Java, in the Greater Sunda group, is the fourth largest of the Indonesian islands, situated between 5⁰52' and 8⁰47'S. and between 105⁰13' and 114⁰37'E. It is south-east of Sumatra and south of Borneo between the Java Sea in the north and the Indian Ocean in the south and west. In the north-west it is separated from Sumatra by the Sunda Strait and in the east from Bali by the Bali Strait. It is 660 miles long with a maximum width of 125 miles.

Java is dominated by a mountain chain running longitudinally from west to east with more than twenty peaks above 8000 feet, the highest being Semeru at 12,060 feet. The mountains are mostly volcanic with about thirteen active or semi-active today.

Despite its closeness to the equator, Java's climate is not very hot: the average temperature is between 78 and 80 degrees Fahrenheit. There is a north-west monsoon from December to March and a south-east monsoon from April to October.

The first Dutch traders arrived in Java in 1596 and, as part of the Dutch East Indies, the island remained under the control of the Netherlands until 1945 when an independent Indonesia was proclaimed.

"JENNY"   Nickname given by the *Bounty* mutineers to TEEHUTEATUAONOA.

JENNY (schooner)   A three-masted schooner from Bristol commanded by Captain James Baker. The *Jenny* arrived at Tahiti on March 25, 1792, and sailed for the north-west coast of America on March 31, carrying with her Captain Matthew Weatherhead and four crew members of the whaler *Matilda*. Vancouver relates that the *Jenny* arrived at Nootka in December 1792.

JOHNSON, Irving McClure   Captain of the brigantine *Yankee*. Johnson was born on July 4, 1905, in Hadley, Massachusetts. He sailed around Cape Horn in the four-masted barque *Peking* in 1929 and was mate of *Shamrock V*, Lipton's America's Cup challenger, on her voyage home in 1930.

Owner and master, first of the schooner and then of the brigantine *Yankee*, Johnson and his family sailed seven times around the world, taking with them a crew of young sailing enthusiasts. On each voyage Johnson made a point of visiting Pitcairn and helping the islanders get *miro* wood (for carving curios) from Henderson Island. In February 1957 he raised the anchor of the *Bounty* which is now mounted in the little square in Adamstown on Pitcairn. Irving Johnson's name is, and will be for generations, remembered with great affection on the island.

Together with his wife Electa, Johnson has written several books about the voyages of the *Yankee*. His earlier books, *Around the Horn in a Square-rigger* and *Shamrock V's Wild Voyage Home*, can be counted among the classics of the sea.

JUNK   Hard salted beef or pork supplied to ships. The word "junk" also referred to old and condemned rope cut into short lengths and used to make swabs, fenders and oakum. Indeed, the second definition was probably the original one and the almost inedible meat derived its name from it.

KAO   Kao is a vast, conically shaped rock only two miles north-east of Tofua. It is the most north-western of the Tonga islands.

Kao is about three miles long, north to south, and one and a half miles wide. Its peak, an extinct volcano, rises to 3380 feet, the tallest mountain in Tonga; on a clear day it is visible from Lifuka. The island is uninhabited at the present time.

Kao was one of the islands on which Lieutenant Robert Corner of the *Pandora* landed in order to investigate possible clues as to the whereabouts of the *Bounty* mutineers.

KAVA See 'AVA.

KEELHAULING A punishment consisting of hauling the offender from one side of a ship under the bottom and up on the other side. Contrary to many popular accounts, keelhauling — which often resulted in death — had been abolished in the British Navy by the time the *Bounty* sailed, although it was still practiced in other navies, such as the French and the Spanish. It was used in the Dutch Navy as late as 1806.

Scott Claver in *Under the Lash* (1954), describes the keelhauling of an English sailor in 1710 for the offense of blasphemy:

> The sailor was ordered to strip off all his clothes except for a strip of cloth round his loins. He was suspended by blocks and pullies, and these were fastened to the opposite extremities of the main yard, and a weight of lead or iron was hung upon his legs to sink him to a competent depth. By this apparatus he was drawn close up to the yard-arm, and thence let fall suddenly into the sea; where, passing under the ship's bottom, he was hoisted up on the opposite side of the ship. And this, after sufficient intervals of breathing, was repeated two or three times.
>
> If the unlucky sailor was drawn too near the ship's bottom, his flesh was torn and scratched by barnacles and such like, which, no doubt, was why he was stripped before the punishment. Uncleanliness and scandalous actions were the other crimes for which keel-hauling was the punishment.

KING GEORGE III ISLAND The name Samuel Wallis gave to Tahiti when he discovered the island on June 24, 1767.

KING'S EVIL (scrofula) A tuberculous constitutional disorder involving swelling and degeneration of the lymphatic glands, especially of the neck, and often inflammation of the joints.

KOEPANG See COUPANG.

KOTU Kotu island is the most western of the Kotu (Lulunga) group in the south-western part of the Haapai group in the Kingdom of Tonga. It is situated at $19^{\circ}57'$S., $174^{\circ}48'$W.

Kotu is a flat, densely wooded island two thirds of a mile long and one third of a mile wide.

At the time of the mutiny, the *Bounty* was sailing on a north-westerly course from Nomuka and was approximately equidistant from Kotu and Tofua. When Bligh was set adrift in the launch together with the loyalists, he decided to head for Tofua rather than Kotu because Tofua was downwind and, being a volcanic island, was more likely to have fresh water and fruit-bearing trees (actually, he found very little of either).

KOTZEBUE, Otto Von Estonian navigator and explorer (1787-1846) who commanded two voyages of circumnavigation. He discovered several minor islands in Polynesia, including Motu One which he named Bellingshausen after his fellow explorer from the Baltic.

Von Kotzebue is of interest in the *Bounty* story primarily because he interviewed Teehuteatuaonoa during his visit on Tahiti in 1824 and reported that she wanted to return to Pitcairn.

KUMARA See 'UMARA.

KUPANG See COUPANG.

LADY PENRHYN After Captain Cook sailed from Tahiti for the last time on September 29, 1777, it was to be almost eleven years until the island was again visited by a European ship. That ship was the *Lady Penrhyn*, which dropped anchor in Matavai Bay on July 10, 1788.

The *Lady Penrhyn*, 340 tons, had been one of the eleven ships in the First Fleet bringing convicts and some free settlers to found a colony in New South Wales. She was now on her way to Macao, but contrary winds had blown her far off course and her crew was severely ill with scurvy. Her commander, Captain William Sever, therefore decided to stop at Tahiti for fresh provisions and to give the crew a chance to rest.

The visit of the *Lady Penrhyn* took place only three months before the arrival of the *Bounty* and Captain Sever and his crew unwittingly gave Bligh some trouble by telling the Tahitians that Cook had died (Bligh managed to convince the Tahitians that it was just an unfounded rumor).

On board the *Lady Penrhyn* was also Lieutenant John Watts who had visited Tahiti in the *Resolution* on Cook's third voyage. He therefore knew chief Tu (Pomare) and noted that Tu still had with him the portrait of Cook which John Webber had painted and which had been given to Tu as a present. This portrait was to be signed on the back by visiting sea captains for many years (see the July 1792 commentary in Part I), although at some point it was lost.

Watts wrote a journal of the voyage in the *Lady Penrhyn* which was published in John Stockdale (ed.): *The Voyage of Governor Phillip to Botany Bay* (1789), but he did not explain why the *Lady Penrhyn* stayed only twelve days at Tahiti. It is possible, of course, that the time was sufficient for the men to regain their health; patients suffering from scurvy tend to respond quickly to the reintroduction of fresh food. Nevertheless, only twelve days in paradise?

On the way to Macao, Captain Sever discovered the lovely atoll Tongareva (now one of the northern Cook islands) and named it Penrhyn Island after the ship. It is still so named on most maps and charts.

Finally, it should be mentioned that Lieutenant Watts described the *Lady Penrhyn* as "a clumsy vessel and a heavy sailer."

LAGOON ISLAND   See TEMATANGI.

LAMB, Robert   Able-bodied seaman and butcher on the *Bounty*; loyalist; went with Bligh; died on the passage from Batavia. Lamb was born in London and was twenty-one years old when he joined the *Bounty*. On December 29, 1788, he was given a dozen lashes for "suffering his Cleaver to be stolen" by Tahitians. He was the only man flogged during the voyage who did not end up as a mutineer.

"End up" is the correct expression here, because Lamb initially joined the mutineers, accepting a musket from Thompson and standing guard over the fore hatchway, but he changed his mind later and went into the launch.

On the open-boat voyage from Tofua to Timor, an incident took place on an island within the Great Barrier Reef which Bligh called Lagoon Key; he describes the event as follows:

> . . . three men went to the East Key to endevour to take some birds, . . . About 12 o'clock the bird party returned with only 12 noddys . . . but if it had not been for the obstinacy of one of the party, who separated from the other two and putting the birds to flight, they might have caught a great number. Thus all my plans were totally defeated, for which on the return of the offender I gave him a good beating —

The offender was Robert Lamb who, upon arrival in Java, confessed that he had alone eaten nine noddies and had frightened the others away.

Lamb died, probably from a tropical disease contracted in Batavia, on the passage from there to Cape Town.

LANDWARD TEVA   See TEVA I UTA.

LARBOARD   Old term for the port side of a ship (the left side when facing forward). The term larboard was discontinued because it could be misheard as its opposite, starboard.

LARKIN (Larkan), John   First lieutenant on the *Pandora*. Not much is known about Larkin, because the surgeon on board, George Hamilton, who wrote an account of the voyage, avoids mentioning him. The little we know about Larkin comes primarily from Morrison's narrative.

He seems to have been a true sadist who enjoyed torturing the *Bounty* men who were imprisoned in "Pandora's box." Morrison gives us an example of how Larkin treated the prisoners:

> . . . Mr. Larkan the First Lieut. in trying the Handcuffs took the Method of setting his foot against our breasts and hauling the Handcuffs over our hands with all his Might, some of which took the Skin off with them, and all that could be hauld off by this Means were reduced, and fitted so close, that there was no possibility of turning the Hand in them, and when our wrists began to swell he told us that "they were not intended to fit like Gloves".

Larkin appears in Nordhoff's and Hall's *Mutiny on the Bounty* as Lieutenant Parkin.

LAU ISLANDS   The Lau group is the most eastern of the Fiji islands. It consists of fifty-seven islands spread over a vast area of the ocean between Viti Levu and the Tonga islands. About half of the islands are inhabited; the most important ones are Lakemba, Vanua Mbalavu, Moala, and Thithia, which all have air service from Nausori.

For the relevance of the Lau group to the *Bounty* story, see ONO-I-LAU and MATUKU.

LEAGUE   Three nautical miles.

LEBOGUE, Lawrence   Sailmaker on the *Bounty*; loyalist; went with Bligh on the open-boat voyage; arrived safely in England; sailed again with Bligh in the *Providence*.

Lebogue was aged forty when mustering on the *Bounty*, one of the oldest men in the remarkably young crew. Glynn Christian in his book *Fragile Paradise* (1982) states that Lebogue was an American from Annapolis, but I do not know his source for the claim.

There is little mention of Lebogue in the literature on the mutiny. He seems to have been highly competent in his craft and a man who went about his work quietly.

On the open-boat voyage from Tofua to Timor, Lebogue and Ledward, the surgeon, came close to dying. On June 10, 1789, Bligh writes: "Lawrence Lebogue and the surgeon cannot live a week longer if I do not get relief . . . the surgeon and Lawrence Lebogue are indeed miserable objects — I issue them a few teaspoonfull of wine out of the little I have remaining, which may secure their existence as long as it lasts."

If the word "indomitable" has any real meaning, it would certainly be in reference to Lebogue, because he volunteered to sail with Bligh again, this time in the *Providence* on the second breadfruit expedition. Again, he is hardly mentioned in the accounts of the voyage, but Bligh, in a letter to Banks, writes that Lebogue had encountered Christian's consort on this voyage and adds: "She went with Christian always untill his last Departure, which was sudden and unknown."

If this is true, it virtually proves that Christian did not have a permanent attachment among the women in Tahiti at the time of the mutiny. If the woman Lebogue met was Christian's consort, why had she not gone with Christian to Tubuai and later to Pitcairn?

The likelihood is that Christian knew both her and Mauatua during his first stay in Tahiti, but that no permanent attachment was formed.

George Mackaness in *The Life of Vice-Admiral William Bligh* (1951), mentions that a friend of the Bligh family once looked up Lebogue and had some grog with him. "Lebogue," said the friend, "this is better than being in the boat." "Oh d—— me," said the sailmaker, "I never think of the boat!"

LEDWARD, Thomas Denman   Surgeon's mate on the *Bounty*; acting surgeon after Huggan's death; loyalist; went with Bligh to Batavia; probably lost at sea during the passage from Batavia to Cape Town.

Bligh had become aware of the chronic drunkenness of his ship's surgeon, Thomas Huggan, long before the *Bounty* sailed from Spithead. He tried to get him replaced, but the Admiralty either refused or could not find a replacement. Bligh then tried to procure an assistant surgeon from one of the ships anchored at Spithead and found Ledward who was a surgeon's mate on board HMS *Triumph*, commanded by Captain Albemarle Bertie. Ledward was interested in coming along on the voyage and his captain was willing to let him go. (Captain Bertie, by the way, would later be one of the judges at the court-martial of the accused mutineers.)

Ledward was a man who went about his duty quietly and conscientiously. What his feelings were about Bligh before the open-boat voyage is questionable, but by the time the loyalists reached Batavia he had only contempt for the pettiness and greed and self-interest of his captain (see Ledward's letter in the November 1789 commentary).

Opposite the name Thomas Ledward the following note is written in the muster book of the *Bounty*: "17th Nov., 1789. Embarked on board the Rotterdam *Welfare*. Q. What became of him?"

The likelihood is that Ledward was lost at sea when the *Welfare* went down without survivors. But, intriguingly, there was a surgeon named Ledward on board Vancouver's ship *Discovery* from 1791 to 1795 (according to Gavin Kennedy in *Bligh*, 1978). We will probably never know if the two are identical.

Nordhoff and Hall use Ledward as the narrator for their epic story of the open-boat voyage, *Men Against the Sea*.

LEEWARD ISLANDS   Huahine, Raiatea, Tahaa, Bora Bora, Maupiti, and Motu Iti. See SOCIETY ISLANDS.

LIND, Anders Cornelius   Anders Lind was a member of the crew of the *Matilda* (see the March 1792 commentary in Part I). He was born in Stockholm, but we know nothing about his life before he arrived on Tahiti (after the *Matilda* had foundered on Mururoa atoll in February 1792).

When Bligh, who was at Tahiti on his second breadfruit expedition, offered the *Matilda*'s crew passage home, six of them elected to stay on Tahiti and of them three, including Lind, fought for Pomare — and three against him — in the wars that were going on. When the Swedish-Finnish seaman Petter Hägersten arrived in the *Daedalus* in 1793, he joined Pomare's "army" and from then on Pomare's victory was assured.

When the missionaries arrived in 1797, they used the services of both Lind and Hägersten as interpreters. They noted that Lind seemed to be about twenty-five years old and Hägersten about forty.

Captain James Wilson of the *Duff*, the ship which had brought the missionaries to Tahiti, seems to have thought that Lind might in some way be harmful to the missionaries. Or perhaps the captain just needed an additional crew member. Be that as it may, when he sailed he simply kidnapped Lind and put him to work as a seaman. Neither one can have been very happy with the other, because when the *Duff* passed the Micronesian island Lamotrek on October 26, 1797, Lind asked to be put ashore and Captain Wilson did not object. Nothing was ever again heard of Anders Lind. By the way, the natives on Lamotrek were cannibals.

LINKLETTER (Lenkletter), Peter   Quartermaster on the *Bounty*; loyalist; went with Bligh; died in Batavia. Linkletter was born in Shetland and was thirty years old when he joined the *Bounty*.

Linkletter is not mentioned much in the literature on the mutiny. We do know that he belonged to the "anti-Bligh group" among the men in the *Bounty*'s launch. According to Alexander McKee in *HMS Bounty* (1962), Linkletter and Purcell had both seen Bligh appropriate extra rations for himself during the voyage and told Bligh so to his face. Bligh retaliated by imprisoning them on a ship in the harbor of Coupang.

Linkletter died of a tropical disease (probably malaria) in Batavia within a fortnight after Bligh's departure for England.

LOBLOLLY BOY   A surgeon's attendant on board a ship.

LORD HOOD'S ISLAND   Captain Edwards' name for MARUTEA.

LOVELY ANN   Brig from London, commanded by Captain Phillip Blythe. In 1826 Jane Quintal, daughter of the mutineer Matthew Quintal, left on this ship for Rurutu in the Austral Islands where she married the local chief and raised a large family. She was the second Pitcairner to leave the island, the first being Teehuteatuaonoa.

LOW ISLANDS   See TUAMOTU.

LUCY ANN   British government barque of 213 tons from Sydney. Commanded by Captain J. Currey and escorted by HMS *Comet*, the *Lucy Ann* carried the entire population of Pitcairn (86) to Tahiti in 1831, leaving Pitcairn on March 7 and arriving in Papeete on March 23.

On the voyage a daughter, named Lucy Ann after the ship, was born to Arthur Quintal (son of mutineer Matthew Quintal and his consort Tevarua) and Catherine McCoy (daughter of mutineer William McCoy and Teio). However, like so many of the Pitcairners, little Lucy Ann died on Tahiti (April 25, 1831).

The ship *Lucy Ann* sailed into literary history under the name of *Julia* in Herman Melville's novel *Omoo*. On August 9, 1842, Melville escaped from the Taipi ("Typee") valley in the Marquesas and boarded the *Lucy Ann* which carried him to Tahiti, arriving on September 20. There was, according to Melville, a mutiny on board — it amounted to some of the crew refusing to obey further orders and insisting on staying in Tahiti. They were then put into the "Calabooza Beretanee" (British jail) where Melville — contrary to what he claims in *Omoo* — joined them voluntarily.

The further adventures of the *Lucy Ann* are not known to me.

LYNX   Merchant ship owned by Duncan Campbell, engaged in trade with the West Indies and commanded by Bligh before he was appointed master of the *Britannia*.

MADEIRA   A rich, strong wine akin to sherry made on the Madeira Islands. It was popular on ship voyages, because it would last much longer than other wines. Bligh took on a large supply of Madeira in Tenerife where he stopped in January 1788 on his way to Cape Horn.

MAHINA   A district in Tahiti about seven miles east of present-day Papeete. It encompasses Point Venus and Orofara. See also HAAPAPE.

MAI ("Omai")   Mai is usually referred to as "Omai" in the literature, the reason being ignorance of the meaning of the particle " 'o" (see that entry). Mai was a Tahitian (actually his home island was Huahine) who volunteered to go to England with Captain Tobias Furneaux, commander of the *Adventure* on Cook's second voyage. The *Adventure*, with Mai on board, left Tahiti on May 14, 1774, and arrived in England on July 14, 1775.

Mai created a real sensation in England, being considered a prime example of a "noble savage." Despite the strangeness of his new surroundings and of the people around him, Mai always carried himself with typical Polynesian dignity and goodnaturedness; he behaved as naturally with King George III as he did with the driver of his carriage. The novelist and diarist Fanny Burney (Frances d'Arblay) wrote:

> Omai, with no tutor but Nature . . . appears in a new world like a man who had all his life studied the Graces and attended with unremitting application and diligence to form his manners, and to render his behaviour politely easy and thoroughly well-bred. . . . Indeed, he seems to shame education, for his manners are so extremely graceful and he is so polite, attentive and easy, that you would have thought he came from some foreign court. . . . I think this shows how much more Nature can do without art than art with all her refining, unassisted by Nature.

Mai spent almost two years in England. He left with Cook on the latter's third voyage and arrived in Tahiti in May, 1777. Mai had been invaluable as an intepreter during the voyage. On October 13, Mai reached Huahine where Cook's carpenters constructed a European-style house for him and filled it with gifts which Mai's friends in England had sent with him. "Omai" died on his home island long before the arrival of the next British ship. But his visit to England had made Tahiti so popular that he can be said to have contributed, indirectly, to the fact that the *Bounty* sailed for the South Seas with all volunteers.

When Bligh sailed from Tahiti in April 1789, he made a special point to sail close to Huahine in order to see whether Mai's house was still standing. Nothing remained, however, except a horse which Cook had given him and which had made a great impression on his fellow islanders.

MAI   Tahitian for "hither" or "in this direction;" often an abbreviation of *Haere mai* which means "Come here."

MAIMITI, "MAINMAST," "MAIMAS"   See MAUATUA.

MAIORO   See VAETUA.

MAITAI   Tahitian for the adjective "good."

MAITEA   See MEHETIA.

MAITITI   Maititi is known in the *Bounty* story as the servant of Charles Churchill and as playing an indirect role in the latter's death (see the March 1790 commentary in Part I).

Maititi was also one of the two Tahitians who sailed to England with Bligh on the second breadfruit expedition. He died on arrival in England on September 4, 1793 (see the July 1792 and September 1793 commentaries in Part I).

MALEWA   See MAREVA.

MAMU   Tahitian word meaning "be quiet" or "shut up." As a result of their long stay in Tahiti, the crew of the *Bounty* had picked up a great number of Tahitian expressions and often used them with each other when conversing. In fact, when Bligh was held at bayonet point on the day of the mutiny and was cursing Christian, the latter told him: "Mamu, sir!"

MANA   Polynesian word for spiritual power. All *mana* emanated from the gods, as we can see from the following chant quoted by Teuira Henry in *Ancient Tahiti* (1928):

> *E mana nui roa to te nu'u atua, E mata ra'a to te atua, E hou'u te ta'ata, e fatiou te mau ra'au, e oriorio, mahe'ahe'a roa, e mimi'o ino to te fenua e to te moana i te mana o to'na rima, i te aho o to'na paoa ihu.*

> All the hosts of gods had great power. Their glance was holy. Man crouched, trees bent down, all on land and in the sea withered, grew pale, and shrank under the power of their hands, before the breath of their nostrils.

J. C. Furnas in *Anatomy of Paradise* (1948), defines *mana* as follows:

> *Mana* was "what it takes," with some aspects of the Latin *virtus*. It was an attribute accorded by the gods to man or tribe; it was the personal force, applied through spells, that enabled the wizard to blast a tree, smash a stone or kill a man at long range. With it came victory, health, wealth, and prestige. The chief had more of it than others, which is why he was chief. His ancestors had passed it on to him, sometimes by an actual ceremony, as when Elijah endowed Elisha with his cloak. This *mana* of the chief's, partaking of, but not necessarily coextensive with, that of the tribe, was what procured him obedience. Obviously it was a great cohesive force. Chief, tribe or wizard could lose *mana* by defeat in war or by anything else that led to loss of prestige, or indicated that the favor of the gods had receded or departed from his doings.

MANARII (Manalii, sometimes Menalee or Minarii)   Manarii was one of the three Tahitian men who joined Christian and his fellow mutineers in their quest for an island refuge (two men from Tubuai and one from Raiatea also came along). When Pitcairn was sighted, Manarii and the other two Tahitians joined Christian in his exploratory shore party.

With the other two men from Tahiti he had to share Mareva. When the two Tubuaians and the man from Raiatea conspired to kill the mutineers at the end of the first year on the island, Manarii participated in killing two of them. On Massacre Day, September 20, 1793, it was he who killed Brown after Teimua had tried to save the gardener's life by shooting at him with a powder charge only and telling him to pretend to be be dead. Brown moved too soon and Manarii clubbed him to death with the butt of his musket.

Soon afterwards, Manarii shot Teimua to death while the latter was accompanying Teraura's singing on his nose flute. The motive was clearly jealousy. After the murder, Manarii ran to the mountains and joined Quintal and McCoy who were still in hiding, fearing for their lives. Some quarrel arose between them, however, and the two mutineers killed Manarii.

Manarii, like the other Polynesians on the island, left no children.

MANGAREVA   The closest inhabited island to Pitcairn. Mangareva is the main island in the Gambier group and is situated at 23°07'S., 134°57'W., 306 miles northwest of Pitcairn. Mangareva and three other inhabited islands in the group are enclosed by a barrier reef almost forty miles in circumference.

Mangareva is near the center of the vast lagoon; the twin-peaked Mount Duff, which rises to 1447 feet, gives the island a highly distinctive and unforgettable appearance. The main port and settlement is Rikitea on the eastern side of the island.

Mangareva was discovered by Captain James Wilson in the *Duff* (the ship which brought the first missionaries to Tahiti) on May 23, 1797. The first European to land on the island was Captain Frederick W. Beechey in HMS *Blossom* on December 29, 1825. There were then 9000 inhabitants altogether on the four islands comprising the group.

On July 16, 1834, Father Louis Jacques Laval, a priest of the Picpus order, arrived on Mangareva and managed to make himself virtual dictator on the island. He ordered the population to start building churches, one more magnificent than the other. The church in Rikitea, for example, looks like Notre Dame in Paris and is three times larger than the cathedral in Papeete. It seats 1200 people.

Father Laval did not only use the population as slave labor; he also starved and worked them to death. They were forbidden to fish or to work their gardens: all their time had to be devoted to building these edifices for the glory of the Christian God. As a result, the inhabitants died like flies; it is estimated that over 5000 perished as a direct result of Father Laval's fanaticism. When a visitor from Tahiti called this to his attention, he said: "True, they are dead, but they have gone to Heaven more quickly!" The Catholic Church waited until 1871 before it moved Father Laval to Tahiti where he died in 1880. He stands as a symbol for the destruction so many missionaries brought to these lovely islands, where they should have gone to learn instead of to teach.

Mangareva today has only 550 inhabitants and that is counting all four islands in the group. In a sense, the French are continuing the work of Father Laval by conducting their atomic tests on nearby Mururoa atoll. To "protect" the population of Mangareva they have built a barn-like structure, so huge that you can hardly see from one end to the other. Into this ugly building the whole population of the four islands is herded — and there they have to stay for days — while the French explode their bombs. Some sprinklers on the roof constitute the alleged protection against radiation.

In 1987, for the first time in history, a Pitcairn longboat made the voyage to Mangareva and back. The boat, christened *Tub*, was a gift from Great Britain and the most sophisticated craft the Pitcairners have ever had, being equipped with dual propellers and also capable of being sailed.

MANIHIKI ISLANDS   Old name for the northern Cook Islands.

MAOHI   Tahitian adjective for indigent, native, Polynesian.

MAPE   A Tahitian type of chestnut, shaped like a kidney (the Tahitian word *mape* also means kidney). The *mape* tree (*Inocarpus edulis*) is generally found growing near river banks. The nuts are very tasty and nutritious and are usually eaten roasted on live coals or baked. The wood of the tree is used for making fences and as firewood.

MARAA   In Tahiti: a promontory on the south-west coast of Tahiti Nui.

MARAAI   Tahitian word for south wind.

MARAE ("morai")

> The maraes were the holiness and the glory of the land,
> They were the pride of the populations of these isles.
> The ornaments of the land were the maraes,
> They were the palaces presented to the gods.
> (Ancient Chant of the Maraes)

A marae is a Polynesian open-air temple. The best description of a marae can be found in the Transactions of the London Missionary Society 1815–1832, written by missionary John Jefferson:

> *Morai*, in the language of the country, signifies a place appropriated to the worship of Eatooa, or deity. As the Otaheiteans have a plurality of deities, so they have many *morais*. They are temporary or permanent. Temporary *morais* are erected before the corpse of the dead agreeable to the fancy of the erector, and (from what I have hitherto seen) are commonly small altars, variously decorated, with leaves and the fruit of palm tree, that grows in abundance, and upon which are placed divers offerings of food. Permanent *morais* are numerous and divers: they are usually enclosed spots of ground surrounded with trees of different kinds, and having in them sundry small pavements of stone: at the head of each stands a stone of larger size, and at the back of the stone is generally fixed a board five or six feet long, with a little rude carving on it; the top divided into five parts, or slits, to represent the fingers of a hand: sometimes the board has the figure of a man or bird carved on its top. At the foot of this pavement the priest worships, with his face directed towards the headstone and plank, and throws his offering, consisting of a young plantain-tree root, green leaves, or the leaf of a cocoa-nut twisted in a peculiar form, upon the pavement. Besides these kinds of oratories within the enclosure, there are altars, on which meat offerings are placed, and before which prayers are made. Altars for the like purpose are scattered up and down the country where there is no *morai*. At one permanent place of worship, there are frequently a plurality of *morais* dedicated to different deities: thus the one I now visited, had in it two others dedicated to as many false gods.

Teuira Henry in *Ancient Tahiti* (1928) lists the different classes of marae:

> There were three classes of marae of public importance: the international, the national, and the local; also five classes of domestic marae: the family, or ancestral marae, the social, the doctors', the canoe-builders', and the fishermen's marae. The marae were built of stone without cement and were made very high, in parallelogram pyramidal form, or low and square, according to the desire of those who erected them. The stones of these structures were considered very sacred and to them are still attached many superstitions.

Henry's book was published in 1928, but what she says about superstitions connected with maraes and the stones of maraes is as true today as it was then. J. Garanger puts it succinctly in *Sacred Stones and Rites of Ancient Tahiti* (1969):

> The time of the *maraes* appears far off to us today. Temples, chapels, and churches seem to have totally replaced the places of worship of the Tahiti of yesteryear; and the Tahitian of today seems to have lost the memory of these sacred rites, whose importance in the religious life of former times we have tried to show.

However! In the districts, many take care not to approach the ruins of these places which their ancestors considered as extremely taboo, and would not dream of touching the stones which have preserved in their eyes some abiding remnants of their former virtue. They know only too well that contacts or profanations would infallibly be followed by irremediable maledictions: disturbances in speech or sight, incurable illnesses, accidents or infirmities.

The *maraes* of the ancestors have disappeared, but the gods of the *maraes* continue despite everything to exercise their supernatural power in the behaviour of their descendants.

The men of the *Bounty* had many occasions to observe ceremonies held at maraes. Part of Morrison's description of such a ceremony is quoted in the February 1791 commentary in Part I.

The missionaries made it a point to destroy all the maraes. Only in the last decades have some of them been restored.

In the district of Paea on Tahiti there is a marae called Arahurahu which has been restored to its original condition. All other maraes on Tahiti have been totally destroyed, even the important Taputapuatea on the north coast and the gigantic Mahaiatea in the south.

Most of the restored maraes are in the Leeward islands, primarily on Huahine and Raiatea, where the Holy Land of the old Polynesians was located. This important work was conceived and supervised by the eminent archeologist Yosihiko H. Sinoto of the Bernice Pauahi Bishop Museum in Honolulu. It is worth a trip to the Leeward islands just to see the magnificent results of Professor Sinoto's work.

MAREVA (Malewa) Mareva may or may not have been kidnapped by the mutineers when the *Bounty* left Tahiti for the last time. On Pitcairn she was shared as a consort by the three Tahitians, Manarii, Teimua, and Niau.

After the Tahitians had been killed, Mareva, together with Tinafanaea, moved into the household of Vahineatua and John Adams. She died sometime between the visit of the *Topaz* (1808) and the *Briton* and the *Tagus* (1814). She left no children.

MARIA The barque, commanded by Captain Thomas Ebriel, on which Joshua Hill arrived at Pitcairn on October 28, 1832.

MARO Tahitian word for a loincloth worn by men; usually a length of *pareu* wound about the waist, passed between the legs, and then tucked in at the waist; it resembles tight, but comfortable, shorts.

MARO URA A *maro*, or a belt of plaited pandanus leaves, decorated with red feathers (sacred to the gods) and sometimes also with yellow and black feathers.

The *maro ura* was used on Tahiti — and on many other islands in eastern Polynesia — as a symbol of royalty, comparable to a royal crown in Europe (see the February 1791 commentary in Part I). A *maro* decorated mainly with yellow feathers was called *maro tea*; it was used mainly on Raiatea.

MARQUESAS ISLANDS The Marquesas lie to the north of the Tuamotu archipelago between the parallels of 7⁰50' and 10⁰35' S., and the meridians of 138⁰25' and 140⁰50' W. They are composed of two rather distinct groups: the north-western group discovered by the American ship *Hope* in 1791 and the south-eastern group discovered in 1595 by Mendana and named Islas de las Marquesas de Mendoza. All of the Marquesas are high islands with majestic mountains; they have a wild and forbidding look about them.

The north-western group consists of: Nuku Hiva, Ua Huka, and Ua Pou. The south-eastern group consists of: Hiva Oa, Fatu Hiva, Tahuata, Motane, Fatu Huku.

Fletcher Christian had originally considered sailing to the Marquesas (he of course knew only about the south-eastern group), but he changed his mind, considering that they were too likely to be visited by other ships.

MARRO Bligh's spelling of MARO.

MARTIN, Isaac Able-bodied seaman on the *Bounty*; mutineer; went with Christian; died on Pitcairn. Martin was born in Philadelphia and was probably American. "Probably," because there is also a small English community near Durham called Philadelphia. He was thirty years old when he signed on the *Bounty*. Bligh's description of Martin, written after the mutiny, reads as follows:

> [ISAAC MARTIN] 30 years, 5 feet, 11 inches high. Sallow complexion, short brown hair, raw-boned. Tattooed on his left breast with a star.

Martin was flogged on Tahiti for striking a native. Bligh's orders to the men were of the "damned if you do and damned if you don't" variety. A man would be flogged if he let a native steal something, but he would also be flogged if he struck one of the thieves. The latter was the case with Martin: he had struck a Tahitian in his effort to get back an iron hoop that the islander had stolen. Bligh sentenced him to twenty-four lashes but reduced them to nineteen after chief Teina and his wife Itia had interceded on Martin's behalf.

A British sailor accepted even severe punishment if he considered it just and did not think less of his commander for it. But if the punishment was unfair, as in Martin's case, it must have left a lingering resentment. During the subsequent mutiny Martin vacillated. He was in Christian's watch and the first man that Christian approached with his plan to take over the ship. Martin refused cooperation. However, after Christian had succeeded in talking Quintal and Churchill into the idea, Martin changed his mind and joined the mutineers.

When Bligh was under guard on the quarterdeck, Martin fed him with a shaddock to relieve his parched mouth with its juice. Bligh later wrote:

> Isaac Martin, one of the guard, I saw I had brought to a sense of his duty, and as he fed me with shaddock . . . we explained to each other by our eyes reciprocally our wishes. This was, however, observed, and Martin was instantly removed from me whose inclination then was to leave the ship, but for a threat of instant death if he did not return out of the boat.

It is possible, even probable, that Martin would not have vacillated, and would have remained a loyalist had it not been for the unfair punishment he had been subjected to in full view of the Tahitians (during an era when a white man's prestige had to be preserved at all times). As it was, he would have remained in the boat if Churchill and Quintal had not threatened to shoot him unless he came back on board.

On Tubuai Martin voted with Christian and joined him on the quest which would finally lead to Pitcairn.

Martin's consort was Teehuteatuaonoa; he had no children with her. On Massacre Day, September 20, 1793, he was the fourth mutineer to be killed by the Polynesians.

MARUTEA (Lord Hood's Island)   A large atoll almost 100 miles north-north-west of Mangareva at 21⁰30'S., 135⁰30'W. It consists of a cluster of islets on which brushwood and some coconut palms grow. There is no entrance into the lagoon. Marutea is inhabited and is periodically visited by Mangarevans for pearl fishing.

Marutea was discovered by Captain Edwards in HMS *Pandora* on March 17, 1791; he named it Lord Hood's Island.

"MARY"   See TEIO.

MARY ANN   The 100-ton brigantine which, commanded by a Captain Wilson, brought the first two families back to Pitcairn from Norfolk after the emigration of the whole population of Pitcairn in 1856.

The *Mary Ann* left Norfolk on her way to Tahiti on December 2, 1858, and arrived at Pitcairn on January 17, 1859. On board were the families of Moses and Mayhew Young, sixteen in all.

They arrived in the nick of time. Only a few days after their homecoming a French man-of-war approached the island with the purpose of annexing it to France. Seeing the Union Jack hoisted, however, the French changed course and left Pitcairn alone.

The returning families found that several houses had been destroyed in their absence. They found a slate in the schoolroom which explained the mystery. On it were written the names of seamen who had used the island as a refuge after their ship, the American clipper *Wild Wave*, 1540 tons, commanded by Captain Josiah Knowles, had foundered on the reef of Oeno atoll seventy-six miles north-west-by-north of Pitcairn. From the planks of the houses and some trees that they felled they had built a boat named *John Adams*, not to honor the mutineer but the President of the United States. Incredibly they managed to reach Nukuhiva in this craft, over a thousand miles to the north-west.

MATAEINAA   Tahitian word for district or chiefdom.

MATAHIAPO   Tahitian word for the first-born child. Thursday October Christian was Fletcher's *matahiapo*.

MATA KI TE RANGI   Although some authorities claim that Mata ki te Rangi (literally "eye toward the sky") is an old Polynesian name for Pitcairn, the great likelihood is that it is an old name for Easter Island (Rapa Nui).

MATAOHU   See TERAURA.

MATAVAI BAY   Situated on the north coast of Tahiti about six miles east of present-day Papeete between One Tree Hill (today's Tahara'a) to the west and Point Venus to the east. Wallis named the bay Port Royal Harbour.

Bengt Danielsson, the renowned expert on the South Seas and member of the famed Kon Tiki expedition, considers Matavai the most beautiful natural harbor in the world. Here is how he describes it in his exciting book *What happened on the Bounty* (1962):

> As is often the case on Tahiti, the shore was covered in rich, coal-black lava sand, over which the white foam of the surf formed ever shifting patterns. Behind the sandy shore was a broad belt of succulent, dark-green breadfruit and coconut palms. But what really gives Matavai Bay its fantastic beauty is not so much the perfectly formed shoreline and unique colour harmonies as the grandiose background of ravines, plateaus and waterfalls which are set off by two mighty peaks rising 7,000 feet against the tropical sky.

Here is where most of the early explorers anchored; this is what greeted the eyes of the seamen weary of a long voyage; this — in addition to the beauty of the Tahitian women — is what the crew of the *Bounty* visualized when they thought back to the island on which they had spent over five wonderful months.

Matavai Bay affords excellent anchorage and good shelter, except when north-westerly gales are blowing, at which time the bay becomes a dangerous lee shore with high surf. This happened in the beginning of December 1788 and that was the reason Bligh moved the *Bounty* to the more sheltered Toaroa harbor towards the end of the month.

MATE See POMARE I.

MATILDA British whaler under the command of Captain Matthew Weatherhead. The *Matilda* had sailed from England on March 27, 1791, and had touched at Port Jackson and Peru before arriving in Tahiti on February 14, 1792, anchoring in Vaitepiha Bay. For some inscrutable reason Captain Weatherhead stayed only three days at Tahiti.

On the night of February 24, 1792, the *Matilda* foundered on Mururoa atoll, 640 miles south-east of Tahiti (see the March 1792 commentary in Part I). All of the crew were saved and reached Tahiti on March 5. Soon afterwards the schooner *Jenny* from Bristol arrived in Tahiti, and when she sailed for America Captain Weatherhead and four members of the crew went with her. Instead of waiting for another ship, three of the men took one of the four whaleboats of the *Matilda*, fitted it with sails of native matting, and sailed for Port Jackson. They were never heard of again.

If they had waited only a few weeks, they could have sailed back to Europe with Captain Bligh in the *Providence*. Bligh arrived on April 10 and when he left a little over three months later, he took fifteen of the *Matilda*'s crew with him. The remaining six wanted to stay on Tahiti. One of them, the Swede Anders Lind, became a kind of military advisor to Pomare I.

In February 1826 Captain Frederick Beechey in HMS *Blossom* found parts of the wreck of the *Matilda* on the northern shore of Mururoa.

MATIVY See MATAVAI.

MATTE Morrison's spelling of Mate. See POMARE I.

MATUKU Matuku is an island in the Lau group in the Fijis, situated about 290 nautical miles almost due west of Tofua at 19°09'S., 179°44'E. It is four and a half miles long, north to south, and three and a half miles wide. Its summit, Ngilligilli, rises to 1262 feet.

Captain Charles Wilkes described Matuku as "the most beautiful of all the islands in the Pacific. There the natives live in perpetual plenty among perennial streams, and could victual the largest ship without feeling any diminution of their stock. In the harbour three frigates could lie in perfect safety, and the people have earned a reputation for honesty and hospitality to passing ships which belongs to the inhabitants of none of the large islands."

The stay at Matuku of master's mate Oliver of the *Pandora* and his crew on the schooner *Resolution* is described in the July 1791 commentary in Part I.

MATYNAH See MATAEINAA.

MAU Tahitian word meaning fixed, solid, established, firm, fastened, basic, real, true. Sometimes an abbreviation of *parau mau* which means "true talk" or "that's true."

MAUATUA (Maimiti, "Mainmast," Isabella) Christian's consort. We do not know when Mauatua was born, but she claimed to remember Cook's first arrival in Tahiti (1769), so she must have been at least twenty-three or twenty-four when the *Bounty* arrived in 1788. There is no evidence that Christian had a serious attachment to her before the mutiny (in fact, it is unlikely), but she did follow him both to Tubuai and later to Pitcairn.

When the loyalists and half of the mutineers had gone ashore on Tahiti on September 22, 1789, Christian left the island the same night. The reason was that Mauatua had found out about a plot among the Tahitians to overpower the nine mutineers and take over the ship (the plot may even have been incited by one or more loyalists, although Morrison does not mention anything about it). If she had not learned about the scheme, or had not told Christian, the *Bounty* story could have had a very different ending and Pitcairn might not be inhabited today.

Mauatua bore Christian two sons, Thursday October and Charles, before he was murdered on Massacre Day, September 20, 1793, and one daughter, Mary Anne, born after his death.

When Christian died, Mauatua became Edward Young's consort (actually she shared him with Toofaiti) and bore him three children: Edward, Polly, and Dorothea.

Mauatua survived the disastrous attempt to migrate to Tahiti in 1831, but saw her first-born child, Thursday October, succumb to the diseases then rampant there to which the Pitcairners had no immunity. She herself died on Pitcairn ten years later — September 19, 1841 — of an epidemic brought by a visiting ship. Of the original settlers on the island, she was survived only by Teraura. In her later years, she was known affectionately as "Maimas," an abbreviation of Mainmast.

MAURUURU (ROA) Tahitian for "thank you (very much);" the literal meaning is "I am (very) satisfied."

McCOY (Mickoy, McKoy), William Able-bodied seaman on the *Bounty*; mutineer; went with Christian; died on Pitcairn. The spelling McCoy has been used throughout this book, because that is how the descendants spell it. In the muster book of the *Bounty*, however, the name is spelled Mickoy.

McCoy was twenty-three years old when he joined the *Bounty*. Together with his buddy Matthew Quintal, he had transferred from HMS *Triumph*. He was a violent man and had been involved in many fights, as evidenced by several scars on his body and face. His physical description, given by Bligh after the mutiny, reads as follows:

> [WILLIAM MICKOY] seaman, aged 25 years, 5 feet 6 inches high, fair complexion, light brown hair, strong made; a scar where he has been stabbed in the belly, and a small scar under his chin; is tatowed in different parts of his body.

The first significant mention we have of McCoy in the *Bounty* literature is that Bligh, in one of his hysterical outbursts, threatened to shoot him if he did not pay attention (to Bligh's incoherent tirade). This was right after the *Bounty* had left Nomuka, in other words, shortly before the mutiny.

McCoy was one of the first to join Christian and took an active part in the mutiny. On Tubuai he voted with Christian and went with him to Pitcairn.

McCoy was one of the three mutineers (the others were Brown and Williams) who, with three Polynesians, went ashore with Christian to explore the island. His consort was Teio whom he called Mary and with whom he had two children, Daniel and Kate. He and Quintal were notorious for the brutality with which they treated the Polynesians.

On Massacre Day, September 20, 1793, McCoy narrowly escaped being murdered and, together with Quintal, fled to the mountains. Together they killed Manarii after he had joined them (see the September 1793 commentary in Part I). Once they had received proof of the death of the remaining Polynesians, they rejoined the village.

McCoy had worked in a brewery in Glasgow and, after much experimentation, he succeeded in distilling a strong liquor from the ti-root. The first bottle was ready for consumption on April 20, 1797. This introduced an era of wild drunkenness on the island. McCoy, especially, became totally addicted to the "Demon's Rum" and developed delirium tremens. Before the end of the year he was dead; during one of his attacks he tied a stone around his neck and jumped to his death from a precipice.

McINTOSH, Thomas   Carpenter's crew on board the *Bounty*; loyalist; kept on board against his will; survived the wreck of the *Pandora*; acquitted at court-martial.

McIntosh was born in North Shields and was twenty-six years old when he joined the *Bounty*. The description Bligh later gave of him reads as follows:

> [THOMAS McINTOSH] Carpenter's Crew. 28 years, 5 feet 6 inches high. Fair complexion, light-brown hair, slender made. Pitted by the smallpox.

McIntosh and Norman were kept on board the *Bounty* by Christian who needed their skills as carpenters; he did not want to force the dour and strong-willed Purcell

ENCYCLOPEDIA

to remain. Neither one had taken part in the mutiny, and both called out to Bligh to remember that they were kept on board against their will.

McIntosh had a woman on Tahiti whom he called Mary. Mary followed him to Tubuai and back and bore him a daughter. When Christian had left with the *Bounty*, McIntosh was the first one that Morrison approached with his plan to build a ship and he, together with Norman, were of invaluable help in carrying through with the project.

When the *Pandora* arrived, McIntosh was the only loyalist who ran up into the mountains to hide with the mutineers. We will never know why. Perhaps he had become attached to his wife and daughter and wanted to remain on Tahiti.

His attempted escape evidently did not count against him. He was one of the three prisoners on the *Pandora* who were released to work the pumps when the ship struck the reef and, once back in England, he did not experience any significant trouble in being acquitted at the court-martial.

When Bligh returned to Tahiti on the second breadfruit expedition, he was approached by "Mary," McIntosh's consort, who showed him a beautiful little girl, about eighteen months old, whose name was Elizabeth and who was McIntosh's daughter. Whether Bligh ever tried to let his former crew-member know about this encounter when he returned to England, is unknown. It seems most unlikely; Bligh could be sentimental about himself but he had little understanding of the feelings of others.

I do not know what happened with McIntosh after the court-martial.

MEHETIA   Mehetia is a small island (three miles at its greatest extent) about sixty miles due east of Tahiti. Situated at 17°53'S., 148°06'W., it is the most eastern of the Society Islands. It was discovered by Samuel Wallis on June 17, 1767; he named it Osnaburgh Island.

In the 1700s Mehetia was inhabited; today islanders visit it occasionally to make copra. The *Bounty*, like most sailing ships, approached Tahiti from the east and Mehetia was the first South Sea island her crew encountered.

MEIA   Tahitian word for banana (*Musa sapientum*).

MENALEE (Menallee)   See MANARII.

MERCURY (Gustaf III)   A brig of 150 tons which most *Bounty* historians have treated as a British ship. This was not strictly true. The *Mercury* was British in origin and had a British crew, but she was actually commissioned as a Swedish privateer with the name *Gustaf III* (after the Swedish King) and sailed under the Swedish flag. Her mission in the Pacific was to raid Russian trading posts on the north-west coast of America. She was commanded by Captain John Henry Cox. An account of her voyage was published by Lieutenant George Mortimer in 1791.

On the night of August 9, 1789, the *Mercury* sailed past Tubuai in the Austral group and saw fires. If she had passed in the daytime, the men on board would have seen the *Bounty* in the lagoon and Captain Cox would certainly have attempted to make contact since European ships were so rare in the Pacific. He would have discovered Christian and his group of mutineers and loyalists in their attempt to found a colony on Tubuai, and, even though Cox of course knew nothing of the mutiny, Christian would have been forced to seek another hide-out. (As it was, Christian abandoned the idea of settling on Tubuai anyway.)

In the darkness of the night the *Mercury* came close to being wrecked on the reef at Tubuai; it is interesting to speculate on what would have happened if such had been the case.

The *Mercury* continued to Tahiti where it marooned one of the seamen, a John Brown (alias Bound), a violent man who came to play an unsavory role in the later history of those men from the *Bounty* who remained on Tahiti. She left the island on September 2 and sailed out of the *Bounty* story.

As far as the real mission of *Gustaf III/Mercury* is concerned, I have not had access to the recently discovered source material. However, the prominent *Bounty* scholar Rolf Du Rietz in Sweden has kindly, in an informal personal communication to me, given the gist of the story. There was no Swede on board the ship, as far as we know. Captain Cox had gained an audience with King Gustaf III while visiting Gothenburg during the Swedish-Russian war (1788–1790) and had arranged to be given a letter of marque with the right to fly the Swedish flag. The idea was that he would attack the Russian fur trade at Bering Strait. Any profit or booty resulting from the raid would go partly to the Swedish crown and partly to Cox.

In the event, nothing came of the project. When Cox arrived at the Russian trading posts, he found the fur traders so poor and miserable that he thought it would be unworthy of the honor of the Swedish flag to rob them of the little they had. The war was over in 1790 and Cox himself died soon afterwards. Lieutenant Mortimer does not mention a word of the project in his narrative; it is only in our days that archival material has been found that throws light on the mystery.

MESS A group of officers who take their meals together.

MICKOY, William See McCOY, WILLIAM.

MIDDLESEX British East Indiaman under the command of Captain John Rogers. Fletcher Christian's older brother Charles was involved in a mutiny on board the *Middlesex* (see the November 1787 commentary in Part I).

MIDSHIPMAN A non-commissioned officer ranking next below a sub-lieutenant in the British Navy. At the time of the *Bounty* expedition, midshipmen were chosen from young men of the nobility and the gentry who aspired to become career officers in the Navy. Acceptance depended a great deal on family influence, although ability also counted heavily. After six years of service — less in times of war — midshipmen were allowed to take an examination for the rank of lieutenant.

MILLS, John Gunner's mate on the *Bounty*; mutineer; went with Christian; was killed on Pitcairn. Mills was born in Aberdeen. David Silverman in *Pitcairn Island* (1967) writes:

> The few scraps of Mills' pre-"Bounty" history gleaned from the record suggests a sadistic bully-boy. On the "Mediator," under Collingwood, Mills was known to send midshipmen on fools' errands in order to steal their food. Once he exacted tribute for retrieving a midshipman's cap from the pump well where he had got the mess boy to hide it.

Captain Bligh described Mills' physical appearance as follows:

> [JOHN MILLS] gunner's mate, aged 40 years, 5 feet 10 inches high, fair complexion, light brown hair, strong made, and raw boned; a scar in his right arm-pit, occasioned by an abscess.

Mills was one of the oldest men on board the *Bounty*. On October 19, 1788, he and William Brown, the gardener, had refused to dance (the daily exercise ordered by Bligh) and had had their grog ration stopped as a consequence. Apart from that incident, there is hardly any mention of Mills in the *Bounty* literature until the day of the mutiny.

Mills was in Christian's watch on that fateful morning, conning the ship with Ellison at the helm. He was one of the men who went below with Christian to arrest Bligh.

On Tubuai, Mills was one of the eight mutineers who voted with Christian and who later sailed with him to Pitcairn. He could hardly have felt much loyalty to Christian, however, because while the latter was ashore exploring the island, he suggested that those aboard the *Bounty* make sail for Tahiti and leave Christian and those who had gone ashore with him to their fate.

Mills was one of the mutineers who treated the Polynesians brutally. His consort was Vahineatua whom he called Prudence and with whom he had two children, Elizabeth and John Jr.

On Massacre Day, September 20, 1793, Mills was the third of the mutineers to be killed.

John Mills Jr. fell from a steep precipice and died when he was twenty-one years old. He had not been married, so the name Mills died out on Pitcairn.

Elizabeth Young, daughter of John Mills, was born in 1792 and witnessed the murder of Quintal in 1799. She migrated to Tahiti in 1831 and to Norfolk in 1856, but she returned to, and died on, Pitcairn at the age of ninety-one on November 6, 1883. She was the last of the second generation descendants of the mutineers.

MILLWARD, John Able-bodied seaman on the *Bounty*; mutineer; stayed on Tahiti; survived the wreck of the *Pandora*; found guilty at the court-martial and hanged. Millward was born in Plymouth and was twenty-one years old when he mustered on the *Bounty*. He was one of the more literate of the seamen on board.

Bligh's description of Millward, written after the mutiny, reads as follows:

> [JOHN MILLWARD] 22 years, 5 feet 5 inches high. Brown complexion. Dark hair, strong made. Tattooed under the pit of the stomach with a taoomy or breastplate of Otaheite.

Millward deserted on Tahiti together with Churchill and Muspratt and, when caught, received forty-eight lashes in two installments with just enough time in between (January 23 to February 4, 1789) for a thin scab to have formed on the exposed flesh of the grisly wound.

In the beginning of the mutiny Millward had been reluctant to join in, at one point saying to Churchill: "No, Charles, you brought me into one Predicament already, and I'll take Care you don't bring me into another." However, although he wavered in choosing sides, he did take up a musket and never made any attempt to get into the launch.

Millward preferred to take his chances on Tahiti rather than go to some unknown island with Christian. He was very friendly with one of chief Poino's wives and actually had a son with her. He was one of the ten men who helped Morrison build the schooner *Resolution* and he took part in the military campaigns designed to help Teina (Mate) gain supremacy over the other districts on the island.

When the *Pandora* arrived, Millward was one of the men who made the futile attempt to hide in the mountains. He survived the wreck of the *Pandora* only to be found guilty at the court-martial and hanged. His speech before the execution was quoted in the October 1792 commentary in Part I of this book.

MINARII Nordhoff's and Hall's name for MANARII.

MIRO (amae, Tahitian rosewood)

> *E mea poiri rumaruma i te ra'au nui o taua mau marae ra;*
> *e o te hau roa i te ra'a o te miro ia, oia te amara.*

> It was dark and shadowy among the great trees of those marae;
> and the most sacred of them all was the *miro* which was the sanctifier.

The *miro* or Tahitian rosewood (*Thespesia populnea*) was a sacred tree, as shown in this old marae chant. The main property of the *miro* (and of the *aito* and the *tamanu*) was that the gods preferred to communicate with the human beings through the rustling of its leaves. It therefore grew on or close to the sites of the maraes. Holding a branch of the *miro* in his hand, the *tahu'a* (priest) could communicate more directly with the gods.

Being a very hard and a very beautiful wood, the *miro* also had its secular uses. But mainly it was used for ornamental purposes because of its striking dark-red color and exquisite grain.

When the missionaries had destroyed the veneration for nature which was an essential part of Tahitian religion, the *miro* trees were cut down for commercial use without any attempt at preservation. As a result, the *miro* is virtually extinct on Tahiti today.

The *miro* also used to grow in abundance on Pitcairn and the most beautiful of the artifacts carved on the island are fashioned from this wood. Although the Pitcairners are trying to preserve the few trees they have left and plant new ones, the *miro* can still be considered virtually extinct on the island. To obtain this wood for their carvings the Pitcairners therefore are forced to go to Henderson Island, 107 miles distant.

MISTELLA   A Spanish wine, actually grape juice which has been prevented from fermenting by the addition of alcohol; often used in the production of vermouth. Mistella was very popular with British sailors who referred to it as "Miss Taylor."

MOALA ("Mywolla")   Island on the western side of the southern Fijis, considered part of the Lau group and situated at 18⁰34'S., 179⁰51'E. It is a volcanic island about seven miles long by five miles wide.

Bligh discovered Moala on the voyage in the launch in May 1789 and identified and charted it on the second breadfruit expedition, August 7, 1792.

MOANA   Tahitian for sea or ocean. The sea had religious significance for the Tahitians, indeed for all Polynesians. In fact, their most prominent god was Ta'aroa (Tangaroa), God of the Ocean. And the sea was considered a temple of the gods, as shown in this ancient chant cited by Teuira Henry in *Ancient Tahiti* (1928):

> *E pure tei te nu'u tai mimiha;*
> *o te moana te marae nui o te ao nei.*

> There was prayer in the moving, rolling ocean;
> the sea was the great temple of the world.

The sea was all-important to the Polynesians; it was, in fact, their last refuge:

On the seaside the wanderer or exile who owned no land worshipped his god. There he presented his son or daughter in marriage, there he offered his newborn child to his tutelar god, and there he presented himself or members of his family when sick or dying to the healing gods, and to Ta'aroa.

Moana is also used as a given name, usually female but sometimes male. Moana was the name of the chief who, together with Ari'ipaea, brought back the deserters from Tetiaroa (see the January 1789 commentary in Part I). Nordhoff and Hall used the name Moana for midshipman Hayward's *taio*, Vaetua.

MOETUA The name given by Nordhoff and Hall to denote Manarii's consort. There was no woman called Moetua on Pitcairn; Manarii's consort was Mareva whom he shared with Teimua and Niau.

HMS *MONMOUTH* On paper, this was the first ship on which Bligh ever served. Her commander, Captain Keith Stewart, consented to enter Bligh on the ship's rolls nominally as his "servant" at the age of seven in order to give Bligh an advantage in seniority later on. The practice was common in the British Navy.

MONOI Scented coconut oil, the fragrance usually being the scent of Tiare Tahiti (*Gardenia tahitiensis*), the Tahitian gardenia. Monoi is used throughout the Society Islands and on many other islands in Eastern Polynesia as body lotion, pomade, perfume, and even as an ointment to soothe mosquito bites! In the memories visitors to the islands carry back with them, the haunting, intoxicating fragrance of monoi plays an important part.

MONTAGU, Sir George Captain of HMS *HECTOR*.

MOOREA (Eimeo, Aimeo, York Island) A volcanic island nine miles west of the north-western part of Tahiti, located at 17°30'S., 149°50'W. Moorea is characterized by steep mountains with numerous peaks, the highest being Mount Tohivea in the south which rises to 3975 feet. Mount Mouaputa (2575 feet) has a huge hole through its top which was caused by the demi-god Pai throwing a spear through it in the dawn of time. The spear landed in Raiatea in the Leeward Islands where the dent it made in one of the mountains can be seen to this day. This legend is told in full by Teuira Henry in *Ancient Tahiti* (1928).

Scenically, Moorea is without a doubt one of the world's most beautiful islands. Mount Rotui (2790 feet) separates what must be the loveliest bays in the world: Pao Pao (Cook's Bay) and Opunohu. Many of the travel posters you will see from Tahiti are photographed in Pao Pao Bay; the 1983 *Bounty* movie by Dino de Laurentiis was filmed there.

Amazingly, Bligh never landed on Moorea, only nine miles away, even though he spent almost half a year on Tahiti during his first expedition and more than three months on his second. After the mutiny, however, some of the *Bounty* men who remained on Tahiti when Christian left for the last time, did visit Moorea in the schooner *Resolution*.

In the later history of Tahiti, and of the South Pacific for that matter, Moorea is notable for having the first printing press in the islands. It was brought by the missionary William Ellis and landed at Afareaitu on March 26, 1817. On June 30 that year the first sheet of any book printed in the South Seas came off the press — the beginning of a spelling primer in Tahitian.

In 1824 the missionaries established a school on Moorea with the ambitious name "The South Seas Academy." One of the first pupils was the very young Pomare III who had been crowned — by the missionaries, really — in 1824. Their efforts to teach him their joyless and humorless creed came to nought when the poor boy died at the age of six and a half.

Today Moorea has 7300 inhabitants. It is studded with hotels along its shores, but they are built in native style and do not really deface the island; its beauty remains reasonably unblemished.

MORAI See MARAE.

MORAYSHIRE The three-masted, full-rigged, 830-ton "emigrant ship" which, under the command of Captain Joseph Mathers, brought the entire population of Pitcairn to Norfolk in 1856.

The *Morayshire* sailed from Pitcairn on May 3 and arrived at Norfolk on June 8. On board were 194 Pitcairners who were soon joined by a baby boy born on May 9. Altogether there were: 48 Christians, 48 Quintals, 21 Youngs, 18 Adamses, 16 McCoys, 20 Buffetts, 13 Nobbses, 11 Evanses.

They brought with them a cannon and the anvil from the *Bounty*, both of which can be seen on Norfolk Island today.

MORRISON, James Boatswain's mate on the *Bounty*; loyalist; stayed on the *Bounty*; survived the wreck of the *Pandora*; returned to England; found guilty at the court-martial; received the King's pardon.

Morrison was born in London and was twenty-seven years old when he mustered on the *Bounty*. He was "of good birth" and well educated. In 1782 he had been a midshipman in HMS *Termagant*, a sloop of war (whose commander, Captain Charles Stirling, was later to write a character reference for Morrison during his court-martial). The main reason Morrison accepted a lesser position on the *Bounty* seems to have been his desire to sail to the South Seas.

After the mutiny, Bligh described Morrison as follows:

[JAMES MORRISON] Boatswain's Mate, 28 years, 5 feet 8 inches high. Sallow complexion. Long black hair. Slender made. Lost the use of the first joint of the forefinger of the right hand. Tattooed with star under his left breast and a garter round his left leg, with the motto *honi soit qui mal y pense*. Has been wounded in one of his arms with a musket ball.

Morrison was in Fryer's watch. At the court-martial, the *Bounty*'s sailing master described him in just a few words: "A steady, sober, attentive, good, Man."

Bligh always portrayed himself as being a perfect commander and his ship as being the happiest that ever sailed an ocean. It is thanks to Morrison that we have a check on Bligh's accuracy. The "cheese incident" was referred to in the February 1788 commentary in Part I. Bligh never mentioned it in his log or journal, but Morrison did. Most of Bligh's comments about the crew of the ship have to be read with several grains of salt. Take, for example, Bligh's entry for March 23, 1788, the day the *Bounty* started her valiant but unsuccessful attempt to round the Horn:

> In the morning I killed a sheep and served it to the ship's company, which gave them a pleasant meal.

Morrison's corresponding entry reads:

> One of the sheep dying, this morning Lieut. Bligh order'd it to be issued in lieu of the day's allowance of pork and pease, declaring that it would make a delicious meal and that it weighed upwards of fifty pounds; it was devided and most part of it thrown overboard, and some dried shark supplyd its place for Sundays dinner, for it was no other than skin and bone.

Morrison did not take part in the mutiny. Later, at the court-martial, he was to say that he had stayed on board in the hope of forming a party to retake the ship. No attempt to do so seems to have been made, however. Christian, by the way, promoted Morrison to boatswain on the *Bounty*.

Morrison was an excellent amateur anthropologist and ethnographer and a natural storyteller. The narrative he later wrote about his experiences on Tahiti and his observations of the life of the Tahitians has become a treasure trove of information for all who are interested in Polynesia.

It was Morrison who initiated and supervised the building of a European-type ship on Tahiti (see the November 1789 and the March and July 1790 commentaries in Part I). In this he was assisted by his *taio* Poino, the chief of Haapape.

On the open-boat voyage after the wreck of the *Pandora* Morrison appears to have been the only one of the prisoners who dared speak up against Edwards' incredibly harsh treatment of the *Bounty* men:

> On the 9th [September] I was laying on the oars talking to McIntosh when

Captn. Edwards ordered me aft. Without assigning any cause, he ordered me to be pinnioned with a cord and lassh'd down in the boat's bottom. Ellison who was then asleep in the boat's bottom was ordered to the same punishment.

I attempted to reason and enquire what I had now done to be thus cruelly treated, urging the distress'd situation of the whole, but received for answer, "Silence, you murdering villain — are you not a prisoner? You piratical dog, what better treatment do you expect?"

I then told him that it was a disgrace to the captain of a British man o' war to treat a prisoner in such an inhuman manner, upon which he started up in a violent rage, and snatching a pistol which lay in the stern sheets threatened to shoot me. I still attempted to speak, when he swore "By God! if you speak another word I'll heave the log with you!"

Finding that he would hear no reason and my mouth being parched so that I could not move my tongue, I was forced to be silent and submit; and was tyed down so that I could not move.

In this miserable situation, Ellison and I remained for the rest of the passage, nor was McIntosh suffered to come near or speak to either of us.

During the court-martial Morrison, like Heywood, was badly damaged by the testimonies of Hayward and Hallett. The fact that he received a King's pardon after being found guilty and condemned to death was certainly not due to family influence. It may, at least in part, be due to the fact that he had written to Reverend Howell (see the December 1792 commentary in Part I), who probably circulated Morrison's writings among the Navy personnel stationed at Portsmouth. Or it may simply be that Morrison and Heywood were recommended to mercy because the court was favorably impressed by them and uncertain about the validity of the evidence against them.

If Morrison's writings had been published, they would have proved quite embarrassing not only to Bligh, but indirectly also to Sir Joseph Banks.

Similarly, Morrison's charges against Edwards could have created a scandal, and it was not in the national interest to have the extraordinary harshness of some Navy commanders exposed, especially at a time when mutiny was "in the air" (erupting only a few years later in the spectacular mutiny at the Nore). Morrison's pardon may even have involved an unofficial agreement that he was not to publish his narrative during his lifetime (he had planned to publish it in February 1793), although this is pure speculation.

Morrison was a good friend of Peter Heywood and gave him a copy of his narrative which, after Heywood's death, was published in part by Heywood's stepdaughter, Lady Diana Belcher, in her book *The Mutineers of the Bounty and their Descendants in Pitcairn and Norfolk Islands* (1870). Extracts had appeared in 1799, 1825 and 1831.

Morrison stayed in the Navy. He made his last voyage as chief gunner in HMS *Blenheim*, the 74-gun flagship of Admiral Sir Thomas Troubridge which was based at Penang in the East India Station. The ship went down with all hands in a violent gale off the Isle of Bourbon (Réunion) on February 1, 1807.

MORTIMER, George   Mortimer was a lieutenant on board the *Mercury* and wrote a narrative of the expedition entitled *Observations and Remarks made during a Voyage . . . in the Brig Mercury* which was published in London in 1791.

For the relevance of the *Mercury*'s voyage to the *Bounty* story, see the August 1789 commentary in Part I and the entry MERCURY.

Mortimer returned to England on October 25, 1790, so it is just possible that he might have had a chance to tell Captain Edwards what he had heard about the *Bounty* in Tahiti (Edwards sailed on November 7). He almost certainly must have told Bligh about it (Bligh did not leave on his second breadfruit expedition until August 3, 1791).

Mortimer later served under Bligh on HMS *Warrior* as Captain of the Marines and testified at Bligh's court-martial in 1805 that the latter "was frequently very violent and passionate and that his conduct was tyrannical and un-officer-like."

MORUROA   See MURUROA.

MOTU (mutu)   Tahitian word for reef island or small island.

MOULTER, William   The heroic boatswain's mate of the *Pandora* who risked his life to save the chained men of the *Bounty* when the ship foundered (see the August 1791 commentary in Part I).

MULBERRY TREE (aute, "cloth plant")   From the bark of this tree (*Broussonetia papyrifera*) most of the strong tapa cloth was made. See TAPA.

MURUROA (Moruroa, ancient name: Hiti-Tautau-Mai)   An atoll in the Tuamotus at 21⁰50'S., 138⁰55'W. It is about fifteen miles long and eight miles wide. Mururoa was discovered by Lieutenant Philip Carteret in HMS *Swallow* in 1767, just a few days after he had discovered Pitcairn. He named Mururoa "Bishop of Osnaburgh Island."

Mururoa has become famous — or, rather, infamous — for the atomic testing that the French have conducted on the atoll since the early 1960s. Because of the atomic tests there are currently about 3000 inhabitants on Mururoa of whom 700 are Polynesians.

It was on Mururoa atoll that the whaler *Matilda* foundered the night of February 24, 1792 (see the March 1792 commentary in Part I). The crew managed to get to Tahiti and Bligh took many of them with him when he sailed from the island on his second breadfruit expedition.

MUSPRATT, William   Able-bodied seaman, tailor, and assistant to the cook on the *Bounty*; mutineer; stayed on Tahiti; survived the wreck of the *Pandora*; was found guilty and condemned to death at the court-martial; released on appeal of verdict.

Muspratt was born in Yarmouth and was twenty-seven years old when he signed on the *Bounty*. Bligh's description of him, written after the mutiny, reads as follows:

> [WILLIAM MUSPRATT] 30 years, 5 feet 6 inches high. Dark complexion, brown hair, slender made. Very strong black beard under his scarred chin. Tattooed in several places.

On Tahiti, Muspratt was the third seaman to be flogged. On December 27, 1788, he received a dozen lashes for an unspecified "neglect of duty." Nine days later, he deserted together with Churchill and Millward. On being caught towards the end of January, he received two dozen lashes on a back that could hardly have been healed by then, and the punishment was repeated on February 4: sixty lashes in less than six weeks. The desertion is described in the January 1789 commentary in Part I.

On the morning of the mutiny, Muspratt and the cook, Thomas Hall, were sitting by the starboard fore scuttle splitting wood for the galley. Muspratt joined the mutineers and armed himself with a musket when ordered to do so by Churchill, although he would later claim at his trial that he had done so only with a view to helping in any attempt the officers might have made to put down the mutiny. He appears to have been vacillating in his loyalty.

Muspratt remained on Tahiti when Christian sailed away for good. He helped Morrison in the building of the schooner *Resolution* and he took part in the military operations designed to help chief Teina (Mate) become supreme ruler over Tahiti.

When the *Pandora* arrived, he and most of the mutineers fled to the mountains in the vain hope of escaping capture. He survived the wreck of the *Pandora* and reached England to stand trial for his role in the mutiny.

Although he, assisted by his excellent attorney Stephen Barney (there is no indication anywhere of how he, alone, among the common seamen, was able to afford an attorney), put on an excellent defense, he was found guilty and sentenced to be hanged. The story of his appeal and its result was told in the September and October 1792 and the February 1793 commentaries in Part I.

The fate of Muspratt after he was freed is unknown to me.

MUTU   See MOTU.

MYDIDDEE   See MAITITI.

MYWOLLA Bligh's spelling of MOALA, name of an island of the Lau group.

NAMUKA See NOMUKA.

NANAI The name used by Nordhoff and Hall for Titahiti's consort. Actually there was no woman named Nanai on Pitcairn. Titahiti's consort was Tinafanaea whom he shared with Oha.

"NANCY" See TOOFAITI.

HMS *NARCISSUS* Captain Edward Edwards was the object of a mutiny on this ship in 1782. The mutiny was quelled, six mutineers were hanged, one received 500 lashes and another 200.

NATIEVA A district on the north-east coast of Tubuai, now called Taahuaia. It was in this district, the chief of which was Ta'aroatohoa, that Fletcher Christian and his men built Fort George.

NAVIGATOR ISLANDS The name given by Bougainville to the Samoa group.

NEGUS A drink composed of wine and hot water, mixed with sugar, nutmeg and lemon juice.

NEHOU, NEHOW See NIAU.

NELSON, David Botanist on the *Bounty*; loyalist; went with Bligh; died on Timor. The King's intention to send out an expedition for the purpose of gathering breadfruit plants for the West Indies was spelled out in a letter to the Lords Commissioners of the Admiralty written by Lord Sydney, a Principal Secretary of State. The letter was dated May 5, 1787, and contained the following paragraph:

> Mr David Nelson and Mr William Brown, Gardeners by Profession, have from their Knowledge of Trees and Plants been hired for the Purpose of selecting such as appear to be of a proper Species and Size and it is His Majesty's Pleasure that your Lordships do order those Persons to be received on board the said Vessel and to be borne for Wages and Victuals during the Voyage.

Nelson knew Bligh from before: they had both sailed with Cook on his third voyage (1776–1780), Nelson on the *Discovery* and Bligh as sailing master in the *Resolution*. He was originally a Kew gardener and had been selected as botanist on Cook's voyage by Sir Joseph Banks who personally paid for his expenses, Captain Charles Clerke, who commanded the *Discovery*, wrot e to Banks that Nelson was "one of the quietest fellows in nature."

Nelson also knew Peckover, of course, that lover of the South Seas who had been on all three of Cook's voyages.

During the voyage Nelson simply went about his business, collecting plants of all sorts in addition to the breadfruit shoots. He seems to have been liked by everyone on board, even by Bligh.

During the mutiny Nelson was kept below deck under guard. Alexander McKee in H.M.S. *Bounty* (1962) quotes Nelson as saying to William Peckover, the veteran gunner: "The ship is taken. It is by our own people, and Mr. Christian at their head. But we know whose fault it is." (See also Du Rietz, 1965, pp. 22-23 and 59.)

Both men chose to go into the launch with Bligh. On the open-boat voyage Nelson was among the weakest and almost died before Timor was reached. On July 20, 1789, Nelson died in Coupang from a tropical fever. Bligh wrote:

> . . . I have had the Misfortune to loose Mr. Nelson the Botanist whose good Conduct in the course of the whole Voyage and Manly fortitude in our late disastrous circumstances deserves this tribute to his Memory.

NEW HOLLAND   The old name for Australia. The Dutch explorer Willem Jansz was probably the first European to reach the coast of Australia (in 1605) and his compatriot Abel Janszoon Tasman was the first to circumnavigate the continent (in 1642) — although he did it unknowingly and never saw the east coast. Captain Cook was the first European to reach the east coast of Australia (in 1770).

NIAU (sometimes misspelled Nehow or Nehou)   Niau was one of the three Tahitian men who accompanied Christian and the other mutineers to Pitcairn (two Tubuaian men and a man from Raiatea were also on board). He seems to have been the youngest of the six Polynesians.

When Pitcairn was sighted, Niau and the other two Tahitians joined Christian in the shore party that explored the island before the decision was made to settle there.

Niau had to share Mareva with the two other Tahitians. He participated in the murders of Tararo and Oha (see the December 1790 commentary in Part I). Before Massacre Day, September 20, 1793, Niau and Teimua had stolen some muskets and hidden themselves in the hills. Sometime after the five mutineers had been killed, Edward Young murdered Niau in cold blood; his reasons for the murder are unknown. Teehuteatuaonoa tells us that "while looking at Young loading his gun, which he [Niau] supposed was for the purpose of shooting hogs, and requested him to put in a good charge, . . . he received the deadly contents."

As was the case with all the Polynesian men on Pitcairn, Niau left no offspring.

NIU   See COCONUT PALM.

NIUAFO'OU (Proby's Island, Good Hope Island, Tin Can Island)   A volcanic island, the most northern of the Tongas, at 15°35'S., 175°38'W. Although the island is inhabited (about 700 inhabitants), volcanic eruptions occur, the most recent one in 1946. Because it has no harbor and only poor anchorage, Niuafo'ou for many years received its mail in kerosene cans thrown from ships to waiting swimmers; hence the name Tin Can Island.

Captain Edwards, while searching for the missing mutineers of the *Bounty*, sighted Niuafo'ou on August 4, 1791, and named it Proby's Island, thinking that he had discovered it. In fact, the island had first been seen on May 14, 1616, by Willem Cornelisz van Schouten (during his voyage around the world 1615–1617 in the ship *Eendracht*) who had named it Good Hope Island.

NIUE (Savage Island)   Niue is an island of coral limestone situated at 19°00'S., 169°50'W., about 240 miles east of the Vavau group in Tonga. It is about twelve miles long, north to south, and about ten miles wide. Its chief distinguishing feature is the large number of enormous caverns, some of which extend a considerable distance inshore.

Niue was discovered by Captain Cook in 1774 on his second voyage. He named it Savage Island because of the hostile reception he received. Bligh passed Niue in April 1789 on his way from Aitutaki to Nomuka.

Today Niue is the world's smallest self-governing state with the exception of the Vatican. It became internally self-governing in free association with New Zealand in 1974; the population (about 3000) is Polynesian (related to Tongans and Samoans) and all are citizens of New Zealand.

NOBBS, George Hunn   Nobbs was an English adventurer who claimed he was born in 1799 as an illegitimate son of the Marquis of Hastings and Jemima Ffrench, daughter of an Irish baronet. He arrived at Pitcairn on November 5, 1828, in a 20-ton sloop from Callao together with a Captain Noah Bunker. Because Bunker was severely ill, John Adams (the old mutineer was still alive, although in bad health) allowed both men to stay and the old, leaking sloop was beached.

On October 18, 1829, Nobbs married Sarah ("Big Salah") Christian, the daughter of Fletcher Christian's second son, Charles, and Sully, the full-blooded Polynesian daughter of Teio. She bore him eleven children, seven boys and four girls. One of them, Ann Naomi Nobbs, lived until 1931.

Nobbs soon became a rival of John Buffett, the English sailor who had offered his services as a teacher in 1823 and remained on Pitcairn. The island population split in their loyalty and two schools and two religious services were conducted simultaneously.

When Joshua Hill established his dictatorship on the island in 1832 (see the entries PITCAIRN ISLAND and HILL, JOSHUA), Nobbs and Buffett became closer since they were both victimized. Together with Buffett's friend Jack Evans they sailed for Tahiti in the whaler *Tuscan* in March 1834. From there they wrote a petition to Commodore Mason in command of the South American Station, complaining of Hill's usurpation of power. In June they returned to Pitcairn in the ship *Pomare* to pick up their families; the Nobbses and the Evanses settled temporarily on Mangareva, the Buffetts on Tahiti.

Nobbs and Evans and their families returned to Pitcairn on October 13, 1834, in the American brig *Olivia* which had brought back the Buffetts a month earlier. In 1837, even before Hill was deported, Nobbs was elected schoolmaster by the whole population.

Nobbs went to England 1852–1853 to be ordained chaplain. With him was his daughter Jane, the first native-born Pitcairner ever to visit England. He thenceforth acted as pastor, surgeon, and schoolmaster for the whole population. He died on Norfolk Island on November 5, 1884, aged eighty-five, leaving a widow, ten children (one had died), sixty-five grandchildren, and nineteen great-grandchildren.

NOGGIN A small quantity of liquor, usually a gill.

NOHU Tahitian word for the highly poisonous stone fish (*Antennarius coccineus*).

NOMUKA (Rotterdam Island) Nomuka Island lies approximately half-way between Tofua and Tongatabu at 20⁰15'S., 174⁰47'W.

It was at Nomuka that the incident occurred that set the stage for the mutiny on the *Bounty* (see the April 1789 commentary in Part I). It was also at Nomuka that Captain Edwards waited in vain for the rendezvous with the schooner *Resolution* (see the June and July 1791 commentaries in Part I).

Nomuka has the shape of an approximately equilateral triangle with each side about two miles in length. Inside the island there is a large salt-water lagoon. The island was discovered by Abel Janszoon Tasman in January 1643; he named it Rotterdam Island.

NORDHOFF, Charles Bernard Nordhoff was born in London on February 1, 1887, but his family was American and soon returned to the States, where they settled in California in the early 1890s. He graduated from Harvard in 1909 and together with his father founded a successful tile- and porcelain-manufacturing business in San Diego.

In 1916, before the United States declared war on Germany, Nordhoff went to France where he at first served as an ambulance driver. He soon became interested in flying, however, and joined the Foreign Legion to get schooling in military aviation. In December 1917 he joined the Escadrille Lafayette.

Nordhoff met James Norman Hall after the end of the war; they had been assigned to write a history of the Corps together. The work on the book was the start of a friendship which was to end only with Nordhoff's death in 1947.

Together they traveled to Tahiti in 1920 in search of Adventure. At the end of the year, on December 4, Nordhoff married a nineteen-year-old Tahitian (actually half-Danish) girl, Christianne Vahine Tua Tearae Smidt, affectionately referred to as Vahine. They settled in the district of Punaauia, about twenty miles from Hall's home in Arue.

Vahine bore Nordhoff seven children. The fourth child was their first-born son, Charles Bernard Jr. When the boy was three and a half years old, he died from an infection which was treated by an incompetent French physician. Nordhoff never fully recovered from this tragedy, and it may have played a role in the subsequent divorce.

Nordhoff's fame as a writer is primarily based on his co-authorship with Hall, but he also had considerable success on his own, writing adventure books for boys, such as *The Pearl Lagoon* (1926) and *The Derelict* (1928).

After divorcing Vahine, Nordhoff had three children with his mistress Teuria; they were all sons whom he never legally recognized. In 1940 he left Tahiti, never to return. On June 12, 1941, he married Laura Grainger Whiley in Santa Barbara. His creative writing days, however, were over. On April 11, 1947, Nordhoff died of an apparent heart attack. Hall, who happened to be in the States at the time, attended the funeral service in Santa Barbara and wept over the fate of his friend.

NORFOLK ISLAND Norfolk Island is situated at 29⁰S., 168⁰E., 3300 miles west of Pitcairn, 930 miles north-east of Sydney, and 630 miles north-west of Auckland. It has a land area of thirteen and a half square miles and a circumference of twenty miles. Norfolk is a rolling, pine-clad island, rather low-lying except for two peaks which rise to somewhat over one thousand feet. On the south coast is the only town, Kingston.

Norfolk was discovered by Captain Cook on October 10, 1774, on his second voyage to the South Pacific. From 1788 to 1856 it was used by the British as a penal colony.

Norfolk is important in the history of Pitcairn as the destination for the second migration of the whole population of the island (see the entry PITCAIRN ISLAND) in 1856.

In 1913 Norfolk became an Australian territory. Today about forty per cent of the close to 2200 inhabitants on Norfolk are descendants of the *Bounty* mutineers. The island gets about 20,000 tourists a year, mostly from Australia but also from New Zealand.

On Norfolk Island, "Bounty Day" is celebrated on June 8, the anniversary of the arrival of the population from Pitcairn.

NORMAN, Charles Carpenter's mate on the *Bounty*; loyalist; kept on board against his will; survived the wreck of the *Pandora*; acquitted at court-martial. Norman was born in Portsmouth and was twenty-four years old when the *Bounty* sailed from Spithead. He was married and had children. His physical description, given by Bligh after the mutiny, reads as follows:

> [CHARLES NORMAN] Carpenter's Mate, 26 years, 5 feet 9 inches high. Fair complexion, light-brown hair, slender made. Pitted by the smallpox, and has a remarkable motion with his head and eyes.

At the court-martial, William Purcell, the *Bounty*'s carpenter and Norman's immediate superior, described him as "sober, diligent, and attentive."

Norman was in Christian's watch during the mutiny and was observing the movements of an enormous shark, unaware that the mutineers were arming themselves. Actually the fact that Norman spotted the shark provided Christian with the perfect excuse to get the key to the arms chest from armorer Coleman: he simply said he was going to shoot a shark.

Christian did not want to force Purcell, the carpenter, to stay on board; Purcell was a very stubborn and difficult man to deal with, as Bligh had found out to his chagrin. But carpenters were needed on board and this is why both Norman and McIntosh, both carpenter's mates, were forced to stay (it is possible that only one would have been kept, if the launch had not been so deeply laden already). Both of them called out to Bligh to remember that they had been kept on board against their will.

On Tahiti, Norman and McIntosh were extremely helpful to Morrison in his ship-building project and they certainly deserve a great deal of the credit for the schooner turning out so well.

When the *Pandora* arrived, Norman was as shocked as the other loyalists when he was put in irons, especially since he and McIntosh had specifically called out to Bligh to remember that they were innocent. The only advantage he received on the *Pandora* — and it may well have saved his life — was that he, together with McIntosh and Coleman (the three whom Bligh had specified as "deserving mercy"), was released to help in manning the pumps when the ship was foundering.

Norman experienced no real difficulties during the court-martial and was acquitted of all complicity in the mutiny. Indirectly and unwittingly, he was instrumental in effecting Muspratt's release on a technicality. Muspratt had asked that Norman, against whom there was no evidence, be released so that he could give testimony in Muspratt's behalf. The court had refused, Muspratt claimed his rights had been violated, and his verdict was overturned on appeal.

Norman's activities after the court-martial are not known to me.

NORTON, John Quartermaster on the *Bounty*; loyalist; went with Bligh; killed by natives on Tofua. Norton was born in Liverpool and was thirty-four years old when the *Bounty* sailed from Spithead. He was one of the six men on board who had sailed with Bligh before and one of the four (the others being Christian, Lebogue, and Ellison) who had been with Bligh in the merchant ship *Britannia*.

Norton went with Bligh in the launch during the mutiny but was killed by the natives on Tofua in the Tonga islands on May 2, 1789, as he attempted to unfasten the sternline of the launch in which Bligh and the loyalists tried to escape. The natives overpowered him and beat him to death with rocks. It was in large part due to his sacrifice that the escape was successful.

According to Purcell, the carpenter, the launch had only a seven and a half inch freeboard and was often in danger of being swamped on the voyage to Timor. No wonder, then, that the Reverend James Bligh, one of the captain's relatives, later wrote:

> I have heard Captain Bligh say it was, with respect to the boat's crew, a fortunate circumstance, for he [Norton] was the stoutest man in the ship, which circumstance would very materially have interfered with the boat's progress and the allowance of provisions.

The place where Norton was killed was henceforth known as "Murderers' Cove." As the surgeon of the *Pandora* later remarked: "Murderers' Cove, in the Friendly Isles, is saying a volume on the subject."

LA NOUVELLE CYTHÈRE   The New Cythera, Bougainville's name for Tahiti. According to legend, Aphrodite was born in the foam of the waves breaking on the shores of Cythera, a Greek island south of the Peloponnesus. It is the scene of Botticelli's "Birth of Venus."

NUGGINGHOUSE   Brothel.

NUKUNONO (Nukunonu, Duke of Clarence Island)   Nukunono is the largest of the three large atolls in the Tokelau (Union) group; it is situated at 9⁰06'S., 171⁰50'W. It is about eight miles long, north to south, and six miles wide. Landing is dangerous.

Nukunono was discovered by Captain Edwards in the *Pandora* on June 12, 1791; he named it Duke of Clarence Island.

Today there are close to 400 inhabitants on Nukunono. They are a mixed race of Polynesians and Micronesians and they are all Catholics.

'O   'O is a Tahitian particle of specification or reference meaning approximately "it is." When the European explorers asked the Tahitians for the name of an island or a district or a person, the answer would be preceded by an '*o*: 'O Tahiti means

"It is Tahiti." This is why the early literature (and some of the later) refers to Tahiti as Otaheite, to Pare as Oparre, to Tu as Otoo, etc. It was only when the missionaries studied the language more closely that the meaning of 'o was realized and Otaheite became, correctly, Tahiti.

In most transcriptions of Tahitian words the glottal stop (') is omitted.

OAITEPEHA   See VAITEPIHA.

OAMO   See AMO.

OATAFU   See ATAFU.

OBEREA (Oberreah, Obarea, Oborea, Opureah)   See PUREA.

OBERREEROAH (Oberroah)   See PUREA-TETUPAIA.

OBUAREI   See PUARAI.

ODIDDY, ODIDEE, OEDIDEEDEE, OEDIDY   See HITIHITI.

OEITEPEHA   Bligh's spelling of VAITEPIHA.

OENO ISLAND   A low atoll situated seventy-six miles north-west-by-north of Pitcairn at 23⁰56'S., 130⁰44'W. It is squarish in shape and a little over two miles wide. The reef varies in width from 200 to 600 yards. The main island is shaped like a figure eight and is about three quarters of a mile long north to south. It is covered by brush and small trees. The lagoon is shallow with many coral heads and filled with many varieties of fish.

The Pitcairners sometimes use Oeno as a "vacation resort," for swimming, fishing, and relaxing.

OHA (sometimes misspelled Oher or Ohoo)   Oha was Titahiti's companion; both were from the same district in Tubuai and both joined Christian and his men.

On Pitcairn, Oha shared Tinafanaea (who may also have been from Tubuai) with Titahiti. When Adams' consort died within a year of the arrival on the island, the mutineers "gave" Tinafanaea to him. This triggered a conspiracy between the two Tubuaians and Tararo (the Raiatean whose consort had also been "given" away) to kill the mutineers. The women betrayed this plan to the white men who sent out the three Tahitians with muskets and orders to kill the conspirators. Oha and Tararo were killed, Titahiti surrendered. Oha, like the other Polynesian men on Pitcairn, left no children.

OLIVER, William Master's mate on the *Pandora*. Captain Edwards put Oliver in command of the little schooner *Resolution* which the *Bounty* men had built in Tahiti. With him were midshipman David Thomas Renouard, quartermaster James Dodds, and six seamen from the *Pandora*. The adventures of Oliver and his men are summarized in the June, July, and October 1791 commentaries in Part I.

OLIVIA American brig from Boston commanded by Captain C. Kendal. It was the *Olivia* which (in September 1834) brought John Buffett and his family and (in October 1834) George Nobbs and John Evans and their families back to Pitcairn after their having been exiled by the "dictator of Pitcairn," Joshua Hill.

OMAI See MAI.

OMAOMAO Tahitian singing bird, about the size of a sparrow, with a call like a nightingale.

ONE TREE HILL (Taharaa) A hill on the Taharaa peninsula rising above the western coastline of Matavai Bay in the district of Arue. Today it is the site of Hotel Taharaa. Captain Cook named it One Tree Hill because of a sole tree, an *'atae* (*Erythrina indica*), growing on its top.

ONO-I-LAU Island (actually a cluster of three islands) in the southern Lau group of Fiji; 20⁰38'S., 178⁰41'W.

On his search for an island refuge, Christian stopped at Ono-i-Lau in late November or early December 1789. This makes him the actual discoverer of the island; until 1956, when Teehuteatuaonoa's accounts of the voyage were found, it was thought that Bellingshausen was the discoverer (in 1820).

OPARRE See PARE.

OPEOWPAH See UPAUPA.

OPUAREI, OPUOLE See PUARAI.

OPUREAH See PUREA.

ORA (aoa, banyan tree) A fig tree (*Ficus prolixa*) whose branches send out roots to the ground, causing the tree to spread out over a wide area. It is found on all high islands in the Society group but is not common.

OREEPYAH, OREPIAH, ORIPAI See ARI'IPAEA.

ORLOP DECK   The lowest deck in a sailing ship, just above the bilge. On the orlop deck the cables were coiled when the anchors were weighed. Here, too, were the powder magazines, the main store rooms, and sometimes cabins for junior officers.

OROHENA (Orofena)   The highest mountain on Tahiti, a sharp pinnacle rising to 7321 feet.

To the old Tahitians, Mount Orohena was sacred. Even though the mountain is extremely difficult to climb (very few white men have accomplished the feat), the old Tahitians built a marae on top of it called Pure Atea (prayer which goes far).

OSNABURGH ISLAND   The name Samuel Wallis gave to MEHETIA when he discovered the island June 17, 1767.

(Bishop of Osnaburgh Island refers to Mururoa.)

OTAHA   See TAHAA.

OTAHEITE   See TAHITI.

OTOO, OTTOO (TU)   See POMARE I and POMARE II.

OTOW   See TEU.

OWHARRE   See FARE.

PAHI   Tahitian word for ship (originally large twin-hulled sailing canoe).

PAITI   See VAETUA.

PALMERSTON ISLAND (Avarau)   The most northern island (atoll) in the Southern Cook group, situated at 18⁰04' S., 163⁰10'W., 270 miles north-west of Rarotonga; discovered by Cook in 1774 on his second voyage.

Sailing westward from Tahiti on his search for the mutineers Captain Edwards found, on the shores of Palmerston, a yard marked "Bounty's Driver Yard" and some spars with "Bounty" written on them. We know today with virtual certainty that they had drifted there from Tubuai, because *(1)* Christian had jettisoned several spars there in order to lighten the ship; *(2)* the prevailing winds and currents would have carried them in that direction; and *(3)* the spars were worm-eaten and had obviously been in the water for a very long time.

PALUDISM   Malaria.

PANDANUS See FARA.

HMS *PANDORA* A British frigate of 24 guns; three-masted; ship-rigged; crew of 120; commanded by Captain Edward Edwards.

The *Pandora* was sent out by the British Admiralty in order to capture the *Bounty* mutineers and, if possible, the ship. Bligh arrived in England on March 14, 1790, and only ten days later the King ordered a ship to be sent out to hunt down the "pirates." On April 1 the following notice appeared in the *London Chronicle*:

> It is said that by the express command of His Majesty two new sloops of war are to be instantly fitted to go in pursuit of the pirates who have taken possession of the *Bounty*. An experienced officer will be appointed to superintend the little command, and the sloops will steer a direct course to Otaheite where, it is conjectured, the mutinous crew have established their rendezvous.

"Two sloops" were changed to one frigate, which was actually an upgrading of sorts. But the term "little command" accurately reflects the fact that to the Admiralty this expedition was of minor importance, especially since war was expected at any moment.

The story of the expedition is told in Part I, starting with the November 1790 commentary and ending with June 1792. The key dates of the voyage were:

November 7, 1790:	Sailed from England.
March 23, 1791:	Arrived at Tahiti.
May 8, 1791:	Sailed from Tahiti.
August 28, 1791:	Struck the Great Barrier Reef and foundered.
September 15, 1791:	Survivors reach Coupang on Timor.
June 19, 1792:	*Bounty* men arrived at Spithead.

In November 1977, the wreck of the *Pandora* was discovered in seventeen fathoms of water on the outer edge of the reef near Cape York. For the story of the discovery and the exploration of the wreck see Luis Marden: "Wreck of H.M.S. Pandora" in *National Geographic Magazine*, October 1985.

PAONIHO Tahitian word (*pao* means to strike or lacerate the head; *niho* means tooth) for a short stick of polished wood, used by women for ceremonial gashing of the head, usually to convey deep sorrow, but sometimes as an expression of extreme joy, such as at weddings or the return of a loved one after a long absence.

When the mutineers and loyalists who had stayed on Tahiti when Christian left were taken prisoners on board the *Pandora*, the women who had become their consorts (and, in some cases, borne them children) would paddle out to the ship and wail and lacerate their heads.

PAORANI   A district (now deserted) on the south-east coast of Tubuai. Its chief during the visit and colonization attempt of Christian and his men was Tinarau.

PAPARA   A district on the south coast of Tahiti Nui east of Paea and west of Atimaono. During the visit of the *Bounty*, Temarii was chief of Papara which was part of the "clandom" Teva i Uta.

PAPEETE   The only town in French Polynesia (although Uturoa on Raiatea is sometimes also counted as a town) and the chief administrative center of the islands. Greater Papeete — also comprising Faaa, Pirae, and Arue — has a population of 65,000. As recently as the early 1960s, Papeete was a sleepy little South Sea port with the most famous bar in the South Pacific, Quinn's Tahitian Hut. Today it is characterized by shopping centers, supermarkets, banks, traffic jams, and a dearth of parking places. Worst of all, there is no more Quinn's!

Teuira Henry, in *Ancient Tahiti* (1928), explains the meaning of the name Papeete:

> This town derives its name from a fine central stream of water named Vai-'ete or Pape-'ete, which gushes from a source at the foot of a hill behind the Government House; *'ete* or *'ete'ete* in old Tahitian, signifies commotion, a shock, or gushing in this sense.

PAPENO'O   A valley and a district on the north coast of Tahiti Nui east of Mahina (Haapape) and west of Tiarei.

PAPER MULBERRY TREE   See MULBERRY TREE.

PAPO   The name of the Tahitian stowaway in the *Providence*. Papo remained in Jamaica in order to help with the planting of the breadfruit trees.

PARAHA ITI   See VAHINEATUA.

PARAI   The Tahitian name for Captain Bligh.

PARE   Pare was a district on the north-west coast of Tahiti which consisted roughly of the eastern half of today's Papeete and all of Pirae. It bordered Te Fana (today's Faaa) on the west and Arue to the east. At the time of the *Bounty*'s arrival, Pare and Arue were combined into a larger district named Te Porionu'u whose chief was Tu (later called Pomare I). When Pare is mentioned in the literature, Te Porionu'u is usually meant (for some reason Arue is seldom mentioned).

Toaroa Bay, to which Bligh moved the *Bounty* from Matavai in late December 1788, is in the district of Pare.

ENCYCLOPEDIA

PAREU   A Tahitian word referring to a length of cloth originally made of *tapa*, but today of brightly colored cotton fabric. A *pareu* can be worn as a sarong or tied around any part of the anatomy or artistically draped into an elegant attire. The modern version is about one yard wide and one and a half yards long. The traditional cotton *pareu* has a lovely pattern of hibiscus and other tropical flowers in white on a primary color field. The favorite is red, but the variants are blue, yellow, green and the rest of the hues of the rainbow. It is a simple, practical, comfortable, and attractive way of dressing in the tropics for women as well as men.

PARKER, John   Captain in command of HMS *Gorgon*.

PARKIN, Lieutenant   The pseudonym used by Nordhoff and Hall for First Lieutenant John Larkin of the *Pandora*.

PASLEY, Sir Thomas   Commodore (later Admiral) Sir Thomas Pasley was Peter Heywood's uncle and staunch friend. It was he who recommended Aaron Graham as Heywood's counsel during the court-martial and kept sending consoling letters to Heywood's sister Nessy. When Heywood received his pardon, Pasley insisted that he serve under his command in HMS *Bellerophon*.

Matthew Flinders, who later became famous for circumnavigating Australia, had also been a midshipman under Sir Thomas's command in the *Bellerophon*.

Only five years after the court-martial of the captured men of the *Bounty*, the then Vice-Admiral Thomas Pasley presided over the court-martial of Richard Parker, the leader of the mutiny at the Nore. Even as an Admiral, Sir Thomas was always referred to as "The Tough Old Commodore."

PASSMORE, George   Sailing master of the *Pandora*. Of Passmore we do not know anything more than that he was a competent surveyor and navigator.

PATI'I   See VAETUA.

PATIRE   Patire was a friend of mutineer Charles Churchill. It was Patire who killed Matthew Thompson after the latter had murdered Churchill (see the March 1790 commentary in Part I).

PAUMOTU   See TUAMOTU.

PECKOVER, William   Gunner on the *Bounty*; loyalist; went with Bligh; arrived safely in England. Peckover was the real "old South Seas hand" on board the *Bounty*. He had been on all three of Cook's voyages and, since Cook visited Tahiti four times (twice on the second voyage), his visit on the breadfruit expedition was his fifth. This, of course, was the reason why Bligh put Peckover in charge of all trading with the Tahitians. He spoke the language fluently and had an excellent understanding of Tahitian customs and ways of thinking.

On the night of the mutiny, Peckover was in charge of the watch from midnight to 4.00 a.m., the one preceding Christian's. When the mutiny broke out he was kept below deck under guard until it was time for the loyalists to go into the launch.

Peckover was a brave man. On Tofua, when ordered by Bligh to single-handedly take the ship's log from the cave to the launch through a hostile crowd of natives armed with spears and slings, he did so without hesitation, boldly pushing his way through the warriors who, judging the book to be something of value, made repeated attempts to wrestle it from him. He succeeded in breaking through with the log; if he had not, we would have known less about the whole affair today, and a brave man would have met a premature death.

At the court-martial, Peckover was one of the witnesses who confirmed Heywood's innocence. Even though Heywood was convicted, it is likely that Peckover's testimony contributed to his being given a King's pardon. Later he was to declare that the facts, as given in Edward Christian's *Appendix*, were substantially accurate.

Peckover loved Tahiti and the South Seas. Even though he did not particularly care for Bligh, he applied for a position as gunner on the *Providence*, but Bligh turned him down. In a letter to Sir Joseph Banks dated July 17, 1791 (two weeks before Bligh sailed on the second breadfruit expedition), he writes:

> Should Peckover my late Gunner ever trouble you to render him further services I shall esteem it a favor if you will tell him I informed you he was a viscious and worthless fellow — He applied to me to render him service & wanted to be appointed Gunner of the *Providence* but as I had determined never to suffer an officer who was with me in the *Bounty* to sail with again, it was for that cause I did not apply for him.

The "viscious and worthless fellow" had been highly esteemed by Captain Cook. The letter shows Bligh's vindictiveness in sharp focus and it had nothing to do with Peckover's testimony in favor of Heywood, nor with his confirmation of the facts in Edward Christian's *Appendix*, since Bligh sailed long before the accused mutineers were brought to England.

Peckover's later fate is unknown to me.

PEERY PEERY See PIRIPIRI.

"PEGGY" The name by which midshipman George Stewart of the *Bounty* called his Tahitian wife who was the daughter of chief Tepahu. She bore Stewart a daughter shortly before the *Pandora* arrived to put an end to their happiness. Peggy died "of a broken heart" a few months after the *Pandora* sailed from Tahiti (in May 1791) with her husband chained like an animal in "Pandora's box" (see the April 1791 commentary in Part I).

The little girl was taken care of by her grandfather, Tepahu. Bligh saw her in April 1792 on his second breadfruit expedition and describes her as follows: "A fine child about twelve months old was brought to me to-day — the daughter of George Stewart, midshipman of the 'Bounty'; it was a very pretty creature, but had been so exposed to the sun as to be little fairer than an Otaheitan." When the missionaries arrived in 1797, they insisted on raising the girl.

In his maudlin poem *The Island or Christian and his Comrades*, Lord Byron calls Peggy "Neuha." But that does not sound like a Tahitian name and we simply do not know what her real name was. Byron writes:

> By Neuha's side he sat and watched the waters,
> Neuha, the sun-flower of the island daughters . . .

His description of "Neuha" is typical of the idealization of the "noble savage" which prevailed at the time:

> There sat the gentle savage of the wild
> In growth a woman, though in years a child
> As childhood dates within our colder clime
> Where naught is ripened rapidly save crime
> The infant of an infant world as pure
> From Nature — lovely, warm and premature.
> With eyes that were a language and a spell
> A form like Aphrodite's in her shell.
> With all her loves around her on the deep
> Voluptuous as the first approach of sleep.

PERETANE Tahitian word for British. Fenua Peretane means Britain.

PEROA See PUREA-TETUPAIA.

PETANIA The current Tahitian name for Pitcairn (Petania also means Seventh-day Adventist).

PIA Tahitian word for arrowroot and also for beer.

PIIMATO Literally "cliff-climber" (from *pii* which means climb and *mato* which means cliff or crag). Tahitian word for men who in pre-Christian times climbed high up into the mountains to secret caves in order to fetch the skulls of ancestors for ceremonial occasions. The office of *piimato* was hereditary.

PILHI   A Pitcairn Island dish made of yams, plantains, bananas, or pumpkin.

PIPON, Philip   Commander of the British frigate *Tagus* which, together with HMS *Briton*, under Commander Sir Thomas Staines, was combing the Pacific for the U.S. Frigate *Essex* which had been attacking British shipping in the area. In the early morning of September 17, 1814, the ships sighted Pitcairn Island.

Folger's discovery of the last hiding place of the mutineers (see FOLGER, MAYHEW) had been reported to the Admiralty but forgotten as unimportant. The men on the ships were therefore surprised when they saw that the island was inhabited, because Carteret, who had discovered it in 1767, had said it was uninhabited. Also, they did not at first realize it was Pitcairn they were seeing. When Carteret calculated its position his defective chronometer caused him to place it almost 200 miles further westward.

Captain Pipon later wrote an article called "The Descendants of the Bounty's Crew," in which he describes the arrival:

> As Pitcairn Island was described as uninhabited, we naturally conjected this in view could not be the place, particularly when, in bringing to, two or three miles off the shore, we observed the natives bring down their canoes on their shoulders, and shortly after darting through a heavy surf and paddling off to the ships; but our astonishment may be better conceived than described on finding that the inhabitants spoke the English language perfectly well.

Among the "natives" coming out in canoes were Thursday October Christian, almost twenty-four years old now and married to Teraura, and George Young, son of Edward Young and Toofaiti, about seventeen or eighteen years old. Both spoke English well and gave a very good impression to the officers and men of the ships. Pipon describes Thursday October as:

> . . . about twenty five years of age, a tall fine young man about six feet high, with dark black hair, and a countenance extremely open and interesting.
>
> He wore no clothes except a piece of cloth round his loins, a straw hat ornamented with black cock's feathers, and occasionally a peacock's, nearly similar to that worn by the Spaniards in South America, though smaller.

Adams should have been about forty-seven years old at this time. The visit of the warships must have caused him a great deal of anxiety, because the British Navy was not known for showing mercy to mutineers and there was no statute of limitations on mutiny. Indeed, if someone like Bligh or Edwards had been in command of the ships, Adams would have been taken to England for trial and, once there, could not have expected any mercy: the law was the law and mutineers were to be hanged.

Luckily for Adams, both Staines and Pipon were compassionate, cultured, and reasonable men who could immediately see that Adams was important for the community and had accomplished a great deal in raising its children to fine human beings (the fact that most of the credit belonged to the Tahitian mothers escapes *Bounty* authors to this day). Adams did volunteer to go back to England, but the community showed such sorrow over that possibility, that the commanders of the ships insisted that he stay.

Perhaps to justify this humane decision to an unfeeling Admiralty, Pipon wrote:

> . . . had we been inclined even to seize on old Adams, it would have been impossible to have conveyed him on board; again, to get to the boats, we had to climb such precipices as were scarcely accessible to any but goats, and the natives and we had enough to do in holding on by the different boughs and roots of trees, to keep on our feet. Besides, from the nature of the island, the inhabitants might retire to such haunts as to defy our utmost search; a measure which they would naturally have had recourse to the moment any intention of seizing any of them had been manifested.

It was an important visit, although it lasted only from morning to evening, because from now on Pitcairn "got on the map" (Folger's discovery had not become widely known). Also, from now on Adams could be reasonably sure that he would not be taken away from the island.

PIRIPIRI   Tahitian word, the literal meaning of which is "sticking or clinging to something," and which is therefore used to mean stingy, one of the worst attributes a person could have, as far as a Tahitian is concerned.

George Hamilton, the surgeon of the *Pandora*, wrote: "The English are allowed by the rest of the world, and I believe with some degree of justice, to be generous, charitable people; but the Otaheitans could not help bestowing the most contemptuous word in their language upon us, which is, Peery, Peery, or Stingy."

PITATE   Tahitian word for jasmine (*Jasminum sambac*).

PITCAIRN ISLAND   Island in the South Pacific situated at 25⁰04'S., 130⁰06'W. The old Polynesians called Pitcairn *Hiti-au-revareva* ("border of passing clouds"). The Polynesians who came with the *Bounty* mutineers referred to it as *Fenua maitai* ("good land"). In modern Tahitian Pitcairn is called *Petania* (which actually means Seventh-day Adventist). The island has also been called Rock of the West.

Pitcairn is the only British Crown Colony left in the South Pacific. Administratively, Pitcairn and the uninhabited Oeno (76 miles to the north-west), Henderson (107 miles to the east-north-east), and Ducie (290 miles due east) islands form the group called Pitcairn Islands.

DISTANCES
FROM PITCAIRN ISLAND

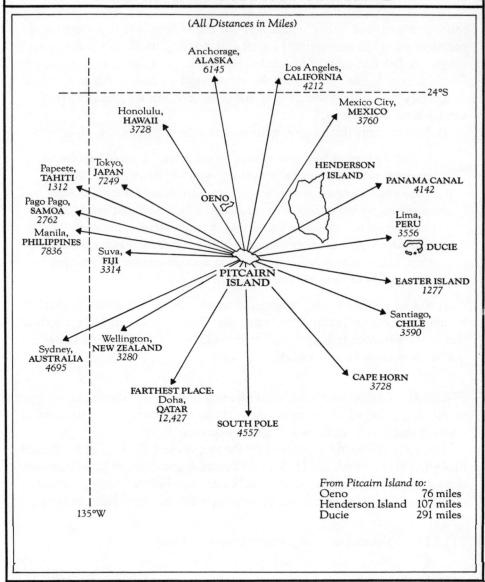

(All Distances in Miles)

Anchorage,
ALASKA
6145

Los Angeles,
CALIFORNIA
4212

Mexico City,
MEXICO
3760

-- -- -- -- -- -- -- -- -- -- -- -- -- -- -- -- 24°S

Honolulu,
HAWAII
3728

Papeete,
TAHITI
1312

Tokyo,
JAPAN
7249

**HENDERSON
ISLAND**

PANAMA CANAL
4142

Pago Pago,
SAMOA
2762

OENO

Lima,
PERU
3556

Manila,
PHILIPPINES
7836

DUCIE

Suva,
FIJI
3314

**PITCAIRN
ISLAND**

EASTER ISLAND
1277

Santiago,
CHILE
3590

Sydney,
AUSTRALIA
4695

Wellington,
NEW ZEALAND
3280

CAPE HORN
3728

FARTHEST PLACE:
Doha,
QATAR
12,427

SOUTH POLE
4557

135°W

From Pitcairn Island to:
Oeno   76 miles
Henderson Island   107 miles
Ducie   291 miles

Pitcairn vies with Easter Island for the honor of being called our planet's most remote inhabited island. In my opinion, Pitcairn wins this contest hands down since it has no airport, no hotel, not even an anchorage. A good idea of its isolation can be gained from the chart above.

Pitcairn is about two miles long and one mile wide with a circumference close to five miles, approximately the same size as Central Park in New York. The maximum elevation is 1076 feet (Pawala Ridge), visible from a distance of 45 miles. Although the soil is fertile, the island's 1120 acres contain only eight per cent flat land. The surface is distributed as follows: 88 acres of flat land; 352 acres of rolling land; 385 acres of steeply sloping land; and 295 acres of cliffs.

At the time of writing (September 1988), the population of Pitcairn is forty-eight plus ten non-Pitcairners. The main settlement is called Adamstown and is situated on the north side of the island 450 feet above sea level. On the same side and to the east is Bounty Bay which is not a bay, nor even a cove, but merely a slight indentation in the steep and rocky coast line.

The earliest history of Pitcairn is impossible to reconstruct. The island was originally settled by Polynesians who most probably came from Mangareva. The mutineers and their Polynesian companions found several traces of the early settlers: maraes (open-air temples), tikis (ancestral stone images), burial places, and petroglyphs, even some stone adzes and chisels. Archeological studies have shown that the early Polynesians arrived at the island some time before 1350 A.D. and probably left during the 1600s. Why they left will probably never be known.

The European discoverer of the island was Philip Carteret on his way around the world in the sloop *Swallow*. The island was sighted on July 2, 1767, and Carteret named it after midshipman Robert Pitcairn who first spotted it. (Robert Pitcairn was a son of John Pitcairn, Major of the Marines, who later at Concord, Massachusetts, gave the order for the first shot to be fired in the American War of Independence. Major Pitcairn was mortally wounded at the Battle of Bunker Hill.) Because of a defective chronometer, Carteret got the longitude of the island wrong, placing it 178 nautical miles farther west than the correct position.

On January 15, 1790, Christian and his companions sighted the island, and its history from that date until September 1793 is told in Part I of this book (January, February, August, October, and December 1790; September 1793).

About two months after the deaths of the last Polynesian men, Edward ("Ned") Young, the former midshipman on the *Bounty*, started writing a journal. It was seen by Captain Beechey in 1825 (who copied some extracts from it) but has since become lost.

The ten women on the island seem to have lived in promiscuity with the four surviving mutineers. They cannot have been happy about their situation, because they made an abortive attempt to leave the island in a small boat which, fortunately for them, capsized soon after it was launched. More ominously, the women on several occasions seem to have conspired to murder the men. They were treated brutally by Quintal and McCoy; it is even said that Quintal bit off Tevarua's ear when she had not caught enough fish for his dinner.

On December 27, 1795, a ship was seen sailing towards the island; however, the weather was rough at the time and no attempt to land was made. By this time, the women seem to have to have accepted their lot and peace reigned on the island until yet another misfortune befell its inhabitants.

McCoy, who had once worked in a brewery in Glasgow, had experimented with making a liquor out of the ti-root and on April 20, 1798, he succeeded in distilling the first bottle. (The kettle from the *Bounty* in which he distilled the spirits is still in the possession of the McCoy family on Norfolk Island.) This ushered in a period of wild drunkenness not only among the men but also among the women. Before the end of the year, McCoy had developed delirium tremens and during one of the attacks had tied a stone around his neck and hurled himself down a cliff to his death.

In early 1799, Quintal's consort Tevarua fell off a cliff while gathering birds' eggs; many thought she had actually committed suicide because of the way she was treated by Quintal. Be that as it may, Quintal now demanded that he be "given" Mauatua who was living with Young. When Young refused, Quintal threatened to kill the children Mauatua had had with Christian. Adams and Young now decided to get rid of Quintal once and for all and, on an occasion when Quintal was drunk, Adams killed him with an axe. Elizabeth Mills, who as a seven-year-old child was an eyewitness to the murder and who lived to the age of ninety-three, often told about the frightening sight of the blood on the walls and the lifeless body on the floor.

Only now was there true peace on the island. By this time there were twenty children in the colony and Young and Adams felt that they should receive some sort of education. Young first taught the almost illiterate Adams to read and write and the two of them started a school of sorts, using Christian's Bible and the Book of Common Prayer as texts. After the murder of Quintal, the alcohol abuse also seems to have stopped, perhaps because of a concern for the children.

Young died on Christmas Day in the year 1800 of some chest ailment, some say asthma, some say "consumption" (tuberculosis). He was the first man on the island to die a natural death.

Adams was now alone with nine women and a large number of children. He appears to have taken a religious turn and to have tried his best to raise the children in the Christian faith.

Vahineatua had become Adams' consort some time after Mills' death and she bore him three daughters. She died a few years after the turn of the century; according to Teehuteatuaonoa, she was "pierced in the bowels by a goat when she was with child." Adams later took Teio as his consort and she bore him a son.

In 1806 a new generation got its start. Thursday October Christian married Teraura, Edward Young's first consort, the ceremony being conducted by Adams with the use of a ring that had belonged to Ned.

Thursday October was only sixteen at the time of the wedding and Teraura must have been at least thirty-one. Their first child was a boy who was named Joseph Christian. Their second child, also a boy, was born in early 1808 and was named

Charles.

On a few occasions during the years ships had been sighted and one of them must even have made a landfall without the Pitcairners knowing about it, because a knife was found on the shore of Bounty Bay which had definitely not come on the *Bounty*. This was the time when whaling ships started plying the Pacific, but Pitcairn was described in the sailing directions as uninhabited and difficult of approach, so the island was not sought out as a stop-over.

On February 6, 1808, the American sealer *Topaz* from Nantucket, commanded by Captain Mayhew Folger, arrived at Pitcairn. Folger was surprised to see smoke rising from the island, since the sailing directions showed the island as uninhabited. An outrigger canoe manned by three young natives (one of them was Thursday October) approached the ship and the captain was even more astonished when he was hailed in English. A conversation ensued and, to his ultimate amazement, Folger found out that he had discovered the last hiding place of the *Bounty* mutineers.

Going ashore he found Adams together with eight Polynesian women and twenty-six children. He did not learn much about the mutiny, however, because Adams was reluctant to talk about it, being afraid that he might be taken off the island by a British warship and taken back to England to hang for his crime. He did not tell Captain Folger much more about the mutiny than that he had been asleep when it took place!

On his return, Folger notified the British Admiralty of his discovery, but England was then embroiled in a major war with France and the matter was totally ignored and immediately forgotten by the Admiralty. (See also FOLGER, MAYHEW.) Six and a half years were to pass until Pitcairn was visited again.

On September 17, 1814, two British warships, HMS *Briton* and HMS *Tagus*, approached the island. Their commanders, Sir Thomas Staines and Philip Pipon, had no knowledge of Folger's report and were equally surprised to find the island inhabited.

Adams was in luck: the two commanders were humane and compassionate men. They were psychologically at the opposite pole from the likes of Captain Edwards and did not do what many other commanders, certainly Edwards, would have done: put Adams in irons and take him to England to be hanged. They felt that Adams had atoned for his crime by helping create a community where kindness and honesty and respect were universal and that his removal from this community would be cruel and unwise. The danger for Adams was over.

It was during this visit that the islanders found out that they had been celebrating the Sabbath on the wrong day (the Seventh-day Adventists were later to say that it was the right day). Having come to the Pacific from the west around the Cape of Good Hope the *Bounty* had gained a day, having crossed what later became the international dateline. Therefore, what they thought was Sunday was really Saturday.

The impact on the islanders must have been strong. In fact, the sketch Lieutenant

John Shillibeer of HMS *Briton* made of Thursday October Christian is entitled Friday October Fletcher Christian. (Thursday October later reverted to his given name.) If anything, it should have been Wednesday October Christian (see CHRISTIAN, THURSDAY OCTOBER).

The island henceforth received visitors with increasing frequency. In 1817 Teehuteatuaonoa left Pitcairn in the American whaler *Sultan*; she wanted to go back to her native Tahiti. She was not only the first but the only original settler to permanently leave Pitcairn; it is said that she later wanted to come back but could not find an opportunity. It is thanks to Teehuteatuaonoa's later interviews, especially the one published by Captain Peter Dillon, that we now know more details about the adventures of the *Bounty* mutineers.

On December 10, 1823, the first immigrant arrived (on the London whaler *Cyrus*), an English sailor by the name of John Buffett who liked the island so much that he stayed. The islanders had nothing against it, especially since Buffett was better educated than Adams and they needed help with the education of the children. A shipmate of Buffett's, John Evans, jumped ship and hid on the island until she had sailed.

On December 4, 1825, HMS *Blossom* arrived, commanded by Captain Frederick W. Beechey. By now Adams really had nothing to fear, so the account he gave to Beechey is probably the most reliable of all the stories he told visiting sea captains over the years. Moreover, Beechey stayed sixteen days at the island, much longer than previous visitors. On December 17 he formally married Adams and Teio who had been his consort during the last years.

As far as we know, Beechey is the only visitor to have seen Young's journal. His *Narrative of a Voyage to the Pacific . . .*, published in 1831, was the first printed account of a visit to Pitcairn.

Before the *Blossom* sailed on December 21, a census was taken of the island population:

		Males	Females
The first settlers consisted of:	White	9	0
	Coloured	6	12
	TOTAL: 27	15	12
Those killed in the quarrel:	White	6	0
	Coloured	6	0
	By accident	1	3
	Died a natural death	1	3
One went away.★	TOTAL DEATHS	14	6

★ Teehuteatuaonoa ("Jenny")

	Males	Females
The original settlers therefore whom we found on the island were	1	5
The children of the white settlers (the men of colour having left none)	10	10
Their grandchildren	22	15
Recent Settlers (Buffett & Evans)	2	0
Child of one of them (Buffett)	1	0
PRESENT POPULATION: 66	36	30

The list does not include four children who had died, two naturally and two through accidents.

On November 5, 1828, a British adventurer named George Hunn Nobbs arrived at the island with the express intention of settling there. The islanders felt uneasy about it, but since Nobbs' friend Noah Bunker was very ill and the islanders were compassionate, they agreed that the men could stay until Bunker recovered. Bunker, however, was in such agony from whatever disease he had that he several times attempted to take his own life and finally he succeeded. By that time Nobbs had become part of island life — he became somewhat of a rival of Buffett's — and was not about to leave.

On January 20, 1829, not long after the arrival of Nobbs and Bunker, the explorer Jacques-Antoine Moerenhout arrived on a small schooner bound for the eastern Tuamotus. He was to become a friend and protector of the Pitcairn islanders and his book *Voyage aux Iles du Grand Ocean,* published in 1837, gives us valuable insights into the early history of the Pitcairn colony. Moerenhout made a sketch of John Adams shortly before the death of the island patriarch.

Adams died on March 5, 1829, followed soon afterwards by his widow, Teio. His gravesite is the only one known of the mutineers; his tombstone can be seen on Pitcairn today.

Only ten days after Adams' death, Pitcairn was visited by HMS *Seringapatam,* commanded by Captain William Waldegrave, bringing clothing and agricultural tools as gifts from the British government.

THE FIRST MIGRATION (1831)

Before his death, Adams had told Captain Beechey of his concern that the island might become overpopulated and Beechey had informed the British government of the potential problem. Actually, there was no problem at the time. All too hastily, without any study of the conditions on the island and without adequate consultation with its inhabitants, the decision was made to move the entire population (eighty-six in all) to Tahiti.

The directors of the London Missionary Society had had a part in promoting the plan, feeling that the population of Pitcairn lacked proper guidance in the Christian faith and that the missionaries stationed on Tahiti would be the best instruments to provide it.

On February 28, 1831, Captain Alexander Sandilands, commander of HMS *Comet* and accompanied by the transport barque *Lucy Ann*, arrived at Pitcairn for the purpose of moving the population to Tahiti. Many of the islanders were reluctant to leave, but they had developed a deep loyalty to the distant British Crown and did not actively resist. They left for Tahiti on March 7, arriving in Papeete on March 23. A girl was born on board and was named Lucy Ann Quintal after the ship.

Four of the Tahitian women who had settled on Pitcairn were still alive and one of them found a sister on Tahiti — after forty-two years!

The migration proved a disaster. The Queen of Tahiti, Pomare IV, was very kind to the Pitcairners and gave them a large piece of land. However, Tahiti was no longer the island which the four oldtimers had left; it had become an Eldorado for whalers and beachcombers. Not only was it morally objectionable to the pious and God-fearing Pitcairners, but Tahiti was rampant with communicable diseases to which they, who had been isolated for so long, had no immunity. Thursday October Christian was the first to die (on April 21) after having been "taken sick with a fever" (probably influenza or dengue) and eleven more were to perish in a short time.

The survivors decided to move back to Pitcairn. They chartered an American whaler, the *Charles Doggett* from Salem, to carry them back, paying for their passage with copper bolts salvaged from the *Bounty*. (The captain of the *Charles Doggett* was William Driver who was later credited with giving the name of "Old Glory" to the flag of the United States.) They arrived at Pitcairn on September 2, 1831, less than six months after they had left their beloved island. Five more of them died after their return from diseases contracted on Tahiti.

For a while the Pitcairners lived in peace and harmony in a thriving community. But then, on October 28, 1832, the barque *Maria* arrived from Tahiti and on board was a man by the name of Joshua Hill who claimed to be the son of the Duke of Bedford and to have authority from the British government to take over the running of the island's affairs. Buffett, Evans, and Nobbs were suspicious of the man's credentials, but the majority of the Pitcairners, being naive and anxious to please the British government, accepted Hill as their leader.

Hill was actually a confidence man, an impostor, with definite psychopathic tendencies. He soon became dictator of the island, usurping power to such an extent that he had islanders flogged for even minor infractions of the (often senseless) rules he had instituted; he even had Buffett and Evans flogged. So powerful was his influence that he was able to drive the three other non-Pitcairners (whom he called "foreigners") from the island in March 1834. For four and a half years he was, in effect, the sole ruler of Pitcairn.

During their exile Buffett, Evans, and Nobbs wrote several letters about Hill to the British government and to various other authorities and they were confident that the dictatorship would not last for much longer. In September 1834 Buffett returned to Pitcairn over Hill's strong protests and Nobbs and Evans returned the next month. But Hill's rule was not threatened until the New Year of 1837.

The end of his reign came in a most ironic manner. On January 10, 1837, HMS *Actaeon* arrived; the commander of the ship was Captain Lord Edward Russell who happened to be the eldest son of the Duke of Bedford! Instead of confirming Joshua as his long-lost brother, he declared him an impostor and, although he did not have the authority to deport Hill from the island, he reported him to the Admiralty. On December 6 of the same year, HMS *Imogene*, commanded by Captain H. W. Bruce, took Hill off the island.

In November 1838, HMS *Fly*, commanded by Captain Russell Elliott, arrived at Pitcairn. The island now had ninety-nine inhabitants and they told Captain Elliott that they felt a need for a governing structure, an agency through which to administer justice and settle disputes. The disastrous experience with Joshua Hill — who had taken advantage of the lack of such a governing body — had made this need all the more evident. The Pitcairners also wanted protection from the crews of passing whalers, some of whom evidently felt they could behave as destructively as they pleased on an island that was not formally under any country's jurisdiction. Some of them had actually mocked the islanders, denying that Pitcairn was under the protection of Great Britain.

Captain Elliott drew up some "hasty regulations" for the islanders which in practice amounted to a constitution of sorts. It provided for a local government headed by an Island Magistrate "to be periodically chosen from among themselves, and answering for his proceedings to Her Majesty." All adults were given the right to vote, making Pitcairn the first community in the world to give women the suffrage. Education was made compulsory — another first in world history.

The date the "regulations" were signed, November 29, 1838, has gone down in Pitcairn history as the time when the island became a British Crown Colony, even though Elliott lacked the power to formally annex the island to the British Empire. Pitcairn celebrated the 150th anniversary of this event in 1988 by issuing its first commemorative coin. It features an engraving of HMS *Fly* on one side and Elizabeth II on the reverse.

On July 15, 1850, Teraura died. She was the last of the settlers who had arrived on the *Bounty*. Half a year before her death she had been present at the first celebration of Bounty Day, January 23, 1850, the sixtieth anniversary of the burning of the *Bounty*. She was the last link with the mutineers and we can only imagine what she must have thought and remembered when she again saw the *Bounty* —

this time represented by a model — burn in Bounty Bay. (The custom of burning a model of the *Bounty* on Bounty Day, January 23, survives to this day.)

On August 11, 1852, George Nobbs boarded HMS *Portland* and sailed to England to be ordained as chaplain. When he returned on May 15, 1853, he brought with him a National Anthem which he had written for Pitcairn during the voyage:

Mid the mighty Southern Ocean
Stands an isolated rock
Blanched by the surf's commotion
Riven by the lightning's stroke.
Hark those strains to heaven ascending,
From those slopes of vivid green,
Old and young their voices blending —
God preserve Britannia's Queen!

In addition to celebrating Bounty Day, the Pitcairners also celebrated Queen Victoria's birthday each May 24 from 1848 to the year of her death, 1901. Nobbs wrote an anthem for this occasion also, to the tune of "The Girl I Left behind me." The concluding stanza proclaimed:

We'll fire the gun, the Bounty's *gun,*
And set the bell a-ringing
And give three cheers for England's Queen
And three for Pitcairn's Island.

By this time many articles and some books had been written about Pitcairn and some of them gave the impression that the island was again becoming overpopulated, that there were not sufficient resources to feed the growing population, that there was a serious water shortage and that the islanders were unhappy about their isolation from the outside world.

THE SECOND MIGRATION (1856)

As a consequence of these allegations, the British government again started seriously considering the removal of the population to another island. The migration to Tahiti had been a disaster, so that island was out of the question; besides, Tahiti was now under French rule. The island selected this time was Norfolk, 4100 miles west-southwest by west of Pitcairn. It was a former penal colony which had recently been evacuated. Again there was no adequate consultation with the Pitcairners themselves about the move.

However, from 1853 to 1855 there happened to be a severe drought on Pitcairn which depends heavily on the usually abundant rain for its water. The drought created a significant water shortage, and this occasioned some of the Pitcairners to think seriously about moving from the island. Another consideration was that the population had increased to such an extent that some families did not have more than half an acre of land. Yet, all of the islanders would not have left their beloved Pitcairn voluntarily, had it not been for the fact that on April 21, 1856, an "emigrant ship," the *Morayshire*, commanded by Captain Joseph Mathers, arrived with orders from the government to transport the whole population — 194 in all — to Norfolk Island.

Friday May 2 was the last morning the Pitcairners had on their island. What their feelings were can be seen from the entry George Hunn Nobbs made in the Island Register for that day:

> *May 2nd* Breakfasted for the last time, on Pitcairns, and that too with heavy hearts. Previous to embarking, many went to the graves, & headstones, which has afforded us the melancholy, & soothing contemplation of the names & years, of those deposited beneath, but now we are about to leave those frail memorials which had become unspeakably dear to us, never to behold them again. These reflections caused our tears to fall, fast, & freely. We were all embarked, at Bounty Bay, & passing safely through the surf, commenced our Exodus. By four o'clock we were all safe on board the "Morayshire," & the ship made sail with a fair breeze. In the dusk of the evening Pitcairns Island receded from view. There were very few of its late Inhabitants who where not on deck, to take, "A long last lingering look" at that much loved & ever to be remembered spot.

When they arrived on Norfolk Island on June 8, each family was given fifty acres of land. All of them, however, did not like the island and almost right away some of them started thinking about going back. Only two and a half years later, on December 2, 1858, two Young families and one McCoy family — 16 in all — embarked on the ship *Mary Ann* and sailed for Pitcairn where they arrived on January 17, 1859.

They had returned in the last moment, because France, which had previously annexed the Society Islands and the surrounding groups, had sent out a warship from Tahiti to claim Pitcairn for France. She arrived soon after the return of the sixteen Pitcairners but, seeing the Union Jack hoisted over the settlement, she turned back to Tahiti.

Four more families arrived from Norfolk in 1863, including Thursday October Christian II and his wife and children.

In 1886 an American sailor, John Tay, arrived on Pitcairn in the British man-of-war HMS *Pelican*. He was a Seventh-day Adventist and brought with him several books expounding his faith. In just six weeks he managed to convert a majority of the islanders to his beliefs and the next year, at a meeting in March 1887, the church recorder noted: "The forms and prayer book of the Church of England laid aside. During the past week, meetings were held to organize our church services on Sabbath [meaning Saturday]." Since Adventists are not allowed to to eat pork, all of the pigs on the island were killed. An unauthenticated but oft-repeated tale has it that they were simply driven over the cliffs into the sea. The story does make sense, however, since the Pitcairners were too poor to waste their hard-earned ammunition on shooting all the pigs.

With contributions from Seventh-day Adventist Sabbath schools a schooner, approximately the size of the *Bounty*, was built at Benicia, California, and christened *Pitcairn*. It was launched in July 1890 and arrived at the island late in the year with six missionaries. The whole island population was now baptized in the Adventist faith.

The next important date in the history of Pitcairn Island is 1914. That was the year the Panama Canal opened, which put Pitcairn squarely in the path of the shipping between Panama and New Zealand and meant that more ships would stop at the island, breaking some of the isolation it had experienced since the end of the era of whaling.

The population continued to increase until a peak of 233 was reached in 1937 after which it has steadily declined.

In 1938 a radio station was built on the island; the first operator was Andrew Young, fifth generation direct descendant of mutineer Edward Young. In 1940 the first Pitcairn postage stamps came out and to this day the sale of stamps constitutes the main source of income for the island, the second source being the sale of artifacts.

In 1948 the first school teacher arrived from New Zealand and since around that time New Zealand has gradually assumed responsibility for the island.

In February 1957 Captain Irving Johnson came to Pitcairn in his famous brigantine *Yankee* on one of his seven globe-circling voyages. Johnson always made it a point to stop at Pitcairn and each time he took the Pitcairners to Henderson Island to enable them to cut a supply of the hard and beautiful *miro* wood for their carvings. (See HENDERSON ISLAND.)

On this visit, one of the crew members of the *Yankee*, while diving, found the twelve-foot anchor of the *Bounty* which today is proudly displayed in front of the little court house in Bounty Square in Adamstown, as the center of the settlement is called. During the *Yankee*'s visit Luis Marden, sponsored by the National Geographic Society, also happened to be on the island and found the site of the wreck.

In 1965 some dirt roads were built with the help of the New Zealand government. At about this time occasional cruise ships started to visit the island, affording the Pitcairners more opportunity to sell their beautiful handicrafts.

In 1983 the first airdrop of supplies was carried out by the Royal New Zealand Air Force, using two C-130 military cargo planes starting from Rarotonga and landing on Easter Island. Some equipment which would otherwise have been difficult or impossible to land, such as a heavy tractor, were dropped with clusters of parachutes. Since the level area of the island is so small, it was a tricky operation, but it was completely successful.

The jetty in Bounty Bay was built in the late 1960s and was strengthened and modified by New Zealand engineers in the mid-1980s.

Pitcairn now has its own flag and coat of arms. The island is governed by a council whose head is the Island Magistrate (at the time of writing, Brian Young), but some people claim that the real power is in the hands of the Seventh-day Adventist Pastor. The council meets in the court house which is really a misnomer, because there is no crime or delinquency on the island.

The main problem of the past was said to be overpopulation. Well, now it is the opposite. If the longboats on Pitcairn today did not have diesel engines, the islanders would be hard put to man the oars of even one of them. Pitcairn faces the same problem as other Pacific islands: the allure for the young people of the glittering urban centers in faraway countries.

It is true that the island is getting less isolated. Since 1986, for example, the islanders can make phone calls to anywhere in the world via satellite. There are several video recorders and cameras on the island, in addition to freezers and three- and four-wheel terrain motorcycles, etc. Supply ships arrive from New Zealand twice, sometimes three times a year. Paradoxically, however, or maybe naturally, the more contact the island has with the outside world, the more interested the young people seem to be in leaving.

The number of ships passing Pitcairn is fairly high, about 30–50 a year. The problem is that most of them are cargo ships and few of them stop, because the owners consider even a short delay in their schedule too costly.

Having visited Pitcairn in 1987 and observed the optimism and resourcefulness of the Pitcairners, I feel certain that the island community will survive. Sad as it seems, however, it may take an infusion of limited tourism, if survival is to be guaranteed. It would be a sad solution to the problem, but it would certainly be preferable to the island being abandoned. At the time of writing (September 1988) a private ferry service between Mangareva and Pitcairn is being discussed.

Those who have seen Pitcairn before such a development (which one hopes will never be necessary), must consider themselves fortunate indeed. My visit to this island will always remain in my memory as a glorious fulfillment of one of my fondest boyhood dreams.

The literature on Pitcairn is voluminous. These four books will be found most helpful and interesting: Robert B. Nicolson: *The Pitcairners* (1965); Frank Clune: *Journey to Pitcairn* (1966); David Silverman: *Pitcairn Island* (1967); Harry L. Shapiro: *The Heritage of the Bounty* (1936).

Finally, there is an excellent booklet, published by the British Consulate General in Auckland and called simply: *A Guide to Pitcairn*.

The best way to get up-to-date information on Pitcairn is to subscribe to the island's monthly newsletter, *Pitcairn Miscellany* (address: Pitcairn Island, South

Pacific, via Auckland, New Zealand). At the time of writing (September 1988) a year's subscription costs US$10.00. You may have to wait for an issue for half a year sometimes, but the interesting information you will receive more than makes up for the long wait.

From the time the first mutineer set foot on the island, one of the most important concerns on Pitcairn has been the arrival of ships. Life on the island could be said to revolve around their arrival and departure and historical events are similarly dated.

For those who have a serious interest in the history of Pitcairn, the following is a list of the ships which visited Pitcairn between 1808 and the end of 1831. The information is primarily from Walter Brodie: *Pitcairn's Island and The Islanders in 1850* (1851), with some minor additions and corrections.

Year	Vessel	From	Captain
1808	Topaz	Boston	Mayhew Folger
1814	HMS Briton	Portsmouth	Sir Thomas Staines
	HMS Tagus	Portsmouth	Philip Pipon
1817	Sultan	Boston	Reynolds
1817	George	Nantucket	?
1819	Hercules	Calcutta	James Henderson
1819	Stanton	Fairhaven	?
1819	Elizabeth	London	Henry King
1820	Surry	London	Thomas Raine
1822	Russell	New Bedford	Frederick Arthur
1823	Cyrus	London	John Hall
1824	Oneo	Nantucket	G. Worth
1824	Maryland	Nantucket	O. Folger
1824	Waverly	Oahu	W. Dana
1825	Waverly	Oahu	W. Dana
1825	Melantho	London	N. Folger
1825	Luna	Nantucket	A. Swain
1825	HMS Blossom	Portsmouth	Frederick W. Beechey
1826	Roscoe	New Bedford	G. Worth
1826	Gov. McQuarrie	?	R. Brimmer
1826	Tahiti	?	?
1826	Lovely Ann	London	Phillip Blythe
1827	Resident	Nantucket	Winslow
1827	Connecticut	Norwich	Chester
1827	Discoverer	Valparaiso	Lindsey
1828	Weymouth	Nantucket	M. Harris

ENCYCLOPEDIA

Year	Vessel	From	Captain
1828	*Discoverer*	Valparaiso	Grimwood
1829	*Ganges*	Nantucket	J. Coffin
1829	*Voladoe*	Valparaiso	J. Clarke
1829	*Independence*	Nantucket	Whippy
1829	*Orion*	Nantucket	Alley
1829	*Connecticut*	Norwich	P. Smith
1829	*Rob Roy*	Boston	T. Percival
1829	*Unity*	?	Madse
1830	HMS *Seringapatam*	Portsmouth	William Waldegrave
1830	*Nelson*	London	E. David
1830	*Courier de Bordeaux*	France	T. Maurac
1830	*Eagle*	London	J. Greave
1831	*Fabius*	Nantucket	Coffin
1831	HMS *Comet*	Portsmouth	Alexander Sandilands
1831	*Lucy Ann*	New South Wales	J. Currey
1831	*Oregon*	Fairhaven	T. Delano
1831	*Charles Doggett*	Salem	William Driver
1831	*Pomare*	Valparaiso	J. Clark

Some of the important ships of subsequent years were:

Year	Vessel	From	Captain
1832	*Maria*	Tahiti	Thomas Ebriel
1834	*Tuscan*	London	Thomas Stavers
1834	*Olivia*	Boston	C. Kendal
1837	HMS *Actaeon*	Portsmouth	Lord Edward Russell
1837	HMS *Imogene*	Portsmouth	H. W. Bruce
1838	HMS *Fly*	Portsmouth	Russell Elliott
1852	HMS *Portland*	Portsmouth	Rear Admiral Fairfax Moresby
1853	HMS *Virago* (The first steamship to visit Pitcairn)	Portsmouth	Prevost
1856	HMS *Morayshire*	Portsmouth	Joseph Mathers
1859	*Mary Ann*	?	Wilson
1864	*St. Kilda*	?	?
1886	HMS *Pelican*	Portsmouth	?
1890	*Pitcairn*	Oakland	J. M. Marsh

Brodie's list of ships ends in 1850; there were 328 ships in all during the first half of the century. A tally of the known home ports shows that well over a third were whalers from New England — New Bedford alone accounted for 55 ships and Nantucket for 48.

For a hundred years now, the Pitcairners have expressed their farewell to each visiting ship by singing the hymn "In the Sweet By and By." As the longboats are raised and lowered by the swells and the last rays of the sun light up Lookout Point, the melody and the words are forever etched in the memory of the departing visitor.

> *To our bountiful Father above,*
> *We will offer a tribute of praise,*
> *For the glorious gift of His love,*
> *And the blessings that hallow our days.*
> *In the sweet by and by,*
> *We shall meet on that beautiful shore;*
> *In the sweet by and by,*
> *We shall meet on that beautiful shore.*

PITCAIRN (vessels)   When the Pitcairners had been converted to the Seventh-day Adventist faith in the late 1880s, the church realized that it would need some reliable way to keep contact with the islanders. For this purpose a two-masted schooner was built in Benicia, California, and christened *Pitcairn*. The vessel was 90 feet long with a beam of 27 feet, in other words, about the size of the *Bounty*.

On her first voyage to Pitcairn, the schooner carried a crew of eight, commanded by Captain J. M. Marsh of Nova Scotia, and five passengers. (The *Bounty* had a complement of 46.) She sailed out of San Francisco Bay on October 20, 1890, and arrived at Pitcairn on November 25.

After several voyages to Pitcairn and one to Norfolk Island, the *Pitcairn* was sold in 1899.

With the help of the British government a cutter, also named *Pitcairn*, was then purchased for the purpose of developing some trade with Mangareva, 306 miles to the north-west. She was manned entirely by Pitcairners and employed in carrying produce to the Mangarevans who paid for it with money they earned in their pearl fisheries. The venture ended, however, when the *Pitcairn* foundered in 1904.

Again with the help of the British government, a cutter named *John Adams* was purchased for £274. She proved unseaworthy, however, and had to be sold — for £60.

The Pitcairners themselves then built a 25-ton schooner in 1919. Named *Messenger*, she made several voyages to Tahiti, but on a return voyage from Mangareva on April 11, 1920, in sight of Pitcairn, she encountered a hurricane and was dismasted. The vessel foundered, but the crew was miraculously saved by the American steamship *Sassenach* which just happened by. Fred Christian, who had gone out to the *Sassenach* and taken part in the rescue, said later, "Before we reached Bounty Bay, the *Messenger* had sunk, and good riddance. She was a terrible job, with a heavy nose, and she went just as fast sideways as forrard!"

PITCAIRNESE Pitcairnese is a language which the Pitcairners use among themselves. It is a mixture of eighteenth-century English and Tahitian, although the Tahitian element is almost unrecognizable, except in the names of plants and fish and a few other words. Harry L. Shapiro describes the probable origin of Pitcairnese in *The Heritage of the Bounty* (1936):

> In many ways the dialect seems as if it had its origin in the efforts of the mutineers to teach the Tahitians the English language. The grammatical breakdown suggests this, as well as the elisions of sounds. I find that it is a common tendency for most of us when confronted with a foreigner, who has little English, to shout a horribly debased kind of English, as though bad grammar and a loud voice could render the language intelligible. (Listen to a customer in a Chinese laundry.) But whatever its precise origin, the Pitcairn dialect today consists of mispronounced English and Tahitian words with a spattering of coined words, the whole employed in a degenerate English syntax.

Here are some examples of Pitcairnese:

Peet-kern •	Pitcairn	*Es stolly* •	It's a lie
O-a •	Yes	*A little sullun* •	A little child
Walley •	Valley	*Bout yawly gwen?* •	Where are you
Malu •	(Tahitian) maro		going?
Musket •	Rifle	*It's darking* •	It's getting dark
I kawa •	I don't know	*I no bin see-um* •	I haven't seen
			him

I see yawl-ey scows segoin'out ah big ship
• I see your boats going out to the big ship
Fut you ally comey diffy and do daffy?
• Why do you come and behave that way?

PLANTAIN See FE'I.

POINO (Poeno, "Poenow") The chief of Haapape during the visits of the *Bounty*. Poino was Morrison's *taio* and the custodian of Webber's portrait of Captain Cook.

POINT VENUS Point Venus is the peninsula forming the eastern shore of Matavai Bay in the old district of Haapape (today's Mahina). It is the northernmost point in Tahiti and lies about six and a half miles east of Papeete. It was here that Captain Cook made his observation of the transit of Venus on June 3, 1769.

It was also here that Captain Bligh established his first shore station for the gathering of breadfruit plants (in November, 1788).

POLYNESIA The word Polynesia comes from the Greek *polys* (many) and *nesos* (island). The Polynesian islands form a rough triangle with Hawaii in the north, New Zealand in the southwest and Easter Island in the east. Altogether the area comprises twelve million square miles, which makes it larger than the continent of Africa. It also contains the most widespread single cohesive culture on earth, although one of the smallest in numbers.

The islands within this triangle range from mountainous volcanic giants to small atolls. Polynesia consists of the following groups:

Easter Island (Rapa Nui)

Pitcairn Islands (geographically counted as part of the Tuamotus)

Gambiers (often counted as part of the Tuamotus)

Tuamotus

Marquesas

Society Islands

Australs

Cook Islands

Phoenix Islands (now part of Kiribati)

Tokelau (Union Islands)

Tuvalu (Ellice Islands)

Samoas (Navigator Islands)

Wallis and Futuna

Niue

Tonga (Tongatabu, Haapai, Vavau)

New Zealand (Aotearoa)

Hawaiian Islands

There are also Polynesian populations on Kapingamerangi, Nukuoro, Tikopia, and Ontong Java.

POMARE I (Tu, Teina, Mate, Vairaatoa) The old Tahitian custom of changing and exchanging names can cause a great deal of confusion when one reads the acounts of the early explorers. Pomare I is an excellent example.

He was probably born in 1751, the first-born son of Teu and his wife Purea-Tetupaia who was the chiefess of Opoa in Raiatea. He was therefore about sixteen years old when Tahiti was "discovered" by Wallis in 1767.

Tu — his name at the time — was the chief of Te Porionu'u, a district which combined Pare (half of today's Papeete plus all of Pirae) and Arue (which adjoins most of the shoreline of Matavai Bay). Because he happened to be the chief who controlled the shores of Matavai, the early explorers thought that Tu was an important, if not the most important, chief on the island of Tahiti.

Bligh knew him as Tu when he first met him in 1777 on Cook's third voyage.

Eleven years later when Bligh came back on the *Bounty*, Tu had changed his name to Teina.

When Christian landed the loyalists and half of the mutineers on Tahiti less than six months after Bligh had said goodbye to Teina, the chief had again changed his name and was now called Mate.

Not long after the *Pandora* had left, Mate changed his name to Pomare and it is under that name he has gone down in history, at the same time establishing a dynasty.

When Bligh came back to Tahiti in 1792 on the second breadfruit expedition, Pomare greeted him as an old friend and was not offended when Bligh insisted on calling him Teina; he must have known by then that Bligh was a most inflexible man.

The missionary William Ellis, who arrived in Tahiti thirteen years after the death of Pomare I, was given an erroneous reason for the birth of the name Pomare. He published it in his *Polynesian Researches* and, as a consequence, you can read it in almost every popular book on Tahiti:

> He (Tynah) was travelling in a mountainous part of Tahiti where it was necessary to spend the night. . . . He took cold and was affected with a cough: this led some of his companions to designate the preceding night by the appellation pomare — night of cough from 'Po' night, and 'Mare' cough. The chief was pleased with the sound of the words, adopted them as his name, and was ever afterwards called Pomare.

Bligh tells us the true story of the origin of the name; he heard it from Pomare himself:

> It surprised me to find that both Iddeah [Itia] and Tynah [Teina] were now called 'Pomarre,' and on inquiring the cause of it I find it is owing to their having lost their eldest daughter Terranaoroa of an illness of that name which they describe to me by coughing. Pomarre is compounded from 'Po,' night, and 'Marre' or 'Morre,' the name of the disease. Whenever a child dies, the parents take the name of the disease; if a dozen children die of different diseases the parents have as many different names, or give them to their relations, and may be called either by the new name or their own. It is a custom common to all ranks of people here.

To make matters even more complicated, the family now referred to as Pomare had earlier adopted the name *Vairaatoa* (grove of toa trees). However, since that was a family name, rather than that of an individual, it does not appear in the accounts of the early explorers. It is found primarily in genealogies.

The Pomare family stemmed from the Tuamotu islands, but it is not clear from the records whether Pomare himself, or his father Teu, or his grandfather, perhaps, was born in the Tuamotus. Whoever it was had, according to some authorities, achieved the status as chief by marrying an heiress to the district of Pare in Porionu'u.

Others claim that Tu, having arrived from Fakarava atoll in the Tuamotus, had become a *hoa* or *taio* (bond-friend) of the chief of Pare, Mauaihiti, and, after his *taio*'s death, became chief himself. Henry Adams writes in *Memoirs of Arii Taimai*:

> Tu of Faarava, having undertaken a visit to the distant land of Tahiti, came in by the Taunoa opening, which is the eastern channel into what is now the harbor of Papeete. Landing at Taunoa a stranger, he was invited to be the guest of Mauaihiti, who seems to have been a chief of Pare. Tu made himself so agreeable, or so useful to his host, that Mauaihiti adopted him as *hoa*, or brother, with the formal ceremonies attached to this custom, which consist in a grand feast, and union of all the families, and offering of all the rights and honors which belong to the host. Tu accepted them, and at the death of Mauaihiti he became heir and successor in the chief's line. He gave up all idea of returning to the Paumotus, and devoted his energy to extending his connections in Tahiti.

Pomare was a large man, over six feet tall and weighing about 300 pounds. His wife Itia (Bligh wrote her name "Iddea") was almost as large and, while Pomare himself was a timid man, Itia was an aggressive, courageous woman who liked manly pursuits; she became skilled in the use of firearms, for example.

In Part I of this book we have shown that the men of the *Bounty* who stayed on the island for one and a half years, from Christian's departure (September 1789) to the arrival of the *Pandora* (March 1791), played a decisive role in Pomare's (then called Mate) rise to power. His position as supreme chief was threatened many times, however, and total consolidation of power for the Pomare dynasty came only with Pomare's son, also named Tu, who became Pomare II.

Pomare I died, probably of a heart attack, when he was paddling his outrigger out to the English ship *Dart* which had just arrived from Port Jackson. The date was September 3, 1803, and Pomare was only a little over fifty years old. Despite the shrewd machinations and clever intrigues engaged in by the missionaries who had arrived six years earlier, Pomare never abandoned his faith in the gods of his forefathers. I like to think that, when he died, he went back to Havaiki, the ancestral land of the Polynesians.

POMARE II (Tu nui ae i te Atua, Tu-nui-aite-atua, "Prince Tu") When the *Bounty* arrived in Tahiti in 1788, Bligh and Peckover who had both been there before were surprised to learn that chief Tu now was called Teina and that his son not only had inherited the name Tu, but was formally the chief despite being only five years old (he was born in 1783).

Tu assumed real power as Pomare II when his father died in 1803. Although Pomare I had come close to achieving supreme power over the island, he had never subdued the powerful Teva chiefs. Pomare II also had severe setbacks and in 1808 he was defeated in a major battle and had to flee to Moorea; many of the missionaries followed him.

Pomare II was a heavy drinker, but he was also shrewd and realized that the most effective way to become supreme ruler over Tahiti was to let himself be baptized in the Christian faith and thus get the backing not only of the missionaries but also of the visiting sea captains who were arriving with increasing frequency.

He asked to be baptized in 1812. The equally shrewd missionaries were well aware that he did so only to achieve power, but they knew their own power would be tied in with his. After a proper period of hesitation they went along with his request.

A bloody war followed which ended with Pomare becoming sole ruler over Tahiti and the island being formally "Christianized" in 1815. The missionaries, whose hypocrisy evidently knew no limits, were among his suppliers of firearms.

In 1819 Pomare II promulgated the so-called Code of Pomare which was based on the laws of England.

Pomare II's first wife was a chiefess named Tetua who died in 1806 from "voluntary abortion" (evidently the deep massage technique used by the Tahitians was not always safe). After her death, he made a very shrewd move in marrying Teritooterai, the eldest daughter of Tamatoa IV, high chief of Raiatea. Raiatea was the Holy Land of all Polynesia and its chiefs carried the highest prestige of all. With Teritooterai, Pomare II had two sons: one died in infancy and the other, named simply Pomare, was to become King of Tahiti as Pomare III.

The marriage was purely political in nature and, long before the two sons were born, Pomare II took up with Teritooterai's younger sister Teremoemoe with whom he had a daughter, named Aimata, in 1813. She was destined to become Queen Pomare IV under whose rule Tahiti lost its independence to the French.

Pomare II died of "excessive drinking" in December 1821.

POMARE III   When Pomare II died in December 1821, his son — also named Pomare — was only eleven months old, but he was still considered King of Tahiti.

The missionaries had achieved a great deal of power under Pomare II, but they had never been able to totally dominate him or to influence his lifestyle which to them was shocking, filled as it was with drinking and singing and dancing and fornicating. Now when he was gone, justly punished for his debauchery by an avenging God, the missionaries had their golden opportunity: they would raise his son to be a creature of their own liking, a somber, humorless, unctuous, automaton who would do their bidding.

The missionaries set to work on little Pomare, shielding him from all other influences and raising him to a life of prayer and devotion. They enrolled him at a very tender age in their "South Seas Academy" on Moorea and kept him away from all frivolous play and other healthy activities. They may well have succeeded in their scheme if the poor boy had not died in 1827 at the age of six and a half.

He was succeeded on the throne by one of the last persons the missionaries would ever have wanted: the vivacious, happy and life-loving Aimata, whom they had despised since she was born out of wedlock.

There had been some important developments during the short "reign" of Pomare III. Firstly, Tahiti got its own flag in 1822. It has three horizontal stripes: a narrow (¼) red stripe at top and bottom and a broad (½) white stripe in the middle. Until very recently, the French authorities forbade the flying — and even the possession — of this flag. George Pritchard, an English missionary who was to strongly oppose the French usurpation of power, arrived in 1824; in the same year a Legislative Assembly was inaugurated; and Papeete replaced Matavai as the principal port in 1826.

POMARE IV (Aimata) Aimata was born on February 28, 1813, as the "illegitimate" (in the eyes of the missionaries) daughter of Pomare II and his consort Teremoemoe. She was the half-sister of Pomare III.

Aimata means "eater of eyes." To the Tahitians, this signified royalty: in the ancient past, the high chiefs had indeed eaten the eyes of human sacrifices during important celebrations in order to add their *mana* (spiritual power) to their own. Even during the stay of the men of the *Bounty* on the island, they had witnessed a symbolic eating of the eyes (see the February 1791 commentary in Part I). The very name Aimata carried tremendous prestige.

Aimata was only fourteen years old when her half-brother died and she became Queen Pomare IV in 1827. She was not yet interested in the duties of a monarch; on the contrary, she wanted to do what the missionaries seemed to hate most: sing and dance and have fun. Moreover, she was pretty and flirtatious, happy and cheerful, and she loved sports and games: in other words, she was the incarnation of sin.

To cure her, she was given into the tutelage of George Pritchard, a missionary who had arrived in Tahiti in 1824. She was lucky. Pritchard was not the typical hypocritical do-gooder that described the average missionary; he was a compassionate and perceptive realist who soon learned to understand the Tahitian psyche and, in the process, learned to speak Tahitian fluently. He was also somewhat of a politician and later became the British Consul on the island.

Under the instruction of Pritchard, Queen Pomare developed into a wise and responsible monarch, even though the fact that she never gave up her informal Tahitian levity often made her seem frivolous to the average visitor.

Queen Pomare, only eighteen years old at the time, was very kind to the Pitcairners when they migrated to Tahiti in 1831. She gave them a large piece of land and did everything to make them feel comfortable and at home. It was not her fault that Tahiti at that time was riddled with diseases brought in by the multitude of ships then visiting the island or that, despite the pious efforts of the missionaries, it had become a rather wild and roisterous place with drunk whalers roaming the streets of Papeete and everything being for sale, including women.

Twelve of the Pitcairners died on Tahiti soon after their arrival and five more succumbed later to illnesses contracted there. The Queen, Pritchard, and several European residents and Tahitians, helped the Pitcairners charter a schooner to take them home. The Pitcairners themselves paid for most of the passage with copper fittings they had brought from the *Bounty*.

Aimata had been married at the age of nine to Tapoa, Prince of Tahaa. The marriage was of course purely political and they divorced in 1834. There were no children from their union. The Queen then married her cousin Tenania of Raiatea who was seven years younger than she. With him she had nine children, the first three of whom died in infancy.

Her eldest and favorite son, Ariiaue, was born in 1838. When he died of tuberculosis in 1855, his younger (by one year) brother Teratane, also named Teriitaria, became Crown Prince, assumed the name Ariiaue, and eventually assumed the throne under the name Pomare V. Tenania survived Queen Pomare by six years.

The history of Queen Pomare's reign is too long and too complicated to be summarized here. The books enumerated at the end of the entry TAHITI provide an excellent summary of the events.

Suffice it to say that Queen Pomare had to live through the tragedy of seeing her beautiful island invaded by ruthless foreign troops and made into an overseas colony of a country on the other side of the world. From 1844 to 1846 the Tahitians fought for their freedom against the French invaders, a fight which in heroism equals the fight of the Finns against the Communist hordes from the East. Unlike the Finns, however, the Tahitians were unable to preserve their independence.

During this final struggle to preserve independence Queen Pomare sought refuge with her cousin, King Tamatoa IV of Raiatea (from 1840 to 1847). She hoped desperately that her "sister," Queen Victoria, who was only six years younger, would come to her rescue. Despite all of Pritchard's efforts, however, England abandoned Tahiti to its fate.

In 1847 Queen Pomare was finally persuaded by her old friend, chiefess Ariitaimai, to return to Tahiti and subject herself to the rule of the French protectorate. She was allowed by the French military commander to stay on as a figurehead. On September 17, 1877, after a reign of fifty years, the sixty-four-year-old Queen died, beloved by her people and by everyone who came to know her, with her dignity unblemished and with her spirit unbroken, a fitting symbol for the greatness of her people.

POMARE V (Teratane, Teriitaria, later: Ariiaue) Teratane (also named Teriitaria) was born to Queen Pomare IV and her consort Tenania on November 3, 1839. When his one-year-older brother Ariiaue, the Crown Prince, died in 1855, Teratane assumed his name. Teratane (now Ariiaue) was married on November 11,

1857, to Temariiateururai, eldest daughter of King and Queen Arii Mate of Huahine. With her he had a daughter and a son, but they died in infancy and Temariiateururai also died soon after the birth of the second child.

On January 28, 1875, Ariiaue married Marau (Joanna Marau-taaroa Tepau Salmon), the daughter of Ariitaimai, the chiefess of the Teva clan. At last the two opposing families were united, but too late to save Tahiti — if it could have been saved, which is doubtful, considering the ruthlessness of the French. With her he had three children.

When his mother, Queen Pomare IV, died on September 17, 1877, Ariiaue assumed the throne as Pomare V. The less said of his "rule" the better.

If you drive eastward from Papeete and stop at 4.7 kilometers, you will find to your left, next to a quaint twelve-sided chapel, a curious steep pyramid with a large letter P and an urn on top that looks a little like a Benedictine bottle. It is the last resting place of Pomare V who died on June 12, 1891, from "an excess in the use of strong liquor."

The place on which the burial vault stands was sacred to the old Tahitians; it was the site of the national marae (open-air temple) Tara-hoi which, like all the other beautiful maraes, was torn down by order of the missionaries.

The urn on top of the vault is *not* meant to symbolize a Benedictine bottle, no matter how much the tourist guides swear to it. It might as well, however, because Pomare V was an alcoholic. He had grown up with mostly French people around him and did not have much understanding or appreciation of the old ways. Moreover, he could see that it was the French that ruled the island and that his "reign" would be meaningless. Even a powerless monarch, however, would have been important as a rallying point and a symbol of the glory of the past for the Tahitian people. Realizing this, the French authorities duped Pomare V into abdicating his throne in the year 1880. He died in 1891.

POMARE (vessel)   The ship which in 1834 carried George Nobbs, John Buffett, and Jack Evans from Tahiti to Pitcairn in order to pick up their families from the island which was then under the dictatorial rule of Joshua Hill. The *Pomare* then took the Nobbs family to Mangareva and the others back to Tahiti.

POMURREY   See POMARE I.

POPA'A   Tahitian for white person.

PORAPORA   See BORA BORA.

PORI   Archaic Tahitian word denoting people, mainly women, who tried to become fat and lighten their skin.

PORIONU'U   See TE PORIONU'U.

PORTLOCK, Nathaniel   Lieutenant Portlock was the commander of the *Assistant* on the second breadfruit expedition. He had sailed as master's mate on the *Discovery* under Captain Charles Clerke on Cook's third voyage; when Cook was killed by the Hawaiians at Kealakekua Bay on February 14, 1779, Portlock was transferred to the *Resolution* to serve under Bligh who was sailing master. He was promoted to lieutenant in 1780.

As commander of the *King George* (1785-1788) Portlock made valuable observations of the islands he visited, especially the Sandwich (Hawaiian) group.

It was difficult for Bligh to praise any of his officers, but he did value Portlock. When Bligh got a recurrence of his malaria (contracted in the East Indies after the open-boat voyage), he had Portlock — rather than his first lieutenant and step-nephew Francis Bond — assume command of the *Providence*.

Portlock was highly regarded by the Admiralty: on the return of the expedition he gained an audience long before Bligh and was promoted to commander. In 1799 he assumed command of the *Arrow* and captured the Dutch ship *Draack*. He died on September 12, 1817.

PORT ROYAL HARBOUR   The name Captain Samuel Wallis gave to MATAVAI BAY.

PORTSMOUTH   Seaport and naval base in Hampshire, England, seventy miles south-west from London. Its current population is about 250,000.

The naval station consists of four towns: Portsmouth, Portsea, Landport, and Southsea. The harbor opens into Spithead, the eastern end of the Solent (the strait between the mainland and the Isle of Wight). (See map, pages 372–73.)

Nelson's flagship, HMS *Victory*, is moored in Portsmouth and is still commissioned but also open to the public as a museum.

"PRINCE TU" ("Prince Otoo")   See POMARE II.

HMS *PRINCESS AMELIA*   The 80-gun ship in which Bligh served as first lieutenant from January 1 to March 19, 1782.

HMS *PROVIDENCE*   The *Providence* was a sixth-rate frigate of 420 tons burden, with three decks, armed with twelve carriage guns and fourteen swivels, and carrying a crew of 134 on Bligh's second breadfruit expedition, August 3, 1791, to August 7, 1793. She was brand new, having been launched at Blackwall on April 23, 1791. The principal officers in the *Providence* were William Bligh (captain), Francis Godolphin Bond (first lieutenant), James Guthrie (second lieutenant), George Tobin

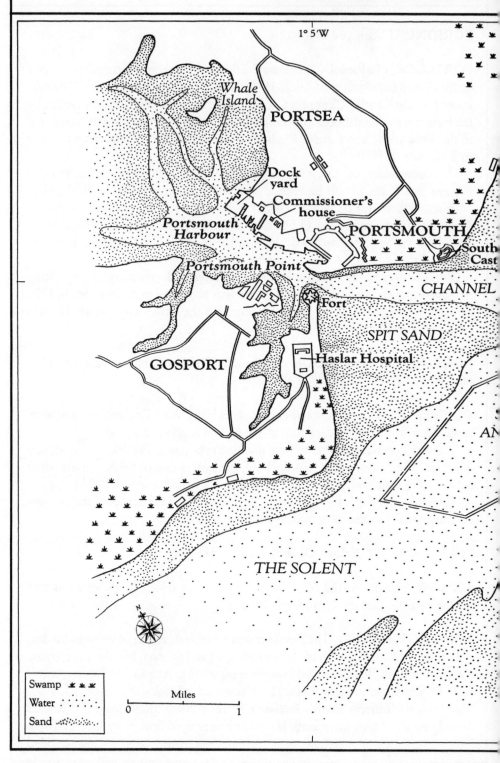

1° 5′W

Whale Island

PORTSEA

Dock yard

Commissioner's house

Portsmouth Harbour

PORTSMOUTH

South Cast

Portsmouth Point

CHANNEL

Fort

SPIT SAND

GOSPORT

Haslar Hospital

AN

THE SOLENT

Swamp

Water

Sand

Miles

0   1

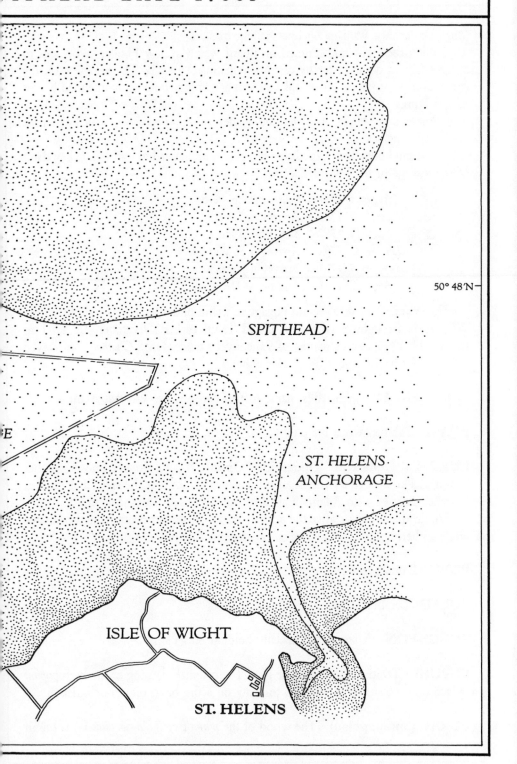

SPITHEAD

50° 48′N—

ST. HELENS
ANCHORAGE

ISLE OF WIGHT

ST. HELENS

(third lieutenant), William Nichols (sailing master).

Among the eight midshipmen on board was Matthew Flinders who was to achieve fame a decade later by circumnavigating Australia. The botanists on the expedition were James Wiles and Christopher Smith, both recommended by Sir Joseph Banks.

Commanding HMS *Assistant*, the tender of the *Providence*, was Lieutenant Nathaniel Portlock.

The second breadfruit expedition has been summarized in Part I. The key dates of the voyage of the Providence are:

August 3, 1791:	Sails from Spithead.
April 9, 1792:	Arrives at Tahiti.
July 19, 1792:	Sails from Tahiti.
January 22, 1793:	Arrives at St Vincent.
February 5, 1793:	Arrives at Jamaica.
August 7, 1793:	Anchors at Deptford.

The *Providence* made a second voyage to Tahiti under the command of Captain William R. Broughton who had visited Tahiti earlier (December 27, 1791 to January 24, 1792) as commander of Vancouver's tender HMS *Chatham*. She stayed in Tahiti from November 28 to December 11, 1795.

"PRUDENCE" John Mills' name for his consort. See VAHINEATUA.

PUA'A Tahitian word for pig.

PUARAI ("Obuarei," "Opuarei," "Opuole") We do not know whether Puarai was kidnapped by Christian and his men or not, but she arrived at Pitcairn as the consort of John Adams who then called himself Alexander Smith.

Within the first year after the arrival, Puarai fell to her death from a precipice while gathering birds or bird eggs. She left no children.

PUEU District in Tahiti on the north coast of the Taiarapu peninsula.

PULAU See PURAU.

PUNCHEON A large cask, usually holding 80 gallons.

PUPUHI Tahitian for musket or gun. The original meaning of the verb *pupuhi* (which now means to shoot) was to blow on a fire or to blow out a flame.

PURAU (burau, pulau) The wood of the *purau* tree (*Hibiscus tiliaceus*) is tough and durable, valuable to the Polynesians as timber for their canoes. An especially straight variety, *purau ahua*, is used for masts and paddles.

PURCELL, William   Carpenter on board the *Bounty*; loyalist; went with Bligh; arrived safely in England. In the *Bounty* literature, Purcell has uniformly been portrayed as a cantankerous man, a perpetual trouble-maker, and somewhat of a "sea-lawyer." It is possible that such was the case and there is no doubt that Purcell was a constant thorn in his captain's side. However, we only have Bligh's description of him, and Bligh disliked him so intensely that he could hardly be seen as an objective judge of Purcell's character and personality. It is just as possible that Purcell simply was "his own man," conscious of his competence and his dignity as a human being, and would not let himself be intimidated by Bligh — an attitude which of course would have infuriated the captain.

Purcell was a loyalist only in the sense that he paid allegiance to the Crown and thereby to Bligh's uniform — but certainly not to Bligh as a person, a man whom he detested.

Purcell was proud of his profession and of his skills and, like Fryer, he was not about to take Bligh's abuse "lying down." In fact, what enraged Bligh the most during the entire voyage — apart from the mutiny of course — was Purcell's assertion on Sunday Island: "I am as good a man as you."

Bligh was a vindictive and petty man, so Purcell was probably not too surprised when Bligh brought charges against him: six counts of misconduct, insubordination, "refractory behaviour," etc. The verdict of the court, which met immediately after Bligh's brief court-martial on October 22, 1790, was that the charges had been proved in part, and Purcell was therefore reprimanded.

During the court-martial of the accused mutineers, Purcell damaged Heywood's case by saying that he had seen the acting midshipman with his hand on the hilt of a cutlass. However, his impression was that Heywood was confused at the time. Also, Heywood had dropped the cutlass immediately when Purcell had asked: "In the name of God, Peter, what do you do with that?" He did not consider Heywood a mutineer.

After the court-martial, Purcell was helpful to Edward Christian in the latter's attempts to gather all the facts pertaining to the mutiny that had been omitted by Bligh. His later pursuits are unknown, but Sir John Barrow, in *The Eventful History of the Mutiny and Piratical Seizure of HMS Bounty*, claims Purcell was in a "madhouse" in 1831, and George Mackaness, in *The Life of Vice-Admiral William Bligh,* says he died at Haslar Hospital on March 10, 1834, "the last survivor of the *Bounty*."

PUREA ("Obarea," "Oberea," "Oberreah," "Oborea," "Opureah")   The wife of Amo, chief of Teva i Uta. Purea visited HMS *Dolphin* when Samuel Wallis "discovered" Tahiti in 1767. Wallis wrote in his journal: "At PM, the Gunner came off with a tall well looking Woman about forty five years old, she had a very Majestic Mein, & he seeing her paid Great respect by the Inhabitants, she being just come there, he made her some presents." Wallis thought she was the "Queen of Tahiti."

Sir Joseph Banks visited Tahiti in 1769 on Cook's first voyage and is said to have had a wild love affair with Purea at the time. Perhaps to guard himself against such an allegation, Banks did not describe her in very flattering terms: ". . . about 40, tall and very lusty, her skin white and her eyes full of meaning, she might have been hansome when young but now few or no traces of it were left."

It was Purea who built the largest marae in Tahiti, Mahaiatea, for her son Teriirere (in the *Bounty* story known as Temarii). It measured 377 by 267 feet. Very little of the temple is left today.

When Dr John Hawkesworth's *An Account of the Voyages of Capts. Byron, Wallis, Carteret and Cook* came out in 1773, the public was titillated by his intimation that Banks had had an intimate liaison with Purea, and someone wrote a poem which became very popular; in fact, it went through five editions within one year. Its title was *An Epistle from Oberea, Queen of Otaheiti, to Joseph Banks, Esq., translated by T. Q. Z., Esq., professor of the Otaheiti language in Dublin and of all the languages of the undiscovered islands in the South Sea.* The first verse went as follows:

> *I Oberea from the Southern main,*
> *Of slighted vows, of injur'd faith complain.*
> *Though now some European maid you woo,*
> *Of waist more taper, and of whiter hue;*
> *Yet oft with me you deign'd the night to pass,*
> *Beyond yon bread-tree on the bending grass.*
> *Oft in the rocking boat we fondly lay*
> *Nor fear'd the drizzly wind, or briny spray.*

Sir Joseph should have been amused. He was not.

PUREA-TETUPAIA (Peroa, "Oberreeroah," "Oberroah") The wife of Teu and mother of Pomare I. Purea-Tetupaia came from the highest nobility, being the eldest child of Tamatoa III, the chief of Opoa (the holiest place in Polynesia) on Raiatea.

QUADRANT The quadrant, developed by John Hadley in 1731, was an instrument used in navigation for measuring the altitude of heavenly bodies. It contained a graduated arc of 90 degrees. After the sextant, capable of measuring angles up to 120 degrees, was developed in 1757, the quadrant gradually fell into disuse, although the *Bounty* carried both instruments.

QUARTERMASTER In the sailing navy, a petty officer whose duty it was to assist the sailing master and his mates in several duties, such as stowing the hold, coiling cables, reading the log line, supervising the heaving of the lead, etc. The *Bounty* had two quartermasters, John Norton and Peter Linkletter.

QUINTAL, Matthew Able-bodied seaman on the *Bounty;* mutineer; went with Christian; murdered by Adams on Pitcairn. The description Bligh wrote of Quintal after the mutiny reads as follows:

> [MATTHEW QUINTAL] seaman, aged 21 years, 5 feet 5 inches high, fair complexion, light brown hair, strong made; very much tatowed on the backside, and several other places.

Quintal, a Cornishman from Padstow, was twenty-one years old when he mustered on the *Bounty*. Together with his crony, William McCoy, he had transferred from HMS *Triumph* which was anchored at Spithead at the time.

Quintal had a brutal nature and was one of the troublemakers on the *Bounty*, the first one to be flogged. On March 11, 1788, Bligh wrote in his logbook:

> Until this afternoon I had hopes I could have performed the voyage without punishment to any one, but I found it necessary to punish Matthew Quintal with 2 dozen lashes for insolence and mutinous behaviour.

The "insolence and mutinous behaviour" had actually been directed at the sailing master, John Fryer, rather than at Bligh.

Quintal could not have had any real animosity towards Fryer, however, because on Nomuka he saved his life. On April 26, 1789 (two days before the mutiny), Fryer headed a watering party on the island. Natives were crowding around the men when Quintal suddenly shouted: "Mr. Fryer, there's a man going to knock you down with his club." Fryer turned around and the native lowered his club and ran away.

Quintal was in Christian's watch. He was the second man Christian turned to with his plan to take over the ship (Isaac Martin had initially refused cooperation). He was immediately for the idea and started to recruit others among the men that he thought could be counted on. He and McCoy and Churchill were probably the most active among the mutineers.

Quintal, unlike Christian, was a born mutineer. Not only was he the first to be flogged on the *Bounty* for insolence and mutinous behavior, but he, together with John Sumner, was also the first to oppose Christian. He and Sumner had gone ashore on Tubuai without leave, and they had spent the night. When they returned to the ship, Christian asked what their reason had been to disobey orders. They then answered, "The ship is moor'd and we are now our own masters." To show them who was master, Christian had them clapped into irons until the next day.

It was Quintal who set fire to the *Bounty* only five days after the arrival on Pitcairn and before the settlers had had a chance to remove everything of value from the ship.

On Pitcairn, Quintal was the leader in the oppression of the Polynesians. On Massacre Day, September 20, 1793, he barely escaped being killed by the Polynesians by fleeing to the mountains together with McCoy.

Quintal was not only cruel to the Polynesian men but he also abused his consort Tevarua. In her book on the history of the island, Rosalind Young tells the story handed down through the years that Tevarua one day went out fishing and did not catch enough to satisfy him, whereupon he punished her by biting off her ear. He could well have been drunk at the time, because he and McCoy were the chief consumers of the ti-root brandy which the latter had succeeded in distilling. Tevarua fell — or, more probably, threw herself — off a cliff and died in 1799.

Captain Beechey, who was the only visitor ever to see Edward Young's journal (in 1825), states that Quintal was executed by Adams and Young later in 1799 after having made an attempt against their lives (another account claims he had threatened to kill the children Mauatua had had with Christian).

With Tevarua ("Sarah"), Quintal had two sons (Matt and Arthur) and two daughters (Jenny and Sarah). A fifth child died at the age of seven days. Quintal also had a posthumous son, Edward, with Teraura, Young's original consort. At the time of writing (September 1988) there are no Quintals on Pitcairn, but many of the descendants have made their home on Norfolk Island and in New Zealand.

RAIATEA (ancient name: Havaiki) Raiatea, located at 16°50'S., 151°25'W., is the second largest island (after Tahiti) in the Society group and the largest of the Leeward Islands. It is about twelve miles long, north to south, and seven and a half miles wide. Its barrier reef also encircles Tahaa, a smaller island only two miles to the north.

Raiatea is the center of the Holy Land of old Polynesia. To the once magnificent marae Taputapuatea at Opoa on Raiatea would come Polynesian pilgrims from as far away as New Zealand (Aotearoa). Teuira Henry writes in *Ancient Tahiti* (1928):

> The great international marae named Taputapuatea at Opoa, on the southeastern side of Ra'iatea, is the most ancient of all royal marae in the Society group. It is said to have been erected by highest royalty in the remotest period of the island's history. It was of widespread fame and was resorted to by many people of eastern Polynesia as the seat of knowledge and religion . . . .To its royal household the highest chiefs throughout the groups are still proud to trace their origin.

Raiatea remained independent until 1888, and the French intruders were not able to crush the resistance of the Raiatean freedom fighters until 1897. Uturoa, a community on the north-eastern coast of the island, is now the administrative center for the Leeward Islands. Five thousand of Raiatea's 7500 inhabitants live in Uturoa.

ENCYCLOPEDIA

On the highest peak of the island, Mount Temehani (3389 feet), grows one of the most remarkable flowers in the world: Tiare Apetahi ("one-sided flower"). It can be found only on the difficult-to-reach, steep slopes around the summit of Temehani; all attempts to transplant it — even just to another mountain on Raiatea — have failed. The five white petals, all positioned on one side of the flower, represent the fingers of a beautiful girl who fell in love with a handsome prince but could not marry him because of her low birth. To this day, the young men of Raiatea climb Temehani to get a Tiare Apetahi for their sweethearts.

Tararo, who sailed to Pitcairn with Christian, was from Raiatea; some sources claim he was a chief on the island.

HMS *RANGER* The ship in which Bligh served as a midshipman (at first he was officially entered as an able-bodied seaman) from September 2, 1774, to March 17, 1776. Three days after his discharge from the *Ranger* Bligh was appointed sailing master of HMS *Resolution*.

RAROTONGA The main island in the Cook group, 21°12'S., 159°47'W.; 620 miles west-south-west of Tahiti.

For a long time it was thought that it was Captain Philip Goodenough who discovered Rarotonga in the schooner *Cumberland* in 1814. Thanks to the finding of Teehuteatuaonoa's accounts in 1956 we now know that it was Fletcher Christian and the mutineers who made this major discovery. This is corroborated by the missionary John Williams who in 1823 heard the Rarotongans speak of a huge floating garden with two waterfalls which had called at the island two generations earlier. This must have been the *Bounty*: it certainly looked like a garden with all the plants on board, it had two pumps ("waterfalls"), and two generations in Polynesia is about thirty to thirty-five years, so the time also agrees with the visit of the *Bounty* in 1789. Rarotonga is a volcanic island about six miles long and four wide. The mountains in the interior are not as spectacular as those on Tahiti, but they are beautiful and covered with dense tropical vegetation. The highest peak is Te Atu Kura which rises to 2110 feet. The island is fringed by a reef which at certain places becomes a barrier reef. On the north side of the island outside the only town, Avarua, high up on the reef, lies the spectacular wreck of the famous brigantine *Yankee* which foundered there with no loss of life in 1964.

A good road encircles the island which is only slightly over twenty miles in circumference. Rarotonga has an international airport. The population on the island is about 10,000, most of them Maoris.

If you are a South Seas buff, you will recognize the name on one of the gravestones outside the coral limestone church on the outskirts of Avarua: Robert Dean Frisbie (1895-1948), writer of several South Sea tales but best known for his *Book of Puka-Puka* (1929).

In the small town of Avarua is the Banana Court, the last "real" South Seas bar in existence, now that Quinn's and La Fayette in Tahiti are gone. When you visit Rarotonga, you must go to the Banana Court to experience the wildness and abandon and joy of life, mixed with sweet nostalgia, that once characterized Polynesian nights and formed part of the romance of the islands.

REMBANG The Dutch East Indiaman in which Captain Edwards and the other survivors of the *Pandora*, including the ten men of the *Bounty*, sailed from Coupang to Batavia. The *Rembang* left Coupang on October 6, 1791. She was dismasted in a cyclone and almost lost (see the October 1791 commentary in Part I) but managed to reach Samarang on October 30; there she found the *Resolution* anchored in the harbor. Accompanied by the *Resolution* she arrived at Batavia on November 7.

RENOUARD, David Thomas Midshipman on the *Pandora*; sailed with master's mate Oliver from Upolu in the Samoas to Samarang on Java in the schooner *Resolution*. Renouard wrote a brief account of the voyage which was published by W. H. Smyth in 1842 and by Henry E. Maude in 1964.

HMS *RESOLUTION* (schooner) Two-masted schooner, 30 feet long with a beam of 9 feet 6 inches, about 16 tons, built on Tahiti by the loyalists and some of the mutineers who had stayed on the island when Christian sailed away on the *Bounty*.

The *Resolution* (named after Cook's flagship on his second and third voyages) was the brainchild of James Morrison, boatswain's mate on the *Bounty*. By April 30, 1790, it had been fully planked and caulked with the gum of the breadfruit tree. On August 5 it was launched with the blessings of the *tahu'as* (native priests). Unfortunately for its builders it could not be sailed long distances, because there was no European sailcloth available and the native matting simply did not hold up for long.

When Captain Edwards left Tahiti on May 8, 1791, he took the *Resolution* along, fitted out with European sails and with a crew of nine men from the *Pandora*, under the command of master's mate William Oliver. On June 22 the two ships became separated and the *Resolution* continued alone to Java where she reached Samarang long before the survivors of the *Pandora* (which had foundered on the Great Barrier Reef) arrived in October.

The subsequent fate of the *Resolution* is not known. It was a well-built, beautiful, fast little vessel and a tribute to the ingenuity and skill of British seamen.

In his excellent history of Tahiti, *Island of Love* (1968), Robert Langdon tells us about one possible fate of the *Resolution*, based on John Marshall's *Royal Naval Biography* (1825); Marshall evidently got the story from Peter Heywood.

According to this version, Captain William R. Broughton, after visiting Tahiti in Bligh's old ship *Providence*, sailed to the coast of Asia where

> he put into Canton for a refit and there bought Morrison's schooner, *Resolution*, which Captain Edwards had sold in Samarang in 1791. The *Resolution* had been employed in the meantime in the sea otter trade, and was reported to have made one of the fastest voyages ever known between China and Hawaii. That was not her final claim to fame. After Broughton had used her for several months as a tender, the little schooner became the means of saving the lives of 112 officers and men in the *Providence* when that vessel was wrecked off the coast of Formosa on May 16, 1797. The *Resolution* then served as Broughton's survey vessel for another twelve months before being sold again in Trincomalee. Her subsequent fate does not appear to have been recorded.

Langdon cautions us, however, that "the known details of the mutineers' schooner do not tally with those recorded by Broughton." It is a romantic tale, nevertheless.

HMS *RESOLUTION* (square-rigger)   Originally a Deptford collier, 462 tons. With a crew of 110 she served as Cook's flagship on his second and third voyages. On the third voyage, Bligh was sailing master of the *Resolution*.

HMS *RESOURCE*   A 34-foot schooner bought by Bligh in Coupang on Timor and armed with four swivel guns and fourteen stand of small arms in order to defend against pirates. Bligh and the surviving loyalists sailed to Batavia in the *Resource* where it was sold together with the *Bounty*'s launch which they had had in tow.

RESTORATION ISLAND   An islet within the Great Barrier Reef close to the Cape York peninsula in Queensland. On the open-boat voyage from Tofua to Timor, this was the first island on which Bligh and the loyalists landed. The date — May 29, 1789 — happened to be the anniversary of the restoration to the throne of King Charles II in 1660. Both for that reason, and in order to celebrate their own salvation, Bligh named it Restoration Island.

ROCK OF THE WEST   A name sometimes used to denote PITCAIRN.

THE ROPE   A steep cliff face on the south-east coast of Pitcairn.

ROSEWOOD, TAHITIAN   See MIRO.

ROTTERDAM ISLAND   Tasman's name for NOMUKA.

ROTUMA (Grenville Island)   Rotuma is an island in the Fiji group approximately 320 miles north-north-west-to-north of Viti Levu at 12⁰30'S., 177⁰05'E. It was discovered by Captain Edwards in the *Pandora* on August 9, 1791. He named it Grenville Island after the current Secretary for Foreign Affairs.

There are approximately 2800 inhabitants on the island today, a mixture of Polynesians and Micronesians.

HMS *ROYAL WILLIAM* Bligh's court-martial, presided over by Admiral Samuel Barrington, took place in this ship, moored at Spithead, on October 22, 1790. The court-martial of William Purcell, the *Bounty*'s carpenter, followed on the same day.

RUSSELL, Lord Edward Captain of HMS *Actaeon*. See the entries for PITCAIRN ISLAND and HILL, JOSHUA.

SAMARANG (Semarang) Harbor on the north coast of Java, Indonesia, 255 miles east of Djakarta (formerly Batavia), the administrative capital of Central Java. Samarang had been a Dutch settlement since 1748 when Bligh and his loyalist crew stopped here in September 1789 on the way from Coupang to Batavia in the schooner *Resource*. Some time in the late summer of 1791 the schooner *Resolution* which had been separated from the *Pandora* arrived with nine members of the latter ship's crew. In October of the same year the survivors of the *Pandora* arrived on their way to Batavia.

One can only wonder what the governor of Samarang must have thought of this steady stream of emaciated and destitute British sailors passing through his domain. It was a sleepy little town then; today Semarang (modern spelling) has over 800,000 inhabitants.

SAMOA ISLANDS (Navigator Islands) The Samoas stretch from 13⁰25'S. to 14⁰30'S. and from 168⁰08'W. to 172⁰46'W. They are composed of the following islands: in American Samoa — Tutuila, Aunuu, Ofu, Olosega, Tau, Rose, Swains (geographically one of the Tokelau islands); in Western Samoa — Upolu, Savaii, Manono, Nuutele, Nuulua, Apolima.

Bougainville discovered Upolu on May 4, 1768, and named the group Navigator Islands because of the numerous seagoing canoes he saw. The Polynesians discovered and populated the group 3000 years ago. The Samoas, especially the Manua group (Ofu, Olosega, Tau), were the probable source for the colonization of the Society Islands and the Marquesas around 300 A.D.

Captain Edwards searched for the *Bounty* mutineers in this group. It was here, off the coast of Upolu, that he lost contact with his tender *Resolution* which was attacked by a large fleet of war canoes (see the June 1791 commentary in Part I).

SAMUEL, John Clerk on the *Bounty*; loyalist; went with Bligh; arrived safely in England. Samuel was born in Edinburgh and was twenty-six years old when the *Bounty* left England. He seems to have been universally disliked on board. In practice he was Bligh's personal servant as much as he was the ship's clerk.

From Tenerife, in January 1788, Bligh wrote to his wife's uncle, Duncan Campbell: ". . . as my pursing [Bligh was also purser on board] depends on much circumspection and being ignorant in it with a worthless clerk, I have some embarrassment, but as I trust nothing to anyone and keep my accounts clear, if I fail in rules of office I do not doubt of getting the better of it."

The "worthless clerk" is Samuel who actually was very efficient and whom Bligh was later to praise in his journal. The "embarrassment" refers almost certainly to the "cheese incident" (see the February 1788 commentary in Part I). When Bligh said two cheeses had been stolen, Hillbrant said they had been taken to Bligh's home on Samuel's orders, a statement which threw Bligh into one of his frequent uncontrollable rages. It is probable that Bligh in his letter wanted to lay the grounds for blaming Samuel if the details of the "pursing" ever were to be questioned by the Admiralty.

At the time of the mutiny, the idea seems to have been only to get rid of Bligh, Hayward, Hallett, and Samuel, the most disliked men on board. The plan had to be abandoned, however, when it turned out that many others preferred leaving the ship to being considered mutineers.

There is no doubt that Samuel was very effective during the mutiny in gathering up as many of Bligh's possessions as he could grab hold of and getting them into the launch past the scrutiny of the mutineers. Yet, when it came to Samuel's turn to enter the launch, he had to be forced overboard.

When Bligh left Batavia on the *Vlydte*, he took only Samuel and John Smith (his steward and personal cook) with him.

SANDILANDS, Alexander A.   Captain Sandilands commanded HMS *Comet* when she escorted the transport barque *Lucy Ann* which carried the population of Pitcairn to Tahiti in 1831. For his two brief reports of this operation see Robert B. Nicolson, *The Pitcairners* (1965).

SANDWICH ISLANDS   Hawaiian Islands. Captain Cook named them after Sir John Montagu, 4th Earl of Sandwich and First Lord of the Admiralty. The Earl of Sandwich had many remarkable achievements to his name, but in Navy circles he was mainly noted for two reasons: *(1)* he invented a snack, today referred to as a sandwich, which allowed him to keep gambling without interrupting the game for supper, and *(2)* he was the only First Lord ever to keep a resident mistress at Admiralty House.

SANGAREE (sangria)   A tropical drink of wine mixed with water and sometimes brandy, sweetened and spiced.

SANTO DOMINGO   Domingo de Boenechea's name for MOOREA.

"SARAH"   Sarah was a nickname used by the mutineers for both TEVARUA and SULLY, Teio's daughter. Some sources also claim that Teatuahitea was called Sarah, in which case there must have been a great deal of confusion on Pitcairn: three out of thirteen Polynesian females referred to as Sarah!

SAVAGE ISLAND   The name Captain Cook gave to NIUE.

SCHOONER   A sailing vessel with two or more masts, all rigged fore and aft. On a two-masted schooner the after mast is the main mast. A topsail schooner carries a square fore topsail.

SCOTCH COFFEE   Burned ship's biscuit dissolved in hot water — a bitter brew indeed.

SCREW PINE   See FARA.

SCROFULA   See KING'S EVIL.

SCUPPER   A drain at the side of the deck designed to let accumulated water drain off into the sea.

SCUTTLEBUTT   A cask or butt containing the day's ration of water. It usually had a square hole or scuttle at the half-full mark to ensure that only half the water would be available for the day. Sailors would often swap gossip around the scuttlebutt.

SEIZING   The thin cord or twine used for tying lines or ropes to each other.

SEMARANG   See SAMARANG.

HMS *SERINGAPATAM*   On March 15, 1830, the British warship *Seringapatam*, commanded by Captain the Honourable William Waldegrave, visited Pitcairn. She brought clothing and agricultural tools as gifts from the British government.

Waldegrave wrote a private journal in which he states: "In the evening we walked to see Christian's and Adams' graves. They are at some distance from each other, — the grave of the former near the spot where he fell, murdered, about one third from the summit of the island; the latter is buried by the side of his Otaheitan wife, at the end of his cottage-garden."

This is interesting, because the spot where Christian was buried is unknown today. The fact that that the grave of the leader of the mutineers could not be pointed out to later visitors has been used to support the theory which holds that Fletcher Christian escaped the island and returned incognito to England.

SEVER, William C.   Captain of the LADY PENRHYN.

SEXTANT   An astronomical instrument used at sea in measuring the altitudes of heavenly bodies in order to determine latitude and longitude.

The sextant was developed in 1757, thirty years before the departure of the *Bounty*, following a suggestion by Captain John Campbell of the British Navy. It was an improvement on the quadrant developed by John Hadley in 1731.

SHADDOCK   The shaddock (*Citrus grandis*) is a fruit from which the grapefruit probably originated. It is native to the Malaysian and also to several Polynesian islands. The fruit, also called *pummelo*, is named after Captain Shaddock who in the seventeenth century brought the seed to the West Indies.

The shaddock grew on Tahiti at the time of the *Bounty*'s visit and was highly appreciated by the crew. Being a citrus fruit, it was of course also a highly effective antiscorbutic. It even played a role in the mutiny. When Bligh had shouted himself hoarse and his mouth was dry, one of the mutineers, Isaac Martin, offered him a shaddock with which to relieve his parched mouth, a gesture for which the captain was very grateful.

SHILLIBEER, John   Lieutenant of the Royal Marines on board HMS *Briton*. When the *Briton*, accompanied by HMS *Tagus*, visited Pitcairn on September 17, 1814, Shillibeer did not go ashore, but he interviewed the young men who came out to the ship. Among them was Thursday October Christian, Fletcher Christian's first born son, and Shillibeer drew a sketch of him, the only one known to exist. Below the sketch he wrote "Friday October Christian."

The international date line was not officially established until 1883. Nevertheless, the *Bounty* had gained a day by sailing eastward to the Pacific, and Thursday October's name should therefore have been "Wednesday October!" Someone had miscalculated somewhere. "Friday October" soon went back to his given name and also named his third son Thursday October (although we do not know if he was born on a Thursday in October).

Shillibeer later wrote *A Narrative of The Briton's Voyage, to Pitcairn's Island* (1817) which, unfortunately, is not very reliable when it deals with past events on Pitcairn but is nevertheless interesting in its description of the visitors on board and their behavior.

SHIP   A sailing vessel with not less than three masts, all square-rigged. The *Bounty* was a ship.

SHIP-RIGGED   Square-rigged on all masts (full-rigged).

SHIP'S LANDING POINT   On Pitcairn Island: a sharp pinnacle of rock rising to 700 feet on the east side of Bounty Bay.

SIMPSON, George   Quartermaster's mate on the *Bounty*; loyalist; went with Bligh; arrived safely in England. Simpson was born in Kendal, Westmorland, and was twenty-seven years old when the *Bounty* sailed from Spithead. He is not mentioned much in the literature about the mutiny, but we do know that he was part of the "anti-Bligh group" in the *Bounty*'s launch. Although he returned to England, he was not present at the court-martial of the accused mutineers, and Heywood mentioned specifically in the summary of his defense that Simpson's absence militated against the successful presentation of his case.

SIVAL, John   The midshipman of the *Pandora* who, together with four crewmen in the ship's cutter, was lost in a squall at Palmerston atoll on May 24, 1791.

SKEDADDLE   To surreptitiously remove oneself from a working party.

SKINNER, Richard   Able-bodied seaman and barber on the *Bounty*; mutineer; stayed on Tahiti; drowned when the *Pandora* sank. Skinner was born in Tunbridge Wells and was twenty-one when he mustered on the *Bounty*. Among his other duties on board he seems to have been Fryer's servant.
   Bligh's description of Skinner, written after the mutiny, reads as follows:

> [RICHARD SKINNER] 22 years, 5 feet 8 inches high. Fair complexion, light-brown hair, very well made. Scars on both ankles and on right shin. Is tattooed, and by trade a Hair Deeper.

Skinner was "badly hurt" at Cape Horn but does not seem to have received any permanent injury.
   He was an active mutineer and seemed to have been on the point of shooting into the launch, probably aiming at Bligh, when someone next to him knocked his musket aside.
   Skinner stayed on Tahiti when Christian and his party sailed in search of an island refuge. He had a daughter with his Tahitian consort.
   Skinner drowned with his hands still manacled when the *Pandora* went down.

SLOP CHEST   A supply of cheap, overpriced clothing, boots, tobacco, etc., sold to seamen during a voyage by the purser who, in the case of the *Bounty*, was Bligh himself.

SLUSH FUND   An illicit fund resulting from the sale of pilfered items (often food from the galley) and used for an important purpose, such as buying an extra ration of rum.

SMITH, Alexander   See ADAMS, JOHN. John Adams appears as Alexander Smith in the *Bounty*'s muster book. Why he chose to sail under this alias will probably never be known (some have assumed he did so in order to hide a criminal past). The somewhat delicate question was apparently not raised by any of the sea captains who interviewed him or, if it was, the answer was not recorded.

SMITH, John   Able-bodied seaman and Bligh's servant on the *Bounty*; loyalist; went with Bligh; arrived safely in England. Smith was thirty-six years old when he mustered on the *Bounty*. He was born in Sterling.

During the mutiny, Christian ordered Smith to serve rum to everyone under arms. It must have galled Bligh to see his own servant being ordered to cater to the mutineers. There is little mention, otherwise, of Smith in the *Bounty* literature. He sailed home to England with his master in the *Vlydte*.

At the court-martial of the accused mutineers, Smith testified that he had seen neither Heywood, nor Morrison, under arms.

His later fate is unknown to me.

SOCIETY ISLANDS   Originally the name Society Islands referred only to the Leeward group north-west of Tahiti (ancient or European names in parenthesis): Huahine, Raiatea (Havai'i), Tahaa (Uporu), Bora Bora (Vavau), Maupiti (Maurua), Motu Iti (Tupai).

On his first voyage, in 1769, Cook visited the Leeward group and named them the Society Islands, not in honor of the Royal Society, as many have claimed, but, as he himself says: "because they lay contiguous to one another."

The Windward group consists of: Tahiti (King George's Island), Moorea (Aimeo, York Island), Mehetia (Osnaburg Island), Tetiaroa, Maiao (Tupuae Manu, Sir Charles Saunders' Island). The Windward Islands were "discovered" and named by Wallis. Gradually they became subsumed under the name Society Islands, as they are known today.

The Society Islands lie between 148°00' and 154°40'W, and between 15°50' and 17°55'S. The group is a possession of France and the administrative center is at Papeete on Tahiti.

SOERABAJA, SOURABAYA   See SURABAYA.

SON OF A GUN   Ladies of pleasure, girlfriends, and wives were permitted to entertain seamen while a ship was in port and the encounters usually took place on a gundeck. The male offspring of such encounters were sons of guns.

SPIKERMAN (first name unknown)   Captain of a British ship at Coupang on Timor; the first officer to greet and help Bligh and his crew on their arrival Sunday June 14, 1789, after the epic open-boat voyage from Tofua.

SPITHEAD   The main base of the British home fleet at the time of the *Bounty* expedition — and for many years before and after. Spithead anchorage is a stretch of water in the east Solent shielded to the north and west by the mainland and Portsmouth and to the south and west by the Isle of Wight.

SPLICING THE MAIN BRACE   Serving out an additional tot of rum or grog to the crew of a ship, usually as a reward for maximum effort.

The main brace is a purchase attached to the main lower yard of a square-rigged ship, and hauling that yard round to the wind required maximum effort from the seamen. This is the probable derivation of the term the meaning of which today requires no explanation.

STAINES, Sir Thomas   Commander of the British warship *Briton* which, together with her consort HMS *Tagus*, was on a mission to track down the U.S. frigate *Essex*, under Commander David Porter, which had been attacking British shipping in the Pacific. In the early morning of September 17, 1814, the two ships sighted Pitcairn Island.

The arrival and some other circumstances are described under the entry PIPON, PHILIP (the commander of the *Tagus* who wrote an account of the voyage).

Both captains went ashore, getting thoroughly wet in the never-ceasing murderous surf in Bounty Bay, and met John Adams, the last surviving mutineer of the *Bounty*. Sir Thomas later wrote that Adams'

> exemplary conduct and fatherly care of the whole of the little colony, would not but command admiration. The pious manner in which all those born on the island have been reared, the correct sense of religion which has been instilled into their young minds by this old man [Adams was about 47 at the time!], has given him the pre-eminence over the whole of them, to whom they look up as the father of the whole and one family.

Adams lied to the visiting captains that he had been sick in bed during the mutiny, but they probably saw through this very understandable deception and yet felt that they should not go "by the book" and arrest him and take him to England to be hanged. They told him that he should stay on the island and continue to take care of the community. In their humanity these captains probably represented the best of the officers of the Royal Navy.

The ships spent only one day at the island and sailed in the evening.

STAVERS, Thomas Captain of the TUSCAN.

STEWART, George Midshipman on the *Bounty*, promoted to acting master's mate when Christian was made acting lieutenant; loyalist; kept on board against his will; drowned when the *Pandora* foundered.

Stewart was well educated and from "a good family" in the Orkneys. Bligh had been well taken care of by Stewart's family when the *Resolution* called at the Orkneys on the way home from the South Pacific, and Bligh had then promised to see what he could do for young George. He seems to have written to the family offering a berth to George when it became clear that he would lead the breadfruit expedition. Initially, Bligh considered Stewart a good seaman who "had always borne a good character."

Stewart was twenty-one years old when he joined the *Bounty*. On board, he ate in Christian's mess together with Peter Heywood and Robert Tinkler.

On Tahiti, Stewart seems to have fallen in love with a woman he called "Peggy," the daughter of a prominent chief called Tepahu. Yet there is absolutely no indication that he wanted to remain on the island or in any way supported or approved of the mutiny.

Stewart was a good friend of Christian's and did his best to dissuade him from putting his suicidal plan to escape on a raft into effect. It was in this connection, however, that he uttered those fatal words which probably triggered the idea of mutiny in Christian's mind: "The men are ripe for anything!" It is virtually certain that Stewart meant these words to appeal to Christian's sense of duty: he, as the most popular officer on board, was needed to control the men.

Heywood, who knew Stewart well and spent a year and a half with him on Tahiti, always became incensed when anyone insinuated that Stewart had meant to suggest mutiny to Christian. Heywood considered it a slur on the memory of a fine officer and so it was and so it is.

During the mutiny, Stewart was kept under guard below deck. Bligh was later to claim that, when the launch was cast off, he saw Stewart come on deck and dance a Tahitian dance. No one else saw it.

Bligh's description of Stewart, written after the mutiny, reads as follows:

> [GEORGE STEWART] midshipman, 23 years, 5 feet 7 inches high. Good complexion, dark hair, slender made, narrow-chested and long-necked — on his left breast tattooed a star and also one on his left arm, on which likewise is tattooed heart with darts — tattooed on backside — very small features.

After the mutiny, Christian appointed Stewart his second in command. The fact that Stewart accepted shows only a sober appraisal of reality; he was needed to navigate the ship, and was not involved in any agreement with Christian in the act of mutiny. He was not very popular with the men, because he was a very strict disciplinarian.

Stewart kept a journal which was later partly abstracted by Captain Edwards; the original was lost with the *Pandora*.

On Tahiti, Stewart and Heywood developed a close relationship. Stewart was formally married in the Tahitian manner to Peggy (we do not know her Tahitian name) and had a daughter with her.

In the April 1791 commentary in Part I of this book we have described the heart-rending scenes that occurred when Stewart and the rest of the *Bounty* men were confined in "Pandora's box" and when the ship left. We will never know if Stewart would have been acquitted or condemned to death at the court-martial, had he survived, but his death with still manacled hands when the *Pandora* foundered will remain an eternal disgrace to Captain Edward Edwards.

ST. KILDA The schooner which brought the second wave of returnees from Norfolk Island to Pitcairn after the second migration of the total population of Pitcairn (see the entry PITCAIRN ISLAND). The *St. Kilda* sailed from Norfolk on December 18, 1863, and arrived at Pitcairn on February 2, 1864.

On board were four families. Among them was Thursday October Christian II with his wife and nine children and Mrs. Christian's mother, Elizabeth Young (née Mills) who was returning to the land of her birth to see her son, Mayhew, who had been named in honor of the re-rediscoverer of Pitcairn, Captain Mayhew Folger.

The other families were Robert Buffett and his wife; Samuel Warren and his wife (the daughter of Thursday October II); and Simon Young and his family.

Samuel Warren was a sailor from Providence, Rhode Island, who had jumped a whaler and joined the colony at Norfolk. The descendants still live on Pitcairn: in December 1987 there were twelve Warrens on the island (one fourth of the total population).

The return of these families, in addition to the sixteen Pitcairners who had returned earlier in the *Mary Ann*, guaranteed the survival of the Pitcairn community.

"SULLY" ("Sarah") Sully was the daughter of Teio and a Tahitian man. We do not know her real name, nor the name of her father. She was only ten months old on arrival at Pitcairn, the only child on board. Island lore has it that she was ferried ashore from the *Bounty* in a barrel.

Sully grew up to marry Fletcher Christian's second son, Charles, in 1810. She bore him eight children: Fletcher, Edward, Charles Jr., Isaac, Sarah, Maria, Mary, and Margaret.

On March 7, 1826, before reaching her thirty-seventh birthday, Sully died of an unknown cause, leaving Charles with four sons and four daughters ranging in age from about fifteen to a little over a year old.

SULTAN American whaler from Boston commanded by a Captain Reynolds. The *Sultan*, as far as can be determined, was the fourth ship to touch at Pitcairn. She arrived sometime in 1817 and the captain traded some iron bars and stores for copper bolts which had been recovered from the *Bounty*. When she left, Teehuteatuaonoa ("Jenny") was on board. Via Chile and the Marquesas she returned to Tahiti, the first of the original settlers to leave the island and the only one who never returned.

SUMNER, John Able-bodied seaman on the *Bounty*; mutineer; stayed on Tahiti; drowned when the *Pandora* foundered. Sumner was born in Liverpool and was twenty-two years old when he signed on the *Bounty*. Bligh's description of Sumner, written after the mutiny, reads as follows:

> [JOHN SUMNER] 24 years, 5 feet 8 inches high. Fair complexion, brown hair. Slender made, a scar on the left cheek and tattooed in several places.

The first significant mention of Sumner in the *Bounty* literature is on April 12, 1789, sixteen days before the mutiny, when he was given twelve lashes for an unspecified "neglect of duty." It was the last flogging on board before the mutiny.

Sumner took an active part in the insurrection; he and Quintal stood guard over Fryer and also kept Peckover and Nelson from coming on deck.

On Tubuai, Sumner and Quintal were the first to disobey orders from Christian (by spending the night on shore without leave) and were, as punishment, clapped into irons for one day.

Sumner elected to stay on Tahiti when Christian sailed from the island for the last time. He accepted an invitation by chief Temarii to settle in Papara and took part in the military campaigns designed to help Pomare I (then called Mate) gain supremacy over Tahiti. When the *Pandora* arrived, he joined the other mutineers in running to the mountains to hide.

John Sumner drowned with his hands still manacled when the *Pandora* went down.

SUNDAY ISLAND The name given by Bligh to a rocky and barren islet within the Great Barrier Reef on which he and the loyalists landed on Sunday, May 31, 1789, on their open-boat voyage from Tofua to Timor. Some oysters and shellfish were found among the rocks.

It was on this islet that Bligh challenged Purcell to a duel (see the June 1789 commentary in Part I).

SURABAYA (Surabaja, Sourabaya, Soerabaja)   The capital of East Java and the principal naval base of Indonesia, situated on the north-eastern coast of Java, 420 miles east-south-east of Djakarta. It is separated from the island of Madura, only one and a half miles to the north-east, by the western end of the Madura Strait.

Surabaya is the largest city in East Java with a population of over two and a half million. It is the second largest city in Indonesia after Djakarta.

Surabaya came under Dutch control in 1743. Bligh and the loyalists stopped at the settlement on their voyage in the schooner *Resource* from Coupang to Batavia. It was here that Bligh again faced a mutiny by some of his men (see the September 1789 commentary in Part I).

"SUSANNAH" ("Susan")   See TERAURA.

HMS *SWALLOW*   The 14-gun sloop with a complement of ninety in which Captain Philip Carteret sailed around the world, discovering Pitcairn in the process. The *Swallow* was old, having been in service many years, and was not fit for a long voyage. She sailed so poorly that Bougainville, when he overtook her in the *Boudeuse* on February 26, 1769, remarked, "His [Carteret's] ship was very small, went very ill, and when we took leave of him, he remained as if it were at anchor. How much he must have suffered in so bad a vessel, may well be conceived."

SWIVEL GUN   The swivel gun was small, throwing shots of only half-a-pound weight. It was mounted on a pedestal so that it could be turned from side to side and up and down. In addition to her four fourpounders, the *Bounty* was armed with ten swivel guns.

TA'AROA

> *O Ta'aroa te tupuna o te mau atua ato'a; na'na te mau mea ato'a i hamani. Mai tahito a iuiu mai o Ta'aroa nui, Tahi-tumu.*

> Ta'aroa (The-unique-one) was the ancestor of all the gods; he made everything. From time immemorial was the great Ta'aroa, Tahi-tumu (The-origin).

> *Na Ta'aroa iho Ta'aroa i tupua toivi noa; oia iho to'na metua, aore to'na metua tane, aore metua vahine.*

> Ta'aroa developed himself in solitude; he was his own parent, having no father or mother.

. . . . .

Tei roto ia Ta'aroa te mau peu ato'a. Te vero, te ua, te tai, tei roto ana'e i to'na 'apu rima.

By Ta'aroa all things existed. The storm, the rain, the sea, were in the hollow of his hand.

Ua hamani ihora Ta'aroa i te tumu nui o te fenua ei tane, e i te papa fenua ei vahine a'e na te Tumu-nui; . . .

Ta'aroa made the great foundation of the earth to be the husband, and the stratum rock to be the wife; . . .

This creation chant is given in its entirety in Teuira Henry's *Ancient Tahiti* (1928). Ta'aroa was the creator of the universe, the primal spirit. He was the father of all the gods. He created the first woman, Hina, before he created the first man, Ti'i (Tiki).

Ta'aroa was worshipped by all Polynesians. In Hawaii, however, where his name was Kanaloa, and in New Zealand and Rarotonga where he was called Tangaroa, he was not the creator of the world but the god of the ocean and seafaring and fishing.

TA'AROAMIVA See TITAHITI.

TA'AROATOHOA The chief of Natieva (now Ta'ahuaia), the small district on Tubuai where Fletcher Christian and his men attempted to establish a colony and started building Fort George. Ta'aroatohoa was the older brother of Ta'aroamiva who, under the name Titahiti, followed Christian to Pitcairn.

TA'ATA Tahitian word for person.

TABOO See TAPU.

TAFANO A slender, tall, and straight tree (*Guettarda speciosa*) with a hard wood, used for the masts of sailing canoes. It is found mostly on Raiatea and in the Tuamotus; at the time of the *Bounty* story it grew on Pitcairn. The *tafano* is treasured by Polynesian women because of its highly fragrant flowers which they weave into their wreaths.

TAFFRAIL The after rail above the stern of a ship.

HMS *TAGUS* British warship commanded by Captain Philip Pipon and accompanying HMS *Briton* on a mission to track down the U.S. frigate *Essex*, under Commander David Porter, which had been attacking British shipping in the Pacific. In the early morning of September 17, 1814, the two ships sighted Pitcairn Island. After establishing contact with the inhabitants they left the same evening. Captain

Pipon later wrote a narrative of the voyage.

See the entries for PIPON and SHILLIBEER (lieutenant on the *Briton*).

TAHAA (ancient name: Uporu)   One of the Leeward Islands in the Society group, situated at 16⁰38'S., 151⁰28'W., only two miles north of Raiatea and sharing the same barrier reef. Tahaa is about half the size of Raiatea, almost round, with a five-mile diameter. Its highest peak, Mount Ohiri, rises to 1936 feet. The principal village, Vaitoare, is on the southeast coast.

Tahaa was one of the islands where Captain Edwards searched for the *Bounty* mutineers in May 1791.

TAHARAA   See ONE TREE HILL.

TAHITI or TAHITI-NUI MARE'ARE'A (Great Tahiti of the Golden Haze)   Tahiti is the main island in the Society group in French Polynesia and is situated at 17⁰38'S., 149⁰25'W. In size it is 388 square miles — about one tenth of Greater Los Angeles — 33 miles long north-west to south-east and 140 miles in circumference. Its shape resembles a figure eight.

At the time of writing (1988) the population is approximately 120,000. The chief administrative center of all French Polynesia (population 180,000) is Papeete which is also the main harbor (on the north-west coast). The chief exports are coconut oil and cultured pearls.

Tahiti is a volcanic island encircled by a barrier reef. The lagoon and immediate surrounding ocean teem with over 300 species of fish. The interior of the island is mountainous with dense tropical vegetation covering the slopes. Some of the mountains rise to spectacular peaks, usually wreathed by clouds. The highest peaks are Orohena (Orofena) which which reaches to 7321 feet, Aorai, 6775 feet, and the most beautiful of them all, Te Tara o Maiao (Diadème), 4340 feet. Lovely waterfalls cascade down several of the steep precipices.

The climate is pleasant with a mean temperature of 80⁰F (26⁰C) and a range from 61⁰–95⁰F (16⁰–35⁰C). The warm and humid season lasts approximately from November to April, the cooler dry season from May to October. The mild trade winds blow almost continuously, so the heat seldom gets oppressive. Due to the prevailing winds, the north-east coast gets almost twice as much rain as the west coast.

Tahiti is without a doubt one of the most beautiful islands in the South Seas. Even Bligh — who was not much given to praise — called it "The Paradise of the

World." In describing Tahiti, Herman Melville wrote in *Omoo*:

> Seen from the sea, the prospect is magnificent. It is one mass of shaded tints of green, from beach to mountain-top; endlessly diversified with valleys, ridges, glens and cascades. Over the ridges, here and there, the loftiest peaks fling their shadows, and far down the valleys. At the head of these, the waterfalls flash out in the sunlight as if pouring through vertical bowers of verdure. Such enchantment, too, breathes over the whole that it seems a fairy land, all fresh and blooming from the hand of the Creator. Upon a nearer approach, the picture loses not its attractions. It is no exaggeration to say, that to a European of any sensibility, who, for the first time, wanders back into these valleys — away from the haunts of the natives — the ineffable repose and beauty of the landscape is such that every object strikes him like something seen in a dream; and, for a time, he almost refuses to believe that scenes like these should have a commonplace existence . . .

The island still looks the way Melville describes it when you approach it from the sea, although of course some of this beauty has been destroyed. The French authorities have built a freeway, a huge industrial center and ugly oil cisterns — the latter now mar what used to be one of the most beautiful harbors in the world.

The tourist brochures do not mention these and other evidences of life in the 1980s, including the sixty-three thousand cars on the island. But, amazingly, Tahiti is still beautiful. The basic beauty and enchantment of the island survives, as even the charms of Hawaii have survived exploitation by the haoles.

Tourism flourishes but does not pose the main danger to the survival of Tahitian culture. The real danger comes from the influx of French immigrants who have the right to vote and who could turn Tahiti into another New Caledonia if they reach a majority. This could be soon, if the tide of immigration is not stemmed. The immigrants take the best and the highest-paying jobs for themselves. As there is no income-tax in Tahiti, they keep growing richer while the Tahitians get poorer. If it were not for the goodnaturedness and patience of the Tahitians, the situation would turn explosive. And, as we know from what happened on Pitcairn (see the September 1793 commentary in Part I), even Tahitian patience can wear thin.

The intruders from overseas have made a deliberate and systematic attempt to destroy the identity and national pride of the Tahitians. Until recently, for example, Tahitian children were not allowed to speak their own language in school; they had to speak French. This led Tahitian mothers, who understandably wanted to see their children succeed, to speak French with them and, as a consequence, Tahitian children today do not know their own language. If you speak Tahitian to a Tahitian child, he will either not understand you or, if he does, he will answer you in French. Now,

MODERN TAHITI

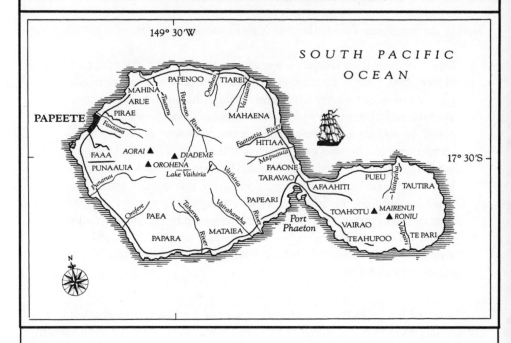

when no children are able to speak the Tahitian language, its use has been permitted again!

Although literature in the Tahitian language is no longer forbidden, the fact that the language is slowly dying makes it difficult for potential publishers to find a market. A Tahitian Academy, *Fare Vana'a* (from *fare,* which means "house," and *vana'a,* which means "oration, counsel, advice"), is now in existence and making heroic efforts to revive the language, but when the French allow only a few hours of Tahitian on radio (mostly religious programs) and only fifteen minutes a day on television, the efforts seem doomed.

There is also strict censorship of anti-French sentiments in books. One example is a book which is the best guide to Polynesia, *South Pacific Handbook* by David Stanley. It cannot be bought in Tahiti because it contains some truthful statements about French rule on the island. There are many other examples.

However, no usurping power will ever defeat the Tahitian spirit. The Tahitians today are as friendly and kind and hospitable as always and they seem to personify the idea that life is to be enjoyed and that you should also make it enjoyable for others. They certainly show this joy in their singing and dancing; no other people could be as musical, except perhaps the Hungarians. They have all the reason in the world to be proud of themselves and their ancestry; after all, their forefathers navigated across the largest ocean of the world and peopled its islands while the Europeans were still hugging their shores, afraid to fall over the edge of the world. (Even the Azores and the Canary islands were not discovered until a thousand years after the Polynesians had populated the Pacific!)

A tremendous strength of the Tahitians lies in their family structure. Family members are close, and that includes the extended family, even distant relatives. Children are loved as nowhere else on earth. The idea of an orphanage is incomprehensible to the vast majority of Tahitians; an orphanage is impossible since everyone loves children and wants to take care of them. A Tahitian child not only has his or her own parents, but also has a set of *fa'a'amu* (feeding) parents, usually not related by blood, but considered as close as the biological parents.

Another strength among the Tahitians is their religious faith. There can be no doubt that the early missionaries caused damage of tragic proportion to the Tahitian people. However, when the London Missionary Society was expelled by the French authorities in 1863 in favor of the French Protestant Mission, the French failed to achieve their purpose: to make the Tahitians French through religion. The Tahitians simply established their own Protestant church, Te Etaretia Porotetani, which today is a significant force in the preservation of Tahitian culture. Moreover, it teaches respect and reverence for the Almighty while at the same time expressing the old Tahitian values of kindness and compassion and joy in which the early missionaries were so lacking.

It seems that the Tahitian people are experiencing a renaissance today. Ever since the great Pouvanaa a Oopa (1895–1977), a World War I hero who was born on Huahine, formed a freedom party in 1947 (for which "crime" he was imprisoned in France), there has developed among the Tahitians a deeper consciousness of their magnificent heritage; a feeling of national unity and a desire for independence seem to be emerging. Until just a few years ago they were forbidden by the French authorities to fly their old Tahitian flag; today the French have been forced to allow them the right to do so — as long as it is hoisted next to the tricolor, of course.

Progress in achieving self-determination in French Polynesia is slow, but will no doubt be achieved some day.

Following is a list of some of the most important dates in the history of Tahiti, many of which are not given in enyclopedias or travel books:

1 million B.C.:	Last volcanic activity.
Around 300 A.D.:	First Polynesians arrive, probably from Samoa.
Around 1760:	The important chiefs of the island were: Vehiatua of Taiarapu (Teva i Tai) Amo of Papara and Vaiare (Teva i Uta) (Temarii was chief of Papara when the *Bounty* arrived)

Hitoti and Paofai of Tiarei (Te Aharoa)
Utami of Punaauia
Potatu of Atehuru
Tu (Teina, Mate, Pomare I) of Pare (Porionuu)
Poino of Haapape
Tepahu of Tefana

June 18, 1767: Samuel Wallis "discovers" Tahiti, names it King George III Island.

April 2, 1768: Visit by Louis de Bougainville who gives Tahiti the name La Nouvelle Cythère.

April 10, 1769: James Cook visits on his first voyage.

November 8, 1772: Visit by Domingo de Boenechea who gives Tahiti the name Amat.

August 17, 1773: Cook's first visit on his second voyage.

April 22, 1774: Cook returns.

1774: Birth of Tati, later the high chief of the Teva clan in Papara. (Death of Louis XV; Louis XVI king of France.)

November 27, 1774: Boenechea's second visit.

October 1775: Visit by Cayetano de Langara.

1776: (American Revolution.)

August 13, 1777: Cook, on his third voyage, visits Tahiti for the last time.

1779: Tu nui ae te Atua ("Prince Tu," later Pomare II) born.

1783: Defeat of Tu (Teina, Mate, Pomare I) at Pare.

July 10, 1788: Captain W. C. Sever arrives in the *Lady Penrhyn*.

October 26, 1788: Bligh arrives in the *Bounty*.

September 22, 1789: *Bounty* mutineers and loyalists debark and stay for one and a half years.

1790–1791: Tu (Teina, Mate, Pomare I) conquers most of Tahiti with the help of the men of the *Bounty*.

March 23, 1791: Edwards arrives in the *Pandora*.

December 30, 1791: Vancouver arrives.

March 7, 1792: The shipwrecked crew of the *Matilda* arrives.

April 10, 1792: Bligh arrives in the *Providence*.

1793–1804: (French Revolution)

March 5, 1797: Protestant missionaries arrive in the *Duff.*

January 24, 1802: George Bass arrives.

1803: Pomare I dies; Pomare II becomes "King."

1804: (Napoleon Emperor.)

1808: Chief Paofai defeats Pomare II who flees to Moorea.

1811: (George III retires; George IV Regent.)

1812: Pomare asks for baptism.

1813: Aimata (later Queen Pomare IV) born.

1814: (Restoration; Louis XVII King of France, Napoleon exiled.)

1815: Pomare II defeats all opponents on Tahiti; the island is "Christianized."

1816: Missionary William Ellis arrives.

1817: Missionaries John Orsmond and John Williams arrive.

1819: Code of Pomare enacted.

1820: Teriitaria (later Pomare III) born. (George III dies; George IV King.)

December 1821: Pomare II dies; Teriitaria King as Pomare III.

1822: First Tahitian flag.

1824: George Pritchard arrives; Legislative Assembly inaugurated. (Louis XVII dies; Charles X King of France.)

1826: Papeete replaces Matavai as main port; treaty with U.S.A.

1827: Pomare III (six and a half years old) dies; his sister Aimata becomes Queen Pomare IV.

1829: Jacques-Antoine Moerenhout arrives.

1830: (Louis Phillipe King of France; George IV dies; William IV King of England.)

1830–1850: Heyday of whaling in the Pacific.

1835: Visit by Charles Darwin.

1836: Catholic missionaries Caret and Laval arrive and are expelled.

1837: George Pritchard becomes British Consul.

1838:	Admiral Abel Dupetit-Thouars arrives for the first visit; Jacques–Antoine Moerenhout becomes French Consul. (Victoria Queen of England.)
1839:	Teratane (later Pomare V) born.
1840:	500 heavily armed French troops land in Papeete, haul down the Tahitian flag; Queen Pomare is forced to flee the island, sails to Raiatea.
1841:	Pritchard leaves for England; Alexander Salmon arrives; visit by Charles Wilkes.
1842:	The French seize the Marquesas Islands, proclaim Tahiti a French protectorate; Herman Melville visits; Paofai dies.
1843:	Pritchard returns; Dupetit-Thouars returns; Queen Pomare IV deposed; Tahiti annexed to France.
1844:	British Consul George Pritchard deported.
1844–1846:	The Tahitians wage a gallant war of liberation against the French invaders, but despite incredible valor are defeated.
1845:	Moerenhout leaves.
1847:	Treaty of Jarnac; Queen Pomare returns from Raiatea, is allowed to reign as figurehead without any real power; Tahiti becomes a French "protectorate."
1847–1880:	Actual power wielded by French military commander.
1848:	Hereditary chiefs abolished by the French.
1851:	English-Tahitian Dictionary published by the missionaries.
1854:	Tati dies; influenza epidemic kills thousands of Tahitians.
1855:	Pomare IV's first son, Ariiaue dies, Teratane becomes Crown Prince and assumes the name Ariiaue.
1861–1865:	(American Civil War.)
1862:	William Stewart arrives.
1863:	French authorities oust the London Missionary Society in favor of the French Protestant Mission.

1864: Stewart imports Chinese coolies for cotton plantation at Atimaono in Papara.

1866: Alexander Salmon dies; Assembly forced to adopt French law.

1872: Julien Viaud (Pierre Loti) visits.

1873: Stewart dies bankrupt.

1875: Teratane married to Marau, daughter of Ariitaimai.

1877: Queen Pomare IV dies; her son Teratane (Ariiaue) becomes the last King of Tahiti as Pomare V.

1880: The French force Pomare V to cede his Kingdom to France; Tahiti becomes a French colony.

1881: The French commence their campaign to conquer the Leeward Islands.

1887: The treaty of Jarnac is revoked.

1888: The Leeward Islands lose their independence to the French; Robert Louis Stevenson visits Tahiti and is given the name Teriitera.

1891: Pomare V dies; Paul Gauguin arrives.

1895: Pouvanaa a Oopa born.

1897: Ariitaimai dies; the French make their final assault on Raiatea.

1898–1899: The gallant leader of the Raiatean freedom fighters, Teraupoo, is captured by the French and exiled; the Leeward Islands are forced into the Colony of French Polynesia with much bloodshed.

1906: Tahiti is hit by a major cyclone.

1908: Jack London visits in the *Snark*.

1914: Over 1000 Tahitians leave to fight for the French (more than 200 lost their lives); Papeete shelled by German raiders SMS *Scharnhorst* and SMS *Gneisenau*; Rupert Brooke visits.

1916: Somerset Maugham visits.

1918: Influenza epidemic kills over 2000 in Tahiti.

1920: James Norman Hall and Charles Nordhoff arrive.

1922: Tahiti participates in World's Fair.

1928: The film *Taboo* is made; Zane Grey arrives to fish

for marlin.

1934: First American film of the *Bounty* mutiny is made on the island; first American tourists arrive.

1940: Election shows the population to side with the "Free French."

1941: Over 300 Tahitians leave for war in Libya, Italy, and France.

1942: American armed forces in Bora Bora (at one time including James Michener).

1947: Pouvanaa a Oopa establishes a freedom party and publishes the newspaper *Te Aratai*; the *Kon Tiki* lands in Raroia with Bengt Danielsson on board who will soon make Tahiti his permanent home; Charles Nordhoff dies (in Santa Barbara).

1951: James Norman Hall dies in Arue.

1958: The French rulers arrest Pouvanaa a Oopa on trumped-up charges and imprison him in France.

1961: The second American film of the *Bounty* mutiny is made in Tahiti.

1962–1963: The international airport at Faaa is completed.

1963: The French nuclear testing program is initiated; an enormous number (around 10,000) of troops and technicians arrive on the island.

1976: The *Hokule'a* arrives (an ocean-going double canoe built according to the ancient Polynesian manner sailing from Hawaii without modern means of navigation).

1977: Pouvanaa a Oopa dies; the French give the local Assembly a minor role in decisions regarding internal affairs.

1984: Somewhat wider powers of self-government are granted by the French authorities, but the governor appointed in Paris still rules and the influx of French settlers continues unabated.

For information not readily available in most publications on Tahiti I refer the reader to the following books which, in my opinion, best describe the island and its history: Robert Langdon, *Island of Love* (1968); David Howarth: *Tahiti: A Paradise Lost* (1985); Edward Dodd: *The Rape of Tahiti* (1983).

For a beautiful and detailed account of old Tahiti, I refer the reader to Teuira Henry's classic *Ancient Tahiti* (1928). For the more scientifically minded, I suggest the mammoth work (three volumes) by Douglas L. Oliver, *Ancient Tahitian Society* (1974).

The foremost expert on Tahiti today, Bengt Danielsson, has written extensively about the island, but unfortunately his monumental work, the definitive history of Tahiti — published in French — still has not appeared in the English language. When it does, I hope that everyone interested in the *Bounty* saga will read it, because without an adequate insight into the history of Tahiti, the story of the *Bounty* cannot be fully appreciated. Meanwhile, the reader of this book will find all of Danielsson's writings on the South Seas interesting, especially his *What Happened on the Bounty* (1962), and, for the visitor to Tahiti, his highly informative book — a fascinating history of the island in itself — *Tahiti: Circle Island Tour Guide*.

Finally, A. Grove Day, the prolific writer and editor of books on the South Seas, has given us a delightful summary of what Tahiti symbolises:

> Ever since I can remember, the name of this island has been one of the most romantic words in the language. Tahiti! The very word is like a bell, tolling the unwary to dreams of an exotic Eden in the far South Seas, where humdrum cares are forgotten and men and women live only for today and each other.

TAHU'A A Tahitian priest. The Tahitians were devout in their religious beliefs and invoked their gods in almost every undertaking. This gave the *tahu'as* almost as much power as was exercised by the secular rulers, the *ari'is*.

There were several healing divinities, such as Hau (the god of peace), Tipa (the healer), and the goddess Aitupuai who was the daughter of the warrior god Oro. Teuira Henry writes in *Ancient Tahiti* (1928):

> The doctors of Hau were famous for their healing powers by massage, accompanying the use of ointment (which they prepared from coconut oil), and for this reason they were named *tahu'a-mori* (anointing-doctors), as well as *tahu'a-ra'au* (medicine-doctors). They were called upon to cast out evil spirits, by invocations and anointing, from persons under the influence of sorcery, and to heal fevers (*fefera*) and aches and pains of the body. They were said to possess great healing or magnetic power. In a little house close to his shrine, the doctor prepared his medicines, from plants chiefly, with great secrecy, for to make them known he thought would take away their virtue. He consecrated them to the deity on the marae.
>
> A woman might be a doctor. The knowledge of remedies was handed down from parent to child, and such persons were regarded with great veneration

as being god-inspired.

Tahu'as exist today as lay healers, somewhat like herb doctors, and are still revered and sought out not only by many Tahitians, but by *popa'as* as well.

TAIARAPU Tahiti consists of two mountainous landmasses, one in the northwest called Tahiti Nui and the other in the south-east called Taiarapu or Tahiti Iti. They are joined by a low, narrow isthmus called Taravao. During the *Bounty's* stay at Tahiti, the main chief in Taiarapu was Vehiatua.

TAIO The archaic Tahitian word *taio* means special friend or, as it has also been translated, bond-friend. The concept of *taio* — and the modern, more general, equivalent *hoa* (friend) or *hoa rahi* ("great" friend) — is described briefly in the February 1789 commentary in Part I.

The closest translation of *taio* or *hoa* was made by Robert Louis Stevenson when he visited Tahiti in his yacht *Casco* in 1888: he interpreted it as "brother in the island mode." Stevenson's host Ori gave him one of his names, Teriitera, and adopted Rui (the Tahitian rendition of Louis) as his own.

Stevenson dedicated his poem *The Song of Rahero* to his host:

> *Ori, my brother in the island mode,*
> *In every tongue and meaning much my friend,*
> *This story of your country and your clan,*
> *In your loved house, your too much honoured guest,*
> *I made in English. Take it, being done;*
> *And let me sign it with the name you gave.*
>
> — *Teriitera.*

TAIORO Tahitian sauce containing grated coconuts, seawater, and shrimps.

TALALO See TARARO.

TAMA'A Tahitian verb for eat (a meal).

TAMA'ARAA Literally a meal, but usually signifying a festive occasion with food and drink and song and dance.

An ancient greeting on Tahiti (and all of the Society Islands) was *Haere mai tama'a* ("Come and eat"). You can still hear it, but it has lost its literal meaning and is slowly dying out.

TAMAHINE Tahitian for girl, girl-child.

TAMARIE   See TEMARII.

TAMARII   Tahitian for children, "kids."

TAMAROA   Tahitian for boy, boy-child.

TAMATOA   The chief of Toerauetoru (today's Mataura), the largest district on Tubuai, actually comprising the whole western half of the island. Tamatoa exchanged names with Fletcher Christian and offered him any land he would want in his district to establish a colony. He was mortified — and became Christian's bitter enemy — when the latter chose to locate in the neighboring district of Natieva instead.

TANE   Tahitian for man. Also the name of a Polynesian god.

TANGAROA   See TA'AROA.

TAOUPITI   See TERAURA.

TAPA   The Tahitians made their cloth from the bark of the mulberry tree (*Broussonetia papyrifera*), in Tahitian *aute*. The finished product was called *tapa*. *Tapa* could also be made from the bark of a kind of breadfruit tree called *pu'upu'u* (*Artocarpus altilis*) or a figlike tree called *aoa* (*Ficus prolaxa*), but the mulberry bark produced the strongest cloth. The procedure used is best described by the boatswain's mate of the *Bounty*, James Morrison:

> Their Cloth, of which the General Names is Ahhoo, is of Different sorts and made from the Bark of different trees but the process of all is the Same. The Best and finest white Cloth Calld Hoboo or Parrawye is made from the Yowte or Cloth Plant and is made thus — The plants having to their proper length (10 or 12 feet) are cut by the Men and brought in by them which is their part of the work, the Weomen then Strip off the bark by entring a pointed Stick between the bark and the Plant and ripping it the whole length on one Side, & the Bark peels off. After they have Stripd all the Plants they take the Bark to the Water where they wash it, [and] spreading it on a board for the Purpose Scrape it Clean, taking off the Outside rind with a large Cockle shell and having freed it from the Sap and Slime it is wrapd in plantain leaves and covered with Grass, where it remains for two three or four days when it becomes Clammy and glutinous, & is then fit for working, it is then spread of a regular thickness of several strips forming a band of 7 or 8 inches broad and of what length the piece is intended to be and the Ground where they intend to work is spread with plantain leaves to keep it from the dirt — the Beans are then placed at

equal distances about 6 feet asunder & at each of them two weomen work, having the Piece between them, beating it with square beetles to its proper breadth; this they perform by a Song given by one & Chorous'd by the rest and keep regular time and Shifting the Piece backwards and forwards till it is all beat out to a regular Breadth and thickness — it is then spread in the sun to Dry for one Day, after which it is bleachd in the Morning Dew till it is perfectly white, being kept from the sun till it is sufficiently bleachd, and then it is spread one or two days in the Sun to dry it and put up for Store or Use.

They make another sort of several Thicknesses which are not placed regular or above half beaten, this is Calld Marro; of this they make their Upper Garments by Striping from one part and pasting on to another till they bring it to a regular breadth & thickness and trim the Fragments off with a piece of split bamboo which answers the purpose of a knife.

Some *tapa* was sun-bleached and almost snow-white, some was decorated with different dyes.

As the settlers on Pitcairn ran out of European cloth, they started wearing clothes made of *tapa*; by the time Captain Folger visited the island in 1808, most Pitcairners were dressed in *tapa* cloth.

TAPATAI Tahitian adjective meaning approximately "fearless of wind and sea," usually applied to fishermen.

TAPU The literal meaning of the Tahitian word *tapu* is "cut" or "cut off." The extended meaning is restriction, something that is "cut off from use." The English language has adopted the word in the latter meaning, spelling it taboo.

A *tapu* denoted a religious restriction in the sense that the gods would be angry if the *tapu* was broken. Some *tapus* were general and perennial, for example women could never eat in the presence of men. Other *tapus*, invoked by the *ari'i rahi* (high chief), were specific or temporary, for example a certain type of fruit could not be picked during a specified season.

An *ari'i rahi* was so holy that every place on which he placed his foot became *tapu*. He therefore had to constantly be carried on the shoulders of a servant.

When the missionaries came and imposed their own taboos on the population, the old *tapus* withered. In today's Tahiti the sign TAPU is rarely seen, and then only on the property of a Frenchman. The (most un-Polynesian) meaning will be KEEP OFF!

TARARO (Talalo, "Talaloo," "Tullaloo") Tararo was from Raiatea; some sources claim he was a chief. He had been in Tahiti when Christian sailed and he decided to join.

On Pitcairn, he was the only Polynesian who had a consort of his own, Toofaiti who was also from the Leeward Islands. But when Williams' consort died within a year of the arrival on the island, the mutineers decided to "give" Toofaiti to him, which of course enraged Tararo. The consort shared by the Tubuaians Titahiti and Oha had also been "given" away, and the three Polynesians now hatched a plan to kill the mutineers. They made the mistake of confiding their scheme to some of the women, however, who informed the mutineers about the conspiracy. The latter sent the three Tahitians on the island, armed with muskets, to kill the conspirators. Tararo was the first one killed (Oha was next, and Titahiti surrendered). The place where Tararo was murdered is still called Talaloo's Ridge. Tararo, like the other Polynesian men on Pitcairn, left no children.

TARAVAO On Tahiti: the isthmus between Tahiti Nui and the Taiarapu peninsula.

TARO The *taro* (*Colocasia antiquorum*), named the "king of roots" by Robert Louis Stevenson, is one of the staple foods in Polynesia. The tuber, either baked in the *hima'a* (earth oven) or boiled, makes a nutritious and pleasant food. The leaves of the plant, called *fafa*, are as good as, or better than, spinach.

TARRAH Bligh's spelling of Taharaa. See ONE TREE HILL.

TASMANIA See VAN DIEMEN'S LAND.

TAUMATA Archaic Tahitian word for a hat or bonnet made from plaited coconut leaves.

TAUMI Ornamented Tahitian breastplate.

TAURUA Nordhoff's and Hall's name for Edward Young's consort TERAURA.

TAUTIRA On Tahiti: a district on the north-east coast of Taiarapu (Tahiti Iti) with a promontory which bears the same name.

TE ARI'I FAATOU See ARI'IPAEA.

TEATUAHITEA ("Sarah") Teatuahitea may or may not have been kidnapped by the mutineers when they left Tahiti for the last time. She arrived at Pitcairn as the consort of William Brown, the gardener on the *Bounty*.

After Brown was killed on Massacre Day, September 20, 1793, Teatuahitea moved in with Teio in the McCoy household. She died of "the dropsy" sometime between the visit of the *Topaz* (1808) and the *Briton* and the *Tagus* (1814). She left no children.

TEEHUTEATUAONOA ("Jenny") Before 1956, our knowledge of what happened with Christian and his companions after they left Tahiti for the last time was based primarily on the accounts of sea captains who had visited Pitcairn and interviewed the last surviving mutineer, John Adams. For some inscrutable reason no one seems to have interviewed the surviving women who, after all, spoke a passable English. It is possible, of course, that Adams did not want the women to be interviewed; he wanted to present what happened in such a way that he did not endanger himself.

Adams, then, told different and conflicting stories to his interviewers who themselves may not have been very careful in their notetaking. We had no check on Adams' stories until 1956 when Professor Henry E. Maude discovered two newspaper articles based on interviews with Teehuteatuaonoa, the first of the settlers — and the only one of the original settlers — to leave Pitcairn permanently.

The first article was by an anonymous author and appeared in the *Sydney Gazette* July 17, 1819. The second article was based on an account dictated to Reverend Henry Nott in the presence of Captain Peter Dillon who had it published in the *Bengal Hurkaru* of October 2,1826. Teehuteatuaonoa had also been interviewed by Otto von Kotzebue in March 1824.

Teehuteatuaonoa's accounts are more reliable than those Adams gave, if for no other reason than that she had nothing to hide. She seems to have been a very intelligent woman and a leader of the women on Pitcairn.

Teehuteatuaonoa was originally the consort of Adams and followed him to Tubuai. In fact, her left arm was tattooed "AS 1789," AS standing for Alexander Smith, the alias of John Adams. On arrival at Pitcairn, however, she was the consort of Isaac Martin and stayed with him until his death on Massacre Day, September 20, 1793. She was very unhappy on the island, perhaps because she had no children, and she left it in 1817 on the whaler *Sultan* in order to go back to her native Tahiti.

We do not know whether Teehuteatuaonoa was still living when the population of Pitcairn briefly emigrated to Tahiti in 1831. Perhaps not, because von Kotzebue indicated that she was homesick for Pitcairn and, if so, she could have gone "home" with the others.

TEE-PLANT See TI-PLANT.

TE FANA (Tetaha) A district on the north-west coast of Tahiti corresponding to today's Faaa. At the time of the *Bounty*'s visit, the chief of Te Fana (Tetaha) was Tepahu.

ENCYCLOPEDIA

TEFANO See TAFANO.

TEIMUA ("Teirnua," "Temua") Teimua was one of the three Tahitian men who accompanied Christian and the other mutineers to Pitcairn (there were also two Tubuaian men and one man from Raiatea on the *Bounty*).

With the other two Tahitians and a few mutineers, Teimua joined Christian in the exploratory shore party when Pitcairn was first sighted.

Teimua had to share Mareva with the other two Tahitians. When the Tubuaians and the Raiatean conspired to kill the mutineers at the end of the first year, he participated in the murders of two of the conspirators.

On Massacre Day, September 20, 1793, it was Teimua who tried to save Brown's life by shooting at him only with a powder charge and telling him to play dead (Brown moved too soon and was beaten to death by Manarii). Sometime afterwards he was sitting with Teraura, accompanying her singing on his nose flute, when he was shot to death by Manarii who was probably jealous.

As was the case with all the Polynesian men on Pitcairn, Teimua left no progeny.

TEINA See POMARE I.

TEIO ("Te'o," "Mary") Teio went to Tubuai as the consort of Thomas McIntosh who was a loyalist and stayed on Tahiti when the *Bounty* sailed away for the last time. Teio was on board, however, but we do not know whether she came along willingly or was kidnapped. She arrived at Pitcairn as the consort of William McCoy and she was the only woman who brought a child with her, a baby daughter whose Tahitian name we do not know, but who was called "Sully" by the mutineers. Sully had had a Tahitian father.

Teio bore McCoy two children: Daniel and Kate. McCoy committed suicide in 1797 by throwing himself off a cliff during an attack of delirium tremens, and we do not know much about what Teio did during the next few years. Sometime after the turn of the century John Adams' consort Vahineatua died and Teio then went to live with him. She bore him his only son George. When Captain Beechey visited the island in 1825, he formally married Teio and Adams.

Teio died only nine days after Adams on March 14, 1829.

"TEIRNUA" See TEIMUA.

TE LAHU See TEATUAHITEA.

TEMARII (Teriirere, Ari'ifaataia, Aromaiterai, "Temmaree," "Terrederrie," "Tomarre") Temarii was the chief of Papara when the men of the *Bounty* lived on the island. Two of the mutineers, Thomas Burkett and John Sumner, accepted his invitation to live in Papara and took part in the military operations against the district of Atehuru (see the September 1790 commentary in Part I).

Temarii was probably born in 1762, the son of Amo and Purea. His mother built him the largest marae on Tahiti at Mahaiatea. Temarii was married to Te Arii na Vaho Roa, the eldest sister of Pomare I; she was thirteen years older than her husband and died in 1788, having borne him no children.

Morrison described him in 1791 as ". . . a Handsom well made man about 27 or 28 years old and about 6 feet high."

Captain Edwards thought Temarii was "the proper king of Otaheite." That he was not, but he was powerful and became important in the history of Tahiti as a staunch friend and supporter of Pomare II. He died in 1798 from injuries received in a gunpowder explosion.

TEMATANGI (Bligh's Lagoon Island)   Tematangi is a low-lying atoll in the Tuamotus about ninety miles west of Mururoa at 21⁰40'S., 140⁰40'W. It was discovered by Bligh in the *Providence* on April 5, 1792. Bligh thought it was uninhabited, but Beechey saw inhabitants there in 1826. The explanation is simply that it sometimes is inhabited and sometimes not. Today, Tuamotuans live on the island periodically while gathering mother-of-pearl.

TEMMAREE   See TEMARII.

TEMUA   See TEIMUA.

TE'O   See TEIO.

TEPAHU   At the time of the *Bounty*'s visit in Tahiti, Tepahu was the chief of Te Fana, the district immediately west of Pare. It was Tepahu who helped Bligh capture the three deserters by pointing out their location. He was a good friend of Peter Heywood and later became the father-in-law of midshipman George Stewart.

TE PORIONU'U   The two ancient districts on the north-west coast of Tahiti, Pare (comprising about half of today's Papeete and all of Pirae) and Arue (most of the shoreline of Matavai Bay) used to be separate chiefdoms. The principal marae of Pare was Raiamanu, in Arue it was Tarahoi.

Sometime before the arrival of the Europeans, the two districts had become combined, perhaps through conquest, under the name of Te Porionu'u with the principal marae being Tarahoi and the hereditary name-title of the "dynasty" being *Tu nui ae i te Atua*. Te Porionu'u bordered Te Fana (today's Faaa) in the west and Haapape (today's Mahina) in the east.

Although Te Porionu'u (in the literature usually referred to as Pare) was small compared to some other districts and district-alliances in Tahiti, it included Matavai Bay where the British preferred to anchor, and Tu (later Pomare I) succeeded in making the early explorers believe that he was the most powerful chief in Tahiti. He thereby received support by, and fire-arms from, the Europeans, which in time actually made him the most powerful chief. In this process he received crucial assistance from the men of the *Bounty* in the time between Christian's final departure (September 1789) and the arrival of the *Pandora* (March 1791).

TEPPAHOO   See TEPAHU.

TERATANE   See POMARE V.

TERAURA (Taoupiti, Mataohu, "Susannah")   We do not know whether Teraura was one of the Tahitian women who were kidnapped by Christian and his companions when the *Bounty* sailed from Tahiti for the last time. She arrived at Pitcairn as the consort of Edward Young.

When the women on the island took their revenge for having lost their male consorts on Massacre Day, Teraura was the one who cut off Tetahiti's head with an axe while he was sleeping with Teatuahitea.

She bore Young no children and when he tired of her, preferring Mauatua and Toofaiti, she seems to have taken up with — or been forced to take up with — Matthew Quintal. We do not know whether this was before or after Quintal's consort Tevarua fell to her death from a precipice in 1799. Teraura was pregnant with Quintal's child when he was murdered later that year by Adams and Young; the child was a boy who was named Edward.

Six years after Young's death, in 1806, she married Fletcher Christian's elder son, Thursday October, when he was sixteen and she was past thirty. She bore him six children: Charles, Joseph, Thursday October II, Mary, Polly, and Peggy.

Teraura survived the disastrous attempt of the population to emigrate to Tahiti in 1831, but she lost her husband there to the diseases against which the Pitcairners had no immunity. She became the last survivor of the original settlers and lived to see the first celebration of Bounty Day, the sixtieth anniversary of the burning of the ship, on January 23, 1850. She died half a year later, on July 15, 1850, almost twenty years after her husband.

TERIIRERE ("Terrederrie")   See TEMARII.

TERIITARIA   See POMARE V.

TETAHA   See TE FANA.

TETAHITI Nordhoff's and Hall's name for TITAHITI.

TETIAROA (Teturoa) Atoll thirty miles north of Tahiti, 17°00'S., 149°34'W., now owned by Marlon Brando.

On January 5, 1789, the three deserters from the *Bounty*, Churchill, Muspratt and Millward, sailed to Tetiaroa in a canoe "borrowed" from the natives. What they had planned to do after reaching the island will probably never be known; suffice to say, they eventually tired of being on constant guard against the natives' attempts to capture them and went back to Tahiti. There Bligh took them prisoner, single-handed, with only a cutlass and not knowing that the muskets' powder was wet.

TETUANUIREIA I TE RAI ATEA See ITIA.

TETUAUNUMAONA See VEHIATUA.

TETUPAIA See PUREA-TETUPAIA.

TE TUPUAI I TE RAI See VAETUA.

TEU ("Tew," "Otow," "Hapai," "Happai," "Whappai") Teu was probably born in 1728. With his wife Tetupaia, chiefess of Opoa in Raiatea, he had eight children, three of whom achieved importance in the history of Tahiti: Tu (later Pomare I), Ari'ipaea, and Vaetua.

Teu himself seems to have played a rather minor role in the political history of Tahiti. In fact, neither Cook, nor Banks, even mentions Teu in the accounts of their visit on the island in 1769 in the *Endeavour*.

Bligh describes Teu as follows: "I found this Old Cheif, who I suppose is about 70 Years of Age, lying under a Small Shed . . . He is a tall Man with weak Eyes and his Skin is much Shrivell'd and Dryed by drinking of that punicious Root the Ava." Teu died in 1803, the same year as his first-born son, Pomare I.

TEVAHITUA I PATEA See AMO.

TEVA I TAI (Seaward Teva) At the time of the *Bounty*'s visit in Tahiti, Teva i Tai was a union of the districts on Taiarapu peninsula: Toahotu, Vairao, Teahupoo, Tautira, Pueu, and Afaahiti.

TEVA I UTA (Landward Teva) At the time of the *Bounty*'s visit in Tahiti, Teva i Uta represented a union of four districts on the south coast of Tahiti Nui: Papara, Atimaono, Vaiuriri (or Papeuriri, today's Mataiea), and Papeari (or Vaiari).

TEVARUA (Tewalua, "Sarah")   Tevarua was the consort of Matthew Quintal who called her "Sarah." Even though she had accompanied him to Tubuai, it is likely that she was one of the Tahitian women who were kidnapped by the mutineers in Tahiti when they left the island for the last time; she must have known Quintal's brutal nature by then. She arrived at Pitcairn as his consort and bore him five children: Matthew, Jenny, Arthur, Sarah and a boy who died unnamed a week after his birth.

Tevarua was without a doubt the most abused woman on Pitcairn. Island tradition has it that Quintal once bit off her ear when she did not bring home enough fish. Even if the story is apocryphal, being Quintal's consort must have been hell on earth.

Tevarua died in 1799 by falling — or more probably, throwing herself — from a precipice.

TEW   See TEU.

TEWALUA   See TEVARUA.

THOMPSON, Matthew   Able-bodied seaman on the *Bounty*; mutineer; killed on Tahiti. Thompson was born on the Isle of Wight and was thirty-seven years old when he signed on the *Bounty*. Bligh's description of Thompson, written after the mutiny, reads as follows:

> [MATTHEW THOMPSON] A.B. 40 years, 5 feet 8 inches high. Very dark complexion, short black hair. Slender made. Has lost the joint of the great toe of his right foot. Is tattooed.

Thompson was perhaps the most brutal man on the *Bounty* and that is saying much when one considers that Churchill and Quintal and McCoy were also on board.

On Tahiti, Thompson was given twelve lashes with the cat-o'-nine-tails for "insolence and disobedience of orders."

During the mutiny Thompson was one of the first to join Christian. It was he who kept guard over the arms chest to prevent the loyalists from arming themselves.

Thompson does not seem to have been liked by anyone on the *Bounty*. Churchill, also a brutal man but with some capacity for friendship, seems to have tolerated him, however, and the two were often seen together on Tahiti.

Thompson may have been the only *Bounty* man who did not have a *taio* and the women, sensing his brutal nature, probably shunned him. On February 8, 1790, Thompson tried to rape the daughter of a chief. Her brother ran to her assistance, knocked Thompson down, and ran off. Thompson in his rage swore that he would kill the first Tahitian he saw. When he came to his hut, there was the usual crowd assembled around it, curious about the doings of *popa'as* (white men) and Thompson told them to disperse. Not understanding him, the crowd remained. Thompson then took his musket and shot into the crowd, killing a father and the baby he was holding and breaking the mother's jaw.

Thompson, fearing reprisals, fled to Taiarapu where Churchill was living with his *taio*, chief Vehiatua. The chief soon died without leaving any male offspring and, in accordance with old Tahitian custom, Churchill succeeded him.

Thompson, incapable of any real friendship, soon became envious of Churchill and moved to another district. Not trusting Thompson, Churchill ordered his servants to steal Thompson's muskets, which they did. Thompson suspected Churchill right away and went to confront him. Churchill swore that he knew nothing about it and the two became "friends" again.

One day, however, Churchill had beaten his servant Maititi mercilessly for some minor offense, and the latter took revenge by telling Thompson the truth about the theft of the muskets. Thompson then killed Churchill.

The killing of a chief had to be avenged, however, so the Tahitians who had been Churchill's subjects — after lulling Thompson into security by pretending that they now recognized him as their new chief — jumped him when he was off guard and bashed his head in with a rock.

TIAIRI   See TUTUI.

TIARABOO   See TAIARAPU.

TIARE   Tahitian for flower.

TIARE TAHITI (Tiare Maohi)   A small white gardenia (*Gardenia tahitiensis*) with a permeating exotic fragrance, a favorite for use in *hei tiares* (flower leis) and *hei upo'os* (head wreaths). It is also a favorite ingredient in *monoi*, a perfumed coconut oil.

Teuira Henry describes the flower (*tiare tahiti* is the modern name for *tiare maohi*) in her book *Ancient Tahiti* (1928):

> The tiare-maohi . . . is a beautiful plant that grows slowly to the height of a small tree and lives to a considerable age. Its bark is smooth. Its strong, gnarled branches are covered with large glossy, obovate leaves, and spangled with snowy-white, waxy-looking stellate flowers, which have a sweet, delicate fragrance. The flowers open in the evening and do not wither for several days . . . The *tiare* has always been regarded as the choicest of Tahitian flowers. When picked in the bud, just ready to bloom, and wrapped closely in their own or other leaves, they retain their odor and freshness for several days and become more flexible to use in making wreaths and other ornaments. In this way they are also used for scenting *monoi* (hair oil), which becomes very softening for the hair and skin. The young buds are also used for internal and external native

medicines. The *tiare* grows from slips on good soil, best on sandy soil, and the largest old plants are found as sweet memorials of the past upon the islets or long sandy points around the high islands, where the ancient kings and chiefs used to have their summer dwellings.

Rupert Brooke named one of his poems *Tiare Tahiti.*

And one thing is certain, the fragrance of *tiare tahiti* will bring back memories of the island even more strongly than will the sounds of Tahitian music.

TIAREI In Tahiti: a district on the north-east coast of Tahiti Nui.

TIARRABU See TAIARAPU.

TIERRA DEL FUEGO Tierra del Fuego ("Land of Fire") is actually the main island at the southern tip of South America, but the name is usually applied to the whole archipelago. The most southern island is Isla de Hornos with Cape Horn. Tierra del Fuego was discovered by Magellan in 1520; it is separated from the mainland by the Straits of Magellan.

Bligh sighted the coast of Tierra del Fuego on March 23, 1788, and almost immediately ran into contrary winds, forcing him to eventually abandon his attempt to round Cape Horn (see the April 1788 commentary in Part I).

TIMOR Timor is the largest and the most eastern of the Nusa Tenggara (or Lesser Sunda) Islands, situated between the Savu Sea in the west and the Timor Sea in the East, stretching from 8⁰19' to 10⁰27'S., and from 123⁰27' to 127⁰18'E. It is about 300 miles long south-west to north-east with a maximum width of about 66 miles. Timor is a mountainous island cut by deep valleys. The climate and vegetation are similar to northern Australia.

The Portuguese started trading with Timor in the first half of the sixteenth century, being particularly interested in the island's rich supply of sandalwood. In the beginning of the seventeenth century the Dutch moved into the East Indies and established a trading post in Coupang which soon developed into the main port on the island. The Portuguese retreated to the north-eastern half of the island and established a settlement, Dili, on the north coast.

Timor remained split between the Dutch and the Portuguese until the Dutch lost their half of the island when Indonesia proclaimed independence in 1945. In 1975 the whole island became part of Indonesia. The population of the island today is approximately one million.

TINAFANAEA ("Tinafornea") Tinafanaea may have been from Tubuai and it is likely that she came along voluntarily when the *Bounty* sailed from Tahiti for the last time. On Pitcairn, she was shared as a consort by the two Tubuaians, Titahiti and Oha. (Some sources claim she was Titahiti's wife but that he shared her with Oha.)

When Adams' consort Puarai died towards the end of the first year on Pitcairn, Tinafanaea was "given" to Adams. Earlier, Tararo's consort Toofaiti had been "given" to Williams. This was more than the Tubuaian men and Tararo could tolerate, and the two outrages combined to set off the bloodshed that eventually wiped out almost all men on the island.

Tinafanaea seems to have stayed in Adams' household even when he, after Mills was killed on Massacre Day, took Vahineatua as his consort.

Tinafanaea died sometime between the visit of the *Topaz* (1808) and the *Briton* and the *Tagus* (1814). She left no descendants.

TINAH Bligh's spelling of Teina. See POMARE I..

TINARAU The chief of the district of Paorani (today deserted) on Tubuai. It was Tinarau and his subjects who had instigated the attack on the *Bounty* when, under Fletcher Christian's command, she had entered the lagoon of Tubuai in May 1789. Tinarau also allied himself with chief Tamatoa against Christian during the latter's attempt to establish a colony on Tubuai.

TINKLER, Robert Able-bodied seaman on the *Bounty*; loyalist; went with Bligh; arrived safely in England. Tinkler was born at Wells-next-the-Sea, Norfolk, in 1770, so he was seventeen years old when he joined the *Bounty*. He was the youngest brother-in-law of the sailing master, John Fryer. Bligh refers to Tinkler as "Boy," but he seems to have actually occupied a position halfway between able-bodied seaman and midshipman and was called Mr. Tinkler by the other seamen. He was in Christian's mess together with Stewart and Heywood.

There is very little mention of Tinkler in the *Bounty* literature. He seems to have been in the anti-Bligh group on the open-boat voyage. Bligh claims that, while at Coupang, Tinkler had been impertinent to William Cole, the boatswain, and that Fryer on that occasion had told his brother-in-law to stick his knife into Cole! The story sounds highly improbable, but perhaps both Tinkler and Fryer were drunk at the time.

Tinkler was present at the Battle of Copenhagen in 1801 as first lieutenant in the *Isis* while Fryer was sailing master in Admiral Parker's flagship *London* and Bligh commanded the *Glatton*. Tinkler was promoted to commander after the engagement.

TI-PLANT The words that follow are taken from the label of an old liquor bottle:

Okolehao Ka Lama Kaulana o
Hawaii Nei, mai ka wa mai o
Kamehameha, Ke Alii Ekahi

Ti Root Okolehao became the
favoured drink of Hawaii during
the reign of Kamehameha I (1795–1819)

O ka Okolehao i loaa mai ke
a-a mai o ke kumu la-i.
Okolehao, Ka Lama
Kaulana o Hawaii!

Only "Oke" made from the root
of the Ti Plant is the original
exotic drink which won world fame
for itself and for Hawaii.

Okolehao was named by the Hawaiians after iron pots used for distilling. The pots came from whaling ships and were used in pairs, each pot having a flat side which when put together resembled the rump of a plump matron. Thus okole for rump, hao for iron. Literally iron bottom or okolehao.

The liquor the bottle once contained, okolehao, has a great deal to do with the *Bounty* story. Teuira Henry, the granddaughter of the missionary to Tahiti, Reverend John M. Orsmond, and also the granddaughter of Reverend William Henry, missionary of the *Duff*, mentions okolehao in her book *Ancient Tahiti* (1928): "In Hawaii, strong spirits are distilled from the ti root by the natives, which they call o-kole-hao, and in the reign of Pomare II 1803–1821 . . . some Hawaiians taught the Tahitians to manufacture the drink."

Before the Hawaiians taught the Tahitians this use, or abuse, of the "Tree of Sin" (as the missionaries called it), the *Bounty* mutineer William McCoy had come upon the secret all by himself on Pitcairn. McCoy had earlier worked in a brewery in Glasgow and was what is sometimes referred to as a "chronically thirsty" man. After much experimentation, he succeeded in distilling a strong liquor from the ti-root, in other words, okolehao; for what happened afterwards, see PITCAIRN.

The abuse of okolehao, then (although it was not known by that name), accounted for at least McCoy's death, but probably also Quintal's, since he seems to have gone totally out of control after starting on the okolehao and this was the reason he was "executed" by Adams and Young.

The word abuse should be stressed, because okolehao is no more dangerous than any other spirits and can taste just as good although — like any other liquor — it can also taste like liquid sandpaper. Captain Charles Fremantle who visited Pitcairn in HMS *Challenger* in 1833 wrote: "It was not unlike whisky and very good!"

Teuira Henry lists thirteen Tahitian varieties of ti (*Cordyline terminalis*) and adds:

The ti is perhaps the most notable of all Polynesian plants; its long glossy leaves of green or brilliant yellow were worn by orators and warriors and enchanters in their official capacities. They were and are still much sought after for decorations and other purposes, and the juice of the root is highly nutritious and pleasant as food.

TIPUTA Tahitian word for a poncho-like garment made of *tapa*.

TITAHITI (Ta'aroamiva) Titahiti's original name was Ta'aroamiva. He was from Tubuai, the younger brother of Ta'aroatohoa, the chief of Natieva (the district is now called Taahuaia). Ta'aroamiva followed Christian and his men to Tahiti (where he changed his name to Titahiti) and to Pitcairn.

On Pitcairn, Titahiti shared Tinafanaea (who may also have been from Tubuai) with his compatriot Oha until she was "given" by the mutineers to Adams whose consort had died within a year of the arrival.

Titahiti was one of the three Polynesians (two from Tubuai, one from Raiatea) who conspired to kill the mutineers towards the end of the first year on the island. The mutineers found out about the plot through the women and sent the three Tahitians to kill the conspirators. Two were killed, but Titahiti surrendered and henceforth lived on the plantation of Isaac Martin as a virtual slave.

On Massacre Day Titahiti borrowed a musket from Martin under the pretext that he was going to shoot a pig for supper. He then joined Teimua and Niau who had stolen some muskets when they fled to the mountains. Some time after the murder of the five mutineers, Titahiti was himself killed by Young's consort Teraura as an act of revenge.

Like the other Polynesian men on Pitcairn, Titahiti left no progeny.

TITERANO The Tahitian name for Fletcher Christian.

TOA See IRONWOOD.

TOAROA Harbor on the north coast of Tahiti in the district of Pare, east of today's Papeete and west of Matavai Bay. It is bordered in the east by the Otueaiai peninsula. This is the harbor to which Bligh moved the *Bounty* on Christmas Day 1788.

Today Toaroa harbor is the main anchorage of the Tahiti Yacht Club.

TOBIN, George Third lieutenant in the *Providence* on the second breadfruit expedition. Tobin was not only a fine navigator but also a good artist who, in his journal of the voyage, made excellent drawings and watercolor sketches of the islands visited, especially Tahiti. He later became a protégé of Admiral Nelson who, through his wife, was connected with Tobin's family.

Tobin was promoted to commander in 1798 and to post captain in 1802. As captain of the *Princess Charlotte,* which he had disguised as a merchantman, he captured the French warship *Cyane* off Tobago in a hard-fought battle.

TOBOOI See TUBUAI.

TOERAUETORU   A district, now called Mataura, comprising the western half of Tubuai but centered on the north coast opposite the lagoon entrance at Bloody Bay. The chief of Toerauetoru during the visit and colonization attempt of Christian and his men was Tamatoa.

TOFUA   Tofua (Bligh spelled it Tofoa) is the most western island in the Haapai group in the Kingdom of Tonga, situated at 19⁰41'S., 173⁰0'W. It lies 45 miles north-north-west-by-north of Nomuka — where the *Bounty* stopped before the mutiny — and less than 100 miles from Tongatabu. It measures four by five miles and has a volcano rising to 1600 feet which was active at the time of the mutiny and still gives off a plume of steam today.

The mutiny took place ten leagues (thirty nautical miles) to the south-west of Tofua and Bligh and the eighteen loyalists sought refuge in a cave on the sheltered north-west coast of the island in an attempt to augment their meager provisions.

In the March 1968 issue of the *National Geographic Magazine*, Luis Marden claims to have found not only Bligh's cave, but also the grave of John Norton, the quartermaster of the *Bounty* who was killed by the Tofuans when the launch made its escape from what surgeon Hamilton in the *Pandora* later described as "Murderers' Cove."

In an article published in the June 1985 issue of the *Pacific Islands Monthly*, Bengt Danielsson shows that Marden was mistaken and describes the actual cave used by Bligh and his men. Marden's cave lies on the exposed south-east coast, whereas Bligh clearly states that the cave was on the sheltered north-west coast (where Danielsson identified it). Moreover, Bligh's description and measurements of the cave and its surroundings match exactly the location found by Danielsson. Finally, it is highly unlikely that the Tofuans would have allotted any gravesite to Norton and, even if that had been the case, it would hardly have been preserved for two centuries. The current inhabitants of Tofua had never heard of the *Bounty* when Danielsson visited the island.

Tofua currently has a population of about fifty who are there primarily to grow *kava (Piper methysticum)* for export to Tongatabu.

TOHOLOMOTA   See TINAFANAEA.

TOKELAU (Union) ISLANDS   The Tokelau group consists of three large atolls: Fakaofo, Nukunono, and Atafu. They are situated approximately 300 miles north-north-west of the Samoas (the word "tokelau" — in Tahitian *to'erau* — means north-north-west) and are a dependency of New Zealand. Geographically, Swains Island (Olohenga), which lies about 125 miles south of Fakaofo, is often counted as one of the Tokelaus, but is politically part of American Samoa.

These are low atolls: at no point is the land higher than fifteen feet above sea level. The combined population at the time of writing is approximately 1700. The inhabitants are a mixed race of Polynesians and Micronesians who speak Tokelauan, a Polynesian language. Since the Bible they use is Samoan, they also understand Samoan well and they learn English in school.

Captain Edwards in the *Pandora* searched for the *Bounty* mutineers in this group during the month of June 1791 at which time he discovered Nukunono (June 12), naming it Duke of Clarence Island.

TOMARRE   Bligh's spelling of TEMARII.

TONGA ISLANDS   The Tonga group lies between 18⁰01' and 21⁰28'S., and between 173⁰54' and 175⁰33'W.; it consists of 169 islands, most of them small. They are usually divided into five groups: Tongatabu, Nomuka, Kotu, Haapai, Vavau.

The outlying islands of Niuatoputapu, Tafahi, and Niuafoo are also counted in this group which forms the independent Kingdom of Tonga, a self-governing state since 1968. The Royal Palace and the seat of government is at Nukualofa on Tongatabu. The population of Tonga is approximately 120,000.

TONGATABU (Amsterdam Island)   The main island in the Kingdom of Tonga; located at 21⁰07'S., 175⁰12'W.

Tongatabu is slightly less than 100 miles south of the island of Tofua where the *Bounty* mutiny took place. When Bligh was set adrift in the *Bounty*'s launch together with the loyalists among the crew, he had originally planned to sail there. However, when he witnessed the savagery of the Tongans at Tofua (see the May 1789 commentary in Part I), he decided against it and set a course for Timor.

From the accounts of Teehuteatuaonoa, we know with reasonable certainty that Christian did stop at Tongatabu to revictual the *Bounty* while sailing on his search for a refuge.

Tongatabu is a rather flat island, eighteen and a half miles long and nine miles wide, ninety-nine square miles in all. Its present population is 13,000. The chief administrative center for all of Tonga, Nukualofa ("the abode of love"), is a quaint South Seas town well worth visiting. It has a Victorian ginger-bread Royal Palace occupied by the present (1988) King Taufaahau Tupou IV, a few streets marked by nasty potholes, and a paucity of hotels.

Tongatabu was discovered by Abel Janszoon Tasman on January 21, 1643, and he called it by the name Bligh knew: Amsterdam Island. Cook visited the island on both his second and third voyages, found the islanders very friendly, and therefore called the whole group the Friendly Isles. He did not know that the islanders had planned to capture his ship and massacre the crew, as they did later with the *Port-au-Prince* and the *Duke of Portland*.

TO'O   Old Tahitian word for pole. On Pitcairn, a shoulder pole used to carry baskets and banana bunches.

TOOBOUAI   See TUBUAI.

TOOFAITI (Toohaiti, Hutia, "Nancy")   We do not know whether Toofaiti was kidnapped by Christian and the other mutineers or whether she came along willingly. On the arrival at Pitcairn, she was the consort of Tararo. Both of them were from the Leeward Islands, she from Huahine, he from Raiatea.

Toofaiti was "given" to John Williams after his consort died; this was the incident that triggered the interracial strife and bloodshed on Pitcairn. According to island tradition, it was Toofaiti who sang the song

Why does black man sharpen axe?
To kill the white men.

which warned the mutineers of the plot by the Tubuaians and the Raiatean Tararo to exterminate them.

After Williams was killed on Massacre Day, September 20, 1793, Toofaiti and Mauatua seem to both have been consorts of Edward Young to whom Toofaiti bore three sons, George, Robert, and William, and one daughter, Nancy.

When the whole population of Pitcairn migrated to Tahiti in 1831, Toofaiti was one of the seventeen who died from a disease contracted on the island. Her death occurred on June 9, 1831.

TOONOEAITEATOOA   Morrison's spelling of Tu nui ae i te Atua. See POMARE II.

TOOTATE   See AITUTAKI.

TOPAZ   A Boston sealer owned by Messrs. Boardman and Pope and commanded by Captain Mayhew Folger.

The *Topaz* sailed from Boston on Sunday April 5, 1807. The main purpose of the voyage was of course to procure seal skins, but the ship also carried gin and rum with which to trade in New Holland (Australia). She arrived in Hobart Town on October 27. Interestingly, Bligh was aware of her dealings, at least afterwards, because in his dispatch to Viscount Castlereagh on June 30, 1808 (in which he reports on his arrest), Bligh includes the report

> That the officers of the *Porpoise* when at the Derwent, commanded by Lieutenant Symons, received from the American Ship *Topaz* . . . upwards of Eight hundred gallons of Rum, and one hundred and fifty of Gin, that about three hundred

was only on account of the Ship, for which Bills were drawn on the Victualling Board, and the remainder was purchased by the Officers on their own private account, and afterwards Sold by them at two and three pounds per gallon.

The *Topaz* continued her voyage into the South Pacific and on February 6, 1808, sighted Pitcairn Island. See also FOLGER, MAYHEW.

TORRES STRAIT   See ENDEAVOUR STRAIT.

TOTTER   Drunkard.

HMS *TRIUMPH*   The ship from which William McCoy and Matthew Quintal had transferred to the *Bounty*.

TU   See POMARE I and POMARE II.

TUAMOTU (Paumotu, Dangerous Archipelago, Low Islands)   The Tuamotu archipelago lies east, east-north-east, and east-south-east of Tahiti. It comprises seventy-eight islands extending over fifteen degrees of longitude. It has a total land mass of 356 square miles. All the islands, except Makatea and Tikei, are low-lying coral atolls.

The Gambier Islands, sometimes referred to as a separate group, are generally considered as part of the Tuamotus. Politically the archipelago is a part of French Polynesia, but geographically the Pitcairn Islands are usually included in the group.

The old appellation "Dangerous Archipelago" comes from the fact that navigation between the islands is hazardous; the waters are reef-infested and the currents are strong and unpredictable. The islands used to be dangerous in another sense also: they were populated by a Polynesian branch of fierce warriors who were said to be cannibals and were feared by the Marquesans to the north-east and the Tahitians to the west.

Living in the Tuamotus was, and is, precarious. Drinking water, if present at all, is brackish; fresh water must be gathered from rain. The range of plant life is narrow, but coconut palms and pandanus grow on the atolls, even some breadfruit here and there. None of the high-island vegetables grow in the Tuamotus and virtually all of the protein comes from fish and shellfish. Hurricanes, although rare, are a significant threat to survival on these low islands.

Most of the inter-island transportation is by "copra boat," usually a small rust-bucket full of cockroaches and copra bugs which looks as if she were going to sink at any moment. A few of the islands, notably Rangiroa, Manihi, and Mangareva, can be reached by air.

The Tuamotus are best known for their pearls and mother-of-pearl. The French conduct their atomic testing here on Mururoa atoll in the south-east.

Captain Bligh discovered one of the islands in the group, Tematangi, on his second breadfruit expedition.

The Pomare family originally came from Fakarava, one of the larger atolls in the Tuamotus.

An excellent description of life on a coral atoll can be found in Nordhoff's and Hall's *The Hurricane* (1936) and in Hall's *Lost Island* (1945).

TUBUAI (Tupuai)   Tubuai is the main island in the Austral group in French Polynesia and lies at 23º23'S., 149º26'W., almost exactly on the Tropic of Capricorn. It is 350 miles due south of Tahiti and 96 miles west-north-west-by-west of Raivavae.

Tubuai is a volcanic island, five by three miles in area, surrounded by a barrier reef. It is a high and well-wooded island; the highest mountain, Taita, rises to 1385 feet.

Tubuai was discovered in 1777 by Cook who sailed past without landing. The men of the *Bounty* who, under Christian's command, arrived at the island on May 24, 1789, were the first Europeans to ever set foot on its soil. Their adventures on the island are described in Part I (in the May to September 1789 commentaries).

The population of Tubuai in the 1780s was about 3000. By 1821 it had dropped to 900 and by 1823 to 300. As was the case on all Polynesian islands, the inhabitants were dying like flies from the diseases brought by the Europeans. Today the population is approximately 1500.

TULLALOO   See TARARO.

TUMU HAARI   See COCONUT PALM.

TU NUI AE I TE ATUA (Tu-nui-aite-atua)   See POMARE II.

TUPUAI   See TUBUAI.

TUSCAN   A 300-ton British whaler which, under the command of Captain Thomas Stavers, arrived at Pitcairn on March 8, 1834, and carried George Nobbs, John Buffett, and John Evans to Tahiti, the three having been exiled by Joshua Hill, the "dictator of Pitcairn."

The surgeon on board the *Tuscan*, Dr. Frederick D. Bennett, has left a fascinating account of the visit in his chapter on Pitcairn in *A Narrative of a Whaling Voyage Round the Globe* (1840).

TUTE   The Tahitian name for Captain Cook.

TUTUI (tiairi, "doodooee," candlenut)   The nuts of the candlenut tree (*Aleurites triloba*) are rich and oily and about the size of a walnut. In old Tahiti they were used for lighting (*tutui* means to kindle a fire or set fire to something). Several nuts were threaded on a rib of a coconut frond, forming a taper which would burn like a candle. Seasoned in black mud the *tutui* takes a high polish and is used for jewelry, especially in Hawaii where the nut is called *kukui*.

Even as recently as half a century ago the *tutui* was used on isolated islands, as reported by H. L. Shapiro in *The Heritage of the Bounty* (1936):

> In the evening, which comes soon after six o'clock on Pitcairn, [the] snug interiors were illuminated by the faltering light of the *doodoee* or candle nut. The use of these nuts for lighting once widespread in Polynesia today still lingers on remote islands such as Rapa. . . .
>
>   . . . as one nut burnt low the next would be ignited, thus producing a candlelike illumination satisfactory except for the cracking and spitting that Beechey found disconcerting.

A reddish brown dye made from the inner bark of the candlenut tree is used to decorate *tapa* cloth and the sap of the tree is used to waterproof it.

TYARRABOO   See TAIARAPU.

TYNAH   See POMARE I.

TYO   See TAIO.

UEA   See UVEA.

UFI (uhi)   Tahitian word for yam.

ULIATEA, ULIETEA, ULITEA   See RAIATEA.

'UMARA   Tahitian for sweet potato (*Ipomoea batatas*). The sweet potato was originally a South American plant and could have come to Polynesia only if transported by man; yet, the early European explorers found it on almost all Polynesian islands. This, and the fact that the Incan name for the plant, *kumara*, is also the name for it in Polynesian languages, proves that there was contact between Polynesians and Incans in old times. That, by the way, only makes sense, because it would seem far-fetched to assume that the Polynesians, in their great migrations eastward, would somehow have stopped their travels when reaching Easter Island and not sailed further.

UNION ISLANDS   Old name for the TOKELAU group.

UPAUPA   Tahitian word for music or musical instrument.

UPOLU   The principal island of Western Samoa; the capital, Apia, is located on the north shore at 13⁰50'S., 171⁰55'W. Upolu lies 36 miles west-north-west of Tutuila and 360 miles due north of Nomuka. The island is 40 miles long, east to west, and 13 miles wide. It is mountainous and its highest peak, Vaaifetu (Fito), rises to 3608 feet.

At the foot of Mount Vaea, a short distance south of Apia, is Vailima, the beautiful residence which Robert Louis Stevenson built when he came to Samoa to stay (in 1889). Close to the summit of Mount Vaea is Stevenson's tomb on which is inscribed:

> *Under the wide and starry sky*
> *Dig the grave and let me lie.*
> *Glad did I live and gladly die*
> *And I laid me down with a will.*
>
> *This be the verse you grave for me:*
> *Here he lies where he longed to be;*
> *Home is the sailor, home from the sea,*
> *And the hunter home from the hill.*

Near this Samoan island, on the evening of June 22, 1791, the *Pandora* lost contact with her tender *Resolution* in a squall and did not see her again. The fate of the *Resolution* remained unknown until four months later when the survivors of the *Pandora* arrived at Samarang and saw the tender anchored in the harbor. The *Resolution* had been attacked by the natives of Upolu and had a narrow escape (see the June 1791 commentary in Part I).

URRIPIAH   See ARI'IPAEA.

'URU   The Tahitian word for BREADFRUIT.

UVEA (Uea, Wallis Island)   Uvea is the main island in the group referred to as Wallis and Futuna Islands, a French overseas territory. Uvea and Futuna lie about 400 miles north-east of Fiji and 200 miles west of Samoa.

Uvea is situated at 13⁰18'S., 176⁰10'W. It is eight miles long, north to south, and three to four miles wide. Its highest mountain, Lulu, is near the center of the island and rises to 475 feet.

There are about 8000 Polynesians on Uvea, mostly descended from Tongan ancestors (the 6000 Futunans stem from Samoa). *South Pacific Handbook* comments: "All the marks of French colonialism are here, from overpaid white officials controlling functionless staff to little French gendarmes in round peaked caps and shorts."

Uvea was discovered by Samuel Wallis on August 16, 1767. It was visited by Francisco Maurelle on April 22, 1781.

On his search for the nine missing mutineers of the *Bounty* Captain Edwards stopped at Uvea and exchanged some presents with the natives.

VA'A   Tahitian for canoe.

VA'A MOTU (va'a ta'ie)   Tahitian one-hull sailing canoe.

VAETUA (Vaitua, Paiti, Pati'i, Maioro, Te Tupuai i te Rai, "Whyeadooa")   Vaetua was born in 1763 and was one of Pomare I's younger brothers. In the *Bounty* story, Vaetua is known primarily as midshipman Thomas Hayward's *taio* on Tahiti.

It was Vaetua who, in the night between the fifth and the sixth of February, 1789, cut the *Bounty*'s anchor cable (or ordered it cut), leaving only one strand to hold the ship. His intention was to free Hayward who was then in irons for having slept on duty. Vaetua had also been ready to kill Bligh, should his friend have been sentenced to be flogged.

Nordhoff and Hall use the name Moana for Vaetua.

VAHINE   Tahitian for woman.

VAHINEATUA (Wahineatua, Paraha Iti, "Balhadi," "Prudence")   We do not know whether Vahineatua was kidnapped by the mutineers or not, but she arrived at Pitcairn as the consort of John Mills to whom she bore two children: Betsy (Elizabeth) and John. The boy died from a fall at a young age.

After Mills had been murdered on Massacre Day, Vahineatua went to live with Adams to whom she bore three daughters: Dina, Rachel, and Hannah. She was pregnant with a fourth child when, according to Teehuteatuaonoa, she "was killed, being pierced in her bowels by a goat."

Mills called Vahineatua "Prudence." Adams referred to her as "Balhadi," which was the closest he could come to pronouncing her second Tahitian name, Paraha Iti.

VAIPO'OPO'O   A valley on the north-west coast of Tahiti; a river with the same name runs through it into the sea at Matavai Bay.

VAIRAATOA   Old name of the Pomare family. See POMARE I.

VAIRAO   On Tahiti: a district on the south-west coast of Taiarapu (Tahiti Iti) south of Toahotu and north of Teahupoo.

VAITEPIHA   A river in the district of Tautira on the north coast of the Taiarapu peninsula on Tahiti. It flows through a valley with the same name and empties in the lagoon east of the Tautira promontory.

Vaitepiha is also the name for the anchorage east of the Tautira promontory. Captain Don Domingo de Boenechea anchored here with the *Aguila* and the *Jupiter* on November 27, 1774. The next year Captain Don Cayetano de Langara, who was then in command of the *Aguila*, used Vaitepiha as his anchorage when he arrived on November 3, 1775.

On his third voyage to the South Seas, Captain Cook anchored in Vaitepiha Bay on May 12, 1777, with his ships *Resolution* and *Discovery*, the latter commanded by Captain Charles Clerke.

VAITUA   See VAETUA.

VALENTINE, James   Able-bodied seaman on the *Bounty*; died from an infection on October 9, 1788, a few weeks before the ship reached Tahiti.

Valentine was born in Montrose and was twenty-eight years old when he joined the *Bounty*. He was one of the strongest and healthiest seamen on board. When the *Bounty* stopped at Adventure Bay, however, he had felt somewhat indisposed (he may have been suffering from asthma) and made the mistake of consulting Dr. Huggan, the alcoholic ship's surgeon. Huggan bled him, his arm became infected, the infection spread, and Valentine got worse with every day.

Bligh was not told about the man's serious condition until he was dying, an example of how incredibly poor communication was on board the small ship. Valentine was buried at sea "with all the decency in our power;" he was the first of the *Bounty*'s crew to die.

VAN DIEMEN'S LAND   The old name for Tasmania. Abel Janszoon Tasman discovered the island on November 24, 1642, and named it after the Governor General of the Dutch East Indies at Batavia, Antony van Diemen. Tasman did not know, however, that Van Diemen's Land was an island. The name Van Diemen's Land was used until 1853.

van ESTE, Willem Adriaan   Governor of Timor at the time Bligh and his men reached Coupang on the voyage in the *Bounty*'s launch. Van Este received the British sailors with great hospitality, but he was at the time dying of "an incurable disease" and most of the arrangements were handled by his son-in-law, Mynheer Timotheus Wanjon.

VANION, Timotheus   See WANJON, TIMOTHEUS.

VANUA LEVU   Second largest island in the Fiji group, situated at 16⁰40'S., 179⁰04'E. On May 6, 1789, Bligh and his men sailed south of Vanua Levu on their voyage from Tofua to Timor in the *Bounty*'s launch.

VAVAU   The ancient name of Bora Bora. Also the most northern island group in Tonga.

VEHIATUA (Tetuaunumaona, "Vayheeadooa")   Vehiatua was born in 1768. During the time of the *Bounty*'s stay at Tahiti he was the paramount chief of the union of districts on Taiarapu called Teva i Tai. He was Pomare I's brother-in-law, being married to Itia's sister Pateamai.

Vehiatua was Charles Churchill's *taio*. In early 1790, at the age of twenty-two he died childless and Churchill succeeded him as chief, the only white man to ever have held that office in eastern Polynesia. Churchill, however, was soon afterwards killed by Matthew Thompson (see the commentaries for February and March 1790 in Part I).

Churchill was succeeded by Teriitapunui, one of Vehiatua's nephews (Pomare II's younger brother).

VI   Tahitian for mango.

HMS *VIRAGO*   The first steamship to visit Pitcairn (January 27, 1853). The visit ended tragically. When the Pitcairners wanted to fire one of the *Bounty*'s cannons in a farewell salute, the ramrod happened to contain a nail which caused a spark that ignited the powder in the cannon, killing the Island Magistrate, Matthew McCoy.

VITI LEVU   Largest island in the Fiji group, 18⁰08'S., 178⁰26'E. On May 6, 1789, Bligh and his loyalists passed north of Viti Levu on the heroic open-boat voyage from Tofua to Timor. Although the discovery of the Fiji islands is officially credited to Tasman (in 1643) and Cook visited them in 1774 on his second voyage, Bligh was the first European to sail through them and the Fijians to this day regard him as the real discoverer of their island group.

VLYDTE   The name of the Dutch East Indiaman, commanded by Captain Peter Couvret, which took Bligh, John Samuel, and John Smith from Batavia to South Africa and on to England.

V. O. C.   Vereenigde Oost-Indische Compagnie, (the Dutch) United East India

Company which controlled the Dutch East Indies at the time of the *Bounty* story.

VREEDENBERG   The Dutch East Indiaman in which Captain Edwards and ten men of the *Bounty* captured on Tahiti traveled from Batavia to Cape Town where they arrived on January 15, 1792.

WAHEATUA, WAHEEATOOA   See VEHIATUA.

WAHINEATUA   See VAHINEATUA.

WAIA   Island in the Yasawa group in the Western Fijis, situated at 17⁰24'S., 176⁰52'E. On May 7, 1789, two large sailing canoes from Waia, filled with warriors (who were cannibals at that time) unsuccessfully pursued Bligh and his crew in the *Bounty*'s launch on their voyage from Tofua to Timor.

WALDEGRAVE, William   Captain of HMS *Seringapatam*. Waldegrave described his visit to Pitcairn in 1830 in a most interesting article entitled "Recent Accounts of the Pitcairn Islanders" (*Royal Geographical Society Journal*, volume 3, 1833). See *SERINGAPATAM*.

WALLIS, Samuel   British navigator and explorer (1728–1795). With orders to search for the unknown southern continent, Terra Australis Incognita, Wallis sailed from England on August 22, 1766, in HMS *Dolphin* accompanied by the sloop *Swallow* commanded by Captain Philip Carteret, the subsequent discoverer of Pitcairn.

The two ships became separated in a fog on April 11, 1767, and did not meet again. Sailing north-west and then west along latitude 20⁰S., Wallis and his crew became the first Europeans to set eyes on Tahiti where they anchored in Matavai Bay on June 24, 1767.

Unfortunately, Wallis was not very interested in describing his discoveries or the people who lived on them, but fortunately his sailing master, George Robertson, wrote an interesting journal of the voyage which has become a goldmine for anthropologists and ethnographers.

Wallis sailed from Tahiti on July 26, 1767, and reached England on May 20, 1768.

WALLIS ISLAND   See UVEA.

WANJON, Timotheus   When Bligh and the loyalists arrived at Coupang on June 14, 1789, it was Mynheer Timotheus Wanjon acting for his father-in-law, Governor van Este, who welcomed them and tried his best to make their stay as comfortable as possible. Wanjon did the same for Captain Edwards and his men and their prisoners from the *Bounty* in September 1791. And he was still there when Bligh returned from his second breadfruit expedition and stopped at Timor on October 2, 1792. Bligh wrote in his log:

> Wednesday, October 3rd. It was a pleasant circumstance to me to find Mr. Timotheus Wanjon, the gentleman who had assisted me so kindly when here in the "Bounty's" Launch, to be now Governor. Out of the little society then living, four were now dead, among whom was the surgeon, Mr. Max, who had attended our sick and dressed our sores.

WARLEY See HMS *CALCUTTA*.

WATTS, John Midshipman in the *Resolution* on Cook's third voyage. Lieutenant in the *Lady Penrhyn.*. See *LADY PENRHYN*.

WEATHERHEAD, Matthew Captain of the whaler *MATILDA*.

WEBBER, John Cook's artist on the third voyage. When the *Resolution* visited Tahiti in 1777, Webber sketched the features of Tu (Pomare) for a full-length painting he was to complete on the return to England. Tu then said that he would like to have a portrait of Captain Cook.

Webber made a painting of Cook, framed and with a box (locked with a key) to keep it in, and presented it to Tu who said he would preserve it forever. As we mentioned in the July 1792 commentary in Part I, the portrait became a kind of "guestbook" for visiting sea captains who all signed it on the back.

When the *Lady Penrhyn* visited Tahiti in 1788, the first ship to do so since the portrait was painted, the painting was still in perfect condition. Bligh, who arrived three months later in the *Bounty*, signed the portrait with these words:

> Lieutenant Bligh of His Britannic Majesty's ship *Bounty* anchored in Matavai Bay, October 25th, 1788, but owing to bad weather was obliged to sail to Oparre, December 25th, where he remained until March 30th, 1789. Was then ready for sea with 1015 breadfruit plants besides many other fruits, and only waiting an opportunity to get to sea, at which time the picture was given up. Sailed April 4th, 1789.

The men in the *Mercury* saw the painting later the same year, as did Captain Edwards in 1791. By this time, Poino, the chief of Haapape had become the custodian of the painting. Vancouver, who visited in 1792, wrote in his journal:

> Poeno, Chief of Matavai, brought with him a portrait of Captain Cook drawn by Mr. Webber in 1777. The picture is always deposited at his house and is

become the public register.

Bligh signed the painting again on his second breadfruit expedition in 1792, a few months after Vancouver. It seems to then have become lost; the missionaries who arrived in 1797 do not mention it.

WHAEATUAH, WHAEEAHTUAH See VEHIATUA.

"WHYEADOOA," "WHYTOOA" See VAETUA.

WHYTOOTACKEE See AITUTAKI.

WILLIAMS, John Able-bodied seaman on the *Bounty*; mutineer; went with Christian; was killed on Pitcairn. Williams was twenty-six years old when he signed on the *Bounty*. Although he put down Stepney in east London as his home, he had grown up on Guernsey and spoke French. Bligh's description of him, written after the mutiny, reads as follows:

> [JOHN WILLIAMS] seaman, aged 25 years, 5 feet 5 inches high, dark complexion, black hair, slender made; has a scar on the back part of his head; is tatowed, and a native of Guernsey; speaks French.

Williams was involved in the famous "cheese incident" (see the February 1788 commentary in Part I). He did not speak up during the confrontation, but it was he who, on the orders of the ship's clerk, Samuel, had delivered the supposedly stolen cheeses — plus a cask of vinegar and "some other things" — in the ship's boat from Long Reach to Bligh's home.

On entering False Bay near Cape Town in South Africa, Bligh found fault with Williams' performance in heaving the lead and sentenced him to six lashes. (Even six lashes left a nasty wound on the back.)

Williams took an active part in the mutiny. On Tubuai, he voted with Christian and he stayed on the *Bounty* when Christian left Tahiti on his search for an island refuge. He was one of the three mutineers who, with three Polynesians, accompanied Christian on his preliminary exploration of Pitcairn.

Williams arrived at Pitcairn with his consort Faahotu whom he called "Fasto." However, she died less than a year after the arrival from "a scrophulous disease which broke out in her neck." Williams then demanded that he be "given" another woman, taken from a Polynesian man.

The mutineers, who, at least in the beginning, seem to have voted on matters affecting the community, realized that granting Williams' request would cause severe problems and they turned it down, suggesting instead that he wait until Sully, the baby girl, reached adulthood (which for a Polynesian meant an age of 13 or 14).

On the *Bounty*, Williams had served as a sort of unofficial armorer's mate, which made his services very important to the mutineers. So vital did Christian feel that the skills of an armorer were that he had even tried to kidnap Coleman when sailing from Tahiti (see the September 1789 commentary in Part I). On Pitcairn, Williams was kept constantly busy with the anvil of the *Bounty* and was therefore exempted from any communal work.

However, he was not about to wait for over a decade for Sully to grow into womanhood and he threatened to leave the island in one of the *Bounty*'s boats. The mutineers then gave in — exactly because they needed his skills — and "gave" him Tararo's consort Toofaiti. It was this decision that triggered the bloodshed which eventually wiped out almost all males on the island.

On Massacre Day, September 20, 1793, Williams was the first of the mutineers to be killed. He left no children by Faahotu, nor by her "replacement," Toofaiti. The anvil from the *Bounty*, however, survives on Norfolk Island.

WILSON, James Captain Wilson was a true adventurer. Having survived hair-raising adventures in India, such as escaping the French by swimming a river full of crocodiles and being imprisoned in a dungeon and escaping again, he had embraced the one and only true faith. Accordingly, the London Missionary Society, not noted for good judgment, for once made an excellent decision: they chose Captain Wilson as the commander of the sailing ship *Duff* which was to carry thirty missionaries, some with wives and children, to the South Seas. Their decision was probably helped along by the fact that the devout Wilson did not charge them anything for his services.

On September 24, 1796, the *Duff* sailed from Portsmouth. She stopped at Rio de Janeiro long enough for the righteous people on board to be horrified by the wrong brand of Christianity that had taken hold there. She then tried to round the Horn, but Wilson was not as rigid as Bligh and, when he saw it was hopeless, he set an eastward course for Tahiti, as Bligh himself had eventually been forced to do.

In the process, Wilson broke a record: he sailed 13,820 miles without sighting land. The first land that was seen was Tubuai on February 21, 1797. What did the missionaries, most of whom had never been outside their own parishes, do during the voyage? One thing they did was study the Tahitian Dictionary which midshipman Peter Heywood of the *Bounty* had compiled.

The *Duff* made a fast voyage. She anchored in Matavai Bay on March 5, 1797, less than five and a half months out of Portsmouth. Eighteen missionaries debarked, eager to spread their message of doom and gloom among the sinfully happy Tahitians. Salvation had arrived on the island at last.

Other missionaries were put ashore on Tongatabu and two were taken to Hivaoa in the Marquesas. One of them, Brother John Harris, had bragged that he would evangelize the whole group alone. He lasted less than twenty-four hours. During his night ashore he awakened surrounded by a group of women who were examining his genitals in order to ascertain whether his lack of interest in sex might be due to some physical deformity. When he let out a scream of fright, the women ran away, taking his clothes with them. Brother Harris spent the rest of the night crying and wailing on the beach, and the next day he persuaded Captain Wilson to take him back to Tahiti, leaving his Brother in the Faith, William Crook, to face the exploration-minded women of Hivaoa alone.

Captain Wilson must be counted among the important explorers of the South Pacific. It was he who discovered the Gambier (Mangareva) group which he named after an admiral who had been helpful in fitting out the *Duff*. He also discovered Timoe atoll which he named Crescent Island and Pukarua (Serle Island). On his way to Macao for a cargo of tea, he made several discoveries in Melanesia, including the Duff group. He anchored in the Thames on July 11, 1798, the cargo of tea being more than enough to pay for the fitting out of the *Duff*.

WINDWARD ISLANDS   Tahiti, Moorea, Mehetia, Tetiaroa, and Maiao. See SOCIETY ISLANDS.

WYETOOA   See VAETUA.

WYTOOTACKEE   See AITUTAKI.

YASAWA   Group of islands in the western Fijis. Bligh traversed the group in early May 1789 on his open-boat voyage from Tofua to Timor, narrowly escaping some pursuing native war canoes.

YORK ISLAND   The name given to MOOREA (then called Aimeo) by Samuel Wallis when he discovered it, together with Tahiti, in 1767.

YOUNG, Brian   At the time of writing (1988) Brian Young, a direct descendant of midshipman Edward Young of the *Bounty*, is Pitcairn Island's magistrate. His Norwegian-born wife, Kari (née Boye), has written an interesting book about Pitcairn called *Den siste mysterist* (*The Last Mutineer*), published in Norwegian in 1982.

YOUNG, Edward ("Ned")   Midshipman on the *Bounty*; mutineer; went with Christian; died on Pitcairn. Young was born on St. Kitts in the West Indies. He was the nephew of Sir George Young and was probably a mulatto. He was twenty-one years old when he signed on the *Bounty*. Bligh's description of him, written after the mutiny, reads as follows:

> [EDWARD YOUNG] midshipman, 22 years, 5 feet 8 inches high. Dark complexion and rather a bad look. Dark-brown hair — strong made — has

lost several of his fore teeth, those that remain are all rotten. A small mole on the left side of the throat, and on the right arm is tattooed a heart and dart through it with "E.Y." underneath, and the date of the year 1788 or 1789, we are not sure.

Young's role in the mutiny is a mystery to this day. He does not seem to have been involved in any of the friction on the *Bounty* and he was the only officer who joined Christian. On the night of April 27, 1789, the night before the mutiny, he was on Peckover's watch, from midnight to 4:00 a.m., the watch immediately preceding Christian's. He seems to have been sleeping when the mutiny broke out; most accounts do not mention him as being on deck.

Some authors see Young as the mastermind behind the mutiny. Madge Darby in *Who Caused the Mutiny on the Bounty?* (1965) thinks that the mutiny must have been planned, that there must have been "a cool, clear brain" behind it, that it had to be an officer, and that the officer was Young. However, she does not address herself to the question of what Young would have had to gain from the mutiny. Other authors have suggested that Young may have joined Christian only after the mutiny was an accomplished fact.

On Tubuai, Young voted with Christian and, when the latter made his emotional speech about sailing away alone in the *Bounty* (see the September 1789 commentary in Part I), Young was the one who said: "We shall never leave you, Mr. Christian, go where you will!"

Young was very popular with the Tahitians and — despite the unattractive description given of him by Bligh — was a special favorite with the women.

Young's consort when he arrived at Pitcairn was Teraura, but he had no children with her. On Massacre Day, when five mutineers were killed by the Polynesian men, Young was not attacked. Some accounts claim he was hidden by the women, but it is highly unlikely that he could have been hidden for any length of time. Incredible as it seems, although he may not have masterminded the mutiny on the *Bounty*, there are indications that he may have masterminded, or at least had foreknowledge of, the massacre on Pitcairn (see the September 1793 commentary in Part I).

In his last years, Young kept a journal which has become lost but was seen by Captain Beechey in 1825. Before his death, he taught the almost illiterate Adams to read and write, thus enabling the latter to educate the children to the extent which the early visitors to Pitcairn found so amazing. Young died of asthma (or perhaps tuberculosis) on Christmas Day 1800, the first man on Pitcairn to die a natural death.

With Toofaiti, Young had four children: Nancy, George, Robert and William. With Mauatua, Christian's widow, he had three children: Edward, Polly and Dorothea. His descendants still live on Pitcairn. The last direct fifth-generation male descendant of the mutineers, Andrew Clarence Young, died on March 17, 1988, almost eighty-nine years old. Other Young descendants live on Norfolk Island and in New Zealand.

YOUNG, Elizabeth (née MILLS)   Elizabeth (Betsy) Mills was born in 1791 or 1792, the daughter of mutineer John Mills and Vahineatua. In 1811 she married Matthew Quintal II who died in 1814. In 1823 she married William Young, the son of mutineer Edward Young and Toofaiti; he died in 1839.

All through her life, Betsy remembered and told of the terror she had experienced as a child in witnessing the murder of Matthew Quintal (see PITCAIRN ISLAND).

Betsy survived both migrations, to Tahiti in 1831 and to Norfolk in 1856. She was in the second group of Pitcairners who, in the schooner St. Kilda, returned from Norfolk Island on February 2, 1864.

Betsy lived to be the last survivor of the children of the mutineers. She died on November 6, 1883, at the age of ninety-one or ninety-two.

A
Sample
of
Literature

ON THE *BOUNTY*

AND RELATED SUBJECTS

LITERATURE

Adams, Henry: *Memoirs of Arii Taimai, Marama of Eimeo, Teriirere of Tooarai, Teriinui of Tahiti, Tauraatua i Amo* (Paris, 1901, Privately Printed).

Adams, Henry: *Letters to a Niece* (London, 1920).

Adams, John: Autographed Narrative Given to Captain Beechey in 1825 (Sydney: Mitchell Library).

Aitkin, R.T.: *Ethnology of Tubuai* (Honolulu: *Bernice P. Bishop Museum Bulletin 70,* 1930).

Alexander, J.H.: *The Islands of the Pacific: From the Old to the New* (1908).

Allen, Edward W.: *The Vanishing Frenchman: The Mysterious Disappearance of La Pérouse* (New York 1959).

Allen, Kenneth S.: *"That* Bounty *Bastard": The True Story of Captain William Bligh* (London: Robert Hale, 1976).

Anderson, C.R.: *Melville in the South Seas* (Columbia University, 1939).

Anderson, Isobel W.: Notes on the Heywood Family of Locarbine, Devonshire, Hampshire and the Isle of Man, Collected By Me, 1966–1967 from Victoria County History, Oliver Heywood's Diaries, Foster Lancashire Pedigrees and Burke's Peerage (Sydney: Mitchell Library, 1967).

Anson, George: *A Voyage Round the World in the Years 1740–44* (London, 1748).

Anstead, A.: *Dictionary of Sea Terms* (Glasgow, 1880).

Anthony, Irvin (ed.): *The Saga of the* Bounty*: Its Strange History as Related by the Participants Themselves* (New York: G.P. Putnam's Sons, 1935).

Anthony, Irvin: *Revolt at Sea: A Narration of Many Mutinies* (New York: G.P. Putnam's Sons, 1937).

Armstrong, Warren: *Mutiny Afloat* (1956).

Askew, J.: *Guide to Cockermouth* 2nd edn. (Cockermouth, 1872).

Australiana Society: *Bligh's Narrative of the Mutiny on Board HMS* Bounty . . . (1790); *Minutes of the Court Martial . . . With an Appendix* (1794); *Bligh's Answers to Certain Assertions* (1794); *Edward Christian's Reply* (1795) (Melbourne, 1952; Facsimiles of Original Pamphlets: Limited Edition).

Baarslag, Karl: *Islands of Adventure* (New York, 1940).

Bach, John: *William Bligh* (Melbourne: Oxford University Press, 1967).

439

Ball, Ian M.: *Pitcairn: Children of the* Bounty (Boston: Little, Brown and Company, 1973).

Ballantyne, R. M.: *The Lonely Island or The Refuge of the Mutineers* (London, 1880).

Bancroft, H.H.: *New Pacific* (New York, 1912).

Banks, Joseph: *The* Endeavour *Journal of Joseph Banks* (ed. J.C. Beaglehole; Sydney, 1962).

Barney, S., and Christian, E.: *Minutes of the Proceedings of the Court Martial Held at Portsmouth, August [sic] 12, 1792 on Ten Persons Charged with Mutiny on Board His Majesty's Ship the* Bounty. *With an Appendix, Containing a Full Account of the Real Causes and Circumstances of that Unhappy Transaction, The Most Material of which have Hitherto been Withheld from the Public* (London: Deighton, 1794).

Barrett, Rev. W.R.: *Bligh's Deposition* (History of Tasmania, 1936).

Barrow, Sir John: *The Eventful History of the Mutiny and Piratical Seizure of H.M.S.* Bounty: *Its Cause and Consequences* (London: John Murray, 1831).

Barrow, Sir John: *The Mutiny & Piratical Seizure of H.M.S.* Bounty *with an Introduction by Admiral Sir Cyprian Bridge, G.C.B.* (Oxford: The World's Classics, 1914; reissue of Barrow, 1831).

Barrow, Sir John: *The Mutiny of the* Bounty (London/Glasgow, 1961; reissue of Barrow, 1831).

Barrow, Sir John: *A Description of Pitcairn's Island and its Inhabitants with an Authentic Account of the Mutiny of the Ship* Bounty *and of the Subsequent Fortunes of the Mutineers* (New York: Haskell House Publishers Ltd., 1972; reissue of Barrow, 1831).

Barrow, Sir John: *The Mutiny of the* Bounty (ed. Gavin Kennedy; Boston: David R. Godine, 1980; reissue of Barrow, 1831).

Barrow, Sir John: "Recent Accounts of the Pitcairn Islanders" *(Journal of the Royal Geographical Society*, vol. E, 1833, pp. 156–67, London).

Baston, Abbé G.A.R: *Narrations d'Omai*, 4 vols. (Rouen: 1790).

Barton, G.B.: *A History of New South Wales from the Records* (Sydney, 1880).

Beaglehole, J.C.: *The Exploration of the Pacific* (London, 1934).

Beaglehole, J.C.: *The Journals of Captain James Cook on his Voyages of Discovery*, vol. 1-2-3, Hakluyt Society Extra Series No. 34–35–36. (Cambridge University Press, 1955–61–67).

Beaglehole, J.C. (ed.): *The* Endeavour *Journal of Joseph Banks 1768–1771*, 2 vols. (Sydney: Angus and Robertson, 1963).

Beaglehole, J.C.: *Captain Cook and Captain Bligh . . .* (Wellington, 1967).

Beaglehole, J.C.: *The Life of Captain James Cook* (London: Adam & Charles Black, 1974).

Beard, William: *"Valiant Martinet" or The Adventures on Sea and Land of Captain William Bligh* (Sydney, 1956).

Beatson, R.: *Naval and Military Memoirs of Great Britain*, 6 vols. (London, 1804).

Bechervaise, Edward: "The Mutiny of the *Bounty* — Lieut. Bligh's Voyage in the Ship's Boat to Timor" (*Victorian Geographical Journal*, vol. 28, pp. 78–87, 1910–11, Melbourne).

Bechervaise, John: *Thirty-Six Years of a Seafaring Life, by an Old Quarter Master* (Portsea, 1839).

Becke, Louis, and Jeffery, Walter: *A First Fleet Family: Based on the Story of the Escaped Convict Bryant and his Wife* (London, 1896).

Becke, Louis, and Jeffery, Walter: *The Mutineer: A Romance of Pitcairn Island* (London: T. Fisher Unwin, 1898).

Becke, Louis, and Jeffery, Walter: *Bligh and the Mutiny on the* Bounty (London, 1899).

Becke, Louis, and Jeffery, Walter: *The Naval Pioneers of Australia* (London, 1899).

Beechey, F.W.: *Narrative of a Voyage to the Pacific and Beering's Strait in His Majesty's Ship* Blossom . . . *in the Years 1825* . . . (London: Henry Colburn & Richard Bentley, 1831).

Behrman, Cynthia Fansler: *Victorian Myths of the Sea* (Ohio University Press, 1977).

Belcher, Lady Diana: *The Mutineers of the* Bounty *and Their Descendants in Pitcairn and Norfolk Islands* (London: John Murray, 1870).

Belcher, Sir Edward: *Narrative of the Voyage of H.M.S.* Samarang, *During the Years 1843–46: Employed Surveying the Islands of the Eastern Archipelago: Accompanied by a Brief Vocabulary of the Principal Languages*, 2 vols. (London, 1848).

Bellingshausen, Thaddeus von: *Voyage to the Antarctic Seas*, 2 vols. (London, 1945).

Bennett, Frederick Debell: "Pitcairn" (in *A Narrative of a Whaling Voyage Round the Globe*, 2 vols., London, 1840).

Benton, Edward Pelham: *The Naval History of Great Britain from the Year 1783 to 1836*, 2 vols. (London, 1937).

Bladen, F.M.: "The Deposition of Governor Bligh" (*Royal Australian Historical Society Journal and Proceedings*, vol. 1, June 1908, pp. 192–200).

Bligh, W.: Letters to Sir Joseph Banks, 30 October 1793 & 16 September 1796 (Sydney: Mitchell Library).

Bligh, W.: Letters to Francis Godolphin Bond, 26 July 1794 & 14 August 1794 (Greenwich: National Maritime Museum).

Bligh, W.: *A Narrative of the Mutiny on Board His Majesty's Ship* Bounty; *and the Subsequent Voyage of Part of the Crew, in the Ship's Boat, from Tofoa, one of the Friendly Islands, to Timor, a Dutch Settlement in the East Indies* (London: George Nicol, 1790; republished at the Sign of the Unicorn, 1901).

Bligh, W., and Burney, J.: *A Voyage to the South Sea, Undertaken by Command of His Majesty for the Purpose of Conveying the Bread-Fruit Tree to the West Indies, in His Majesty's Ship the* Bounty *Commanded by Lieutenant William Bligh. Including an Account of the Mutiny on Board the Said Ship, and the Subsequent Voyage of Part of the Crew in the*

Ship's Boat, from Tofoa, one of the Friendly Islands to Timor, a Dutch Settlement in the East Indies, with Seven Charts, Diagram and a Portrait (London: George Nicol, 1792; republished New York, 1965 as *The Mutiny on the* Bounty).

Bligh, William: *Bligh's Voyage in the* Resource *from Coupang to Batavia, Together with the Log of his Subsequent Passage to England in the Dutch Packet* 'Vlydte' *and his Remarks on Morrison's Journal* (All Printed for the First Time from the Manuscripts in the Mitchell Library of New South Wales, with an Introduction and Notes by Owen Rutter, & Engravings on Wood by Peter Barker-Hill, London: Golden Cockerel Press, 1937, Limited Edition).

Bligh, William: *An Answer to Certain Assertions Contained in the Appendix to a Pamphlet, Entitled Minutes of the Proceedings on the Court-Martial Held at Portsmouth, August [sic] 12th, 1792, on Ten Persons Charged with Mutiny on Board his Majesty's Ship the* Bounty (London, 1794).

Bligh, William: "Remarks on Morrison's Journal" (Manuscript, Sydney: Mitchell Library).

Bligh, William: "Miscellaneous Letters" (in *Historical Records of New South Wales*, vols. 6 and 7 Sydney, 1898–1901).

Bligh, Capt. W.: *The Log of H.M.S.* Providence (Facsimile, London, 1976).

Bolton, W.W.: "An Impudent Fraud: How 'Lord' Hill Governed Pitcairn Is." (*Pacific Islands Monthly*, December 1936, pp. 37–38).

Bolton, W.W.: "A Link with the *Bounty*" (*Pacific Islands Monthly*, April 1945, pp. 25–28).

Bond, F.G.: Letter Fragment to Thomas Bond, December 1792, & Notes Relating to Michael Byrne (of the *Bounty*) (Greenwich: National Maritime Museum).

Bonner, Smith, D.: "Some Remarks About the Mutiny of the *Bounty*" (*Mariner's Mirror*, London, April 1936).

Bonner Smith, D.: "More Light on Bligh and the *Bounty*" (*Mariner's Mirror*, London, April 1937).

Boswell, James: *Life of Dr. Samuel Johnson* (ed. G.B. Hill; Oxford, 1934).

Bougainville, Louis Antoine de: *A Voyage Round the World* (English translation by John Reinhold Forster; London, 1772).

Bowden, Keith MacRae: *George Bass* (Melbourne, 1952).

Brault, M.: "La Reine Pomaré, 1822–1877" (*Les Contemporains* No. 202, 1896).

Brenton, E.P.: *The Naval History of Great Britain*. 2 vols. (London, 1837).

Brewster, A.B.: *The Hill Tribes of Fiji* (London, 1922).

Briand, Jr., Paul L.: *In Search of Paradise: The Nordhoff-Hall Story* (Duell, 1966).

Bricaire de La Dixième: Le Sauvage de Taiti aux Français (Paris, 1770).

The British Consulate-General: *A Guide to Pitcairn* (Published for the Government of the Islands of Pitcairn, Auckland, 1982).

LITERATURE

Brodie, Walter: *Pitcairn's Island and the Islanders in 1850* (London: Whittaker & Co., 1851).

Brooke, Rupert: *Collected Poems* (New York, 1948).

Brosses, Charles de: *Histoire des Navigations aux Terres Australes*, 2 vols (Paris, 1756).

Broughton, William Robert: *A Voyage of Discovery* (London, 1804).

Brown, J.M.: *Peoples and Problems of the Pacific*, vol. 1 (1927).

Bryant, Rev. J.: "A Lonely Isle and a Curious People" [Pitcairn Island], (*The Scottish Geographical Magazine*, vol. 30, no. 2, February 1914).

Buck, Sir Peter H. (Te Rangi Hiroa): "The Feather Cloak of Tahiti" (*Journal of the Polynesian Society*, 52, 1943).

Buck, Sir Peter H. (Te Rangi Hiroa): *Explorers of the Pacific* (Honolulu: Bernice P. Bishop Museum, 1953).

Buck, Sir Peter H. (Te Rangi Hiroa): *Vikings of the Sunrise* (Christchurch, 1954).

Buffett, John: "A Narrative of Twenty Years' Residence on Pitcairn's Island" (*The Friend* vol. 4, Honolulu, 1845–6).

Bullocke, J.G.: "Mutiny of the *Bounty* . . . 1789" (in *Sailors' Rebellion: A Century of Naval Mutinies*, London: Eyre & Spottiswoode, 1938).

Burrows, M.: *Pitcairn's Island* (London, 1853).

Byron, Lord: *The Island; or Christian and His Comrades. A Poem; Based Partly on the Account of the Mutiny of the Bounty, and Partly on Mariner's Account on the Tonga Islands. With appropriate Extracts from the Voyage, by Capt. Bligh.* (London, 1823).

Caillot, A.C.E.: *Les Polynesiens Orientaux au Contact de la Civilization* (Paris: Ernest Leroux, 1909).

Caillot, A.C.E.: *Histoire de la Polynésie Oriental* (Paris: Ernest Leroux, 1910).

Calderon, George: *Tahiti by 'Tihoti'* (London, 1921).

Callender, Geoffrey: "The Portraiture of Bligh" (*Mariner's Mirror*, vol. 22, no. 2, April 1936).

Cameron, Hector Charles: *Sir Joseph Banks* (London, 1952).

Cameron, Ian: *Lost Paradise* (Topsfield, Massachusetts: Salem House Publishers, 1987).

Campbell, Gordon: *Captain James Cook R.N., F.R.S.* (London, 1936).

Campbell, J.: *Lives of the British Admirals*, 8 vols. (London, 1817).

Campbell, J.: *Maritime Discovery and Christian Missions* (London, 1840).

Campbell, J.: *Norfolk Island and its Inhabitants* (1870).

Carteret, Philip: "An Account of a Voyage Round the World" (in *Hawkesworth's Voyages*, London, 1773).

Carteret, Philip: "Passage from Masasuero to Queen Charlotte's Islands, 1767" (in *Hawkesworth's Voyages* vol. 2, 1823).

Casey, Robert J.: "Pitcairn: The Breed of the Bounty Mutineers" (in *Easter Island: Home of the Scornful Gods*, London, 1932).

Cater, Harold Dean: *Henry Adams and his Friends* (Boston, 1947).

Chamier, Frederick: *Jack Adams, The Mutineer*, 3 vols. (London, 1838).

Chandler, J.E.: *Beloved, Respected and Lamented: A Story of the Mutiny of the* Bounty (Marlborough: The Author, 1973).

Chauvel, Charles: *In the Wake of the* Bounty *to Tahiti and Pitcairn Island* (Sydney: The Endeavour Press, 1933).

Chomley, C.H.: *A Successful Rebellion; Tales of Old Times* (Melbourne, 1903).

Christian, Ada M.: "Early Ships at Pitcairn Island" (*Pacific Islands Monthly*, October 1940, p. 30).

Christian, Edward: "An Appendix Containing a Full Account of the Real Causes and Circumstances of the Unhappy Transaction the Most Material of Which have been hitherto Withheld from the Public" (in Stephen Barney, *Minutes of the Proceedings*, London, 1794).

Christian, Edward: *A Short Reply to Captain William Bligh's Answer* (London: J. Deighton, 1795; also in *Australiana Facsimiles*, vol. 2, Australiana Society, 1952).

"Christian Fletcher" (?): *Letters from Mr. Fletcher Christian, Containing a Narrative of the Transactions on Board His Majesty's Ship* Bounty, *Before and After the Mutiny, With His Subsequent Voyages and Travels in South America* (London, 1796).

"Christian, Fletcher" (?): *Voyages and Travels of Fletcher Christian and a Narrative of the Mutiny on Board H.M.S.* Bounty *at Otaheite, With a Succinct Account of the Proceedings of the Mutineers, With a Description of the Manners, Customs . . . and Every Interesting Particular Relating to the Society Islands* (London, 1798).

Christian Glynn: *Fragile Paradise: The Discovery of Fletcher Christian*, Bounty *Mutineer* (Boston: Little, Brown and Company, 1982).

Clark, Roy P.: "How *Bounty*'s Rudder was Found" (*Pacific Islands Monthly*, April 1934, p. 5).

Clark, Thomas Blake: *Omai, First Polynesian Ambassador to England* (San Francisco, 1940).

Clarke, J.S., and Macarthur, J.: *Life of Admiral Lord Nelson*, 2 vols. (London, 1809).

Clarke, Marcus: *The Rum Rebellion* (Sydney: Angus & Robertson).

Clarke, Peter: *Hell and Paradise: The Norfolk–Bounty–Pitcairn Saga* (New York: Viking, 1986).

Claver, Scott: *Under the Lash* (London: Torchstream Books, 1954).

Clowes, Sir William Laird: *The Royal Navy: A History from the Earliest Times to the Present*, 7 vols (London, 1877–1903).

Clune, Frank: *A Tale of Tahiti* (Sydney: Angus & Robertson, 1958).

Clune, Frank: *Journey to Pitcairn* (Sydney: Angus & Robertson, 1966).

Clune, Frank: *The Norfolk Island Story* (Sydney: Angus & Robertson, 1967).

Collins, D.: *An Account of the English Colony in New South Wales,* 2 vols. (London, 1798–1802).

Connecticut Historical Society: "The 'Bounty' Bible" (*Conn. Hist. Soc. Bulletin,* vol. 19, no. 2, May 1959).

Conrad, Barnaby: "What Happened to Mister Christian of H.M.S. *Bounty?*" (*Smithsonian,* February 1988).

Conrad, Joseph: "Geography and Some Explorers" (Washington: *National Geographic Magazine,* March 1924).

Cook, James: *A Voyage to the Pacific Ocean Undertaken by the Command of His Majesty, for Making Discoveries in the Northern Hemisphere, to Determine the Position and Extent of the West Side of North America, Its Distance from Asia, and the Practicability of a Northern Passage to Europe, Performed under the Direction of Captains Cook, Clerke and Gore, in His Majesty's Ships the* Resolution *and* Discovery, *in the Years 1776, 1777, 1778, 1779 and 1780,* vol. 2, book 3 (London: G. Nichol and T. Cadell, 1784).

Cooper, Gordon: *Isles of Romance and Mystery* (1949).

Copplestone, B.: *The Boat Voyage of* Bounty *Bligh* (Oxford, 1925).

Corney, Bolton G. (ed.): *The Quest and Occupation of Tahiti by Emissaries of Spain During the Years 1772–6,* 3 vols. (London: Hakluyt Society, Works, 1913–19).

Couper, J.M.: *The Book of Bligh* (Melbourne, 1969).

Covit, Bernard: *Official Directory and Guide Book for Tahiti* (San Francisco, Latest Edition).

Craig, Robert D., and King, Frank P. (eds.): *Historical Dictionary of Oceania* (Westport, Connecticut: Greenwood Press, 1981).

Cumming, C.F. Gordon: *A Lady's Cruise Aboard a French Man of War* (London, 1882).

Cunningham, C.: *A Narrative of Occurrences that Took Place During the Mutiny at the Nore* . . . (Chatham, 1829).

Currey, C.H.: "An Outline of the Story of Norfolk Island and Pitcairn's Island 1788–1857" (*Royal Australian Historical Society Journal and Proceedings,* vol. 44, part 8, 1958).

Currey, C.H.: *The Transportation, Escape and Pardoning of Mary Bryant (née Broad)* (Sydney: Angus & Robertson, 1963).

Dakin, W.J.: *Whalemen Adventurers* (Sydney: Angus & Robertson, 1934).

Dampier, William: *Collection of Voyages,* 4 vols. (London, 1729).

Danielsson, Bengt: *Love in the South Seas* (London: George Allen and Unwin, 1956).

Danielsson, Bengt (& Rolf E. Du Rietz): *What Happened on the* Bounty? (London: George Allen and Unwin, 1962).

Danielsson, Marie-Thérèse and Bengt: "Bligh's Cave: 196 Years On" (*Pacific Islands Monthly,* June 1985).

Darby, Madge: *Who Caused the Mutiny on the* Bounty? (Sydney: Angus & Robertson, 1965).

LITERATURE

Darby, Madge: *The Causes of the* Bounty *Mutiny: A Short Reply to Mr. Rolf Du Rietz's Comments (Studia Bountyana,* vol. 2, Uppsala: Dahlia Books, 1966).

D'Auvergne, E.B.: *Pierre Loti* (London, 1926).

David, Andrew C.F.: *The Surveyors of the* Bounty: *A Preliminary Study of the Hydrographic Surveys of William Bligh, Thomas Hayward and Peter Heywood and the Charts Published from them* (Taunton, 1976).

David, Andrew C.F: "Broughton's Schooner and the *Bounty* Mutineers" (*Mariner's Mirror,* vol. 63, 1977, pp. 207–13).

David, Andrew C.F.: "The Surveys of William Bligh" (*Mariner's Mirror,* vol. 63, no. 1, February 1977, pp. 69–70).

Davis, Louise: "The Wintry Ordeal and the Tropical Trial" (*The Tennessean,* Sunday, September 5, 1976).

Daws, Gavan: "Kealakekua Bay Re-Visited" (*Journal of Pacific History,* 1968, vol. 13, pp. 21–3).

Dawson, W.R. (ed.): *The Banks Letters: A Calendar of the Manuscript Correspondence of Sir Joseph Banks Preserved in the British Museum, and Other Collections in Great Britain* (London, 1958).

Day, A. Grove: *Rogues of the South Seas* (Honolulu: Mutual Publishing Co., 1986).

Day, A. Grove: *Mad About Islands* (Honolulu: Mutual Publishing Co., 1987).

Day, A. Grove (ed.): *The Lure of Tahiti* (Honolulu: Pacific Trade Group, 1988).

DeBovis, Edmond: *Etat de la Société Tahitienne à l'arrivée des Européens* (Papeete, 1909).

DeKerchove, Rene: *International Maritime Dictionary* (Princeton, N.J.: Van Nostrand, 1961).

Delano, Amasa: *A Narrative of Voyages and Travels, in the Northern and Southern Hemispheres: Comprising Three Voyages Round the World; Together with a Voyage of Survey and Discovery, in the Pacific Ocean and Oriental Islands* (Boston: Amasa Delano, 1817).

Delano, Amasa: *Pitcairn's Island* (1819).

Delessert, E.: *Voyages Dans les Deux Océans* (Paris, 1848).

Dening, G.M.: "The Geographical Knowledge of the Polynesians and the Nature of Inter-Island Contact" (in *Polynesian Navigation* edited by Jack Golson, Supplement to the *Journal of the Polynesian Society* 71 pp. 102–53, 1962).

Department of Territories (Australia): *Norfolk Island Centenary Celebrations 1856–1956.*

Dick, W.H.: *Mutiny of the* Bounty (1882).

Diderot, Denis: *Supplément au Voyage de Bougainville* (ed. G. Chinard, Baltimore, 1935).

Dillon, Peter: *Narrative and Successful Result of a Voyage in the South Seas, Performed by Order of the Government of British India, to Ascertain the Actual Fate of La Pérouse's Expedition, Interspersed with Accounts of the Religion, Manners, Customs and Cannibal Practices of the South Seas Islanders. By the Chevalier Capt. P. Dillon,* 2 vols. (London, 1829).

Dillon, Peter (ed.): "Pitcairn's Island — The *Bounty's* Crew" (*United Services Journal*, February 1829).

Dillon, Peter: "Captain Dillon's Story of Jenny Martin" (*United Services Journal*, November 1829).

Dodd, Edward: *The Rape of Tahiti* (New York: Dodd, Mead & Company, 1983).

Dorling, H.T.: "The Mutiny of the *Bounty* by 'Taffrail'" (*Chambers's Journal*, November 1928).

Drollet, Alexandre: "Légende du Marae de Arahurahu" (*Bulletin de la Société d'Etudes Océaniennes* 9, pp. 336–345).

Dugan, James: *The Great Mutiny* (New York: G.P. Putnam's Sons, 1965).

Duncan, Archibald: "Narrative of the Loss of the *Bounty* through a Conspiracy" (*The Mariner's Chronicle*; vol. 4, pp. 21–35, 1811) and "Narrative of the Total Loss of his Majesty's Ship the *Bounty*, including the Transactions of the Mutineers, After they Gained Possession of the Vessel. Extracted from the Letters of Lieutenant Christian" (pp. 49–62). Also "Loss of the *Pandora* Frigate", (vol. 5, pp. 271–3).

DuPetit-Thouars, Abel Aubert: *Voyage Autour du Monde sur la Fregate* la Venus, 4 vols (Paris, 1840–5).

Du Rietz, Rolf E.: "William Bligh" (*Finsk Tidskrift* No. 6, 1955).

Du Rietz, Rolf E.: "Three Letters from James Burney to Sir Joseph Banks, A Contribution to the History of William Bligh's 'A Voyage to the South Sea'" (*Ethnos*, Stockholm, 1962).

Du Rietz, Rolf E.: "The Voyage of H.M.S. *Pandora*, 1790–1792: Some Remarks upon Geoffrey Rawson's Book on the Subject" (*Ethnos* vols. 2–4, Stockholm, 1963).

Du Rietz, Rolf E.: *The Causes of the* Bounty *Mutiny. Some Comments on a book by Madge Darby (in Studia Bountyana*, vol. 1, Uppsala: Dahlia Books, 1979).

Du Rietz, Rolf E.: *Thoughts on the present state of Bligh Scholarship* (*Banksia*, vol. 1, Uppsala: Dahlia Books, 1979).

Du Rietz, Rolf E.: *Fresh light on John Fryer of the* Bounty (*Banksia*, vol. 2, Uppsala: Dahlia Books, 1981).

Du Rietz, Rolf E.: *Peter Heywood's Tahitian Vocabulary and the Narratives by James Morrison: Some Notes on Their Origin and History* (*Banksia* vol. 3, Uppsala: Dahlia Books, 1986).

Dyall, Valentine: *A Flood of Mutiny* (London, 1957).

Edmonds, I.G.: *The* Bounty's *Boy* (London, 1964).

Edwards, Edward, and Hamilton, George: *Voyage of* H.M.S. Pandora, *Dispatched to Arrest the Mutineers of the* Bounty *in the South Seas, 1790–91, Being the Narratives of Captain Edward Edwards R.N., the Commander, and George Hamilton, the Surgeon; With Introduction and Notes by Sir Basil Thomson* (London: Francis Edwards, 1915).

Elder, John Rawson (ed.): *The Letters and Journals of Samuel Marsden, 1765–1838* (Dunedin, 1932).

Ellis, M.H.: *John Macarthur* (Sydney: Angus & Robertson, 1955).

Ellis, M.H.: "The Mutiny on the *Bounty*: Bligh Whitewashed Again" (Sydney: *The Bulletin*, 16 February, 1963).

Ellis, William: *An Authentic Narrative of a Voyage Performed by Captain Cook and Captain Clerke, in His Majesty's Ships* Resolution and Discovery, *during the Years 1776, 1777, 1778, 1779, and 1780, in Search of a North-West Passage between the Continents of Asia and America, Including a Faithful Account of All Their Discoveries, and the Unfortunate Death of Captain Cook*, 2 vols. (London: G. Robinson, J. Sewell, and J. Debrett, 1782).

Ellis, William: *Polynesian Researches*, 4 vols. 2nd edn. (London: Fisher, Son and Jackson, 1829).

Ellis, William: *The History of the London Missionary Society, Comprising an Account of the Origin of the Society, Biographical Notices of Some of its Founders and Missionaries; with a Record of Its Progress at Home and its Operations Abroad. Compiled from Original Documents in the Possession of the Society*, vol. 1 (London: John Snow, 1844).

Ellison, Joseph W.: *Tusitala of the South Seas* (New York, 1953).

Emory, Kenneth P.: "Traditional History of Maraes in the Society Islands" (Honolulu: unpublished manuscript in the Bernice P. Bishop Museum, N.D.).

Eskridge, R.L.: *Mangareva, The Forgotten Island* (Indianapolis, 1931).

Evatt, H.V.: *Rum Rebellion: A Study of the Overthrow of Governor Bligh by John Macarthur and the New South Wales Corps* (Sydney: Angus & Robertson, 1965).

Ferdon, Edwin N. Jr.: "Pitcairn Island, 1956" (*Geographical Review*, vol. 48, January 1958).

Ferdon, Edwin N. Jr.: *Early Tahiti: As the Explorers Saw It 1767–1797* (Tucson: University of Arizona Press, 1981).

Ferguson, J.A.: *Bibliography of Australia*, 3 vols. (Sydney: Angus & Robertson, 1963, 1965, 1969).

Ferris, N.A.: *The Story of Pitcairn's Island* (Washington, 1957).

Findlay, A.G.: *A Directory for the Navigation of the Pacific Ocean* (London, 1851).

Finney, Ben R.: "Notes on Bond-Friendship in Tahiti" (*Journal of the Polynesian Society* 1964, vol. 73, no. 4, pp. 431-5).

Finney, Ben R.: *Hokule'a: The Way to Tahiti* (New York: Dodd, Mead & Company, 1979).

Fletcher, William: *Fletcher Christian and the Mutineers of the* Bounty (Carlisle: Transactions of the Cumberland Association for the Advancement of Literature and Science, part 2, 1876-7).

Flinders, M.: *A Voyage to Terra Australis*, 2 vols. (London, 1814).

LITERATURE

Folger, Mayhew: "Log of the Topaz 1807–9" (Manuscript, Nantucket: The Whaling Museum).

Folger, Mayhew: "Letter to Admiralty, London, from Nantucket, 1 March 1813" (in *Quarterly Review*, April 1815; also in *Annual Register* 1818; and *The Naval Chronicle*, January 1816).

Folger, Mayhew: "Letter to Amasa Delano" (*Quarterly Review of Science and Arts*, vol. 1, 1819).

Ford, Herbert: *Pitcairn* (La Crescenta, California: An Anchor Title, 1972).

Ford, Herbert: *The Miscellany of Pitcairn's Island* (Mountain View, California: Pacific Press Publishing Association, 1980).

Forster, Georg Adam: *A Voyage Round the World in His Britannic Majesty's Sloop, Resolution, Commanded by Captain James Cook, During the Years 1772, 3, 4 and 5*, 2 vols (London: B. White, J. Robson, P. Elmsly and G. Robinson).

Forster, Johann Reinhold: *Observations made During a Voyage Round the World on Physical Geography, Natural History and Ethic Philosophy*, part 6: "The Human Species" (London: G. Robinson, 1778).

Fox, U.: "*Bounty*'s Launch" (in *Sailing, Seamanship and Yacht Construction*, book 2, pp. 137–9, London, 1935).

Francis, B.: *Isles of the Pacific* (1882).

Fryer, John: *Narrative* (Facsimile, London, 1979).

Fryer, Mary Ann: *John Fryer of the* Bounty: *Notes on His Career Written by his Daughter Mary Ann. With an Introduction and Commentary by Owen Rutter and Wood-Engravings by Averil Mackenzie-Grieve* (London: Golden Cockerel Press, 1939).

Fullerton, W.Y.: *The Romance of Pitcairn Island* (London: The Carey Press, 1923).

Furnas, J.C.: *Anatomy of Paradise* (New York: William Sloane Associates, Inc., 1948).

Gaffarel, P.: *L'Affaire Pritchard* (Société Bourguignonne de Géographie et D' Histoire, 1912).

Garanger, J.: *Sacred Stones and Rites of Ancient Tahiti* (Paris: Société des Océanistes, Dossier 2, 1969).

Gauguin, Paul: *Letters to Georges Daniel DeMonfried* (London, 1923).

Gauguin, Paul: *Letters to his Wife and Friends* (Cleveland/New York, 1949).

Gauguin, Paul: *Noa Noa* (New York, 1920).

Gazzard, Albert: *The* Bounty *and After* (1943).

Gessler, C.: *The Leaning Wind* (1943).

Gill, Conrad: *The Naval Mutinies of 1797* (Manchester: Manchester University Press, 1913).

Gill, Wyatt: "Extracts from Dr. Wyatt Gill's Papers, No. 13. The Coming of Goodenough's Ship to Rarotonga in 1820" (*Journal of The Polynesian Society*, 20, 1911).

Goddard, R.H.: "Captain Thomas Raine of the *Surry*" (*Royal Australian Historical Society Journal*, vol. 26, part 4, 1940).

Godwin, George: *Vancouver: A Life, 1757–1798* (London, 1930).

Goldhurst, William: "Martinet or Martyr" (New York, *Horizon*, vol. 5, no. 7, September 1963, pp. 42–8).

Goldman, Irving: "The Evolution of Polynesian Societies" (in *Culture in History*, Stanley Diamond (ed.), New York: Columbia University Press, 1960).

Goldman, Irving: *Ancient Polynesian Society* (Chicago: The University of Chicago Press, 1970).

Good, T.C.: "The *Pandora* and the *Bounty*" (*The Journal for AutoCAD Users*, vol. 3, no. 2, 1986).

Gosset, R.W.G.: "Notes on the Discovery of Rarotonga" (*The Australian Geographer*, 3, 1940).

Gould, R.T. (ed.): "Bligh's Notes on Cook's Last Voyage" (*Mariner's Mirror*, vol. 14, no. 4, October 1928).

Gould, R.T.: *Captain Cook* (London, 1935 and 1978).

Gravelle, Kim: "Bligh's Cave Revisited" (*Pacific Islands Monthly*, September 1985).

Greatheed, S.: "Authentic History of the Mutineers of the *Bounty*" (*The Sailor's Magazine and Naval Miscellany*, vols. 1–2, 1820, London).

Griffin, J.: *Memoirs of Captain James Wilson* (London, 1930).

Gunson, Niel: "Great Women and Friendship Contract Rites in pre-Christian Tahiti" (*Journal of the Polynesian Society* vol. 73, pp. 53–69).

Gwyther, J.: *Captain Cook and the South Pacific* (Cambridge, U.S.A., 1955).

Hale, E.E.: *Stories of the Sea* (1880).

Hall, James Norman: *Shipwreck: An Account of a Voyage in the Track of the* Bounty *from Tahiti to Pitcairn Island in 1933* (London, 1935).

Hall, James Norman: *My Island Home* (Boston: Little, Brown and Co., 1952).

Hamilton, George: *A Voyage Round the World in His Majesty's Frigate* Pandora, *Performed Under the Direction of Captain Edwards in the Years 1790, 1791, and 1792; With Discoveries Made in the South Sea and . . . A Voyage of Eleven Hundred Miles in Open Boats, Between Endeavour Straits and The Island of Timor* (Berwick, 1793).

Hamond, Captain: "Account of the Proceedings of the *Bounty* Court Martial" (*Gentleman's Magazine*, December 1792).

Hancock, W.K.: *Politics in Pitcairn* (London, 1947).

Hannay, David: *Some Naval Mutinies* (London, 1900).

Hannay, David: *Naval Courts Martial* (Cambridge: Cambridge University Press, 1914).

Hanson, Lawrence and Elizabeth: *The Noble Savage* (London, 1954).

Hattersley, Roy: *Nelson* (London, 1974).

Harding, George L., and Kroepelien, B.: *The Tahitian Imprints of the London Missionary Society* (Oslo, 1950).

Hassall, C.: *Rupert Brooke* (London, 1964).

Haweis, Thomas: *A Missionary Voyage to the Southern Pacific Ocean Performed in the Years 1796, 1797, 1798, in the Ship Duff, Commanded by Captain James Wilson* (London: T. Chapman, 1799).

Hawkesworth, John: *An Account of the Voyages Undertaken by Order of His Present Majesty for Making Discoveries in the Southern Hemisphere, and Successfully Performed by Commodore Byron, Captain Wallis, Captain Carteret and Captain Cook. In the* Dolphin, *the* Swallow, *and the* Endeavour: *Drawn up from the Journals which were kept by the Several Commanders. And from the Papers of Joseph Banks, Esq,* 3 vols. (London, 1773).

Hawkey, Arthur: *Bligh's Other Mutiny* (London, 1975).

Hay, R.G.: "One Aspect of the Deposition of Governor Bligh" (*Journal and Proceedings of the Parramatta and District Historical Society*, 1935, vol. 4).

Henderson, G.C.: *The Discoverers of the Fiji Islands: Tasman, Cook, Bligh, Wilson, Bellingshausen* (London, 1933).

Henry, Teuira: "The Oldest Great Tahitian Maraes and the Last One Built in Tahiti" (*Journal of the Polynesian Society*, vol. 21, 1913, pp. 77-8).

Henry, Teuira: *Ancient Tahiti* (Honolulu: *Bernice P. Bishop Museum Bulletin 48*, 1928).

Herbert, David: *Great Historical Mutinies, Comprising the Story of the Mutiny of the Bounty, the Mutiny at Spithead, the Mutiny at the Nore, Mutinies in Highland Regiments and the Indian Mutiny* (London/Edinburgh, 1876).

Heyerdahl, Thor: *American Indians in the Pacific* (London, 1952).

Heywood, P.: Manuscript, *Transcript of a Selection of Heywood Family Papers Relating to the* Bounty (Chicago: Newberry Library).

Hill, Joshua: "Memorandum 1841" (Dixon Library).

Hirn, Yrjö: Ön I Världshavet (Helsingfors, 1928).

Hoare, Merval: *Norfolk Island. An Outline of its History 1774-1981* (1982).

Home, Rev. C.S.: *The Story of the London Missionary Society 1795-1895* (London, 1894).

Hort, Dora: *Tahiti, The Garden of the Pacific* (London, 1891).

Hough, Richard: *Captain Bligh and Mr. Christian* (Hutchinson & Co. Ltd, 1972).

Hough, Richard: *A History of Fighting Ships* (Octopus Books, 1975).

Houston, Neil B.: "Fletcher Christian and the Rhyme of the Ancient Mariner" (*The Dalhousie Review*, Winter 1965-6, vol. 45, no. 55, pp. 431-46).

Houston, Neil B.: "The Mutiny on the *Bounty*: An Historical and Literary Bibliography" (*Bulletin of Bibliography and Magazine Notes*, April–June 1969, vol. 26, no. 2, pp. 37–41, Westwood, Mass.).

Howard, Ed: "Pitcairn and Norfolk — The Saga of *Bounty*'s Children" (*National Geographic Magazine*, October 1983).

Howarth, David: *Tahiti: A Paradise Lost* (New York: Viking Penguin, 1983).

Howay, F.W.: "Some Lengthy Open-Boat Voyages in the Pacific Ocean" (*American Neptune*, January 1944, pp. 53–7, Salem, Mass.).

Howe, F.H.: *Life and Death on the Ocean* (Cincinnati, Ohio, 1865).

Howell, Rev. W.: *Original Autograph MS Sermon Preached on the Sunday After the Execution of Three Mutineers on the Text: Hebrew 13v. 17. 16 pp. 4to.* (Portsmouth, 1792).

Hughes, E.A. (ed.): *Bligh of the* Bounty: *Being the Narrative of the Mutiny of the* Bounty *and the Voyage in the Open Boat* (London, 1928).

Hughes, Edward: *North Country Life in the 18th Century*, 2 vols (Oxford, 1965).

Humble, Richard: *Captain Bligh* (London: Arthur Barker Ltd., 1976).

Hurd, E.T.: *The Wreck of the* Wild Wave (1942).

Jackson, G.G.: *Romance of Exploration* (1930).

Jacolliot, L.: *La Vérité sur Tahiti* (Paris, 1869).

Jarman, Robert: *Journal of a Voyage to the South Seas in the* Japan (London, 1838).

"Jenny": "First Narrative" (*Sydney Gazette*, 17 July, 1819); "Second Narrative" (*Bengal Hurkaru*, 2 October 1816; *United Services Journal*, November 1829, part 2, pp. 589–93).

Johnson, Irving & Electa: *Westward Bound in the Schooner* Yankee (New York: W.W. Norton, 1936).

Johnson, Irving & Electa: *Sailing to See* (New York: W.W. Norton, 1939).

Johnson, Irving & Electa: *The* Yankee's *Wander-World* (New York: W.W. Norton, 1949).

Johnson, Irving & Electa: "The *Yankee's* Wander-World" (*National Geographic Magazine*, January 1949, pp. 1–50).

Johnson, Irving & Electa, and Edes, Lydia: Yankee's *People and Places* (New York: W.W. Norton, 1956).

Jore, L.: *Essai de Bibliographie du Pacifique* (Paris, 1931).

Jore, L.: *George Pritchard, L'Adversaire de la France* (Paris, 1940).

Jose, Arthur W.: *History of Australia from the Earliest Times to the Present Day* (Sydney: Angus & Robertson, 1924).

Jourdain, Commandant P.: *Ancient Tahitian Canoes* (Société des Océanistes, Dossier 4, 1970, Paris).

Källgard, Anders: *Myteristernas Ättlingar* (Arboga, Sweden: Textab förlag, 1986).

Keable, Robert: *Tahiti: Isle of Dreams* (London. N.D.).

LITERATURE

Kemp, Peter (ed.): *History of the Royal Navy* (London, 1969).

Kemp, Peter: *The Oxford Companion to Ships and the Sea* (Oxford University Press, 1976).

Kemp, Peter (ed.): *Encyclopaedia of Ships and Seafaring* (New York: Crown Publishers, Inc.. 1980).

Kennedy, Gavin: *Bligh* (London: Gerald Duckworth & Co. Ltd., 1978).

Kennedy, Gavin: *The Death of Captain Cook* (London, 1978).

Kennedy, Gavin (ed.): *Sir John Barrow, The Mutiny of the* Bounty (Boston: David R. Godine, 1980).

Kennedy, Ludovic: *Nelson's Captains* (Norton Co., 1951).

Kennedy, Sir William: *Hurrah for the Life of a Sailor!* (Edinburgh: Blackwood, 1900).

Kent, W.G.C., R.N.: *Courtmartial on Charges Exhibited Against Him, by Captain William Bligh, R.N.* (Portsmouth, 1811).

Kerr, R.: *General History and Collection of Voyages and Travels*, 18 vols. (Edinburgh: William Blackwood, 1811–24).

King, Agnes Gardner: *Islands Far Away* (London, 1920).

King, Henry: "Extract from the Journal of Captain Henry King of the *Elizabeth*" [Visit to Pitcairn Island] (*Edinburgh Philosophical Journal*, 1820, vol. 3, no. 6, article 22, pp. 380–8).

King, Jonathan: *Australia's First Fleet: The Voyage and the Re-Enactment 1788/1988* (Sydney: Fairfax-Robertsbridge, 1988).

Kinnane, Janet: "People of Pitcairn" (*Oceans*, September 1983).

Kippis, Andrew: *A Narrative of the Voyages Round the World, Performed by Captain James Cook. With an Account of his Life, During the Previous and Intervening Periods*, 2 vols. (London, 1788).

Kirch, Patrick V.: "Polynesia's Mystery Islands" (*Archeology*, May/June 1988, vol. 41, no. 3, p. 26).

Kitson, A.: *The Life of Captain James Cook* (London, 1912).

Knight, C.: "H.M. Armed Vessel *Bounty*" (*Mariner's Mirror*, vol. 22, no. 2, April 1936).

Knowles, J.: *Crusoes of Pitcairn Island — Diary of the Wreck of the* Wild Wave (Los Angeles, 1957).

Koivistoinen, Eino: "Tahitin Kuninkaan Suomalainen Sotapäällikkö" (*Seura*, Helsinki, 1963).

Koskinen, Aarne A.: "Ariki the First Born. An Analysis of a Polynesian Chieftain Title" (*Folklore Fellows*, Communication no. 181, 1960, Helsinki).

Kotzebue, Otto von: *A New Voyage Round the World*, 2 vols. (London: Sir Richard Phillips & Co., 1830).

Labillardière, J.J. Houtou de: *An Account of a Voyage in Search of La Pérouse, Undertaken by Order of the Constituent Assembly of France, and Performed in the Years 1791, 1792, and 1793, In the* Recherche *and* Espérance, *Ships of War, Under the*

Command of Rear-Admiral Bruni d'Entrecasteaux, 2 vols. (translated from the French of M. Labillardière, London, 1800).

La Farge, John: *Reminiscences of the South Seas* (London, 1914).

Langdon, Robert: *Tahiti: Island of Love* (London: Cassell and Company Ltd., 1959).

Langdon, Robert: "Ancient Cornish Inn is Link with the *Bounty*" (*Pacific Islands Monthly*, April, 1961).

Langdon, Robert: "New Light on the *Bounty* Mutiny: Lost *Pandora* Logbook Turns Up in U.K. after 170 Years" (*Pacific Islands Monthly*, April 1965).

Langdon, Robert: "The Lost Tahitian Vocabulary of Peter Heywood" (*Pambu*, Canberra, October 1968).

Langdon, Robert: "Tahiti, as the Early Explorers Saw It" (*Pacific Islands Monthly*, March 1982).

Lanyon-Orgill, Peter A.: *Captain Cook's South Sea Island Vocabularies* (London: the author, 1979).

La Pérouse, J.F.G. de: *Voyage de La Pérouse*, 4 vols. (Paris: 1798).

La Place, Cyril Pierre Theodore: *Campagne de Circumnavigation de la Frégate* L'Artemise, 6 vols. (Paris, 1841).

Laughton, John Knox (ed.): *Letters and Dispatches of Horatio, Viscount Nelson, K.B., Duke of Bronte, Vice-Admiral of the White Squadron* (London, 1886).

Ledward, Thomas D.: "Letters to his Family" (*Notes and Queries*, 9th Series, vol. 12, 26 December, 1903).

Lee, Ida: *Captain Bligh's Second Voyage to the South Sea* (London: Longmans, Green and Co., 1920).

Lee, Ida: "The Morrison Myth" (Review in *Mariner's Mirror*, vol. 25, no. 4, October, 1939).

Lesson, René Primavere: *Voyage Autour de Monde sur la Corvette*, La Coquille, 2 vols. (Paris, 1838–9).

L'Estrange, Alfred G.L.: *Lady Belcher and Her Friends* (London, 1891).

Lewis, Michael: *British Ships and British Seamen* (London: Longmans, Green & Co., 1942).

Lewis, Michael: *England's Sea-Officers: The Story of the Naval Profession* (London: George Allen & Unwin, 1948).

Lewis, Michael: *The Navy of Britain* (London: George Allen & Unwin, 1948).

Lewis, Michael: *A Social History of the Navy 1793–1815* (London: George Allen & Unwin, 1960).

Lindsay, Philip: *Bligh in New South Wales* (London: Ruffians Hall, 1931).

Lloyd, Christopher: *Pacific Horizons* (London, 1946).

Lloyd, Christopher: *The Nation and the Navy: A History of Naval Life and Policy* (London: The Cresset Press, 1954).

Lloyd, Christopher: *The British Seaman 1200–1860: A Social Survey* (London: Collins, 1968).

Lloyd, Christopher: *Mr. Barrow of the Admiralty: A Life of Sir John Barrow 1764–1848* (London, 1970).

Lloyd, Christopher, and Coulter, J.L.S.: *Medicine and the Navy*, 4 vols. (London, 1957–63).

London Missionary Society: *Narrative of the Mission at Otaheite and the Other Islands in the South Seas* (London, 1818).

London Missionary Society: *Quarterly Chronicle of the Transactions of the London Missionary Society, 1815–1832*, 4 vols. (London: London Missionary Society, 1821–1833).

Lonsdale, H.: *Worthies of Cumberland* (London, 1876).

Lord, Clive: "Notes on Captain Bligh's Visits to Tasmania" (*Papers and Proceedings of the Royal Society of Tasmania*, 1922).

Lord, Mary Alice: Letter to the Editor of the *Smithsonian* concerning the *Bounty* Bible (*Smithsonian*, March 1988).

Loti, Pierre: *The Marriage of Loti* (English translation by Clara Bell, London, 1925).

Lovett, Richard: *History of the London Missionary Society 1795–1895* (London, 1899).

Lowis, Geoffrey L.: *Fabulous Admirals and Some Naval Fragments* (London: Putnam, 1957).

Lucas, Sir Charles (ed.): *The Pitcairn Island Register Book* (London, 1929).

Lucett, Edward: *Rovings in the Pacific* (London, 1852).

Luke, Sir Harry: *Islands of the South Pacific* (London, 1962).

Lutteroth, Henri: *O'Taiti, Histoire et Enquête* (Paris, 1845).

Macarthur, John: *A Treatise of the Principles and Practice of Naval Courts-Martial, with an Appendix, Containing Original Papers and Documents Illustrative of the Text, Opinions of Counsel upon Remarkable Cases, the Forms Preparatory to Trial, and Proceedings of the Court to Judgment and Execution.* (London, 4th edn. 1813).

McCoy, Emily: "The Pitcairn Island Miracle in Ethnology" (*Independent*, vol. 57, September 1904).

McCoy, F.H.: "Pitcairn: New Angles on the Old Story of the *Bounty*" (*Pacific Islands Monthly*, July 1942, p. 13).

MacDonald, A.C.: "Discovery of Pitcairn Island; Mutiny of the *Bounty*; Life of the Mutineers on Pitcairn and Their Removal to Norfolk Island" (*Australasian Association for the Advancement of Science*, 1901).

McFarland, A.: *Mutiny in the* Bounty *and the Story of the Pitcairn Islanders* (Sydney, 1884).

McGilchrist, J.: *The Mutineers: A Poem* (Edinburgh, 1859).

Mackaness, George: *The Life of Vice-Admiral William Bligh*, 2 vols. (Sydney: Angus & Robertson, 1931; new and revised edn., 1951).

Mackaness, George: *Sir Joseph Banks: His Relations with Australia* (Sydney: Angus & Robertson, 1936).

Mackaness, George (ed.): *Captain William Bligh's Discoveries and Observations in Van Diemen's Land* (Sydney, 1943).

Mackaness, George (ed.): *Some Correspondence of Captain William Bligh, R.N. with John and Francis Godolphin Bond, 1776–1811* (Sydney, 1949).

Mackaness, George (ed.): *Fresh Light on Bligh: Being Some Unpublished Correspondence of Captain William Bligh, R.N., and Lieutenant Francis Godolphin Bond, R.N., with Lieutenant Bond's Manuscript Notes Made on the Voyage of H.M.S.* Providence, *1791–1795* (Sydney, 1953).

Mackaness, George (ed.): "Extracts from a Log-Book of H.M.S. *Providence* Kept by Lieut. Francis Godolphin Bond, R.N., on Bligh's Second Bread-Fruit Voyage, 1791-3, Made, with Descriptive Commentary and Abstracts, by His Son, Rev. Frederick Hookey Bond, from the Craigfoot Family Papers" (*Journal and Proceedings of the Royal Australian Historical Society*, 46, pp. 24–66).

Mackaness, G., and Kennedy, G. (eds.) *A Book of the* Bounty *by William Bligh and Others* (London: J.M. Dent, 1981).

MacKay, David: "Banks, Bligh and Breadfruit" (*New Zealand Journal of History*, 8, 1974).

McKee, Alexander: *The Truth About the Mutiny on the* Bounty (London, 1961).

McKee, Alexander: *H.M.S.* Bounty (New York: William Morrow and Company, 1962).

McKinnes, George: *Biography of William Bligh* (Sydney, 1931).

MacPherson, R.C.: "A Link with the *Bounty*" (*Pacific Islands Monthly*, November 1944, pp. 38–39).

Mahan, A.T.: *Types of Naval Officers Drawn from the History of the British Navy* (London: Sampson Low, Marston & Company Ltd., 1902).

Maiden, J.H.: *Sir Joseph Banks, the 'Father of Australia'* (London/Sydney, 1909).

Manwaring, G.E.: *My Friend the Admiral: The Life, Letters, and Journals of Rear-Admiral James Burney* (London, 1931).

Manwaring, G.E. and Dobrée, Bonamy: *The Floating Republic: An Account of the Mutinies at Spithead and the Nore in 1797* (London: Geoffrey Bles, 1935).

Marden, Luis: "I found the Bones of the *Bounty*" (*National Geographic Magazine*, December 1957).

Marden, Luis: "Huzza for Otaheite!" (*National Geographic Magazine*, April 1962).

Marden, Luis: "Tahiti: Finest Island in the World" (*National Geographic Magazine*, July 1962).

Marden, Luis: "Wreck of H.M.S. *Pandora* found on Australia's Great Barrier Reef" (*National Geographic Magazine*, October 1985).

LITERATURE

Mariner, W.: *An Account of the Natives of the Tonga Islands*, 2 vols. (ed. J. Martin, London, 1817).

Marks, Percy J.: *Norfolk Island and the Bounty Mutiny* (Sydney: private printing, 1935).

Marrington, Pauline: *In the Sweet Bye and Bye* (1981).

Marsden, J.B. (ed.): *Memoirs of the Life and Labours of the Rev. Samuel Marsden, of Parmatte, Senior Chaplain of New South Wales; and His Early Connexion with the Missions to New Zealand and Tahiti* (London, 1958).

Marshall, Donald Stanley: *A Working Bibliography of the Society Islands, Particularly Tahiti* (Auckland, 1951).

Marshall, J.: *Royal Naval Biography* (Article on Peter Heywood, vol. 2, part 2, London, 1823–35).

Martin, J.: *Memorandoms* [sic.] (ed. C. Blount, London, 1937).

Masefield, John: *Sea Life in Nelson's Time* (London: Methuen & Co., 1905; new edn, London: Conway Maritime Press Ltd., 1971).

Massachusetts Sabbath School Society: *Aleck and the Mutineers of the Bounty* (Boston, 1855).

Maude, Henry E.: "In Search of a Home: From the Mutiny to Pitcairn Island (1789-1790)" (*Journal of the Polynesian Society*, June 1958, vol. 67, no. 2, Wellington).

Maude, Henry E.: "Tahitian Interlude: The Migration of the Pitcairn Islanders to the Motherland in 1831" (*Journal of the Polynesian Society*, June 1959, vol. 68, no. 2).

Maude, Henry E.: "The Voyage of the *Pandora's* Tender" (*Mariner's Mirror*, Aug. 1964).

Maude, Henry E.: "The Edwards Papers" (*Journal of Pacific History*, vol. 1, 1966, pp. 184–5).

Maude, Henry E.: *Of Islands and Men* (Melbourne: Oxford University Press, 1968).

Melville, Herman: *Omoo* (New York, 1847).

Michener, James A., and Day, A. Grove: *Rascals in Paradise* (New York: Random House, 1957).

Miller, Stanley: *Mr. Christian! The Journal of Fletcher Christian, Former Lieutenant of His Majesty's Armed Vessel* Bounty (A novel; London: Macmillan Publishing Co., 1973).

Mitchell, Carleton: *Beyond Horizons* (New York: W.W. Norton & Co., 1953).

Mitchell, R. Else: "George Caley: His Life and Work" (*Royal Australian Historical Society Journal and Proceedings*, 1939, vol. 25: "The Bligh Rebellion").

Mitford, Mary Russell: *Christina, The Maid of the South Seas: a poem* (London, 1811).

Moerenhout, J.A.: *Voyages aux Iles du Grand Océan*, 2 vols. (Paris: Arthus Bertrand, 1837).

Montgomerie, H.S.: *William Bligh of the Bounty in Fact and in Fable* (London: Williams & Norgate, 1937).

Montgomerie, H.S.: *The Morrison Myth: A Pendant to "William Bligh of the Bounty in Fact and in Fable"* (London: private printing, 1938).

LITERATURE

Moore, A.W.: *Manx Worthies, or Biographies of Notable Manx Men and Women* (Douglas: Isle of Man, 1901).

Moore, A.W.: *Nessy Heywood* (Isle of Man: Douglas, 1913).

Moorehead, Alan McCrae: *The Fatal Impact* (London: Hamish Hamilton, 1966).

Moorman, M.: *William Wordsworth*, (London, 1957).

Morrison, James: *The Journal of James Morrison Boatswain's Mate of the* Bounty *Describing the Mutiny & Subsequent Misfortunes of the Mutineers Together With an Account of the Island of Tahiti. With an Introduction by Owen Rutter and Five Engravings by Robert Gibbings* (London: Golden Cockerel Press, 1935).

Morrison, James: "Memorandums and Particulars Respecting the Bounty and her Crew" (Manuscript 1, Sydney: Mitchell Library).

Morrison, James: "Narrative of the *Bounty* Expedition of Tubuai and Tahiti" (Manuscript 2, Sydney: Mitchell Library).

Morrison, James: *Journal de James Morrison, Second Mâitre à Bord de la* Bounty (Papeete: Société des Etudes Océaniennes, 1981).

Mortimer, George: *Observations and Remarks Made During a Voyage to the Islands of Tenerife, Amsterdam, Maria's Islands near Van Diemen's Land; Otaheite, Sandwich Islands; Owhyhee, The Fox Islands on the North West Coast of America, Tinian, and from thence to Canton, in the Brig* Mercury (London, 1791).

Mudie, J.: *The Felonry of New South Wales* (London, 1837).

Muir, H.: "The Literature of the *Bounty*" (in Charles Barnet, *The Pacific: Ocean of Islands*, Melbourne, 1950).

Murray, Hugh: *Adventures of British Seamen in the Southern Ocean, Displaying the Striking Contrasts which the Human Character Exhibits in an Uncivilized State* (Edinburgh, 1827).

Murray, Rev. Thomas Boyles: *Pitcairn: The Island, the People and the Pastor; With a Short Account of the Mutiny of the* Bounty (London, 1853).

Newbury, Colin: *The History of the Tahitian Mission, 1799–1830, Written by John Davies* (London: Cambridge University Press, 1961).

Newbury, Colin: "Aspects of Cultural Change in French Polynesia: The Decline of the Ari'i" (*Journal of the Polynesian Society* 1967b, vol. 76, pp. 477–514).

Newbury, Colin: *Tahiti Nui: Change and Survival in French Polynesia 1767-1945* (Honolulu: The University Press of Hawaii, 1980).

Newell, G.: "First Officer of the *Sultan*" (*New-England Galaxy*, vol. 4, January 12, 1821).

Nichols, G.R.: "Governor Bligh's Farm" (*Historical Notes on the Hawkesbury*, Sydney, 1904–18).

Nicholson, Joyce: *Man Against Mutiny: The Story of Vice Admiral William Bligh* (London, 1961).

Nicolson, Robert B.: *The Pitcairners* (Sydney: Angus & Robertson, 1965).

Nield, R.A.: *Mutiny of the* Bounty *and Story of Pitcairn Island, 1790–1814* (London).

Nordhoff, Charles, and Hall, James Norman: *Faery Lands of the South Seas* (New York: Harper & Brothers, 1921).

Nordhoff, Charles, and Hall, James Norman: *Mutiny on the* Bounty (Boston: Little, Brown and Co., 1932).

Nordhoff, Charles, and Hall, James Norman: *Men Against the Sea* (Boston: Little, Brown and Co., 1935).

Nordhoff, Charles, and Hall, James Norman: *Pitcairn's Island* (Boston: Little, Brown and Co., 1935).

O'Brien, Frederick: *White Shadows in the South Seas* (New York: The Century Co., 1919).

O'Brien, Frederick: *Mystic Isles of the South Seas* (New York: The Century Co., 1921).

O'Brien, Frederick: *Atolls of the Sun* (London: Hodder and Stoughton, 1922).

O'Hara, J.: *History of New South Wales* (London, 1817).

Oliver, Douglas L.: *Ancient Tahitian Society*, 3 vols. (Honolulu: The University Press of Hawaii, 1974).

Oliver, Douglas L.: *The Pacific Islands* revised edn. (Honolulu: The University Press of Hawaii, 1988).

Oliver, Douglas L.: *Return to Tahiti: Bligh's Second Breadfruit Voyage* (Carlton, Victoria: Melbourne University Press, 1988).

Oman, Carola: *Nelson* (London, 1947).

O'Reilly, Patrick: *Pomare, Queen of Tahiti* (Société des Océanistes, Dossier 13, 1972).

O'Reilly, Patrick: *Dancing: Tahiti* (Nouvelles Editions Latines, Dossier 22).

O'Reilly, Patrick and Reitman, Edouard: "Bibliographie de Tahiti et de la Polynésie Française" (*Publications de la Société des Océanistes* no. 14, 1967).

Oster, Gerald, and Oster, Selmaree: "The Great Breadfruit Scheme" (*Natural History*, March 1985).

Pacific Islands Monthly (Authors Unknown):
"*Bounty* Relic: Recovered from Sea Bottom" (December 1933, p. 4).
"*Bounty* Relics: Taken from Pitcairn Island" (April 1937, p. 6).
"Pitcairners on Norfolk" (June 1937, p. 75).
"The Homesickness of Polynesians: Pitcairners Who Went Home" (April 1938, p. 58).
"Pitcairn Island: Death of Fletcher Christian's Great Grandson" (June 1938, p. 19).
"*Bounty* Men's Graves" (December 1938, p. 6).

Padfield, Peter: *Guns at Sea* (London, 1973).

Paine, Ralph D.: *Lost Ships and Lonely Seas* (London, 1921).

Parkinson, Sydney: *Journal of a Voyage to the South Seas in His Majesty's Ship the* Endeavour, *Faithfully Transcribed from the Papers of the Late Sydney Parkinson, Draughtsman to Sir Joseph Banks, Esq. on His Late Expedition with Dr. Solander, Round*

LITERATURE

the World (London: Stanfield Parkinson, 1773).

Pears, G.: Journal Kept on H.M.S. *Blossom*, Captain Beechey, in 1825 (Manuscript, London: British Museum).

Perkins, Edward: *Na Motu, or Reef Rovings in the South Seas* (New York, 1854).

Pilling, H.G.: *Report on a Visit to Pitcairn Island . . . 1929* (1930).

Pipon, Philip: "Descendants of the *Bounty's* Crew" (*United Services Journal*, 1834, vol 63).

Pitcairn, A Guide to the Government of the Islands of Pitcairn (1982).

The Pitcairn Island Register Book: (ed. Sir Charles Lucas, London, 1929).

Pool, Bernard: *Navy Board Contracts 1660–1832: Contract Administration Under the Navy Board* (London, 1966).

Pope, Dudley: *The Black Ship* (London: Weidenfeld and Nicolson, 1963).

Pope, Dudley: *Life in Nelson's Navy* (Annapolis, Maryland: Naval Institute Press, 1981).

Pottle, F.A.: *The Girl from Botany Bay* (New York: Viking Press, 1937).

Powell, Dulcie: *The Voyage of the Plant Nursery, H.M.S.* Providence *1791–1793* (Institute of Jamaica, 1973).

Pritchard, George: *The Missionary's Reward* (London, 1844).

Pritchard, W.T.: *Polynesian Reminiscences* (London, 1844).

Raine, Thomas: "Captain Raine's Narrative of a Visit to Pitcairn's Island in the Ship *Surry*, 1821" (*The Australian Magazine*, 1821, vol. 1; also in *Naval Chronicle*, July 1821).

Ramsay, Doctor: Scrap Book of the Log of the Ship *Surry*, quoted in R.B. Nicolson's *The Pitcairners* (Sydney: Angus & Robertson, 1965).

Ramsden, Eric: "The Pitcairners Return to Tahiti" (*Pacific Islands Monthly*, August 1936, pp. 41–2).

Rawson, Geoffrey: *Bligh of the* Bounty (London: Philip Allan & Co. Ltd., 1930).

Rawson, Geoffrey: *The Strange Case of Mary Bryant* (London: Philip Allan & Co., Ltd, 1935).

Rawson, Geoffrey: Pandora's *Last Voyage* (New York: Harcourt, Brace & World, Inc., 1963).

Renouard, David T.: "*Pandora*'s Tender 1791" (*The United Service Magazine*, 1842, part 3, pp. 1–3; *Mariner's Mirror*, 1964, vol. 50, no. 3).

Reybaud, L.: L'Artémise à Tahiti (Paris, 1840).

Ribourt, P.: *Etat de l'Ile Taiti Pendant les Années 1847–48* (Papeete, 1863).

Richerie, E. Gaultier de la: *Etablissements Françaises de l'Océanie* (Paris, 1865).

Richerie, E. Gaultier de la: "Souvenirs de Tahiti" (*Bulletin de la Société de Géographie*, Paris, 1866).

Rientis, Rex and Thea: *The Voyages of Captain Cook* (London: The Hamlyn Publishing Group Ltd., 1968).

LITERATURE

Roberts, Stephen H.: *History of French Colonial Policy*, vol. 2 (London, 1929).

Robertson, George: *The Discovery of Tahiti* (ed. Hugh Carrington, London, 1929).

Robertson, George: *The Discovery of Tahiti* (ed. Hugh Carrington, London: Hakluyt Society, 1948).

Robinson, A.H.W.: "Captain William Bligh R.N., Hydrographic Surveyor" (*Empire Survey Review*, 1952, vol. 9, no. 85, pp. 301-6).

Rodwell, Sir C.: "Report on a Visit to Pitcairn Island" (*Colonial Reports* no. 93, London, 1921).

Ropiteau, André: "Légende Des Deux Amies" (*Bulletin de la Société d'Etudes Océaniennes* 3: pp. 289-91, 1929).

Ropiteau, André: "Notes sur l'Ile Maupiti" (*Bulletin de la Société d'Etudes Océaniennes* 5: pp. 113-29).

Ross, Allan S.C., and Moverly, A.W.: *The Pitcairnese Language* (London, 1964).

Roughley, T.C.: "*Bounty* Descendants Live on Remote Norfolk Island (*National Geographic*, October 1960).

Rowe, Newton A.: *Voyage to the Amorous Islands: The Discovery of Tahiti* (London: Andre Deutsch, 1955).

Russell, A.: *Aristocrats of the South Seas* (London, 1961).

Rutter, Owen: *Cain's Birthday* (A novel based on the character of Fletcher Christian, London, 1930).

Rutter, Owen (ed.): *The Court-Martial of the* Bounty *Mutineers* (Edinburgh: William Hodge & Co., 1931).

Rutter, Owen: "Travels of Fletcher Christian" (*Blue Peter*, June 1932, London).

Rutter, Owen: "Vindication of William Bligh" (*Quarterly Review*, October 1933).

Rutter, Owen (ed.): *The Voyage of the* Bounty's *Launch as Related in William Bligh's Dispatch to the Admiralty and the Journal of John Fryer* (London, 1934).

Rutter, Owen (ed.): *The Journal of James Morrison, Boatswain's Mate of the* Bounty, *Describing the Mutiny & Subsequent Misfortunes of the Mutineers, Together with an Account of the Island of Tahiti* (London: Golden Cockerel Press, 1935).

Rutter, Owen: "Bligh's Log" (*Mariner's Mirror*, April 1936, vol. 22, no. 2).

Rutter, Owen: *Turbulent Journey: A Life of William Bligh, Vice-Admiral of the Blue* (London, 1936).

Rutter, Owen: *The True Story of the Mutiny of the* Bounty (London, 1936).

Rutter, Owen (ed.): *The Log of the* Bounty: *Being Lieutenant William Bligh's Log of the Proceedings of His Majesty's Armed Vessel* Bounty *on a Voyage to the South Seas, to Take the Breadfruit from the Society Islands to the West Indies* 2 vols. (London: 1936-7).

Rutter, Owen (ed.): *Bligh's Voyage in the* Resource *From Coupang to Batavia, Together with the Log of his Subsequent Passage to England in the Dutch Packet* Vlydte *and his Remarks on Morrison's Journal* (London: Golden Cockerel Press, 1937).

Rutter, Owen (ed.): *John Fryer of the* Bounty*: Notes on his Career Written by his Daughter Mary Ann* (London: Golden Cockerel Press, 1939).

Salmon, Marau Taaroa [Queen Marau Taaroa]: "Légende de Ariitaumatatini" (*Bulletin de la Société D'Etudes Océaniennes* 2: pp. 119–23, 1926).

Samwell, David: *A Narrative of the Death of Captain James Cook* (London, 1786).

Samwell, David: *Captain Cook and Hawaii* (London, 1786).

Sargeant, Charles L.: *The Life of Alexander Smith* (London, 1819).

Sawyer, Beryl: "New *Bounty* Brings Film-Makers to Eager Tahiti" (*Pacific Islands Monthly*, January 1961, p. 27).

Scott, Ernest; *La Pérouse* (Sydney: Angus & Robertson, 1912).

Scott, Ernest: *The Life of Captain Matthew Flinders, R.N.* (Sydney: Angus & Robertson, 1914).

Seale, Alvin: *Narrative of Trip to South Sea Islands, with Notes on Voyages, Islands and People 1901–1902* (Honolulu: Bernice P. Bishop Museum Library, 1902).

The Seaman's Church Institute of New York: "A Tale of Two Bibles" (*The Lookout*, May 1959).

Shadbolt, Maurice, and Ruhen, Olaf: "Isles of the South Pacific" (Washington, D.C.: *National Geographic Special Publications Division*, 1968).

Shafter, Richard A.: "Pitcairn Island Through Native Eyes" (*Travel*, vol. 90, January 1948).

Shapiro, H.L.: *Robinson Crusoe's Children* (1928).

Shapiro, H.L.: *Descendants of the Mutineers of the* Bounty (Honolulu: Bernice P. Bishop Museum, 1929).

Shapiro, H.L.: *The Heritage of the* Bounty*, The Story of Pitcairn Through Six Generations* (New York: Simon & Schuster, 1936).

Shapiro, H.L.: "Pitcairniana — A Commentary on the Mutiny of the *Bounty* and its Sequel on Pitcairn Island" (*Natural History*, January 1938, vol. 41, pp. 34–45).

Sharp, Andrew: *Ancient Voyagers in Polynesia* (Sydney: Angus and Robertson Publishers, 1963).

Shillibeer, J.: *A Narrative of the* Briton's *Voyage to Pitcairn's Island* (London: Law & Whittaker, 1817).

Shipley, Conway: *Sketches in the Pacific* (London, 1851).

Shipp, John: *Flogging and its Substitute* (London, 1831).

Silverman, David: *Pitcairn Island* (Cleveland: World Publishing Company, 1967).

Simons, R.T.: "Report on Pitcairn Island" (*Colonial Reports*, London, 1905).

Slocum, V.: "Voyage of the *Bounty*'s Launch" (*Yachting*, July 1926, vol. 40).

Smith, Bernard: "Coleridge's 'Ancient Mariner' and Cook's Second Voyage" (*Journal of the Warburg and Courtauld Institutes*, 1956, vol. 19, no. 1–2, pp. 117–54).

L I T E R A T U R E

Smith, Bernard: *European Vision and the South Pacific 1768–1850: A Study in the History of Art and Ideas* (Oxford, 1960).

Smith, D. Bonner: See Bonner Smith, D.

Smith, E.: *Life of Sir Joseph Banks* (London, 1911).

Smith, S. Percy: "The Genealogy of the Pomare Family of Tahiti, from the Papers of the Rev. J.M. Orsmond" (*Journal of the Polynesian Society* 2: pp. 25–42, 1893).

Smith, S. Percy: *Hawaiki: The Original Home of the Maori*, 3rd edn. (London: Whitcomb and Tombs, 1910).

Smyth, William Henry: "Sketch of the Career of the Late Capt. Peter Heywood, R.N." (*United Services Journal*, no. 29, April 1831).

Smyth, William Henry: "Capt. Beechey's Narrative" (*United Services Journal*, no. 29, April 1831).

Smyth, William Henry: "The *Bounty* Again!" (*United Services Journal*, no. 36, November 1831).

Smyth, William Henry: "The *Pandora* Again!" (*United Services Journal*, no. 172, March 1843).

Snow, Philip, and Waine, Stefanie: *The People from the Horizon* (Oxford: Phaidon Press Ltd, 1979).

South Pacific Commission: *A Guide to Pitcairn* (Suva Fiji, 1963).

Sparks, J.: *Memoirs of the Life and Travels of John Ledyard* (London, 1828).

Spence, S.A.: *Captain William Bligh, R.N. (1754–1817) & Where to Find Him: Being a Catalogue of Works Wherein Reference is Contained to this Remarkable Seaman* (London: private printing, 1970).

Spruson, J.J.: *Norfolk Island: Outline of its History from 1788 to 1884* (Sydney, 1885).

Squire, John: "Was Fletcher Christian the Ancient Mariner?" (*Illustrated London News*, 9 May 1953, vol. 222, p. 732).

Stackpole, Edouard A.: *The Sea Hunters* (New York, 1953).

Stackpole, Edouard A.: "Nantucket and Pitcairn: An Islander Unravels an Island Mystery Half a World Away" (*Sea History*, Winter 1986–87).

Staines, Sir T., and Pipon, P.: *Interesting Report on the Only Remaining Mutineer of His Majesty's Ship Bounty, resident on Pitcairn's Island in the Pacific Ocean* (Sydney: Mitchell Library, 1940).

Stanley, David: *South Pacific Handbook* (Chico California: Moon Publications, 1985).

Steven, M.J.E.: "Robert Campbell and the Bligh Rebellion 1808" (*Canberra and District Historical Society*, March 1962; Sydney, 1952).

Stevenson, Robert Louis: *Works* (London, 1911–12).

Stuart, R.P., and Naylor, T.B.: *The Botany Bay of 1846* (1979).

Suttor, H.M.: *Australian Milestones*, vol. 2 (1925).

"Taffrail" [H.T. Dorling]: "The Mutiny of the *Bounty*" (*Chamber's Journal*, 20 October,' 1928, vol. 18).

Tagart, E.: *A Memoir of the Late Captain Peter Heywood, R.N., with Extracts from his Diaries and Correspondence* (London, 1832).

Tasman, A.J.: *Abel Janszoon Tasman's Journal of his Discovery of Van Diemen's Land* (Amsterdam, 1898).

Taylor, A.H.: "William Bligh at Camperdown" (*Mariner's Mirror*, October 1937, vol. 23, no. 4).

Taylor, C.R.H.: *A Pacific Bibliography* (Wellington, 1951).

Teehuteatuaonoa (or Jenny): "First Narrative" (*Sydney Gazette*, 17 July 1819). "Second Narrative" (*Bengal Hurkaru*, 2 October, 1826; and *The United Services Journal*, November 1829, part 2, pp. 589–93).

Tench, Captain Watkin: *A Narrative of the Expedition to Botany Bay* (London, 1879).

Thiery, M.: *The Life and Voyages of Captain Cook* (London, 1929).

Thomas, Marcel: *L'Affaire du* Bounty. *Documents Originaux Traduits et Presentés* (Paris, 1958).

Thomson, Sir Basil (ed.): *E. Edwards and G. Hamilton, Voyage of H.M.S.* Pandora, *Dispatched to Arrest the Mutineers of the* Bounty *in the South Seas, 1790–91, Being the Narratives of Captain Edwards, R.N., the Commander, and George Hamilton, Surgeon* (London: Francis Edwards, 1915).

Thomson, Robert: "History of Tahiti" (unpublished Manuscript in the London Missionary Society Archives, N.D.).

Tobin, G.: Letter to Francis Godolphin Bond, 15 December 1917 (Greenwich: National Maritime Museum).

Topliff, Samuel: "Visit of *Sultan* to Pitcairn, 1817" (*New-England Galaxy*, January 1821, vol. 4).

Turnbull, John: *A Voyage Around the World*, 3 vols. (London: A. Maxwell, 1813).

Valtiala, Robin: "Drömmen om en ö" (Helsingfors: *Hufvudstadsbladet*, January 12, 1988).

Vancouver, George: *A Voyage of Discovery to the North Pacific Ocean, and Round the World; in which the Coast of North-West America has been Carefully Examined and Accurately Surveyed. Undertaken by His Majesty's Command, Principally with a View to Ascertain the Existence of any Navigable Communication betweeen the North Pacific and North Atlantic Oceans; and Performed in the Years 1790, 1791, 1792, 1793, 1794 and 1795, in the Discovery Sloop of War, and Armed Tender* Chatham, *under the Command of Captain George Vancouver*, 3 vols. (London, 1798).

Vason, James: *An Authentic Narrative of Four Years' Residence at Tongatapoo* (London, 1810).

Vaucaire, Michel: *Les Révoltes de la* Bounty *Récit Historique* (Paris, 1947).

Verne, Jules: *Les Révoltés de la* Bounty suivi de *Un Drame au Méxique* (Paris, 1880).

Verne, Jules: *The Begun's Fortune; with an Account of the Mutineers of the* Bounty

LITERATURE

(Translated by W.H.G. Kingston, London 1880).

Verne, Jules: "*Bounty* Mutiny" (*Bekannte und Unbekannte Welten*, 1882, vols. 37–8, pp. 250–3).

Vesilind, Priit J.: "The Society Islands, Sisters of the Wind" (*National Geographic Magazine*, June 1979).

Vidil, Charles: *Histoire des Mutins de la* Bounty *et de L'Ile Pitcairn 1789–1930* (Paris, 1932).

Villiers, Alan: *Men, Ships, and the Sea* (Washington, D.C., 1962).

Villiers, Alan: *Captain James Cook* (New York: Charles Scribner's Sons, 1967).

Villiers, Alan: "Captain Cook: The Man who Mapped the Pacific" (*National Geographic Magazine*, September 1971).

Volk, Winifried: *Die Entdeckung Tahitis und das Wünschbild der seligen Insel in der Deutschen Literatur* (Heidelberg: Kranz und Heinrichmöller, 1934).

Wahlroos, Sven: "Happy Birthday H.M.S. *Bounty*" (*Pacific Islands Monthly*, March 1988, p. 58).

Wahlroos, Sven: "Den psykologiska gåtan William Bligh, befälhavare i Hans Majestäts skepp *Bounty*" (*Longitude* No. 24, 1989).

Waldegrave, Captain W.: "Recent Accounts of the Pitcairn Islanders" (*Royal Geographical Society Journal*, vol. 3, 1833).

Wales, William: *Remarks on Mr. Forster's Account of Captain Cook's Last Voyage Round the World, in the Years 1772, 1773, 1774, and 1775.* (London: J. Nourse, 1778).

Walker, C.F.: *Young Gentlemen: The Story of Midshipmen from XVIIth Century to the Present Day* (London, 1938).

Wallis, Captain S.: *The History of Wallis's and Carteret's Voyage Round the World* (London, 1784).

Walpole, Frederick: *Four Years in the Pacific* (Paris, 1850).

Walters, Stephen: "The Literature of Bligh" (*Sea Breezes: The Magazine of Ships and the Sea*, October 1976, vol. 50, no. 370, pp. 608–11).

Walters, Stephen (ed.): *The Voyage of the* Bounty *Launch: John Fryer's Narrative* (Guildford: Genesis Publications, 1979).

Ward, John M.: *British Policy in the South Pacific*, parts 3, 5–6 (Sydney, 1948).

Warren, Samuel: "The Paradise in the Pacific" (*Works*, 1855, vol. 5, London/Edinburgh).

Watson, James: "The Mutiny on the *Bounty*" (Chapter 4 in *Stamps and Ships* London: 1959).

Weate, Philip, and Chapman, Caroline: *Captain William Bligh* (Sydney, 1972).

Webb, A.J.: *The History of Fiji* (Sydney, 1885).

Webber, James: *Views in the South Seas* (London, 1808).

Welsby, T.: "*Bounty* Mutiny" (in *Discoverers of the Brisbane River*, London, 1913).

Whipple, A.B.C.: *Yankee Whalers in the South Seas* (1954).

White, Ralph Gardner, and Ariihau A Terupe: *Linguistic Check-Sketch for Tahitian* (Tahiti: Te Fare Vana'a, 1985).

Whymper, T.: "Mutiny of the *Bounty*" (in *The Sea 1878–1880*, London).

Wilder, Gerrit P.: "The Breadfruit of Tahiti" (Honolulu: *Bernice P. Bishop Museum Bulletin* no. 50, 1928).

Wilkie, A.: *Governor Bligh: A Tale of Old Sydney* (Sydney, 1930).

Wilkinson, C.S.: *The Wake of the* Bounty (London, 1953).

Wilks, Mark: *Tahiti* (1844).

Williams, John: *Narrative of Missionary Enterprise in the South Sea Islands* (London: J. Snow, 1838).

Williamson, James Alexander: *Capt. Cook and the Opening of the Pacific* (London, 1946).

Willson, Erle: *Adams of the* Bounty (Sydney: Angus & Robertson, 1958).

Wilson, James A.: *A Missionary Voyage to the Southern Pacific Ocean, Performed in the Year 1796, 1797, 1798, in the Ship* Duff, *Commanded by Captain James Wilson. Compiled from Journals of the Officers and the Missionaries; and Illustrated with Maps, Charts, and Views, Drawn by Mr. William Wilson, and Engraved by the most Eminent Artists* (London, 1799).

Wilson, P. and Others: *"Voyages to the South Seas" (New . . . Collection of Authentic and Entertaining Voyages*, London, 1794).

Wise, Henry, A.: *Los Gringos: or an Inside View of Polynesia* (New York, 1949).

Wood, G.A: *The Discovery of Australia* (London, 1922).

Wood, G.A.: *Voyage of the* Endeavour (Melbourne, 1925).

Woof, R. (ed.): *Wordsworth's Hawkshead by T.W. Thompson* (London, 1970).

Yonge, C.D.: *The History of the British Navy: From the Earliest Period to the Present Time*, 2 vols. (London, 1863).

Young, Sir George: "H.M.S. *Bounty*" (in *Young of Formosa*, London, 1928).

Young, J.L.: "The Origin of the Name Tahiti, as Related by Marerenui, A Native of Faaiti Island, Paumotu Group". (*Journal of the Polynesian Society* 7: pp. 109–11, 1898).

Young, Kari Boye: *Den siste myterist* (Oslo: H. Aschehoug & Co., 1982).

Young, Rosalind Amelia, — *A Native Daughter: Mutiny of the* Bounty *and Story of Pitcairn Island, 1790–1894* (Mountain View, California: Pacific Press Publishing Assn., 1894).

Index

(Compiled by Judy Fifer)

Index

Index

Index

Index

Index

Index

Index

Index

Dyce, Andrew, 165

Easter Island, 133, 295, 316, 348, 358, 364, 424

East India, 217

East India Company, 13, 260

East Indiaman, 13, 242, 290, 321

East India Station, 329

East Indies, see Dutch East Indies

Ebriel, Captain Thomas, **263**, 313

Eddia, Edea, see Itia

Edgar, Thomas, 254, 256

Edge, The, 95, **263**, 293

Edwards, Captain Edward, 34, 73, 111, 121–123, 127, 133–135, 137, 138, 139, 140, 141, 142, 143, 144, 145, 147, 152, 153, 154, 155, 156, 157, 158, 159, 161, 162, 167, 169, 171, 172, 173, 181, 183, 189, 210, 215, 219, 229, 234, 258, 260, 261, 262, **263–264**, 267, 281, 286, 288, 291, 294, 296, 307, 315, 327–328, 329, 331, 333, 334, 337, 339, 340, 341, 346, 351, 380–381, 382, 390, 394, 398, 410, 420, 426, 429–430

Eendracht, 333

Eimeo, **264**; see Moorea

Elephant, HMS, **264**, 281

Elizabeth, **264**, 289

Elizabeth I, 218

Elizabeth II, 355

Elizabeth Island, see Henderson Island

Ellice Islands, see Tuvalu Islands

Elliott, Russell, **265**, 274, 355, 361

Ellis, William, 212, 254, 326, 365

Ellison, Thomas, 15, 28, 62, 65, 84, 181–184, 185–186, 235, 237, 251, **265–266**, 291, 322, 328, 337

Elphinstone, William, 14, 59, 64, 87, **266**

"E Maoruuru a vau," 57

Emea, see Moorea

Endeavour, HMS, 127, 216, 227, 252, 412

Endeavour Strait, 43, 59, 139, 143, 147, 179, 181, 185, 227, 240, **266–267**

England, 3, 27, 33, 34, 35, 36, 37, 38, 40, 58, 59, 61, 62, 67, 82, 87, 88, 89, 91, 95, 98, 99, 101, 102, 105, 111, 119, 120, 121, 125, 128, 135, 147, 160, 161, 169, 170, 171, 172, 173, 177, 181, 185, 187, 189, 191, 193, 195, 197, 208, 219, 220, 223, 226, 228, 246, 250, 253, 254, 255, 262, 276, 277, 278, 279, 283, 285, 287, 291, 292, 296, 297, 298, 304, 306, 308, 309, 320, 326, 330, 334, 341, 343–344, 345, 346–347, 351–358, 360–361, 369, 375, 383, 384, 385, 386, 387, 388, 416, 428, 429

England, John, 164

England, Thomas, 165

English

"Epistle from Oberea, Queen of Otaheiti, to Joseph Banks, Esq..." 376

Esperance, 209

Essex, 233, 346, 388, 393

Etoile, 127

Etuati, **267**

Europe, 33, 37, 42, 63, 77, 78, 159, 217, 283, 317

Europeans, 68, 89, 96, 98, 105, 109, 113, 117, 127–129, 131, 143, 173, 177, 198, 201, 206, 213, 217, 229, 298, 302, 310, 321, 327 332, 337–338, 369, 380, 406, 410–411, 423, 424

"discovery" of Fiji Islands, 179, 269–270, 339, 428

"discovery" of Pitcairn Island, 349

"discovery" of Tahiti, 173, 261, 301, 364, 429

"discovery" of Tubuai, 423

in Polynesia, 105–107, 127–129, 143, 169–170, 172, 198–202, 213, 229, 302, 310, 349

Index

169-170, 172, 229
view of Polynesians, 96, 111, 345
Eurydice, HMS, 29, 244-245, 259, **267**
Evans, John, 235, 236, 259, **267-268**, 292, 326,
334, 339, 352-355, 370, 423
*Eventful History of the Mutiny and Piratical Seize
of HMS Bounty: Its Cause and Consequences,
The*, 36, 218, 290, 375
execution, see hanging; death sentence
Explorers of the Pacific, 240

Faaa, see Te Fana
faaata, **268**
Faahotu, 112, 125, **268**, 431-432
Faaone, **268**
Fabulous Admirals, 271
Faery Lands of the South Seas, 283
Fahutu, see Faahotu "Fair Maid of the South
Seas," 247
Fakaofo, 215, 419
Fakarava, 366, 423
Falconer's Marine Dictionary, 240
False Bay, 27, 29, 33, 35, 431
family therapy, 203
fara, **268**
fare, **269**
Fare, Vana'a 297, 395-396
Fasto, see Faahotu
fathom, **269**
Fatu Hiva, 314
Fatu Huku, 314
Feejee, see Fiji Islands
fe'i, **269**
Fenua, **269**
Fenua Maitai, 3, **269**, 347
Ferai Hill, 284
Fergusson, Captain John, 221
fever, see disease
Ffrench, Jemima, 333
fiddler, see Byrne, Michael
fig tree, see ora
figgy-dowdy, **269**
Fiji Islands, 68, 88, 143, 179, 227, **269-270**, 304,
317, 324, 339, 381, 425, 428, 429, 433
films of *Mutiny on the Bounty*, 17, 63, 231, 325,
401-402
Finland, people of, 170
Finnish sailor, see Hagersten, Petter
fire, on board *Bounty*, 92
firearms, see *Bounty*, weapons; muskets;

weapons
First Fleet, 34, 51, 217, 231, 302
First Fleet Family, A, 156
fish, 69
fishline, 69
Fito, see Vaaifetu
Fitzmaurice, Lieutenant William, 278
fleas, 79
Fleet prison, 34
Flinders, Matthew, 164, 266, **270-271**, 343, 374
flip, **271**
flogging, 1, 23, 35, 40, 42, 45, 46, 50, 51, 54,
55, 56, 207, 234, **271-274**, 303, 314, 330, 331,
354, 377, 391
Fly, HMS, 265, **274**, 355, 361
Foley, Captain Thomas, 280
Folger, Captain Mayhew, 119, 226, 232, 260,
274-278, 346-347, 351, 360, 390, 406, 421
Ford, Commodore, 195
Forster, George, 253, 376
Forster, Johann Reinhold, 253
Fort George, 74-75, 78, 79, 82, **278-279**, 331,
393
map of, 72
moat, 79
Fragile Paradise, see Christian, Glynn
France, 34, 121, 127, 147, 223, 229, 297, 315,
357, 387, 397, 401, 402
King Charles X of, 261
National Convention of, 195
war with England, 195, 223, 277
Franklin, Richard, 164
freeboard, **279**
Fremantle, Captain Charles, 417
French, 113, 168, 223, 228, 229, 260, 279, 297,
311, 315, 367-370, 378, 395-397
Revolution, 276
ships, 127, 195, 223, 228, 301, 418
French Polynesia, 113, 342, 356-357, 367-370,
378, 387, 394-397, 400-402, 422-423, 425-426
French Protestant Mission, 397, 400
Friendly Islands, 57, 67, 102, 144; map, 60; see
also Tonga
frigate, **279**
Frisbie, Robert Dean, 379
Fryer, Harrison, 264
Fryer, John, 14, 23, 31, 39, 40, 46, 49, 55, 56,
64, 68, 71, 73, 77, 81, 120, 182, 188, 243,
250, 264, 266, **279-281**, 327, 377, 386, 391,
416

Index

Index

Index

Index

Index

Index

Index

muskets, 67, 81, 97, 116, 126, 141, 170, 183, 198-202, 248, 323, 330, 332, 338, 374-375, 407, 414, 418

Muspratt, William, 15, 46, 49, 50, 53, 63, 65, 84, 88, 152, 181-184, 185, 193, 211, 218, 237, 243, 245, 248, 272-274, 280, 285, 323, **330**, 336, 412

Mutineer, The, 219-220

mutineers, 28, 29, 33, 46, 50, 51, 53, 54, 63, **65**, 67, 73, 78, 79, 82, 83, **84**, 86, 88, 89, 90, 92, 95, 97, 99, 105, 111, 112, 113, 116, 117, 120, 121, 122, 125-126, 134, 137, 139, 140, 141, 144, 145, 147, 153, 154, 155, 157, 158, 161, 163, 169, 172, 175, 181, 182, 187, 188, 189, 193, 198-202, 207, 208, 215, 218, 219, 220, 226, 234, 235, 236, 237, 242, 243, 244, 246, 248, 251, 258, 259, 260, 263, 264, 265, 269, 275-278, 280, 281, 283, 287, 288, 291, 293, 296, 297, 300, 301, 303, 305, 310, 314, 315, 318, 319-320, 321, 322, 323, 330, 332, 333, 335, 338, 341, 344, 346, 349-351, 353, 355, 365, 375, 377, 379, 380-381, 382, 383, 385, 386, 387, 388, 391, 394, 407, 409, 411, 413-414, 416, 417, 418, 420, 421, 426, 431, 432, 433, 435

consorts of, 112, 113, 125-126, 131, 198-202, 207-208, 237, 251, 260, 305, 318, 319, 338, 349-356, 378, 407-408, 409, 411, 413, 415-416, 418

Mutineers of the Bounty and Their Descendants in Pitcairn and Norfolk Islands, The, 220, 328

"Mutineers Turning Bligh and His Men Adrift in the *Bounty's* Launch, The," 261

mutiny, 13, 33, 34, 35, 121, 144, 154, 163, 226, 328, 346

mutiny, against English rule, 244

mutiny, *Bounty*, 1, 2, 3, 13, 19, 21, 23, 24, 26, 29, 34, 35, 36, 37, 46, 50 51, 53, 54, 56, 58-66, 67, 69, 71, 85, 89, 99, 100, 101, 103, 105, 109, 119, 120, 121, 137, 161, 163, 181-182, 183-186, 187, 188, 189, 191, 193-194, 203-204, 206, 207, 210, 211, 215, 218, 220, 224, 226, 231, 235, 236, 237, 238, 242, 243, 248, 250, 265, 272-274, 275-278, 285, 287, 289, 294, 304, 314-315, 318, 319-320, 321, 322, 323, 326, 330, 332, 334, 336, 337, 344, 351, 377, 383, 386, 387, 389-390, 391, 413, 419, 420, 431, 433-434

mutiny, *Hermione*, 1-2, 272

mutiny, *Lucy Ann*, 307

mutiny, *Middlesex*, 13, 242, 321

mutiny, *Narcissus*, 122, 263, 331

Mutiny of the Bounty, 290

Mutiny on the Bounty, 3, 237, 283, 284, 328, 343

mutiny, Nore, 34, 225, 261

mutu, see motu

Mydiddee, see Maititi

Myers, Daniel, 165

Mywolla, **331**

Nadi, 270

Namuka, see Nomuka

Nanai, **331**

Nancy, see Toofaiti

Nantucket, 274, 351, 360-362

Napoleon, 276

Narcissus, HMS, 122, 263, **331**

Narrative of the Briton's Voyage to Pitcairn's Island, 385

Narrative of the Death of Captain James Cook, A, 256

Narrative of the Mutiny on board His Majesty's Ship "Bounty"; and the subsequent voyage of part of the crew in the ship's boat from Tofoa, one of the Friendly Islands, to Timor, a Dutch Settlement in the East Indies, 21, 105

Narrative of a Voyage to the Pacific...in His Majesty's Ship Blossom, 220, 352

Narrative of Voyages and Travels, A, 260, 278

Narrative of a Whaling Voyage Round the Globe, 423

Nassau, 257

Natieva, 278, **331**, 393, 418

National Geographic Magazine, 267, 341, 419

National Geographic Society, 278, 358

National Maritime Museum, Greenwich, 277

Nausori, 304

Nautical Magazine, 277

navigation, see Bligh, William, navigational skill of

navigational equipment, 68, 271, 376

Navigator Islands, **331**; see also Samoas

Navy, British, see Navy, Royal

Navy, Royal, 11, 13, 19, 21, 23, 24, 27, 33, 34, 36, 50, 119, 121, 179, 181, 184, 186, 189, 195, 201, 203, 218, 223, 229, 239, 240, 246, 255, 259, 261, 263, 265, 267, 270, 271, 272, 278, 280, 282, 290, 292, 297, 301, 322, 325,

Index

Oha, 112, 113, 208, 331, 332, **338**, 407, 416, 418
Oher, Ohoo, see Oha
Okeolehao, 417
Oliver, Douglas L., 215, 233, 294, 403
Oliver, William, 139, 142, 143, 158, 269-270, 318, **339**, 380
Olivia, 236, 268, 334, **339**
Olohenga, see Swain's Island
Olosega, 382
Omai, see Mai
omaomao, 339
Omoo, 307, 394-395
One Tree Hill, 316, **339**
Ono-i-Lau, 88, 269, 304, **339**; see also Fiji Islands
Ontong Java, 364
Oparre, see Pare
open-boat voyage
    of *Bounty*, see Bligh, William, open-boat voyage
    of escaped convicts, 156
    of *Pandora*, 155-156, 157, 327-328
Opeowpah, see Upaupa
Opoa, 364, 378, 412
Opuarei, Opuole, see Puarai
Opunohu, 325
ora, **339**
orange, 86
Oreepyah, Orepiah, Oripai, see Ari'ipaea
O'Reilly, Peter, 288
orlop deck, **340**
'Oro, 211-212
Orofara, 307
Orofena, Orohena, **340**, 394
Orsmond, Reverend John M., 417
Osnaburgh Island, 221, 320, **340**, 387; see also MehetiaOtago, 266
Otaha, see Tahaa
Otaheite, see Tahiti
Otoo, Ottoo, see Tu
Otow, see Teu
Otueaiai peninsula, 418
outrigger canoes, see canoes
overcrowding on *Bounty*, see *Bounty*, overcrowding on
Owharre, see Fare
Oxford, 216

Pacific, see South Pacific
Pacific Islands Monthly, 419
Paea, 215, 313, 342
pahi, **340**
Pai, 325
Paine, Thomas, 33
Paiti, see Vaetua
Palmerston Island, 140, 141, 257, 263, 294, **340**, 386
paludism, **340**
Panama Canal, 169, 358
pandanus, 131, 422; see also fara
Pandora, HMS, 3, 41, 62, 73, 88, 106, 111, 121-123, 125, 127, 129, 131, 133-135, 137, 138, 144, 147, 152, 153, 154, 155, 157, 159, 161, 171, 181, 183, 184, 185, 219, 220, 234, 236, 237, 238, 250, 251, 258, 260, 261, 262, 263-264, 265, 269, 279, 281, 282, 285-286, 287, 288, 290, 291, 293, 294, 300, 304, 315, 318, 319, 320, 323, 326, 327, 329, 330, 336, 337, 339, **341**, 343, 344-345, 347, 365, 366, 380, 382, 386, 389-390, 391, 398, 411, 419, 420, 425
    crew of, 121-122, 139, 140, 153, 154, 155, 159, 258, 260, 264
    jolly boat of, 140, 141
    map of voyage of, 148-151
    officers of, 121-123, 139, 140, 287
"Pandora's box," 137, 139, 141, 144, 152, 263-264, 286, 294, 304, 345, 390
Pandora's Last Voyage, 122
paoniho, **341**
Pao Pao, 325
Paorani, **342**, 416
Papara, 116, 211, 237, **342**, 391, 397, 409-410, 412
Papeari, 268, 412
Papeete, 49, 297, 307, 310, 316, **342**, 354, 364, 366, 368, 369, 370, 387, 394, 396, 400, 410, 418
Papeno'o, 284, **342**
paper mulberry tree, see mulberry tree
Papeuriri, 412
Papo, 193, **342**
Paradise Island, see Tahiti
Paraha Iti, see Vahineatua
Parai, 173, **342**
Pare, 43, 83, 88, 98, 102, 103, 115, 116, 117, 132, 170, 172, 173, 211, 214, **342**, 364-366,

486

Index

Index

Index

253, 254, 256, 302, 371, 379, **381**, 389, 430
Resource, HMS, 30, 77, 79, 81, 85, 219, 224,
   258, **381**, 382, 392
   weapons on, 77
Restoration Island, 69, **381**
Reunion, 221, 329
revolution, 34
Reynolds, Captain, 391
Rickman, John, 254, 256
Ridgeway, Robert, 164
rigging, 25, 27
Rikitea, 310
Rio de Janeiro, 125, 127, 432
Riou, Edward, 254
Rix Dollars, 30, 77
Roaring Forties, 39
Robertson, George, 127, 429
Rock of the West, 347, **381**; see also Pitcairn
   Island
Rogers, Captain John, 321
Rope, The, **381**
Rose, 382
rosewood, Tahitian, see miro
Rotterdam Island, 334, **381**; see also Nomuka
Rotterdam *Welfare*, see *Welfare*
Rotuma, 147, **381-382**
Round Island, 69
Royal Academy, 261
Royal Geographical Society Journal, 429
Royal Naval Biography, 380
Royal Navy, see Navy, Royal
Royal Pardon, 185, 297
Royal Society of the Arts, 38, 198, 216, 387
Royalty Theatre, 101
Royal William, HMS, 119, **382**
rum, 18, 21, 40, 49, 59, 61, 69, 171, 225-226,
   234, 282, 296, 319, 387, 388, 421
Rum Corps, 175
Rururu, 307
Russia
   at war with Sweden, 79, 320-321
   settlements in Alaska, 79
Russell, Lord Edward, 207, 355, 361, **382**
Rutter, Owen, 184, 227, 355

Sabbath, 351
Sacred Stones and Rites of Ancient Tahiti, 312-313
sailcloth, 110, 139, 380
sailing master

on *Assistant*, see Watson, George
on *Bounty*, see Fryer, John
on *Dolphin*, see Robertson, George
on *Pandora*, see Passmore, George
on *Providence* see Nichols, William
sailmaker, on *Bounty*, see Lebogue, Lawrence
sails, 25, 27, 49, 50, 63, 89, 95, 110, 250, 380
St. Augustine's Bay, 187
St. Helena, 187, 189
St. John, Professor Hardold, 289
St. Kilda, **390**, 435
St. Paul, 106
St. Paul Island, 33
St. Vincent, 191, 225, 374
Salem, 241, 354, 361
Sally, see Sully
Samarang, 81, 157, 159, 264, 380-381, **382**, 425
Samoa Islands, 141-142, 157, 206, 257, 261,
   331, 364, 380, **382**, 397, 419-420, 425; see
   also Navigator Islands
   people of, 333
Samuel, John, 15, 21, 59, 64, 85, 160, 294, **382-**
   383, 428, 431
Samwell, David, 254, 256
Sandilands, Captain Alexander A., 251, 354,
   361, **383**
Sandwich Islands, 371, **383**; see also Hawaiian
   Islands
Sandwich, Earl of, see Sandwich Islands
sangaree, sangria, **383-384**
Santa Cruz, 19
Santa Cruz Islands, 147
Santo Domingo, **384**
Sarah, **384**; see also Sully, Tevarua,
   Teatuahitea
Sassenach, 363
Saunders, Sir Charles, Island, see Maiao
Savage Island, 333, **384**
Savaii, 141, 382
Savu Sea, 415
schooner, **384**
   built by *Bounty* crewmen on Tahiti, see
      Resolution
   built by Seventh-day Adventists, see
      Pitcairn (vessels)
   purchased by Bligh, see *Resource*
Scotch coffee, **384**
Scott, Robert, 165
screw pine, see fara

Index

scrofula, 105, 125, 268, 301, 431; see also King's Evil

scupper, **384**

scurvy, 255, 271, 303

scuttlebutt, 384

"sea lawyer," 36, 375

Seale, Alvin, 278

sealing, 274, 351

seamen on *Bounty*, see *Bounty*, crew of

Sedgwick, Ellery, 284

seizing, **384**

Semarang, see Samarang

Semeru, 299

Seringapatam, HMS, 353, 361, **384-385**, 429

Serle Island, see Pukarua

Seventh-day Adventists, 209, 345, 347, 351, 357-359, 362

Sever, Captain William C., 128, 302-303, **385**

sextant, 68, 376, **385**

sexual, sexuality, see homosexual relationship; *Bounty*: marital status of crew; prostitutes, relationships with; women, relationships with

shaddock, **385**

Shaddock, Captain, 385

Shamrock V, 300

Shamrock V's Wild Voyage Home, 300

Shapiro, Larry L., 137, 359, 363, 424

sharks, 159

Sharon, 289

Shillibeer, Lieutenant John, 233-234, 247, 351-352, **385**, 394

ship, **386**

ship-rigged, **386**

"ship's fever," see typhus ship's landing point, 386

shore leave, 49

shore operations, 58

Short Reply to Capt. William Bligh's Answer, 243

Shovel, Sir Clowdisley, 271

Silverman, David, 322, 359

Simonstown, see False Bay

Simpson, George, 14, 64, **386**

Sinoto, Professor Yosihiko, 289, 313

Sivall, John, 140, **386**

skedaddle, **386**

Skinner, Richard, 15, 65, 84, 133, 152, 153-154, **386**

slavery, 11, 34, 37

slave labor, 11, 34, 37, 195

slop chest, **386-387**

slush fund, **387**

Smith, Adam, 221

Smith, Alexander, **387**; see Adams, John

Smith, Christopher, 165, 167, 173, 178, 187, 374

Smith, John, 15, 64, 85, 183, 243, 383, **387**, 428

Society Islands, 39, 106, 212, 228, 257, 297, 306, 320, 325, 357, 364, 378, 382, **387**, 394, 433

Soerabaja, see Surabaya

Solander, Dr. Daniel, 37, 216, 252, 255

Solent, 371, 388

Solomon Islands, 147, 260, 263

son of a gun, **388**

Song of Rahero, The, 404

Sourabaya, see Surabaya

South Africa, 85, 428, 431

South America, 260, 334, 415, 424

Southern Cook islands, 58, 257, 340

South Pacific, 3, 43, 63, 69, 122, 127, 139, 169, 171, 177, 181, 219, 223, 233, 240, 246, 274, 317, 320, 321, 326, 335, 342, 347, 351, 359, 388, 389, 393, 422, 433

South Pacific Handbook, 396, 425-426

Southsea, 371

South Seas, 2, 4, 11, 13, 96, 109, 127, 128, 144, 147, 157, 161, 195, 197, 198, 204, 210, 216, 219, 220, 240, 241, 252, 257, 283, 308, 316, 320, 326, 332, 342, 343-344, 379-380, 394, 403, 420, 427, 432

"South Seas Academy," 326, 367

Spain, 121, 223, 228, 277, 278

ships of, 127, 128, 228, 301

wine from, 324

Sparrman, Anders, 253

Sparrowhawk, HMS, 277

Spence, Charles, 260

Spikerman, Captain, 77, **388**

Spithead, 13, 88, 119, 175, 181, 186, 189, 218, 224, 226, 235, 237, 244, 262, 264, 273, 281, 288, 297, 305, 336, 337, 341, 371, 374, 377, 382, **388**

splicing the main brace, **388**

Sporing, Herman, 252

Staines, Sir Thomas, 208, 233, 234, 278, 346-347, 351, 360, **388-389**

Stanley, David, 396

Index

Index

Index

Index

Index

Index